Effective Leadership *and* Management *in* Nursing

BRIEF CONTENTS

Seventh Edition

Effective Leadership *and* Management *in* Nursing

ELEANOR J. SULLIVAN

PHILLIP J. DECKER

PEARSON

Prentice
Hall

Pearson Education International

Publisher: Julie Levin Alexander
Publisher's Assistant: Regina Bruno
Editor-in-Chief: Maura Connor
Senior Acquisitions Editor: Pamela Fuller
Editorial Assistant: Jennifer Aranda
Development Editor: Patricia Gillivan
Managing Production Editor: Patrick Walsh
Production Liaison: Cathy O'Connell
Production Editor: Lynn Steines, S4Carlisle Publishing Services
Manufacturing Manager: Ilene Sanford
Art Director: Maria Guglielmo
Cover and Interior Designer: Wanda España
Director of Marketing: Karen Allman

Senior Marketing Manager: Francisco Del Castillo
Marketing Specialist: Michael Sirinides
New Media Project Manager: Stephen Hartner
Director, Image Resource Center: Melinda Patelli
Manager, Rights and Permissions: Zina Arabia
Manager, Visual Research: Beth Brenzel
Manager, Cover Visual Research & Permissions: Karen Sanatar
Image Permission Coordinator: Ang'john Ferreri
Composition: S4Carlisle Publishing Services
Printer/Binder: CJ Krehbiel
Cover Printer: Phoenix Color Corp/Hagerstown
Cover Illustration: Getty Images/Chad Baker

Notice: Care has been taken to confirm the accuracy of information presented in this book. The authors, editors, and the publisher, however, cannot accept any responsibility for errors or omissions or for consequences from application of the information in this book and make no warranty, express or implied, with respect to its contents.

The authors and publisher have exerted every effort to ensure that drug selections and dosages set forth in this text are in accord with current recommendations and practice at time of publication. However, in view of ongoing research, changes in government regulations, and the constant flow of information relating to drug therapy and drug reactions, the reader is urged to check the package inserts of all drugs for any change in indications of dosage and for added warnings and precautions. This is particularly important when the recommended agent is a new and/or infrequently employed drug.

If you purchased this book within the United States or Canada you should be aware that it has been wrongfully imported without the approval of the Publisher or the Author.

Pearson Education Ltd., London
Pearson Education Singapore, Pte. Ltd.
Pearson Education Canada, Inc.
Pearson Education—Japan

Pearson Education Australia PTY, Limited
Pearson Education North Asia Ltd., Hong Kong
Pearson Educación de Mexico, S.A. de C.V.
Pearson Education Malaysia, Pte. Ltd.
Pearson Education, Upper Saddle River, New Jersey

ISBN-10:   0-13-208304-3
ISBN-13: 978-0-13-208304-1

ABOUT THE AUTHOR

Eleanor J. Sullivan, PhD, RN, FAAN, is the former dean of the University of Kansas School of Nursing, past president of Sigma Theta Tau International, and previous editor of the *Journal of Professional Nursing*. She has served on the board of directors of the American Association of Colleges of Nursing, testified before the U.S. Senate, served on a National Institutes of Health council, presented papers to international audiences, been quoted in *Chicago Tribune, St. Louis Post-Dispatch*, and *Rolling Stone Magazine*, and named to "Who's Who in Health Care" by *Kansas City Business Journal*. She earned nursing degrees from St. Louis Community College, St. Louis University, and Southern Illinois University and holds a PhD from St. Louis University.

Dr. Sullivan is known for her publications in nursing, including this award-winning textbook, *Effective Leadership & Management in Nursing*, and *Becoming Influential: A Guide for Nurses* from Prentice Hall. Other publications include *Creating Nursing's Future: Issues, Opportunities and Challenges* and *Nursing Care for Clients with Substance Abuse*.

Today Dr. Sullivan is a professional speaker and mystery author. Her mystery series (*Twice Dead, Deadly Diversion, Assumed Dead*) features nurse sleuth Monika Everhardt. By showing nursing realistically, she hopes that readers will understand the complexity of nursing care and the skills and knowledge involved in being a nurse.

Visit her at www.EleanorSullivan.com

PREFACE

Leading and managing are essential skills for all nurses in today's rapidly changing health care arena. New graduates find themselves managing unlicensed assistive personnel, and experienced nurses are managing groups of health care providers from a variety of disciplines and educational levels. Declining revenues and increasing costs mandate that every organization use its resources efficiently. Thus, nurses are challenged to manage effectively with fewer resources. Never has the information presented in this textbook been needed more. *Effective Leadership & Management in Nursing*, Seventh Edition, can help both student nurses and those with practice experience acquire the skills needed to ensure success in today's dynamic health care environment.

Features of the Seventh Edition

Effective Leadership & Management in Nursing has made a significant and lasting contribution to the education of nurses and nurse managers in its six previous editions. Used worldwide, this award-winning textbook is now offered in an updated and revised edition to reflect changes in the current health care system and in response to suggestions from the book's users. The Seventh Edition builds upon the work of previous contributors to provide the most up-to-date and comprehensive learning package for today's busy students and professionals.

This book has been a success for many reasons. It combines practicality with conceptual understanding; is responsive to the needs of faculty, nurse managers, and students; and taps the expertise of contributors from a variety of disciplines, especially management professionals whose work has been adapted by nurses for current nursing practice. The expertise of management professors in schools of business and practicing nurse managers is seldom incorporated into nursing textbooks. This unique approach provides students with invaluable knowledge and skills and sets the book apart from others.

Student-Friendly Learning Tools

Designed with the adult learner in mind, the book focuses on the application of the content presented with specific guidelines for implementing the skills included. To further illustrate and emphasize key points, each chapter in this edition includes these features:

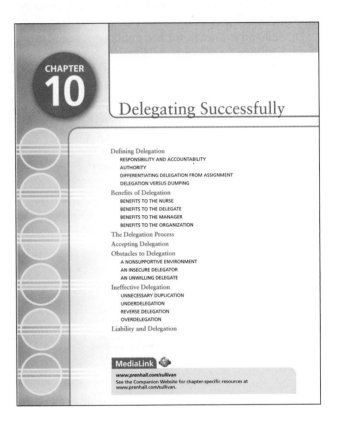

- Chapter outline and preview
- New MediaLink boxes in each chapter introduce readers to resources and activities on the Companion Website at www.prenhall.com/sullivan.
- MediaLink tabs in the chapter margins encourage students to use the website activities.

Key Terms

Accountability *p135*	Delegation *p135*	Reverse delegation *p142*
Assignment *p136*	Overdelegation *p142*	Underdelegation *p142*
Authority *p136*	Responsibility *p135*	

- Key terms are defined in the glossary at the end of the book

- What You Know Now lists at the end of each chapter
- A list of "tools," or key behaviors, for using the skills presented in the chapter
- Questions to Challenge You to help students relate concepts to their experiences
- Up-to-date references

What You Know Now

- Delegation is a contractual agreement in which authority and responsibility for a task is transferred by the person accountable for the task to another individual.
- Delegation involves skill in identifying and determining the task and level of responsibility, determining who has the requisite skills and abilities, describing expectations clearly, reaching mutual agreement, and monitoring performance and providing feedback.
- Delegatable tasks are personal, routine tasks that the delegator can perform well; that do not involve discipline, highly technical tasks, or confidential information; and that are not controversial.
- Delegation benefits the delegator, delegate, the organization.
- Various organizational, delegator, and delegate barriers can prevent effective delegation.
- Ineffe
  resp
- Adhe
  deleg
- Deleg

Tools for Delegating Successfully

1. Delegate only tasks for which you have responsibility.
2. Transfer authority when you delegate responsibility.
3. Be sure you follow state regulations, job descriptions, and agency policies when delegating.
4. Follow the delegation process and key behaviors for delegating described in the chapter.
5. Accept delegation when you are clear about the task, time frame, reporting, and other expectations.
6. Confront your fears about delegation; recognize those that are realistic and those that are not.

Questions to Challenge You

1. Review your state's nurse practice act. How is delegation defined? What tasks can and cannot be delegated? How is supervision defined? Are there any other guidelines for supervision? Are responsibilities regarding advanced practice delineated? How does the scope of practice differ between registered and licensed practical/vocational nurses? What is the scope of practice of other health care providers?
2. What are your agency's policies on delegation?

someone else. Did you follow the steps of
come positive? If not, what went wrong?
a task to you. Did your delegator explain
on? Not enough? Was supervision appropriate
tcome?
shown in Box 10-1? What did you learn about

CASE STUDY 10-1   Delegation

Lisa Ford is a school nurse for a suburban school district. She has responsibility for three school buildings, including a middle school, a high school, and a vocational rehabilitation workshop for mentally and physically handicapped secondary students. Her management responsibilities include providing health services for 1,000 students, 60 faculty members, and 25 staff members, and supervising 2 unlicensed school health aides and 3 special education health aides. The logistics of managing multiple school sites results in the delegation of many daily health room tasks, including medication administration, to the school-based health aides.

Nancy Andrews is an unlicensed health aide at the middle school. This is her first year as a health aide and she has a limited background in health care. The nurse practice act in the state allows for the delegation of medication administration in the school setting. Lisa is responsible for training Nancy to safely administer medication to students, documenting the training, evaluating Nancy's performance, and providing ongoing supervision. Part of Nancy's training will also include a discussion of those medication-related decisions that must be made by a registered nurse.

Manager's Checklist

The nurse manger is responsible to:

- Understand the state nurse practice act and its applicability to the school setting
- Implement school district policies related to health services and medication administration
- Develop and implement an appropriate training program
- Limit opportunities for error and decreasing liability by ensuring that unlicensed health aides are appropriately trained to handle delegated tasks
- Maintain documentation related to training and observation of medication administration by unlicensed staff
- Audit medication administration records to ensure accuracy and completeness
- Conduct several "drop in" visits during the school year to track competency of health aides
- If necessary, report any medication errors to administration and follow up with focused training and closer supervision

- Case Studies with Manager's Checklist to demonstrate application of content

Organization

The text is organized into four sections that address the essential information and key skills that nurses must learn to succeed in today's volatile health care environment.

Part 1. Understanding Nursing Management and Organizations. Part 1 introduces the concepts of organizations and organizational theory and design with an emphasis on health care system mergers, integrated care networks, and managed care. Leadership is presented within a theoretical framework, and management functions are explained. Also included in Part 1 is information about initiating and managing change, improving quality, and power and politics, all necessary for nurses to succeed and prosper.

Part 2. Learning Key Skills in Nursing Management. Essential skills for today's managers comprise Part 2. These include thinking critically, making decisions, solving problems, communicating with a variety of individuals and groups, delegating, working in teams, resolving conflicts, and managing time.

Part 3. Managing Resources. Knowing how to manage resources is essential for nurses today. They must be adept at budgeting fiscal resources; recruiting and selecting staff; handling staffing and scheduling; motivating and developing staff; evaluating staff performance; coaching, disciplining and terminating staff; reducing turnover and retaining staff; managing absenteeism; and handling the inevitable personnel problems. In addition, collective bargaining and preventing workplace violence are included in Part 3.

Part 4. Taking Care of Yourself. Nurses are their own most valuable resource so Part 4 shows how to manage stress and to advance in their careers.

Resources for Learning and Teaching

COMPANION WEBSITE

Students and instructors can use the updated and greatly enhanced Companion Website at www.prenhall.com/sullivan to apply textbook concepts to real practice scenarios experienced in a variety of health care settings. This free online Study Guide is designed to help students apply the concepts presented in the book. Each chapter-specific module features Objectives, NCLEX Review with rationales, Chapter Outlines for lecture notes, Critical Thinking Activities, Current Event Activities, MediaLinks, Glossary, and more. Additionally, each chapter in the Companion Website features Nursing Leadership & Management in Action activities, such as "Managing Staff Resources," "Identifying Variance," and "Personal Motivation." These activities serve as an excellent tool designed to enhance the understanding of leadership and management principles and to apply the theoretical concepts of leadership and management in a safe environment.

ONLINE COURSE MANAGEMENT

Online companions are available for schools using course management systems. The online course management solutions feature all instructor and student online course materials for this book, such as interactive assessment modules, electronic test bank, PowerPoint slides, online grade books, communication between students and instructors, and much more. For more information about adopting an online course management system to accompany *Effective Leadership & Management in Nursing*, Seventh Edition, please contact your Prentice Hall Sales Representative or go to the appropriate website below:

http://cms.prenhall.com/webct/index.html
http://cms.prenhall.com/blackboard/index.html

INSTRUCTOR'S RESOURCE CD-ROM

To assist instructors in using this book, the Instructor's Resource CD-ROM provides an electronic test bank, PowerPoint slides, and a complete Instructor's Resource Manual in Word with chapter outlines, discussion questions, and guidelines for using the Companion Website and online course management (i.e., Blackboard, WebCt) in the course. The Instructor's Resource Manual is also available through secure download only to instructors at www.prenhall.com/nursing. Please contact your Prentice Hall Sales Representative for more information.

ACKNOWLEDGMENTS

The success of previous editions of this book has been due to the expertise of many contributors. Nursing administrators, management professors, and faculty in schools of nursing all made significant contributions to earlier editions. I am enormously grateful to them for sharing their knowledge and experience to help nurses learn leadership and management skills. Without them, this book would not exist.

At Prentice Hall Health, Editor Pamela Fuller and Development Editor Patricia Gillivan guided this revision throughout. Editorial Assistant Jennifer Aranda was especially helpful with this revision. The production staff, including Patrick Walsh, Cathy O'Connell, and Maria Guglielmo, helped bring this book to publication. Allison V. Level, college liaison librarian for the Warner College of Natural Resources at Colorado State University–Ft. Collins provided excellent reference support.

Because health care continues to change, reviewers who are using the book in their management practice and in their classes provided invaluable comments and suggestions (see list on pages xi–xii).

I am especially grateful to experienced Nurse Manager Elaine Level for her expert research assistance, ability to generate real-life examples, and her talent to create case scenarios to exemplify the experience of nurses in management roles. In addition, she assisted throughout with ideas and suggestions.

To everyone who has contributed to this fine book over the years, I thank you.

Eleanor J. Sullivan, PhD, RN, FAAN www.EleanorSullivan.com

DEDICATION

This book is dedicated to my family for their continuing love and support.

Eleanor J. Sullivan

SUPPLEMENT CONTRIBUTORS AND REVIEWERS

Supplement Contributors

Gail Bromley, RN, PhD
Assistant Professor
College of Nursing
Kent State University
Kent, Ohio
Instructor's Resource CD-ROM

Heather Lane Carlton, RN, MSN
Staff Development Specialist
University of Kentucky Hospital
Lexington, Kentucky
Companion Website

Vera Dauffenbach, RN, MSN, EdD
Associate Professor
Director of the Graduate Program
Bellin College of Nursing
Green Bay, Wisconsin
Companion Website

Rhonda Hutton Gann, RN, MSN
Nursing Informatics Lab Manager
State Fair Community College
Sedalia, Missouri
Companion Website

Rauda Gelazis, RN, PhD, CS, CTN
Instructor's Resource CD-ROM

Amy Herrington, RN, MSN, CEN
Staff Development Specialist
University of Kentucky Healthcare
Lexington, Kentucky
Companion Website

Jane Walker, BBA, RN, MSN
Associate Professor of Nursing
Walkers State Community College
Instructor's Resource CD-ROM

Jan Weust, RN, MSN
Chief Nurse Officer
Sullivan County Community Hospital
Sullivan, Indiana
Instructor's Resource CD-ROM

Reviewers

Magdeline Aagard, EdD, RN
Second Level Faculty
North Hennepin Community College
Brooklyn Park, Minnesota

Stoerm Anderson, EdD, MSN, RN
RN-BS/MS Program Coordinator
Texas Woman's University
College of Nursing
Denton, Texas

B. Michael Barbour, RN, MSN
Faculty, Associate in Nursing
Florida State University
Panama City, Florida

Brenda A. Becker, BSN, MA, RN
Nursing Faculty
North Hennepin Community College
Brooklyn Park, Minnesota

Gail Bromley, PhD, RN
College of Nursing
Kent State University
Kent, Ohio

Theresa G. Buxton, RN, PhD
Instructor
Washington State University's
Intercollegiate College of Nursing
Spokane, Washington

Mary Ann Camann, PhD, APRN, BC
Associate Professor
Kennesaw State University
WellStar School of Nursing
Kennesaw, Georgia

Jesus (Jessie) Casida, PhD, RN,
CCRN-CSC, APN,C
Assistant Professor Adult Health Nursing
Wayne State University College of Nursing
Detroit, Michigan

Connie Lynn Clark, RN, PhD
Professor
Mercy College of Health Sciences
Des Moines, Iowa

Ann Cook, RN, PhD
Professor; Director, Assessment and
Evaluation
Columbia College of Nursing
Milwaukee, Wisconsin

Kim Cooper, RN, MSN
Associate of Science Nursing Program Chair
Ivy Tech State College
Terre Haute, Indiana

Mary Curtis, PhD, APRN, BC
Associate Professor of Nursing
Maryville University
St. Louis, Missouri

Erlinda N. Dubal, MBA, MA,
BSN, RN, BC
Director: MS Executive Program for
Nursing and Healthcare Management
Long Island University
Brooklyn, New York

Lori A. Escallier, PhD, RN CPNP
Clinical Associate Professor
State University of New York
at Stony Brook
School of Nursing
Stony Brook, New York

Linda Freeman, RN, BSN, MN
Assistant, Professor Nursing
John Tyler Community College
Chester, Virginia

Julia A. Goodwin, PhD, RN
Clinical Assistant Professor
College of Nursing
University of Arkansas for
Medical Sciences
Little Rock, Arkansas

Sharon Guillet
Associate Professor and Chair
BSN Program
Marymount University
Arlington, Virginia

Janet Harden, PhD, RN
Assistant Professor
Wayne State University
College of Nursing
Detroit, Michigan

Peggy L. Hawkins, PhD, RN, BC, CNE
Associate Dean of Health Professions and
Professor of Nursing
College of Saint Mary
Omaha, Nebraska

Alice Kempe PhD, CS
Associate Professor
Ursuline College
Pepper Pike, Ohio

Carol A. Mannahan, EdD, RN, CNAA
Executive Director, Leadership Programs
University of Oklahoma College of Nursing
Oklahoma City, Oklahoma

Rebecca Matthews, DNP, MNSc,
IBCLC, RN
Assistant Professor
Arkansas State University, College of
Nursing and Health Professions
Jonesboro, Arkansas

Tammie Mann McCoy, RN, PhD
Chair Baccalaureate Nursing Program
Mississippi University for Women
Columbus, Mississippi

Eileen M. McGee, RN, PhD
Assistant Professor Nursing
Simmons College
Boston, Massachusetts

Susan Meyer, MSN, RN, PHN
Director BSN Program
Mount Saint Mary's College

Ava S. Miller, EdD, RN, AHN-BC
Associate Professor
The University of Texas at Brownsville
Brownsville, Texas

Polly A. Royal, MS, RN-BC
Clinical Assistant Professor
Purdue University
West Lafayette, Indiana

Rose Sherman, EdD, RN, CNAA, BC
Director, Nursing Leadership Institute
Coordinator, Nursing Administration
Boca Raton, Florida

Cheryl Slaughter Smith, PhD, RN
Associate Professor of Nursing
Arkansas Tech University
Russellville, Arkansas

Mary S. Tilbury, EdD, RN, CNAA, BC
Associate Professor
University of Maryland
Baltimore, Maryland

Robin Toms, PhD, RN, CS, CNAA, BC
Assistant Professor
Texas Woman's University
College of Nursing
Houston, Texas

Judith Valloze, ARNP, MSN
Professor
Daytona Beach Community College
Daytona Beach, Florida

Patricia A. Varvel, MS, RN
Assistant Professor
Houston Baptist University College
of Nursing
Houston, Texas

Ann H. White, RN, PhD, MBA, CNA, BC
Assistant Dean for Nursing
University of Southern Indiana
Evansville, Indiana

Kathleen M. White, PhD, RN, CNAA, BC
Associate Professor and Director, Master's
Program
The Johns Hopkins University School of
Nursing
Baltimore, Maryland

Kristi A. Wilkerson, RN, MSN
Nursing Faculty-Clinical Nursing Instructor
Southeastern Community College
West Burlington, Iowa

Odette P. Willis, RN, MN, MBA
Assistant Professor
George Mason University
College of Nursing and Health Science
Fairfax, Virginia

CONTENTS

Part 2   Learning Key Skills in Nursing Management   103

Part 4   Taking Care of Yourself   303

Understanding Nursing Management and Organizations

Introducing Nursing Management

Learning Outcomes

After completing this chapter, you will be able to:

1. Describe the forces that are changing the health care system.
2. Explain how quality improvement and benchmarking can reduce medical errors.
3. Discuss how cultural and generational differences affect the health care environment.
4. Describe how evidence-based practice is changing nursing.
5. Explain what emerging technologies will mean for nursing.
6. Explain why preparation is the best defense against disasters.
7. Discuss the changes and challenges that nurses will face in the future.

MediaLink

www.prenhall.com/sullivan

See the Companion Website for chapter-specific resources at
www.prenhall.com/sullivan.

Key Terms

Benchmarking *p5*
Electronic health record *p6*
Evidence-based practice *p6*

Integrated health care
    networks *p3*
Leapfrog Group *p4*

Quality management *p4*
Remote care *p7*
Robotics *p7*

Today, all nurses are managers. Whether you work in a freestanding clinic, an ambulatory surgical center, a critical unit in an acute care hospital, or in hospice care for a home care agency, you must learn to work effectively and efficiently with staff, other nurses, and unlicensed assistive personnel. To survive in the current health care environment, you must be vigilant about costs. Additionally, to manage well, you must understand the health care system and how the organization where you work functions. You need to recognize what external forces affect your work and how to influence those forces. You need to know what motivates people and how you can help create an environment that inspires and sustains the individuals who work in it. You must be able to collaborate with others, as a leader, a follower, and a team member, in order to become confident in your ability to be a leader and a manager.

This book is designed to provide new graduates or novice managers with the information they need to become effective managers and leaders in health care. More than ever before, today's rapidly changing health care environment demands highly refined management skills and superb leadership.

Forces Changing Health Care

Today's health care system is continuing to undergo significant changes. Costly lifesaving medicines, robotics, remote care, and innovations in imaging technologies, noninvasive treatments, and surgical procedures have combined to produce the most sophisticated and effective health care ever—and the most expensive. Skyrocketing costs and inaccessibility to health care are ongoing concerns for employers, health care providers, policy makers, and the public at large. A number of factors are forcing change on the health care system.

THE HEALTH CARE BUSINESS

That health care is a business is no longer disputed. Health care is a commodity that some people (insured, government subsidized, or the wealthy) can buy and others (poor, unemployed, or underemployed) cannot. For some, this is a temporary situation, due to changing jobs. Many others continue to go without health care because they work part-time without benefits or because they have a preexisting health condition that makes them ineligible for coverage. When the uninsured receive care, it is often provided at great expense in emergency rooms, often after the condition has progressed, which then requires more complex and long-term care. Some of the costs of this unnecessarily expensive care are borne by the health care organization, and some costs are passed on to other payers, such as Medicare and private insurance companies, who pass on their costs to their constituents: taxpayers and customers.

In spite of concerted efforts to contain costs, the United States spends more money on health care than any other country, and health care spending continues to rise. Health care consumed 16 percent of the gross domestic product (the measure of output of goods and services) in the United States in 2006 (Forbes, 2007). In addition, federal forecasters predict that U.S. health care spending will double by 2016 to $4.1 trillion per year (Forbes, 2007).

Health care is now a competitive, market-based enterprise. This change has transformed health care from an industry with a service orientation to one with a business orientation. Scrutinizing costs is a way of life in health care today. Every expenditure, including supplies, equipment, and most importantly, how staff utilize their time, are being closely examined.

HEALTH CARE NETWORKS

Integrated health care networks emerged as organizations struggled to find ways to survive in today's

MediaLink ⊕ Health Care Change

cost-conscious environment. Integrated systems encompass a variety of model organizational structures, but certain characteristics are common. Network systems

- Deliver a whole continuum of care;
- Provide geographic coverage for the buyers of health care services; and
- Accept the risk inherent in taking a fixed payment in return for providing health care for all persons in the selected group, such as all employees of one company.

To provide such services, networks of providers emerged to encompass hospitals and physician practices. Most importantly, the focal point for care is primary care rather than the hospital. The goal is to keep patients healthy by treating them in the setting that incurs the lowest cost and thereby reducing expensive hospital treatments. A former goal was to keep hospital beds filled. It is now the goal of the health care industry to keep patients out of them!

As a result of the need to contain cost, a variety of other arrangements have emerged, varying from loose affiliations between hospitals to complete mergers of hospitals, clinics, and physician practices. These arrangements continue to move and shift as alliances fail, return to separate entities, or form new affiliations. Regardless, providing care through systems and networks is expected to continue throughout the 21st century.

DEMAND TO REDUCE ERRORS

Medical Errors

When the Institute of Medicine (IOM, 1999) reported that 98,000 deaths occurred each year from preventable medical mistakes in hospitals, health care organizations and the public alike were astounded. In addition, medical injuries have been found to increase length of stay and patients' costs as well as increase the risk of mortality (Zhan & Miller, 2003). Health care organizations have been working hard to design and develop systems to prevent such errors. One example is a computerized system for pharmacy that will alert staff to possible drug interactions or adverse reactions based on the patient's condition or other medications. Computerized medication administration records and patient identification bands with bar codes are additional ways to prevent errors.

To add impetus to efforts to reduce medical errors, the Centers for Medicare and Medicaid Services (CMS) decided that, beginning in fiscal year 2008, they would no longer reimburse hospitals for the costs related to

hospital-acquired infections or medical errors (CMS, 2006). According to the Centers for Disease Control and Prevention (CDC), approximately 2 million people suffer from hospital-acquired infections, 100,000 die of these infections, and the added costs are nearly $27.5 billion (CDC, 2007).

As positive an impact as such a change might have, it could also result in unintended consequences. Staff might be more likely to use restraints—chemical or physical—to reduce liability. In addition, there is still the problem of who will pay for costs incurred from medical errors. Will hospitals absorb them in order to avoid the chance they might be sued? Or will they charge the patient? These issues remain unanswered.

The Leapfrog Group

The **Leapfrog Group** is a consortium of public and private purchasers that provide benefits to more than 37 million Americans in all 50 states (Leapfrog Group, 2007a). The organization uses its mammoth purchasing power to leverage quality care for its consumers by rewarding health care organizations that demonstrate quality outcome measures. The quality indicators they focus on include: increasing computer physician order entry systems; using evidence-based hospital referrals; and using ICU physician intensivists staff. These three practices have demonstrated the most significant impact on preventing medical errors. They estimate that if these three patient safety practices were implemented, more than 65,000 lives could be saved, more than $41 billion dollars could be saved, and more than 900,000 medical errors could be avoided (Leapfrog Group, 2007b).

Quality Management

Quality management is a preventive approach designed to address problems before they become crises. The quality movement began in post–World War II Japan, when Japanese industries adopted a system that W. Edwards Deming designed to improve the quality of manufactured products. Its philosophy is that the consumers' needs should be the focus and that employees should be empowered to evaluate and improve quality. In addition to other industries in the United States and abroad, the U.S. health care industry has also adopted total quality management or variations of it.

Built into the system is a mechanism for continuous improvement of products and services through constant evaluation of how well the consumers' needs are met and then devising plans to perfect the process. Patient satisfaction surveys exemplify how health care organizations evaluate their customers' needs.

Benchmarking

In contrast to quality management, which compares internal measures across comparable units, **benchmarking** compares an organization's data with similar organizations. Outcome indicators are identified that can be used to compare performance across disciplines or organizations. Once the results are known, health care organizations can address areas of weakness and enhance areas of strength.

CULTURAL AND GENERATIONAL DIFFERENCES

Immigrant Populations and Cultural Diversity

According to the U.S. Census Bureau, the nation's minority population reached 100 million in 2007. A year ago, minorities comprised 98 million. Hispanics remain the largest minority group at 44 million; African Americans were next at 40 million (U.S. Census Bureau, 2007). Hispanics are also the fastest growing minority, followed by Asians.

One barrier for both native- and foreign-born minorities is socioeconomic status. If you can pay for health care, access is not an issue; but for those who can't, health care is not readily available. The challenge for health care policy makers and the public is to find ways to provide universal access to care regardless of race, ethnic origin, or socioeconomic status.

The influx of immigrants means that health care must assume a transcultural focus. Those who decide health care policies and those who offer clinical services must consider the values, beliefs, and lifestyles of a number of diverse cultures. This is no small challenge. Becoming aware of the differences and similarities among cultures, being sensitive to different perspectives, and providing care within the cultural belief system of the patient requires commitment, respect, and persistence.

The cultural diversity seen in the general population is also reflected in nursing. The Health Resources and Services Administration (HRSA, 2007) reports that 81.8 percent of nurses identify themselves as Caucasian in their most recent (2004) survey. The remaining 18.2 percent were assumed to be from minority populations (up from 12 percent in 2000); however, 7.5 percent of the 2004 respondents did not identify their racial or ethnic background. African American and Hispanic backgrounds are the most frequently reported minorities.

The gender mix of people who are nurses, though, differs from the general population with women greatly outnumbering men. Only 5.4 percent of nurses were men in the 2000 HRSA survey (2000). Although the number has grown slightly to 5.7 percent in 2004 (HRSA, 2007), the talents of nearly half the population are not available to nursing at a time when nursing shortages threaten to intensify.

Sensitivity to cultural differences among staff as well as patients and responsiveness to these differences in the work environment is essential today.

Generational Diversity

In the past it was rare for multiple generations to work together. Seeing four generations working side by side in today's workplace is common. These generations, termed traditionals, baby boomers, generation X, and millenials, have different values and expectations in the workplace (Sherman, 2006). Traditionals value loyalty and respect authority. Baby boomers value professional and personal growth and expect that their work will make a difference.

Generation X members desire a positive work environment. They also want their work to have worth. They want independence, fun, and to have a balance between work and other important areas of their lives, which include personal relationships, child rearing, and pleasurable pursuits. They value independence, and they tend to focus on outcomes rather than processes.

Millenials (also called generation Y) are technically savvy, responsible, and competent. Already experts in connecting online, they may prefer to participate in collaborative structures discussed in Chapter 2. Millenials also value contributing to the collective good, a factor seen in the growth in applications to nursing schools (AACN, 2005).

Changes in the workplace can also add to the conflict due to the generations' different expectations (Weston, 2006). Bureaucracies, common to the traditionals, have given way to quality management teams. The industrial model, where knowledge came from the top down, has transformed into the information age where knowledge is available to any nurse with Internet access (Weston, 2006). Managing employees from different generations can significantly affect the organization's culture (Hersey, Blanchard, & Johnson, 2007). This is discussed more fully in Chapter 2.

The challenge for managers is to avoid stereotyping within the generations, to value the unique contributions of each generation, to encourage mutual respect for differences, and to leverage those differences to enhance teamwork (Kupperschmidt, 2006; Sherman, 2006; Weston, 2006).

Diversity in groups is valuable, posits Surowiecki (2005) in *The Wisdom of Crowds*. In contrast to worries that a crowd will become a like-thinking group (see Chapter 8 on groupthink), he suggests that a diverse group generates a range of ideas that result in better outcomes.

AGING PATIENTS, AGING NURSES

Aging Patients

The older population, which is defined as persons 65 years or older, numbered 37 million in 2006. They represented 12 percent of the U.S. population, or approximately one in every eight Americans. By 2030, there will be more than 71 million older adults, or more than twice their number than in 2000. The population of people 65 and older is expected to grow to be 20 percent of the population by 2030 (DHHS, Administration on Aging, 2007).

The demand for health care for aging patients will continue to grow, not only because people are living longer, but because health care technologies are enabling many people to survive previously fatal diseases and conditions. Additionally older patients often require ongoing care for chronic illnesses as well as for acute episodes of illness.

Increases in life expectancy, older workers retiring later, and good health practices (e.g., exercise, healthy eating, screenings) has increased the number of people wanting to live longer and to remain as healthy and mobile as possible. These people will also require episodic and chronic care. The burden on the health care system is not expected to abate.

Aging Nurses

Just as the population is aging and requiring more and more care, nurses, too, are growing older. The average age of the registered nurse is 46.8 years (HRSA, 2007) compared with 45.2 years in 2000 and 44.3 years in 1996. The percent of nurses over 54 years of age increased to 25.2 percent in 2004, compared to 20.3 percent in 2000 and 16.9 percent in 1980.

What does this mean for the nurses and nurse managers today? It means that the current shortage of nurses will continue and grow worse as more and more aging nurses retire from practice. At the same time the demand for nurses will increase, according to the U.S. Department of Labor (Heckler, 2004). They predict that positions for registered nurses will be the second largest occupation through 2014. (The largest is retail salespersons.)

More Change on the Way

Just when you thought it was safe to go back into the forest . . . more change is coming. Technology, climate, and terrorism threats are driving the additional changes.

EVIDENCE-BASED PRACTICE

Using **evidence-based practice** (EBP) a nurse applies the best scientific evidence to a patient's unique diagnosis, condition, and situation to make clinical decisions. EBP grew out of the movement in medicine in the mid-1990s to use scientific evidence as a basis for decision making (Sackett, Rosenberg, Gray, Haynes, & Richardson, 1996). The term has been confused with research, but they are not the same.

EBP shifts the traditional nursing focus from clinical experience, knowledge of pathophysiology, and intuition to scientific evidence, patient values and preferences, and the clinical situation (Salmond, 2007).

The process of EBP is:

1. Identify the clinical question.
2. Find the evidence to answer the question.
3. Evaluate the evidence.
4. Apply the evidence.
5. Evaluate the outcome (Moyer & Elliott, 2004).

Opponents of EBP criticize the absence of theory to guide decision making as well as the lack of time, expertise, and resources for nurses to implement the practice (Oermann, Floyd, Galvin, & Roop, 2006). Several strategies are suggested to overcome opposition and encourage staff to implement EBP. Vratny and Shriver (2007) suggest that educating staff and an enthusiastic manager can help increase staff participation. One large health care system that has implemented EBP is the U.S. Veterans Health Administration (VA). They have linked evidence-based practice with quality improvement to care for the 5.2 million patients they treat annually (Francis & Perlin, 2006). Regardless of opposition and difficulty in implementing EBP, it is expected to remain a constant in the future.

ELECTRONIC HEALTH RECORDS

An **electronic health record** integrates health information from all medical sources and can be accessed from multiple locations by authorized providers (Simpson, 2007). Computerization of medical records, however, has been slow for a number of reasons. Privacy and confidentiality concerns are major obstructions, and federal regulations to address these concerns adequately are lacking (Steward, 2005). It has been estimated that the cost of implementing a nationwide system in the United States would top $156 billion and require $48 billion in annual operating costs (Kaushal et al., 2005).

Electronic records, however, would reduce redundancies, improve efficiency, decrease medical errors, and lower health care costs (Steward, 2005). While banks, retailers, airlines, and other industries rely on fully-integrated systems to manage communication and reduce redundancies, health care has continued to rely on voluminous paper records duplicated in multiple locations.

The pressure to create a national system of electronic health records is increasing (Kleinke, 2005). System design and appropriate regulations and supervision can address the problems of privacy and confidentiality. A system to monitor record access, for example, is easily designed. Since the inplementation of the Health Insurance Portability and Accountability Act of 1996 (HIPAA) the federal government's regulations have not kept pace with the transfer to electronic records (Steward, 2005).

Fully integrated systems allow for collective data analysis across clinical conditions, health care organizations, or worldwide. Furthermore, such systems facilitate a common nursing language (Simpson, 2007) and support evidence-based decision making (Kirkley, 2004).

Another form of electronic health records is a personal health record that patients maintain. These online systems allow the patient to track medications, record medical interventions, and update their own medical information as needed.

In addition to electronic health records, point-of-care systems and handheld devices speed accurate record keeping (Poissant, Pereira, Tamblyn, & Kawasumi, 2005).

ROBOTICS AND REMOTE CARE

Another technological advance is the use of robots to transport supplies and to deliver remote care. These systems allow supplies and medications to be ordered electronically and filled by laser-guided robots. These robots deliver the requested supplies to nursing units via their own elevators more efficiently, accurately, and in less time than individuals could (Meyers, 2007).

Physicians in remote locations can access patients using wireless video connections in robots at the bedside (Vaughan, 2007). Nurses and physicians alike appreciate

how these interactions enhance their communication and planning. Some robots offer electronic stethoscopes and other diagnostic devices. Physicians may use remote systems even within their own institution, such as following up on lab results between cases instead of after the day's procedures (Meyers, 2007).

TERRORISM AND DISASTER PREPAREDNESS

Recent national disasters, such as the tsunami in Southeast Asia and Hurricane Katrina, as well as the ongoing threat of terrorism in the United States, and pandemics such as the avian flu, demonstrate that few official agencies or health care organizations are prepared to respond to mass casualties (Bartlett, 2006; Vinson, 2007; Caskey, 2006). Events such as these, unfortunately, are likely. Health care institutions must prepare for potential massive emergencies or an influx of patients into an already overcrowded system that will overwhelm the capabilities of health care workers and endanger their health and lives as well (Secor-Turner & O'Boyle, 2006).

Being abandoned following a bioterrorism disaster is nurses' greatest fear, and organizations' readiness plans must address this concern (O'Boyle, Robertson, & Secor-Turner, 2006a). Extensive staff training is required. These include computer simulations, video demonstrations, disaster drills, and clear understanding of communication systems and the incident command center (AHRQ, 2004). Organizations must also include assessing nurses' concerns and providing accessible information, support, and opportunities for debriefing (O'Boyle, Robertson, & Secor-Turner, 2006b). A natural disaster, an attack of terrorism, or an epidemic may occur, and all health care organizations must be prepared to reduce the impact on its patients as well as on its staff.

EVEN MORE CHANGE . . .

What does the future hold for health care? Change is the one constant. Health care will continue to move beyond hospital walls into less-expensive settings, including homes, ambulatory clinics, and assisted living facilities. Technologies of care and information will continue to evolve. Accountability demands will continue to force quality implementation. Access to care will continue to drive policy decisions.

Tim Porter-O'Grady (2003) challenges nursing leaders to help staff "close the door" on allegiance to past practices and turn toward emerging practice opportunities. Leaders themselves must learn new skills as well as convey enthusiasm and commitment for change. Everyone in health care must learn to live with ambiguity and be flexible enough to adapt to the changes it brings.

Challenges Facing Nurses

Every nurse must be prepared to manage. Specific training in management skills is needed in nursing school as well as in the work setting. Most important, however, is that nurses must be able to transfer their newly acquired skills to the job itself. Thus, nurse managers must be experienced in management and must be able to assist their staff in developing adequate management skills. Management training for nurses at all levels is essential for any organization to be efficient and effective in today's cost-conscious and competitive environment.

The challenge for nurse managers and administrators is how to manage in a constantly changing system. Working with teams of administrators and providers to deliver quality health care in the most cost-effective manner offers opportunity as well. Nurses' unique skills in communication, negotiation, and collaboration position them well for the system of today and for the future.

Nurse managers today are challenged to manage with decreasing resources, to help design new systems of care, to supervise teams of professionals and nonprofessionals from a variety of cultures, and, finally, to teach personnel how to function well in the new system. This is no small task. It requires that nurses and their managers be committed, involved, enthusiastic, flexible, and innovative; above all else, it requires that they have good mental and physical health. Because the nurse manager of today is responsible for others' work, the nurse manager must also be a coach, a teacher, and a facilitator. The manager works through others to meet the goals of individuals, of the unit, and of the organization. Most importantly, the nurse manager must be a leader who can motivate and inspire.

Nurse managers must address the interests of both administrators and employees. Both want the same result—quality care. Administrators, however, must focus on cost and efficiency in order for the organization to compete and survive. Employees want to be supported in their work with adequate staffing, supplies, equipment, and, most of all, time. Therein lies the conflict. Between the two is the nurse manager, who must balance the needs of both. Being a nurse manager today is one of the most challenging opportunities in health care. This book is designed to prepare you to meet these challenges.

What You Know Now

- Health care is radically changing today and will continue to change in the foreseeable future.
- Health care is a business, and cost competes with quality in today's health care system.
- The tension between providing adequate nursing care and paying for that care will continue.
- Reducing medical errors is a priority.
- Cultural and generational diversity will continue to demand nurses' attention and shape nursing's workforce.
- Evidence-based practice will guide nursing decisions into the future.
- Electronic health records, robotics, and remote care are just a few of the many technologies on the horizon for health care.
- Threats of natural disasters, terrorism, and pandemics require all health care organizations to plan and prepare for mass casualties.
- Nurses are challenged to manage in a constantly changing environment.

Questions to Challenge You

1. What would you suggest to reduce the cost of health care without compromising patients' health and safety? Name three changes. Consider how you could help make these changes.
2. What mechanisms could you suggest to improve and ensure the quality of care? (Don't just suggest adding nursing staff!)
3. How could you help reduce medical errors? What can you suggest that a health care organization could do?
4. Is evidence-based practice the way you make decisions? If not, why?
5. What are some ways that nurses could take advantage of emerging technologies in health care and information systems? Think big.

6. Have you participated in a disaster drill? Did you notice ways to improve the organization's readiness for mass casualties? Think about suggesting those changes to administration.

7. What steps do you plan to take to transfer the knowledge and skills you learn in this book into your work setting?

Explore MediaLink 🌐

Additional interactive resources for this chapter can be found on the Website at http://www.prenhall. com/sullivan. Click on Chapter 1 to select activities for this chapter.

- Video Overview
- NCLEX® Review Questions
- Critical Thinking Activities
- Current Events
- Nursing Leadership and Management in Action
- MediaLinks

References

Agency for Healthcare Research and Quality (AHRQ). (2004). *Training of Hospital Staff to Respond to a Mass Casualty Incident,* Structured Abstract. April 2004. Agency for Healthcare Research and Quality, Rockville, MD. Retrieved July 2007 from http://www.ahrq.gov/clinic/tp/hospmcitp. htm

American Association of Colleges of Nursing (AACN). (2005). *With enrollments rising for the 5th consecutive year, US nursing schools turn away more than 30,000 applicants in 2005.* Retrieved July 2007 from www.aacn.nche.edu

Bartlett, J. G. (2006). Planning for avian influenza. *Annals of Internal Medicine, 145*(2), 141–144.

Caskey, C. R. (2006). The rule of law and bioterrorism. *Clinical Laboratory Science, 19*(4), 196–202.

Centers for Disease Control (CDC). (2007). Monitoring hospital-acquired infections to promote patient safety—United States, 1990–1999. Retrieved December 2007 from http://www.cdc. gov/epo/mmwr/preview/mmwrhtml/mm4908a1.htm

Centers for Medicare and Medicaid Services (CMS). (2006). *Eliminating serious, preventable, and costly medical errors: Never events.* Retrieved November 2007 from http://www.cms.hhs.gov/apps/media/press/factsheet.asp?Counter= 1863&intNumPerPage=10&checkDate=&checkKey=& srchType=2&numDays=0&srchOpt=0&srchData=medical+ error&srchOpt=0&srchData=medical+error&keywordType= All&chkNewsType=6&intPage=&showAll=1&pYear=&year= 0&desc=&cboOrder=date

Department of Health and Human Services, Administration on Aging. (2007). *Statistics on the Aging Population.* Retrieved July 2007 from http://www.aoa.gov/prof/Statistics/profile/2006/ 2.asp

Forbes. (2007). *U.S. health-care costs to top $4 trillion by 2016.* (news release) Retrieved June 2007 from http://www.forbes. com/forbeslife/health/feeds/hscout/2007/02/21/hscout602078. html

Francis, J., & Perlin, J. B. (2006). Improving performance through knowledge translation in the Veterans Health Administration. *Journal of Continuing Education in the Health Professions, 26*(1), 63–71.

Health Resources and Services Administration (HRSA). (2000). *National sample survey of registered nurses 2000.* Retrieved September 2003 from http://bhpr.hrsa.gov

Health Resources and Services Administration (HRSA). (2007). *The registered nurse population: Findings from the March 2004 national sample survey of registered nurses.* Washington, DC: U.S. Department of Health and Human Services.

Heckler, D. E. (2004). *Occupational employment projections to 2012.* Washington, DC: U.S. Department of Labor, Bureau of Labor Statistics.

Hersey, P., Blanchard, K. H., & Johnson, D. E. (2007). *Management of organizational behavior* (9th ed.). Upper Saddle River, NJ: Prentice Hall.

Institute of Medicine (IOM). (1999). *To err is human: Building a safer health system.* Washington, DC: National Academy Press.

Kausal, R. et al. (2005). The costs of a national health information network. *Annals of Internal Medicine, 143*(3), 165–173.

Kirkley, D. (2004). Clinical IT: Powering up data analysis for the nurse executive. *Nursing Economic$, 22*(3), 147–151.

Kleinke, J. D. (2005). Dot-gov: Market failure and the creation of a national health information technology system. *Health Affairs, 24*(5), 1263–1265.

Kupperschmidt, B. R. (2006). Addressing multigenerational conflict: Mutual respect and carefronting as strategy. *Online Journal of Issues in Nursing, 11*(2), posted 06/27/2006.

Leapfrog Group. (2007a). *The Leapfrog Group: Informing choices. Rewarding excellence. Getting health care right.* Retrieved July 2007 from http://www.leapfroggroup.org

Leapfrog Group. (2007b). *The Leapfrog Group: Hospital performance measurement initiatives.* Retrieved July 2007 from http://www.leapfroggroup.org

Meyers, S. (2007). Robots become RNs' little helpers. *Nurseweek,* May–June 2007, 12–13.

Moyer, V. A., & Elliott, E. J. (Eds.). (2004). *Evidence-based pediatrics and child health* (2nd ed.). London: BMJ Publishing Group.

O'Boyle, C., Robertson, C., & Secor-Turner, M. (2006a). Public health emergencies: Nurses' recommendations for effective actions. *American Association of Occupational Health Nurses Journal, 54*(8), 347–353.

O'Boyle, C., Robertson, C., & Secor-Turner, M. (2006b). Nurses' beliefs about public health emergencies: Fear of abandonment. *American Journal of Infection Control, 34*(6), 351–357.

Oermann, M. H., Floyd, J. A., Galvin, E. A., & Roop, J. C. (2006). Brief reports for disseminating systematic reviews to nurses. *Clinical Nurse Specialist, 20*(5), 233–240.

Poissant, L., Pereira, J., Tamblyn, R., & Kawasumi, Y. (2005). *Journal of the American Medical Informatics Association, 12*(5), 505–516.

Porter-O'Grady, T. (2003). A different age for leadership, Part 2: New rules, new roles. *Journal of Nursing Administration, 33*(3), 173–178.

Sackett, D. L., Rosenberg, W. M. C., Gray, J., Haynes, R. B., & Richardson, W. S. (1996). Evidence-based medicine: What it is and what it isn't. *British Medical Journal* (312), 71–72.

Salmond, S. W. (2007). Advancing evidence-based practice: A primer. *Orthopaedic Nursing, 26*(2), 114–125.

Secor-Turner, M., & O'Boyle, C. (2006). Nurses and emergency disasters: What is known. *American Journal of Infection Control, 34*(7), 414–420.

Sherman, R. O. (2006). Leading a multigenerational nursing workforce: Issues, challenges, and strategies. *Online Journal of Issues in Nursing, 11*(2), posted 06/29/2006.

Simpson, R. L. (2007). Easing the way for the electronic health record. *American Nurse Today, 2*(2), 48–50.

Steward, M. (2005). Electronic medical records: Privacy, confidentiality, liability. *Journal of Legal Medicine, 26*(4), 491–506.

Surowiecki, J. (2005). *The wisdom of crowds.* New York: Anchor Books.

U.S. Census Bureau. (2007). *Minority population tops 100 million.* U.S. Census Bureau News released May 17, 2007. Retrieved July 2007 from http://www.census.gov/Press-Release/www/releases/archives/population/010048.html

Vaughan, D. (2007). Bari closes patient care gap: Hospital robot allows immediate doctor-patient interaction. *Nursing Spectrum, 19A*(2).

Vinson, E. (2007). Managing bioterrorism mass casualties in an emergency department: Lessons learned from a rural community hospital disaster drill. *Disaster Management & Response, 5*(1), 18–21.

Vratny, A., & Shriver, D. (2007). A conceptual model for growing evidence-based practice. *Nursing Administration Quarterly, 31*(2), 162–170.

Weston, M. J. (2006). Integrating generational perspectives in nursing. *Online Journal of Issues in Nursing, 11*(2), posted 06/29/2006.

Zhan, C., & Miller, M. R. (2003), Excess length of stay, charges, and mortality attributable to medical injuries during hospitalization. *Journal of the American Medical Association, 290*(14), 1868–1874.

Designing Organizations

MediaLink

www.prenhall.com/sullivan

See the Companion Website for chapter-specific resources at
www.prenhall.com/sullivan.

Strategic Planning

Organizational Environment and Culture

Becoming a Magnet Hospital

Learning Outcomes

After completing this chapter, you will be able to:

1. Describe how organizational theories differ.
2. Describe the different types of health care organizations.
3. Explain how health care organizations are structured.
4. Demonstrate how strategic planning guides the organizational decision making.
5. Discuss how organizational environment affects success.
6. Explain how to become a magnet hospital.

Key Terms

Bureaucracy *p13*
Capitation *p23*
Chain of command *p13*
Diversification *p24*
Goals *p26*
Hawthorne effect *p14*
Heterarchy *p21*
Horizontal integration *p24*
Joint venture *p24*
Line authority *p13*

Magnet recognition program *p28*
Mission *p26*
Objectives *p27*
Organization *p12*
Organizational culture *p27*
Organizational environment *p27*
Philosophy *p26*
Redesign *p25*
Reengineering *p26*

Restructuring *p26*
Shared governance *p20*
Span of control *p13*
Staff authority *p13*
Strategic planning *p26*
Strategies *p27*
Values *p26*
Vertical integration *p24*
Vision statement *p26*

Within our society are numerous organizations—schools, churches, businesses, and so on. An **organization** is a collection of people working together under a defined structure to achieve predetermined outcomes using financial, human, and material resources. The justification for developing organizations is both rational and economic. Coordinated efforts capture more information and knowledge, purchase more technology, and produce more goods, services, opportunities, and securities than individual efforts. This chapter discusses organizational theory, structures, and functions.

Organizational Theories

The earliest recorded example of organizational thinking comes from the ancient Sumerian civilization, around 5000 B.C. The early Egyptians, Babylonians, Greeks, and Romans also gave thought to how groups were organized. Later, Machiavelli in the 1500s and Adam Smith in 1776 established the management principles we know as specialization and division of labor (Cannon, 1925). Nevertheless, organizational theory remained largely unexplored until the Industrial Revolution during the late 1800s and early 1900s when a number of approaches to the structure and management of organizations developed. The early philosophies are traditionally labeled classical theory and humanistic theory while later approaches include systems theory, contingency theory, chaos theory, and complexity theory.

CLASSICAL THEORY

The classical approach to organizations focuses almost exclusively on the structure of the formal organization. The main premise is efficiency through design. People are seen as operating most productively within a rational and well-defined task or organizational design. Therefore, one designs an organization by subdividing work, specifying tasks to be done, and only then fitting people into the plan. Classical theory is built around four elements: division and specialization of labor, chain of command, organizational structure, and span of control.

Division and Specialization of Labor

Dividing the work reduces the number of tasks that each employee must carry out, thereby increasing efficiency and improving the organization's product. This concept lends itself to proficiency and specialization. Therefore, division of work and specialization are seen as economically beneficial. In addition, managers can standardize the work to be done, which in turn provides greater control.

Chain of Command

The **chain of command** is the hierarchy of authority and responsibility within the organization. Authority is the right or power to direct activity, whereas responsibility is the obligation to attain objectives or perform certain functions. Both are derived from one's position within the organization and define accountability. The line of authority is such that higher levels of management delegate work to those below them in the organization.

One type of authority is **line authority**, the linear hierarchy through which activity is directed. Another type is **staff authority**, an advisory relationship; recommendations and advice are offered, but responsibility for the work is assigned to others. In ***Figure 2-1***, the relationships among the chief nurse executive, nurse manager, and staff nurse are examples of line authority. The relationship between the acute care nurse practitioner and the nurse manager illustrates staff authority. Neither the acute care nurse practitioner nor the nurse manager is responsible for the work of the other; instead, they collaborate to improve the efficiency and productivity of the unit for which the nurse manager is responsible.

Organizational Structure

Organizational structure describes the arrangement of the work group. It is a rational approach for designing an effective organization. Classical theorists developed the concept of departmentalization as a means to maintain command, reinforce authority, and provide a formal system for communication. The design of the organization is intended to foster the organization's survival and success.

Characteristically, the structure takes shape as a set of differentiated but interrelated functions. Max Weber (1958) proposed the term **bureaucracy** to define the ideal, intentionally rational, most efficient form of organization. Today this word has a negative connotation, suggesting long waits, inefficiency, and red tape.

Span of Control

Span of control addresses the pragmatic concern of how many employees a manager can effectively supervise. Complex organizations usually have numerous departments that are highly specialized and differentiated; authority is centralized, resulting in a tall organizational

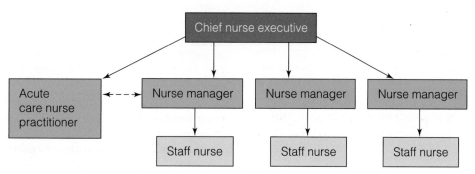

Figure 2-1 ● Chain of authority.

structure with many small work groups. Less complex organizations have flat structures; authority is decentralized, with several managers supervising large work groups. ***Figure 2-2*** depicts the differences.

In the professional bureaucracy, the operating core of professionals is the dominant feature. Decision making is usually decentralized, and the technostructure is underdeveloped. The support staff, however, is well developed. Most hospitals are professional bureaucracies.

The *divisionalized form* is characterized by a number of independent divisions that are joined by a mutual administration. Decision making is decentralized; both technostructure and support staffs are minimal. A multiorganizational health system is an example of the divisionalized design.

Adhocracy represents a fluid structure in which management, staff, and experts work together on teams. Power, coordination, and control are constantly shifting. Relationship-oriented structures (discussed later in this chapter) are particularly prone to change, and as relationships among and between health care providers shift and evolve so do power, coordination, and control.

Organizational theories suggest organizational structures. Traditional structures (described later in the chapter) operationalize the tenets of classic theory.

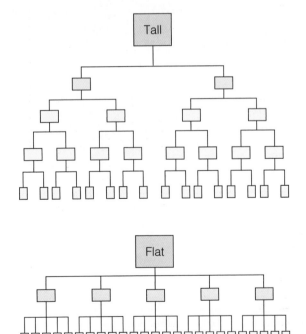

Figure 2-2 ● Contrasting spans of control. *From Managing Health Services Organizations and Systems, 4th ed. (p. 124), by B. B. Longest, J. S. Rakich, and K. Darr, 2000, Baltimore: Health Professions Press. Reprinted by permission.*

HUMANISTIC THEORY

Criticism of classical theory led to the development of humanistic theory, an approach identified with the human relations movement of the 1930s. A major assumption of this theory is that people desire social relationships, respond to group pressures, and search for personal fulfillment. This theory was developed as the result of a series of studies conducted by the Western Electric Company at its Hawthorne plant in Chicago. The first study was conducted to examine the effect of illumination on productivity. However, this study failed to find any relationship between the two. In most groups, productivity varied at random, and in one study productivity actually rose as illumination levels declined. The researchers concluded that unforeseen "psychological factors" were responsible for the findings. Further studies of working conditions, such as rest breaks and the length of the workweek, still failed to reveal a relationship to productivity. The researchers concluded that the social setting created by the research itself—that is, the special attention given workers as part of the research—enhanced productivity. This tendency for people to perform as expected because of special attention became known as the **Hawthorne effect**.

Although the findings are controversial, they led organizational theorists to focus on the social aspects of work and organizational design. (See Chapter 17 for a description of motivational theories.) One important assertion of this school of thought was that individuals cannot be coerced or bribed to do things they consider unreasonable; formal authority does not work without willing participants (Barnard, 1938).

SYSTEMS THEORY

Organizational theorists who maintain a systems perspective view productivity as a function of the interplay among structure, people, technology, and environment. Like nursing theories based on systems theory (such as those of Roy and Neuman), organizational theory defines system as a set of interrelated parts arranged in a unified whole (Robbins, 1983). Systems can be closed or open. Closed systems are self-contained and usually can be found only in the physical sciences. An open system, in contrast, interacts both internally and with its environment, much like a living organism.

An organization is a complex, sociotechnical, open system. This theory provides a framework by which the interrelated parts of the system and their functions can be studied. Resources, or input, such as employees, patients, materials, money, and equipment, are imported from the environment. Within the organization, energy and resources are utilized and transformed; work, a process called throughput, is performed to produce a product. The product, or output, is then exported to the environment. An organization, then, is a recurrent cycle of input, throughput, and output. Each health care organization—whether a hospital, ambulatory surgical center, or a home care agency, and so on—requires human, financial, and material resources. Each also provides a variety of services to treat illness, restore function, provide rehabilitation, and protect or promote wellness.

In this model, the manager is the catalyst for the input–throughput–output process. Managers are responsible for integrating information and other stimuli from the environment, such as legislation or changes in health care delivery, to coordinate and facilitate the work of the organization. *Figure 2-3* depicts a systems model of a health care organization.

Systems theorists have provided great insight into important organizational and human variables. However, systems theory does not recognize the vast complexity of organizations or the interactive effects of many variables.

CONTINGENCY THEORY

Contingency theorists believe organizational performance can be enhanced by matching an organization's structure to its environment. The environment is defined as the people, objects, and ideas outside the organization that influence the organization. The environment of a health care organization includes patients and potential patients; third-party payers, including Medicare and managed-care companies; regulators; competitors; and suppliers of physical facilities, personnel (such as schools of nursing and medicine), equipment, and pharmaceuticals.

Health care organizations are unique with respect to the kinds of products and services they offer. However,

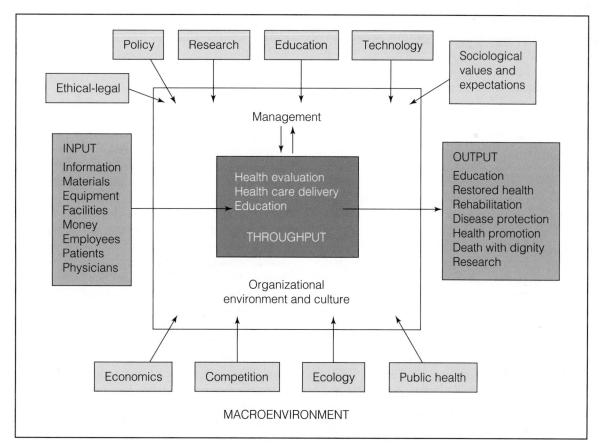

Figure 2-3 • The health care organization as an open system.

like all other organizations, health care organizations are shaped by external and internal forces. These forces stem from the economic and social environment, the technologies used in patient care, organizational size, and the abilities and limitations of the personnel involved in the delivery of health care, including nurses, physicians, technicians, administrators, and, of course, patients.

Given the variety of health care services and patients served today, it should come as no surprise that organizations differ with respect to the environments they face, the levels of training and skills of their caregivers, and the emotional and physical needs of patients. It is naive to think that the form of organization best for one type of patient in one type of environment is appropriate for another type of patient in a completely different environment. Think about the differences in the environment of a substance abuse treatment center compared to a women's health clinic. Thus, the optimal form of the organization is contingent on the circumstances faced by that organization.

CHAOS THEORY

Chaos theory, which was inspired by the finding of quantum mechanics, challenges us to look at organizations and the nature of relationships and proposes that nature's work does not follow a straight line. The elements of nature often move in a circular, ebbing fashion; a stream destined for the ocean, for example, never takes a straight path. In fact, very little in life operates as a straight line; people's relationships to each other and to their work certainly do not. This notion challenges traditional thinking regarding the design of organizations. Organizations are living, self-organizing systems that are complex and self-adaptive.

The life cycle of an organization is fully dependent on its adaptability and response to changes in its environment. The tendency is for the organization to grow. When it becomes a large entity, it tends to stabilize and develop more formal standards. From that point, however, the organization tends to lose its adaptability and responsiveness to its environment.

Chaos theory suggests that the drive to create permanent organizational structures is doomed to fail. The set of rules that guided the industrial notions of organizational function and integrity must be discarded, and newer principles that ensure flexibility, fluidity, speed of adaptability, and cultural sensitivity must emerge. The role of leadership in these changing organizations is to build resilience in the midst of change, to maintain a balance between tension and order, which promotes creativity and prevents instability.

This theory requires us to abandon our attachment to any particular model of design and to reflect instead on creative and flexible formats that can be quickly adjusted and changed as the organization's realities shift.

COMPLEXITY THEORY

Complexity theory originated in the computational sciences when scientists noted that random events interfered with expectations. No longer could linear cause and effect explain outcomes. They realized that it is more difficult to solve a problem than to check if the solution was correct. Additionally, the more complex the task, the less likely the solution is an absolute one (Goldreich, 2005).

The theory is useful in health care because the environment is rife with randomness and complex tasks. Patients' conditions change in an instant; necessary staff are not available; or equipment fails, all without warning. Tasks involve intricate interactions between and among staff, patients, and the environment. Managing in such ambiguous circumstances requires considering every aspect of the system as it interacts and adapts to changes.

Complexity theory explains why health care organizations, in spite of concerted efforts, struggle with patient safety. Unlike the airline industry, for example, that has been successful in eliminating system errors, health care continues to focus on patient care providers rather than the system as a whole. Using high reliability teams to recognize even minor variations in expected outcomes and intervene has been effective in preventing serious errors in health care settings (McKeon, Oswaks, & Cunningham, 2006).

Hierarchy is less important in complexity theory. Every encounter between a patient and a caregiver offers information about possible solutions to problems, according to Bleich and Kosiak (2007). Encouraging the flow of information between and among all members of the team, leaders and followers, whether top-down, bottom-up, or sideways, is the manager's task. Relationship-oriented structures (explained later in the chapter) facilitate this task.

All of the theories that consider an organization as a total system, including contingency, chaos, and complexity theory, value individual contributions to the organization. In a review of research covering more than 50 years, however, Mick and Mark (2005) found that nurses' contributions to the internal work processes in health care organizations were few. Relationship-oriented structures (discussed later in the chapter) offer opportunities for nurses to participate appropriately in organizational decision making.

Traditional Organizational Structures

The optimal organizational structure integrates organizational goals, size, technology, and environment. When structure is not aligned with organizational needs, the organization's response to environmental change diminishes; decisions are delayed, overlooked, or poor; conflict results; and performance deteriorates (Porter-O'Grady, 1994). Organizational structure is an important tool through which managers can increase organizational efficiency. Reorganization occurs in response to changes in organizational goals, size, technology, or environment.

FUNCTIONAL STRUCTURE

In *functional structures,* employees are grouped in departments by specialty, with similar tasks being performed by the same group, similar groups operating out of the same department, and similar departments reporting to the same manager. In a functional structure, all nursing tasks fall under nursing service; the same is true of other functional areas. Functional structures tend to centralize decision making because the functions converge at the top of the organization.

Functional structures have several weaknesses. Coordination across functions is poor. Decision-making responsibilities can pile up at the top and overload senior managers, who may be uninformed regarding day-to-day operations. Responses to the external environment that require coordination across functions are slow. General management training is limited because most employees move up the organization within functional departments. Functional structures are uncommon in today's rapidly changing health care environment.

SERVICE-LINE STRUCTURE

Service-line structures also are called product-line or service-integrated structures. In a service-line structure, all functions needed to produce a product or service are grouped together in self-contained units (*Figure 2-4*). A large health care institution that acquires a smaller clinic may operate it as a self-contained unit. The service-integrated structure is decentralized; units are based on product, service, geographical location, or type of customer.

Integrated structures are preferred in large and complex organizations because the same activity (for example, hiring) is assigned to several self-contained units, which can respond rapidly to the unit's immediate needs. This is extremely appropriate when environmental uncertainty is high and the organization requires frequent adaptation and innovation.

One of the strengths of the service-line structure is its potential for rapid change in an unstable environment. Because each division is specialized and its outputs can be tailored to the situation, client satisfaction is high. Coordination across function (nursing, dietary, pharmacy,

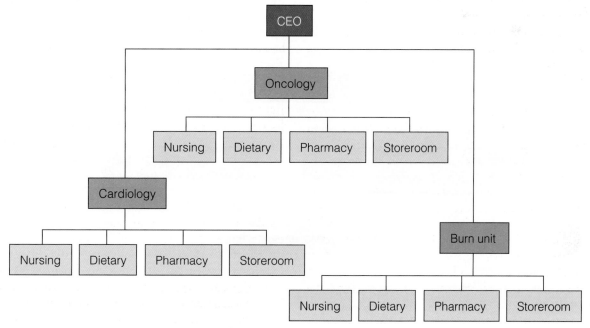

Figure 2-4 ● Service-line structure.

and so on) occurs easily; work partners identify with their own service and can compromise or collaborate with other service functions to meet service goals and reduce conflict. Service goals receive priority under this organizational structure because employees see the service outcomes as the primary purpose of their organization.

The major weaknesses of service-integrated structures include possible duplication of resources (such as ads for new positions) and lack of in-depth technical training and specialization. Coordination across service categories (oncology, cardiology, and the burn unit, for example) is difficult; services operate independently and often compete. Each service category, which is independent and autonomous, has separate and often duplicate staff and competes with other service areas for resources.

With a service-line structure, a department of nursing may not be shown on the organizational chart. This presents a challenge to nursing administrators and managers to maintain nursing standards across service lines (Fitzpatrick, McElroy, & DeWoody, 2001).

HYBRID STRUCTURE

When an organization grows, it typically organizes both self-contained units and functional units; the result is a hybrid organization (**Figure 2-5**).

The strengths of the hybrid structure are that it:

- Provides simultaneous coordination within product divisions while maintaining the quality of each function
- Improves the alignment between corporate and service or product goals
- Fosters better adaptation to the environment while still maintaining efficiency.

The weakness of hybrid structures is conflict between top administration and managers. Managers often resent administrators' intrusions into what they see as their own area of responsibility. Over time, organizations tend to accumulate large corporate staffs to oversee divisions in an attempt to provide functional coordination across service or product structures.

MATRIX STRUCTURE

The matrix structure is unique and complex (**Figure 2-6**); it integrates both product and functional structures into one overlapping structure. In a matrix structure, different managers are responsible for function and product. For example, the nurse manager for the oncology clinic may report to the vice president for nursing as well as the vice president for outpatient services.

Matrices tend to develop where there are strong outside pressures for a dual organizational focus on product and function. The matrix is appropriate in a highly uncertain environment that changes frequently but also requires organizational expertise.

A major weakness of the matrix structure is its dual authority, which can be frustrating and confusing for departmental managers and employees. Excellent interpersonal skills are required from the managers involved. A matrix organization is time consuming, because frequent meetings are required to resolve problems and conflicts; the structure will not work unless participants can see beyond their own functional area to the big organizational picture. Finally, if one side of the matrix is more closely aligned with organizational objectives, that side may become dominant.

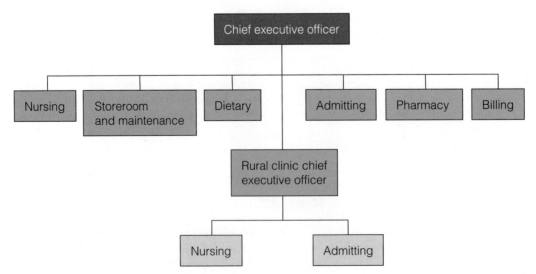

Figure 2-5 ● Hybrid structure.

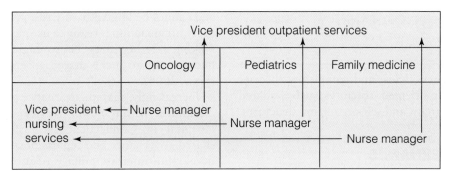

Figure 2-6 ● Matrix structure.

PARALLEL STRUCTURE

Parallel structure is a structure unique to health care. It is the result of complex relationships that exist between the formal authority of the health care organization and the authority of its medical staff. In a parallel structure, the medical staff is separate and autonomous from the organization. The result is an organizational dilemma: two lines of authority. One line extends from the governing body to the chief executive officer and then to the managerial structure; the other line extends from the governing body to the medical staff. These two intersect in departments such as nursing, in which decision making involves both managerial and clinical elements.

Parallel structures are found in health care institutions with a functional structure and separate medical governance structure (**Figure 2-7** ●). Parallel structures are becoming less successful as health care organizations integrate into newer models that incorporate physician practice under the organizational umbrella.

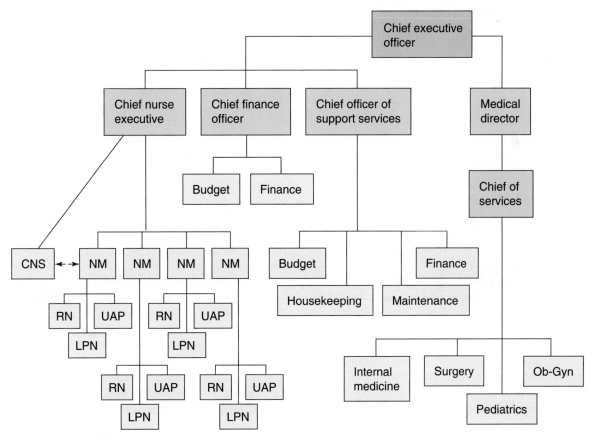

Figure 2-7 ● Parallel structure.

Relationship-Oriented Structures

Systems, contingency, chaos, and complexity theories suggest relationship-oriented structures, such as shared governance, heterarchy, and self-organizing structures.

SHARED GOVERNANCE

Shared governance is based on a philosophy that nursing practice is best determined by nurses. Shared governance, however, is a concept, not a structure (Porter-O'Grady, 2004). Shared governance has evolved from the desire to build accountable decision making in hospitals, especially among the nursing staff. Participative decision making is the hallmark of shared governance. Interdependence and accountability are the basis for constructing a network of making nursing practice decisions in a decentralized environment. As a result, nurses gain significant control over their practice, efficiency and accountability are improved, and feelings of powerlessness are mitigated.

Shared governance allows staff nurses significant control over major decisions about nursing practice. These systems usually are built on a foundation of primary nursing, peer review, and some provision for clinical advancement. Most shared governance systems are similar to and reflect the principles often found in academic or medical governance models. For example, nurses may elect a council to represent the nursing staff collectively. Other councils may exist, such as a human resources council in charge of staffing levels, recruitment, and retention; a nursing council in charge of care standards, audit criteria, research, and staff education; and individual unit councils.

Some shared governance systems incorporate elected advisory boards for each service or clinical department. From these boards is elected a senate or congress that meets several times a year to decide larger policy issues.

The ultimate outcome of shared governance is that nurses participate in an accountable forum to control their own practice within the health care organization. The assumption is that nursing staffs, like medical staffs, will predetermine the clinical skills of staff nurses and monitor the work of each through peer review while deciding on other practice issues through accountable forums or councils.

Shared governance is by design and concept an invitational process. Because of its dynamic nature, it cannot be contained or owned in any exclusive framework and cannot be limited to any specific work group. Not every organization is ready to use participative decision making or they may be so highly structured and bureaucratic to make shared governance not feasible (Hess, 2004).

Increasingly, shared governance principles integrate disciplines within newer service settings. Hartford Hospital in Connecticut successfully implemented shared governance and reports positive experiences in developing interdisciplinary relationships (Caramanica, 2004).

As the continuum of care and the linkage of services become more important components of organizational design, shared governance provides a process and structure that supports decision making, quality imperatives, and collaboration among disciplines. Departmental and divisional structures are disappearing, and soon discipline-specific structures may give way to service configurations that address the continuum of care in a large health plan. Shared governance principles are increasingly being used as a framework for the models of structure that will integrate the organization's functions and structures.

Partners in care include all the professional and technical workers that operate within the patient care continuum. This group includes physicians, who have historically been viewed as working independently of the functional relationship of institutional providers. Because partnership is the driving theme of shared leadership and decision making, bringing the physician into the partnership creates the essential relationship necessary to initiate effective service arrangements, evaluate care, and build effective supporting structures.

Integrative care models and multidisciplinary team approaches to care further facilitate the demand for an organizational structure more supportive of team members than that which is currently available in the more traditional hospital hierarchies. Creating more collateral structures that reflect the relationship of the players to each other acts more clearly in concert with interdisciplinary work than do more traditional structures.

Implications for altering service, operations, and governance are considerable. The fact that principles of shared governance reflecting partnership, equity, accountability, and ownership form the basis for these newer approaches indicates the strong foundations that shared governance has established in successfully structuring an empowered nursing organization. It is natural to assume that these processes would expand as the health system moves to point-of-service design and constructs the empowerment processes necessary to make these more integrated systems function effectively.

The continuum of care and the structures that support it will have a major impact on nurses and the design of patient service organizations of the future. The configuration of these systems will be radically different from those found in the past. New foundations for building knowledge and conducting research will emerge as newer organizational forms take shape.

HETERARCHY STRUCTURE

One such innovative structure has been suggested by organizational consultant, nurse Tim Porter-O'Grady (Porter-O'Grady & Malloch, 2002). **Heterarchy** is a relational design based on the concept of connections (see *Figure 2-8*●). In contrast to organizational structures based on industrial models, heterarchy acknowledges the linkages among people and their relationships.

SELF-ORGANIZING STRUCTURES

A self-organizing (self-renewing) structure is flexible and able to respond to both internal and external change. The only requirement of this structure is self-reference; that is, future structures are consistent with the previously established identity and its past. Rigid, permanent structures are avoided; the organizational structure changes when the need arises. Roles and structures are created out of need and interest; relationships, exchanges, and connections among employees are nurtured as the primary source of organizational creativity and success.

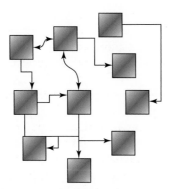

Figure 2-8 ● Heterarchy structure. *From* Quantum Leadership: A Textbook of New Leadership, *by T. Porter-O'Grady and K. Malloch, 2002, Sudbury, MA: Jones and Bartlett Publishers (www. jbpub.com). Reprinted with permission.*

Health Care Organizations

TYPES OF HEALTH CARE ORGANIZATIONS

Today's health care organizations differ in ownership, role, activity, and size. Ownership can be either private or government, voluntary (not for profit) or investor-owned (for profit), and sectarian or nonsectarian (*Figure 2-9*●). Private organizations are usually owned by corporations or religious entities, whereas government organizations are operated by city, county, state, or federal entities, such as the Indian Health Service. Voluntary organizations are usually not for profit, meaning that surplus monies are reinvested into the community. Investor-owned, or for-profit corporations, distribute surplus monies back to the investors, who expect a profit. Sectarian agencies have religious affiliations.

Hospitals

Hospitals are frequently classified by length of stay and type of service. Most hospitals are acute (short-term or episodic) care facilities, and they may be classified as general or special care facilities, such as pediatric, rehabilitative, and psychiatric facilities. Many hospitals also serve as teaching institutions for nurses, physicians, and other health care professionals.

The term teaching hospital commonly designates a hospital associated with a medical school that maintains a house staff of residents on call 24 hours a day. Nonteaching hospitals, in contrast, have only private physicians on staff. Because private physicians are less accessible than house staff, the medical supervision of patient care differs, as may the role of the nurse. This designation is changing dramatically as new forms of physician groups and allied practices emerge in partnerships with hospitals and medical schools. Some organizations hire hospitalists, physicians who provide care only to hospital inpatients; those who care for patients in intensive care are known as intensivists.

Long-Term Care Facilities

Long-term care facilities provide professional nursing care and rehabilitative services. They may be freestanding or part of a hospital, and length of stay is limited. Residential care facilities, also known as nursing homes, are sheltered environments in which the care is provided by nursing assistants with supervision from licensed professional or registered nurses.

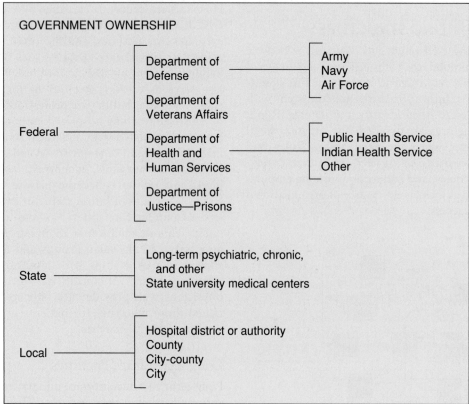

Figure 2-9 ● Types of ownership in health care organizations. *From* Managing Health Services Organizations and Systems, *4th ed. (p. 173), by B. B. Longest, J. S. Rakich, and K. Darr, 2000, Baltimore: Health Professions Press. Reprinted by permission.*

Ambulatory Care Centers

A growing proportion of health care is delivered in ambulatory settings. Physician's offices, emergency rooms, surgical centers, birthing centers, clinics in pharmacies, diagnostic imaging centers, and family planning clinics are just a few examples of the variety of ambulatory services available. Many hospitals offer both on- and off-campus outpatient sites to compete in this growing area of health care.

Home Health Care Agencies

Another growth area is in home health care. Home health care is the intermittent, temporary delivery of health care in the home by skilled or unskilled providers. With shortened lengths of hospital stay, more acutely ill patients are discharged to recuperate at home. Furthermore, more people are surviving life-threatening illnesses or trauma and require extended care. The primary service provided by home care agencies is nursing care; however, larger home care agencies also offer other professional services, such as physical or occupational therapy, and durable medical equipment, such as ventilators, hospital beds, home oxygen equipment, and other medical supplies. Hospice care for the final days of a patient's terminal illness may be provided by a home care agency or a hospital.

Free-standing Clinics

Clinics that provide ambulatory care have sprung up in shopping centers, pharmacies, and discount stores. Staffed by nurse practitioners, these clinics provide physicals or treat walk-in patients for common and recurring minor illnesses, such as colds or sore throats.

Temporary Service Agencies

An outgrowth of the home health care industry is the temporary service agency. These agencies provide nurses and other health care workers to hospitals that are temporarily short-staffed; they also provide private duty nurses to individual patients either at home or in the hospital.

Managed Health Care Organizations

The managed health care organization is a system in which a group of providers is responsible for delivering services (that is, managing health care) through an organized arrangement with a group of individuals (for example, all employees of one company, all Medicaid patients in the state). Different types of managed-care organizations exist: health maintenance organizations (HMOs), preferred provider organizations (PPOs), and point-of-service plans (POS).

The HMO is a geographically organized system that provides an agreed-on package of health maintenance and treatment services. There are four different types of HMOs:

1. **Staff Model.** Physicians are HMO employees paid a salary.
2. **Independent Practice Association (IPA).** Physicians maintain individual or group practices, but contract with an HMO to serve enrollees for a negotiated fee.
3. **Group Model.** The HMO contracts with a multispecialty group to provide enrollees' services for a negotiated fee.
4. **Network Model.** The HMO contracts with two or more IPAs (independent or group practices) to provide enrollee services at a fixed monthly fee per enrollee, called **capitation**.

In a PPO, the managed-care organization contracts with independent practitioners to provide enrollees with established discounted rates. If an enrollee obtains services from a nonparticipating provider, significant copayments are usually required.

Point-of-service (POS) is considered to be an HMO–PPO hybrid. In a POS, enrollees may use the network of managed-care providers to go outside the network as they wish. However, use of a provider outside the network usually results in additional costs in copayments, deductibles, or premiums.

The current decade has seen a decline in managed-care organizations as both patients and providers have become dissatisfied with its limitations and inflexibility. Patients are restricted to a limited provider group, and providers are pressured to constrain costs, often by cutting time spent with patients, ordering fewer tests, and reducing referrals that they fear may be denied by the organization's administrators.

INTERORGANIZATIONAL RELATIONSHIPS

With increased competition for resources and public and governmental pressures for better efficiency and effectiveness, organizations have been forced to establish relationships with one another for their continued survival. Multihospital systems and multiorganizational arrangements, both formal and informal, are mechanisms by which these relationships have formed.

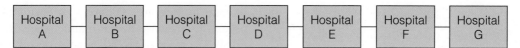

Figure 2-10 ● Horizontal integration.

Arrangements between or among organizations that provide the same or similar services are examples of **horizontal integration**. For instance, all hospitals in the network provide comparable services, as shown in *Figure 2-10*●.

Vertical integration, in contrast, is an arrangement between or among dissimilar but related organizations to provide a continuum of services. An affiliation of a health maintenance organization with a hospital, pharmacy, and nursing facility represents vertical integration (see *Figure 2-11*●).

Besides enhancing survival, vertical integration is thought to improve coordination of services, quality, cost effectiveness, efficiency, and bargaining power; promote continuity of care and improve community service; expand services, which enhances competition; strengthen education and research opportunities; and use human resources more efficiently (Newhouse & Mills, 1999).

Numerous arrangements using horizontal and vertical integration can be found, and these models likely will become the common structure for delivery of health care. Examples of such arrangements include affiliations, consortia, alliances, mergers, and consolidations. An assortment of health care agencies under the umbrella of a corporate network is shown in the example in *Figure 2-12*●.

DIVERSIFICATION

Diversification provides another strategy for survival in today's economy. Diversification is the expansion of an organization into new arenas. Two types of diversification are common: concentric and conglomerate.

Concentric diversification occurs when an organization complements its existing services by expanding into new markets or broadening the types of services it currently has available. For example, a children's hospital might open a day-care center for developmentally delayed children or offer drop-in facilities for sick child care.

Conglomerate diversification is the expansion into areas that differ from the original product or service. The purpose of conglomerate diversification is to obtain a source of income that will support the organization's product or service. For example, a long-term care facility might develop real estate or purchase a company that produces durable medical equipment.

Another type of diversification common to health care is the **joint venture**. A joint venture is a partnership in which each partner contributes different areas of expertise, resources, or services to create a new product or service. In one type of joint venture, one partner (general partner) finances and manages the venture, whereas the other partner (limited partner) provides a needed service. Joint ventures between

Figure 2-11 ● Vertical integration.

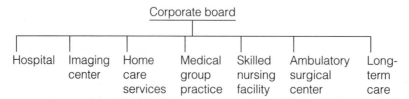

Figure 2-12 ● Corporate health care network.

health care organizations and physicians are becoming increasingly common. Integrated health care organizations, hospitals, and clinics seek physician and/or practitioner groups they can bond (capture) in order to obtain more referrals. The health care organization as financier and manager is the general partner, and physicians are limited partners.

A joint venture also might involve two organizations with different areas of expertise who join together to create a new product or service. An alliance between the Cerner Corporation who supplies hospital information systems and the University of Kansas School of Nursing to develop a clinical system for teaching students evidence-based practice is an example of combining resources of both organizations to develop an innovative new product (Connors, Weaver, Warren, & Miller, 2002).

Redesigning, Restructuring, and Reengineering

Health care is a dynamic environment with multiple factors impinging on continuity and stability. Changes in reimbursement, supply of staff, political shifts, and the economy are just a few of the factors that make workplace redesign, restructure, and reengineering a reality today (Edens, 2005).

In **redesign**, the distribution of activities, role overlap, excess specialization, and waste are examined. The goal is to design each job according to appropriate tasks and necessary qualifications and to have all jobs fit together so that the organization's work gets done in the most efficient and effective manner. Redesign usually focuses on the individual jobs in one clinical specialty area, although each area may be undergoing job redesign simultaneously or consecutively (see job analysis in Chapter 15).

BARRIERS TO JOB REDESIGN

Some common problems emerge in the redesign of jobs. For example, the nurse manager's role may change from leader and director of unit staff to that of coordinator of staff activities. Somehow, the notion of coordinator seems inconsistent with our cultural stereotypes of leadership. We usually think of a leader as the person in charge, or the boss. That stereotype of leadership tends to include the unilateral and unquestioned use of power with objectives, strategies, and evaluation defined strictly from the leader's perspective.

A number of factors other than the power afforded by virtue of job title and reporting relationships are involved in effective leadership. Effective leadership is accepted leadership, and there are many ways to foster acceptance of the nurse manager's legitimate organizational power (see Chapter 7). If effectiveness means being a coordinator as opposed to being the boss, then the strategies and techniques involved in carrying out that role are what the nurse manager should use.

Another barrier to job redesign is that the values implicit in job redesign may be at odds with those of the organization's administration. The notion of providing autonomy, feedback, greater responsibility, and self-direction in the performance of jobs may not be in tune with the philosophy and history of the organizational hierarchy—matters that are not under the nurse manager's immediate discretion or control. However, different management areas afford different degrees of responsibility, and there may be a good deal of flexibility within the limits of the organization's rules, especially with the flux in today's environment. Job redesign is just another tool to use within the limits of the situation at hand.

In some cases, staff members are reluctant to engage in job redesign or other motivational efforts because they fear that increased productivity may have implications for their job security. They are concerned that if productivity increases sufficiently, some people may lose their jobs because they are no longer needed to accomplish the work. Increased productivity, however, not only eases the workload but also, if properly managed (for example, rewarded), is likely to result in greater satisfaction and organizational commitment as well as less absenteeism and turnover. Also, fears regarding job security usually focus solely on the quantity of work and ignore the quality of work as a separate, but equally important, dimension. Motivating staff members involves both of these dimensions, but job enrichment most consistently increases job satisfaction and work quality rather than the quantity of work produced. The fourth major barrier to job redesign is that not everyone desires change or growth in his or her job. Some people prefer to have their work clearly prescribed, unvarying in its content or procedure, and highly predictable from day to day.

Still another major barrier to job redesign is the lack of exact specifications of what is to be accomplished by redesigning an individual's job. For that reason, organizations may restructure and reengineer systems.

RESTRUCTURING AND REENGINEERING

Job redesign focuses on individual jobs; **restructuring** and **reengineering** examine the entire health organization's structure with a goal of improving the organization's functioning and productivity.

Organizations restructure to improve efficiency and enhance effectiveness by changing the way the organization is structured. The administrative structure changes, as do reporting relationships and communication channels. Restructuring naturally follows organizational affiliations, mergers, and the establishment of integrated health care systems as efforts to reduce duplication among the network's various entities ensue. In restructuring, coordination of work effort is stressed and interdependence valued. Organizationally based models, such as case management, total quality management, and product-line management, are used in system reorganization.

Reengineering involves examining and improving the process by which health care is delivered. Reengineering usually involves the entire organization and is collaborative, data driven, and patient focused. Reengineering results in major change in the workplace (Edens, 2005).

Reengineering is very complex and often radical. A new approach to the organization of patient care is adopted. Nurses, physicians, and other health care professionals develop different teams and the use of patient outcomes are integral parts of restructuring and reengineering. Working in collaborative teams and using a multidisciplinary approach requires open communication, the ability to accept and give criticism, clarity about responsibilities, and accountability by all. Adopting these behaviors is challenging and stressful, and some individuals resist it. The challenge for nurse managers is to help staff members understand the ultimate goal, participate in the process, and use their professional expertise to contribute to the well-being of the organization's patients, both now and in the future.

Nurse managers are key players in the redesign efforts. They are expected not only to initiate change while reducing costs, maintaining or improving quality of care, coaching and mentoring, and team building, but also to do so in an ever-changing environment full of ambiguities while their own responsibilities are expanded.

Strategic Planning

Successful organizations, both for profit and not for profit, have learned that they must focus their resources on a limited number of activities. The competitive health care environment requires organizations to respond to consumer demands for quality and accountability and to market their expertise to the public.

Strategic planning is the organization's process to:

- Identify a preferred future
- Recognize potential environmental changes
- Analyze current strengths and weaknesses
- Determine goals, objectives, specific actions, responsible persons or groups, how met goals will be evaluated, and a time line for successful completion
- Establish a plan for ongoing evaluation of progress and reexamination of goals, objectives, and activities.

This is a time-consuming and demanding process and should not be undertaken hurriedly. Put in use, however, a well-thought-out strategic plan guides the organization toward its goals, helps all the staff stay directed, and prevents the organization from responding to inappropriate requests.

A strategic plan projects the organization's goals and activities into the future, usually 2 to 5 years ahead. Based on the organization's philosophy and leaders' assessment of their organization and the environment, strategic planning guides the direction the organization is to take.

The **philosophy** is a written statement that reflects the organizational values, vision, and mission. **Values** are the beliefs or attitudes one has about people, ideas, objects, or actions that form a basis for behavior. Organizations use value statements to identify those beliefs or attitudes esteemed by the organizational leaders.

A **vision statement** describes the goal to which the organization aspires. The vision statement is designed to inspire and motivate employees to achieve a desired state of affairs. "Our vision is to be a regional integrated health care delivery system providing premier health care services, professional and community education, and health care research," is an example of a vision statement for a health care system.

The **mission** of an organization is a broad, general statement of the organization's reason for existence. Developing the mission is the necessary first step to designing a strategic plan. "Our mission is to improve the health of the people and communities we serve," is an example of a mission statement that guides decision making for the organization. Purchasing a medical equipment company, for example, might not be considered because it fails to meet the mission of improving the community's health.

Once the environment and mission of the organization has been clarified, goals are determined. **Goals** are specific statements of what outcome is to be achieved. Goals describe outcomes that are measurable and precise. "Every patient will be satisfied with his or her care" is an example of a goal.

Goals apply to the entire organization, whereas **objectives** are specific to an individual unit. A nursing objective to meet the above goal might be "Provide appropriate information and education to patients from preadmission to discharge." **Strategies** follow objectives and specify what actions will be taken. "Implement patient education classes for prenatal patients" is an example of a strategy to meet the patient satisfaction objective.

Other categories in a strategic plan include the personnel responsible for each activity, the projected cost, criteria to establish that the goal has been met, expected date of completion, and the current status.

The process of doing strategic planning involves gathering a planning committee composed of (at least):

- Top-level administrators
- Representatives of those closest to the work
- Staff to collect data and distribute information
- Willingness by all involved to contribute.

People who are enthusiastic, experienced, and committed to the organization are the best representatives to the planning committee. Naysayers can be included once some parts of the plan are formulated. Everyone in the organization must be involved even peripherally. "Buy-in" is critical to the plan's success.

Strategic planning is an ongoing process, not an end in itself. It requires meticulous attention to how the organization is meeting its goals and, if goals are not met, what the reasons are for the variance. Maybe the goal needs to change, or possibly other personnel should be assigned to the task. Perhaps a change in the environment (reimbursement) or within the organization (shortage of key personnel) requires the goal to be abandoned. Continual evaluation will help the organization target its resources best.

Organizational Environment and Culture

The terms **organizational environment** and **organizational culture** both describe internal conditions in the work setting. Organizational environment is the systemwide conditions that contribute to a positive or negative work setting. The American Association of Critical-Care Nurses (2005) named six characteristics of a healthy work environment. They are:

- Skilled communication
- True collaboration
- Effective decision making
- Appropriate staffing
- Meaningful recognition
- Authentic leadership.

A positive environment directly affects better patient outcomes (Aiken et al., 2002). The nurse manager plays a key role in maintaining a positive environment. Cummings (2006) found that resonant (defined as emotionally intelligent) leaders maintained a positive environment for nurses who remained employed after organizational restructuring. Conversely, the researchers found negative effects if the leaders were dissonant.

One way to assess the organizational environment is to evaluate the qualities of those hired for key positions in the organization. An organization in which nursing leaders are innovative, creative, and energetic will tend to operate in a fast-moving, goal-oriented fashion. If humanistic, interpersonal skills are sought in candidates for leadership positions, the organization will focus on human resources, employees, and patient advocacy (Hersey, Blanchard, & Johnson, 2007).

Organizational culture, on the other hand, are the basic assumptions and values held by members of the organization (Kaissi, 2006). These are often known as the unstated "rules of the game" (Sullivan, 2004). For example, who wears a lab coat? When is report given? To whom? Is tardiness tolerated? How late is acceptable?

Like environment, organizational culture varies from one institution to the next and subcultures and even countercultures, groups whose values and goals differ significantly from those of the dominant organization, may exist. A subculture is a group that has shared experiences or like interests and values. Nurses form a subculture within health care environments. They share a common language, rules, rituals, dress, and have their own unstated rules. Individual units also can become subcultures.

Besides organizational cultures differing between institutions, culture may differ between the organization and its subculture. If the subculture's norms and traditions are in agreement with the organization's, then consonance occurs; if not, dissonance occurs. Evaluating an organization's culture is essential when a merger is being considered. Ignoring issues of organizational culture can result in one culture becoming dominant (McConnell, 2000). Unintended consequences

MediaLink Determining an Organizational Philosophy

may result, including poor morale and, ultimately, loss of employees. More than one merger, established for financial reasons without consideration of people issues, has failed.

Becoming a Magnet Hospital

Developed in 1994 by the American Nurses Credentialing Center (ANCC), the **magnet recognition program** designates organizations that "recognize health care organizations that provide nursing excellence" (ANCC, 2007). To qualify for recognition as a magnet hospital the organization must demonstrate that they are:

- Promoting quality in a setting that supports professional practice
- Identifying excellence in the delivery of nursing services to patients/residents
- Disseminating "best practices" in nursing services.

Becoming a magnet hospital requires a significant investment of time and financial resources. Nonethe-less, 251 health care organizations in 44 states have received this prestigious recognition (ANCC, 2007). Even among those institutions unlikely to achieve magnet status, using selected criteria can help to improve nursing care and retain valued nurses (McClure, 2005). Additionally, providing a strong nursing support system pays off. In spite of a national nursing shortage, magnet hospitals have been successful in retaining and recruiting nurses (Aiken, Havens, & Sloane, 2000).

Systems involving participatory management and shared governance create organizational environments that reward decision making, creativity, independence, and autonomy. These organizations retain and recruit independent, accountable professionals. Organizations that empower nurses to make decisions will better meet consumer requests. As the health care environment continues to evolve, more and more organizations are adopting consumer-sensitive cultures that require accountability and decision making from nurses.

What You Know Now

- The schools of organizational theory are classical theory, humanistic theory, systems theory, contingency theory, chaos theory, and complexity theory.
- Organizations can be viewed as social systems consisting of people working in a predetermined pattern of relationships who strive toward a goal. The goal of health care organizations is to provide a particular mix of health services.
- Traditional organizational structures are functional, service-line, hybrid, matrix, and parallel structures.
- Relationship-oriented structures include shared governance, heterarchy, and self-organizing.
- Integration, diversification, and joint ventures are strategies used by organizations to survive in today's competitive environment.
- Shared governance provides the framework for empowerment and partnership within the health care organization.
- Organizational restructure and redesign characterize changing dynamics in health care.
- Strategic planning is a process used by organizations to focus their resources on a limited number of activities.
- Organizational environment and culture affect the internal conditions of the work setting.
- The magnet hospital recognition program identifies hospitals that provide excellent nursing care.

Questions to Challenge You

1. Secure a copy of the organizational chart from your employment or clinical site. Would you describe the organization the same way the chart depicts it? If not, redraw a chart to illustrate how you see the organization.
2. What organizational structure would you prefer? Think about how you might go about finding an organization that meets your criteria.

3. Organizational theories explain how organizations function. Which theory or theories describes your organization's functioning? Do you think it is the same theory your organization's administrators would use to describe it? Explain.
4. Have you been involved in strategic planning? If so, explain what happened and how well it worked in directing the organization's activities.
5. Using the six characteristics of a healthy work environment in the chapter, evaluate the organization where you work or have clinicals. How well does it rate? What changes would improve the environment?

Explore MediaLink

Additional interactive resources for this chapter can be found on the Website at http://www.prenhall. com/sullivan. Click on Chapter 2 to select activities for this chapter.

- Video Overview
- NCLEX® Review Questions
- Critical Thinking Activities
- Current Events
- Nursing Leadership and Management in Action
- MediaLinks

References

Aiken, L. H., Clarke, S. P., Sloane, D. M., Sochalski, J., & Silber, J. H. (2002). Hospital nurse staffing and patient mortality, nurse burnout, and job dissatisfaction. *Journal of the American Medical Association, 288*(16), 1987–1993.

Aiken, L. H., Havens, D., & Sloane, D. (2000). The magnet nursing services recognition program: A comparison of two groups of magnet hospitals. *American Journal of Nursing, 100*(3), 26–35.

American Association of Critical-Care Nurses (ANCC). (2005). *AACN standards for establishing and sustaining health work environments: A journey to excellence.* Retrieved July 2007 from www.aacn.org

American Nurses Credentialing Center. (2007). *Magnet recognition program.* Retrieved July 2007 from http://www .nursecredentialing.org/magnet/index.html

Barnard, C. I. (1938). *The functions of the executive.* Cambridge, MA: Harvard University Press.

Bleich, M. R., & Kosiak, C. P. (2007). Managing, leading, and following. In *Leading and Managing in Nursing* (4th ed.), by P. S. Yoder-Wise. St. Louis, MO: Mosby Elsevier.

Cannon, E. (Ed.). (1925). *Adam Smith, An inquiry into the nature and causes of the wealth of nations* (4th ed.). London: Methuen. (Original work published 1776)

Caramanica, L. (2004). Shared governance: Hartford Hospital's experience. *Online Journal of Issues in Nursing, 9*(1), retrieved December 2007 at http://www.nursingworld.org/ MainMenuCategories/ANAMarketplace/ANAPeriodicals/OJIN/ TableofContents/Volume92004/Number1January31/ HartfordHospitalsExperience.aspx

Connors, H. R., Weaver, C., Warren, J., & Miller, K. L. (2002, September–October). An academic-business partnership for advancing clinical informatics. *Nursing Education Perspectives,* 228–233.

Cummings, G. G. (2006). Hospital restructuring and nursing leadership: A journey from research question to research program. *Nursing Administration Quarterly, 30*(4), 321–329.

Edens, P. S. (2005). Workplace reengineering, reorganization, and redesign from nursing management: Principles and practice. *Medscape Critical Care, 6*(2), posted 09/13/2005.

Fitzpatrick, M. J., McElroy, M. J., & DeWoody, S. (2001). Building a strong nursing organization in a merged, service-line structure. *Journal of Nursing Administration, 31*(1), 24–32.

Goldreich, O. (2005). A brief overview of complexity theory. Lecture notes retrieved July 2007 from http://www.wisdom.weizmann.ac.il/ ~oded/cc-over.html

Hersey, P., Blanchard, K. H., & Johnson, D. E. (2007). *Management of organizational behavior* (9th ed.). Upper Saddle River, NJ: Prentice Hall.

Hess, R. G. (2004). From bedside to boardroom: Nursing shared governance. *Online Journal of Issues in Nursing, 9*(1), retrieved December 2007 at http://www.nursingworld.org/ MainMenuCategories/ANAMarketplace/ANAPeriodicals/OJIN/ TableofContents/Volume92004/Number1January31/ FromBedsidetoBoardroom.aspx

Kaissi, A. (2006). An organizational approach to understanding patient safety and medical errors. *The Health Care Manager, 25*(4), 292–305.

McClure, M. L. (2005). Magnet hospitals: Insights and issues. *Nursing Administration Quarterly, 29*(3), 198–201.

McConnell, C. R. (2000). The manager and the merger: Adaptation and survival in the blended organization. *Health Care Manager, 19*(1), 1–11.

McKeon, L. M., Oswaks, J. D., & Cunningham, P. D. (2006). Safeguarding patients: Complexity science, high reliability organizations, and implications for team training in healthcare. *Clinical Nurse Specialist, 20*(6), 298–306.

Mick, S. S., & Mark, B. A. (2005). The contribution of organization theory to nursing health services research. *Nursing Outlook, 53*(6), 317–323.

Newhouse, R. P., & Mills, M. E. (1999). Vertical systems integration. *Journal of Nursing Administration, 29*(10), 22–29.

Porter-O'Grady, T. (1994). Re-engineering the nursing profession. *Aspen's Advisor for the Nurse Executive, 9*(7), 7–8.

Porter-O'Grady, T. (2004). Shared governance: Is it a model for nurses to gain control over their practice? *Online Journal of Issues in Nursing, 9*(1), retrieved December 2007 at http://www.nursingworld.org/MainMenuCategories/ANAMarketplace/ANAPeriodicals/OJIN/TableofContents/Volume92004/Number1January31/Overview.aspx

Porter-O'Grady, T., & Malloch, K. (2002). *Quantum leadership: A textbook of new leadership*. Gaithersburg, MD: Aspen.

Robbins, S. P. (1983). *Organizational theory*. Englewood Cliffs, NJ: Prentice-Hall.

Sullivan, E. J. (2004). *Becoming influential: A guide for nurses*. Upper Saddle River, NJ: Prentice Hall.

Weber, M. (1958). *From Max Weber: Essays in sociology*. H. Gerth & C. W. Mills (Eds.). New York: Oxford University Press.

Delivering Nursing Care

Traditional Models of Care

    FUNCTIONAL NURSING

    TEAM NURSING

    TOTAL PATIENT CARE

    PRIMARY NURSING

Integrated Models of Care

    PRACTICE PARTNERSHIPS

    CASE MANAGEMENT

    CRITICAL PATHWAYS

    DIFFERENTIATED PRACTICE

    PATIENT-CENTERED CARE

    CLINICAL MICROSYSTEMS

    OTHER INNOVATIVE SYSTEMS

Learning Outcomes

After completing this chapter, you will be able to:

1. Describe how the delivery system structures nursing care.
2. Describe what types of nursing care delivery systems exist.
3. Discuss the positive and negative aspects of different systems.
4. Describe the new types of delivery systems that have emerged.
5. Explain what skills are required to use the system effectively.

MediaLink

www.prenhall.com/sullivan

See the Companion Website for chapter-specific resources at
www.prenhall.com/sullivan.

Key Terms

Case management *p36*

Clinical microsystems *p41*

Critical pathways *p37*

Differentiated practice *p39*

Functional nursing *p32*

Patient-centered care *p39*

Practice partnership *p35*

Primary nursing *p34*

Team nursing *p33*

Total patient care *p34*

MEDIALINK ❖ American Nurses Association

The core business of a hospital is nursing care (McClure, 2005). The challenge for the hospital is how to efficiently organize that care so that patients receive the care they need 24 hours a day.

The purpose of a nursing care delivery system is to provide a structure that enables nurses to deliver nursing care to a specified group of patients. The delivery of care includes assessing care needs, formulating a plan of care, implementing the plan, and evaluating the patient's responses to interventions. This chapter describes how nursing care is organized to ensure quality care in an era of cost containment.

Since World War II, nursing care delivery systems have undergone continuous and significant changes (Box 3-1). Over the years, various nursing care delivery systems have been critiqued. Debates regarding the pros and cons of each method have focused on identifying the perfect delivery system for providing nursing care to patients with varying degrees of need. This ongoing evaluation has been spurred by changes in availability of nursing personnel, reductions in reimbursement for patient care and hospital revenue, changes in acuity levels of patients, shorter lengths of stay, demands by health care consumers for quality care at a reduced rate, and demands by nurses, physicians, and other health care professionals for a more effective delivery system. The major challenges of any nursing care delivery system include effectiveness, cost efficiency, quality, and the needs of consumers and practitioners.

Traditional Models of Care

FUNCTIONAL NURSING

Functional nursing, also called task nursing, began in hospitals in the mid-1940s in response to a national nursing shortage (see **Figure 3-1**●). The number of reg-

---

BOX 3-1 Job Description of a Floor Nurse (1887)

Developed in 1887 and published in a magazine of Cleveland Lutheran Hospital.

In addition to caring for your 50 patients, each nurse will follow these regulations:

1. Daily sweep and mop the floors of your ward, dust the patients' furniture and window sills.

2. Maintain an even temperature in your ward by bringing in a scuttle of coal for the day's business.

3. Light is important to observe the patient's condition. Therefore, each day fill kerosene lamps, clean chimneys, and trim wicks. Wash windows once a week.

4. The nurse's notes are important to aiding the physician's work. Make your pens carefully. You may whittle nibs to your individual taste.

5. Each nurse on day duty will report every day at 7 A.M. and leave at 8 P.M., except on the Sabbath, on which you will be off from 12 noon to 2 P.M.

6. Graduate nurses in good standing with the Director of Nurses will be given an evening off each week for courting purposes, or two evenings a week if you go regularly to church.

7. Each nurse should lay aside from each pay a goodly sum of her earnings for her benefits during her declining years, so that she will not become a burden. For example, if you earn $30 a month you should set aside $15.

8. Any nurse who smokes, uses liquor in any form, gets her hair done at a beauty shop, or frequents dance halls will give the Director of Nurses good reason to suspect her worth, intentions, and integrity.

9. The nurse who performs her labor, serves her patients and doctors faithfully and without fault for a period of five years will be given an increase by the hospital administration of five cents a day providing there are no hospital debts that are outstanding.

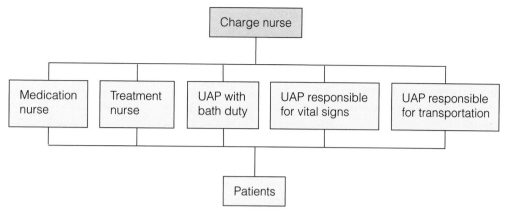

Figure 3-1 ● Functional nursing.

istered nurses (RNs) serving in the armed forces during World War II depleted the supply of nurses at home. As a result of this loss of RNs, the composition of nursing staffs in hospitals changed. Staff that had been composed almost entirely of RNs gave way to the widespread use of licensed practical nurses (LPNs) and unlicensed assistive personnel (UAPs) to deliver nursing care.

In functional nursing, the needs of a group of patients are broken down into tasks that are assigned to RNs, LPNs, or UAPs so that the skill and licensure of each caregiver is used to his or her best advantage. Under this model an RN assesses patients whereas others give baths, make beds, take vital signs, administer treatments, and so forth. As a result the staff become very efficient and effective at performing their regular assigned tasks.

Disadvantages of functional nursing include:

- Uneven continuity
- Lack of holistic understanding of the patient
- Problems with follow-up.

Because of these problems, functional nursing care is used infrequently in acute care facilities and only occasionally in long-term care facilities.

TEAM NURSING

Team nursing (*Figure 3-2* ●) evolved from functional nursing and has remained popular since the middle to late 1940s. Under this system, a team of nursing personnel provides total patient care to a group of patients. In some instances, a team may be assigned a certain number of patients; in others, the assigned patients may be grouped by diagnoses or provider services.

The size of the team varies according to physical layout of the unit, patient acuity, and nursing skill mix. The team is led by an RN and may include other RNs, LPNs, and UAPs. Team members provide patient care under the direction of the team leader. The team, acting as a unified whole, has a holistic perspective of the needs of each patient. The team speaks for each patient through the team leader.

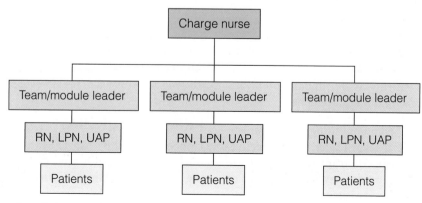

Figure 3-2 ● Team/modular nursing.

Typically, the team leader's time is spent in indirect patient care activities, such as:

- Developing or updating nursing care plans
- Resolving problems encountered by team members
- Conducting nursing care conferences
- Communicating with physicians and other health care personnel.

With team nursing, the unit nurse manager consults with team leaders, supervises patient care teams, and may make rounds with all physicians. To be effective, team nursing requires that all team members have good communication skills. A key aspect of team nursing is the nursing care conference, where the team leader reviews with all team members each patient's plan of care and progress.

Advantages of team nursing are:

- It allows the use of LPNs and UAPs to carry out some functions (e.g., making beds, transporting patients, collecting some data) that do not require the expertise of an RN.
- It allows patient care needs requiring more than one staff member, such as patient transfers from bed to chair, to be easily coordinated.
- The geographical boundaries of team nursing help save steps and time.

Disadvantages of team nursing are:

- The time needed for the team leader to communicate, supervise, and coordinate team members.
- Continuity of care may suffer due to changes in team members, leaders, and patient assignments.
- No one person considers the total patient.
- Role confusion and resentment against the team leader who staff may view as more focused on paperwork and less directed at the physical or real needs of the patient.
- Nurses have less control over their assignments due to the geographical boundaries of the unit.
- Assignments may not be equal if they are based on patient acuity or monotonous if nurses continuously care for patients with similar conditions (e.g., all patients with hip replacements).

Skills in delegating, communicating, and problem solving are essential for a team leader to be effective. Open communication between team leaders and the nurse manager is also important to avoid duplication of effort, overriding of delegated assignments, or competition for control or power. Problems in delegation and

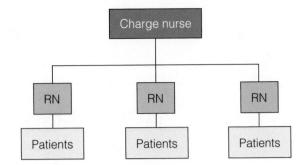

Figure 3-3 ● Total patient care.

communication are the most common reasons why team nursing is less effective than it theoretically could be.

TOTAL PATIENT CARE

The original model of nursing care delivery was **total patient care**, also called case method (**Figure 3-3** ●), in which a registered nurse was responsible for all aspects of the care of one or more patients. During the 1920s, total patient care was the typical nursing care delivery system. Student nurses often staffed hospitals, whereas RNs provided total care to the patient at home. In total patient care, RNs work directly with the patient, family, physician, and other health care staff in implementing a plan of care.

The goal of this delivery system is to have one nurse give all care to the same patient(s) for the entire shift. Total patient care delivery systems are typically used in areas requiring a high level of nursing expertise, such as in critical care units or post-anesthesia recovery areas.

The advantages of a total patient care system include:

- Continuous, holistic, expert nursing care
- Total accountability for the nursing care of the assigned patient(s) for that shift
- Continuity of communication with the patient, family, physician(s), and staff from other departments.

The disadvantage of this system is that RNs spend some time doing tasks that could be done more cost-effectively by less skilled persons. This inefficiency adds to the expense of using a total patient care delivery system.

PRIMARY NURSING

Conceptualized by Marie Manthey and implemented during the late 1960s after two decades of team nursing, **primary nursing** (**Figure 3-4** ●) was designed to place the registered nurse back at the patient's bedside (Manthey, 1980). Decentralized decision making

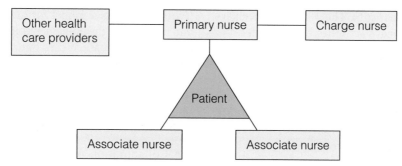

Figure 3-4 ● Primary nursing.

by staff nurses is the core principle of primary nursing, with responsibility and authority for nursing care allocated to staff nurses at the bedside. Primary nursing recognized that nursing was a knowledge-based professional practice, not just a task-focused activity.

In primary nursing, the RN maintains a patient load of primary patients. A primary nurse designs, implements, and is accountable for the nursing care of patients in the patient load for the duration of the patient's stay on the unit. Actual care is given by the primary nurse and/or associate nurses (other RNs).

Primary nursing advanced the professional practice of nursing significantly because it provided:

- A knowledge-based practice model
- Decentralization of nursing care decisions, authority, and responsibility to the staff nurse
- 24-hour accountability for nursing care activities by one nurse
- Improved continuity and coordination of care
- Increased nurse, patient, and physician satisfaction.

Primary nursing also has some disadvantages, including:

- It requires excellent communication between the primary nurse and associate nurses.
- Primary nurses must be able to hold associate nurses accountable for implementing the nursing care as prescribed.
- Because of transfers to different units, critically ill patients may have several primary care nurses, disrupting the continuity of care inherent in the model.
- Staff nurses are neither compensated nor legally responsible for patient care outside their hours of work.
- Associates may be unwilling to take direction from the primary nurse.

Although the concept of 24-hour accountability is worthwhile, it is a fallacy. When primary nursing was first implemented, many organizations perceived that it required an all–RN staff. This practice was viewed as not only expensive but also ineffective because many tasks could be done by less skilled persons. As a result, many hospitals discontinued the use of primary nursing. Other hospitals successfully implemented primary nursing by identifying one nurse who was assigned to coordinate care and with whom the family and physician could communicate, and other nurses or unlicensed assistive personnel assisted this nurse in providing care.

Integrated Models of Care

PRACTICE PARTNERSHIPS

The **practice partnership** (*Figure 3-5* ●) was introduced by Marie Manthey in 1989 (Manthey, 1989). In the practice partnership model, an RN and an assistant—UAP, LPN, or less experienced RN—agree to be practice partners. The partners work together with the same schedule and the same group of patients. The senior RN partner directs the work of the junior partner within the limits of each partner's abilities and within limits of the state's nurse practice act.

The relationship between the senior and junior partner is designed to create synergistic energy as the two

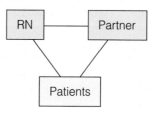

Figure 3-5 ● Practice partnerships.

work in concert with patients. The senior partner performs selected patient care activities but delegates less specialized activities to the junior partner. The partners can achieve the workload or outcomes that previously were achieved by two RNs (Manthey, 1989).

When compared to team nursing, practice partnerships offer more continuity of care and accountability for patient care. When compared to total patient care or primary nursing, partnerships are less expensive for the organization and more satisfying professionally for the partners.

Disadvantages of this model are:

- Organizations tend to increase the number of UAPs and decrease the ratio of professional nurses to non-professional staff. If, for example, one UAP is assigned to more than one RN, the UAP must follow the instructions of several people, making a synergistic relationship with any one of them difficult.
- Another problem is the potential for the junior member of the team to assume more responsibility than appropriate. Senior partners must take caution not to delegate inappropriate tasks to junior partners.

Practice partnerships can be applied to primary nursing and used in other nursing care delivery systems, such as team nursing, modular nursing, and total patient care. As organizations restructured, practice partnerships offered an efficient way of using the skills of a mix of professional and nonprofessional staff with differing levels of expertise.

CASE MANAGEMENT

Following the introduction and impact of prospective payments, nursing case management, used for decades in community and psychiatric settings, was adopted for acute inpatient care. Nursing **case management**

(**Figure 3-6**●) is a model for identifying, coordinating, and monitoring the implementation of services needed to achieve desired patient care outcomes within a specified period of time. Nursing case management organizes patient care by major diagnoses or diagnosis-related groups (DRGs) and focuses on attaining predetermined patient outcomes within specific time frames and resources.

Nursing case management requires:

- Collaboration of all members of the health care team
- Identification of expected patient outcomes within specific time frames
- Use of principles of continuous quality improvement (CQI) and variance analysis
- Promotion of professional practice.

Case management has been particularly successful with disability management, helping injured employees to return to work (Salazar, 2000). Likewise home care and ambulatory settings lend themselves to case management as well. The case manager, who may be called a care coordinator, usually does not provide direct patient care but rather supervises the care provided by licensed and unlicensed nursing personnel. Patient involvement and participation is key to successful case management (Aliotta, 2002).

In response to the nursing shortage, differentiated practice (see later section), and prospective payment restrictions, the Robert Wood Johnson University Hospital developed the professionally advanced care team (ProACT) model that used a clinical care manager and a primary nurse (Cohen & Cesta, 2005). Over time the model evolved from unit-based to become a service orientation.

In an acute care setting the case manager has a caseload of 10 to 15 patients and follows patients' progress through the system from admission to discharge,

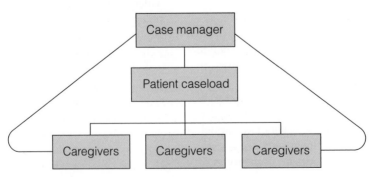

Figure 3-6 ● Case management.

accounting for variances from expected progress. One or more nursing case managers on a patient care unit may coordinate, communicate, collaborate, problem solve, and facilitate patient care for a group of patients. Ideally, nursing case managers have advanced degrees and considerable experience in nursing.

After a specific patient population is selected to be "case managed," a collaborative practice team is established. The team, which includes clinical experts from appropriate disciplines (e.g., nursing, medicine, physical therapy) needed for the selected patient population, defines the expected outcomes of care for the patient population. Based on expected patient outcomes, each member of the team, using his or her discipline's contribution, helps determine appropriate interventions within a specified time frame.

To initiate case management, specific patient diagnoses that represent high-volume, high-cost, and high-risk cases are selected. High-volume cases are those that occur frequently, such as total hip replacements on an orthopedic floor. High-risk cases include patients or case types who have complications, stay in a critical care unit longer than 2 days, or require ventilatory support. Patients also may be selected because they are treated by one particular physician who supports case management. Whatever patient population is selected, baseline data must be collected and analyzed first. These data provide the information necessary to measure the effectiveness of case management. Essential baseline data include length of stay, cost of care, and complication information.

Five elements are essential to successful implementation of case management:

- Support by key members of the organization (administrators, physicians, nurses)
- A qualified nurse case manager
- Collaborative practice teams
- A quality management system
- Established critical pathways (see next section).

In case management, all professionals are equal members of the team; thus, one group does not determine interventions for other disciplines. All members of the collaborative practice team agree on the final draft of the critical pathways, take ownership of patient outcomes, and accept responsibility and accountability for the interventions and patient outcomes associated with their discipline. The emphasis must be on managing interdisciplinary outcomes and building consensus with physicians. In addition, outcomes must be specified in measurable terms.

CRITICAL PATHWAYS

Successful case management relies on **critical pathways** to guide care. The term *critical path,* also called a *care map,* refers to the expected outcomes and care strategies developed by the collaborative practice team. Again, interdisciplinary consensus must be reached and specific, measurable outcomes determined.

Critical paths provide direction for managing the care of a specific patient during a specified time period. Critical paths are useful because they accommodate the unique characteristics of the patient and the patient's condition. Critical paths use resources appropriate to the care needed and, thus, reduce cost and length of stay. Critical paths are used in every setting where health care is delivered.

A critical path quickly orients the staff to the outcomes that should be achieved for the patient for that day. Nursing diagnoses identify the outcomes needed. If patient outcomes are not achieved, the case manager is notified and the situation analyzed to determine how to modify the critical path.

Altering time frames or interventions is categorized as a variance, and the case manager tracks all variances. After a time, the appropriate collaborative practice teams analyze the variances, note trends, and decide how to manage them. The critical pathway may need to be revised or additional data may be needed before changes are made.

Some features are included on all critical paths, such as specific medical diagnosis, the expected length of stay, patient identification data, appropriate time frames (in days, hours, minutes, or visits) for interventions, and patient outcomes. Interventions are presented in modality groups (medications, nursing activity, and so on). The critical path must include a means to identify variances easily and to determine whether the outcome has been met.

Table 3-1 is an example of a collaborative critical path for patients having a total hip replacement. Normally a patient would be expected to be discharged on the sixth day after surgery. This path describes expectations for days 1 through 3.

A recent evolution of critical paths is the incorporation of actual and potential nursing diagnoses with specific time frames into the critical pathway (the lower section of Table 3-1). Education paths are also excellent tools for planning patient and family education (Table 3-2). A copy of this form is given to the patient and the family, and the nurse reviews the information

TABLE 3-1	**Critical Path with Actual/Potential Nursing Diagnoses for Total Hip Replacement**

Collaborative Critical Path
Case Type: Total Hip Replacement

Patient Name: _____

Record Number: _____

DRG: <u>209</u>

Expected LOS: <u>6 days</u>

	DAY 1 / OR	**Y/N**	**DAY 2 / POSTOPERATIVE DAY 1**	**Y/N**	**DAY 3 / POSTOPERATIVE DAY 2**	**Y/N**
Patient Activity	Bed rest	—	Begin mobility plan;	—	Cont mobility plan	—
	T-DB q2h	—	T-DB q2h	—	T-DB q2h	—
	Initiate skin protection protocol	—	Cont skin protection protocol	—	Cont skin protection protocol	—
Nursing	VS qh × 4, then q4h	— —	VS q4h	—	VS q8h	—
	Assess cir/neuro legs qh × 4, then q4h;	— —	Assess cir/neuro q4h	—	D/C assessment	—
	Check drainage/ Hemovac qh × 4, then q4h;	— —	Check drainage/ Hemovac q4h	—	D/C Hemovac; Check drainage q8h	—
	I & O (Foley/ Hemovac) q8h;	—	I & O (Foley/ Hemovac) q8h	—	I & O q8h D/C Foley; urinates within 8h	—
	Thigh-hi elastic hose	—	Cont elastic hose	—	Cont elastic hose	—
Medications	Antibiotic	—	Cont antibiotic	—	Cont antibiotic	—
	Pain control:		Cont pain control	—	PO pain control	—
	PCA pump	—				
	Stool softener	—	Cont stool softener	—	Cont stool softener	—
	Cont home Rx;	—	Cont home Rx	—	Cont home Rx	—
	IVs	—	IVs cont	—	IV to heparin lock	—
			Coumadin	—	Cont coumadin	—
			Sleeping Rx	—	Sleeping Rx	—
Physical Therapy	Preop instructions	—	Evaluate mobility progress	—	Evaluate mobility progress	—
Diagnostic Tests	H & H 2h postop	—	H & H Prothrombin time	— —	Prothrombin time	—
Nutrition	NPO—Cl liq as tol	—	Diet as tolerated	—	Diet as tolerated	—
Teaching	*Preop:* Pain control	—	Repeat teaching if nec	—	Repeat teaching if nec	—
	Use of assist devices	—				
	Gait control	—				
	Incentive spirometry	—				
	Mobility plan	—				
	Pt/family crit plan given & reviewed	—	Review pt/family crit plan if nec	—	Review pt/family crit plan if nec	—
Discharge Plan	SNU evaluation	—			Review transfer discharge needs	—
	Home Health evaluation	—				

TABLE 3-1	Continued

Patient Problems and Outcomes for Total Hip Replacement

NURSING DIAGNOSIS	DAY 1 / OR	Y/N	DAY 2 / POSTOPERATIVE DAY 1	Y/N	DAY 3 / POSTOPERATIVE DAY 2	Y/N
Knowledge deficit: medications; use of assistive devices; treatments	Appropriately uses: PCA pump, incentive spirometry, assistive devices; Verbalizes mobility plan	— — —	Uses all devices appropriately	—	Verbalizes additions to care	—
Pain related to surgery, physical injury	Pain managed	—	Pain managed	—	Pain managed	—
Risk for infection related to invasive procedures, immobility	Remains afebrile No skin breakdown	— —	Remains afebrile No skin breakdown	— —	Remains afebrile	—
Impaired physical mobility related to surgery, prosthesis	Verbalizes mobility plan Verbalizes role of staff providing assistance	— —	Meeting mobility expectations	—	Participates in transfer/discharge plans, decisions	—
Risk for injury related to altered tissue perfusion, altered mobility, and prosthesis	Explains need for frequent assessments Verbalizes need for early mobility and hose	— —	Circulation to extremities good Leg maintained in proper alignment	— —	Circulation to extremities normal Leg in proper alignment	— —

with them. Thus, both the patient and the family know what to expect during an anticipated, uncomplicated hospitalization.

DIFFERENTIATED PRACTICE

Differentiated practice is a method that maximizes nursing resources by focusing on the structure of roles and functions of nurses according to their education, experience, and competence. Differentiated practice is designed to identify distinct levels of nursing practice based on defined abilities that are incorporated into job descriptions.

In differentiated practice, the responsibilities of RNs (mainly those with bachelor's and associate degrees) differ according to the competence and training associated with the two education levels as well as the nurses' experience and preferences. The scope of nursing practice and level of responsibility are specifically defined for each level. Some organizations differentiate roles,

responsibilities, and tasks for professional nurses, licensed practical nurses, and unlicensed assistive personnel, which are incorporated into their respective job descriptions.

PATIENT-CENTERED CARE

Patient-centered care is a model of nursing care delivery in which the role of the nurse is broadened to coordinate a team of multifunctional unit-based caregivers. In patient-centered care, all patient care services are unit-based, including admission and discharge, diagnostic and treatment services, and support services, such as environmental and nutrition services and medical records. The focus of patient-centered care is decentralization, the promotion of efficiency and quality, and cost control.

In this model of care the number of caregivers at the bedside is reduced, but their responsibilities are increased so that service and waiting times are decreased.

TABLE 3-2	Patient/Family Education Path for Total Hip Replacement		
	DAY 1 / OR	**DAY 2 / POSTOPERATIVE DAY 1**	**DAY 3 / POSTOPERATIVE DAY 2**
Unit	Admission process; surgery & recovery areas; then Orthopedic Unit	Orthopedic Unit	Orthopedic Unit (Possible transfer next day to SNU or Rehab Unit)
Patient Activity and Safety Issues	Bed rest first 24 h; leg exercises qh (q4h); T-DB q2h; explain skin protection plan; give copy of mobility plan; assist c̄ bath; thigh-hi elastic support hose	Up in chair c̄ help; Leg exercises q2h; T-DB q2h; cont skin protect plan; cont mobility plan; assist c̄ bath; cont thigh-hi elastic support hose	Up in chair and walking as outlined in mobility plan; T-DB q2h; cont skin protection plan; assist c̄ bath; cont thigh-hi elastic support hose
Nursing Care	Frequency of taking vital signs (BP-P-R-T); check drainage on dressing; check circulation and sensations to legs; intake & output measured q8h; Foley and Hemovac in for 48 h	Vital sign checks q4h; dressing, circulation, and sensation checks to legs q4h; I & O (Foley and Hemovac) measured q8h	Vital sign checks q8h; D/C Foley and Hemovac; I & O q8h; urinate with in 8 h; D/C dressing, circulation, and sensation checks to legs
Medications	Verify list of home Rx so physician can order; pain medication and PCA pump; IVs and need for arm restraint; other drugs that will be ordered (e.g., antibiotics; stool softener)	Cont pain management c̄ PCA pump; IVs; cont arm restraint; cont antibiotic and other drugs (sleeping assistance)	Oral pain management; IV to heparin lock; cont antibiotic and other drugs
Diet	NPO before OR; clear liquids, ice chips	Diet as tolerated	Diet as tolerated
Tests	Blood test: Hemoglobin and hematocrit 2 h after OR	Blood tests: H & H and prothrombin time	Blood test: prothrombin time
Teaching	Pain management; use of assistive devices (trapeze, walker) and incentive spirometry; mobility plan reviewed: how to transfer from bed to chair, and so on	Clarify questions	Clarify questions
Discharge Plan	Discuss purpose of Skilled Nursing Unit and Rehab Unit; identify need for Home Health Service after discharge	Cont with discussion of SNU, Rehab, and Home Health Services	Clarify questions and needs with transfer/discharge plans

A typical team in a unit providing patient-centered care consists of:

- Patient care coordinators (RNs)
- Patient care associates or technicians who are able to perform delegated patient care tasks
- Unit support assistants who provide environmental services and can assist with hygiene and ambulation needs
- Administrative support personnel who maintain patient records, transcribe orders, coordinate admission and discharge, and assist with general office duties.

The patient-centered care model also may be used in outpatient and home care settings. Patients with chronic conditions are appropriate candidates for patient-centered care approaches, including the use of complementary and alternative medicine therapies (Parkman, 2000).

The nurse manager's role in patient-centered care requires considerable time. No longer is the manager doing rounds and assisting with patient care. Instead, being responsible for a staff that is more diverse with fewer professional RN staff demands a strong leader proficient to interview, hire, train, and motivate staff. Some organizations share assistive staff between units, also increasing the need for more communication and coordination with other managers.

CLINICAL MICROSYSTEMS

Clinical microsystems are a recent addition to care delivery structures. Clinical microsystems evolved from the belief that decision making is best given to those involved in the smallest unit of care. Thus, a clinical microsystem is a small unit of care that maintains itself over time.

The clinical microsystem is being viewed as a positive change in nursing care delivery systems. Top-performing units are dynamic, interactive, self-aware, interdependent, and led by skilled leaders (Nelson et al., 2001). A large neonatal intensive care unit developed a microsystems approach and found a positive effect on patients and staff alike. Specifically, the model improved teamwork, communication, and continuity of care in a 40-bed unit (Goldschmidt, 2006).

OTHER INNOVATIVE SYSTEMS

Other innovative systems of care reported by Kimball, Joynt, Cherner, and O'Neil (2007) include:

- The 12-bed hospital model used at Baptist Hospital of Miami that segments its hospital into smaller units
- The Primary Care Team model at Seton Family of Hospitals in Austin, Texas
- The population-based Collaborative Patent Care Management model at High Point Regional Health System in High Point, North Carolina
- The Transitional Care model created at the University of Pennsylvania originally for older adults
- The Hospital at Home model from Johns Hopkins Bayview Medical Center for acutely ill patients at home.

No delivery system is perfect. Most organizations use a combination or modification of various nursing care delivery systems to meet the unique demands of different patient care units. Different systems are even within the same organization (Minnick, Mion, Johnson, & Catrambone, 2007). The organization or unit's goals, characteristics, and needs as well as costs determine the most appropriate nursing care delivery system.

MediaLink Agency for Healthcare Research and Quality

What You Know Now

- Nursing care delivery systems provide a structure for nursing care. Most organizations use a combination of nursing care delivery systems or modify one or more systems to meet their own needs.
- Integrated models of care use the best combination of staff based on patient needs and staff qualifications.
- Case management is a collaborative patient care system that uses case managers (RNs) who are responsible for facilitating patient interventions and achieving patient outcomes from admission to discharge.
- Critical paths are used to designate specific patient outcomes within specified time frames.
- Differentiated practice and patient-centered care are two systems that use nurses and support personnel based on expertise of staff and needs of patients.
- Clinical microsystems use a structure that puts decision making in small units of those who provide the care.
- Health care organizations are adapting delivery systems to meet their unique patient care needs.

Questions to Challenge You

1. Describe the patient care delivery system(s) at your place of work or clinical placement site. How functional is it? Can you suggest a better system?
2. Pretend that you are designing a new nursing care delivery system. Select the system or combination of systems you would use. Explain your rationale.
3. Why have different systems been used in earlier times? Would any of them be useful today? Explain what characteristics of the health care system today would make them appropriate or inappropriate to use.

4. As a manager, which system would you prefer? Why?
5. If you were a patient, which system do you think would provide you with the best care?

Explore MediaLink

Additional interactive resources for this chapter can be found on the Website at http://www.prenhall.com/sullivan. Click on Chapter 3 to select activities for this chapter.

- Video Overview
- NCLEX® Review Questions
- Critical Thinking Activities
- Current Events
- Nursing Leadership and Management in Action
- MediaLinks

References

Aliotta, S. (2002). Direct outcomes of case management: Involvement/participation, empowerment, and knowledge. *Case Manager, 13*(4), 67–71.

Cohen, E. L., & Cesta, T. G. (2005). Dimensions of nursing case management. In E. L. Cohen & T. G. Cesta *Nursing Case Management* (4th ed.). St. Louis, MO: Elsevier.

Goldschmidt, K. A. (2006). A model of nursing care microsystems for a large neonatal intensive care unit. *Advanced Neonatal Care, 6*(2), 81–88.

Kimball, B., Joynt, J., Cherner, D., & O'Neil, E. (2007). The quest for new innovative care delivery models. *Journal of Nursing Administration, 37*(9), 392–398.

Manthey, M. (1980). *The practice of primary nursing*. St. Louis: Mosby.

Manthey, M. (1989). Practice partnerships: The newest concept in care delivery. *Journal of Nursing Association, 19*(2), 33–35.

McClure, M. L. (2005). Magnet hospitals: Insights and issues. *Nursing Administration Quarterly, 29*(3), 198–201.

Minnick, A. F., Mion, L. C., Johnson, M. E., & Catrambone, C. (2007). How unit level nursing responsibilities are structured in US hospitals. *Journal of Nursing Administration, 37*(10), 452–458.

Nelson, E. C., Batalden, P. B., Godfrey, M. S., Headrick, L. A., Huber, T. P., Mohr, J. J., & Wasson, M. D. (2001). *Executive summary for health care leaders microsystems in health care: The essential building blocks of high performing systems.* Retrieved August 2007 from http://www.dartmouth.edu/~cecs/hcild/downloads/RWJ_MS_Exec_Summary.pdf

Parkman, C. A. (2000). The patient-centered plan of care. *Case Manager, 11*(6), 25–27.

Salazar, M. K. (2000). Maximizing the effectiveness of case management service delivery. *Case Manager, 11*(3), 58–63.

Leading, Managing, Following

MediaLink

www.prenhall.com/sullivan
See the Companion Website for chapter-specific resources at
www.prenhall.com/sullivan.

Followership: An Essential Component of Leadership

What Makes a Successful Leader?

    AUTHENTIC LEADERS

    EMOTIONAL LEADERS

Learning Outcomes

After completing this chapter, you will be able to:

1. Explain why every nurse is a manager and can be a leader.
2. Differentiate between leaders and managers.
3. Discuss how different theories explain leadership and management.
4. Describe what management roles nurses fill in practice.
5. Discuss how followership is essential to leadership.
6. Describe what makes a leader successful.

Key Terms

Achievement-oriented leadership *p52*
Autocratic leadership *p46*
Bureaucratic leadership *p46*
Charge nurse *p60*
Charismatic leadership *p53*
Clinical nurse leader *p61*
Contingency planning *p56*
Controlling *p56*
Democratic leadership *p46*
Directing *p56*
Directive leadership *p52*

Expectancy *p52*
First-level manager *p60*
Followership *p61*
Formal *p45*
Informal *p45*
Instrumentality *p52*
Laissez-faire leadership *p46*
Leader *p45*
Manager *p45*
Organizing *p56*
Participative leadership *p52*
Planning *p55*

Quantum leadership *p53*
Relational (connective) leadership *p54*
Servant leadership *p55*
Shared leadership *p54*
Strategic planning *p56*
Supportive leadership *p52*
Transactional leadership *p53*
Transformational leadership *p53*
Valence *p52*

Managers are essential to any organization. A manager's functions are vital, complex, and frequently difficult. They must be directed toward balancing the needs of patients, the health care organization, employees, physicians, and self. Nurse managers need a body of knowledge and skills distinctly different from those needed for nursing practice, yet few nurses have the education or training necessary to be managers (Grossman & Valiga, 2005). Frequently, managers depend on experiences with former supervisors, who also learned supervisory techniques on the job. Often a gap exists between what managers know and what they need to know. Today, all nurses are managers, not in the formal organizational sense but in practice. They direct the work of nonprofessionals and professionals in order to achieve desired outcomes in patient care. Acquiring the skills to be both a leader and a manager will help the nurse become more effective and successful in any position.

This chapter delineates the difference between leaders and managers, explains how leadership and management theories guide practice, and discusses qualities that make leaders successful.

Leaders and Managers

Manager, leader, supervisor, and *administrator* are often used interchangeably, yet they are not the same. A **leader** is anyone who uses interpersonal skills to influence others to accomplish a specific goal. The leader exerts influence by using a flexible repertoire of personal behaviors and strategies. The leader is important in forging links—creating connections—among an organization's members to promote high levels of performance and quality outcomes.

The functions of a leader are to achieve a consensus within the group about its goals, maintain a structure that facilitates accomplishing the goals, supply necessary information that helps provide direction and clarification, and maintain group satisfaction, cohesion, and performance.

A **manager**, in contrast, is an individual employed by an organization who is responsible and accountable for efficiently accomplishing the goals of the organization. Managers focus on coordinating and integrating resources, using the functions of planning, organizing, supervising, staffing, evaluating, negotiating, and representing. Interpersonal skill is important, but a manager also has authority, responsibility, accountability, and power defined by the organization. The manager's job is to:

- Clarify the organizational structure
- Choose the means by which to achieve goals
- Assign and coordinate tasks, developing and motivating as needed
- Evaluate outcomes and provide feedback.

All good managers are also good leaders—the two go hand in hand. However, one may be a good manager of resources and not be much of a leader of people. Likewise, a person who is a good leader may not manage well. Both roles can be learned; skills gained can enhance either role.

Leadership

Leadership may be formal or informal. Leadership is **formal** when practiced by a nurse with legitimate authority conferred by the organization and described in a job description (e.g., nurse manager, supervisor, coordinator, case manager). Formal leadership also depends on personal skills, but it may be reinforced by organizational authority and position. Insightful formal leaders recognize the importance of their own informal leadership activities and the informal leadership of others who affect the work in their areas of responsibility.

Leadership is **informal** when exercised by a staff member who does not have a specified management role. A nurse whose thoughtful and convincing ideas substantially influence the efficiency of work flow is exercising leadership skills. Informal leadership depends primarily on one's knowledge, status (e.g., advanced practice nurse, quality improvement coordinator, education specialist, medical director), and personal skills in persuading and guiding others.

Leadership Theories

Research on leadership has a long history, but the focus has shifted over time from personal traits to behavior and style, to the leadership situation, to change agency (the capacity to transform), and to other aspects of leadership. Each phase and focus of research has contributed to managers' insights and understandings about leadership and its development. This chapter discusses four categories of leadership theories: trait theories, behavioral theories, contingency theories, and contemporary theories.

TRAIT THEORIES

In the earliest studies researchers sought to identify inborn traits of successful leaders. Stogdill (1974) developed a profile of successful leaders and traits. Bass (1990) added more traits, which he classified into three categories: intelligence, personality, abilities. Gilbert (1975), in examining the personalities of nursing graduate students, found that potential leaders were more likely to exhibit traits such as dominance, aggressiveness, ambition, high capacity to attain status, poise, self-confidence, tolerance for others' views, high need to achieve, orderly thinking, sensitivity to others, and flexibility. Although inconclusive, these early attempts to specify unique leadership traits provided benchmarks by which most leaders continue to be judged.

BEHAVIORAL THEORIES

Research on leadership in the early 1930s focused on what leaders do. In the behavioral view of leadership, personal traits provide only a foundation for leadership; real leaders are made through education, training, and life experiences.

MEDIALINK Nursing Leadership and Management in Action

MEDIALINK Separating "Leading" from "Managing" Can Be Destructive

Leadership Styles

Behavior-based theories assume that effective leaders acquire a pattern of learned behaviors. Initial studies of teams of teenage boys identified three patterns or *styles* of leadership: autocratic, democratic, and laissez-faire (Lewin & Lippit, 1938; Lewin, Lippit, & White, 1939). The **autocratic leadership** style assumes that individuals are motivated by external forces, such as power, authority, and need for approval; the leader makes all the decisions and uses coercion, punishment, and direction to change followers' behavior and achieve results.

The **democratic leadership** style assumes that individuals are motivated by internal drives and impulses, want active participation in decisions, and want to get the task done; the leader uses participation and majority rule in setting goals and working toward achievement. The **laissez-faire leadership** style also assumes that individuals are motivated by internal drives and impulses and that they need to be left alone to make decisions about how to complete the work; the leader provides no direction or facilitation.

Jenkins and Henderson (1984) added a fourth style, the **bureaucratic leadership** style. The bureaucrat assumes that employees are motivated by external forces. This leader trusts neither followers nor self to make decisions and therefore relies on organizational policies and rules to identify goals and direct work processes. Table 4-1 compares the four leadership styles.

By the early 1950s, leadership styles in work settings began to be explored (Katz & Kahn, 1952; Stogdill & Coons, 1957). Two major dimensions of behavioral style were identified: initiating structure and consideration. *Initiating structure* refers to the behaviors that managers use to organize and define the goals of work, work patterns and methods, channels of communication, and roles. For example, administration develops a manual of job descriptions, personnel policies, and procedures for granting time off, implementing a new policy on intravenous tubing changes, or family visiting.

Consideration, the employee-centered dimension, refers to behavior that conveys mutual trust, respect, friendship, warmth, and rapport between the manager and the staff. When the leader is considerate, the employee learns to expect that the manager will hear a concern openly and without reprisal, will involve employees in decision making, and will attend to the needs of the work group as a whole. The manager is alert to employees' responses to stress, the effects of personal crises on their work, and the social dynamics of the work group.

Followers' and managers' perceptions of managers' leadership style often differ; attempts to enhance a manager's style in one area or the other do not necessarily

TABLE 4-1	Comparison of Leadership Styles	
LEADERSHIP STYLE	**ASSUMED EMPLOYEE MOTIVATORS**	**LEADER CHARACTERISTICS**
Authoritarian (autocratic)	External forces, e.g., power and authority, needs for approval	Concerned with task accomplishment rather than relationships Uses directive behavior Makes decisions alone Expects respect and obedience of staff Lacks group support generated by participation Exercises power with coercion Proves useful (even necessary) in crisis situations
Democratic (participative)	Internal drives and impulses	Is primarily concerned with human relations and teamwork Fosters communication that is open and usually two-way Creates a spirit of collaboration and joint effort that results in staff satisfaction
Permissive (laissez-faire)	Internal drives and impulses	Tends to have few established policies; abstains from leading Is not generally useful in highly structured organizations (e.g., health care institutions)
Bureaucratic	External forces	Lacks a sense of security and depends on established policies and rules Exercises power by applying fixed, relatively inflexible rules Tends to relate impersonally to staff Avoids decision making without standards or norms for guidance

result in higher employee performance or improved goal achievement; equally effective leaders might possess strength in consideration or structure or both.

With the realization that different combinations of leader behaviors might produce different effects, researchers began searching for an optimal mix of behaviors that would produce optimal employee performance. As these models evolved, researchers began to recognize the complexity and range of the approaches managers use to produce results in organizations.

System 4 Management

Likert (1967) developed the System 4 model of management based on the premise that involving employees in decisions about work is central to effective leadership.

The model is composed of four dimensions based on increasing levels of employee involvement. *Autocratic leaders* have little trust in employees and systematically exclude them from decision making. *Benevolent leaders* are kind to employees but still do not involve them in decision making. *Consultative leaders* seek employees' advice about decisions. *Participative* or *democratic leaders* value employee involvement, teamwork, and team building; they also have high levels of confidence in employees and seek consensus in decision making. In doing so, the participative leader shares power.

The Managerial Grid

Another model for depicting leadership along a continuum is the managerial grid (***Figure 4-1***). Five

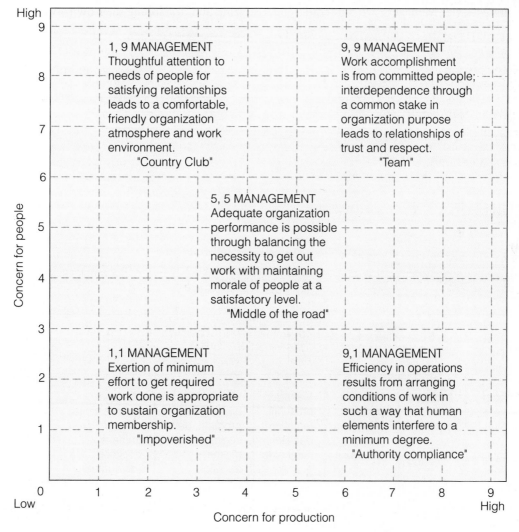

Figure 4-1 ● The managerial grid. *From* Leadership Dilemmas—Grid Solutions, *by R. R. Blake and A. A. McCanse, 1991, Austin, TX: Grid International. Reprinted with permission.*

leadership styles are plotted in four quadrants of a two-dimensional grid. The grid depicts various degrees of leader concern for production (structure) and concern for people (consideration). Leadership styles are labeled "impoverished" (low concern for both production and people), "authority compliance" (high concern for production, low concern for people), "country club" (high concern for people, low concern for production), "middle of the road" (moderate concern for both production and people), and "team" (high concern for both production and people).

Continuum of Leadership Behavior

Leadership behavior also is depicted as occurring along a continuum. This model focuses specifically on the decision-making style of managers. As displayed in **Figure 4-2**●, the left end of the continuum reflects a manager-centered style. Managers are autocratic and directive and simply make and announce decisions. At the right end of the continuum, managers are employee-centered; they use a laissez-faire style and permit employees to set their own goals and function within established parameters. No single leadership style is correct or appropriate for every management situation.

Sellgren, Ekvall, and Tomson (2006) suggest that leaders must use more authority with less experienced followers (see later section on Followership) but that as followers become more accomplished, the need for leaders to exert authority diminishes.

The numerous variations of the multidimensional, behavioral approach have contributed significantly to our understanding of managers' performance and effectiveness. Nurses may use these perspectives as a basis for analyzing the leadership styles of others and analyzing and developing their own styles.

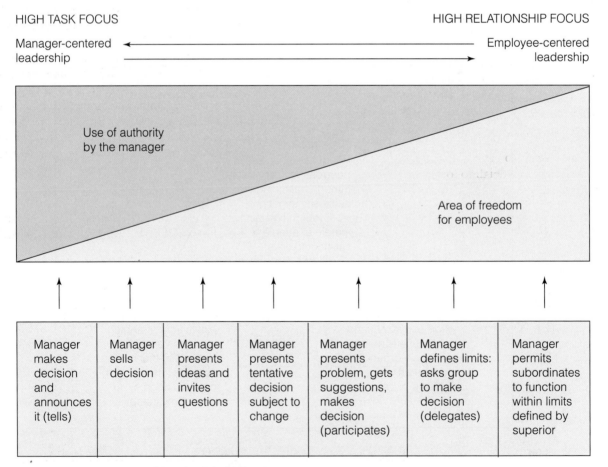

Figure 4-2 ● Continuum of leadership behavior. *From "How to Choose a Leadership Pattern," by R. Tannenbaum and W. H. Schmidt, 1973, Harvard Business Review, 51, p. 164. Reprinted by permission. Copyright © 1973 by the Harvard Business School Publishing Corporation; all rights reserved.*

CONTINGENCY THEORIES

Contingency approaches suggest that managers adapt their leadership styles in relation to changing situations. According to contingency theory, leadership behaviors range from authoritarian to permissive and vary in relation to current needs and future probabilities. A nurse manager may use an authoritarian style when responding to an emergency situation such as a cardiac arrest but use a participative style to encourage development of a team strategy to care for patients with multiple system failure. The manager might delegate to a highly competent and eager follower group decision making and task completion in designing a new patient intake form. The most effective leadership style for a nurse manager is the one that best complements the organizational environment, the tasks to be accomplished, and the personal characteristics of the people involved in each situation. Numerous contingency models have been developed. Four are discussed in this chapter: Fiedler's contingency theory, situational leadership theory, Vroom–Yetton expectancy model, and House–Mitchell path–goal theory.

Fiedler's Contingency Theory

Fiedler (1967) proposed that a leader is most effective when he or she matches leadership style (relationship-oriented or task-oriented) to situational factors. Fiedler described three situational factors of leadership, which are listed in decreasing order of importance:

- Manager–follower relationship (good to poor)
- Task structure (high to low)
- Manager power (strong to weak).

Manager–follower relations reflect the degree to which the leader enjoys the loyalty and support of subordinates. Task structure is the degree to which the task or result is clearly described and/or standard operating procedures guarantee successful completion and evaluation of the quality of the task. Position power is the degree to which leaders are able to administer rewards and punishment by virtue of their positions (that is, legitimate power).

Figure 4-3 illustrates how the task-motivated leader will be more effective under high and low structures and the relationship-motivated leader will have greater effectiveness under in-between situations.

Situational Leadership® Theory

Hersey, Blanchard, and Johnson (2007) expanded Fiedler's contingency model by considering the followers' readiness and willingness to perform the assigned tasks. In their theory of Situational Leadership®, four distinct leadership styles (S) are prescribed according to the readiness and ability of followers (R) (***Figure 4-4***).

Leaders use a telling style (S1—high task, low relationship) with followers who are unable and unwilling or insecure about performing the task (R1). Leaders use a selling style (S2—high task, high relationship) with followers who are unable but are willing or confident in performing the task (R2). Leaders use a participating style (S3—low task, high relationship) with followers who are able but unwilling or lacking in confidence in performing the task (R3). Finally, leaders use a delegating style (S4—low task, low relationship) with followers who are both able and willing and have confidence in performing the task (R4).

Vroom–Yetton Expectancy Model

Vroom and Yetton (1973) developed a prescriptive model for determining the amount of participation

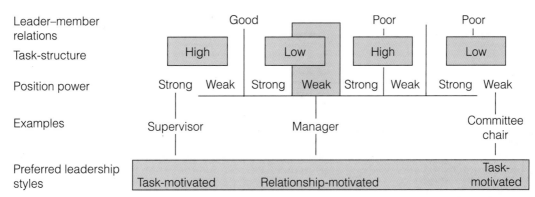

Figure 4-3 ● Fiedler's situational variables and their preferred leadership styles. *From* Organizational Behavior, *8th ed. (p. 291), by J. R. Schermerhorn, Jr., J. G. Hunt, and R. N. Olson, 2003, New York: Wiley. This material is used by permission of John Wiley & Sons, Inc.*

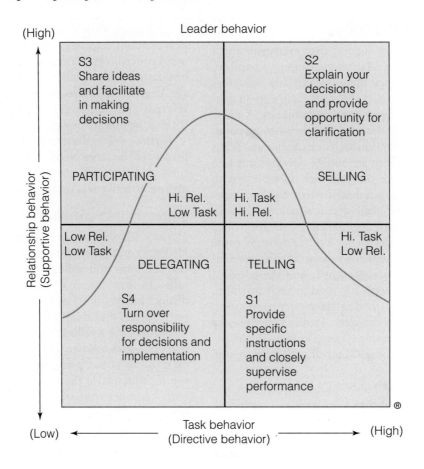

Figure 4-4 ● Situational Leadership® Model. *© Copyright 2006. Reprinted with permission of the Center for Leadership Studies, Inc., Escondido, CA 92025. All rights reserved.*

leaders should seek from employees in decision making. This model, depicted in **Figure 4-5**●, helps managers decide how to make a decision contingent on the task to be accomplished and needs of both managers and employees.

Three questions guide the manager's selection of an appropriate leadership style and the extent of participation employees should have in decision making.

1. Is all the information available to make the decision?
2. Is the staff's acceptance of the decision required for effective implementation?
3. Would the group make a decision the leader could live with?

Vroom and Yetton (1973) identified five leadership styles: tell, sell, consult, join, and delegate. Here

Manager has all of the information
needed to make the decision

	Yes	No
Yes Acceptance of subordinates needed to effectively implement?	Use some participation	Participation absolutely required
No	Need no participation	Use some participation

Figure 4-5 ● Variables affecting use of participation in leadership.

are their guidelines to decide which leadership style to use:

Use a telling style to assess a problem, make a decision independently, and inform followers.

Use a selling style to gather information from followers about a problem, make a decision independently, and persuade followers to implement it.

Use a consultative style to seek advice from followers individually, make the decision independently, and inform followers.

Use a joining style to join the group, seek suggestions, independently make a decision, and inform followers.

Use a delegation style to work with followers in developing solutions to the problem and facilitate consensus-building toward a group solution, which generally is accepted and implemented as the group wishes.

The manner in which managers make decisions directly reflects their leadership style. A model or framework that addresses the many contingencies in a decision-making situation helps managers analyze how to make decisions successfully. It also helps managers demonstrate a consistent, predictable decision-making style, which enables coworkers to anticipate the manager's expectations and perform accordingly.

An example of the Vroom-Yetton model of decision-making is shown in Box 4-1.

BOX 4-1   Example of Vroom–Yetton Model of Decision Making

Administration wants to pilot a model of self-directed teams on one unit in the hospital. One of the nurse managers, Martina Duchek, volunteers. She analyzes the staff's responses. Martina addresses the following questions:

1. Is the information needed to make the decision available? The manager needs to know, for example, how much the staff know about self-directed teams, how they feel about them, and what they would need by way of training and development to implement them. The answer to question 1 is no.

2. Is the staff's acceptance required for implementation? In this case, the answer to question 2 is clearly yes.

3. If the decision to adopt self-directed work teams is delegated to the staff, will they make a decision acceptable to Martina? She thinks not and realizes that it is the manager's responsibility to make a final decision with extensive staff involvement. Therefore, the answer to question 3 is no.

Martina could participate with the staff in a meeting to consider the costs and benefits of moving to self-directed teams, facilitate group decision making about what might be required to implement them, and create an implementation plan. Alternatively, she could discuss the pros and cons of implementing self-directed teams with individual staff members, gather information, analyze potential costs and other possible consequences to the unit, seek staff recommendations, and then make a decision.

House–Mitchell Path–Goal Theory

Path–goal theory applies a theory of human motivation and task performance to leadership effectiveness (House & Mitchell, 1974). Because a primary function of leadership is to motivate others to attain goals, path–goal theory proposes that removing obstacles to goal attainment, coaching, and providing personal rewards for achievement will result in high levels of performance and productivity. The leader affects performance by influencing employees' perceptions of their work and personal goals and facilitating the process by which employees achieve goals.

The motivational functions of leadership derive directly from the expectancy theory of motivation (Porter & Lawler, 1968; Vroom, 1964; also see Chapter 19). Employees work for rewards they find attractive and that result from successful performance.

Three concepts are central to expectancy theory:

Expectancy is the perceived probability that effort will result in successful performance.

Instrumentality is the perceived probability that performance will lead to desired outcomes.

Valence is the perceived value of an outcome.

The manager exercises leadership by defining and clarifying expectancies, instrumentalities, and valences associated with specific tasks and employees' personal goals.

Path–goal theory specifies four leader behaviors (House, 1971):

Directive leadership involves telling employees what is expected, giving specific guidance, ensuring adherence to rules and procedures, and scheduling and coordinating work efforts. This type of leadership is most effective for employees who are marginally trained or prepared and are performing partially routine and ambiguous tasks.

Supportive leadership focuses on the needs of employees, displays concern for their well-being, and creates a friendly climate in the work environment. Supportive leadership behavior is most effective for employees who are performing routine work or are very experienced with the work.

Participative leadership involves consultation with subordinates and requests for opinions and suggestions, which the leader takes into consideration when making decisions. This style works best for employees who have moderate skill levels and are performing somewhat ambiguous work. Involvement of employees encourages mutual clarification of objectives and specification of mutually helpful work processes.

Achievement-oriented leadership includes setting challenging goals, seeking performance improvements, emphasizing excellence in performance, and showing confidence that employees will attain high levels of performance. It is indicated for employees who are skilled and perform highly innovative and ambiguous work. By setting challenging goals and pointing out valued rewards, managers fulfill a strong motivating role.

Staff members interpret and respond to leader behavior in different ways, depending on personal characteristics and characteristics of the task and environment. Specifically, employees' needs for achievement, affiliation, power, competence, autonomy, and personality traits form a context within which leaders function. As in situational leadership, the effect of leadership behavior on employee satisfaction and effort depends on the task and the work situation.

Path–goal theory is interesting because it suggests that there are substitutes for direct leader–follower interaction. On the one hand, the manager can influence employee performance directly by clarifying the route to desired goals. On the other hand, actions that clarify objectives, specify roles, increase the value of rewards, provide needed support to complete tasks successfully, and facilitate performance might be viewed as substitutes for direct leadership activity.

The application of any contingency theory to leadership practice requires continuous monitoring of employees' expectancies, abilities, and motivations and an understanding of the task and options for completing it. Managers must also thoroughly consider the consequences of their actions on employee performance. For every leader's action, a predictable employee reaction is likely to occur. A nurse manager must carefully observe the cause-and-effect relationships that exist between leader behavior and employee response and continuously take into account the multitude of environmental factors that influence leader–employee interactions.

Contemporary Theories

Leaders in today's health care environment place increasing value on collaboration and teamwork in all aspects of the organization. They recognize that as health systems become more complex and require integration, personnel who perform the managerial and clinical work must cooperate, coordinate their efforts, and produce joint results. Leaders must use additional skills, especially group and political leadership skills, to create collegial work environments.

QUANTUM LEADERSHIP

Trait, behavioral, and contingency theories represent conventional approaches to leadership and have provided important foundations for leadership. Current views of leadership are neither complete reformulations nor simple refinements of conventional perspectives. Evolved from the principles of quantum mechanics, effective leadership today reflects a remarkable fusion of trait, behavior, and contingency approaches.

Quantum leadership is based on the concepts of chaos theory (see Chapter 2). Reality is constantly shifting, and levels of complexity are constantly changing. Movement in one part of the system reverberates throughout the system. Roles are fluid and outcome oriented. It matters little what you did; it only matters what outcome you produced. Within this framework, employees become directly involved in decision making as equitable and accountable partners, and managers assume more of an influential facilitative role, rather than one of control (Porter-O'Grady & Malloch, 2002).

Quantum leadership demands a different way of thinking about work and leadership. Change is expected. In fact, the leader's role is to encourage employees to "close the door on receding practices and challenge them to simply turn around and squarely confront the opportunities and challenges of emerging practice" (Porter-O'Grady, 2003, p. 177).

Informational power, previously the purview of the leader, is now available to all. Patients and staff alike can access untold amounts of information. The challenge, however, is to assist patients, uneducated about health care, how to evaluate and use the information they have. Because staff have access to information only the leader had in the past, leadership becomes a shared activity, requiring the leader to possess excellent interpersonal skills.

CHARISMATIC LEADERSHIP

Charismatic leadership is based on personal qualities such as charm, persuasiveness, personal power, self-confidence, extraordinary ideas, and strong (often unconventional) convictions. The leader's personality arouses great affection and emotional commitment, first to the leader and secondarily to the beliefs and causes the leader espouses. Few leaders possess genuine charisma. Those who do often use their powerful personalities to advance revolutionary goals.

TRANSACTIONAL LEADERSHIP

Transactional leadership is based on the principles of social exchange theory (Homans, 1958; Thibaut & Kelley, 1959). The primary premise of social exchange theory is that individuals engage in social interactions expecting to give and receive social, political, and psychological benefits or rewards. The exchange process between leaders and followers is viewed as essentially economic. Once initiated, a sequence of exchange behavior continues until one or both parties finds that the exchange of performance and rewards is no longer valuable. The nature of these transactions is determined by the participating parties' assessments of what is in their best interests; for example, staff respond affirmatively to a nurse manager's request to work overtime in exchange for granting special requests for time off. Leaders are successful to the extent that they understand and meet the needs of followers and use incentives to enhance employee loyalty and performance. Transactional leadership is aimed at maintaining equilibrium, or the status quo, by performing work according to policy and procedures, maximizing self-interests and personal rewards, emphasizing interpersonal dependence, and routinizing performance.

TRANSFORMATIONAL LEADERSHIP

Transformational leadership goes beyond transactional leadership to inspire and motivate followers (Aarons, 2006). Transformational leadership emphasizes the importance of interpersonal relationships (Ward, 2002). Transformational leadership is not concerned with the status quo, but with effecting revolutionary change in organizations and human service. Whereas traditional views of leadership emphasize the differences between employees and managers, transformational leadership focuses on merging the motives, desires, values, and goals of leaders and followers into a common cause. The goal of the transformational leader is to generate employees' commitment to the vision or ideal rather than to themselves.

Transformational leaders appeal to individuals' better selves rather than these individuals' self-interests. They foster followers' inborn desires to pursue higher values, humanitarian ideals, moral missions, and causes.

Transformational leaders also encourage others to exercise leadership. The transformational leader inspires followers and uses power to instill a belief that followers also have the ability to do exceptional things. McGuire and Kennerly (2006) found that transformational leaders were more likely than transactional leaders to have committed followers willing to put extra effort into their work, thus enhancing the organization's overall performance.

Transformational leadership may be a natural model for nursing managers, because nursing has traditionally been driven by its social mandate and its ethic of human service. Transformational leadership can be used effectively by nurses with clients or coworkers at the bedside, in the home, in the community health center, and in the health care organization.

RELATIONAL LEADERSHIP

Relational leadership, also known as relationship-oriented leadership or connective leadership, recognizes that today we are all connected and that relationships form the cornerstone of contemporary leadership. Klakovich (1994) proposed a connective leadership paradigm for nursing. This paradigm acknowledges the need for more flexible systems in health care that empower employees, their interdisciplinary colleagues, clients, and families. Klakovich explains that contemporary nursing leadership skills should include the ability to create interconnections between and across caregiving settings and among multiple constituencies.

The purpose of relational leadership is to better coordinate and integrate patient care services in a caring, noncompetitive manner. The focus is to link professionals, communities, governing groups, and voluntary agencies to improve patient-centered care. Connective leaders use their interpersonal skills to broker alliances, encourage collaboration, and integrate systems. Klakovich stresses the importance of collegiality among health care professionals in achieving patient care and organizational goals.

The nurse manager applies relational leadership principles when convening a group of physicians, administrators, nursing staff, and representatives of other disciplines to plan a new patient care program, for example, or bring nursing staff members together to develop a staff orientation program or seek the assistance of an external expert to help in the professional development of the nursing staff. Hierarchical relationships break down and leadership develops at all levels in the organization.

Relational leadership requires both content and process skills (such as the task and relationship skills discussed earlier). Both power and political tactics may be needed (see Chapter 7). The ability to manage groups and team interactions is essential. (Teams and team building are discussed in Chapter 11.) In addition, leaders must recognize that integrating the activities of diverse participants in health care involves creating connections that extend beyond well-defined groups.

The process of developing relationships and creating connections requires the leader to:

- Identify actual and potential collaborators
- Communicate and sell a potential shared vision to those in varied settings and under disparate conditions
- Describe the value each collaborator could bring to the endeavor, both to the individual and others
- Facilitate communication by sharing information, preparing for interactions, and following up on communications exchanges
- Build and maintain social interaction and comfort
- Define and sell roles and assignments
- Track and reward contributions
- Formalize an integrated effort at the right time.

SHARED LEADERSHIP

Reorganization, decentralization, and the increasing complexity of problem solving in health care have forced administrators to recognize the value of **shared leadership**, which is based on the empowerment principles of participative and transformational leadership. Essential elements of shared leadership are relationships, dialogues, partnerships, and understanding boundaries. The application of shared leadership assumes that a well-educated, highly professional, dedicated workforce is comprised of many leaders. It also assumes that the notion of a single nurse as the wise and heroic leader is unrealistic and that many individuals at various levels in the organization must be responsible for the organization's fate and performance.

Different issues call for different leaders, or experts, to guide the problem-solving process. A single leader is not expected always to have knowledge and ability beyond that of other members of the work group. Appropriate leadership emerges in relation to the current challenges of the work unit or the organization. Individuals in formal leadership positions and their colleagues are expected to participate in a pattern of reciprocal influence processes. Examples of shared leadership in nursing include:

- **Self-directed work teams.** Work groups manage their own planning, organizing, scheduling, and day-to-day work activities.
- **Shared governance.** The nursing staff are formally organized at the service area and organizational levels to make key decisions about clinical practice standards, quality assurance and improvement, staff development, professional development, aspects of unit operations, and research. Decision making is conducted by representatives of the nursing staff who have been authorized by the administrative hierarchy and their colleagues to make decisions about important matters.
- **Co-leadership.** Two people work together to execute a leadership role. This kind of leadership has become more common in service-line management, where the skills of both a clinical and administrative leader are needed to successfully direct the operations of a multidisciplinary service. For example, a nurse manager provides administrative leadership in collaboration with a clinical nurse specialist, who provides clinical leadership. The development of co-leadership roles depends on the flexibility and maturity of both individuals, and such arrangements usually require a third party to provide ongoing consultation and guidance to the pair.

SERVANT LEADERSHIP

Servant leadership is based on the premise that leadership originates from a desire to serve and that in the course of serving, one may be called to lead. According to Greenleaf (1991), servant leadership occurs when other people's needs take priority, when those being served "become healthier, wiser, freer, more autonomous, and more likely themselves to become servants" (p. 7). The servant leader must address the question of whether the least advantaged in society benefit from the leader's service.

Campbell and Rudisill (2005) suggest that servant leaders must have these skills:

- Listening—the most important skill
- Awareness—of a situation or individual need
- Persuasion—to convince, do, or believe
- Foresight—a visionary to create change
- Stewardship—take responsibility and be accountable
- Commitment—to the growth of individuals.

Servant leadership appeals to nurses for two reasons. First, our profession is founded on principles of caring, service, and the growth and health of others. Second, nurses serve many constituencies, often quite selflessly, and consequently bring about change in individuals, systems, and organizations.

Health care environments require innovations in care delivery and therefore innovative leadership approaches. Quantum, charismatic, transactional, transformational, relational, shared, and servant leadership comprise a new generation of leadership styles that have emerged in response to the need to humanize working environments and improve organizational performance. In practice, leaders tap a variety of styles culled from diverse leadership theories.

Management Functions

CLASSICAL DESCRIPTION

In 1916, French industrialist Henri Fayol first described the functions of management as planning, organizing, directing, and controlling. These are still relevant today.

Planning

Planning is a four-stage process to:

- Establish objectives (goals)
- Evaluate the present situation and predict future trends and events
- Formulate a planning statement (means)
- Convert the plan into an action statement.

Planning is important on both an organizational and a personal level and may be an individual or group process that addresses the questions of what, why, where, when, how, and by whom. Decision making and problem solving are inherent in planning. Numerous computer software programs and databases are available to help facilitate planning.

Organization-level plans, such as determining organizational structure and staffing or operational budgets, evolve from the mission, philosophy, and goals of the organization. The nurse manager plans and develops specific goals and objectives for her or his area of responsibility.

Antonio, the nurse manager of a home care agency, plans to establish an in-home phototherapy program, knowing that part of the agency's mission is to meet the health care needs of the child-rearing family. To effectively implement this program, he would need to address:

- *How the program supports the organization's mission*
- *Why the service would benefit the community and the organization*
- *Who would be candidates for the program*
- *Who would provide the service*
- *How staffing would be accomplished*
- *How charges would be generated*
- *What those charges should be.*

Planning can be contingent or strategic. Using **contingency planning** the manager identifies and manages the many problems that interfere with getting work done. Contingency planning may be reactive, in response to a crisis, or proactive, in anticipation of problems or in response to opportunities. What would you do if two registered nurses called in sick for the 12-hour night shift? What if you were a manager for a specialty unit and received a call for an admission, but had no more beds? Or what if you were a pediatric oncology clinic manager and a patient's sibling exposes a number of immunocompromised patients to chickenpox? Planning for crises such as these are examples of contingency planning.

Strategic planning refers to the process of continual assessment, planning, and evaluation to guide the future. Its purpose is to create an image of the desired future and design ways to make those plans a reality. A nurse manager might be charged, for example, with developing a business plan to add a time-saving device to commonly-used equipment, presenting the plan persuasively, and developing operational plans for implementation, such as acquiring devices and training staff.

Organizing

Organizing is the process of coordinating the work to be done. Formally, it involves identifying the work of the organization, dividing the labor, developing the chain of command, and assigning authority. It is an ongoing process that systematically reviews the use of human and material resources. In health care, the mission, formal organizational structure, delivery systems, job descriptions, skill mix, and staffing patterns form the basis for the organization.

In organizing the home phototherapy project, Antonio develops job descriptions and protocols, determines how many positions are required, selects a vendor, and orders supplies.

Directing

Directing is the process of getting the organization's work done. Power, authority, and leadership style are intimately related to a manager's ability to direct. Communication abilities, motivational techniques, and delegation skills also are important. In today's health care organization, professional staff are autonomous, requiring guidance rather than direction. The manager is more likely to sell the idea, proposal, or new project to staff rather than tell them what to do. The manager coaches and counsels to achieve the organization's objectives. In fact, it may be the nurse who assumes the traditional directing role when working with unlicensed personnel.

In directing the home phototherapy project, Antonio assembles the team of nurses to provide the service, explains the purpose and constraints of the program, and allows the team to decide how they will staff the project, giving guidance and direction when needed.

Controlling

Controlling involves comparing actual results with projected results. This includes establishing standards of performance, determining the means to be used in measuring performance, evaluating performance, and providing feedback. The efficient manager constantly attempts to improve productivity by incorporating techniques of quality management, evaluating outcomes and performance, and instituting change as necessary.

Today, managers share many of the control functions with the staff. In organizations using a formal quality improvement process, such as continuous quality improvement (CQI), staff participate in and lead the teams. Some organizations use peer review to control quality of care.

When Antonio introduces the home phototherapy program, the team of nurses involved in the program identify standards regarding phototherapy and their individual performances. A subgroup of the team routinely reviews monitors designed for the program and identifies ways to improve the program.

Planning, organizing, directing, and controlling reflect a systematic, proactive approach to management. This approach is used widely in all types of organizations, health care included. Timmereck (2000) found that health care managers used these classic functions extensively.

Mintzberg's Behavioral Description

A newer model is based on a behavioral approach to management. Mintzberg (1973) believed that much of a manager's activity involves human relations, a premise that is supported by the contemporary leadership theories discussed previously. Mintzberg also believed managers were more reactive than proactive. As a result of these two premises, he identified three categories of managerial roles: interpersonal roles, informational roles, and decisional roles.

Interpersonal Roles

Mintzberg describes three interpersonal roles that reflect the formal authority inherent in the manager's position: the figurehead, the leader, and the liaison. The *figurehead role* reflects the ceremonial performance of duties, such as welcoming new employees at orientation or attending social events. As a *leader,* the manager defines the work environment of the organization and is responsible for the work of associates—motivating, training, and disciplining as needed. The manager, as a leader, is responsible to see that the organization's goals are accomplished efficiently. The third interpersonal role, *liaison,* deals with expanding the manager's information sources and networks outside the organization. National conferences, local coalitions, and professional meetings are valuable resources for obtaining information and expanding networks.

Informational Roles

Mintzberg also describes three informational roles. As a *monitor,* the manager informally seeks information about the organization through internal networks, gossip, and observations. Tours of the organization, as well as formal and informal meetings, allow the manager to find out how the organization is functioning and what else might be needed to improve it. In the *disseminator* role, managers either share information between work units or share information from outside the organization. Information is a source of power; sharing information empowers employees and improves job satisfaction. As a *spokesperson*, the manager shares information with individuals outside the organization and provides visibility for the organization. Attending community meetings, offering continuing education, and participating in professional organizations are examples of ways in which the manager serves as a spokesperson.

Decisional Roles

Mintzberg describes four decisional roles. The *entrepreneur* constantly seeks ways to solve problems and make improvements in the organization. Reorganizing supplies, redesigning staff assignments, or creating new roles are all examples of entrepreneurship. The *disturbance handler* responds to unforeseen circumstances, such as replacement of staff for sick call, nosocomial outbreaks, or missing equipment. As *resource allocators*, managers schedule their own time, assign staff, and manage financial resources. Finally, the *negotiator* deals with outside forces mediating resources and decisions, such as resolving collective bargaining disputes or helping decide on major capitol purchases.

A CONTEMPORARY MODEL OF MANAGERIAL WORK

In 1994 Mintzberg proposed another model to describe managerial functions depicted in *Figure 4-6* (Mintzberg, 1994). In this model, managerial work is envisioned as occurring on three levels represented by concentric circles: *information, people,* and *action.* The manager, in the center, brings to the position a set of values, experiences, knowledge, and competencies. The manager conceives the frame, which includes the purpose of the job, the work needed, and how it should be done. Managing involves:

- Communicating and controlling at the information level
- Leading and linking at the people level
- Doing at the action level.

The first level of work, informational processing, includes communicating and controlling. *Communicating* involves receiving and sharing information with others, whereas controlling is using information to manage the work of others.

The second level of managerial work involves leading and linking people in order to encourage people to take action. *Leading* involves encouraging and enabling others—individually, as a team, or as an entire organization—to take effective action. *Linking* is establishing networks outside the unit in order to relay needs and exchange influence.

At the third and most concrete level, the focus is on managing action by doing. *Doing* includes taking supervisory actions—directing change, handling disturbances, and negotiating with other departments.

Using this framework for an analysis of nursing management, Mintzberg (1994) found that the roles previously described are blended into an intricate, caring management style.

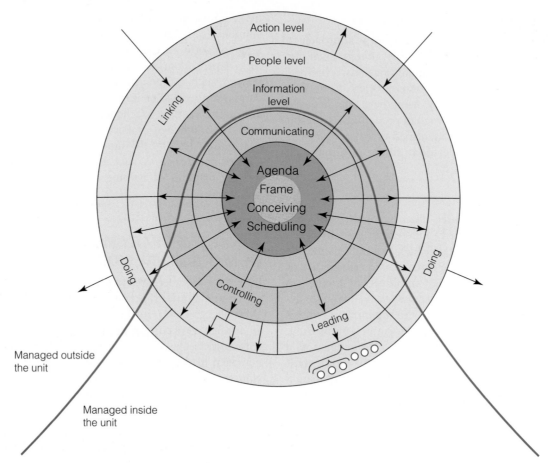

Figure 4-6 ● A model of managerial work. *From "Managing as Blended Care" by H. Mintzberg, 1994,* Journal of Nursing Administration, 24, p. 30.

Nurse Managers in Practice

Putting nursing management into practice in the dynamic health care system of today is a challenge. Organizations are in flux, structures are changing, and roles and functions of nurse managers become moving targets.

Titles for nurse managers vary as widely as do their responsibilities. The first line manager may also be titled first-line manager or unit manager. A middle manager might be deemed a department manager. The top-level nursing administrator could be named executive manager, chief nursing officer, or vice president of patient care. In addition, clinical titles might include professional practice leaders who are clinical nurse specialists or nurse practitioners. Regardless of their titles, all nurse managers must hold certain competencies.

NURSE MANAGER COMPETENCIES

The American Organization of Nurse Executives (AONE), an organization for the top nursing administrators in health care, identified five areas of competency necessary for nurses at all levels of management (AONE, 2005). Nurse managers must be skilled communicators and relationship-builders, have a knowledge of the health care environment, exhibit leadership skills, display professionalism, and demonstrate business skills (see Table 4-2). These characteristics intersect to provide a common core of leadership competencies (see ***Figure 4-7*** ●).

STAFF NURSE

Although not formally a manager, the staff nurse supervises LPNs, other professionals, and assistive

TABLE 4-2 AONE Five Areas of Competency

AONE BELIEVES THAT MANAGERS AT ALL LEVELS MUST BE COMPETENT IN THE FOLLOWING:

COMMUNICATION AND RELATIONSHIPS-BUILDING COMPETENCIES INCLUDE:

- Effective communication
- Relationship management
- Influence of behaviors
- Ability to work with diversity
- Shared decision-making
- Community involvement
- Medical staff relationships
- Academic relationships

KNOWLEDGE OF THE HEALTH CARE ENVIRONMENT INCLUDES:

- Clinical practice knowledge
- Patient care delivery models and work design knowledge
- Health care economics knowledge
- Health care policy knowledge
- Understanding of governance
- Understanding of evidence-based practice
- Outcome measurement
- Knowledge of and dedication to patient safety
- Understanding of utilization/case management
- Knowledge of quality improvement and metrics
- Knowledge of risk management

LEADERSHIP SKILLS INCLUDE:

- Foundational thinking skills
- Personal journey disciplines
- The ability to use systems thinking
- Succession planning
- Change management

PROFESSIONALISM INCLUDES:

- Personal and professional accountability
- Career planning
- Ethics
- Evidence-based clinical and management practice
- Advocacy for the clinical enterprise and for nursing practice
- Active membership in professional organizations

BUSINESS SKILLS INCLUDE:

- Understanding of health care financing
- Human resource management and development
- Strategic management
- Marketing
- Information management and technology

Copyright © 2005 by the American Organization of Nurse Executives. Address reprint permission requests to aone@aha.org.

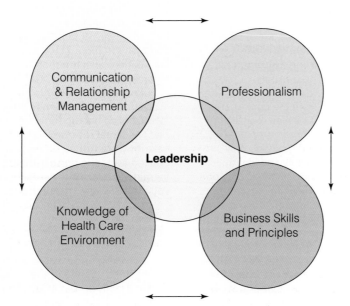

Figure 4-7 ● Core of leadership competencies. *Copyright © 2005 by the American Organization of Nurse Executives. Address reprint permission requests to aone@aha.org.*

personnel and so is also a manager who needs management and leadership skills. Communication, delegation, and motivation skills are indispensable.

In some organizations, shared governance has been implemented and traditional management responsibilities are allocated to the work team. In this case, staff nurses have considerable involvement in managing the unit. More information about shared governance and other innovative management methods is provided in Chapter 2.

FIRST-LEVEL MANAGEMENT

The **first-level manager** is responsible for supervising the work of nonmanagerial personnel and the day-to-day activities of a specific work unit or units. With primary responsibility for motivating the staff to achieve the organization's goals, the first-level manager represents staff to upper administration, and vice versa. Nurse managers have 24-hour accountability for the management of a unit(s) or area(s) within a health care organization. In the hospital setting, the first-level manager is usually the head nurse, nurse manager, or an assistant. In other settings, such as an ambulatory care clinic or a home health care agency, a first-level manager may be referred to as a coordinator. Box 4-2 describes a first-level manager's day.

CHARGE NURSE

Another role that does not fit the traditional levels of management is the **charge nurse**. The charge nurse

---

BOX 4-2	A Day in the Life of a First-Level Manager

As the manager for a surgical intensive care unit (SICU), Jamal Johnson is routinely responsible for supervising patient care, trouble shooting, maintaining compliance with standards, and giving guidance and direction as needed. In addition, he has fiscal and committee responsibilities and is accountable to the organization for maintaining its philosophies and objectives. The following exemplifies a typical day.

As Jamal came on duty, he learned that there had been a multiple car accident and that three of the victims were currently in surgery and destined for the unit. The assistant manager for nights had secured more staff for days: two part-time SICU nurses and a staff nurse from the surgical floor. However, she had not had time to arrange for two more patients to be moved out of the unit. From their assigned nurses, Jamal obtained an update on the patients who were candidates for transfer and, in consultation with his assistant, made the appropriate arrangements for the transfers.

Other staffing problems were at hand: In addition to the nurse who had been pulled from the floor, there were two orientees, and the staff needed to attend a safety in-service. As soon as the charge nurse came in, Jamal apprised her of the situation. Together, they reviewed the operating room schedule and identified staffing arrangements. Fortunately, Jamal had only one meeting today and would be available for backup staffing. In the meantime, he would work on evaluations.

After his discussions with the charge nurse, Jamal met with each of the night nurses to get an update on the status of the other patients. Then he went to his office to review his messages and plan his day. Tamera, an RN, had just learned she was pregnant, but she stated that she planned to work until delivery. Jamal learned that his budget hearing had been scheduled for the following Monday at 10 A.M. A pharmaceutical representative wanted to provide an in-service for the unit. Fortunately, there were no immediate crises.

Jamal called his supervisor to inform her of the status of affairs on the unit and learned that two other individuals in the accident had been transported to another hospital; one had since died. They discussed the ethical and legal ramifications. Jamal would need to review the policies on relations with the press and law enforcement and to update his staff.

As the first patient returned from surgery, Jamal went to help admit the patient and receive a report. Learning that the patient was stable, he informed Lucinda, the charge nurse, that the patient they had just received was likely to be charged with manslaughter and reviewed media and legal policies with her. They also discussed how the staff were doing. There were some equipment problems in room 2110; Lucinda had temporarily placed the patient on a transport monitor and was waiting for a biomedical technology staff member to check the monitor. Could Jamal follow up? Jamal agreed and commended Lucinda for her problem solving. She reminded Jamal they would need backup for lunch and in-services.

As Jamal returned to his office, he noted that the alarms were turned off on one of the patients. He pulled aside the nurse assigned to the patient and reminded her of the necessity to keep the alarms on at all times. Finally, back in his office he called biomedical technology to ascertain their plans to check the monitor and made notes regarding the charge nurse's problem-solving abilities and the staff nurse's negligence.

He reviewed staffing for the next 24 hours and noted that an extra nurse was needed for both the evening and night shifts because of the increased workload. After finding staff, he was able to finish one evaluation before covering for the in-services and lunch and then attending the policy and procedure team meeting.

position is an expanded staff nurse role with increased responsibility. The charge nurse functions as a liaison to the nurse manager, assisting in shift-by-shift coordination and promotion of quality patient care as well as efficient use of resources. The charge nurse often troubleshoots problems and assists other staff members in decision making. Role modeling, mentoring, and educating are additional roles that the charge nurse often assumes. Therefore, the charge nurse usually has extensive experience, skills, and knowledge in clinical practice and is familiar with the organization's standards and practices.

The charge nurse's job differs, though, from that of the first-level manager. The charge nurse's responsibilities are confined to a specific shift or task, whereas the first-level manager has 24-hour responsibility and accountability for all unit activities. Also the charge nurse has limited authority; the charge nurse functions as an agent of the manager and is accountable to the manager for any actions taken or decisions made.

Although often involved in planning and organizing the work to be done, the charge nurse has a limited scope of responsibility, usually restricted to the unit for a specific time period. In the past, the charge nurse had limited involvement in the formal evaluation of performance, but in today's climate of efficiency, the charge nurse may be involved in evaluations as well. With the trend toward participative management, charge nurses are assuming more of the roles and functions traditionally reserved for the first-level manager.

In some organizations, the position may be permanent and assigned and thus a part of the formal management team; in other organizations, the job may be rotated among experienced staff. The charge nurse, who switches from serving as a manager one day and a staff nurse the next, is especially challenged to balance the rotating roles (Leary & Allen, 2005). In some organizations, a differential amount of compensation is paid to the person performing charge duties; in others, no differential is paid because the position is shared equally among staff or represents a higher rung of a career ladder (possibly the first rung of a management ladder).

The charge nurse is often key to a unit's successful functioning (Leary & Allen, 2005). A charge nurse usually has considerable influence with the staff and may actually have more informal power than the manager. Therefore, the charge nurse is an important leader and can benefit by developing the skills considered necessary for a manager. Acting as charge nurse is often the first step toward a formal management position.

CLINICAL NURSE LEADER

The American Association of Colleges of Nursing (AACN), along with partners in practice, is spearheading an initiative to create a new nursing role, that of a **clinical nurse leader** (CNL) (Harris, Tornabeni, & Walters, 2006). The CNL is not a manager, per se, but instead is a lateral integrator of care responsible for a specified group of clients within a microsystem of the health care setting (AACN, 2007). The CNL role is designed to respond more effectively to challenges in today's rapidly changing, complex technological environment. Prepared at the master's level, the CNL "designs, implements, and evaluates client care by coordinating, delegating and supervising the care provided by the health care team, including licensed nurses, technicians, and other health professionals" (AACN, 2007, p. 6). AACN, ANA, and AONE are working on implementing the role into care delivery.

In the meantime a pilot study using clinical nurse leaders in one institution found that the role was effective in promoting positive outcomes for individual patients but not necessarily patients in the aggregate (Bowcutt, Wall, & Goolsby, 2006). Also the report raised the question if nurses prepared as nurse practitioners could fill the role of a CNL.

Followership: An Essential Component of Leadership

Leaders cannot lead without followers in much the same way that instructors need students to teach. Nor is anyone a leader all the time; everyone is a follower as well (Frisina, 2005). Even the hospital CEO follows the board of directors' instructions.

Followership is interactive and complementary to leadership, and the follower is an active participant in the relationship with the leader. A skilled, self-directed, energetic staff member is an invaluable complement to the leader and to the group (Grossman & Valiga, 2005). Most leaders welcome active followers; they help leaders accomplish their goals and the team succeed.

Followers are powerful contributors to the relationship with their leaders. Followers can influence leaders in negative ways, as government coverups, Medicare fraud, and corporate law-breaking attest (Offermann, 2004). The reverse is also true. Poor managers can undermine good followers by direct and indirect ways, such as criticizing, belittling, or ignoring positive contributions to the team. To counter such behaviors, you should note incidents that you experience, enlist others to help, and remain in control of yourself (Korn, 2004). (More about teams in Chapter 11.)

Miller (2007) describes followership along two continuums: participative and thinking. Participation can vary from passive (ineffective follower) to active (successful follower). Thinking can fluctuate between dependent and uncritical to independent and critical. Courage to be active contributors to the team and the leader characterize the effective follower.

Followership is fluid in another way. The nurse may be a leader at one moment and become a follower soon afterward. In fact, the ability to move along the continuum of degrees of followership is a must for successful teamwork. The nurse is a leader with subordinate staff and a follower of the nurse manager, possibly at the same time.

A constructive follower has several positive characteristics:

- Self-directed
- Proactive
- Supportive
- Commitment
- Initiative
- Candid, willing to criticize (Grossman & Valiga, 2000; Solovy, 2005; Spreitzer & Quinn, 2001).

Many of these qualities are the same ones that make an excellent leader, discussed next.

What Makes a Successful Leader?

Leadership success is an elusive quality. Some people seem to be natural leaders, and others struggle to attain leadership skills. Alas, subordinates often rate their nurse managers lower on leadership skills than the managers did themselves on all three dimensions studied: initiating change; maintaining positive relationships with employees; and creating order, structure, and clarity (Sellgren, Ekvall, & Tomson, 2006).

Leaders are skilled in empowering others, creating meaning and facilitating learning, developing knowledge, thinking reflectively, communicating, solving problems, making decisions, and working with others. Leaders generate excitement; they clearly define their purpose and mission. Leaders understand people and their needs; they recognize and appreciate differences in people, individualizing their approach as needed.

Leaders also have the capacity to earn and hold trust. They have a genuine concern for others and help others achieve their potential (Kerfoot, 2000). Leader-

ship is relationship management. The organizational structure heterarchy, described by Porter-O'Grady and Malloch (2002) and displayed in Figure 2-13 (see Chapter 2), exemplifies the importance of the leader's relationship skills.

Leadership requires attending to and acknowledging others and being personally authentic and accountable (Lewin & Regine, 2000). The leader must have enthusiasm, energy, and commitment, but most of all, the leader must be able to inspire others to commit to the goals of the organization.

AUTHENTIC LEADERS

Authentic leadership is a term recently added to the concept of excellence in leadership (Farber, 2004; George, 2003; Goffee & Jones, 2005). George (2003) posits a sense of purpose distinguishes an authentic leader. Farber (2004) adds that authentic leaders must be willing to take risks, even to the point of failing, but that creating an environment to inspire others is the authentic leader's most important imperative.

Authentic leadership is one of the American Association for Critical-Care Nurses requirements to establishing and sustaining a healthy work environment (AACN, 2005; Shirey, 2006). Authentic leaders, according to Kerfoot (2006), must be connected to the real pressures of front-line staff, be passionate about creating a quality work environment for them, and be able to generate the energy to push themselves to do the impossible.

EMOTIONAL LEADERS

Emotional intelligence has gained acceptance in the business world and more recently in health care (Herbert & Edgar, 2004). Goleman, Boyatzis, and McKee (2002) countered commonly accepted wisdom that emotions are best ignored in the work setting by asserting that the main job of leadership is emotional. Emotional intelligence involves personal competence, which includes self-awareness and self-management, and social competence, which includes social awareness and relationship management that begins with authenticity. (See Table 4-3.)

Goleman (2006) continues the discussion of emotional intelligence to include the social environment, asserting that attachment to others is an innate trait of human beings. Thus, emotions are "catching" with a pleasant day and an otherwise innocuous event turning into a negative experience that spills over into future interactions. Or the reverse. A positive experience lightens the mood and affects the next encounter. In a study also mentioned in Chapter 2, emotionally

TABLE 4-3	Emotional Intelligence Domains and Associated Competencies

PERSONAL COMPETENCE: These capabilities determine how we manage ourselves.

SELF-AWARENESS
- *Emotional self-awareness:* Reading one's own emotions and recognizing their impact; using "gut sense" to guide decisions
- *Accurate self-assessment:* Knowing one's strengths and limits
- *Self-confidence:* A sound sense of one's self-worth and capabilities

SELF-MANAGEMENT
- *Emotional self-control:* Keeping disruptive emotions and impulses under control
- *Transparency:* Displaying honesty and integrity; trustworthiness
- *Adaptability:* Flexibility in adapting to changing situations or overcoming obstacles
- *Achievement:* The drive to improve performance to meet inner standards of excellence
- *Initiative:* Readiness to act and seize opportunities
- *Optimism:* Seeing the upside in events

SOCIAL COMPETENCE: These capabilities determine how we manage relationships.

SOCIAL AWARENESS
- *Empathy:* Sensing others' emotions, understanding their perspective, and taking active interest in their concerns
- *Organizational awareness:* Reading the currents, decision networks, and politics at the organizational level
- *Service:* Recognizing and meeting follower, client, or customer needs

RELATIONSHIP MANAGEMENT
- *Inspirational leadership:* Guiding and motivating with a compelling vision
- *Influence:* Wielding a range of tactics for persuasion
- *Developing others:* Bolstering others' abilities through feedback and guidance
- *Change catalyst:* Initiating, managing, and leading in a new direction
- *Conflict management:* Resolving disagreements
- *Building bonds:* Cultivating and maintaining a web of relationships
- *Teamwork and collaboration:* Cooperation and team building

From *Primal Leadership* (2002) by D. Goleman, R. Boyatsis, and A. McKee. Boston: Harvard Business School Press, p. 39.
Copyright © 2002 by the Harvard Business School Publishing Corporation; all rights reserved.

intelligent leaders maintained a positive environment for nurses who remained employed after organizational restructuring (Cummings, 2006). When people feel good, they work more effectively.

Nurses, with their well-honed skills as compassionate caregivers, are aptly suited to this direction in leadership that emphasizes emotions and relationships with others as a primary attribute for success. These skills fit better with the more contemporary relationship-oriented theories as well. Thus, the workplace is a more complex and intricate environment than previously suggested. The following chapters show you how to put these skills to work.

What You Know Now

- A leader employs specific behaviors and strategies to influence individuals and groups to attain goals.
- Managers are responsible for efficiently accomplishing the goals of the organization.
- Leadership approaches are not static; they can be adapted for different situations, tasks, individuals, and future expectations.
- Trait theories attempt to identify the inborn characteristics of successful leaders, whereas behavioral theorists focus on learned leadership abilities and behaviors.
- Contingency theorists contend that leaders should adapt their style in relation to changing situations.
- Contemporary theorists assert that reality is fluid, complex, and interrelated and that interpersonal relationships are core to successful leadership.
- Traditional management functions include planning, organizing, directing, and controlling.
- Contemporary management requires communication, leadership, and action.
- Both leaders and followers contribute to the effectiveness of their relationship.
- Successful leaders are authentic, emotionally intelligent people who attend to, inspire, and empower others.

Tools for Leading, Managing, and Following

1. Pay attention to the context: Are you leading, managing, or following in this situation?
2. Recognize that each situation requires a specific skill set. Each is described in the chapter.
3. Notice others whose leadership style you admire and try to incorporate their behaviors in your own leadership if the situation is appropriate.
4. Evaluate yourself at regular opportunities in order to find ways to improve your abilities to lead, manage, and follow.

Questions to Challenge You

1. Think about people you know in management positions. Are any of them leaders as well? Describe the characteristics that make them leaders.
2. Think about people you know who are not in management positions but are leaders nonetheless. What characteristics do they have that make them leaders?
3. Describe the manager to whom you report. (If you are not employed, use the first-level manager on a clinical placement site.) Evaluate this person using the management functions described in the chapter.
4. Think about yourself as a manager whether you are in a management position or not. What skills do you possess that help you? What skills would you like to improve?
5. Evaluate yourself as a follower. Find at least one characteristic listed in the chapter that you would like to develop or improve. During the next week, try to find opportunities to practice that skill.
6. Evaluate yourself as a leader. How would you like to improve?

Explore MediaLink 🌐

Additional interactive resources for this chapter can be found on the Website at http://www.prenhall.com/sullivan. Click on Chapter 4 to select activities for this chapter.

- Video Overview
- NCLEX® Review Questions
- Critical Thinking Activities
- Current Events
- Nursing Leadership and Management in Action
- MediaLinks

References

American Association of Colleges of Nursing. (2007). *White paper on the education and role of the clinical nurse leader*. Retrieved July 2007 from www.aacn.nche.edu/Publications/pdf/CNLDRAFT.pdf

American Association of Critical-Care Nurses. (2005). *AACN standards for establishing and sustaining health work environments: A journey to excellence*. Retrieved July 2007 from www.aacn.org/aacn/pubpolcy.nsf/Files/ExecSum/$file/ExecSum.pdf

American Organization of Nurse Executives. (2005). *Nurse executive competencies*. Retrieved August 2007 from www.aone.org/aone/pdf/February%20Nurse%20Leader—final%20draft—for%20web.pdf

Aarons, G. A. (2006). Transformational and transactional leadership: Association with attitudes toward evidence-based practice. *Psychiatric Services, 57*(8), 1162–1169.

Bass, B. (1990). *Bass and Stogdill's handbook of leadership: Theory, research and managerial applications* (3rd ed.). New York: Free Press.

Bowcutt, M., Wall, J., & Goolsby, M. J. (2006). The clinical nurse leader: Promoting patient-centered outcomes. *Nursing Administration Quarterly, 30*(2), 156–161.

Campbell, P. T., & Rudisill, P. T. (2005). Servant leadership: A critical component for nurse leaders. *Nurse Leader, 3*(3), 27–29.

Cummings, G. G. (2006). Hospital restructuring and nursing leadership: A journey from research question to research program. *Nursing Administration Quarterly, 30*(4), 321–329.

Farber, S. (2004). *The radical leap: A personal lesson in extreme leadership*. Chicago: Dearborn Trade Publishing.

Fiedler, F. E. (1967). *A theory of leadership effectiveness*. New York: McGraw-Hill.

Frisina, M. E. (2005). Learn to lead by following. *Nursing Management, 36*(3), 12.

George, B. (2003). *Authentic leadership: Rediscovering the secrets to creating lasting value*. San Francisco: Jossey-Bass.

Gilbert, M. A. (1975). Personality profiles and leadership potential of medical-surgical and psychiatric nursing graduate students. *Nursing Research, 24*, 125–130.

Goffee, R., & Jones, G. (2005). Managing authenticity. *Harvard Business Review, 83*(12), 85–94.

Goleman, D. (2006). *Social intelligence: The new science of human relationships*. New York: Bantam Books.

Goleman, D., Boyatzis, R., & McKee, A. (2002). *Primal leadership: Realizing the power of emotional intelligence*. Boston: Harvard Business School Press.

Greenleaf, R. K. (1991). *The servant as leader*. Indianapolis: Robert K. Greenleaf Center.

Grossman, S. C., & Valiga, T. M. (2005). *The new leadership challenge: Creating the future of nursing* (2nd ed.). Philadelphia: F. A. Davis.

Harris, J. L., Tornabeni, J., & Walters, S. E. (2006). The clinical nurse leader: A valued member of the healthcare team. *Journal of Nursing Administration, 36*(10), 446–447.

Herbert, R., & Edgar, L. (2004). Emotional intelligence: A primal dimension of nursing leadership? *Canadian Journal of Nursing Leadership, 17*(4), 56–63.

Hersey, P., Blanchard, K. H., & Johnson, D. E. (2007). *Management of organizational behavior* (9th ed.). Upper Saddle River, NJ: Prentice Hall.

Homans, G. (1958). Social behavior as exchange. *American Journal of Sociology, 63*(6), 597–606.

House, R. J. (1971). A path–goal theory of leader effectiveness. *Administrative Science Quarterly, 16*(3), 321–338.

House, R. J., & Mitchell, T. R. (1974). Path–goal theory of leadership. *Journal of Contemporary Business, 3*, 81–98.

Jenkins, R. L., & Henderson, R. L. (1984). Motivating the staff: What nurses expect from their supervisors. *Nursing Management, 15*(2), 13–14.

Katz, D., & Kahn, R. L. (1952). Some recent findings in human relations research. In G. E. Swanson, E. M. Newcomb, & R. E. Hartley (Eds.), *Readings in social psychology*. New York: Holt, Rinehart and Winston.

Kerfoot, K. (2000). On leadership: Leading from the inside out. *Nursing Economics, 18*(6), 6–7.

Kerfoot, K. (2006). On leadership: Authentic leadership. *Dermatology Nursing, 18*(6), 595–596.

Klakovich, M. D. (1994). Connective leadership for the 21st century: A historical perspective and future directions. *Advances in Nursing Science, 16*(4), 42–54.

Korn, M. (2004). Toxic cleanup: How to deal with a dangerous leader. *Fast Company, 88*, 117.

Leary, C., & Allen, S. (2005). *A charge nurse's guide: Navigating the path of leadership*. Cleveland, OH: Center for Leader Development.

Lewin, K., & Lippitt, R. (1938). An experimental approach to the study of autocracy and democracy: A preliminary note. *Sociometry, 1*, 292–300.

Lewin, K., Lippitt, R., & White, R. K. (1939). Patterns of aggressive behavior in experimentally created social climates. *Journal of Social Psychology, 10*, 271–301.

Lewin, R., & Regine, B. (2000). *The soul at work: Listen. Respond. Let go*. New York: Simon & Schuster.

Likert, R. (1967). *The human organization: Its management and value*. New York: McGraw-Hill.

McGuire, E., & Kennerly, S. M. (2006). Nurse managers as transformational and transactional leaders. *Nursing Economic$, 24*(4), 179–186.

Miller, L. A. (2007). Followership. *Journal of Perinatal & Neonatal Nursing, 21*(1), 76.

Mintzberg, H. (1973). *The nature of managerial work*. New York: Harper & Row.

Mintzberg, H. (1994). Managing as blended care. *Journal of Nursing Administration, 24*, 29–36.

Offermann, L. R. (2004). When followers become toxic. *Harvard Business Review, 82*(1), 55–60.

Porter, L. W., & Lawler, E. E. (1968). *Managerial attitudes and performance*. Homewood, IL: Irwin-Dorsey.

Porter-O'Grady, T. (2003). A different age for leadership, Part 2: New rules, new roles. *Journal of Nursing Administration, 33*(3), 173–178.

Porter-O'Grady, T., & Malloch, K. (2002). *Quantum leadership: A textbook of new leadership*. Gaithersburg, MD: Aspen.

Sellgren, S., Ekvall, G., & Tomson, G. (2006). Leadership styles in nursing management: Preferred and perceived. *Journal of Nursing Management, 14*(5), 348–355.

Shirey, M. R. (2006). Authentic leaders: Creating healthy work environments for nursing practice. *American Journal of Critical Care, 15*(3), 256–268.

Solovy, A. (2005). Followership. *Hospital & Health Networks, 78*(5), 32.

Spreitzer, G. M., & Quinn, R. E. (2001). *A company of leaders: Five disciplines for unleashing the power in your workforce*. San Francisco: Jossey-Bass.

Stogdill, R. M. (1974). *Handbook of leadership: A survey of the literature*. New York: Free Press.

Stogdill, R. M., & Coons, A. E. (Eds.). (1957). *Leadership style: Its description and measurement*. Research Monograph O. 88. Columbus, OH: Bureau of Business Research, Ohio State University.

Thibaut, J. W., & Kelley, H. H. (1959). *The social psychology of groups*. New York: Wiley.

Timmereck, T. C. (2000). Use of the classical functions of management by health services midmanagers. *Health Care Manager, 19*(2), 50–67.

Vroom, V. H. (1964). *Work and motivation*. New York: Wiley.

Vroom, V. H., & Yetton, P. W. (1973). *Leadership and decision making*. Pittsburgh: University of Pittsburgh Press.

Ward, K. (2002). A vision for tomorrow: Transformational nursing leaders. *Nursing Outlook, 50*(3), 121–126.

CHAPTER 5

Initiating and Implementing Change

Learning Outcomes

After completing this chapter, you will be able to:

1. Explain why nurses need to be change agents.
2. Describe how different theorists explain change.
3. Discuss how the change process is similar to the nursing process.

MediaLink

www.prenhall.com/sullivan

See the Companion Website for chapter-specific resources at
www.prenhall.com/sullivan.

4. Differentiate among change strategies.
5. Describe the manager's role in change.
6. Discuss how to handle resistance to change.

Key Terms

Change *p67*

Change agent *p67*

Driving forces *p68*

Empirical–rational model *p71*

Normative–reeducative strategy *p72*

Power-coercive strategies *p71*

Restraining forces *p68*

Transitions *p75*

Why Change?

Leading change is an art (Bruhn, 2004), never needed more in the rapidly evolving system of health care. Organizational change is essential for adaptation; creative change is mandatory for growth. This climate for change produces new opportunities for nurses. Nurses are rethinking the way health care is organized and delivered. Innovation is in. The participatory approach is popular because status quo management will not work when a whole system is in transition. Transitional times demand new ways of thinking, creative strategies, and fresh opinions.

Change is inevitable, if not always welcome. Change is necessary for growth, although it often produces anxiety and fear. Even when planned, it can be threatening and a source of conflict because **change** is the process of making something different from what it was. There is a sense of loss of the familiar, the status quo. This is particularly true when change is unplanned or beyond human control. Even when change is expected and valued, a grief reaction still may occur. Those who initiate and manage change often encounter resistance from those experiencing unease and, possibly, symptoms of anxiety and grief.

Change is a continually unfolding process rather than an either/or event. The process begins with the present state, is disrupted, moves through a transition period, and ultimately comes to a desired state. Once the desired state has been reached, however, the process begins again.

Although nurses should understand and anticipate these reactions to change, they need to develop and exude a different approach. They can view change as a challenge and encourage their colleagues to participate. They can become uncomfortable with the status quo and be willing to take risks.

The Nurse as Change Agent

A **change agent** is one who works to bring about a change. Being a change agent, however, is not easy. Although the end result of change may benefit nurses and patients alike, initially it requires time, effort, and energy, all in short supply in the high-stress environment of health care.

A change agent can be a role model for others by touting the positive outcomes of change—improved patient care (Leary & Allen, 2006). The nurse, as an integral part of the system, is key to stimulating the need for change and crucial for the success of planned change (Mathena, 2002).

Changes will continue at a rapid pace with or without nursing's expert guidance. Nurses, like organizations, cannot afford merely to survive changes. If they are to exist as a distinct profession that has expertise in helping individuals respond to actual or potential health problems, they must be proactive in shaping the future. Opportunities exist now for nurses, especially those in management positions, to change the system about which they so often complain. On the other hand, managers should not initiate change just for the sake of change or to show that they are "managing" (McConnell, 2002).

Change Theories

Because change occurs within the context of human behavior, understanding how change occurs (or doesn't) is helpful to learn how to initiate or manage change. Four theorists, Lewin, Lippitt, Havelock, and Rogers, explain the change process from a social-psychological viewpoint. Table 5-1 compares the four.

Lewin (1951) proposes a force-field model, shown in **Figure 5-1** . He sees behavior as a dynamic balance

MEDIALINK   The Institute for Change Leadership

TABLE 5-1	Comparison of Change Models		
LEWIN	**LIPPITT**	**HAVELOCK**	**ROGERS**
1. Unfreezing	1. Diagnose problem	1. Building a relationship	1. Knowledge
2. Moving	2. Assess motivation	2. Diagnosing the problem	2. Persuasion
3. Refreezing	3. Assess change agent's motivations and resources	3. Acquiring resources	3. Decision
	4. Select progressive change objects	4. Choosing the solution	4. Implementation
	5. Choose change agent role	5. Gaining acceptance	5. Confirmation
	6. Maintain change	6. Stabilization and self-renewal	
	7. Terminate helping relationships		

of forces working in opposing directions within a field (such as an organization). **Driving forces** facilitate change because they push participants in the desired direction. **Restraining forces** impede change because they push participants in the opposite direction. To plan change, one must analyze these forces and shift the balance in the direction of change through a three-step process: unfreezing, moving, and refreezing. Change

Example:

Restraining forces

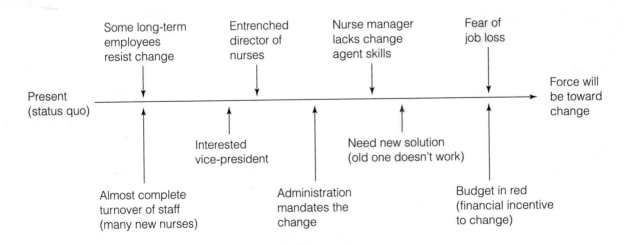

Driving forces

Figure 5-1 ● Lewin's force-field model of change. *Adapted from* Resolving Social Conflicts and Field Theory in Social Science *by K. Lewin. Copyright © 1997, by the American Psychological Association. Adapted with permission.*

occurs by adding a new force, changing the direction of a force, or changing the magnitude of any one force. Basically, strategies for change are aimed at increasing driving forces, decreasing restraining forces, or both.

Lewin's model has been used successfully in health care settings (Baulcomb, 2003). The image of people's attitudes thawing and then refreezing is conceptually useful. This symbolism helps to keep theory and reality in mind simultaneously.

Lippitt and colleagues (1958) extended Lewin's theory to a seven-step process and focused more on what the change agent must do than on the evolution of change itself. (See Table 5-1 for a comparison of four change theories.) They emphasized participation of key members of the target system throughout the change process, particularly during planning. Communication skills, rapport building, and problem-solving strategies underlie their phases.

Havelock (1973) described a six-step process, also a modification of Lewin's model. Havelock describes an active change agent as one who uses a participative approach.

Rogers (1983) takes a broader approach than Lewin, Lippitt, or Havelock (see Table 5-1). His five-step innovation–decision process details how an individual or decision-making unit passes from first knowledge of an innovation to confirmation of the decision to adopt or reject a new idea. His framework emphasizes the reversible nature of change: Participants may initially adopt a proposal but later discontinue it, or the reverse—they may initially reject it but adopt it at a later time. This is a useful distinction. If the change agent is unsuccessful in achieving full implementation of a proposal, it should not be assumed the issue is dead. It can be resurrected, perhaps in an altered form or at a more opportune time.

Rogers stresses two important aspects of successful planned change: Key people and policy makers must be interested in the innovation and committed to making it happen.

The Change Process

The change process follows the same path as the nursing process: assessment, planning, implementation, and evaluation (see Table 5-2).

ASSESSMENT

Emphasis is placed on the assessment phase of change for two reasons. Without data collection and analysis, planned change will not proceed past the "wouldn't it be a good idea if" stage.

TABLE 5-2	**Steps in the Change Process**

1. Identify the problem or opportunity.
2. Collect necessary data and information.
3. Select and analyze data.
4. Develop a plan for change, including time frame and resources.
5. Identify supporters or opposers.
6. Build a coalition of supporters.
7. Help people prepare for change.
8. Prepare to handle resistance.
9. Provide a feedback mechanism to keep everyone informed of the progress of change.
10. Evaluate effectiveness of the change and, if successful, stabilize the change.

Identify the Problem or the Opportunity

Change is often planned to close a discrepancy between the desired and actual state of affairs. Discrepancies may arise because of problems in reaching performance goals or because new goals have been created.

Opportunities demand change as much as (or more than) problems do, but they are often overlooked. Be it a problem or an opportunity, it must be identified clearly. If the issue is perceived differently by key individuals, the search for solutions becomes confused.

Start by asking the right questions, such as:

1. Where are we now? What is unique about us? What should our business be?
2. What can we do that is different from and better than what our competitors do?
3. What is the driving stimulus in our organization? What determines how we make our final decisions?
4. What prevents us from moving in the direction we wish to go?
5. What kind of change is required?

This last question generates integrative thinking on the potential effect of change on the system. Organizational change involves modifications in the system's interacting components: technology, structure, and people.

Introducing new technology changes the structure of the organization. The physical plant may altered if new services are added and then relationships among the people who work in the system change when the structure is changed. New units open; others close. New rules and regulations, new authority structures, and new budgeting methods may emerge. They, in turn,

MEDIALINK Initiating Change

change staffing needs, requiring people with different skills, knowledge bases, attitudes, and motivations.

Collect Data

Once the problem or opportunity has been clearly defined, the change agent collects data external and internal to the system. This step is crucial to the eventual success of the planned change. All driving and restraining forces are identified so the driving forces can be emphasized and the restraining forces reduced. It is imperative to assess the political pulse. Who will gain from this change? Who will lose? Who has more power and why? Can those power bases be altered? How?

Assess the political climate by examining the reasons for the present situation. Who is in control who may be benefiting now? Egos, commitment of the involved people, and personality likes and dislikes are as important to assess as the formal organizational structures and processes. The innovator has to gauge the potential for resistance.

The costs and benefits of the proposed change are obvious focal points. Also assess resources—especially those the manager can control. A manager who has the respect and support of an excellent nursing staff has access to a powerful resource in today's climate.

Analyze Data

The kinds, amounts, and sources of data collected are important, but they are useless unless they are analyzed. The change agent should focus more energy on analyzing and summarizing the data than on just collecting it. The point is to flush out resistance, identify potential solutions and strategies, begin to identify areas of consensus, and build a case for whichever option is selected. When possible, a statistical analysis should be made; it is worth the effort, especially when the change agent will need to persuade persons in power. The case should be presented cogently and succinctly using visual aids (e.g., bar graphs and charts) if needed.

At a not-for-profit hospital in the process of seeking Magnet status, each service line is looking for opportunities to improve standards of care, efficiency, and patient safety. In the ambulatory surgery center, the process of preoperative services was often slow and inefficient. The surgery center nurses were charged with finding ways to improve efficiency.

PLANNING

Planning the who, how, and when of the change is a key step. What will be the target system for the change?

Members from this system should be active participants in the planning stage. The more involved they are at this point, the less resistance there will be later. Lewin's unfreezing imagery is relevant here. Present attitudes, habits, and ways of thinking have to soften so members of the target system will be ready for new ways of thinking and behaving. Boundaries must melt before the system can shift and restructure.

This is the time to make people uncomfortable with the status quo. Plant the seeds of discontent by introducing information that may make people feel dissatisfied with the present and interested in something new. This information comes from the data collected (e.g., research findings, quantitative data, and patient satisfaction questionnaires or staff surveys). Couch the proposed change in comfortable terms as far as possible, and minimize anxiety about the new change.

Managers need to plan the resources required to make the change and establish feedback mechanisms to evaluate its progress and success. Establish control points with people who will provide the feedback and work with these people to set specific goals with time frames. Develop operational indicators that signal success or failure in terms of performance and satisfaction.

Three surgery center nurses designed a flow chart of how the process could flow better, took it to administration, and then were put in charge of implementation.

IMPLEMENTATION

The plans are put into motion (Lewin's moving stage). Interventions are designed to gain the necessary compliance. The change agent creates a supportive climate, acts as energizer, obtains and provides feedback, and overcomes resistance. Managers are the key change–process actors. Some methods are directed toward changing individuals in an organization, whereas others are directed toward changing the group.

Methods to Change Individuals

The most common method used to change individuals' perceptions, attitudes, and values is information giving (Katz & Kahn, 1978). Providing information is prerequisite to change implementation, but it is inadequate unless lack of information is the only obstacle to effecting change. Providing information does not address the motivation to change.

Training is often considered a method to change individuals. Training combines information-giving with skill practice. Training typically shows people how they are to perform in a system, not how to change it. Therefore, it is a strategy to help make the transition to a planned chance rather than a mechanism to initiate change.

Selecting and placing personnel or terminating key people often is used to alter the forces for or against change. When key supporters of the planned change are given the authority and accountability to make the change, their enthusiasm and legitimacy can be effective in leading others to support the change. Conversely, if those opposed to the change are transferred or leave the organization, the change is more likely to succeed.

Methods to Change Groups

Some implementation tactics use groups rather than individuals to attain compliance to change. The power of an organizational group to influence its members depends on its authority to act on an issue and the significance of the issue itself. The greatest influence is achieved when group members discuss issues that are perceived as important and make relevant, binding decisions based on those discussions. Effectiveness in implementing organizational change is most likely when groups are composed of members who occupy closely related positions in the organization.

Individual and group implementation tactics can be combined. Whatever methods are used, participants should feel their input is valued and should be rewarded for their efforts. Some people are not always persuaded before a beneficial change is implemented. Sometimes behavior changes first, and attitudes are modified later to fit the behavior. In this case, the change agent should be aware of participants' conflicts and reward the desired behaviors. It may take some time for attitudes to catch up.

The surgery center nurses worked with physician offices, insurance companies, and other hospital departments to implement the new process of preoperative services.

EVALUATION

Evaluate Effectiveness

At each control point, the operational indicators established are monitored. The change agent determines whether presumed benefits were achieved from a financial as well as a qualitative perspective, explaining the extent of success or failure. Unintended consequences and undesirable outcomes may have occurred.

Stabilize the Change

The change is extended past the pilot stage, and the target system is refrozen. The change agent terminates the

helping relationship by delegating responsibilities to target system members. The energizer role is still needed to reinforce new behaviors through positive feedback.

Over the next 3 months, the preoperative services department was able to show a 90 percent decrease in duplicate test orders, a 50 percent decrease in patient waiting time, and an 80 percent increase in physician satisfaction with the process.

Change Strategies

Regardless of the setting or proposed change, the four-step change process should be followed. However, specific strategies can be used, depending on the amount of resistance anticipated and the degree of power the change agent possesses.

POWER-COERCIVE STRATEGIES

Power-coercive strategies are based on the application of power by legitimate authority, economic sanctions, or political clout. Changes are made through law, policy, or financial appropriations. Those in control enforce changes by restricting budgets or creating policies. Those who are not in power may not even be aware of what is happening. Even if they are aware, they have little power to stop it. The prospective payment system for Medicare (DRGs) was a power-coercive strategy by the federal government. Similarly managed care has changed economic incentives in health care.

The change process continues through the seven steps, but there is little, if any, participation by the target system members. Resistance is handled by authority measures: Accept it, or leave.

Power-coercive strategies are useful when a consensus is unlikely despite efforts to stimulate participation by those involved. When much resistance is anticipated, time is short, and the change is critical for organizational survival, power-coercive strategies may be necessary.

EMPIRICAL–RATIONAL MODEL

In the **empirical–rational model** of change strategies, the power ingredient is knowledge. The assumption is that people are rational and will follow their rational self-interest if that self-interest is made clear to them. It is also assumed that the change agent who has knowledge has the expert power to persuade people to accept a rationally justified change that will benefit them. The flow of influence moves from those who know to those who do not know. New ideas are invented and communicated or diffused to all participants. Once enlightened, rational people will either accept or reject the idea based on its merits and consequences. Empirical–rational strategies are often effective when little resistance to the proposed change is expected and the change is perceived as reasonable.

Introduction of new technology that is easy to use, cuts nursing time, and improves quality of care would be accepted readily after in-service education and perhaps a trial use. The change agent can direct the change. There is little need for staff participation in the early steps of the change process, although input is useful for the evaluation and stabilization stages. The benefits of change for the staff and perhaps research findings regarding patient outcomes are the major driving forces. Well-researched, cost-effective technology can be implemented using these strategies.

NORMATIVE–REEDUCATIVE STRATEGIES

In contrast to the rational–empirical model, **normative–reeducative strategies** of change rest on the assumption that people act in accordance with social norms and values. Information and rational arguments are insufficient strategies to change people's patterns of actions; the change agent must focus on noncognitive determinants of behavior as well. People's roles and relationships, perceptual orientations, attitudes, and feelings will influence their acceptance of change.

In this mode, the power ingredient is not authority or knowledge, but skill in interpersonal relationships. The change agent does not use coercion or nonreciprocal influence, but collaboration. Members of the target system are involved throughout the change process. Value conflicts from all parts of the system are brought into the open and worked through so change can progress.

Normative–reeducative strategies are well suited to the creative problem solving needed in nursing and health care today. With their firm grasp of the behavioral sciences and communication skills, nurses are comfortable with this model. Changing from a traditional nursing system to self-governance or initiating a home follow-up service for hospitalized patients are examples of changes amenable to the normative–reeducative approach. In most cases, the normative–reeducative approach to change will be effective in reducing resistance and stimulating personal and organizational creativity. The obvious drawback is the time required for group participation and conflict resolution throughout the change process. When there is adequate time or when group consensus is fundamental to successful adoption of the change, the manager is well advised to adopt this framework.

Resistance to Change

Resistance to change is to be expected for a number of reasons: lack of trust, vested interest in the status quo, fear of failure, loss of status or income, misunderstanding, and belief that change is unnecessary or that it will not improve the situation (Yukl, 2005; Hellriegel, Jackson, & Slocum, 2002). In fact, if resistance does not surface, the change may not be significant enough (Morjikian, Kimball, & Joynt, 2007).

Employees may resist change because they dislike or disapprove of the person responsible for implementing the change or they may distrust the change process. Regardless, managers continually deal with change— both the change that they themselves initiate and change initiated by the larger organization.

Resistance varies from ready acceptance to full-blown resistance. Rogers (1983) identified six responses to change:

- *Innovators* love change and thrive on it.
- Less radical, *early adopters* are still receptive to change.
- The *early majority* prefers the status quo, but eventually accept the change.
- The *late majority* are resistive, accepting change after most others have.
- *Laggards* dislike change and are openly antagonistic.
- *Rejecters* actively oppose and may even sabotage change.

The change agent should anticipate and look for resistance to change. It will be lurking somewhere, perhaps where least expected. It can be recognized in such statements as:

- We tried that before.
- It won't work.
- No one else does it like that.
- We've always done it this way.
- We can't afford it.
- We don't have the time.
- It will cause too much commotion.
- You'll never get it past the board.
- Let's wait awhile.
- Every new boss wants to do something different.
- Let's start a task force to look at it; put it on the agenda.

Expect resistance and listen carefully to who says what, when, and in what circumstances. Open resisters are easier to deal with than closet resisters. Look for nonverbal signs of resistance, such as poor work habits and lack of interest in the change.

Resistance prevents the unexpected. It forces the change agent to clarify information, keep interest level high, and establish why change is necessary. It draws attention to potential problems and encourages ideas to solve them. Resistance is a stimulant as much as it is a force to be overcome. It may even motivate the group to do better what it is doing now, so that it does not have to change.

On the other hand, resistance is not always beneficial, especially if it persists beyond the planning stage and well into the implementation phase. It can wear down supporters and redirect system energy from implementing the change to dealing with resisters. Morale can suffer. Galpin (1996) suggests that communication is key to lowering resistance.

To manage resistance, use the following guidelines:

1. Talk to those who oppose the change. Get to the root of their reasons for opposition.
2. Clarify information, and provide accurate feedback.
3. Be open to revisions but clear about what must remain.
4. Present the negative consequences of resistance (e.g., threats to organizational survival, compromised patient care).
5. Emphasize the positive consequences of the change and how the individual or group will benefit. However, do not spend too much energy on rational analysis of why the change is good and why the arguments against it do not hold up. People's resistance frequently flows from feelings that are not rational.
6. Keep resisters involved in face-to-face contact with supporters. Encourage proponents to empathize with opponents, recognize valid objections, and relieve unnecessary fears.
7. Maintain a climate of trust, support, and confidence.
8. Divert attention by creating a different disturbance. Energy can shift to a more important problem inside the system, thereby redirecting resistance. Alternatively, attention can be brought to an external threat to create a bully phenomenon. When members perceive a greater environmental threat (such as competition or restrictive governmental policies), they tend to unify internally.

A nurse manager in a home health care agency used change management strategies to overcome resistance as shown in Case Study 5-1.

The Nurse's Role

INITIATING CHANGE

Contrary to popular opinion, change often is not initiated by top-level management (Yukl, 2005), but rather emerges as new initiatives or problems are identified. In fact, Ingersoll et al. (2002) found that mid-level managers had more effect on staff nurses' perception of change than did the executives. Likewise, Crow (2006) suggests that a partnership between staff and administrators is more effective in producing change than the traditional top-down approach.

Staff nurses often think that they are unable to initiate and create change, but that is not so.

Home health nurses were often frustrated by not having appropriate supplies with them when seeing a patient for the first time. A team of nurses completed a chart audit to identify commonly used supplies and equipment. Each nurse was then supplied with a small plastic container to keep in his or her car with these items. Frustration decreased and efficient use of nursing time was improved.

The manager, as well, may resist leading change. Afraid of "rocking the boat," fearful that no one will join our efforts, recalling that past efforts at change had failed, or even the reluctance to become involved may prevent the nurse from initiating change (Grindel, 2006).

Making change is not easy, but it is a mandatory skill for managers. Successful change agents demonstrate certain characteristics that can be cultivated and mastered with practice. Among these are:

- The ability to combine ideas from unconnected sources
- The ability to energize others by keeping the interest level up and demonstrating a high personal energy level
- Skill in human relations: well-developed interpersonal communication, group management, and problem-solving skills
- Integrative thinking: the ability to retain a big picture focus while dealing with each part of the system
- Sufficient flexibility to modify ideas when modifications will improve the change, but enough persistence to resist nonproductive tampering with the planned change
- Confidence and the tendency not to be easily discouraged
- Realistic thinking

CASE STUDY 5-1 Encouraging Change

Peter Beasley is nurse manager of pediatric home care for a private home health care agency. Last year the agency completed a pilot of wireless devices for use in documenting home visits. As nurses complete the documentation, charges for supplies and medical equipment are also generated. The agency director informed the nurse managers that all nurses will be required to use the wireless devices within the next 3 months.

Charlene Ramirez has been a pediatric nurse for 18 years, working for the home health care agency for the past 5 years. Charlene has been active in updating the pediatric documentation and training staff when new paper-based documentation was implemented in the past. Although she was part of the pilot, Charlene is very much opposed to using the new wireless devices. She has rarely used a computer and complains she can barely visualize text on a regular monitor. At a recent staff meeting, Charlene stated she would rather quit than learn to use the new wireless devices.

Peter empathizes with Charlene's reluctance to use the new handheld computers. He also recognizes how much Charlene contributes in expertise and leadership to the department. However, he knows that the new performance standards require all employees to use the wireless devices. After three mandatory training sessions, Charlene repeatedly tells coworkers "We've tried things like this before, it never works. We'll be back on paper within 6 months, so why waste my time learning this stuff?" The program trainer reports that Charlene was disruptive during the class and failed her competency exam.

Peter meets privately with Charlene to discuss her resistance to the new technology. Charlene again states that she fails to see the need for wireless devices in delivering quality patient care. Peter reviews the new performance standards with Charlene, emphasizing the technology requirements. He asks Charlene if she has difficulty understanding the application or just in using the device. Charlene admits she cannot see the text on the screen and therefore cannot determine what exactly she is documenting. Peter informs Charlene that the agency's health benefits include vision exams and partial payment for corrective lenses. He suggests she talk with an optometrist to see if special glasses would help her see the screen. Peter also makes a note to speak with the technology specialist to see if there are aids to assist staff in viewing data on the device.

Manager's Checklist

The nurse manager is responsible to:

- Communicate openly and honestly with employees who oppose change.
- Understand resistance to change.
- Maintain support and confidence in staff even if they are resistive to change.
- Emphasize the positive outcomes from initiating change.
- Find solutions to problems that are obstacles to change.

- Trustworthiness: a track record of integrity and success with other changes
- The ability to articulate a vision through insights and versatile thinking
- The ability to handle resistance.

Energy is needed to change a system. Power is the main source of that energy. Informational power, expertise, and possibly positional power can be used to persuade others.

To access optimum power, use the following strategies:

1. Analyze the organizational chart. Know the formal lines of authority. Identify informal lines as well.

2. Identify key persons who will be affected by the change. Pay attention to those immediately above and below the point of change.
3. Find out as much as possible about these key people. What are their "tickle points"? What interests them, gets them excited, turns them off? What is on their personal and organizational agendas? Who typically aligns with whom on important decisions?
4. Begin to build a coalition of support before you start the change process. Identify the key people who will be affected by the change. Talk informally with them to flush out possible objections to your idea and potential opponents. What will

the costs and benefits be to them—especially in political terms? Can your idea be modified in ways that retain your objectives but appeals to more key people?

5. Follow the organizational chain of command in communicating with administrators. Don't bypass anyone to avoid having an excellent proposal undermined.

This information helps you develop the most sellable idea or at least pinpoint probable resistance. It is a broad beginning to the data-collection step of the change process and has to be fine-tuned once the idea is better defined. The astute manager keeps alert at all times to monitor power struggles.

Although a cardinal rule of change is: Don't try to change too much too fast, the savvy manager develops a sense of exquisite timing by pacing the change process according to the political pulse. For example, the manager unfreezes the system during a period of coalition building and high interest, while resistance is low or at least unorganized.

You may decide to stall the project beyond a pilot stage if resistance solidifies or gains a powerful ally. In this case, do whatever you can to reduce resistance. If resistance continues, two options should be considered:

- The change is not workable and should be modified to meet the strongest objections (compromise).
- The change is fine-tuned sufficiently, but change must proceed now and resistance must be overcome.

IMPLEMENTING CHANGE

In addition to initiating change, nurses and nurse managers are called on to assist with change in other ways. They may be involved in the planning stage, charged with sharing information with coworkers, or they may be asked to help manage the transition to planned change.

Planning Change

One magnet-recognized hospital engaged all of its nurses in planning for the desired future of clinical nursing in their organization (Capuano, Dirishin, Millard, & Hitchings, 2007). Using the American Nurses Association's *Nursing's Agenda for the Future* (2002) as a framework, they held a series of group events to solicit ideas and opinions. Every nurse—executive, manager, or staff nurse—had an equal vote to approve or veto a proposed change. Their process illustrates the normative–reeducative process of change.

Managing Transitions to Change

Transitions are those periods of time between the current situation and the time when change is implemented (Bridges, 2004). They are the times ripe for a change agent to act. As a leader or a follower, the nurse can help other staff adapt, accept losses, and retain or regain their passion for the work (Porter-O'Grady, 2003). Just as initiating change is not easy, neither is transitioning to changed circumstances.

Letting go of long-term, comfortable activities is difficult. The tendency is to:

- Add new work to the old
- Make individual decisions about what to add and what to let go
- Toss out everything done before (Bridges, 2004)

Accepting loss and honoring the past with respect is essential. Passion for the work is based on results, not activities, regardless of their necessity or effectiveness.

A large national for-profit health care system purchased a new hospital clinical information system. Because all paper charting would be eliminated, nurses would be directly affected. Their participation could spell success or failure for the new system. To help the transition occur smoothly, nurses from each department met together for a demonstration of the new clinical information system and provided feedback to the IT department about nursing process and integrating patient care with the new system. Then a few nurses on each unit were selected to be trained as experts in the new technology and they, in turn, trained other staff members, communicating with the IT department when concerns arose.

Handling Constant Change

Change has always occurred; what's different today is both the pace of change and that an initial change causes a chain reaction of more and more change (Bridges, 2004). Change, rather than an occasional event, has become the norm.

Regardless of their position in an organization, nurses find themselves constantly dealing with change. Whether they thrive in such an atmosphere is a function of both their own personal resources and the environment in which change occurs.

If you don't like the current situation, you may look forward to change. As Midwesterners are fond of saying when asked about the weather: "If you don't like it today, just wait until tomorrow. It will change."

What You Know Now

- In today's health care system, change is inevitable, necessary, and constant.
- With change occurring rapidly, nurses are in a pivotal position to initiate and participate in change.
- For change to be positive for nurses, they must develop change agent skills.
- Critical evaluation of change theories provides guidance and direction for initiating and managing change.
- The change process is similar to the nursing process: assessment, planning, implementation, and evaluation.
- Change strategies differ depending on resistance expected and the change agent's power.
- Resistance to change is to be expected, and it can be a stimulant as well as a force to be overcome.
- The manager may be involved in change by initiating it or participating in implementing change.
- Handling constant change is a function of nurses' resources and the environment in which change occurs.

Tools for Initiating and Managing Change

1. Communicate openly and honestly with employees who oppose change.
2. Maintain support and confidence in staff even if they are resistive to change.
3. Emphasize the positive outcomes from initiating change.
4. Find solutions to problems that are obstacles to change.
5. Accept the constancy of change.

Questions to Challenge You

1. Identify a needed change in the organization where you practice. Using the change process, outline the steps you would take to initiate change.
2. Consider your school or college. What change do you think is needed? Explain how you would change it to become a better place for learning.
3. Have you had an experience with change occurring in your organization? What was your initial reaction? Did that change? How well did the change process work? Was the change successful?
4. Do you have a behavior you would like to change? Using the steps in the change process, describe how you might effect that change.
5. How do you normally react to change? Choose from the following:
   a. I love new ideas, and I'm ready to try new things.
   b. I like to know that something will work out before I try it.
   c. I try to avoid change as much as possible.
6. Did your response to the above question alter how you would like to view change? Think about this the next time change is presented to you.
7. Remember your first time on a clinical unit. Picture it in your mind. How did you feel? Overwhelmed? Afraid of failing? That's the feeling that people have when facing change. Try to remember how you felt when you encounter resistance to change.

Explore MediaLink 🌐

Additional interactive resources for this chapter can be found on the Website at http://www.prenhall.com/sullivan. Click on Chapter 5 to select activities for this chapter.

- Video Overview
- NCLEX® Review Questions
- Critical Thinking Activities
- Current Events
- Nursing Leadership and Management in Action
- MediaLinks

References

American Nurses Association. (2002). *Nursing's agenda for the future: A call to the nation.* Washington, DC: American Nurses Publishing.

Baulcomb, J. S. (2003). Management of change through force field analysis. *Journal of Nursing Management, 11*(4), 275–280.

Bridges, W. (2004). *Managing transitions* (2nd expanded edition). Cambridge, MA: Da Capo Press.

Bruhn, J. G. (2004). Leaders who create change and those who manage it: How leaders limit success. *The Health Care Manager, 23*(7), 132–140.

Capuano, T., Durishin, L. D., Millard, J. L., Hitchings, K. S. (2007). The desired future of nursing doesn't just happen—engaged nurses create it. *Journal of Nursing Administration, 37*(2), 61–63.

Crow, G. (2006). Diffusion of innovation: The leaders' role in creating the organizational context for evidence-based practice. *Nursing Administration Quarterly, 30*(3), 236–242.

Galpin, T. J. (1996). *The human side of change.* San Francisco: Jossey-Bass.

Grindel, C. (2006). The nurse's responsibility in creating a "nurse-friendly" culture in the workplace. *MEDSURG Nursing, 15*(3), 125–126.

Havelock, R. (1973). *The change agent's guide to innovation in education.* Englewood Cliffs, NJ: Educational Technology Publications.

Hellriegel, D., Jackson, S. E., & Slocum, Jr., J. W. (2002). *Management: A competency-based approach* (9th ed.). Eagan, MN: South-Western.

Ingersoll, G. L., Wagner, L., Merck, S. E., Kirsch, J. C., Hepworth, J. T., & Williams, M. (2002). Patient-focused redesign and employee perception of work environment. *Nursing Economic$, 20*(4), 163–170.

Katz, D., & Kahn, R. (1978). *The social psychology of organizations* (2nd ed.). New York: Wiley.

Leary, C., & Allen, S. J. (2006). *A charge nurse's guide: Navigating the path of leadership.* Cleveland, OH: Center for Leader Development Press.

Lewin, K. (1951). *Field theory in social science.* New York: Harper & Row.

Lippitt, R., Watson, J., & Westley, B. (1958). *The dynamics of planned change.* New York: Harcourt & Brace.

Mathena, K. A. (2002). Nursing manager leadership skills. *Journal of Nursing Administration, 32*(3), 136–142.

McConnell, C. R. (2002). Know when to manage less, not more. *The Health Care Manager, 20*(4), iv–vi.

Morjikian, R. L., Kimball, B., & Joynt, J. (2007). Leading change: The nurse executive's role in implementing new care delivery models. *Journal of Nursing Administration, 37*(9), 399–404.

Porter-O'Grady, T. (2003). A different age for leadership, Part 2: New rules, new roles. *Journal of Nursing Administration, 33*(3), 173–178.

Rogers, E. (1983). *Diffusion of innovations* (3rd ed.). New York: Free Press.

Yukl, G. (2005). *Leadership in organizations* (6th ed.). Upper Saddle River, NJ: Prentice Hall.

CHAPTER 6

Managing and Improving Quality

Learning Outcomes

After completing this chapter, you will be able to:

1. Describe how total quality management, continuous quality management, Six Sigma, and Lean Six Sigma address quality.
2. Describe the efforts that are being made to improve the quality of health care.
3. Point out how nurses are involved in reducing risks.
4. Explain how the nurse manager is key to reducing risks.
5. Discuss how to create a blame-free environment.

MediaLink

www.prenhall.com/sullivan
See the Companion Website for chapter-specific resources at
www.prenhall.com/sullivan.

Key Terms

Benchmarking *p81*
Concurrent audit *p82*
Continuous quality
  improvement (CQI) *p80*
Incident report *p85*
Indicator *p81*
Lean Six Sigma *p83*

Outcome standards *p81*
Outcomes management *p82*
Peer review *p82*
Process standards *p81*
Reportable incident *p85*
Retrospective audit *p82*
Risk management *p84*

Six Sigma *p82*
Standards *p81*
Structure standards *p81*
Total quality management
  (TQM) *p79*
Utilization reviews *p82*

I n today's highly competitive health care environment, each member of the health care organization must be accountable for the quality and cost of health care. Concern about quality gained national attention after publication of the Institute of Medicine's (IOM) reports on medical errors in 1999 (IOM, 1999) and their later recommendations for health professionals' education (IOM, 2003). Additionally, concern about cost continues unabated. Both quality and cost containment are found in the concept of total quality management, which has evolved into a model of continuous quality improvement designed to improve system and process performance. Risk management is integrated within a quality management program.

Quality Management

Quality management moved health care from a mode of identifying failed standards, problems, and problem people to a proactive organization in which problems are prevented and ways to improve care and quality of care are sought. This paradigm shift involves all in the organization and promotes problem solving and experimentation.

A quality management program is based on an integrated system of information and accountability. Clinical information systems can provide the data needed to enable organizations to track activities and outcomes. For example, data from clinical information systems can be used to track patient wait times from admitting to outpatient testing to admission in an inpatient care unit. Delays in the process can be identified so appropriate staff and resources are available at the right time to decrease delays and increase efficiency and patient satisfaction. Methods to discover problems in the system without blaming the "sharp end," the last

individual in the chain to act (e.g., the nurse gives a wrong medication). The system must be accepted and used by the entire staff.

TOTAL QUALITY MANAGEMENT

Total quality management (TQM) is a management philosophy that emphasizes a commitment to excellence throughout the organization. The creation of Dr. W. Edwards Deming, TQM was adopted by the Japanese and helped transform their industrial development after World War II. Dr. Deming based his system on principles of quality management that were originally applied to improve quality and performance in the manufacturing industry. They are now widely used to improve quality and customer satisfaction in a number of service industries, including health care.

TQM Characteristics

Four core characteristics of total quality management are:

- Customer/client focus
- Total organizational involvement
- Use of quality tools and statistics for measurement
- Key processes for improvement identified.

Customer/Client Focus An important theme of quality management is to address the needs of both internal and external customers. Internal customers include employees and departments within the organization, such as the laboratory, admitting office, and environmental services. External customers of a health care organization include patients, visitors, physicians, managed-care organizations, insurance companies, and regulatory agencies, such as the Joint Commission, which accredits health care organizations, and public health departments.

Under the principles of TQM, the nurses must know who the customers are and endeavor to meet their needs. Providing flexible schedules for employees, adjusting routines for A.M. care to meet the needs of patients, extending clinic hours beyond 5 P.M., and putting infant changing tables in restrooms are some health care examples. Putting the customer first requires creative and innovative methods to meet the ever-changing needs of internal and external customers.

Total Organizational Involvement The goal of quality management is to involve all employees and empower them with the responsibility to make a difference in the quality of service they provide. This means all employees must have knowledge of the TQM philosophy as it relates to their job and the overall goals and mission of the organization. Knowledge of the TQM process breaks down barriers between departments. The phrase "That's not my job" is eliminated. Departments work together as a team. On occasion, nursing personnel might clean a bed for a new admission from the emergency room or an administrator might transport a patient to the radiology department. Sharing processes across departments and patient care functions increases teamwork, productivity, and patient positive outcomes.

Use of Quality Tools and Statistics for Measurement A common management adage is, "You can't manage what you can't (or don't) measure" (Chaiken & Holmquest, 2003). There are many tools, formats, and designs that can be used to build knowledge, make decisions, and improve quality. Tools for data analysis and display can be used to identify areas for process and quality improvement, and then to benchmark the progress of improvements. Deming applied the scientific method to the concept of TQM to develop a model he called the PDCA cycle (Plan, Do, Check, Act) depicted in *Figure 6-1●*.

Identification of Key Processes for Improvement All activities performed in an organization can be described in terms of processes. Processes within a health care setting can be:

- Systems-related (e.g., admitting, discharging, and transferring patients)
- Clinical (e.g., administering medications, managing pain)
- Managerial (e.g., risk management and performance evaluations).

Processes can be very complex and involve multidisciplinary or interdepartmental actions. Processes involving multiple departments must be investigated in detail by members from each department involved in the activity so that they can proactively seek opportunities to reduce waste and inefficiencies and develop ways to improve performance and promote positive outcomes.

CONTINUOUS QUALITY IMPROVEMENT

TQM is the overall philosophy, whereas **continuous quality improvement (CQI)** is the process used to improve quality and performance. TQM and CQI often are used synonymously. In health care organizations, CQI is the process used to investigate systematically ways to improve patient care. As the name implies, continuous quality improvement is a never-ending endeavor (Hedges, 2006).

CQI means more than just meeting standards and thresholds or solving problems. It involves evaluation, actions, and a mind-set to strive constantly for excellence. This concept is sometimes difficult to grasp because patient care involves the synchronization of activities in multiple departments. Therefore, the importance of developing and implementing a well-thought-out process is key to a successful CQI implementation.

There are four major players in the CQI process:

- Resource group
- Coordinator
- Team leader
- Team

The resource group is made up of senior management (e.g., CEO, vice presidents). It establishes overall CQI policy, vision, and values for the organization and actively involves the board of directors in this process, thereby ensuring that the CQI program has sufficient emphasis and is provided with the training resources needed. The CQI coordinator is often appointed by

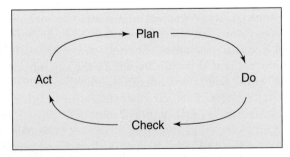

Figure 6-1 ● PDCA cycle. *From* Improving Quality Performance, *by P. Schroeder, 1994, St. Louis, MO: Mosby.*

the CEO to provide day-to-day management of the CQI process and related activities (e.g., training programs).

CQI teams are designated to evaluate and improve select processes. They are formally established and supported by the resource group. CQI teams range in size from 5 to 10 people, representing all major functions of the process being evaluated.

Each CQI team is headed by a team leader who is familiar with the process being evaluated. The leader organizes team meetings, sets the agenda, and guides the group through the discussion, evaluation, and implementation process.

Continuous quality improvement was integrated with patient feedback in one study (Hyrkas & Lehti, 2003). Results revealed that nurses and patients were more satisfied when the evaluations of the quality of their care agreed. The researchers concluded that integrating CQI with team supervision improved the quality of patient care as well.

COMPONENTS OF QUALITY MANAGEMENT

A comprehensive quality management program includes:

- **A comprehensive quality management plan.** A quality management plan is a systematic method to design, measure, assess, and improve organizational performance. Using a multidisciplinary approach, this plan identifies processes and systems that represent the goals and mission of the organization, identifies the customers, and specifies opportunities for improvement. Critical paths, which are described in Chapter 3, are an example of a quality management plan. Critical paths identify expected outcomes within a specific time frame. Then variances are tracked and accounted for.
- **Set standards for benchmarking. Standards** are written statements that define a level of performance or a set of conditions determined to be acceptable by some authorities. Standards relate to three major dimensions of quality care:
  - Structure
  - Process
  - Outcome

Structure standards relate to the physical environment, organization, and management of an organization. **Process standards** are those connected with the actual delivery of care. **Outcome standards** involve the end results of care that has been given.

An **indicator** is a tool used to measure the performance of structure, process, and outcome standards. It is measurable, objective, and based on current knowledge. Once indicators are identified, **benchmarking**, or comparing performance using identified quality indicators across institutions or disciplines, is the key to quality improvement.

In nursing, both generic and specific standards are available from the American Nurses Association and specialty organizations; however, each organization and each patient care area must designate standards specific to the patient population being served. These standards are the foundation on which all other measures of quality are based.

An example of a standard is: Every patient will have a written care plan within 12 hours of admission.

- **Performance appraisals.** Based on requirements of the job, employees are evaluated on their performance. This feedback is essential for employees to be professionally accountable. (See Chapter 18 for more on performance appraisals.)
- **A focus on intradisciplinary assessment and improvement.** There will always be a need for groups to assess, analyze, and improve their own performance. Methods to assess performance should, however, focus on the CQI philosophy, which involves group or intradisciplinary performance. Peer review, discussed later in the chapter, is an example of intradisciplinary assessment.
- **A focus on interdisciplinary assessment and improvement.** Multidisciplinary, patient-focused teamwork emphasizing collaboration, communication, coordination, and integration of care is the core of CQI in health care. It is important not to disband departmental quality functions, such as patient satisfaction, utilization review, or infection control, but rather to refocus information on improving the process.

Resources are used to collect data, such as the number of postoperative infections or the number of return clinic visits, to guide the decision-making process. Throughout the evaluation and implementation process, the team's focus is the patient. Implementation is continually evaluated using a patient satisfaction survey, which is just one of the methods used to monitor nursing care. For example, some organizations follow up outpatient surgery clients with direct phone calls from nursing staff to ensure patients understand discharge instructions and that pain was controlled following discharge. Any potential complications are referred to the surgeon.

Other methods include the nursing audit, peer review, and utilization review.

Nursing Audits

A nursing audit can be retrospective or concurrent. A **retrospective audit** is conducted after a patient's discharge and involves examining records of a large number of cases. The patient's entire course of care is evaluated and comparisons made across cases. Recommendations for change can be based on the experiences of many patients with similar care problems as well as on the spectrum of care considered.

A **concurrent audit** is conducted during the patient's course of care; it examines the care being given to achieve a desired outcome in the patient's health and evaluates the nursing care activities being provided. Changes can be made if patient outcomes so indicate.

Peer Review

Peer review occurs when practicing nurses assess and judge the performance of professional peers against predetermined standards. In this case, nurses are the experts at determining what the indicators of quality care are and when such care has been provided. Their expertise is especially useful in complicated cases; sometimes more than one expert's opinion is used for comparisons. For example, the Women's Health service line committee brought together experienced nurses from all departments: obstetrics, gynecology, and reproductive services to evaluate the standards of care for high risk pregnancies.

Utilization Review

Utilization reviews are based on the appropriate allocation of resources and are mandated by the Joint Commission. Such a review is not specifically directed toward nursing care, but it may provide information on nursing practices that require further investigation.

Once standards have been set, criteria established, and methods for evaluating adherence to the standards determined, the organization is prepared to examine its risk in relation to its accountability. Risk management programs in health care organizations involve two important areas: patient and/or family incident review, and employee and visitor safety. (See later section on risk management.)

Outcomes Management

Outcomes management is a new technology in which costs and quality are concurrently and retrospectively measured and evaluated in order to improve clinical practice. Internal or external data from the literature or other health care providers are used as benchmarks against which process, quality, and financial goals can be set and achieved. Additionally, data from internal clinical information systems can be used to provide a linear view of patient care delivery and associated cost. Collaborative practice teams consisting of physicians, nurses, dietitians, pharmacists, social workers, and finance experts develop research-based standardized practice models such as order sets or critical pathways. These models are implemented and patient outcomes measured. The outcomes are statistically analyzed. Care is redesigned based on the outcomes analysis and the new processes implemented. The cycle continues, constantly evaluating whether desired outcomes have been achieved.

SIX SIGMA

Six Sigma is another quality management program that uses, primarily, quantitative data to monitor progress (Pande & Holpp, 2002). Six Sigma is a *measure*, a *goal*, and a *system of management*.

- **As a measure.** Sigma is the Greek letter—ó—for standard, meaning how much performance varies from a standard. This is similar to how CQI monitors results against an outcome measure.
- **As a goal.** One goal might be accuracy. How many times, for example, is the right medication given in the right amount to the right patient at the right time by the right route?
- **As a management system.** Compared to other quality management systems, Six Sigma involves management to a greater extent in monitoring performance and ensuring favorable results.

The system has six themes:

- Customer (patient) focus
- Data driven
- Process emphasis
- Proactive management
- Boundary-less collaboration
- Aim for perfection; tolerate failure.

The first three themes are similar to other quality management programs. The focus is on the object of the service, in nursing's case—the patient. Data provide the evidence of results and the emphasis is on the processes used in the system.

The latter three themes, however, differ from other programs. Management is actively involved and

MEDIALINK   Six Sigma

boundaries breached (e.g., the disconnect between departments). More radically, Six Sigma tolerates failure (a necessary condition for creativity) while striving for perfection.

LEAN SIX SIGMA

Lean Six Sigma focuses on improving process flow and eliminating waste (Martin, 2007). Waste occurs when the organization provides more resources than are required. For example, most managers respond to increased census by adding staff but tend not to reduce staff when census declines (Caldwell, 2006). Because the goal of Lean Six Sigma is to identify and reduce waste it provides tools that can be used with a Six Sigma management system.

Improving the Quality of Care

TQM, CQI, Six Sigma, and Lean Six Sigma are quantifiable systems that measure performance against set standards, but they are not a panacea for all of health care's problems. For example, health maintenance organizations, promulgated by Paul Ellwood in the 1970s, tried to "manage" health care with prepaid service. (See Chapter 1 for more information about managed care.) He neglected, however, to account for unintended consequences. The result that Ellwood sought was to encourage prevention but the reverse happened: physicians were incentivized to limit or reduce care (Bruhn, 2004).

In contrast to Ellwood, Donald Berwick (2002) used an organizational approach to health care's problems by focusing on the patient, not the physician. Similarly, Kaissi (2006) proposes that a culture of safety, rather than a culture of blame, characterizes an organization where everyone accepts responsibility for patient safety. Errors are opportunities to improve by focusing on "what happened" as opposed to "who did it." Wojner (2002) agrees. She states that providers and administrators must partner to reduce errors and improve safety and that organizational transparency should be the goal of patient safety initiatives.

NATIONAL INITIATIVES

A culture of safety and quality permeates many efforts at the national level. The Institute of Medicine has focused on safety since the late 1990s with the publication of *To Err Is Human: Building a Safer Health System* (IOM,

1999) and continued with numerous other initiatives to improve safety and quality of healthcare (IOM, 2006a). Joint Commission has adopted mandatory national patient safety goals (Joint Commission, 2007), including a requirement to assess the organization's culture of safety and quality (Adamski, 2007).

In addition, the Institute of Healthcare Improvement (IHI) offers programs to assist organizations in improving the quality of care they provide (IHI, 2007). Their goals are:

- No needless deaths
- No needless pain or suffering
- No helplessness in those served or serving
- No unwanted waiting
- No waste.

Measured standards are used extensively in industrial settings to reveal errors, but the same cannot be said when measuring human behavior, which can vary and still be effective (Borckardt et al., 2006). Also, if the organization embraces these systems to such an extent that all variance is discouraged, then innovation is also suppressed (Harris & Zeisler, 2002). Improvement in quality is sacrificed at the expense of innovative ideas and processes; organizations fail to allow input, then become stagnant, and cease to be effective. This is the danger of all living systems that depend on outside input for survival. This is not to say that quality systems are not essential. They are. Organizations must find ways to foster creativity and innovation without compromising quality management.

HOW COST AFFECTS QUALITY

Quality measures can also reduce costs (Nolan & Bisognano, 2006). Wasted resources is an example. These include the time nurses waste looking for missing supplies or lab results, the costs of overtime pay and agency nurses because of unfilled positions, and delay in patient discharge due to lack of coordination or an adverse event (e. g., medication error).

NURSE STAFFING

Evidence is growing that increased nurse staffing results in better patient outcomes (American Nurses Association, 2007). A comprehensive review of studies from 1990 to 2006 in the United States and Canada found that a higher RN-to-patient ratio resulted in reduced patient mortality and shortened lengths of stay (Reeves, 2007). Likewise, another study reported that as the number of nurses rises, infection rates fall (Reeves, 2007).

MediaLink ● To Err is Human: Building a Safer Health System

REDUCING MEDICATION ERRORS

To reduce medication errors, the Institute of Medicine (2006b) suggests that patients must become more involved in managing their own care and that providers must help educate patients as well as helping them to educate themselves. The IOM also advises using point-of-care technology to access drug reference information and that medication names should be unique to avoid unnecessary confusion. Nurses can also provide education to patients and their families regarding proper medication administration and encourage them to ask their physician and pharmacist for clarification when they have questions regarding their medications.

Risk Management

Whereas quality management is a prevention-focused approach, **risk management** is problem focused. It is a component of quality management, but its purpose is to identify, analyze, and evaluate risks and then to develop a plan for reducing the frequency and severity of accidents and injuries. Risk management is a continuous daily program of detection, education, and intervention.

A risk management program involves all departments of the organization. It must be an organization-wide program, with the board of directors' approval and input from all departments. The program must have high-level commitment, including that of the chief executive officer and the chief nurse.

A risk management program:

1. Identifies potential risks for accident, injury, or financial loss. Formal and informal communication with all organizational departments and inspection of facilities are essential to identifying problem areas.
2. Reviews current organization-wide monitoring systems (incident reports, audits, committee minutes, oral complaints, patient questionnaires), evaluates completeness, and determines additional systems needed to provide the factual data essential for risk management control.
3. Analyzes the frequency, severity, and causes of general categories and specific types of incidents causing injury or adverse outcomes to patients. To plan risk intervention strategies, it is necessary to estimate the outcomes associated with the various types of incidents.
4. Reviews and appraises safety and risk aspects of patient care procedures and new programs.

5. Monitors laws and codes related to patient safety, consent, and care.
6. Eliminates or reduces risks as much as possible.
7. Reviews the work of other committees to determine potential liability and recommend prevention or corrective action. Examples of such committees are infection, medical audit, safety/security, pharmacy, nursing audit, and productivity.
8. Identifies needs for patient, family, and personnel education suggested by all of the foregoing and implementing the appropriate educational program.
9. Evaluates the results of a risk management program.
10. Provides periodic reports to administration, medical staff, and the board of directors.

NURSING'S ROLE IN RISK MANAGEMENT

In the organizational setting, nursing is the one department involved in patient care 24 hours a day; nursing personnel are therefore critical to the success of a risk management program. The chief nursing administrator must be committed to the program. Her or his attitude will influence the staff and their participation. After all, it is the staff, with their daily patient contact, who actually implement a risk management program.

An innovative program to reduce risk was instituted at one midwest health care organization (Kerfoot, Rapala, Ebright, & Rogers, 2006). Under the direction of the risk manager, the purpose of the Safe Passage Program was to create a safe passage for patients and a supportive environment for staff. Staff were selected as safe passage nurses to serve as unit-based experts on patient and staff safety and, more importantly, proactively looked for potential problem areas.

High-risk areas in health care fall into five general categories:

- Medication errors
- Complications from diagnostic or treatment procedures
- Falls
- Patient or family dissatisfaction with care
- Refusal of treatment or refusal to sign consent for treatment.

Nursing is involved in all areas, but the medical staff may be primarily responsible in cases involving refusal of treatment or consent to treatment.

Medical records and incidence reports serve to document organizational, nurse, and physician accountability. For every reported occurrence, however, many more are unreported. If records are faulty, inadequate, or omitted, the organization is more likely to be sued and more likely to lose. **Incident reports** are used to analyze the severity, frequency, and causes of occurrences within the five risk categories. Such analysis serves as a basis for intervention.

Incident Reports

Accurate and comprehensive reporting on both the patient's chart and in the incident report is essential to protect the organization and caregivers from litigation. Incident reporting is often the nurse's responsibility. Reluctance to report incidents is usually due to fear of the consequences. This fear can be alleviated by

- Holding staff education programs that emphasize objective reporting;
- Omitting inflammatory words and judgmental statements;
- Having a clear understanding that the purposes of the incident reporting process are documentation and follow-up; and
- Never using the report, under any circumstances, for disciplinary action. Nursing colleagues and nurse managers should not berate another employee for an incident, and never in front of other staff members, patients, or patients' family members.

A **reportable incident** should include any unexpected or unplanned occurrence that affects or could potentially affect a patient, family member, or staff. The report is only as effective as the form on which it is reported, so attention should be paid to the adequacy of the form as well as to the data required.

Reporting incidents involves the following steps:

1. **Discovery.** Nurses, physicians, patients, families, or any employee or volunteer may report actual or potential risk.
2. **Notification.** The risk manager receives the completed incident form within 24 hours after the incident. A telephone call may be made earlier to hasten follow-up in the event of a major incident.
3. **Investigation.** The risk manager or representative investigates the incident immediately.
4. **Consultation.** The risk manager consults with the referring physician, risk management committee member, or both to obtain additional information and guidance.
5. **Action.** The risk manager should clarify any misinformation to the patient or family, explaining exactly what happened. The patient should be

referred to the appropriate source for help and, if needed, be assured that care for any necessary service will be provided free of charge.
6. **Recording.** The risk manager should be sure that all records, including incident reports, follow-up, and actions taken, if any, are filed in a central depository.

EXAMPLES OF RISK

The following are some examples of actual events in the various risk categories.

Medication Errors

A reportable incident occurs when a medication or fluid is omitted, the wrong medication or fluid is administered, or a medication is given to the wrong patient, given at the wrong time, in the wrong dosage, or by the wrong route. Here are some examples.

Patient A. *Weight was transcribed incorrectly from emergency room sheet. Medication dose was calculated on incorrect weight; therefore, patient was given double the dose required. Error discovered after first dose and corrected. Second dose omitted.*

Patient B. *Tegretol dosage written in Medex as "Tegretol 100 mg chewable tab—50 mg po BID." Tegretol 100 mg given po at 1400. Meds checked at 1430 and error noted. 50 mg Tegretol should have been given. Doctor notified. Second dose held.*

Patient C. *During rounds at 3:30 P.M. found .9% sodium chloride at 75 c.c.'s per hour hanging. Order was D5W. Fluids last checked at 2:00 P.M. Changed to correct fluid. Doctor notified.*

Diagnostic Procedure

Any incident occurring before, during, or after such procedures as blood sample stick, biopsy, X-ray examination, lumbar puncture, or other invasive procedure is categorized as a diagnostic procedure incident.

Patient A. *When I checked the IV site, I saw that it was red and swollen. For this reason, I discontinued the IV. When removing the tape, I noted a small area of skin breakdown where the tape had been. There was also a small knot on the medial aspect of the left antecubital above the IV insertion site. Doctor notified. Wound dressed.*

Patient B. *Patient found on the floor after lumbar puncture. Right side rail down. Examined by a physician, BP 120/80, T 98.6, P 72, R 18. No injury noted on exam.*

Medical-Legal Incident

If a patient or family refuses treatment as ordered and prescribed or refuses to sign consent forms, the situation is categorized as a medical-legal incident.

Patient A. *After a visit from a member of the clergy, patient indicated he was no longer in need of medical attention and asked to be discharged. Physician called. Doctor explained potential side effects if treatment was discontinued. Patient continued to ask for discharge. Doctor explained "against medical advice" (AMA) form. Patient signed AMA form and left at 1300 without medications.*

Patient B. *Patient refused to sign consent for bone marrow biopsy. States side effects not understood. Doctor reviewed reasons for test and side effects three different times. Doctor informed the patient that without consent he could not perform the test. Offered to call in another physician for second opinion. Patient agreed. After doctor left, patient signed consent form.*

Patient or Family Dissatisfaction with Care

When a patient or family indicates general dissatisfaction with care and the situation cannot be or has not been resolved, then an incident report is filed.

Patient A. *Mother complained that she had found child saturated with urine every morning (she arrived around 0800). Explained to mother that diapers and linen are changed at 0600 when 0600 feedings and meds are given. Patient's back, buttocks, and perineal areas are free of skin breakdown. Parents continue to be distressed. Discussed with primary nurse.*

Patient B. *Mr. Smith obviously very angry. Greeted me at the door complaining that his wife had not been treated properly in our emergency room the night before. Wanted to speak to someone from administration. Was unable to reach the administrator on call. Suggested Mr. Smith call administrator in the morning. Mr. Smith thanked me for my time and assured me that he would call the administrator the next day.*

ROLE OF THE NURSE MANAGER

The nurse manager plays a key role in the success of any risk management program. Nurse managers can reduce risk by helping their staff view health and illness from the patient's perspective. Usually, the staff's understanding of quality differs from the patient's expectations and perceptions. By understanding the meaning of the course of illness to the patient and the family, the nurse will manage risk better because that understanding can enable the nurse to individualize patient care. This individualized attention produces respect and, in turn, reduces risk.

A patient incident or a patient's or family's expression of dissatisfaction regarding care indicates not only some slippage in quality of care but also potential liability. A distraught, dissatisfied, complaining patient is a high risk; a satisfied patient or family is a low risk. A risk management or liability control program should therefore emphasize a personal approach. Many claims are filed because of a breakdown in communication between the health care provider and the patient. In many instances, after an incident or bad outcome, a quick visit or call from an organization's representative to the patient or family can soothe tempers and clarify misinformation.

In the examples given, prompt attention and care by the nurse manager protected the patients involved and may have averted a potential liability claim. Once an incident has occurred, the important factors in successful risk management are:

- Recognition of the incident
- Quick follow-up and action
- Personal contact
- Immediate restitution (where appropriate).

Most patients' and their family's concerns can and should be handled at the unit level. When that first line of communication breaks down, however, the nurse manager needs a resource—usually the risk manager or nursing service administrator.

Handling Complaints

Handling a patient's or family member's complaints stemming from an incident can be very difficult. These confrontations are often highly emotional; the patient or family member must be calmed down, yet have their concerns satisfied. Sometimes just an opportunity to release the anger or emotion is all that is needed.

The first step is to listen to the person to hear concerns and to help defuse the situation. Arguing or interrupting only increases the person's anger or emotion. After the patient or family member has had his or her say, the nurse manager can then attempt to solve the problem by asking what is expected in the form of a solution. The nurse manager should ensure immediate patient care and safety needs are met, collect all facts relevant to the incident, and if possible, comply with the patient or family member's suggested resolution. Sometimes, a simple apology from a staff member or moving a patient to a different room on the unit, can resolve a difficult situation. If the patient and/or family member's requested resolution exceeds the nurse manager's authority, the nurse manager should seek the assistance of a nurse administrator or hospital legal counsel. Offering vague solutions (e.g., "everything will be taken care of") may only lead to more problems later on if expectations as to solution and timing differ.

All incidents must be properly documented. Information on the incident form should be detailed and include all the factors relating to the incident, as demonstrated in the previous examples. The documentation in the chart, however, should be only a statement of the facts and of the patient's physical response; no reference to the incident report should be made, nor should words such as *error* or *inappropriate* be used.

When a patient receives 100 mg of Demerol instead of 50 mg as ordered, the proper documentation in the chart is, "100 mg of Demerol administered. Physician notified." The remainder of the documentation should include any reaction the patient has to the dosage, such as "Patient's vital signs unchanged." If there is an ad-verse reaction, a follow-up note should be written in the chart, giving an update of the patient's status. A note related to the patient's reaction should be written as frequently as the status changes and should continue until the patient returns to his or her previous status.

The chart must never be used as a tool for disciplinary comments, action, or expressions of anger. Notes such as "Incident would never have occurred if Doctor X had written the correct order in the first place" or "This carelessness is inexcusable" are totally inappropriate and serve no meaningful purpose. Carelessness and incorrect orders do indeed cause errors and incidents, but the place to address and resolve these issues is in the risk management committee or in the nurse manager's office, not on the patient chart.

Handling a complaint without punishing a staff member is a delicate situation. The manager must determine what happened in order to prevent another occurrence, but using an incident report for discipline might result in fewer or erroneous incident reports in the future. Learn how one manager handled a situation of this kind in Case Study 6-1.

CASE STUDY 6-1   Risk Management

Yasmine Dubois is the nurse manager for the cardiac catheterization lab and special procedures unit in a suburban hospital. The hospital has an excellent reputation for its cardiac care program, including the use of cutting-edge technology. The cath lab utilizes a specialized computer application that records the case for the nursing staff, requiring little handwritten documentation at the end of a procedure.

Last month, a 56-year-old woman was brought from the ER to the cath lab at approximately 1900 for placement of a stent in her left anterior descending coronary artery. During the procedure, the heart wall was perforated, the patient coded and was taken in critical condition to the OR, where she died during surgery.

Two days following the incident, the patient's husband requested a review of his wife's medical records. During his review, he pointed out to the medical records clerk that the documentation from the cath lab stated that his wife ". . . tolerated the procedure well and was taken in satisfactory condition to the recovery area." The documentation was signed, dated, and timed by Elizabeth Clark, RN. The medical records director notified the hospital's risk manager of the error. The risk manager investigated the incident and determined that Elizabeth Clark's charting was in error.

Following her meeting with the risk manager, Yasmine met with Elizabeth to discuss the incident. She showed Elizabeth a copy of the cath lab report. Elizabeth asked Yasmine if she could have the chart from medical records so she could correct her mistake. Yasmine informed Elizabeth that she couldn't correct her charting at this point in time. But, she could, however, write an addendum to the chart, with today's date and time, to clarify the documentation. Yasmine also told Elizabeth that the addendum would be reviewed by the risk manager and the hospital's attorney prior to inclusion in the chart.

To ensure compliance with the hospital's documentation standards and to determine if Elizabeth or any other cath lab nurse had committed any similar charting errors, Yasmine requested charts for all patients in the past 12 months who had been sent to surgery from the cath lab due to complications during a procedure. She conducted a retrospective audit and determined that this had been an isolated incident.

A Caring Attitude

The nurse manager sets the tone with employees that contributes to a safe and low-risk environment. One of the most important ways to reduce risk is to instill a sense of confidence in both patients and families by emphasizing and recognizing that they will receive personalized attention and that their needs will be attended to with competence. This confidence is created environmentally and professionally.

Examples of environmental factors include cleanliness, attention to patients' privacy, promptly responding to patient and family member's requests, an orderly looking unit, and minimal social conversations in front of patients. One example of portraying professional confidence is to provide patients and families with the name of the person in charge. A sincere visit by that person is reassuring. Also, a thorough orientation creates independence for the patient and confidence in an efficient unit.

The nurse manager needs to foster the attitude that any mistake that does occur is perceived as an opportunity to improve a system or a process rather than to punish an individual. If the nurse manager has developed a patient-focused atmosphere in which patients believe their best interests are a priority, the potential for risk will be reduced.

CREATING A BLAME-FREE ENVIRONMENT

Most errors in health care are due to system failures, according to the Institute of Medicine's 1999 report. Thus, reducing errors and preventing potential errors (near misses) requires a systemwide solution.

The goal of dealing with adverse events is to correct system failures, prevent future mistakes, and ensure patient safety (Mace, 2005). Reprisal for mistakes, on the other hand, discourages reporting, which can lead to continuation of the problem area or exacerbation of the problem. Conversely, staff should be encouraged to report adverse events and to help discover solutions to prevent mistakes in the future.

To create a blame-free environment the organization must put in place organization-wide, equitable policies for reporting. Mace (2005) recommends dealing with exceptions to the blame-free environment with a separate disciplinary policy. Exceptions include failure to report an adverse event or error, criminal acts, false reporting, or refusing to participate in a system designed to prevent errors.

Managing and improving quality requires ongoing attention to systemwide processes and individual actions. The nurse manager is in a key position to identify problems and encourage a culture of safety and quality.

What You Know Now

- Total quality management is a philosophy committed to excellence throughout the organization.
- Continuous quality improvement is a process to improve quality and performance.
- Six Sigma is another quality management program that uses measures, has goals, and is a management system.
- Lean Six Sigma provides tools to identify waste and can be used with a Six Sigma management system.
- Efforts to improve quality include a focus on a culture of safety and quality, eliminating waste, and creating a blame-free environment.
- A risk management program focuses on reducing accidents and injuries and intervening if either occurs.
- Nurses, on the front line of care, are critical to the success of a risk management program by reporting problems promptly. Nurses also can be proactive in identifying potential problem areas and helping craft solutions to them.
- The nurse manager can reduce risks by helping staff view health and illness from the patient's perspective.
- An incident report should never be used for discipline but rather should be an opportunity for learning and improvement.
- A caring attitude and prompt attention to complaints help to reduce risk.
- To create a blame-free environment requires systemwide policies for reporting that exclude reprisals.

Tools for Managing and Improving Quality

1. Remember: quality management is a system. When something goes wrong, it is usually due to a flaw in the system.
2. Become familiar with standards and outcome measures and use them to guide and improve your practice.
3. Strive for perfection but be prepared to tolerate failure in order to encourage innovation.
4. Be sure that performance appraisals and incident reports are not used for discipline but rather are the bases for improvements to the system and/or development of individuals.
5. Remind yourself and your colleagues that a caring attitude is the best preventative of problems.

Following an incident:

1. Meet with the risk manager and hospital attorney to review documentation and determine staff to be interviewed regarding the incident.
2. Provide any requested information to administration in a timely manner.
3. Audit documentation and processes to determine if an incident is part of a pattern or an isolated incident.
4. Provide the results of any audits or discussions with staff to appropriate administrators.
5. Educate staff as appropriate.
6. Determine if disciplinary action is required.
7. Follow up with risk management, nursing administration, and human resources as appropriate.
8. Continue to cooperate with the hospital attorney if the incident results in litigation.

Questions to Challenge You

1. Imagine that an organization is debating among several quality management programs. What would you recommend? Why?
2. Do you know what standards and outcome measures are used in the organization where you work or have your clinical experiences? How are data handled? Are they shared with employees?
3. What comparable groups, both internal and external, are used for benchmarking performance in your organization?
4. Universities also use benchmarking. What institutions does your college or university use to benchmark its performance? Find out.
5. Have you, a family member, or a friend ever had a serious problem in a health care organization that resulted in injury? What was the outcome? Is this how you would have handled it? What will you do in the future in a similar situation?
6. Have you or anyone you know ever made a mistake in a clinical setting? What happened? Would you assess the organization as a blame-free environment?

Explore MediaLink

Additional interactive resources for this chapter can be found on the Website at http://www.prenhall.com/sullivan. Click on Chapter 6 to select activities for this chapter.

- Video Overview
- NCLEX® Review Questions
- Critical Thinking Activities
- Current Events
- Nursing Leadership and Management in Action
- MediaLinks

References

Adamski, P. (2007). Leadership chapter revisions: Everybody wins. *Nursing Management, 38*(11), 10.

American Nurses Association. (2007). Infections and deaths down, quality up: Evidence for having appropriate nurse staffing mounts. *American Journal of Nursing, 107*(4), 19.

Berwick, D. M., Godfrey, A. B., & Roessner, J. (2002). *Curing health care: New strategies for quality improvement.* Hoboken, NJ: Jossey-Bass.

Borckardt, J. J., Nash, M. R., Hardesty, S., Herbert, J., Cooney, H., & Pelic, C. (2006). How unusual are the "unusual events" detected by control chart techniques in healthcare settings? *Journal for Healthcare Quality: Promoting Excellence in Healthcare, 28*(4), 4–9.

Bruhn, J. G. (2004). Leaders who create change and those who manage it: How leaders limit success. *The Health Care Manager, 23*(7), 132–140.

Caldwell, C. (2006). Lean-Six Sigma: Tools for rapid cycle cost reduction. *Healthcare Financial Management, 60*(10), 96–98.

Chaiken, B. P., & Holmquest, D. L. (2003). Patient safety: Modifying processes to eliminate medical errors. *Nursing Outlook, 51*(3), S21–S24.

Harris, S. D., & Zeisler, S. (2002). Weak signals: Detecting the next big thing. *The Futurist, 36*(6), 21–28.

Hedges, C. (2006). Research, evidence-based practice, and quality improvement. *AACN Advanced Critical Care, 17*(4), 457–458.

Hyrkas, K., & Lehti, K. (2003). Continuous quality improvement through team supervision supported by continuous self-monitoring of work and systematic patient feedback. *Journal of Nursing Management, 11*(3), 177–188.

Institute for Healthcare Improvement. (2007). *About us.* Retrieved December 2007 from http://www.ihi.org/IHI

Institute of Medicine. (1999). *To err is human: Building a safer health system.* Washington, DC: National Academy Press.

Institute of Medicine. (2003). *Health professions education: A bridge to quality.* Washington, DC: National Academy Press.

Institute of Medicine. (2006a). *Crossing the Quality Chasm: The IOM Health Care Quality Initiative.* Retrieved December 2007 from http://www.iom.edu/?id=35957

Institute of Medicine. (2006b). *Preventing medication errors.* Washington, DC: National Academy Press.

Joint Commission. (2007). Facts about the 2008 national patient safety goals. Retrieved December 2007 from http://www.jointcommission.org/PatientSafety/NationalPatientSafetyGoals/08_npsg_facts.htm

Kaissi, A. (2006). An organizational approach to understanding patient safety and medical errors. *The Health Care Manager, 25*(4), 292–305.

Kerfoot, K. M., Rapala, K., Ebright, P., & Rogers, S. M. (2006). The power of collaboration with patient safety programs: Building safe passage for patients, nurses, and clinical staff. *Journal of Nursing Administration, 36*(12), 582–588.

Mace, K. A. (2005). Is employee discipline the solution for patient safety? *Nursing Management, 36*(12), 57–59.

Martin, W. F. (2007). Quality models: Selecting the best model to deliver results. *The Physician Executive, 33*(3), 24–29.

Nolan, R., & Bisognano, M. (2006). Finding the balance between quality and cost. *Healthcare Financial Management, 60*(4), 67–72.

Pande, P., & Holpp, L. (2002). *What is Six Sigma?* New York: McGraw-Hill.

Reeves, K. (2007). New evidence report on nurse staffing and quality of patient care. *MEDSURG Nursing, 16*(2), 73–74.

Wojner, A. W. (2002). Capturing error rates and reporting significant data. *Critical Care Nursing Clinics of North America, 14*(4), 375–384.

Understanding Power and Politics

Learning Outcomes

After completing this chapter, you will be able to:

1. Define power.
2. Describe how power is used.
3. Discuss how image is a source of power.
4. Develop a plan to increase your power.
5. Discuss how politics influence policy.
6. Explain how to be politically savvy.

MediaLink

www.prenhall.com/sullivan

See the Companion Website for chapter-specific resources at
www.prenhall.com/sullivan.

As a nurse, do you want power? Do you need power? Do you have power? Are you politically savvy? Should you be more involved in the politics of nursing and health care? These are essential questions for nurses to consider. Although many nurses believe their work should be apolitical, failure to recognize the politics of patient care and nursing management can result in poor quality of care for the patient and frustration for the nurse.

This chapter identifies sources and uses of power, discusses the principles of power and politics, discusses strategies for effective political action, and applies these principles to the practice of the staff nurse, the role of the nurse manager, and the role of nurse leaders in the community.

Why Power?

Power emerges in every human encounter, whether you choose to acknowledge it or not. Often, the content, meaning, and purpose of power use or abuse are misunderstood or ignored. Power needs to be your ally, and you must seek to understand its dynamic qualities.

Power is the potential ability to influence (Hersey, Blanchard, & Johnson, 2007). Power also is defined as the potential to achieve goals.

It is also important to understand why power is used. The most common reasons are to gain a competitive advantage, acquire information, motivate, communicate, improve performance, and improve processes. By developing a power base, you gain the potential for maximum influence. The willingness to use power increases a nurse's ability to acquire the resources needed to improve patient care.

Regardless of when, why, and where care takes place, power centers around an individual's ability to influence others or the behavior of others. To acquire power, maintain it effectively, and use it skillfully, nurses must be aware of the sources and types of

power that they will use to influence and transform patient care.

Power and Leadership

Real power—principle-centered power—is based on honor, respect, loyalty, and commitment. Principle-centered power is not forced; it is invited (Covey, 1992). It is defined by the capacity to act and to make choices and decisions. How you choose and what you choose is based on deeply held values. If you choose to live up to your own values and potential, you have an infinite amount of power available. By recognizing your power and the capacity to use it, you can influence and lead others in promoting and creating changes in health care and in your community.

Leadership power then becomes the capacity to create order from conflict, contradictions, and chaos. Leadership power comes from the ability to sustain proactive influence because followers trust and respect the leader to do the right thing for the right reason. As leaders in health care, nurses must understand and select behaviors that activate principle-centered leadership:

- **Get to know people.** Understanding what other people want is not always simple.
- **Be open.** Keep others informed. Trust, honor, and respect spread just as equally as fear, suspicion, and deceit.
- **Know your values and visions.** The power to define your goals is the power to choose.
- **Sharpen your interpersonal competence.** Actively listen to others, and learn to express your ideas well.
- **Use your power to enable others.** Be attentive to the dynamics of power, and give attention to ground rules, such as encouraging dissenting voices and respecting disagreement.
- **Enlarge your sphere of influence and connectedness.** Power sometimes grows out of someone else's need.

Power: How Managers and Leaders Get Things Done

Classically, managers in health care institutions relied on authority to rouse employees to perform tasks and accomplish goals. In contemporary health care organizations, managers use persuasion, enticement, and inspiration to mobilize the energy and talent of a work group and to overcome resistance to change.

A leader's use of power alters attitudes and behavior by addressing individual needs and motivations. There are seven generally accepted types of interpersonal power used in organizations to influence others (French & Raven, 1959; Hersey, Blanchard, & Natemeyer, 1979).

1. **Reward power** is based on the inducements the manager can offer group members in exchange for cooperation and contributions that advance the manager's objectives. The degree of compliance depends on how much the follower values the expected benefits. For example, a nurse manager may grant paid educational leave as a way of rewarding staff nurses for implementing a new patient database system. Reward power often is used in relation to a manager's formal job responsibilities.

2. **Punishment**, or coercive, **power** is based on the penalties a manager might impose on an individual or a group. Motivation to comply is based on fear of punishment or withholding of rewards. For example, the nurse manager might make undesirable job assignments, mete out a formal reprimand, or recommend termination for a nurse who engages in disruptive behavior. Punishment or coercion is used in relation to a manager's perceived authority to determine employment status.

3. **Legitimate power** stems from the manager's right to make a request because of the authority associated with job and rank in an organizational hierarchy. Followers comply because they accept a manager's prerogative to impose requirements, sanctions, and rewards in keeping with the organization's mission and aims. For instance, staff nurses will comply with a nurse manager's directive to take time off without pay when the workload has dropped below projected levels because they know that the manager is charged with maintaining unit expenses within budget limitations.

4. **Expert power** is based on possession of unique skills, knowledge, and competence. Nurse managers, by virtue of experience and advanced education, often are the best qualified to determine what to do in a given situation. Employees are motivated to comply because they respect the manager's expertise. Expert power relates to the development of personal abilities through education and experience. Newly graduated nurses might ask the nurse manager for advice in learning clinical procedures or how to resolve conflicts with coworkers or other health professionals.

5. **Referent power** is based on admiration and respect for an individual. Followers comply because they like and identify with the manager. Referent power relates to the manager's likeability and success. For example, a new graduate might ask the advice of a more experienced and admired nurse about career planning.

6. **Information power** is based on access to valued data. Followers comply because they are motivated by a desire for information that will meet personal needs and facilitate decision making. Information power depends on a manager's organizational position, connections, and communication skills. For example, the nurse manager is frequently privy to information obtained at meetings with administrators about pending organizational changes that affect employees' work situations. A nurse manager may exercise information power by sharing significant information at staff meetings, thereby improving attendance.

7. **Connection power** is based on an individual's formal and informal links to influential or prestigious persons within and outside an area or organization. Followers comply because they want to be linked to influential individuals. Connection power also relates to the status and visibility of the individual as well as the position. In some cases, nurse managers have personal relationships with an organization's board members that followers believe will protect or advance their work situation.

These power bases are available to managers and may be classified more simply as personal or position power. **Position power** is determined by the job description, assigned responsibilities, recognition, advancement, authority, the ability to withhold money, and decision making. Legitimate, coercive, and reward power are positional because they relate to the "right" to influence others based on rank or role. The extent to which managers mete out rewards and punishment usually is dictated by organizational policy. Information and legitimate power are directly related to the manager's role in the organizational structure.

Expert, referent, information, and connection power are based, for the most part, on personal traits.

Personal power refers to one's credibility, reputation, expertise, experience, control of resources or information, and ability to build trust. The extent to which one may exercise expert, referent, information, and connection power relates to personal skills and positive interpersonal relationships, as well as employees' needs and motivations. Box 7–1 illustrates that nurses can learn to use power in organizations.

Using Power

Despite an increase in pride and self-esteem that comes with using power and influence, some nurses still consider power unattractive. The association of power with aggression and coercion remains strong. In a profession that prides itself on care and compassion, power is viewed as alien. How, then, can nurses bridge the disparity between power as good versus power as bad?

Power grabbing, which has been the traditionally accepted means of relating to power for one's own self-interests and use, is how nurses often think of power. Rather, nurses tend to be more comfortable with power sharing and empowerment: power "with" rather than power "over" others. Although nurses need power to ensure that patients have access to cost-effective quality nursing care, nurses can help transform health care organizations by using power that embraces equality and caring.

BOX 7-1   Guidelines for the Use of Power in Organizations

Guidelines for Using Legitimate Authority

- Make polite, clear requests.
- Explain the reasons for a request.
- Don't exceed your scope of authority.
- Verify authority if necessary.
- Follow proper channels.
- Follow up to verify compliance.
- Insist on compliance if appropriate.

Guidelines for Using Reward Power

- Offer the type of rewards that people desire.
- Offer rewards that are fair and ethical.
- Don't promise more than you can deliver.
- Explain the criteria for giving rewards and keep it simple.
- Provide rewards as promised if requirements are met.
- Use rewards symbolically (not in a manipulative way).

Guidelines for Using Coercive Power

- Explain rules and requirements, and ensure that people understand the serious consequences of violations.
- Respond to infractions promptly and consistently without showing any favoritism to particular individuals.
- Investigate to get the facts before using reprimands or punishment, and avoid jumping to conclusions or making hasty accusations.
- Except for the most serious infractions, provide sufficient oral and written warnings before resorting to punishment.

- Administer warnings and reprimands in private, and avoid making rash threats.
- Stay calm and avoid the appearance of hostility or personal rejection.
- Express a sincere desire to help the person comply with role expectations and thereby avoid punishment.
- Invite the person to suggest ways to correct the problem, and seek agreement on a concrete plan.
- Maintain credibility by administering punishment if noncompliance continues after threats and warnings have been made.

Guidelines for Using Expert Power

- Explain the reasons for a request or proposal and why it is important.
- Provide evidence that a proposal will be successful.
- Don't make rash, careless, or inconsistent statements.
- Don't exaggerate or misrepresent the facts.
- Listen seriously to the person's concerns and suggestions.
- Act confidently and decisively in a crisis.

Ways to Acquire and Maintain Referent Power

- Show acceptance and positive regard.
- Act supportive and helpful.
- Use sincere forms of ingratiation.
- Defend and back up people when appropriate.
- Do unsolicited favors.
- Make self-sacrifices to show concern.
- Keep promises.

Adapted from *Leadership in Organizations*, 6th ed. (pp. 150–156), by G. Yukl, 2007, Upper Saddle River, NJ: Prentice Hall. Reprinted by permission.

IMAGE AS POWER

A major source of power for nurses is an image of power. Even if one does not have actual power from other sources, the perception by others that one is powerful bestows a degree of power. The same is true for the profession as a whole. If the public sees the profession of nursing as powerful, the profession's ability to achieve its goals and agendas is enhanced.

Images emerge from interactions and communications with others. If nurses present themselves as caring and compassionate experts in health care through their interactions and communications with the public, then a strong, favorable image develops for both the individual nurse and the profession. Nurses, as the ambassadors of care, must understand the importance and benefit of positive therapeutic communications and image. Developing a positive image of power is important for both the individual and the profession.

Individual nurses can promote an image of power by a variety of means.

1. Appropriately introducing yourself by saying your name, using eye contact, and shaking hands can immediately establish you as a powerful person. If nurses introduce themselves by first name to the physician, Dr. Smith, they have immediately set forth an unequal power relationship unless the physician also uses his or her first name. Although women are not socialized to initiate handshakes, it is a power strategy in male-dominated circles, including health care organizations. In Western cultures, eye contact conveys a sense of confidence and connection to the individual to whom one is speaking. These seemingly minor behaviors can have a major impact on whether the nurse is perceived as competent and powerful.

2. Appropriate attire can symbolize power and success. Although nurses may believe that they are limited in choice of attire by uniform codes, it is in fact the presentation of the uniform that can hold the key to power. For example, a nurse manager needs a powerful image both with unit staff and with administrators and other professionals who are setting organizational policy. An astute nurse manager might wear a suit rather than a uniform to work on the day of a high-level interdisciplinary committee meeting. Certainly, attention to details of grooming and uniform selection can enhance the power of the staff nurse as well.

3. Conveying a positive and energetic attitude sends the message that you are a "doer" and someone to be sought out for involvement in important issues. Chronic complaining conveys a sense of powerlessness, whereas solving problems and being optimistic promote a "can do" attitude that suggests power and instills confidence in others.

4. Pay attention to how you speak and how you act when you speak. Nonverbal signs and signals say more about you than words. Make sure your words are reflected in your body language. In other words, keep your facial expression consistent with your message. Stand erect and move energetically. Speak with an even pace and enunciate words clearly. Use only body movements and gestures necessary to make your point.

5. Use facts and figures when you need to demonstrate your point. Policy changes usually evolve from data presented in a compelling story. To position yourself as a powerful player requires the ability to collect and analyze data. Data can be obtained to describe nursing care issues, activities, or concerns. These include patient acuity, daily census, length of stay, overtime budgets, or any data that reflect nursing's overall contribution. Remember that power is a matter of perception; therefore, you must use whatever data are available to support your judgment.

6. Knowing when to be at the right place at the right time is crucial to gain access to key personnel in the organization. This means being invited to events, meetings, and parties not necessarily intended for nurses. It means demanding to sit at the policy table when decisions affecting staffing and patient care are made. Influence is more effective when it is based on personal relationships and when people see others in person: "If I don't see you, I can't ask you for needed information, analysis, and alternative recommendations." Become visible. Be available. Offer assistance. You can be invaluable in providing policy makers with information, interpreting data, and teaching them about the nursing side of health care.

7. In dealing with people outside of nursing, it is important to develop powerful partnerships. Be very careful to use "we" instead of "they". Learn how to share both credit and blame. When working on collaborative projects, be clear about what is needed. If something isn't working well, say so. Never accept another's opinion as fact. Facts can be easily manipulated to fit one's personal agenda. Learn how to probe and obtain additional information. Don't assume you have all the information. Beware of unsolicited commentary.

of giving strong criticism, but always put criticisms in context. Before giving any criticism, give a compliment, if appropriate. Also, make sure your partners are ready to hear all sides of the issue. It's never superfluous to ask, "Do you want to talk about such and such right now?" Once an issue is decided—really decided—don't raise it again.

8. Make it a point to get to know the people who matter in your sphere of influence. Become a part of the power network so that when people are discussing issues or seeking people for important appointments of leadership, your name comes to mind. Be sure to deal with senior people. The more contact you have with the "power brokers," the more support you can generate in the future should the need arise. The more power you use, the more you get.

9. Know who holds the power. Identify the key power brokers. Develop a strategy for gaining access to power brokers through joining alliances and coalitions. Learn how to question others and how to become part of the organizational infrastructure. There is an art to determining when, what, and how much information is exchanged and communicated at any one time and to determining who does so. Powerful people have a keen sense of timing. Be sure to position yourself to be at the right place at the right time. Any strategy will involve a good deal of energy and effort. Direct influence and efforts toward issues of highest priority or when greatest benefits are likely to result.

10. Use power appropriately to promote consensus in organizational goals, develop common means to achieve these goals, and enhance a common culture to bind organizational members together. As the health care providers closest to the patient, nurses best understand patients' needs and wants. In the hospital, nurses are present on the first patient contact and thereafter for 24 hours a day, 7 days a week. In the clinic, the nurse may be the person the patient sees first and most frequently. By capitalizing on the special relationship that they have with patients, nurses can use marketing principles to enhance their position and image as professional caregivers.

Nursing as a profession must market its professional expertise and ability to achieve the objectives of health care organizations. From a marketing perspective, nurses must to ensure that identified markets (e.g., patients, other health professionals, community members) have a clear understanding of what

nursing is, what it does, and what it is going to do. In doing so, nursing is seen as a profession that gives expert care with a scientific knowledge base.

Nursing care often is seen as an indicator of an organization's overall quality. Regardless of the setting, quality nursing care is something that is desired and valued. Through understanding patients' needs and preferences for programs that promote wellness and maintain and restore health, nurses become the organization's competitive edge to enhancing revenues. Marketing an image of expertise linked with quality and cost can position nursing powerfully and competitively in the health care marketplace.

USING POWER APPROPRIATELY

Using power not only affects what happens at the time, but also has a lasting effect on your relationships. Therefore, it is best to use the least amount of power necessary to accomplish your goals. Also, use power appropriate to the situation (Sullivan, 2004). Table 7-1 lists rules for using power.

Improper use of power can destroy a manager's effectiveness. Power can be overused or underused. Overusing power occurs when you use excessive power relative to the situation. If you fail to use power when it is needed, you are underusing your power. In addition to the immediate loss of influence, you may lose credibility for the future.

Power plays are another way that power is used inappropriately. **Power plays** are attempts by others to diminish or demolish their opponents. Table 7-2 describes several common power plays and their consequences. It

TABLE 7-1   **Rules for Using Power**
1. Use the least amount of power you can to be effective in your interactions with others.
2. Use power appropriate to the situation.
3. Learn when not to use power.
4. Focus on the problem, not the person.
5. Make polite requests, never arrogant demands.
6. Use coercion only when other methods don't work.
7. Keep informed to retain your credibility when using your expert power.
8. Understand you may owe a return favor when you use your connection power.

From *Becoming Influential: A Guide for Nurses* (p. 35), by E. J. Sullivan, 2004, Upper Saddle River, NJ: Prentice Hall. Reprinted by permission.

TABLE 7-2	Power Plays
POWER PLAY	**RECIPIENT'S RESPONSE**
"Let's be fair."	Feelings of insecurity; insecure about choices because power game is played by someone else's rules.
"Can you prove that?"	Embarrassed by inability to defend self.
"Be specific."	Feelings of incompetence if facts and figures cannot be generated to support position.
"It's either this or that; which is it? Take your pick."	Angered at being forced to choose between limited options.
"But you said . . . and now you say . . ."	Confused about what was meant; believe your position is illogical.

is essential that nurses not accept these statements at face value. Often, restating one's initial point in a firm manner is a useful strategy. It is not necessary to respond directly to statements such as those shown in Table 7-2.

Nursing must perceive power for what it really is—the ability to mobilize and focus energy and resources. What better position can nurses be in but to assume power to face new problems and responsibilities in reshaping nursing practice to adapt to environmental changes? Power is the means, not the end, to seek new ways for doing things in this uncertain and unsettling time in health care.

POWER PLUS VISION

The key to understanding and gaining power is to identify what you and other people really desire. Once you have decided what you want, look at the total situation or encounter. Take into account, for example, the whole organization, not just your workplace or unit. Rank your wants or needs in order of importance. Determine who controls what you want and who or what stands in your way of achieving it. Identify the resources you control and the individuals who might desire those resources. Power resides not in aggressiveness or assertiveness but in the ability to make a conscious choice. Focus on the choice, not the action.

By making choices about what you want, you develop a strong sense of self-confidence and are aware of and feel good about your true capabilities. Your self-respect depends not on maintaining your role or position of power, but rather on your sense of purpose and direction. A clear vision pulls it all together by building consensus and support; identifying present capabilities; determining success factors; and identifying resources of people, time, and money.

Once you understand how power influences what choices are made and how these choices affect behaviors and feelings, you can appreciate its usefulness. In a constantly dynamic universe, power is a fundamental ingredient. You must ask yourself: Are you willing to use your power to know yourself, set goals, ignite the imagination, direct nursing care, build teams, and reach beyond the unknown into what could be? To use power to change and improve patient care is to recognize that power is natural and desirable.

Politics: The Art of Influencing

Politics is the art of influencing the allocation of scarce resources, which includes money, time, personnel, and materials (Mason, Leavitt, & Chaffee, 2006). Politics is a means to an end, a means for influencing events and the decisions of others. Nurses who renounce politics are essentially saying they do not want to influence events in their everyday work.

Politics:

- Is an interpersonal endeavor
- Is a collective activity
- Requires analysis and planning
- Involves image.

As an *interpersonal endeavor*, politics uses the skills of communication and persuasion. Nurses' communication skills make them particularly effective in political activities. Nurses understand the importance of rapport and how to create meaningful connections with people. They understand the importance of time in developing these connections. They also understand the need to appeal to the other person's needs and interests if the goal is going to be reached. At a "Nurses Night" telephone bank to solicit support for a congressional candidate, the candidate's manager told the nurse organizer of the event, "You nurses are wonderful at this! I was listening to one nurse talking on the phone with a man who I thought must be her uncle or someone she knew well—it was a stranger, but they were talking as if they were old friends!"

As a *collective activity*, politics often requires the support and action of many people to bring effective politics to bear on a situation or issue. Furthermore, working with others for political action can be invigorating, more creative, and simply more effective because there are more people to do the work and provide the emotional support that may be needed to sustain long-term political action.

The politically astute nurse develops and carefully uses a support base that crosses the hierarchical lines of each sphere. In the workplace, this means developing connections to other nurses, the maintenance people, top administrators, the social work department, physicians, and other workers at all levels of the organization. Certainly, this takes time, but it can and should be a part of the nurse's everyday work. For example, greet and speak to the person who is cleaning the floor every morning, sit with different people at lunch, and invite the new chief of the medical staff for a cup of coffee. It involves going to professional nursing meetings and exchanging business cards with those you meet. It involves providing support for others' agendas, knowing that they may be able to support you on an issue in the future. And it involves being able to organize and mobilize groups of nurses and coalitions of diverse groups.

It is helpful to have a target list of people with whom you would like to connect to build your support base, remembering that the secretary to the chief officer in the organization may be one of the most powerful persons in the organization by virtue of his or her ability to control access to the top administrator.

Politics is also about *analysis and planning*. Just as the nursing process requires a thorough assessment, good politics arises from a careful and insightful political analysis of the situation, issue, or problem. A political analysis includes assessing the structure and functioning of the sphere in which you are operating. What is the organizational structure? What are the formal and informal lines of communication? Who holds legitimate power? Who holds informal power? What are the stated and unstated missions and agendas of the organization? What individuals are involved in the issue or situation? From a systems perspective, one change on the system can have far-reaching effects on the rest of the system. What are the values, interests, beliefs, priorities, and agendas of these players? What connections and power bases do they have? What is the current context of the situation or issue? What is the climate for change? What outside forces might be influencing the situation or potential solutions or changes? What recent events might influence how others view the situation and their openness to change?

A good political analysis also includes a thorough assessment of the issue or problem itself. Why does the issue exist? What are the contributing factors? Who is affected by the issue? Do efforts need to be devoted to creating an audience interested in the issue? What beliefs and feelings do people hold about the issue? Are more data needed?

Effective political action involves planning. Based on the analysis just described, a group trying to influence an issue or situation would brainstorm about alternative solutions and evaluate their risks and benefits. But the group also would develop a plan for introducing its alternative and persuading others to support its position. Political analysis tells you who can be counted on to play what role in this process. For example, who should introduce the alternative to the person with the formal authority to make the decision to adopt it? Sometimes, the most politically astute approach is not to have the originator of the alternative introduce it, but rather the individual who is most likely to be accepted by the decision maker(s). Is collective action needed? What coalitions need to be formed? The political analysis also will suggest strategies related to timing. Should the alternative be proposed now or in 2 months? Should it be proposed as a pilot project or demonstration project? Should it be gradually phased in or implemented fully at one time? Should group pressure be brought to bear now or later? Timing is often crucial to the effectiveness of political action. People usually are more willing to accept something as a trial or test. Pilot projects also enable those affected to adjust to the change gradually.

Politics is also about *images*. Do people think you can make the change? Do people think the change will be harmful to them? Do people trust you? Do people identify positively with the coalition involved? Your future ability to be politically effective may hinge on the image that others have of you or the group. For example, it is well known that when a workers' contract is settled in a collective-bargaining dispute, both the union and management sides try to come out of the negotiations with the appearance of having won the most. Even losses can be seen as victories, particularly if the effort resulted in the mobilization and empowerment of nurses so that the whole group's power and likelihood of future success are enhanced. Defining the message you want others to receive and effectively marketing that message can create the image needed to further your political agenda.

Policy and Political Action

Policy can be defined as the decisions that govern action. Policies determine an organization's relationships, activities, and goals. Policies result from political action.

Politics is often referred to negatively, but is not. Politics, itself, is neutral. It is the art of influencing others to achieve a goal (Mason, Chaffee, & Leavitt, 2006).

Nurses may think that political skill is only required of the top administrators. Again, they would be wrong (Middaugh & Robertson, 2005). Every nurse, every manager, in fact, every employee can influence the organization's future.

Are you political? Test your skills by answering the questions in Table 7-3.

Political skill, per se, is not included in nursing education (nor is it tested on state board exams) yet it is a vital skill for nurses to acquire (Vestal, 2007). Green and Chaney (2006) suggest that political skill is built on relationships with others. To improve your political skill they advise you to:

- Learn self-promotion—report your accomplishments appropriately.
- Be honest and tell the truth—say what you mean and mean what you say.
- Use compliments—recognize others' accomplishments.
- Discourage gossip—silence is the best response.
- Learn and use quid pro quo—do and ask for favors.
- Remember: appearance matters—attend to grooming and attire.
- Use good manners—be courteous.

By using strategic alliances nurses can become political entrepreneurs (Hughes, Duke, Bamford, & Moss, 2006). Look for solutions to problems and for "windows of opportunity," they suggest, and then build coalitions of others whose goals fit with yours. Similarly, Middaugh and Robertson (2005) challenge nurses to identify their **stakeholders**, those people or groups who have a direct interest in the work of an organization, such as physicians, other health care providers, administrators, patients and their families, to name a few. Work with stakeholders to accomplish mutually beneficial goals, they advise.

Health care involves multiple special-interest groups all competing for their piece of a limited pool of resources. The delivery of nursing services occurs at many levels in health care organizations. The effectiveness of care delivery is linked to the application of power, politics, and marketing. Nurses belong to a complex organization that is continually confronted with limited resources and is in competition for those resources.

The steps in political action are shown in Table 7-4. You must first decide what you want to accomplish. Is it realistic? Will you have supporters? Who will be the detractors?

Try to find out what other people involved want. Maybe you could piggyback on their ideas. Congress does this all the time by adding amendments to proposed bills in an attempt to satisfy their opponents.

Start telling your supporters about your idea and see if they will join with you in a coalition. This is not necessarily a formal group but intended for you to know who you can count on in the discussions.

Find out exactly what objections your opponents have and try to figure out a way to alter your plan accordingly or help them understand how your proposal might help them. Political action is never easy, but the most politically astute people accomplish goals far more often than those who don't even try.

A case study that exemplifies a nurse using organizational politics is shown in Case Study 7-1.

What happens in the workplace both depends on and influences what is happening in the larger community, professional organizations, and government. The effective nurse manager understands the connections among these groups and uses them to the advantage of nursing, patients, and the health care organization. Developing

---

TABLE 7-3 Test for Political Savvy

Take the following test to determine your political savvy.
- Do you get credit for your ideas?
- Do you know how to deal with a difficult colleague?
- Do you have a mentor?
- Are you "in the loop"?
- Can you manage and influence others' perceptions of you and your work?
- Are you able to convert enemies to friends?
- Do your ideas get a fair hearing?
- Do you know when and how to present them?

Adapted from *It's All Politics, Winning in a World Where Hard Work and Talent Aren't Enough* by Kathleen Kelley Reardon, PhD, copyright © 2005 by Kathleen Kelley Reardon, PhD. Used by permission of Doubleday, a division of Random House, Inc.

TABLE 7-4 Steps in Political Action

1. Determine what you want.
2. Learn about the players and what they want.
3. Gather supporters and form coalitions.
4. Be prepared to answer opponents.
5. Explain how what you want can help them.

From *Becoming Influential: A Guide for Nurses* (p. 35), by E. J. Sullivan, 2004, Upper Saddle River, NJ: Prentice Hall. Reprinted by permission.

Juanita Pascheco has been nurse manager of medical and surgical ICUs in a large, urban, for-profit hospital for the past 7 years. Two years ago, Juanita completed her master's degree in nursing administration. Her thesis research centered on the acceptance of standardized and computerized documentation methods for critical care units. Juanita is well respected in her current role and is a member of several key committees addressing the need for a replacement health information system (HIS) for the hospital. She reports directly to the director of critical care services.

Although Juanita enjoys her work as nurse manager, she believes she is ready to assume additional responsibilities on a director level. Through her work on the hospital's HIS selection team and as the nursing representative to the physician's technology committee, Juanita identifies the need for a clinical informatics director role. One of Juanita's responsibilities on the HIS selection team is to identify talent from clinical areas who could support the HIS implementation. Juanita has also agreed to chair several working committees that will assist in determining required clinical functionality for the HIS.

During her tenure at the hospital, Juanita has cultivated solid working relationships with several key decision makers within the organization. The human resources director, Ken Harding, has worked with Juanita on several large projects over the past 2 years, including implementation of multidisciplinary teams in the ICUs. Juanita schedules a lunch with Ken to discuss growth opportunities in the information technology department, the process for creating new roles, and in particular, who will determine the need for and approval of new information technology positions. Using this knowledge and her experience on the HIS selection team and the physicians'

technology committee, Juanita develops a proposal for the clinical informatics director position.

As the HIS selection team draws closer to selecting a final vendor and an implementation timeline is established by the information technology department, Juanita approaches her supervisor, Sherrie Wright, with her proposal. Juanita also provides Sherrie with an overview of the clinical support that will be necessary for successful implementation of the HIS product. Since the critical care units are targeted for the initial phase of implementation, Sherrie is aware that Juanita's high interest in technology and her clinical expertise in the ICU would be invaluable for successful implementation. As a strong manager, Juanita can build acceptance among the nurses, physicians, and other members of the health care team.

Sherrie agrees to take Juanita's proposal to the chief nursing officer for formal consideration.

Manager's Checklist

The nurse manager is responsible to:

- Know and understand the formal lines of authority within the organization.
- Identify key decision makers and understand their priorities and how those priorities affect any new initiatives.
- Recognize the importance of timing when initiating change.
- Be ready to take advantage of new opportunities.
- Build strong and credible working relationships with decision makers.
- Be willing to take on new and challenging tasks that may lead to more responsibility.

influence in each of these three groups takes time and a long-range plan of action. Although the nurse's first priority should be to establish influence in the workplace, the nurse can gradually increase connections and influence with other groups and, later on, make these other groups a priority.

POLITICAL ACTION IN THE COMMUNITY

The workplace, government, and organizations all interact with the community, whether local, regional, national, or international. One nurse found that her leadership in a community effort to eliminate improper

garbage dumping in her town enabled her to develop important connections to government officials on both state and local levels. It also brought her to the attention of her hospital administrator in a positive and powerful way. The administrator knew that she had developed a positive reputation in the community and made significant connections to other persons of influence as a result of her actions. For many nurses who have children, an important forum for developing their political skills and power is the school's PTA or school board. An identity as a nurse in these groups can and should be made known. The connections developed can be used to further other purposes in the future.

This framework suggests that nurses need to understand the connections between what they do in their everyday work and what takes place in the rest of the community, nation, and world. Such a macroscopic view is particularly needed for the nurse manager. Although the nurse manager is rightfully concerned about how the work group is functioning, she or he must recognize that it does not function in a vacuum. Understanding and considering the broader context in which the unit is functioning makes the difference in whether the nurse manager is seen as visionary, whether the unit is on the cutting edge of nursing practice, and whether the unit sets the standard for excellence in the organization.

Using Power and Politics for Nursing's Future

Kelly (2007) suggests that apathy prevents nurses from using their political skills. Becoming active in professional associations, learning the legislative issues that affect nursing, gaining political skills, and being willing to advocate for nursing's causes are necessary for the profession to flex its considerable political muscles. All nurses can participate to some extent in these activities.

Nurses can have a tremendous impact on health care policy. The best impact is often made with a bit of luck and timing, but never without knowledge of the whole system. This includes knowledge of the policy agenda, the policy makers, and the politics that are involved. Once you gain this knowledge, you are ready to move forward with a political base to promote nursing.

To convert your policy ideas into political realities, consider the following power points:

- **Use persuasion over coercion.** Persuasion is the ability to share reasons and rationale when making a strong case for your position while maintaining a genuine respect for another's perspective.
- **Use patience over impatience.** Despite the inconveniences and failings caused by health care restructuring, impatience in the nursing community can be detrimental. Patience, along with a long-term perspective on the health care system, is needed.
- **Be open-minded rather than closed-minded.** Acquiring accurate information is essential if you want to influence others effectively.
- **Use compassion over confrontation.** In times of change, errors and mistakes are easy to pinpoint. It takes genuine care and concern to change course and make corrections.
- **Use integrity over dishonesty.** Honest discourse must be matched with kind thoughts and actions. Control, manipulations, and malice must be pushed aside for change to occur.

To manage nursing care in the future, nurses must come to realize that nursing expertise and clinical judgment are the best combination to effectively influence nursing practice and policy changes. By applying power and politics to the workplace, nurses increase their professional influence. Using influence, knowledge, and expertise can make the health care delivery system work.

(For a how-to guide on political action see *Becoming Influential: A Guide for Nurses*, by Eleanor Sullivan, from Prentice Hall, 2004.)

What You Know Now

- Power enables nurses and nurse managers to accomplish their goals.
- Exercise of power is an essential aspect of leadership. Power is positional or personal and is based on several different sources, including control over rewards, punishment, information, institutional authority, expertise, personal likeability, or connections.
- Power can be overused, underused, or used inappropriately.
- To be effective, the power used must be appropriate to the situation.
- Image is a source of power.
- Politics is the ability to influence the allocation of scarce resources and events in our everyday world.
- Policies result from political action.
- Nurses can use political action to influence policies in the organization, the community, and to advance nursing's goals.

Tools for Using Power and Politics

1. Learn the formal lines of authority within the organization.
2. Identify key decision makers and build strong and credible relationships with them.
3. Identify decision makers' priorities and how those affect any new initiatives.
4. Learn the rules for using power and put them into practice.
5. Prepare to combat power plays (Table 7-2) by role playing better responses.
6. Offer solutions to problems and take advantage of new opportunities.
7. Exhibit a willingness to take on new and challenging tasks that may lead to more responsibility.
8. Pay attention to people who are influential and adopt their strategies if appropriate.

Questions to Challenge You

1. Consider a person you believe to have power. What are the bases of that person's power?
2. Evaluate how the person you named uses his or her power. Is it positive or negative?
3. Have you observed people using power inappropriately? Describe what they did and what happened as a result.
4. Assess your own power using the seven types of power discussed in the chapter. Name three ways you could increase your power.
5. How did you score on the test for political savvy? Did you discover areas to challenge you?
6. Have you been involved in developing policies or political activities in your organization or school, community, or profession? Explain.

Explore MediaLink 🌐

Additional interactive resources for this chapter can be found on the Website at http://www.prenhall.com/sullivan. Click on Chapter 7 to select activities for this chapter.

- Video Overview
- NCLEX® Review Questions
- Critical Thinking Activities
- Current Events
- Nursing Leadership and Management in Action
- MediaLinks

References

Covey, S. (1992). *Principle-centered leadership*. New York: Simon & Schuster.

French, J. R. P., & Raven, B. (1959). The bases of social power. In C. Cartwright & A. Zander (Eds.), *Studies of social power*. Ann Arbor, MI: Institute for Social Research.

Green, C. G., & Chaney, L. H. (2006). The game of office politics. *Supervision, 67*(8), 3–6.

Hersey, P., Blanchard, K. H., & Johnson, D. E. (2007). *Management of organizational behavior*. Upper Saddle River, NJ: Prentice Hall.

Hersey, P., Blanchard, K., & Natemeyer, W. E. (1979). Situational leadership perception and the impact of power. *Group and Organizational Studies, 4*(4), 418–428.

Hughes, F., Duke J., Bamford, A., & Moss, C. (2006). Enhancing nursing leadership through policy, politics, and strategic alliances. *Nurse Leader, 4*(2), 24–27.

Kelly, K. (2007). From apathy to political activism. *American Nurse Today, 2*(8), 55–56.

Mason, D. J., Leavitt, J. K., & Chaffee, M. W. (2006). *Policy and politics in nursing and health care* (5th ed.). St. Louis, MO: Saunders.

Middaugh, D. J., & Robertson, R. D. (2005). Politics in the workplace. *Nursing Management, 14*(6), 393–394.

Sullivan, E. J. (2004). *Becoming influential: A guide for nurses*. Upper Saddle River, NJ: Prentice Hall.

Vestal, K. (2007). The power and intrigue of workplace politics. *Nurse Leader, 5*(1), 6–7.

Learning Key Skills in Nursing Management

CHAPTER 8

Thinking Critically, Making Decisions, Solving Problems

Critical Thinking
    USING CRITICAL THINKING
    CREATIVITY

Decision Making
    TYPES OF DECISIONS
    DECISION-MAKING CONDITIONS
    THE DECISION-MAKING PROCESS
    DECISION-MAKING TECHNIQUES
    GROUP DECISION MAKING
    STUMBLING BLOCKS

Problem Solving
    PROBLEM-SOLVING METHODS
    THE PROBLEM-SOLVING PROCESS
    GROUP PROBLEM SOLVING

Learning Outcomes

After completing this chapter, you will be able to:

1. Describe why critical-thinking skills are essential to nurses.
2. Describe how to become more creative.
3. Develop a plan to improve your decision-making and problem-solving skills.
4. Compare and contrast individual and collective decision-making processes in various situations.
5. Describe how to work with individuals and groups to solve problems.

MediaLink

www.prenhall.com/sullivan
See the Companion Website for chapter-specific resources at
www.prenhall.com/sullivan.

Key Terms

Nurse managers are expected to use knowledge from various disciplines to solve problems with patients, staff, and the organization, as well as problems in their own personal and professional lives. They also must make decisions in dynamic situations, such as:

- Do the advantages of the primary nursing care delivery system outweigh proposed advantages of expanded use of unlicensed personnel?
- Would a new model of differentiated practice be more useful?
- Is the present policy requiring 12-hour shifts adequate for both patients and nurses?
- Which is the best staffing pattern to prevent turnover and ensure quality patient care?

Critical thinking helps nurses examine all aspects of an issue and look for different and exciting ways to solve new and old problems. This chapter explains and differentiates critical thinking, problem solving, and decision making and describes processes and techniques for using each.

Critical Thinking

Critical thinking is the process of examining underlying assumptions, interpreting and evaluating arguments, imagining and exploring alternatives, and developing a reflective criticism for the purpose of reaching a conclusion that can be justified. Critical thinking is not the same thing as criticism, though it does call for inquir-

ing attitudes, knowledge about evidence and analysis, and skills to combine them.

Critical-thinking skills can be used to resolve problems rationally. Identifying, analyzing, and questioning the evidence and implications of each problem stimulate and illuminate critical thought processes. Critical thinking is also an essential component of decision making. However, compared to problem solving and decision making, which involve seeking a single solution, critical thinking is broader and involves considering a range of alternatives and selecting the best one for the situation (Ignatavicius, 2001). Critical thinking is a higher-level cognitive process that includes creativity, problem solving, and decision making (**Figure 8-1**●).

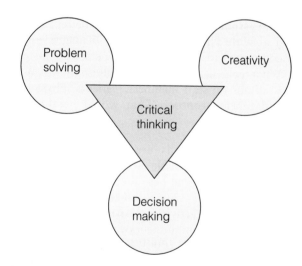

Figure 8-1 ● Critical-thinking model.

USING CRITICAL THINKING

The critical-thinking process seems abstract unless it can be related to practical experiences. One way to develop this process is to consider a series of questions when examining a specific problem or making a decision, such as:

1. **What are the underlying assumptions?** Underlying assumptions are unquestioned beliefs that influence an individual's reasoning. They are perceptions that may or may not be grounded in reality. For example, some people believe the AIDS epidemic is punishment for homosexual behavior. This attitude toward people with AIDS could alter one's approach to care for an AIDS patient.
2. **How is evidence interpreted?** What is the context? Interpretation of information also can be value laden. Is the evidence presented completely and clearly? Can the facts be substantiated? Are the people presenting the evidence using emotional or biased information? Are there any errors in reasoning?
3. **How are the arguments to be evaluated?** Is there objective evidence to support the arguments? Have all value preferences been determined? Is there a good chance that the arguments will be accepted? Are there enough people to support decisions? Health care organizations were able to change to smoke-free environments once societal values favored nonsmokers, and a strong majority supported the movement.
4. **What are possible alternative perspectives?** Using different basic assumptions and paradigms can help the critical thinker develop several different views of an issue. Compare how a nurse manager who assumes that more RNs equal better care will deal with a budget cut with a manager who is committed to adding assistive personnel instead. What evidence supports the alternatives? What solutions do staff members, patients, physicians, and others propose? What would be the ideal alternative?

Critical-thinking skills are used throughout the nursing process (see Table 8-1). Managers need to build on the knowledge base they began acquiring in school to make the critical-thinking process a conscious one in daily activities. Learning to be a critical thinker requires a commitment over time, but the skills can be learned (Ward, 2006). Ignatavicius (2001) describes the characteristics of an expert critical thinker in Box 8-1.

TABLE 8-1	Critical Thinking Through the Nursing Process
THE NURSING PROCESS	**CRITICAL-THINKING SKILLS**
Assessment	Observing
	Distinguishing relevant from irrelevant data
	Distinguishing important from unimportant data
	Validating data
	Organizing data
	Categorizing data
Diagnosis	Finding patterns and relationships
	Making inferences
	Stating the problem
	Suspending judgment
Planning	Generalizing
	Transferring knowledge from one situation to another
	Developing evaluative criteria
	Hypothesizing
Implementation	Applying knowledge
	Testing hypotheses
Evaluation	Deciding whether hypotheses are correct
	Making criterion-based evaluations

From *Nursing Process in Action: A Critical Thinking Approach* (p. 29), by J. Wilkinson, 1992, Redwood City, CA: Addison-Wesley Nursing.

CREATIVITY

Creativity is an essential part of the critical-thinking process. **Creativity** is the ability to develop and implement new and better solutions. Creativity demands a certain amount of exposure to outside contacts, receptiveness to new and seemingly strange ideas, a certain amount of freedom, and some permissive management.

Most nurses, however, are employed in bureaucratic settings that do not foster creativity. Control is exercised over staff, and rigid adherence to formal channels of communication jeopardizes innovation. In addition, there is little room for failure, and when failures do occur they are not tolerated very well. When staff are afraid of the consequences of failure, their creativity is inhibited and innovation does not take place.

MEDIALINK   Developing Critical Thinking Skills

BOX 8-1	Characteristics of an Expert Critical Thinker

- Outcome-directed
- Open to new ideas
- Flexible
- Willing to change
- Innovative
- Creative
- Analytical
- Communicator
- Assertive

- Persistent
- Caring
- Energetic
- Risk-taker
- Knowledgeable
- Resourceful
- Observant
- Intuitive
- "Out of the box" thinker

From "Six Critical Thinking Skills for At-the-bedside Success," by D. D. Ignatavicius, 2001, *Nursing Management, 32*(1), pp. 37–39.

Maintaining a certain level of creativity is one way to keep an organization alive. New employees, who are not encumbered with details of accepted practices often can make suggestions based on their prior experiences or insights before they get set in their ways or have their innovative ideas "turned off." The advantages offered by new employees should be explored because all staff gain from such use of valuable human resources.

The climate must promote the survival of potentially useful ideas. The nurse manager can foster a climate of support by giving new ideas a fair and adequate hearing, and thereby reduce the tendency to discourage the creative process in individuals and within groups. The challenge for nurse managers is to know when, for whom, and to what extent control is appropriate. If creativity does have a priority in the health care setting, then the reward system should be geared to and commensurate with that priority.

Creativity has four stages: preparation, incubation, insight, and verification. Even people who think they are not naturally creative can learn this process (*Figure 8-2*).

1. **Preparation.** A carefully designed planning program is essential. First, acquire information necessary to understand the situation. Individuals can do this on their own or groups can work together.

    The process follows this sequence:
    - Pick a specific task
    - Gather relevant facts
    - Challenge every detail
    - Develop preferred solutions
    - Implement improvements

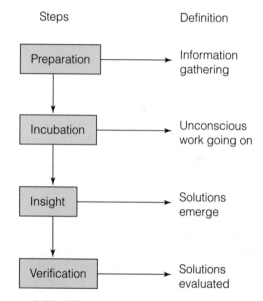

Figure 8-2 ● The creative process.

2. **Incubation.** After all the information available has been gathered, allow as much time as possible to elapse before deciding on solutions.
3. **Insight.** Often solutions emerge after a period of reflection that would not have occurred to anyone without this time lapse.
4. **Verification.** Once a solution has been implemented, evaluate it for effectiveness. You may need to restart the process or go back to another step and create a different solution.

Case Study 8-1 describes how one nurse manager used creativity to solve a problem.

CASE STUDY 8-1   Creative Problem Solving

Jeffrey was just promoted to manager of an acute care clinic, which recently expanded its hours from 6 A.M. until 10 P.M. Jeffrey has realized that staff nurses are reluctant to sign up and do quality chart audits. He gathers information about quality improvement, reviews the literature on motivation and incentives, and discusses the issue with other nurse managers (preparation). He continues to manage the clinic, thinking about the information he has gathered but does not consciously make a decision or reject new ideas (incubation). When working on a new problem, self-scheduling for the change in hours, he realizes a connection between the two problems. Many nurses complain that by the time they receive the schedule the day shifts are filled. Jeffrey states that he will review the chart audits and that those nurses who regularly participate in quality improvement projects will receive a "perk." They will be allowed, on a rotating basis, first choice at selecting the schedule they want to work (this is the insight stage). He discusses the plan with the staff and proposes a 2-month trial period to determine whether the solution is effective (verification).

Manager's Checklist

The nurse manager is responsible to:

- Identify problem areas
- Generate ideas that might serve as possible solutions
- Check with others for advice
- Select motivators
- Implement a solution
- Evaluate the results

Decision Making

Considering all the practice individuals get in making decisions, it would seem they might become very good at it. However, the number of decisions a person makes does not correspond to the person's skill at making them. The assumption is that decision making comes naturally, like breathing. It does not.

The decision-making process described in this chapter provides nurses with a system for making decisions that is applicable to any decision. It is a useful procedure for making practical choices. A decision not to solve a problem is also a decision.

The label *decision making* is used inconsistently and often interchangeably with *problem solving*. Although the two processes appear similar and may in some instances depend on one another, they are not synonymous. The main distinctions between the two are that **decision making** may or may not involve a problem, but it always involves selecting one of several alternatives, each of which may be appropriate under certain circumstances, whereas **problem solving** involves diagnosing a problem and solving it, which may or may not entail deciding on one correct solution.

Most of the time, decision making is a subset of problem solving. However, some decisions are not of a problem-solving nature, such as decisions about scheduling, equipment, in-services, or other matters that do not involve problem solving as a deliberate process.

Also, habit and tradition may be modes of decision making, such as holding onto the wall when walking down a wet hospital corridor or scheduling patient care activities in traditional ways (e.g., giving every patient a bath every morning).

Research has discredited the early belief that decisions are choices people make after extensive evaluation of all options in order to find an optimal solution. Simon (1955) and others recognized that evaluation is seldom extensive and virtually never exhaustive. In the 1970s it was recognized that decision makers have a variety of strategies for making choices and a variety of aims in addition to utility. Most often, past experiences provide ways of dealing with problems. Making a deliberate choice is relatively rare and usually is done by screening out the unacceptable options and choosing the best option from the remainders.

TYPES OF DECISIONS

The types of problems nurses and nurse managers encounter and decisions they must make vary widely and determine the problem-solving or decision-making methods they should use. Relatively well defined, common problems can usually be solved with routine decisions, often using established rules, policies, and procedures. For instance, when a nurse makes a medication error, the manager's actions are guided by policy and the report form. **Routine decisions** are more often made by first-level managers than by top administrators.

Adaptive decisions are necessary when both problems and alternative solutions are somewhat unusual and only partially understood. Often they are modifications of other well-known problems and solutions. Managers must make **innovative decisions** when problems are unusual and unclear and when creative, novel solutions are necessary.

DECISION-MAKING CONDITIONS

The conditions surrounding decision making can vary and change dramatically. Consider the total system. Whatever solutions are created will succeed only if they are compatible with other parts of the system. Decisions are made under conditions of certainty, risk, or uncertainty.

Decision Making under Certainty

When you know the alternatives and the conditions surrounding each alternative, a state of certainty is said to exist. Suppose a nurse manager on a unit with acutely ill patients wants to decrease the number of venipunctures a patient experiences when an IV is started, as well as reduce costs resulting from failed venipunctures. Three alternatives exist:

- Establish an IV team on all shifts to minimize IV attempts and reduce costs
- Establish a reciprocal relationship with the anesthesia department to start IVs when nurses experience difficulty
- Set a standard of two insertion attempts per nurse per patient although this does not substantially lower equipment costs

The manager knows the alternatives (IV team, anesthesia department, standards) and the conditions associated with each option (reduced costs, assistance with starting IVs, minimum attempts and some cost reduction). A condition of strong certainty is said to exist and the decision can be made with full knowledge of what the payoff probably will be.

Decision Making under Uncertainty and Risk

Seldom do decision makers know everything there is to know about a subject or situation. If everything was known, the decision would be obvious for all to realize.

Most critical decision making in organizations is done under conditions of *uncertainty* and *risk*. The individual or group making the decision does not know all the alternatives, attendant risks, or possible consequences of each option. Uncertainty and risk are inevitable because of the complex and dynamic nature of health care organizations. Successful decisions, McConnell (2000) asserts, are dependent on human knowledge, experience, and judgment.

Here is an example: If the weather forecaster predicts a 40 percent chance of snow, the nurse manager is operating in a situation of risk when trying to decide how to staff the unit for the next 24 hours.

In a risk situation, availability of each alternative, potential successes, and costs are all associated with probability estimates. **Probability** is the likelihood, expressed as a percentage, that an event will or will not occur. If something is certain to happen, its probability is 100 percent. If it is certain not to happen, its probability is 0 percent. If there is a 50-50 chance, its probability is 50 percent.

Suppose a nurse manager decides to use agency nurses to staff a unit during heavy vacation periods. Two agencies look attractive, and the manager must decide between them. Agency A has had modest growth over the past 10 years and offers the manager a 3-month contract, freezing wages during that time. In addition, the unit will have first choice of available nurses. Agency B is much more dynamic and charges more but explains that the reason they have had a high rate of growth is that their nurses are the best and the highest paid in the area. The nurse manager can choose Agency A, which will provide a safe, constant supply of nursing personnel, or B, which promises better care but at a higher cost.

The key element in decision making under conditions of risk is to determine the probabilities of each alternative as accurately as possible. The nurse manager can use a **probability analysis**, whereby expected risk is calculated or estimated. Using the probability analysis shown in Table 8-2, it appears as though Agency A offers the best outcome. However, if the second agency had a 90 percent chance of filling shifts and a 50 percent chance of fixing costs, a completely different situation would exist.

TABLE 8-2	Probability Analysis
PROBABILITY ANALYSIS	
Agency A	60% Filling shifts 100% Fixed wages
Agency B	50% Filling shifts 70% Fixed wage

The nurse manager might decide that the potential for increased costs was a small tradeoff for having more highly qualified nurses and the best probability of having the unit fully staffed during vacation periods. **Objective probability** is the likelihood that an event will or will not occur based on facts and reliable information. **Subjective probability** is the likelihood that an event will or will not occur based on a manager's personal judgment and beliefs.

Janeen, a nurse manager of a specialized cardiac intensive care unit, faces the task of recruiting scarce and highly skilled nurses to care for coronary bypass patients. The obvious alternative is to offer a salary and benefit package that rivals that of all other institutions in the area. However, this means Janeen will have costly specialized nursing personnel in her budget who are not easily absorbed by other units in the organization. The probability that coronary bypass procedures will become obsolete in the future is unknown. In addition, other factors (e.g., increased competition, government regulations regarding reimbursement) may contribute to conditions of uncertainty.

THE DECISION-MAKING PROCESS

The **rational decision-making model** is a series of steps that managers take in an effort to make logical, well-grounded rational choices that maximize the achievement of objectives. First identify all possible outcomes, examine the probability of each alternative, and then take the action that yields the highest probability of achieving the most desirable outcome. Not all steps are used in every decision nor are they always used in the same order. The rational decision-making model is thought of as the ideal but often cannot be fully used.

Individuals seldom make major decisions at a single point in time and often are unable to recall when a decision was finally reached. Some major decisions are the result of many small actions or incremental choices the person makes without regarding larger issues. In addition, decision processes are likely to be characterized more by confusion, disorder, and emotionality than by rationality. For these reasons, it is best to develop appropriate technical skills and the capacity to find a good balance between lengthy processes and quick, decisive action.

The **descriptive rationality model**, developed by Simon in 1955 and supported by research in the 1990s (Simon, 1993), emphasizes the limitations of the rationality of the decision maker and the situation. It recognizes three ways in which decision makers depart from the rational decision-making model:

- The decision maker's search for possible objectives or alternative solutions is limited because of time, energy, and money
- People frequently lack adequate information about problems and cannot control the conditions under which they operate
- Individuals often use a satisficing strategy.

Satisficing is not a misspelled word; it is a decision-making strategy whereby the individual chooses an alternative that is not ideal but either is good enough (suffices) under existing circumstances to meet minimum standards of acceptance or is the first acceptable alternative.

Many problems in nursing are ineffectively solved with satisficing strategies.

Elena, a nurse manager in charge of a busy neurosurgical floor with high turnover rates and high patient acuity levels, uses a satisficing alternative when hiring replacement staff. She hires all nurse applicants in order of application until no positions are open. A better approach would be for Elena to replace staff only with nurse applicants who possess the skills and experiences required to care for neurosurgical patients, regardless of the number of applicants or desire for immediate action. Elena also should develop a plan to promote job satisfaction, the lack of which is the real reason for the vacancies.

Individuals who solve problems using satisficing may lack specific training in problem solving and decision making. They may view their units or areas of responsibility as drastically simplified models of the real world and be content with this simplification because it allows them to make decisions with relatively simple rules of thumb or from force of habit.

The **political decision-making model** describes the process in terms of the particular interests and objectives of powerful stakeholders, such as hospital boards, medical staffs, corporate officers, and regulatory bodies. Power is the ability to influence or control how problems and objectives are defined, what alternative solutions are considered and selected, what information flows, and, ultimately, what decisions are made (see Chapter 7).

The decision-making process begins when a gap exists between what is actually happening and what should be happening, and it ends with action that will narrow

BOX 8-2	Steps in Decision Making

1. Identify the purpose: Why is a decision necessary? What needs to be determined? State the issue in the broadest possible terms.

2. Set the criteria: What needs to be achieved, preserved, and avoided by whatever decision is made? The answers to these questions are the standards by which solutions will be evaluated.

3. Weight the criteria: Rank each criterion on a scale of values from 1 (totally unimportant) to 10 (extremely important).

4. Seek alternatives: List all possible courses of action. Is one alternative more significant than another? Does one alternative have weaknesses in some areas? Can these be overcome? Can two alternatives or features of many alternatives be combined?

5. Test alternatives: First, using the same methodology as in step 3, rank each alternative on a scale of 1 to 10. Second, multiply the weight of each criterion by the rating of each alternative. Third, add the scores and compare the results.

6. Troubleshoot: What could go wrong? How can you plan? Can the choice be improved?

7. Evaluate the action: Is the solution being implemented? Is it effective? Is it costly?

or close this gap. The simplest way to learn decision-making skills is to integrate a model into one's thinking by breaking the components down into individual steps. The seven steps of the decision-making process (Box 8-2) are as applicable to personal problems as they are to nursing management problems. Each step is elaborated by pertinent questions clarifying the statements, and they should be followed in the order in which they are presented.

DECISION-MAKING TECHNIQUES

Decision-making techniques vary according to the nature of the problem or topic, the decision maker, the context or situation, and the decision-making method or process. For routine decisions, choices that are tried and true can be made for well-defined, known situations or problems. Well-designed policies, rules, and standard operating procedures can produce satisfactory results with a minimum of time. **Artificial intelligence**, including programmed computer systems such as **expert systems** that can store, retrieve, and manipulate data, can diagnose problems and make limited decisions.

For adaptive decisions involving moderately ambiguous problems and modification of known and well-defined alternative solutions, there are a variety of techniques. Many types of decision grids or tables can be used to compare outcomes of alternative solutions. Decisions about units or services can be facilitated, with analyses comparing output, revenue, and costs over

time or under different conditions. Analyzing the costs and revenues of a proposed new service is an example.

Regardless of the decision-making model or strategy chosen, data collection and analysis are essential. In many health care organizations, quality teams are using a variety of tools to gather, organize, and analyze data about their work such as cause-and-effect diagrams, flow charts, Pareto charts, run charts, histograms, control charts, and scatter diagrams. These tools help nurses understand facts and relationships in processes they are examining. ***Figure 8-3*** illustrates a cause-and-effect diagram that a team of nurses created to help them improve the documentation process for their ambulatory oncology unit.

GROUP DECISION MAKING

The widespread use of participative management, quality improvement teams, and shared governance in health care organizations requires every nurse manager to determine when group, rather than individual, decisions are desirable and how to use groups effectively. A number of studies have shown that professional people do not function well in a micromanaged environment. As an alternative, group problem solving of substantial issues casts the manager in the role of facilitator and consultant. Compared to individual decision making, groups can provide more input, often produce better decisions, and generate more commitment. Several group decision-making techniques can be used.

MEDIALINK Group Decision Making

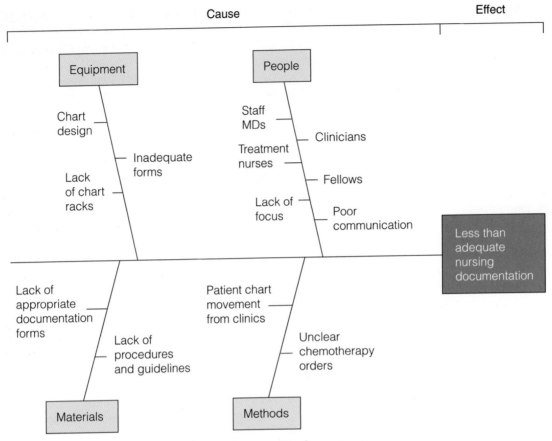

Figure 8-3 ● Brainstorming session of a nursing quality focus team.

Nominal Group Technique

The **nominal group technique (NGT)**, developed by Delbecq, VandeVen, and Gustafson (1975), is a structured and precise method of eliciting written questions, ideas, and reactions from group members. NGT is a group process in name only because no direct exchange occurs among members. NGT consists of:

- Silently generating ideas in writing
- Round-robin presentation by group members of their individual ideas in a terse phrase on a flip chart
- Discussion of each recorded idea for clarification and evaluation
- Voting individually on priority ideas, with the group solution being derived mathematically through rank ordering or rating using the group's decision rule

Delphi Technique

In the **Delphi technique**, judgments on a particular topic are systematically gathered from participants who do not meet face to face. Ideas are collected through a carefully designed sequence of questionnaires interspersed with summaries of information and opinions derived from previous questionnaires. The process may involve many iterations but normally does not exceed three. This technique can rely on the input of experts widely dispersed geographically. It can be used to evaluate the quality of research proposals or to make predictions about the future based on current scientific knowledge. This technique is useful when expert opinions are needed and expense would prohibit bringing them together.

For fact-finding problems with no known solution, the NGT and the Delphi technique are superior to other group techniques. Both NGT and the Delphi technique minimize the chances of more vocal members dominating discussion and allow independent consideration of ideas.

Statistical Aggregation

Like the Delphi technique, **statistical aggregation** does not require a group meeting. Individuals are polled regarding a specific problem, and their responses are tallied. It is a very efficient technique, but it is limited to problems for which a quantifiable answer can be obtained. One disadvantage of both statistical aggregation and the Delphi technique is that no opportunity exists for group members to strengthen their interpersonal ties or for the generative effect of group interaction.

Brainstorming

In **brainstorming**, group members meet together and generate many diverse ideas about the nature, cause, definition, or solution to a problem without consideration of their relative value. A premium is placed on generating lots of ideas as quickly as possible and on coming up with unusual ideas. Most importantly, members do not critique ideas as they are proposed. Evaluation takes place after all the ideas have been generated. Members are encouraged to improve on each other's ideas. These sessions are very enjoyable but are often unsuccessful because members inevitably begin to critique ideas, and as a result, meetings shift to the ordinary interacting group format. Criticisms of this approach are the high cost factor, the time consumed, and the superficiality of many solutions.

STUMBLING BLOCKS

The leader's personality traits, inexperience, lack of adaptability, and preconceived ideas may be obstacles to problem solving and decision making.

Personality

The leader's personality can and often does affect how and why certain decisions are made. Many nurse managers are selected because of their expert clinical, not management skills. Inexperienced in management, they may resort to various unproductive activities. On the one hand, a nurse manager who is insecure may base decisions primarily on approval seeking. When a truly difficult situation arises, the manager, rather than face rejection from the staff, makes a decision that will placate people rather than one that will achieve the larger goals of the unit and organization.

On the other hand, a nurse manager who demonstrates an authoritative type of personality might make unreasonable demands on the staff, fail to reward staff for long hours because he or she has a "workaholic" attitude, or give the staff no control over patient care activities. Similarly, an inexperienced manager may

cause a unit to flounder because the manager is not inclined to act on new ideas or solutions to problems. Optimism, humor, and a positive approach are crucial to energizing staff and promoting creativity.

Rigidity

Rigidity, an inflexible management style, is another obstacle to problem solving. It may result from ineffective trial-and-error solutions, fear of risk taking, or inherent personality traits. You can avoid ineffective trial-and-error problem solving by gathering sufficient information and determining a means for early correction of wrong or inadequate decisions. Also, to minimize risk in problem solving, understand alternative risks and expectations.

The person who uses a rigid style in problem solving easily develops tunnel vision—the tendency to look at new things in old ways and from established frames of reference. It then becomes very difficult to see things from another perspective, and problem solving becomes a process whereby one person makes all of the decisions with little information or data from other sources. In the current changing health care setting, rigidity can be a barrier to effective problem solving.

Preconceived Ideas

Effective leaders do not start out with the preconceived idea that one proposed course of action is right and all others wrong. Nor do they assume that only one opinion can be voiced and others will be silent. They start out with a commitment to find out why others disagree. If the staff, other professionals, or patients see a different reality or even a different problem, leaders need to integrate this information into developing additional problem-solving alternatives.

Problem Solving

People use problem solving when they perceive a gap between an existing state (what is going on) and a desired state (what should be going on). How one perceives the situation influences how the problem is identified or solved. Therefore, perceptions need to be clarified before problem solving can occur.

PROBLEM-SOLVING METHODS

A variety of methods can be used to solve problems. People with little management experience tend to use the **trial-and-error method**, applying one solution after another until the problem is solved or appears to be improving. These managers often cite lack of experience and of time and resources to search for alternative solutions.

In a step-down unit with an increasing incidence of medication errors, Max, the nurse manager, uses various strategies to decrease errors, such as asking nurses to use calculators, having the charge nurse check medications, and posting dosage and medication charts in the unit. After a few months, by which time none of the methods has worked, it occurs to Max that perhaps making nurses responsible for their actions would be more effective. Max develops a point system for medication errors: When nurses accumulate a certain amount of points, they are required to take a medication test; repeated failure of the test may eventually lead to termination. Max's solution is effective, and a low level of medication errors is restored.

As the above example shows, a trial-and-error process can be time consuming and may even be detrimental. Although some learning can occur during the process, the nurse manager risks being perceived as a poor problem solver who has wasted time and money on ineffective solutions.

Experimentation, another type of problem solving, is more rigorous than trial and error. Pilot projects or limited trials are examples of experimentation. Experimentation involves testing a theory (hypothesis) or hunch to enhance knowledge, understanding, or prediction. A project or study is carried out in either a controlled setting (e.g., in a laboratory) or an uncontrolled setting (e.g., in a natural setting such as an outpatient clinic). Data are collected and analyzed and results interpreted to determine whether the solution tried has been effective.

Lin, a nurse manager of a pediatric floor, has received many complaints from mothers of children who think the nurses are short-tempered. Lin has a hunch that 12-hour shifts, which have been recently implemented on her floor, are contributing to the problem; she believes that nurses who must interact frequently with families would perform better on 8-hour shifts. She can test her theory by setting up a small study comparing the two staffing patterns with patient satisfaction.

Experimentation may be creative and effective or uninspired and ineffective, depending on how it is used. As a major method of problem solving, experimentation may be inefficient because of the amount of time and control involved. However, a well-designed experiment can be persuasive in situations in which an idea or activity, such as a new staffing system or care procedure, can be tried in one of two similar groups and results objectively compared.

Still other problem-solving techniques rely on *past experience* and *intuition*. Everyone has various and countless experiences. Individuals build a repertoire of these experiences and base future actions on what they considered successful solutions in the past. If a particular course of action consistently resulted in positive outcomes, the person will try it again when similar circumstances occur. In some instances, an individual's past experience can determine how much risk he or she will take in present circumstances. The nature and frequency of the experience also contribute significantly to the effectiveness of this problem-solving method. How much the person has learned from these experiences, positive or negative, can affect the current viewpoint and can result in either subjective and narrow judgments or very wise ones. This is especially true in human relations problems. A nurse manager who has an unfortunate experience with a nurse recovering from chemical dependency may, in the future, judge all nurses with acknowledged chemical dependency negatively. Intuition relies heavily on past experience and trial and error. The extent to which past experience is related to intuition is difficult to determine, but nurses' wisdom, sensitivity, and intuition are known to be valuable in solving problems.

Some problems are self-solving: If permitted to run a natural course, they are solved by those personally involved. This is not to say that a uniform laissez-faire management style solves all problems. The nurse manager must not ignore managerial responsibilities, but often difficult situations become more manageable when participants are given time, resources, and support to discover their own solutions. This typically happens, for example, when a newly graduated nurse joins a unit where most of the staff are associate degree RNs who resent the new nurse's level of education as well as the nurse's lack of experience. If the nurse manager intervenes, a problem that the staff might have worked out on their own becomes an ongoing source of conflict. The important skill required here is knowing when to act and when not to act. (See Chapter 12 for a discussion of conflict.)

THE PROBLEM-SOLVING PROCESS

Many nursing problems require immediate action. Nurses don't have time for formalized processes of research and analysis specified by the scientific method. Therefore, learning an organized method for problem

BOX 8-3	Steps in Problem Solving

1. Define the problem.
2. Gather information.
3. Analyze the information.
4. Develop solutions.
5. Make a decision.
6. Implement the decision.
7. Evaluate the solution.

solving is invaluable. One practical method for problem solving is to follow this seven-step process, which is also outlined in Box 8-3.

1. **Define the problem.** The definition of a problem should be a descriptive statement of the state of affairs, not a judgment or conclusion. If one begins the statement of a problem with a judgment, the solution may be equally judgmental, and critical descriptive elements could be overlooked.

   Suppose a nurse manager reluctantly implements a self-scheduling process and finds that each time the schedule is posted, evenings and some weekend shifts are not adequately covered. The manager might identify the problem as the immaturity of the staff and their inability to function under democratic leadership. The causes may be lack of interest in group decision making, minimal concern over providing adequate patient coverage, or, perhaps more correctly, a few nurses' lack of understanding of the process.

   If the nurse manager defines the above problem as immaturity and reverts to making out the schedules without further fact-finding, a minor problem could develop into a full-blown crisis.

   Premature interpretation can alter one's ability to deal with facts objectively. For example, are there other explanations for the apparent behavior that do not entail negative assumptions about the maturity of the staff? Premature interpretations can be avoided by using reflective inquiry.

   Schmieding (1999) describes four characteristics of *reflective inquiry*:
   - Objective data are tested against one's thoughts and feelings.

- Past experiences and knowledge are used to evaluate the situation.
- Ideas about the problem are validated or refuted based on empirical evidence through a serial rather than a linear process.
- The facts and ideas generated are verified through deliberate investigation.

   Accurate assessment of the scope of the problem also determines whether the manager needs to seek a lasting solution or just a stopgap measure. Is this just a situational problem requiring only intervention with a simple explanation, or is it more complex, involving the leadership style of the manager? The manager must define and classify problems in order to take action.

   In defining a problem, determine the area it covers and ask:
   - Do I have the authority to do anything about this myself?
   - Do I have all the information? The time?
   - Who else has important information and can contribute?
   - What benefits could be expected? A list of potential benefits provides the basis for comparison and choice of solutions. The list also serves as a means for evaluating the solution.

2. **Gather information.** Problem solving begins with collecting facts. This information gathering initiates a search for additional facts that provides clues to the scope and solution of the problem. This step encourages people to report facts accurately. Everyone involved can provide information. Although this may not always provide objective information, it reduces misinformation and allows everyone an opportunity to tell what he or she thinks is wrong with a situation.

   Experience is another source of information—one's own experience as well as the experience of other nurse managers and staff. Everyone involved usually has ideas about what should be done about a problem, and many of these ideas provide good information and valuable suggestions. Yet information gathered may never be complete. Some data will be useless, some inaccurate, but some will be useful to develop innovative ideas worth pursuing.

3. **Analyze the information.** Analyze the information only when all of it has been sorted into some orderly arrangement as follows:
   - Categorize information in order of reliability.
   - List information from most important to least important.

- Set information into a time sequence. What happened first? Next? What came before what? What were the concurrent circumstances?
- Examine information in terms of cause and effect. Is A causing B, or vice versa?
- Classify information into categories: *human factors,* such as personality, maturity, education, age, relationships among people, and problems outside the organization; *technical factors,* such as nursing skills or the type of unit; *temporal factors,* such as length of service, overtime, type of shift, and double shifts; and *policy factors,* such as organizational procedures or rules applying to the problem, legal issues, and ethical issues.
- Consider how long the situation has been going on.

   Because no amount of information is ever complete or comprehensive enough, critical-thinking skills are important to the manager's ability to examine the assumptions, evidence, and potential value conflicts.

4. **Develop solutions.** As an individual or a group analyzes information, numerous possible solutions will suggest themselves. Do not consider only simple solutions, because that may stifle creative thinking and cause over concentration on detail. Developing alternative solutions makes it possible to combine the best parts of several solutions into a superior one. Also, alternatives are valuable in case the first-order solutions prove impossible to implement.

   When exploring a variety of solutions, maintain an uncritical attitude toward the way the problem has been handled in the past. Some problems have had a long-standing history by the time they reach you, and attempts may have been made to resolve them over a long period of time. "We tried this before and it didn't work," is often said and may apply—or more likely, may not apply—in a changed situation. Past experience may not always supply an answer, but it can aid the critical-thinking process and help prepare for future problem solving.

5. **Make a decision.** After reviewing the list of potential solutions, select the one that is most applicable, feasible, satisfactory, and has the fewest undesirable consequences. Some solutions have to be put into effect quickly; matters of discipline or compromises in patient safety, for example, need immediate intervention. You must have legitimate authority to act in an emergency and know the penalties to be imposed for various infractions.

   If the problem is a technical one and its solution brings about a change in the method of doing work (or using new equipment), expect resistance. Changes that threaten individuals' personal security or status are especially difficult. In those cases, the change process must be initiated before solutions are implemented. If the solution involves change, the manager should fully involve those who will be affected by it, if possible, or at least inform them of the process. (See Chapter 5 for discussion of the change process.)

6. **Implement the decision.** Implement the decision after selecting the best course of action. If unforeseen new problems emerge after implementation, evaluate these impediments. Be careful, however, not to abandon a workable solution just because a few people object; a minority always will. If the previous steps in the problem-solving process have been followed, the solution has been carefully thought out, and potential problems have been addressed, implementation should move forward.

7. **Evaluate the solution.** After the solution has been implemented, review the plan instituted and compare the actual results and benefits to those of the idealized solution. People tend to fall back into old patterns of habit, only giving lip service to change and carrying out the same old behavior. Is the solution being implemented? If so, are the results better or worse than expected? If they are better, what changes have contributed to its success? How can we ensure that the solution continues to be used and to work? Such a periodic checkup gives you valuable insight and experience to use in other situations and keeps the problem-solving process on course.

See Case Study 8-2 to learn how one nurse manager used critical thinking to solve a problem.

GROUP PROBLEM SOLVING

Traditionally, managers solved most problems in isolation. This practice, however, is outdated. Both the complexity of problems and the staff's desire for meaningful involvement at work create the impetus for using group approaches to problem solving. Today consensus-based problem solving is more often the norm.

Advantages of Group Problem Solving

Groups collectively possess greater knowledge and information than any single member and may access more strategies to solve a problem. Under the right circumstances and with appropriate leadership, groups

CASE STUDY 8-2 — Critical Thinking and Problem Solving

Latonia Wilson is nurse manager for a busy 20-bed telemetry unit. In addition to providing postsurgical care for cardiac patients, nurses also prepare patients for cardiac lab procedures. Latonia's staff includes eight graduate nurses, almost half of her nursing staff. The new nurses have attended most of the required nursing orientation for the hospital.

Three times in one month, telemetry unit patients who had orders for heparin drips were instead administered heparin flush. Premixed IV bags for heparin drips as well as heparin flush for indwelling arterial catheters are stocked on the IV solutions cart in the medication room. While no adverse patient outcomes had been reported, procedures have been delayed.

Geena Donati is a graduate nurse on the telemetry unit. Recently, she took a bag of heparin drip from the IV cart and started to attach it to the IV tubing. She noticed that the label stated heparin flush instead of heparin. Upon returning to the med room, she checked the heparin drip bin and found heparin flush bags mixed in with the heparin drip. The pharmacy technician came into the med room and began stocking the IV cart. Geena noticed that the pharmacy technician put extra heparin drip bags in the heparin flush bin. She questioned the pharmacy technician and he told Geena that since the unit used a lot of heparin solution, he had started bringing extra to decrease his trips to the unit.

Geena met with Latonia later during her shift. She told her manager about the extra heparin bags being mixed into the wrong bins. Latonia asked Geena if she would be interested in working with two other RNs on the unit to develop new procedures to decrease heparin medication errors. Geena and the task force worked with the pharmacy department to change the label color for heparin drip and heparin flush solutions, physically separated the bins on the IV cart onto different shelves, and provided a short educational segment at the monthly staff meeting. Since the new procedures were developed, no further heparin errors have occurred on the telemetry unit.

Manager's Checklist

The nurse manager is responsible to:

- Track and identify reoccurring negative performance issues on the unit
- Analyze adverse outcomes to determine what factors contributed to the outcome
- Empower staff to improve work processes on the unit
- Understand the organizational structure and assist staff to work with other departments within the organization

---

can deal with more complex problems than a single individual, especially if there is no one right or wrong solution to the problem. Individuals tend to rely on a small number of familiar strategies; a group is more likely to try several approaches.

Group members may have a greater variety of training and experiences and approach problems from more diverse points of view. Together, a group may generate more complete, accurate, and less biased information than one person. Groups may deal more effectively with problems that cross organizational boundaries or involve change that requires support from all departments affected. Participative problem solving has additional advantages: It increases the likelihood of acceptance and understanding of the decision, and it enhances cooperation in implementation.

Disadvantages of Group Problem Solving

Group problem solving also has disadvantages: It takes time and resources and may involve conflict. Group problem solving also can lead to the emergence of benign tyranny within the group. Members who are less informed or less confident may allow stronger members to control group discussion and problem solving. A disparity in participation may contribute to a power struggle between the nurse manager and a few assertive group members.

Also managers may resist using groups to make decisions. They may fear that they may not agree with the decision the group makes or that they will not be needed if all decisions are made by the group. Neither is the case. Some decisions are rightfully the managers (e. g., handling the budget), others are staff decisions (e.g., peer review, self-scheduling), and some are shared (e.g., joint hiring decisions). *Figure 8-4* illustrates this (Shiparski, 2005).

Group problem solving also can be affected by **groupthink**. Groupthink is a negative phenomenon that occurs in highly cohesive groups that become isolated. Through prolonged close association, group members

Figure 8-4 ● Shared decision making goal. *From "Engaging in Shared Decision Making: Leveraging Staff and Management Expertise," by L. A. Shiparski (2005). Nurse Leader, 3(1), p. 40.*

come to think alike and have similar prejudices and blind spots, such as stereotypical views of outsiders. They exhibit a strong tendency to seek concurrence, which interferes with critical thinking about important decisions. In addition, the leadership of such groups suppresses open, free-wheeling discussion and controls what ideas will be discussed and how much dissent will be tolerated. Groupthink seriously impairs critical thinking and can result in erroneous and damaging decisions.

Two phenomena are associated with groupthink (Forsyth, 1983): premature concurrence seeking, and illusions and misperceptions. **Premature concurrence seeking** is evidenced in several features of groupthink, such as:

- High pressure to conform and taboos against expressing dissent or criticizing ideas presented by the majority, a leader, or some other powerful member
- Self-censorship of dissenting opinions, in which members with questions or concerns remain silent
- **Mindguards**, who use "gatekeeping" to protect the group from controversial information and discourage dissent by diverting doubts about the group's decisions or beliefs
- Apparent unanimity, reflected in the illusion that the group is in concurrence despite objections and concerns

Misperceptions and illusions are also characteristic of groupthink. They may include:

- A belief that the group is morally correct, which encourages members to ignore the ethical and moral consequences of their decisions
- Rationalization of warnings and other forms of negative feedback
- Biased perceptions of the out-group
- Collective rationalization of contradictory information (Janis, 1982)

Use the following tactics to prevent groupthink in cohesive groups:

1. Promote open inquiry by assigning the crucial evaluator role to each member. Encourage the group to give high priority to airing objections and doubts. Reinforce by accepting criticism.
2. The leader initially should delay stating his or her preferences and expectations until others' views have been fully disclosed.
3. The leader may set up several independent work groups to tackle the same issue. The groups then reconvene to explore a variety of approaches to problem solving and to hammer out differences.
4. Each member of the decision-making group should discuss periodically the group's deliberations with trusted associates in his or her own unit of the organization and report back nonmembers' views and reactions.
5. One or more outside experts within the organization who are not core members of the problem-solving group should be invited to each meeting on a rotating basis to challenge the views of the core members.
6. At every problem-solving meeting, at least one group member should be assigned the role of "devil's advocate" by attempting to find fault with any argument that might be considered valid.
7. Whenever problem solving involves relations with a rival, all warning signals from the rival should be analyzed and possible interpretations of the rival's intentions examined.
8. After reaching a preliminary consensus (agreement that everyone can support, arrived at without formal voting) about the best alternative, the problem-solving group should hold a second chance meeting at which every member is expected to express as vividly as possible all residual doubts and to rethink the entire issue before making a final choice (Janis, 1982).

Although managing dissent may be complicated, time consuming, and at times unpleasant, conflict is not always dysfunctional, and it is often necessary for quality decision making.

Dialectical inquiry is another technique to minimize groupthink. In dialectical inquiry, advocates of a plan and a counterplan undertake a formal debate. This technique formalizes conflict by allowing disagreement, encourages the exploration of alternative solutions, and reduces the emotional aspects of conflict. The benefits from this method come from the presentation and debate of the basic assumptions underlying proposed courses of action. Any false or misleading assumptions become apparent, and the process promotes better understanding of problems and leads to higher levels of confidence in a decision. Some potential drawbacks to this method are that it can lead to an emphasis on who won the debate rather than what the best decision is or it can lead to inappropriate compromise.

Risky Shift

Groups tend to make riskier decisions than individuals. Groups are more likely to support unusual or unpopular positions (e.g., public demonstrations). Groups tend to be less conservative than individual decision makers and frequently display more courage and support for unusual or creative solutions to problems. This phenomenon is referred to as **risky shift** (Napier & Gershenfeld, 1981).

Several factors contribute to this phenomenon. Individuals who lack information about alternatives may make a safe choice, but after group discussion they acquire additional information and become more comfortable with a less secure alternative. The group setting also allows for the diffusion of responsibility. If something goes wrong, others also can be assigned the blame or risk. In addition, leaders may be greater risk takers than individuals, and group members may attach a social value to risk taking because they identify it with leadership.

When to Use Groups for Problem Solving

Vroom and Jago (1974, 1988) developed a model for determining when to use a group for problem solving. In practice, several factors determine the degree of participation in group problem solving:

- Who initiates ideas
- How much support from subordinates is required to implement a solution
- How completely an employee is involved in each phase of problem solving (identifying the problem, analyzing the problem, finding alternatives, estimating consequences, and making choices)
- How much weight the nurse manager attaches to the ideas received
- How much the nurse manager knows about the issue

Generally, groups should be used for problem solving when time and deadlines allow for a group decision; the problem is complex or unstructured; the group members share the organization's goals; there is need for acceptance, or at least understanding, of the decision if it is to be implemented properly; and the process will not lead to unacceptable conflict.

Using critical thinking and creativity, along with change strategies and appropriate techniques, will enable nurses and their managers to solve problems and make decisions in the least time and with the best outcomes.

What You Know Now

- Critical thinking requires examining underlying assumptions about current evidence, interpreting information, and evaluating the arguments presented to reach a new and exciting conclusion.
- The creative process involves preparation, incubation, insight, and verification, which can be learned by individuals and groups.
- Problem-solving and decision-making processes use critical-thinking skills.
- The decision-making process may employ several models: rational, descriptive rationality, satisficing, and political.
- Decision-making techniques vary according to the problem and the degree of risk and uncertainty in the situation.
- Methods of problem solving include trial and error, intuition, experimentation, past experience, tradition, and recognizing that some problems are self-solving.
- The problem-solving process involves defining the problem, gathering information, analyzing information, developing solutions, making a decision, implementing the decision, and evaluating the solution.
- Group problem solving can be positive, providing more information and knowledge than an individual. It can also be negative if it generates disruptive conflict or groupthink.

Tools for Making Decisions and Solving Problems

1. Identify problem areas.
2. Ask questions, interpret data, and consider alternatives to make decisions and solve problems.

3. Evaluate the level of certainty, uncertainty, and risk, and consider appropriate alternatives.
4. Identify opportunities to use groups appropriately to make decisions and solve problems.
5. Follow the problem-solving process described in the chapter.

Questions to Challenge You

1. Identify someone you believe has critical-thinking skills. What critical thinking attributes does this person possess?
2. Describe a situation when you made an important decision. What content in the chapter applied to that situation? What was the outcome?
3. Have you been involved in group decision making at school or work? What techniques were used? Were they effective?
4. From the models discussed in the chapter, describe fictional or real situations using these models.
5. A number of ways that problem solving might fail were discussed in the chapter. Name three more.

Explore MediaLink 🌐

Additional interactive resources for this chapter can be found on the Website at http://www.prenhall.com/sullivan. Click on Chapter 8 to select activities for this chapter.

- Video Overview
- NCLEX® Review Questions
- Critical Thinking Activities
- Current Events
- Nursing Leadership and Management in Action
- MediaLinks

References

Delbecq, A. L., VandeVen, A. H., & Gustafson, D. H. (1975). *Group techniques for program planning.* Glenview, IL: Foresman.

Forsyth, D. R. (1983). *An introduction to group dynamics.* Monterey, CA: Brooks/Cole.

Ignatavicius, D. D. (2001). Six critical thinking skills for at-the-bedside success. *Nursing Management, 32*(1), 37–39.

Janis, I. L. (1982). *Groupthink: Psychological studies of policy decisions and fiascoes* (2nd ed.). Boston: Houghton Mifflin.

McConnell, C. R. (2000). The anatomy of a decision. *Health Care Manager, 18*(4), 63–74.

Napier, R. W., & Gershenfeld, M. K. (1981). *Groups: Theory and experience.* Boston: Houghton Mifflin.

Schmieding, N. J. (1999). Reflective inquiry framework for nurse administrators. *Journal of Advanced Nursing, 30*(3), 631–639.

Shiparski, L. A. (2005). Leveraging staff and management expertise. *Nurse Leader, 3*(1), 36–41.

Simon, H. A. (1955). A behavioral model of rational choice. *Quarterly Journal of Economics, 69,* 99–118.

Simon, H. A. (1993). Decision making: Rational, nonrational, and irrational. *Education Administration Quarterly, 29*(3), 392–411.

Vroom, V. H., & Jago, A. G. (1974). Decision making as a social process: Normative and descriptive models of leader behavior. *Decision Sciences, 5,* 743–769.

Vroom, V. H., & Jago, A. G. (1988). *The new leadership.* Englewood Cliffs, NJ: Prentice Hall.

Ward, C. W. (2006). Developing critical thinking in nursing. *Med-Surg Matters, 5*(5), 1–3.

Communicating Effectively

Learning Outcomes

After completing this chapter, you will be able to:

1. Identify the factors that influence communication.
2. Discuss how communication can be distorted and misunderstood.

MediaLink

www.prenhall.com/sullivan
See the Companion Website for chapter-specific resources at
www.prenhall.com/sullivan.

3. Choose which communication mode to use depending on the message and the relationship.
4. Explain how communication strategies vary according to the situation and those involved.
5. Determine how to communicate with difficult people.
6. Develop a plan to enhance your communication skills.

Key Terms

Communication *p122*
Diagonal communication *p123*
Downward communication *p123*
Fogging *p127*

Intersender conflict *p123*
Intrasender conflict *p123*
Lateral communication *p123*
Metacommunications *p123*

Negative assertion *p127*
Negative inquiry *p127*
Upward communication *p123*

What if you could see a video of yourself right now? Would viewers see a confident professional? Would they see a conscientious student? Would your words convey what you mean? In today's environment with cell phone cameras always at the ready, you could find yourself on a video, not one you'd like to see online. So, present your best self by learning and using the communication skills offered here.

Communication

Communication is a complex, ongoing, dynamic process in which the participants simultaneously create shared meaning in an interaction. The goal of communication is to approach, as closely as possible, a common understanding of the message sent and the one received. At times, this can be difficult because both participants are influenced by past conditioning, the present situation, each person's purpose in the current communication, and each person's attitudes toward self, the topic, and each other. It is important that participants construct messages as clearly as possible, listen carefully, monitor each other's response, and provide feedback.

MODES OF COMMUNICATION

Messages may be oral (face-to-face, one-on-one, or in groups; by telephone; on voice mail) or written (handwritten or typed) and sent by mail, e-mail, text, or fax.

The purpose of the message determines the best mode to use. In general, the more important or delicate the issue, the more intimate the mode should be. Any difficult issue should be communicated face-to-face, such as terminating an individual's employment. Conflict or confrontation also is usually best handled in person so that the individual's response, especially nonverbal signals (discussed later), can be seen and answered appropriately.

What mode to use depends on the level of intimacy required based on the person, your relationship, and the message. The levels of intimacy, in descending order, are:

- in person
- on the telephone
- voice mail
- e-mail, instant messaging, or by texting
- memos, faxes, and written mail

Meeting someone face-to-face is the most intimate contact. The individual can see your face, your body movements, and your words simultaneously. The telephone is slightly less intimate than in-person communication. Tone of voice, for instance, can be conveyed and may facilitate cooperation. Voice mail is the next level of communication. Voice mail is useful to convey information that is not necessarily sensitive and may or may not require a reply. The time and place of an upcoming meeting, for example, can be communicated by voice mail, which has the added advantage of avoiding "phone tag." E-mail is useful for information similar to that conveyed by voice mail and, like some voice mail systems, can be broadcast to large groups at once. The dates and times for a blood drive are a good example of a broadcast message. Conveying complicated information that may require thought before the receiver replies is another value of using e-mail.

The level of formality of the communication also affects the mode used. Applying for a position requires a written format even if the letter is e-mailed rather than mailed. The relationship between the sender and receiver also affects the mode. If a staff nurse, for example, wants to nominate a coworker for an award given by the hospital board of directors, a written letter or e-mail is required. Memos are less formal than written messages and can be e-mailed, faxed, or mailed.

DISTORTED COMMUNICATION

Oral messages are accompanied by a number of nonverbal messages known as **metacommunications**. These behaviors include head or facial agreement or disagreement; eye contact; tone, volume, and inflection of the voice; gestures of the shoulders, arms, hands, or fingers; body posture and position; dress and appearance; timing; and environment.

Nonverbal communication is more powerful than the words one speaks and can distort the meaning of the spoken words. When a verbal message is incongruent with the nonverbal message, the recipient has difficulty interpreting the intended meaning; this results in **intrasender conflict**. For example, a manager who states, "Come talk to me anytime," but keeps on typing at the keyboard while you talk, sends a conflicting message to the staff. **Intersender conflict** occurs when a person receives two conflicting messages from differing sources. For example, the risk manager may encourage a nurse to report medication errors, but the nurse manager follows up with discipline over the error. The nurse is caught between conflicting messages from the two.

Other common causes of distorted communication are:

- Using inadequate reasoning
- Using strong, judgmental words
- Speaking too fast or too slowly
- Using unfamiliar words
- Spending too much time on details

Distortion also occurs when the recipient is busy or distracted, bases understanding on previous unsatisfactory experience with the sender, or has a biased perception

of the meaning of the message or the messenger. Consider the example of distortion of written communication provided in Box 9-1.

E-mail is particularly fraught with opportunities for misunderstanding. From the greeting (e.g., dear, hi, hello) to the sign-off (e.g., warm regards, best wishes, or the curt "best"), the sender conveys more than the choice of words. A speedy reply is expected and encourages a response, sometimes without adequate thought. Finally, the possibility of sending the message to the wrong person, especially the dreaded "reply to all," is another chance for your message to be misinterpreted. Texting shares many of the same dangers as e-mail and has added pressure for a faster response.

DIRECTIONS OF COMMUNICATION

Formal or informal communication may be downward, upward, lateral, or diagonal. **Downward communication** (manager to staff) is often directive. The staff is told what needs to be done or given information to facilitate the job to be done. **Upward communication** occurs from staff to management or from lower management to middle or upper management. Upward communication often involves reporting pertinent information to facilitate problem solving and decision making. **Lateral communication** occurs between individuals or departments at the same hierarchical level (e.g., nurse managers, department heads). **Diagonal communication** involves individuals or departments at different hierarchical levels (e.g., staff nurse to chief of the medical staff). Both lateral and diagonal communication involve information sharing, discussion, and negotiation.

An informal channel commonly seen in organizations is the grapevine (e.g., rumors and gossip). Grapevine communication is usually rapid, haphazard, and prone to distortion. It can also be useful. Sometimes the only way you learn about a pending change is through the grapevine. One problem with grapevine communication is that no one is accountable for any misinformation that is relayed. Keep in mind, too, that information gathered this way is a slightly altered version of the truth, changing as the message passes from person to person.

GENDER DIFFERENCES IN COMMUNICATION

Men and women communicate differently, according to linguist Deborah Tannen (2001). They have become socialized through communication patterns that reflect their societal roles. Men tend to talk

MediaLink · Men and Women in Conversation

BOX 9-1	Distortion in Written Communication

There is ample opportunity for distortion in the complicated process of sending, receiving, and responding to messages, as demonstrated by the following correspondence between a plumber and an official of the National Bureau of Standards (Donaldson & Scannell, 1979).

Bureau of Standards
Washington, D.C.
Gentlemen:
   I have been in the plumbing business for over 11 years and have found that hydrochloric acid works real fine for cleaning drains. Could you tell me if it's harmless?

> Sincerely,
> Tom Brown, Plumber

Mr. Tom Brown, Plumber
Yourtown, U.S.A.
Dear Mr. Brown:
   The efficacy of hydrochloric acid is indisputable, but the chlorine residue is incompatible with metallic permanence!

> Sincerely,
> Bureau of Standards

Bureau of Standards
Washington, D.C.
Gentlemen:
   I have your letter of last week and am mightily glad you agree with me on the use of hydrochloric acid.

> Sincerely,
> Tom Brown, Plumber

Mr. Tom Brown, Plumber
Yourtown, U.S.A.
Dear Mr. Brown:
   We wish to inform you we have your letter of last week and advise that we cannot assume responsibility for the production of toxic and noxious residues with hydrochloric acid and further suggest you use an alternate procedure.

> Sincerely,
> Bureau of Standards

Bureau of Standards
Washington, D.C.
Gentlemen:
   I have your most recent letter and am happy to find you still agree with me.

> Sincerely,
> Tom Brown, Plumber

Mr. Tom Brown, Plumber
Yourtown, U.S.A.
Dear Mr. Brown:
Don't use hydrochloric acid, it eats the hell out of pipes!

> Sincerely,
> Bureau of Standards

For communication among more than two people, the chance of distortion increases proportionally.

more, longer, and faster, whereas women are more descriptive, attentive, and perceptive. Women tend to use tag questions (e.g., "I can take off this weekend, can't I?") and tend to self-disclose more than men. Women tend to ask more questions and solicit more input than their male counterparts. Men tend to be more aggressive, express their opinion, and disagree more than women managers (Davidhizar & Cramer, 2000). In unpleasant situations, men talk more whereas women withdraw. Table 9-1 lists some of the differences in the ways that men and women communicate.

Using gender-neutral language in communication helps bridge the gap between men's and women's ways of communicating. Men and women can improve their ability to communicate with each other by following the recommendations for gender-neutral communication found in Table 9-2.

GENERATIONAL AND CULTURAL DIFFERENCES IN COMMUNICATION

Generational differences, discussed in Chapter 1, affect communication styles, patterns, and expectations. Traditionals tend to be more formal, following the chain of command without question. Baby boomers question more. They enjoy the process of group problem solving and decision making. Independent generation X are just the opposite and want decisions made without unnecessary discussion. Collegial millenials (generation Y) expect immediate feedback to their messages. E-mail, text, or voice mail is the best way to connect with them (Sherman, 2006). Mutual respect and understanding of the unique differences between and among groups will help to minimize conflict and maximize satisfaction for both managers and staff (Kupperschmidt, 2006).

TABLE 9-1	Gender Differences in Communication	
MEN TEND TO		**WOMEN TEND TO**
Interrupt more frequently		Wait to be noticed
Talk more, longer, louder, and faster		Use qualifiers (prefacing and tagging)
Disagree more		Use questions in place of statements
Focus on the issue more than the person		Relate personal experiences
Boast about accomplishments		Promote consensus
Use banter to avoid a one-down position		Withdraw from conflict

From *Becoming Influential: A Guide for Nurses* (p. 52), by E. J. Sullivan, 2004, Upper Saddle River, NJ: Prentice Hall. Reprinted by permission.

Cultural attitudes, beliefs, and behaviors also affect communication. Such elements as body movement, gestures, tone, and spatial orientation are culturally defined. A great deal of misunderstanding results from people's lack of understanding of each other's cultural expectations. For example, people of Asian descent take great care in exchanges with superiors so that there is no conflict or "loss of face" for either person.

Understanding the cultural heritage of employees and learning to interpret cultural messages is essential to communicate effectively with staff from diverse backgrounds. Personal and professional cultural enrichment training is recommended. This includes reading the literature and history of the culture; participating in open, honest, respectful communication; and exploring the meaning of behavior. It is important to recognize, however, that subcultures exist within all cultures; therefore, what applies to one individual will not be true for everyone else in that culture.

DIFFERENCES IN ORGANIZATIONAL CULTURE

As discussed in Chapter 2, the customs, norms, and expectations within an organization are powerful forces that shape behavior. Focusing on relevant issues regarding the organizational culture can identify failures in communication. Poor communication is a frequent source of job dissatisfaction as well as a powerful determinant of an organization's effectiveness. Just as violation of other norms within the organization results in repercussions, so does violation of communication rules.

To discover what rules affect communication in your organization, ask yourself:

- Who has access to what information? Is information withheld? Is it shared widely?
- What modes of communication are used for which messages? Are they used appropriately?
- How clear are the messages? Or are they often distorted?

TABLE 9-2	Recommendations for Gender-Neutral Communication	
MEN MAY NEED TO		**WOMEN MAY NEED TO**
Listen to objections and suggestions		State your message clearly and concisely
Listen without feeling responsible		Solve problems without personalizing them
Suspend judgment until information is in		Say what you want without hinting
Explain your reasons		Eliminate unsure words ("sort of") and nonwords ("truly")
Not yell		Not cry

From *Becoming Influential: A Guide for Nurses* (p. 52), by E. J. Sullivan, 2004, Upper Saddle River, NJ: Prentice Hall. Reprinted by permission.

- Does everyone receive the same information?
- Do you receive too much information? Not enough?
- How effective is the message?

The Role of Communication in Leadership

Although communication is inherent in the manager's role, the manager's ability to communicate often determines his or her success as a leader. Leaders who engage in frank, open, two-way communication and whose nonverbal communication reinforces the verbal communication are seen as informative. Communication is enhanced when the manager listens carefully and is sensitive to others. The major underlying factor, however, is an ongoing relationship between the manager and employees.

Successful leaders are able to persuade others and enlist their support. The most effective means of persuasion is the leader's personal characteristics. Competence, emotional control, assertiveness, consideration, and respect promote trustworthiness and credibility. A participative leader is seen as a careful listener who is open, frank, trustworthy, and informative.

Communicating with Different Populations

SUBORDINATES

Depending on the organization's policies, the nurse manager's responsibilities may include selecting, interviewing, evaluating, counseling, and disciplining employees; handling their complaints; and settling conflicts. The principles of effective communication are especially pertinent in these activities because good communication is the adhesive that builds and maintains an effective work group.

Giving direction is not, in itself, communication. If the manager receives an appropriate response from the subordinate, however, communication has occurred. To give directions and achieve the desired results, develop a message strategy. The techniques that follow can help improve effective responses from others.

- **Know the context of the instruction.** Be certain you know exactly what you want done, by whom, within what time frame, and what steps should be followed to do it. Be clear in your own mind what information a person needs to carry out your instruction, what the outcome will be if the instruction is carried out, and how that outcome can or will be evaluated. When you have thought through these questions, you are ready to give the proper instruction.
- **Get positive attention.** Avoid factors that interfere with effective listening. Informing the person that the instructions will be given is one simple way to try to get positive attention. Highlighting the background, giving a justification, or indicating the importance of the instructions also may be appropriate.
- **Give clear, concise instructions.** Use an inoffensive and nondefensive style and tone of voice. Be precise, and give all the information receivers need to carry out your expectations. Follow a step-by-step procedure if several actions are needed.
- **Verify through feedback.** Make sure the receiver has understood your specific request for action. Ask for a repeat of the instructions.
- **Provide follow-up communication.** Understanding does not guarantee performance. Follow up to discover if your instruction is clear and if the person has any questions.

The nurse manager is responsible both for the quality of the work life of individual employees and for the quality of patient care in the entire unit. To carry out this job, acknowledge the needs of individual employees, especially if the needs of one conflict with needs of the unit, speak directly with those involved, and state clearly and accurately the rationale for the decisions made.

SUPERIORS

The manager's interaction with higher administration is comparable to the interaction between the manager and a subordinate, except that the manager is now the subordinate. Higher administration is responsible for the consequences of decisions made for a larger area, such as all of nursing service or the entire organization. The principles used in communicating with subordinates are equally appropriate. Managers should be organized and prepared to state their needs clearly, explain the rationale for requests, suggest benefits for the larger organization, and use appropriate channels. Listen objectively to your supervisor's response and be willing to consider reasons for possible conflict with needs of other areas.

Working effectively with a supervisor is important because this person directly influences personal success in a career and within the organization. Managing a supervisor, or managing upward, is a crucial skill for nurses. To manage upward, remember that the relationship requires participation from both parties. Managing upward is successful when power and influence move in both directions. Rules for managing your supervisor are found in Box 9-2.

One aspect of managing upward is to understand the supervisor's position from her or his frame of reference. This will make it easier to propose solutions and ideas that the supervisor will accept. Understand that a supervisor is a person with even more responsibility and pressure. Learn about the supervisor from a personal perspective: What pressures, both personal and professional, does the supervisor face? How does the supervisor respond to stress? What previous experiences are liable to affect today's issues? This assessment will allow you to identify ways to help your supervisor with his or her job and for your supervisor to help you with yours.

Influencing Your Supervisor

Nurses need to approach their supervisor to exert their influence on a variety of issues and problems. Support for the purchase of capital equipment, for changes in staffing, or for a new policy or procedure all require communicating with your supervisor. Your rationale, choice of form or format, and possible objections all are important factors to consider as you prepare to make such a request. Timing is critical; choose an opportunity when the supervisor has time and appears receptive. Also, consider the impact of your ideas on other events occurring at that time.

Should ideas be presented in spoken or written form? Usually some combination is used. Even if you have a brief meeting about a relatively small request, it is a good idea to follow up with an e-mail, detailing your ideas and the plans to which you both agreed. Sometimes the procedure works in reverse. If you provide the supervisor a written proposal prior to a meeting, both

of you will be familiar with the idea at the start. In the latter case, careful preparation of the written material is essential.

What can be done if, in spite of careful preparation, your supervisor says no? First, make sure you have understood the objections and associated feelings. **Negative inquiry** (e.g., "I don't understand") is a helpful technique to use. Do not interrupt or become defensive or distraught; remain diplomatic. **Fogging**, agreeing with part of what was said, or **negative assertion**, accepting some blame, are two additional techniques that you can use.

The next step is confrontation. Keep your voice low and measured; use "I" language; and avoid absolutes, why questions, put-downs, inflammatory statements, and threatening gestures. Finally, if you feel you have lost and compromise is unlikely, table the issue by saying, "Could we continue discussing this at another time?" Then, think through your supervisor's reasoning and evaluate it.

Afterward ask yourself: "What new information did I get from the supervisor?" "What are ways I can renegotiate?" "What do I need to know or do to overcome objections?" Once you can answer these questions, approach your supervisor again with the new information. This behavior shows that the proposal is a high priority, and the new information may cause him or her to reevaluate.

Managers often succeed in influencing superiors through persistence and repetition, especially if supporting data and documentation are supplied. If the issue is important enough, you may want to take it to a higher authority. If so, tell your supervisor you would like an administrator at a higher level to hear the proposal. Keep an open mind, listen, and try to meet objections with suggestions of how to solve problems. Be prepared to compromise, which is better than no movement at all, or to be turned down.

BOX 9-2   Rules for Managing Your Supervisor

- Give immediate positive feedback for good things that the supervisor does; positive feedback is a welcome change.
- Never let your supervisor be surprised; keep her or him informed.
- Always tell the truth.
- Find ways to compensate for weaknesses of your supervisor. Fill in weak areas tactfully. Volunteer to do something the supervisor dislikes doing.

- Be your own publicist. Don't brag, but keep your supervisor informed of what you achieve.
- Keep aware of your supervisor's achievements and acknowledge them.
- If your supervisor asks you to do something, do it well and ahead of the deadline if possible. If appropriate, add some of your own suggestions.
- Establish a positive relationship with the supervisor's assistant.

Taking a Problem to Your Supervisor

No one wants to hear about a problem, and your boss is no different. Nonetheless, work involves problems, and the manager's job is to solve them. Go to your supervisor with a goal to problem solve together. Have some ideas about solving the problem in hand if you can but do not be so wedded to them that you are unable to listen to your supervisor's ideas. Keep an open mind. Use the following steps to take a problem to your supervisor:

- Find an appropriate time to discuss a problem, scheduling an appointment if necessary.
- State the problem succinctly and explain why it is interfering with work.
- Listen to your supervisor's response and provide more information if needed.
- If you agree on a solution, offer to do your part to solve it. If you cannot discover an agreeable solution, schedule a follow-up meeting or decide to gather more information.
- Schedule a follow-up appointment.

By solving the problem together and, if necessary, by taking active steps together, you and your supervisor are more likely to accept the decision and be committed to it. Setting a specific follow-up date can prevent a solution from being delayed or forgotten.

If All Else Fails . . .

Sometimes no matter what you do, working with your supervisor seems nearly impossible. Kimura (2003) calls such supervisors "toxic." Toxic managers foster a negative work environment, and employees become dissatisfied, angry, and depressed. High absenteeism and turnover result. As a manager you are charged with supporting your superior. If working with that superior is too difficult for you to manage your work satisfactorily, you may have to transfer elsewhere or leave.

PEERS

Interactions with peers are inevitable. Relationships can vary from comfortable and easy to challenging and complex. Peers often share similar concerns. Camaraderie may be present; peers can exchange ideas and address problems creatively. Peers can provide support, and the strengths of one can be developed in the other.

Conversely, there may also be competition or conflicts (e.g., battles over territory, personality clashes, differences of opinion) and affected by history, the organization's mores, or generational or cultural differences. Even when there are conflicts, peers should interact on a professional level; tactics for communicating with difficult people and negotiating may be helpful. Both topics are discussed later in the chapter.

MEDICAL STAFF

Communication with the medical staff may be difficult for the nurse manager because the relationship of physicians and nurses has been that of superior and subordinate. Gender-based differences in nursing (although less so in medicine today) may add to the difficulty. Furthermore, physician training in communication skills has largely been absent (Cegala & Lenzmeier-Broz, 2002).

Complicating physician–nurse relationships is the employee status of the medical staff. They may not be employees of the organization but still have considerable power because of their ability to attract patients to the organization, and, finally, the medical staff is in itself diverse, consisting of physicians who are organizational employees, residents, physicians in private practice, and consulting physicians.

Nurse managers are role models and leaders for establishing nurse–physician relationships on their units. Nurse–physician communication has been shown to affect patient outcomes in two landmark studies. Lower-than-expected death rates in intensive care units were related to excellent coordination and communication among the nurse–physician staff in one study (Knaus, Draper, Wagner, & Zimmerman, 1986), and lack of communication and coordination among health care providers was related to unnecessarily high-cost stays for patients in another (Gavett, Drucker, McCrum, & Dickenson, 1985). Nurse managers have important reasons, then, for setting a positive tone that fosters mutual respect among nurses and physicians on their units.

In today's competitive health care marketplace, it also is necessary to view the physician as a nursing service customer. Organizations are competing for patients, and physicians (as well as insurers) are sources of patients. The product of nursing service is patient care; physicians help provide the patients.

What do physicians want? Physicians first want quality staff—nurses, health care workers, and other physicians. They want up-to-date facilities and equipment, quality care, and adequately trained nursing personnel. Physicians also want respect (as do nurses and others who work in health care) and regard patient care as their primary concern. These are many of the same goals that nurses have.

To support greater collaboration between nurses and physicians and to improve the product of nursing service—patient care—keep these principles in mind:

- Respect physicians as persons, and expect them to respect you.
- Consider yourself and your staff equal partners with physicians in health care.
- Build your staff's clinical competence and credibility. Ensure that your staff has the clinical preparation necessary to meet required standards of care.
- Actively listen and respond to physician complaints as customer complaints. Create a problem-solving structure. Stop blaming physicians exclusively for communication problems.
- Use every opportunity to increase your staff's contact with physicians and to include your staff in meetings that include physicians. Remember that limited interactions contribute to poor communication.
- Establish a collaborative practice committee on your unit whose membership is composed equally of nurses and physicians. Identify problems, develop mutually satisfactory solutions, and learn more about each other. Emphasize similarities and the need for quality care. Begin with those physicians who have a positive attitude toward collaboration.
- Serve as a role model to your staff in nurse–physician communication.
- Support your staff in participating in collaborative efforts by words and by your actions.

But if you are confronted with power plays or intimidation, what is the best way to respond? Intimidation results from vulnerability and a threat to self-worth (Lindeke & Sieckert, 2005). Intimidation can be counteracted by increasing self-confidence and personal feelings of power. Four ways that generate power are:

1. With words:
   - Use the other person's name frequently.
   - Use strong statements.
   - Avoid discounters, such as "I'm sorry, but . . . ?"
   - Avoid clichés, such as "hit the nail on the head," "goes without saying," "easier said than done."
   - Avoid fillers (such as "ah," "uh," and "um").
2. Through delivery:
   - Be enthusiastic.
   - Speak clearly and forcefully.
   - Make one point at a time.
   - Do not tolerate interruptions.
3. By listening:
   - For facts.
   - For emotions.
   - For what is not being said (e.g., body language, mixed messages, hidden messages).
4. Through body posture and body language:
   - Sit next to your antagonist; turn 30 degrees toward the person when you address that person.
   - Lean forward.
   - Expand your personal space.
   - Use gestures.
   - Stand when you talk.
   - Smile when you are pleased, not in order to please.
   - Maintain eye contact, but do not stare.

One nurse manager handled a problem with a physician as shown in Case Study 9-1. Additional techniques to counteract intimidation and threat are included in Chapter 12.

OTHER HEALTH CARE PERSONNEL

The nurse manager has the overwhelming task of coordinating the activities of a number of personnel with varied levels and types of preparation and different kinds of tasks. The patient may receive regular care from a registered nurse, unlicensed assistive personnel, a respiratory therapist, a physical therapist, and a dietitian, among others. The nurse manager may supervise all of them. Regardless, the manager needs considerable skill to communicate effectively with diverse personnel, recognize their commonalities, and deal with their differences.

PATIENTS AND FAMILIES

Nurse managers deal with many difficult issues. Patient or family complaints about the delivery of care (e.g., complaints about a staff member, violations of policy) are one example. When dealing with patient or family complaints, keep the following principles in mind:

- **The patient (and family) are the principal customers of the organization.** Treat patients and families with respect; keep communication open and honest. Dissatisfied customers fail to continue to use a service and also inform their friends and families about their negative experiences. Handle complaints or concerns tactfully and expeditiously. Many times lawsuits can be avoided if the patient or family feels that someone has taken the time to listen to their complaints. (See the section on risk management in Chapter 6.)

CASE STUDY 9-1   Communication

Josie Randolph is nurse manager of a perioperative unit, including responsibility for the preoperative testing unit, 18 OR suites, preop holding, and sterile processing. The OR department supports the hospital's Level I trauma service as well as all other surgical services.

Dr. Jonas Welborne is a plastic surgeon with a history of aggressive behavior. He has several cases on today's OR schedule. While he is in his first surgery, a trauma case is brought to the OR. Susan Richardson, the OR charge nurse, decides to bump Dr. Welborne's second case out of OR #3 to make room for the trauma case. When Dr. Welborne has finished his first case, he is informed of the delay in his second case. Dr. Welborne storms into the OR scheduling office and begins yelling at Susan. The situation quickly escalates to the point where Dr. Welborne uses obscenities and throws several charts on the floor. Loretta Donnelly, an OR tech, runs to Josie's office and asks her to come immediately to the OR scheduling office.

Susan and Dr. Welborne continue to yell at one another, in full view of patients in the preop area. Josie immediately steps between Dr. Welborne and Susan and firmly asks both of them to lower their voices. She instructs Susan to wait in the staff lounge while she speaks with Dr. Welborne. Josie asks Dr. Welborne to step into her office so they can calmly discuss the situation. Dr. Welborne is still visibly agitated but agrees to discuss the problem. After hearing his side of the story, Josie apologizes for the inconvenience, but reminds him of the OR policies. Emergent cases take precedence over elective cases, and no other elective cases were on the schedule at that time. She asks Dr. Welborne if there are alternatives to scheduling his cases that would minimize delays or bumps. As they talk, Dr. Welborne becomes calmer. Josie informs Dr. Welborne that his earlier behavior is unacceptable. Within a few minutes, he apologizes to Josie and asks to speak with Susan. He also apologizes to Susan. Josie and Susan discuss the incident and ways Susan can help diffuse similar situations in the future. As with Dr. Welborne, Josie indicates that Susan's behavior was unprofessional.

Manager's Checklist

The nurse manager is responsible to:

- Mediate conflict in a timely manner
- Know organizational policies and procedures that support staff decisions
- Allow open and complete discussion of the problem
- Actively listen to both participants
- Use assertive communication to facilitate problem solving

- **Most individuals are unfamiliar with medical jargon.** Use words that are appropriate to the recipient's level of understanding. However, take care not to be condescending or intimidating. It is just as important to assess the person's knowledge base and level of understanding as it is to know his or her vital signs or liver status.
- **Maintain privacy and identify a neutral location for dealing with difficult interactions.**
- **Make special efforts to find interpreters if a patient or family does not speak English.** Have readily available a list of individuals who are able to communicate in a variety of languages. The list also should include individuals experienced in sign language and Braille. Another resource is AT&T's language line service (1-800-752-6096), which provides interpreters for over 140 languages 24 hours a day.
- **Recognize cultural differences in communicating with patients and their families.** People in some

cultures do not ask questions for fear of imposing on others. Some cultures prefer interpreters from their own culture; others do not. Cultural education for the staff can help identify some of these differences and teach them appropriate, culturally sensitive responses.

Communicating with Difficult People

Difficult personalities exist in all groups of people—subordinates, superiors, physicians, other health care team members, patients, and family members alike. Strategies for coping with difficult people follow (Nations, 1990a, 1990b, 1990c).

1. **Put physical distance between you and the difficult person.** A common method to achieve physical

distance is to limit the time you spend with the individual. Match the person's energy level in speed, pitch, and volume; this conveys awareness and empathy. This technique is particularly effective with hostile, aggressive individuals. However, negative behavior, such as yelling and tantrums, should not be mirrored; instead, remain calm but assertive.

2. **Psychologically distance yourself from the individual.** View the person from a different perspective; try "putting on his shoes." Also "lose the shoulds" (for example, "Who does he think he is? He shouldn't be allowed to talk to us like that.") Ask: What does this person's behavior accomplish? What type of personality trait is being exhibited?

3. **Identify the individual's feelings and information level.** Then validate those feelings and information as well as your relationship, but don't patronize. This technique is particularly successful with a "know-it-all" who may be under the illusion that only he or she is right.

4. **Ask extensional questions.** Questions that begin with "how" or "what" often help the person to focus on his or her concerns and rethink what has just been said. Focusing on holes in the individual's argument provides an opportunity for a graceful retreat.

5. **Use physical movement.** Lead an upset individual to your office or another neutral location, or suggest that the two of you go for a cup of coffee. Physical activity often diminishes stress and hostility.

6. **Try humor.** If the situation is not too serious, humor is an excellent method to defuse anger and frustration; however, be careful to avoid sarcasm or putdowns.

(Difficult people include those who bully. How to deal with bullies is included in Chapter 12, "Handling Conflict.")

Enhancing Your Communication Skills

Communication skills can be learned. At one program offered at Memorial Sloan Kettering Hospital, oncology nurses improved their abilities to communicate in an assertive manner, manage conflict, motivate others, and delegate appropriately after training (Walczak &

TABLE 9-3	Improving Communication

1. Consider your relationship to the receiver.
2. Craft your message, including your goal and how to answer responses.
3. Decide on the medium based on your relationship, the content, and the setting.
4. Check your timing.
5. Deliver your message.
6. Attend to verbal or written responses.
7. Reply appropriately.
8. Conclude when both parties' messages have been understood.
9. Evaluate communication process.

Absolon, 2001.) Suggestions to improve your communication skills are shown in Table 9-3.

To communicate effectively, first consider your relationship to the receiver (e.g., boss or patient). Then craft your message. Be clear about your goal in your mind so that you can communicate it appropriately. Then think about what the other person is liable to say and consider how you might respond.

Next decide on the medium. Is this message best conveyed in person, by phone, or e-mail? Should you leave a message if the person isn't available? Note the personal intimacy content earlier in the chapter for guidance.

Timing plays a critical role in successful communication. Catch your boss in the midst of planning for a budget shortfall and you are less apt to get a receptive hearing.

Be prepared when you deliver your message. The best-crafted message, delivered by the appropriate medium can misfire by a sender who fails to listen carefully, avoids responding out of fear of consequences, or undermines the message with qualifiers, such as "I don't know if you're interested."

The effort to develop excellent communication skills is well worth the effort. As Porter-O'Grady (2003) reminded us, today's relationship-oriented environments require superb interpersonal skills. A facilitative leadership style encourages others, empowers them to do their best work, and supports them when problems and conflict inevitably emerge.

(For more information on communicating effectively, see *Becoming Influential: A Guide for Nurses*, by Eleanor Sullivan.)

MEDIALINK Developing Assertiveness

What You Know Now

- Communication is a complex, ongoing, dynamic process.
- How to deliver a message depends on the purpose, the content, and the relationship.
- Messages can be distorted or misconstrued.
- Gender, cultural background, and the organizational culture influence communication and its outcome.
- Expert communication skills are essential for a leader to be successful.
- Communication strategies vary according to the situation and the roles of people involved.
- Communicating with difficult people is challenging, and specific skills can help.
- Nurses can enhance their communication skills with effort and practice.

Tools for Communicating Effectively

1. Identify and use the appropriate method (in person, phone, voice mail, e-mail, letter) for your communications.
2. Evaluate your communication skills in various situations. Think of ways to improve.
3. Practice using the skills described in specific situations, such as with your supervisor, with the medical staff, or with difficult people.
4. Become sensitive to others' responses, both verbal and nonverbal, and craft your messages appropriately.
5. Gather feedback and continue to assess the effectiveness of your communications.
6. Strive to improve your communication skills.

Questions to Challenge You

1. Consider a recent interaction you witnessed.
   - Did the sender express the message clearly?
   - Use the appropriate medium?
   - Listen and respond to questions and comments?
   - What was the outcome?
2. Now think about a recent interaction where you were the sender using the above criteria. If you could replay the interaction, what would you do differently?
3. How well does communication function in your workplace, school, or clinical site?
4. To improve your communication, practice the skills described in the chapter by role playing or recording yourself (Sullivan, 2004).

Explore MediaLink

Additional interactive resources for this chapter can be found on the Website at http://www.prenhall.com/sullivan. Click on Chapter 9 to select activities for this chapter.

- Video Overview
- NCLEX® Review Questions
- Critical Thinking Activities
- Current Events
- Nursing Leadership and Management in Action
- MediaLinks

References

Cegala, D. J., & Lenzmeier-Broz, S. (2002). Physician communication skills training: A review of theoretical backgrounds, objectives and skills. *Medical Education, 36*(1), 1004–1017.

Davidhizar, R., & Cramer, C. (2000). Gender differences in leadership in the health professions. *Health Care Manager, 18*(3), 18–24.

Donaldson, L. & Scannell, E. (1979). Human response development: The new trainer's guide. Reading, MA: Addison-Wesley.

Gavett, J. W., Drucker, W. R., McCrum, M. S., & Dickenson, J. C. (1985). *A study of high cost inpatients in Strong Memorial Hospital.* Rochester, NY: Rochester Area Hospital Corporation and University of Rochester.

Kimura, H. (2003). Overcome toxic management. *Nursing Management, 34*(1), 26–29.

Knaus, W. A., Draper, E. A., Wagner, D. P., & Zimmerman, J. E. (1986). An evaluation of outcome from intensive care in major medical centers. *Annals of Internal Medicine, 104,* 410–418.

Kupperschmidt, B. R. (2006). Addressing multigenerational conflict: Mutual respect and carefronting as strategy. *Online Journal of Issues in Nursing, 11*(2), posted 06/27/2006.

Lindeke, L. L., & Sieckert, A. M. (2005). Nurse-physician workplace collaboration. *Online Journal of Issues in Nursing, 10*(1). Accessed on 09/20/2007 from: http://nursingworld.org/ MainMenuCategories/ANAMarketplace/ANAPeriodicals/ OJIN/TableofContents/Volume102005/No1January31/ tpc26_416011.aspx

Nations, K. H. (1990a). Coping with difficult people. Part 1. *Medical Laboratory Observer, 22*(9), 22–25.

Nations, K. H. (1990b). Coping with difficult people. Part 2: Dealing with know-it-alls even if you are one yourself. *Medical Laboratory Observer, 22*(10) 29–30, 32.

Nations, K. H. (1990c). Coping with difficult people. Part 3: Effective ways to deflect hostility. *Medical Laboratory Observer, 22*(11), 40–42.

Porter-O'Grady, T. (2003). A different age for leadership, Part 1: New context, new content. *Journal of Nursing Administration, 32*(2), 105–110.

Sherman, R. O. (2006). Leading a multigenerational nursing workforce: Issues, challenges, and strategies. *Online Journal of Issues in Nursing, 11*(2), posted 06/29/2006.

Sullivan, E. J. (2004). *Becoming influential: A guide for nurses.* Upper Saddle River, NJ: Prentice Hall.

Tannen, D. (2001). *Talking from 9 to 5: Women and men at work.* New York: Harper.

Walczak, M. B., & Absolon, P. L. (2001). Essentials for effective communication in oncology nursing: Assertiveness, conflict management, delegation, and motivation. *Journal for Nurses in Staff Development, 17*(3), 159–162.

CHAPTER 10

Delegating Successfully

MediaLink

www.prenhall.com/sullivan
See the Companion Website for chapter-specific resources at
www.prenhall.com/sullivan.

Learning Outcomes

After completing this chapter, you will be able to:

1. Describe how delegation involves responsibility, accountability, and authority.
2. Describe how effective delegation benefits the delegator, the delegate, and the organization.
3. Discuss how to be an effective delegator.
4. Identify obstacles that can impede effective delegation.
5. Explain how liability affects delegation.

Key Terms

Accountability *p135*
Assignment *p136*
Authority *p136*

Delegation *p135*
Overdelegation *p142*
Responsibility *p135*

Reverse delegation *p142*
Underdelegation *p142*

R eport is over. Where do you begin? Assessments. Patients to prepare for surgery. Medicines to give. Breakfast trays to deliver and set up. Baths to give. Treatments to do. An admission coming. Charting. Too much to do and so little time. Have you ever felt this way? How can you get it all done, be efficient, provide quality care, and survive the day? Delegate!

It is easy to say delegate, but delegation is a difficult leadership skill for nurses to learn and one that may not be taught in undergraduate education. Given the confusion over what tasks unlicensed assistive personnel (UAP) can perform and what are those that are the unique purview of registered nurses (Kleinman & Saccomano, 2006), nurses and nurse managers may be reluctant to delegate. Never before, however, has delegation been as critical a skill for nurses and nurse managers to perfect as it is today, with the emphasis on doing more with less.

Defining Delegation

Delegation is the process by which responsibility and authority for performing a task (function, activity, or decision) is transferred to another individual who accepts that authority and responsibility. Although the delegator remains accountable for the task, the delegate is also accountable to the delegator for the responsibilities assumed. Delegation can help others to develop or enhance their skills, promotes teamwork, and improves productivity. Delegation skills can be learned.

RESPONSIBILITY AND ACCOUNTABILITY

Although *responsibility* and *accountability* are often used synonymously, the two words represent different concepts that go hand in hand. **Responsibility** denotes an obligation to accomplish a task, whereas **accountability** is accepting ownership for the results or lack thereof. Responsibility can be transferred, but accountability is shared.

You can delegate only those tasks for which you are responsible. If you have no direct responsibility for the task, then you can't delegate that task. For instance, if a manager is responsible for filling holes in the staffing schedule, the manager can delegate this responsibility to another individual. However, if staffing is the responsibility of a central coordinator, the manager can make suggestions or otherwise assist the staffing coordinator, but cannot delegate the task.

Likewise, if an orderly who is responsible for setting up traction is detained and a nurse asks a physical therapist on the unit to assist with traction, this is not delegation, because setting up traction is not the responsibility of the nurse. However, if the orderly (the person responsible for the task) had asked the physical therapist to help, this could be an act of delegation if the other principles of delegation are met.

MEDIALINK Differentiating Responsibility, Accountability, and Authority

AUTHORITY

Along with responsibility, you must transfer authority. **Authority** is the right to act. Therefore, by transferring authority, the delegator is empowering the delegate to accomplish the task. Too often this principle of delegation is neglected. Nurses retain authority, crippling the delegate's abilities to accomplish the task, setting the individual up for failure, and minimizing efficiency and productivity. This pitfall is discussed later in the chapter.

DIFFERENTIATING DELEGATION FROM ASSIGNMENT

Delegation is often confused with work allocation. Delegation involves transfer of responsibility and authority. In **assignment** no transfer of authority occurs. Instead, assignments are a bureaucratic function that reflect job descriptions and patient or organizational needs. Effective delegation benefits the delegator, the delegate, and the organization.

DELEGATION VERSUS DUMPING

You should delegate because it is the best use of time, both yours and the delegates, not to dump an undesirable task or to reward a productive employee with even more work. Managers can role model this behavior, and they can teach their staff to do likewise. One way is to have RNs and UAPs exchange part of a shift with each other (Cohen, 2004). Of course UAPs cannot do RNs' work, but they can learn what all is involved when nurses give medications, for example. Similarly, RNs can learn how UAPs handle delegation from several nurses, possibly simultaneously. Trying to accomplish those tasks could bring a new-found appreciation for the work of UAPs. Role modeling delegation and giving staff opportunities to experience delegation from another's point of view can improve the work of the team.

Benefits of Delegation

BENEFITS TO THE NURSE

Nurses also benefit from delegation. If the nurse is able to delegate some tasks to UAPs, more time can be devoted to those tasks that cannot be delegated, especially complex patient care. Thus, patient care is enhanced, the nurse's job satisfaction increases, and retention is improved.

Nancy, RN, has three central line dressing changes to complete as well as transfer two patients to another unit before the end of shift in 1 hour. Nancy delegates the transfer duties to Shelley, LPN, and completes the central line dressing changes.

BENEFITS TO THE DELEGATE

The delegate also benefits from delegation. The delegate gains new skills and abilities that can facilitate upward mobility. In addition, delegation can bring trust and support, and thereby build self-esteem and confidence. Subsequently, job satisfaction and motivation are enhanced as individuals feel stimulated by new challenges. Morale improves; a sense of pride and belonging develops as well as greater awareness of responsibility. Individuals feel more appreciated and learn to appreciate the roles and responsibilities of others, increasing cooperation and enhancing teamwork.

BENEFITS TO THE MANAGER

Delegation also yields benefits for the manager. First, if staff are using UAPs appropriately, the manager will have a better functioning unit. Also the manager may be able to delegate some tasks to staff members and devote more time to management tasks that cannot be delegated. With more time available, the manager can develop new skills and abilities, facilitating the opportunity for career advancement.

BENEFITS TO THE ORGANIZATION

As teamwork improves, the organization benefits by achieving its goals more efficiently. Overtime and absences decrease. Subsequently, productivity increases, and the organization's financial position may improve. As delegation increases efficiency, the quality of care improves. As quality improves, patient satisfaction increases.

The Delegation Process

The delegation process has five steps:

1. **Define the task.** Delegate only an aspect of your own work for which you have responsibility and authority. These include:
   - Routine tasks
   - Tasks for which you do not have time
   - Tasks that have moved down in priority

Define the aspects of the task. Ask yourself:
- Does the task involve technical skills or cognitive abilities?
- Are specific qualifications necessary?
- Is performance restricted by practice acts, standards, or job descriptions?
- How complex is the task?
- Is training or education required?
- Are the steps well defined, or are creativity and problem solving required?
- Would a change in circumstances affect who could perform the task?

While you are trying to define the complexity of the task and its components, it is important not to fall into the trap of thinking no one else is capable of performing this task. Often others can be prepared to perform a task through education and training. The time taken to prepare others can be recouped many times over. Also know well the task to be delegated.

An alternative would be to subdivide the task into component parts and delegate the components congruent with the available delegate's capabilities. For example, developing a budget is a managerial responsibility that cannot be delegated, but someone else could explore the types of tympanic thermometers on the market, their costs, advantages, and so on. A committee of staff nurses could evaluate the options and make a recommendation that you could include in the budget justification.

But how do you know what should not be delegated?

Before a task is delegated, determine what areas of authority and what resources you control to achieve the expected results. A unit manager who is responsible for maintaining adequate supplies needs budget authority. The authority to spend money on supplies, however, may be limited to a specific amount for specific supplies or may be allocated to supplies in general.

Certain tasks should never be delegated. Discipline should not be delegated nor should a highly technical task. Also any situation that involves confidentiality or controversy should not be delegated to others.

2. **Decide on delegate.** Match the task to the individual. Analyze individuals' skill levels and abilities to evaluate their capability to perform the various tasks; also determine characteristics that might prevent them from accepting responsibility for the task. Conversely experience and individual characteristics, such as initiative, intelligence, and enthusiasm, can expand the individual's capabilities.

A rule of thumb is to delegate to the lowest person in the hierarchy who has the requisite capabilities and who is allowed to do the task legally and by organizational policy.

Next determine availability. For example, Su Ling might be the best candidate, but she leaves for vacation tomorrow and won't be back before the project is due. Then ask who would be willing to assume responsibility. Delegation is an agreement that is entered into voluntarily.

3. **Determine the task.** The next step in delegation is to clearly define your expectations for the delegate. Also plan when to meet. Attempting to delegate in the middle of a crisis is not delegation; that is directing. Provide for enough time to describe the task and your expectations and to entertain questions. Also, meet in an environment as devoid of distractions as possible.

Key behaviors in delegating tasks are:

a. Describe the task using "I" statements, such as "I would like . . ." and appropriate nonverbal behaviors—open body language, face-to-face positioning, and eye contact. The delegate needs to know what is expected, when the task should be completed, and where and how, if that is appropriate. The more experienced delegates may be able to define for themselves the where and how. Decide whether written reports are necessary or if brief oral reports are sufficient. If written reports are required, indicate whether tables, charts, or other graphics are necessary. Be specific about reporting times. Identify critical events or milestones that might be reached and brought to your attention. In patient care tasks, it also important to determine who has responsibility and authority to chart certain tasks; UAPs can enter vital signs, but if they observe changes in patient status, the RN must investigate and chart her assessment.

b. Describe the importance to the organization, you, the patient, and the delegate. Provide the delegate with an incentive for accepting both the responsibility and the authority to do the task.

c. Clearly describe the expected outcome and the timeline for completion. Establish how closely the assignment will be supervised. Monitoring is important because you remain accountable for the task, but controls should never limit an individual's opportunity to grow.

d. Identify any constraints for completing the task or any conditions that could change. For example, you may ask an assistant to feed a

CASE STUDY 10-1   Delegation

Lisa Ford is a school nurse for a suburban school district. She has responsibility for three school buildings, including a middle school, a high school, and a vocational rehabilitation workshop for mentally and physically handicapped secondary students. Her management responsibilities include providing health services for 1,000 students, 60 faculty members, and 25 staff members, and supervising 2 unlicensed school health aides and 3 special education health aides. The logistics of managing multiple school sites results in the delegation of many daily health room tasks, including medication administration, to the school-based health aides.

Nancy Andrews is an unlicensed health aide at the middle school. This is her first year as a health aide and she has a limited background in health care. The nurse practice act in the state allows for the delegation of medication administration in the school setting. Lisa is responsible for training Nancy to safely administer medication to students, documenting the training, evaluating Nancy's performance, and providing ongoing supervision. Part of Nancy's training will also include a discussion of those medication-related decisions that must be made by a registered nurse.

Manager's Checklist

The nurse manger is responsible to:

- Understand the state nurse practice act and its applicability to the school setting
- Implement school district policies related to health services and medication administration
- Develop and implement an appropriate training program
- Limit opportunities for error and decreasing liability by ensuring that unlicensed health aides are appropriately trained to handle delegated tasks
- Maintain documentation related to training and observation of medication administration by unlicensed staff
- Audit medication administration records to ensure accuracy and completeness
- Conduct several "drop in" visits during the school year to track competency of health aides
- If necessary, report any medication errors to administration and follow up with focused training and closer supervision

patient for you as long as the patient is coherent and awake, but you would feed the patient if he were confused.

e. Validate understanding of the task and your expectations by eliciting questions and providing feedback.

4. **Reach agreement.** Once you have outlined your expectations, you must be sure that the delegate agrees to accept responsibility and authority for the task. You need to be prepared to equip the delegate to complete the task successfully. This might mean providing additional information or resources or informing others about the arrangement as needed to empower the delegate. Before meeting with the individual, anticipate areas of negotiation, and identify what you are prepared and able to provide.

5. **Monitor performance and provide feedback.** Monitoring performance provides a mechanism for feedback and control that ensures that the delegated tasks are carried out as agreed. Give careful thought to monitoring efforts when objectives are established. When defining the task and

expectations, clearly establish the where, when, and how. Remain accessible. Support builds confidence and reassures the delegate of your interest in the delegate and negates any concerns about dumping undesirable tasks.

Monitoring the delegate too closely, however, conveys distrust. Analyze performance with respect to the established goal. If problem areas are identified, privately investigate and explain the problem, provide an opportunity for feedback, and inform the individual how to correct the mistake in the future. Provide additional support as needed. Also, be sure to give the praise and recognition due, and don't be afraid to do so publicly.

See how a school nurse handled delegation in Case Study 10-1.

Accepting Delegation

When you accept delegation, it is important to understand what is being asked of you. First, acknowledge the delegator's confidence in you, but realistically examine whether you have the skills and abilities for the task and the time to do it. If you do not have the skills, you must inform the delegator. However, it does not mean you cannot accept the responsibility. See whether the person is willing to train or otherwise equip you to accomplish the task. If not, then you need to refuse the offer.

Accepting delegation means that you accept full responsibility for the outcome and its benefits or liabilities. Just as the delegator has the option to delegate parts of a task, you also have the option to negotiate for those aspects of a task you feel you can accomplish. Recognize, however, that this may be an opportunity for growth. You may decide to capitalize on it, obtaining new skills or resources in the process.

Once you agree on the role and responsibilities you are to assume, make sure you are clear on the time frame, feedback mechanisms, and other expectations. Don't assume anything. As a minimum, repeat to the delegator what you heard said; better yet, outline the task in writing.

Throughout the project, keep the delegator informed. Report any concerns you have as they come up. Foremost, complete the task as agreed. Successful completion can open more doors in the future.

If you are not qualified or do not have the time, do not be afraid to say no. Thank the delegator for the offer and clearly explain why you must decline at this time. Express your interest in working together in the future.

Obstacles to Delegation

Although delegation can yield many benefits, there are potential barriers. Some barriers are environmental; others are the result of the delegator's or delegate's beliefs or inexperience (Table 10-1).

A NONSUPPORTIVE ENVIRONMENT

Organizational Culture

The culture within the organization may restrict delegation. Hierarchies, management styles, and norms may all preclude delegation. Rigid chains of command and autocratic leadership styles do not facilitate delegation and rarely provide good role models. The norm is to do the work oneself because others are not capable or skilled. An atmosphere of distrust prevails as well as a poor tolerance for mistakes. A norm of crisis management or poorly defined job descriptions or chains of command also impede successful delegation.

Personal Qualities

Poor communication and interpersonal skills can also be a barrier to delegation. Thomas and Hume (1998) note that in addition to good communication skills and respecting and treating staff fairly, a willingness to work with the other, to be open to suggestions, to provide feedback and acknowledgment for work well done is essential. They also note that delegates must be reliable and willing to follow instructions.

TABLE 10-1 Potential Obstacles to Delegation

ENVIRONMENTAL	DELEGATOR	DELEGATE
Practice acts	Lack of trust and confidence	Inexperience
Standards	Believe others incapable	Fear of failure and reprisal
Job descriptions	Believe self indispensable	Lack of confidence
Policies	Fear of competition	Overdependence on others
Organizational structure	Fear of criticism	Avoidance of responsibility
Management styles	Fear of liability	
Norms	Fear of blame for others' mistakes	
Resources	Fear of loss of control	
	Fear or overburdening	
	Fear of decreased job satisfaction	
	Insecurity	
	Inexperience in delegation	
	Inadequate organizational skills	

Reprinted with permission from "Delegation: How to deliver care through others," R. Hansten and M. Washburn, 1992, *American Journal of Nursing, 92*(3), pp. 87–88.

Resources

Another difficulty frequently encountered is a lack of resources. For example, there may be no one to whom you can delegate. Consider the sole registered nurse in a skilled nursing facility. If practice acts define a task as one that only a registered nurse can perform, there is no one else to whom that nurse can delegate that task.

Financial constraints also can interfere with delegation. For instance, someone from your department must attend the annual conference in your nursing specialty area. However, the organization will only pay the manager's travel and conference expenses, which precludes anyone else from attending.

Educational resources may be another limiting factor. Perhaps others could learn how to do a task if they could practice with the equipment, but the equipment or a trainer is not available.

Time can also be a limiting factor. For example, it is Friday and the schedule needs to be posted Monday. No one on your staff has experience developing schedules and you need to go out of town for a family emergency, so there is no one else to do the schedule.

AN INSECURE DELEGATOR

The majority of the barriers to delegation arise from the delegator. Reasons people give to fail to delegate include:

"I can do it better."
"I can do it faster."
"I'd rather do it myself."
"I don't have time to delegate."

Often underlying these statements are erroneous beliefs, fears, and inexperience in delegation. Certainly, the experienced person can do the task better and faster. Indeed, delegation takes time, but failing to delegate is a time waster. Time invested in developing staff today is later repaid many times over.

Common fears are:

- **Fear of competition or criticism.** What if someone else can do the job better or faster than I? Will I lose my job? Be demoted? What will others think? Will I lose respect and control? This fear is unfounded if the delegator has selected the right task and matched it with the right individual. In fact, the delegate's success in the task provides evidence of the delegator's leadership and decision-making abilities.
- **Fear of liability.** Some individuals are not risk takers and shy away from delegation for this reason. There are risks associated with delegation, but the delega-

tor can minimize these risks by following the steps of delegation. A related concern is a fear of being blamed for the delegate's mistakes. If the delegator used prudence in selecting the task and delegate, then the responsibility for any mistakes made are solely those of the delegate; it is not necessary to take on guilt for another's mistakes.

To help keep this issue in perspective, it is important to recall the benefits of delegation and balance the rewards with the risks while making the delegation decision. Managers really need to clearly delineate what tasks can be delegated and to whom. Additionally, RNs, LPNs and UAPs need to understand what tasks can be delegated under the state's nurse practice act as well as abiding by organizational policies. RNs often fear blame from management if something goes wrong when a task has been delegated to an LPN or UAP, but those fears can be relieved if state law, organizational policies, and job descriptions are followed.

- **Fear of loss of control.** Will I be kept informed? Will the job be done right? How can I be sure? The more one is insecure and inexperienced in delegation, the more this fear is an issue. This is also a predominant concern in individuals who tend toward autocratic styles of leadership and perfectionism. The key to retaining control is to clearly identify the task and expectations and then to monitor progress and provide feedback.
- **Fear of overburdening others.** They already have so much to do; how can I suggest more? Everyone has work to do. Such a statement belittles the decisional capabilities of others. Recall that delegation is a voluntary, contractual agreement; acceptance of a delegated task indicates the availability and willingness of the delegate to perform the task. Often, the delegate welcomes the diversion and stimulation, and what the delegator perceives as a burden is actually a blessing. The onus is on the delegator to select the right person for the right reason.
- **Fear of decreased personal job satisfaction.** Because the type of tasks recommended to delegate are those that are familiar and routine, the delegator's job satisfaction should actually increase with the opportunity to explore new challenges and obtain other skills and abilities.

Additional hindrances to delegation include inadequate organizational skills, such as poor time management, and inexperience in delegation. Test your delegation skills by completing the delegation assessment in Box 10–1.

BOX 10-1	**Delegation Assessment**

1. Mr. Jones, a bedridden but stable patient, needs a complete bed bath. You
   a. Assign the task to the nurse assistant.
   b. Work together with the nursing assistant to give the bath.
   c. Do the job yourself because Mr. Jones is a VIP and you know you'll do the best job.

2. You are the charge nurse, and one of your team members is a float nurse who has never worked on the unit before. You
   a. Spend 15 minutes with her assessing her abilities and providing a brief orientation to the unit so that she can take the full assignment.
   b. Give her three of the "easiest patients" and pick up the rest of the assignment yourself.
   c. Call the supervisor and tell her that you have no time to orient someone and the float will be more trouble than she's worth.

3. Another new admission is arriving on your unit. You
   a. Assign the patient to the LPN, recognizing that one of the registered nurses will be overseeing and completing the admission assessment.
   b. Ask the nursing assistant to get the vital signs, and you complete the admission before assigning the patient to another RN.
   c. Take the admission yourself because everyone else seems too busy.

4. You and a nursing assistant are assigned to 10 patients on a medical surgical floor. You
   a. Spend 15 minutes making walking rounds with the nursing assistant, then decide how to distribute patient care tasks.
   b. Assign tasks according to the assignment board from yesterday.

   c. Send the nursing assistant to take vital signs without further information or communication.

5. You are uncertain about a nursing assistant's skill in giving a cleansing enema. You
   a. Review the hospital procedure with the nursing assistant and observe him performing the task so that next time he can do it alone.
   b. Give the enema yourself today, promising that the next time you'll teach the nursing assistant.
   c. You never assign him to give an enema.

6. Your manager tells you that the care delivery system on your unit is changing and you'll need to use assistive personnel. You
   a. Welcome the opportunity to free up some of your time to do more of your professional duties.
   b. Keep an open mind and wait to review the job description of the new assistants.
   c. Take a wait-and-see attitude, but if it doesn't work out in the next two weeks, you'll apply to another hospital in town where you can still be a "real nurse."

If you answered mostly "a"s, congratulations! You have overcome many of the typical barriers to delegation. You can be a mentor to your coworkers who are learning the skill.

If you answered mostly "b"s, you are on the way to overcoming your personal barriers to delegation. Keep an open mind and read on.

If you answered mostly "c"s, oops! You have strong objections to sharing your work load with others. Read on. Learning this skill and applying it will enhance your daily work life.

Reprinted with permission from "Delegation: How to deliver care through others," R. Hansten and M. Washburn, 1992, *American Journal of Nursing, 92*(3), pp. 87–88.

AN UNWILLING DELEGATE

Inexperience and fear of failure can motivate a potential delegate to refuse to accept a delegated task. Much reassurance and support are needed. In addition, the delegate should be equipped to handle the task. If proper selection criteria are used and the steps of delegation followed, then the delegate should not fail. The delegator can boost the delegate's lack of confidence by building on simple tasks. The delegate needs to be reminded that everyone was inexperienced at one time. Another common concern is how mistakes will be handled. When describing the task, the delegator should provide clear guidelines for handling problems, guidelines that adhere to organizational policies.

Another barrier is the individual who avoids responsibility or is overdependent on others. Success breeds success; therefore, it is important to use an enticing incentive to engage the individual in a simple task that guarantees success.

Ineffective Delegation

When the steps of delegation are not followed or barriers remain unresolved, delegation is often ineffective. Inefficient delegation can result from unnecessary duplication, underdelegation, reverse delegation, and overdelegation.

UNNECESSARY DUPLICATION

If staff are duplicating the work of others, related tasks may have been given to too many people (Barter, 2002). To avoid unnecessary duplication, try to delegate associated tasks to as few people as possible. This allows the person to complete the assignment without spending time negotiating with others about which task should be done by which person. Also reporting is simplified for both the delegate and the delegator.

To prevent work duplication, Barter (2002, p. 57) suggests that you ask:

- How often does staff duplicate an activity that someone else has recently performed?
- Why does this duplication occur and is it necessary?
- How could nurses delegate to prevent duplication?

UNDERDELEGATION

Underdelegation occurs when

- The delegator fails to transfer full authority to the delegate;
- The delegator takes back responsibility for aspects of the task; or
- The delegator fails to equip and direct the delegate.

As a result, the delegate is unable to complete the task, and the delegator must resume responsibility for its completion.

Sharon, RN, is a school nurse with three separate buildings under her direction. UAPs, called health clerks, operate in the school health office when Sharon is at another building. Joye, a first year health clerk, has had minimal medication administration instruction and experience. During the first week of school, Joye tries to "speed up" the medication administration process and sets out all of the noon medications in individual, unlabeled cups for the students. The cups are rearranged by students trying to find their meds and Joye cannot identify what meds belong to which students. Sharon is called back to the school to administer the correct medications, students are late to class, and Joye is frustrated that she couldn't handle the task.

REVERSE DELEGATION

In **reverse delegation**, someone with a lower rank delegates to someone with more authority.

Thomas is a nurse practitioner for the burn unit. He recently arrived on the unit to find several patients whose dressing changes have not been completed due to a code situation earlier in the morning. Dawn, LPN, asks Thomas to complete a few dressing changes to help the staff complete dressing changes before physician rounds begin.

OVERDELEGATION

Overdelegation occurs when the delegator loses control over a situation by providing the delegate with too much authority or too much responsibility. This places the delegator in a risky position, increasing the potential for liability.

Ellen, GN, is in her sixth week of orientation in the trauma ICU. Her mentor, Dolores, RN, notes that Mr. Anderson is scheduled for an MRI off the unit. Dolores delegates the task of escorting Mr. Anderson to the MRI unit. Ellen is not ACLS certified. During the MRI, Mr. Anderson is accidentally extubated and suffers respiratory and cardiac arrest. A code is called in the MRI suite and ER nurses must respond since an ACLS certified nurse is not with the patient.

Liability and Delegation

Fear of liability often keeps nurses from delegating. State nurse practice acts determine the legal parameters for practice, professional associations set practice standards, and organizational policy and job descriptions define delegation appropriate to the specific work setting.

Also several guidelines can help. The National Council of State Boards of Nursing (2007) identified the five rights of delegation:

- Right task (task is one that can be delegated for specific patient)
- Right circumstances (setting is appropriate and resources are available)
- Right person (give the right task to the right delegate for the right patient)
- Right direction and communication (describe objectives, limits, and expectations)
- Right supervision (monitor, evaluate, give feedback, and intervene if necessary)

In addition, the American Nurses Association and the National Council of State Boards of Nursing issued a joint statement on delegation to explain both the profession's practice guidelines and the legal requirements for delegation (ANA & NCSBN, 2006). *Figure 10-1* shows a decision tree for delegation from the joint statement.

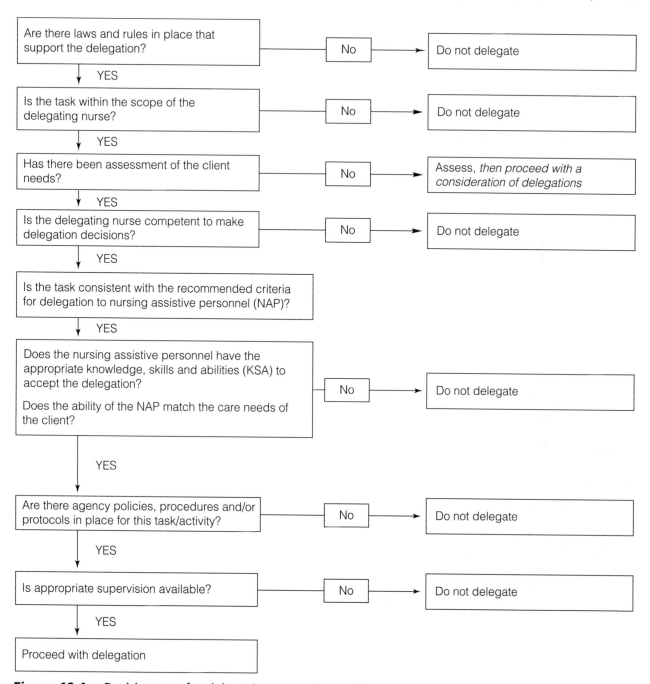

Figure 10-1 ● Decision tree for delegation to nursing assistive personnel. *Adapted from National Council of State Boards of Nursing. (2006). Joint statement on delegation. Retrieved December 2007 from* www.ncsbn.org/Joint_statement.pdf

One situation that may present a challenge to the manager is when the staff receives written or verbal orders from a physician's office nurse (Austin, 2004). The same legal guidelines for the nurse giving the orders apply to the staff receiving them. If the nurse's license allows prescribing privileges, such as a nurse practitioner, the staff can accept appropriate orders. Otherwise, the orders must also be verified by the prescribing physician. The staff put their own licenses in jeopardy if not.

Delegation is a skill that can be learned. Like other skills, delegating successfully requires practice. Sometimes it seems it might be easier to do it yourself. But it is not. Once you learn how to delegate, you will extend your ability to accomplish more by using others' help. No one in health care today can afford not to delegate.

What You Know Now

- Delegation is a contractual agreement in which authority and responsibility for a task is transferred by the person accountable for the task to another individual.
- Delegation involves skill in identifying and determining the task and level of responsibility, determining who has the requisite skills and abilities, describing expectations clearly, reaching mutual agreement, and monitoring performance and providing feedback.
- Delegatable tasks are personal, routine tasks that the delegator can perform well; that do not involve discipline, highly technical tasks, or confidential information; and that are not controversial.
- Delegation benefits the delegator, delegate, the organization.
- Various organizational, delegator, and delegate barriers can prevent effective delegation.
- Ineffective delegation usually results from inadequate or inappropriate transference of authority or responsibility.
- Adhering to the steps of delegation—in particular, prudently selecting a qualified person as delegate and providing appropriate supervision—minimizes the risk of liability.
- Delegation is essential in health care today.

Tools for Delegating Successfully

1. Delegate only tasks for which you have responsibility.
2. Transfer authority when you delegate responsibility.
3. Be sure you follow state regulations, job descriptions, and agency policies when delegating.
4. Follow the delegation process and key behaviors for delegating described in the chapter.
5. Accept delegation when you are clear about the task, time frame, reporting, and other expectations.
6. Confront your fears about delegation; recognize those that are realistic and those that are not.

Questions to Challenge You

1. Review your state's nurse practice act. How is delegation defined? What tasks can and cannot be delegated? How is supervision defined? Are there any other guidelines for supervision? Are responsibilities regarding advanced practice delineated? How does the scope of practice differ between registered and licensed practical/vocational nurses? What is the scope of practice of other health care providers?
2. What are your agency's policies on delegation?
3. Describe a situation when you delegated a task to someone else. Did you follow the steps of delegation explained in the chapter? Was the outcome positive? If not, what went wrong?
4. Describe a situation when someone else delegated a task to you. Did your delegator explain what to do? Did you receive too much information? Not enough? Was supervision appropriate to the task and to your abilities? What was the outcome?
5. How did you score on the delegation assessment shown in Box 10-1? What did you learn about how to improve your delegation skills?

Explore MediaLink 🌐

Additional interactive resources for this chapter can be found on the Website at http://www.prenhall.com/sullivan. Click on Chapter 10 to select activities for this chapter.

- Video Overview
- NCLEX® Review Questions
- Critical Thinking Activities
- Current Events
- Nursing Leadership and Management in Action
- MediaLinks

References

American Nurses Association (ANA) & National Council of State Boards of Nursing (NCSBN). (2006). *Joint statement on delegation.* Retrieved December 2007 from https://www.ncsbn.org/Joint_statement.pdf

Austin, S. (2004). Respect the scope of your license and practice. *Nursing Management, 35*(12), 18, 20.

Barter, M. (2002). Follow the team leader. *Nursing Management, 33*(10), 54–57.

Cohen, S. (2004). Delegating vs. dumping: Teach the difference. *Nursing Management, 35*(10), 14, 18.

Kleinman, C. S., & Saccomano, S. J. (2006). Registered nurses and unlicensed assistive personnel: An uneasy alliance. *The Journal of continuing Education in Nursing, 37*(4), 162–170.

National Council of State Boards of Nursing. (2007). The five rights of delegation. Retrieved December 2007 from www.ncsbn.org/Joint_statement.pdf

Thomas, S., & Hume, G. (1998). Delegation competencies: Beginning practitioners' reflections. *Nurse Educator, 23*(1), 38–41.

CHAPTER 11

Building and Managing Teams

Learning Outcomes

After completing this chapter, you will be able to:

1. Differentiate between groups and teams.
2. Describe the characteristics of different types of groups.

MediaLink

www.prenhall.com/sullivan

See the Companion Website for chapter-specific resources at www.prenhall.com/sullivan.

3. Discuss how groups form, function, and end.
4. Explain why the nurse manager is a team leader.
5. Discuss how to manage groups, task forces, and patient care conferences.

Key Terms

Additive task *p155*
Adjourning *p150*
Cohesiveness *p154*
Committees or task forces *p148*
Competing groups *p148*
Conjunctive task *p155*
Disjunctive task *p155*
Divisible task *p155*
Formal committees *p157*
Formal groups *p147*
Forming *p149*

Group *p147*
Hidden agendas *p152*
Informal committees *p157*
Informal groups *p148*
Norming *p150*
Norms *p152*
Ordinary interacting groups *p149*
Performing *p150*
Pooled interdependence *p155*
Productivity *p154*
Real (command) groups *p148*

Reciprocal interdependence *p156*
Re-forming *p150*
Role *p152*
Sequential interdependence *p155*
Status *p153*
Status incongruence *p153*
Storming *p150*
Task forces *p157*
Task group *p148*
Team building *p151*
Teams *p148*

Most often, nursing occurs in a team environment. Work groups that share common objectives function in a harmonious, coordinated, purposeful manner as teams. High-performance teams require expert leadership skills. In a health care delivery system integrated across settings, a team environment becomes increasingly essential. Nurse managers must skillfully orchestrate the activity and interactions of interdisciplinary teams as well as conventional nursing work groups. Understanding the nature of groups and how groups are transformed into teams is essential for the nurse to be effective.

Because staff nurses work in close proximity and frequently depend on each other to perform their work, the quality of group leadership and interaction is vital. A positive climate is one in which there is mutual high regard and in which group members safely may discuss work-related concerns, critique and offer suggestions about clinical practice, and comfortably experiment with new behaviors. Maintaining a positive work group climate and building a team is a complex and demanding leadership task.

Differentiating Groups from Teams

A **group** is an aggregate of individuals who interact and mutually influence each other. Both formal and informal groups exist in organizations. **Formal groups** are clusters of individuals designated temporarily or permanently by an organization to perform specified organizational tasks. Formal groups may be structured laterally, vertically, or diagonally. Task groups, teams, task forces, and committees may be structured in all of these ways, whereas command groups generally are structured vertically.

Group members include:

- Individuals from a single work group (e.g., nurses on one unit) or individuals at similar job levels from more than one work group (e.g., all professional staff)
- Individuals from different job levels (e.g., nurses and UAPs)
- Individuals from different work groups and different job levels in the organization (e.g., committee to review staff orientation classes)

Groups may be permanent or temporary. Command groups, teams, and committees usually are permanent, whereas task groups and task forces are often temporary.

Informal groups evolve naturally from social interactions. Groups are informal in the sense that they are not defined by an organizational structure. Examples of informal groups include individuals who regularly eat lunch together or who convene spontaneously to discuss a clinical dilemma.

Real (command) groups accomplish tasks in organizations and are recognized as a legitimate organizational entity. Its members are interdependent, share a set of norms, generally differentiate roles and duties among themselves, are organized to achieve ongoing organizational goals, and are collectively held responsible for measurable outcomes. The group's manager has line authority in relation to group members individually and collectively. The group's assignments are usually routine and designed to fulfill the specific mission of the agency or organization. The regularly assigned staff who work together under the direction of a single manager constitute a command group.

A **task group** is composed of several persons who work together, with or without a designated leader, and are charged with accomplishing specific time-limited assignments. A group of nurses selected by their colleagues to plan an orientation program for new staff constitute a task group. Usually, several task groups exist within a service area and may include representatives from several disciplines (e.g., nurse, physician, dietitian, social worker).

Other special groups include **committees or task forces** formed to deal with specific issues involving several service areas. A committee responsible for monitoring and improving patient safety or a task force assigned to develop procedures to adhere to patient privacy regulations are examples of special work groups. Health care organizations depend on numerous committees, which nurses participate in and often lead. Some of these committees are mandated by accrediting and regulatory bodies, such as committees for education, standards, disaster, and patient care evaluation. Others are established to meet a specific need (e.g., to formulate a new policy on substance abuse).

Teams are real groups in which individuals must work cooperatively with each other in order to achieve some overarching goal. Teams have command or line authority to perform tasks, and membership is based on the specific skills required to accomplish the tasks. Similar to groups described above, teams may include individuals from a single work group or individuals at similar job levels from more than one work group, individuals from different job levels, or individuals from different work groups and different job levels in the organization. They may have a short life span or exist indefinitely.

Metropolitan Hospital has established a clinical ladder system for nursing staff. Each quarter, members of the clinical excellence committee meet to review applications from staff nurses who are seeking promotion to the next clinical level. The committee is made up of staff nurses and nurse managers from each service line. Each applicant is responsible for completing a comprehensive application. The committee members evaluate each application and make recommendations to the vice president for patient care on those nurses who should be considered from promotion.

Not all work groups, however, are teams. For example, groups of individuals who perform their tasks independently of each other are not teams. **Competing groups**, in which members compete with each other for resources to perform their tasks or compete for recognition, also are not teams.

A work group becomes a team when the individuals must apply group process skills to achieve specific results. They must exchange ideas, coordinate work activities, and develop an understanding of other team members' roles in order to perform effectively. Members appreciate the talents and contributions of each individual on the team and find ways to capitalize on them. Most work teams have a leader who maintains the integrity of the team's function and guides the team's activities, performance, and development. Teams may be self-directed, that is, led jointly by group members who decide together about work objectives and activities on an ongoing basis.

In a given service area, the entire staff might not function as a team, but a subgroup may. For example, case managers for the inpatient and ambulatory cystic fibrosis population in a children's medical center might be called a team. Individual members of an interdisciplinary team, such as this one, may report formally to different managers, but in delivering care to the cystic fibrosis population there is no designated individual in charge. In meetings, the team members discuss clients' problems and jointly decide on plans of action.

Many different types of groups and teams are used throughout the organization. Examples are ad hoc task groups, quality improvement teams, quality circles, self-directed work teams, councils, and focus groups.

Nurse managers at a large university hospital are responsible for educating their staff about patient satisfaction. Patient satisfaction surveys are sent to randomly selected patients. Results are compiled and each department receives a detailed report of the results. Staff members review the data at monthly staff meetings, using both positive and negative comments to guide their patient care activities. As needed, department standards and protocols are updated to reflect improved processes.

Most groups are considered **ordinary interacting groups**. These groups usually have a designated formal leader, but they may be leaderless. Most work teams, task groups, and committees are ordinary interacting groups. Discussions usually begin with a statement of the problem by the group leader followed by an open, unstructured conversation. Normally, the final decision is made by consensus (without formal voting; members indicate concurrence with a group agreement that everyone can live with and support publicly). The decision also may be made by the leader or someone in authority, majority vote, an average of members' opinions, minority control, or an expert member. Interacting groups enhance the cohesiveness and *esprit de corps* among group members. Participants are able to build strong social ties and will be committed to the solution decided on by the group.

Infection control nurses have been tracking occurrences of MRSA infections among patients in their hospital system. In addition to implementing patient care protocols as recommended by federal and state infectious disease agencies, the nurses track compliance in high risk units and tailor education programs to meet the needs of nursing and assistive staffs.

Ordinary interacting groups, however, may be dominated by one or a few members. If the group is highly cohesive, its decision-making ability may be affected by groupthink, discussed in Chapter 8. Groupthink results in pressure for every member to conform, usually to the leader's beliefs, even to violating personal norms.

Sometimes groups spend excessive time dealing with socioemotional relationships, reducing the time spent on the problem and slowing consensus. Ordinary groups may reach compromise decisions that may not really satisfy any of the participants. Because of these problems, the functioning of ordinary groups is very dependent on the leader's skills.

Each type of group presents unique opportunities and challenges. An important role of the nurse manager is to link service areas with groups at higher levels in the organization. This link facilitates problem solving, coordination, and communication throughout the organization. Leadership roles in work groups are important and also may be either formal or informal.

For example, the nurse manager formally leads the unit or service area staff but may also informally lead a support group of nurse managers.

The leader's influence on group processes, formal or informal, and the ability of the group to work together as a team often determines whether the group accomplishes its goals. Nurse managers may effectively manage work groups and turn them into teams by understanding principles of group processes and applying them to group decision making, team building, and leading committees and task forces.

Group and Team Processes

The modified version of Homans' (1950, 1961) social system conceptual scheme presented in *Figure 11-1* provides a framework for understanding group inputs, processes, and outcomes. The schematic depicts the effects of organizational and individual background factors on group leadership, including dynamics (tasks, activities, interactions, attitudes) and processes (forming, storming, norming, performing, adjourning). Elements of the required group system and processes influence each other and the emergent group system and social structure.

This system determines the productivity of the group as well as members' quality of work life, such as job satisfaction, development, growth, and similarity in thinking. The framework distinguishes required factors that are imposed by the external system from factors that emerge from the internal dynamics of the group.

According to Homans' framework, the three essential elements of a group system are activities, interactions, and attitudes. Activities are the observable behaviors of group members. Interactions are the verbal or nonverbal exchanges of words or objects among two or more group members. Attitudes are the perceptions, feelings, and values held by individual group members, which may be both positive and negative. To understand and guide group functioning, a manager should analyze the activities, interactions, and attitudes of work group members.

Homans' framework indicates that background factors, the manager's leadership style, and the organizational system influence the normal development of the group. Groups, whether formal or informal, typically develop in the phases: form, storm, norm, perform, and adjourn or re-form. In the initial stage, **forming**, individuals assemble into a well-defined cluster. Group members are cautious in approaching each other as they come together as a group and begin to understand requirements

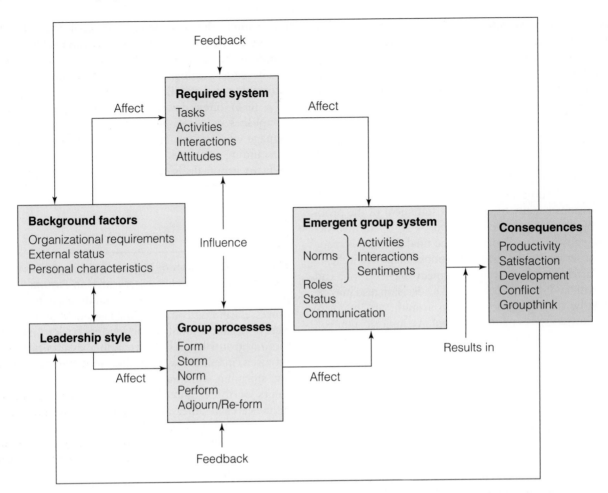

Figure 11-1 ● Conceptual scheme of a basic social system. *Adapted from* The Human Group *by G. Homans, 1950, New York: Harcourt Brace Jovanovich; and* Social Behavior: Its Elementary Forms *by G. Homans, 1961, New York: Harcourt Brace. By permission of Transaction Publishers.*

of group membership. At this stage, the members often depend on a leader to define purpose, tasks, and roles.

As the group begins to develop, **storming** occurs. Members wrestle with roles and relationships. Conflict, dissatisfaction, and competition arise on important issues related to procedures and behavior. During this stage, members often compete for power and status, and informal leadership emerges. During the storming stage, the leader helps the group to acknowledge the conflict and to resolve it in a win-win manner.

In the third stage, **norming**, the group defines its goals and rules of behavior. The group determines what are or are not acceptable behaviors and attitudes. The group structure, roles, and relationships become clearer. Cohesiveness develops. The leader explains standards of performance and behavior, defines the group's structure, and facilitates relationship building.

In the fourth stage, **performing**, members agree on basic purposes and activities and carry out the work.

The group's energy becomes task-oriented. Cooperation improves, and emotional issues subside. Members communicate effectively and interact in a relaxed atmosphere of sharing. The leader provides feedback on the quality and quantity of work, praises achievement, critiques poor work and takes steps to improve it, and reinforces interpersonal relationships within the group.

The fifth stage is either **adjourning** (the group dissolves after achieving its objectives) or **re-forming**, when some major change takes place in the environment or in the composition or goals of the group that requires the group to refocus its activities and recycle through the four stages. When a group adjourns, the leader must prepare group members for dissolution and facilitate closure through celebration of success and leave-taking. If the group is to refocus its activities, the leader will explain the new direction and provide guidance in the process of re-forming.

Team Building

Team building focuses on both task and relationship aspects of a group's functioning and is intended to increase efficiency and productivity. The group's work and problem-solving procedures, member–member relations, and leadership are analyzed, and exercises are prescribed to help members modify their patterns of interaction or processes of decision making.

Team-building activities may include outside intervention to build team cohesiveness, use internal consultative services, be manager driven, and/or involve the training and development of the group's members and/or leader.

Team building involves:

- Gathering data through individual interviews, questionnaires, and/or group meetings about the team and its functioning
- Diagnosing the team's strengths and areas in need of development
- Holding semistructured retreat sessions, usually directed by an experienced facilitator, aimed at addressing priority team problems

Team building may occur over months during specially arranged retreats or may be confined to "quick fix" activities during regular work time. Most team building involves simulated real-life activities aimed at improving the team's functioning through observing and intervening in the team's actual performance rather than through training. Some of these strategies are depicted in Table 11-1.

Retreat sessions ideally are conducted away from the workplace over a period lasting from one day to several days and are insulated from professional or personal interruptions of the participants. Retreat-style team building is intended to create intense, prolonged interactions that force conflicts and unhealthy group processes to the surface so that they can be examined and improved under the guidance of an objective, skilled third party. Follow-up in the work setting is often overlooked, but it is an essential final step to ensure application of new collaborative behaviors and ongoing commitments to team development.

Retreats may be directed by either internal or external leaders. Internal leaders know and are known in the organization, understand the culture and policies, and have an institutional memory. External leaders, on the other hand, are more likely to be considered unbiased and objective and bring past experience with a variety of clients and situations. Sometimes the best solution is to use a combination of both internal and external leaders (McNally & Lukens, 2006).

The most important initial activities in team building are data gathering and diagnosis. Questions must be asked about the group's context (organizational structure, climate, culture, mission, and goals); characteristics of the group's work, including group members'

TABLE 11-1	Strategies for Team Management
PROBLEM	**SOLUTION**
Member isn't a Team Player	• Consider why you want person on team. • Approach person in an assertive manner. • Give person an opportunity to provide feedback on problematic situations. • If person is unable to communicate with other team members, leader might approach for one-to-one dialogue. • Listen actively, using all senses to assess both verbal and nonverbal messages. • Avoid blaming and shaming, which tend to create defensiveness and cause arguments.
Member Lacks Sense of Personal Accountability	• Explain how failure to take responsibility affects team as a whole. (For example, "Mary, last week when you didn't present your part of the report, it set team goals back a week.") • Without blaming or shaming, provide feedback from all team members.
Team Lacks Clear Goals	• Brainstorm to clarify short-term goals and develop action plan. • Arrive at consensus regarding mission and goals. • Define member responsibilities. • Determine resources needed to accomplish goals, including staff, financial and administrative support, time, and equipment. • Periodically review team progress and goal attainment.
Roles and Boundaries are Unclear	• With member input, leader must clarify boundaries. • All team members' roles and responsibilities must be defined, including leader's. • Periodically review team development.

From D. Antai-Otong, 1997, "Team Building in a Health Care Setting," *American Journal of Nursing, 97*(7), pp. 48–51.

MediaLink ● Team Building

roles, styles, procedures, job complexity; and the team, its problem-solving style, interpersonal relationships, and relations with other groups.

The following questions may be asked:

1. To what extent do the team's members understand and accept the goals of the organization?
2. What, if any, hidden agendas interfere with the group's performance? **Hidden agendas** are members' individual unspoken objectives that interfere with commitment or enthusiasm.
3. How effective is the group's leadership?
4. To what extent do group members understand and accept their roles?
5. How does the group make decisions?
6. How does the group handle conflict? Are conflicts dealt with through avoidance, forcing, accommodating, compromising, competing, or collaborating?
7. What personal feelings do members have about each other?
8. To what extent do members trust and respect each other?
9. What is the relationship between the team and other units in the organization?

Only after diagnosing the problems of the team can the leader take actions to improve team functioning. A nurse manager may decide to assume personal responsibility for team building when the team is basically functional and simply needs some fine-tuning to deal more effectively with minor interpersonal issues or changing circumstances.

Thoughtful team-building strategies allow group members to acknowledge the developmental process and respond to it in constructive ways. Team-building activities may also be used to facilitate the normal stages of group development (forming, storming, norming, performing, and adjourning or re-forming), an important process in managing teams.

Team-building techniques also may be used to intervene in traditional work groups that are experiencing problems or in any other type of group, such as a task force or committee. Numerous techniques and commercial resources are available for managers or an intervention specialist to use.

Characteristics of Groups

NORMS

Norms are the informal rules of behavior shared and enforced by group members. Norms emerge whenever humans interact. Groups develop norms that members

believe must be adhered to for fruitful, stable group functioning. Nursing groups often establish norms related to how members deal with absences that affect the workload of colleagues. Norms may include not calling in sick on weekends, readily accommodating requests for trading shifts, and returning from breaks in a timely manner. In a team environment, norms are more likely to be linked to each team member's expected contribution to the performance and products of the team's efforts. If an individual agrees to take on a specific assignment on the team's behalf and fails to complete the assignment on time, a group norm has been violated.

Group norms are likely to be enforced if they serve to facilitate group survival, ensure predictability of behavior, help avoid embarrassing interpersonal problems, express the central values of the group, and clarify the group's distinctive identity.

Groups go through several stages in enforcing norms with deviant members. First, members use rational argument, or present reasons for adhering to the norms to the deviant individual. Second, if rational argument is not effective, members may use persuasive or manipulative techniques, reminding the deviant of the value of the group. The third stage is attack. Attacks may be verbal or even physical and sometimes include sabotaging the deviant's work. The final stage is ignoring the deviant.

It becomes increasingly difficult for a deviant to acquiesce to the group as these strategies escalate. Agreeing to rational argument is easy, but agreeing after an attack is very difficult. When the final stage (ignoring) is reached, acquiescence may be impossible because group members refuse to acknowledge the deviant's surrender. A nurse manager has a responsibility to help groups deal with members who violate group norms related to performance, including counseling the employee and preventing destructive conflict.

ROLES

Norms apply to all group members, whereas roles are specific to positions in the group. A **role** is a set of expected behaviors that fit together into a unified whole and are characteristic of persons in a given context. Roles commonly seen in groups can be classified as either task roles or socioemotional (nurturing) roles. Often, individuals fill several roles. Individuals performing task roles attempt to keep the group focused on its goals.

Task roles include:

- **Initiator-contributor.** Redefines problems and offers solutions, clarifies objectives, suggests agenda items, and maintains time limits

- **Information seeker.** Pursues descriptive bases for the group's work
- **Information giver.** Expands information given by sharing experiences and making inferences
- **Opinion seeker.** Explores viewpoints that clarify or reflect the values of other members' suggestions
- **Opinion giver.** Conveys to group members what their pertinent values should be
- **Elaborator.** Predicts outcomes and provides illustrations or expands suggestions, clarifying how they could work
- **Coordinator.** Links ideas or suggestions offered by others
- **Orienter.** Summarizes the group's discussions and actions
- **Evaluator critic.** Appraises the quantity and quality of the group's accomplishments against set standards
- **Energizer.** Motivates group to accomplish, qualitatively and quantitatively, the group's goals
- **Procedural technician.** Supports group activity by arranging the environment (e.g., scheduling meeting room) and providing necessary tools (e.g., ordering visual equipment)
- **Recorder.** Documents the group's actions and achievements

Nurturing roles facilitate the growth and maintenance of the group. Individuals assuming these roles are concerned with group functioning and interpersonal needs.

Nurturing roles include:

- **Encourager.** Compliments members for their opinions and contributions to the group
- **Harmonizer.** Relieves tension and conflict
- **Compromiser.** Submits own position to maintain group harmony
- **Gate-keeper.** Encourages all group members to communicate and participate
- **Group observer.** Takes note of group processes and dynamics and informs group of them
- **Follower.** Passively attends meetings, listens to discussions, and accepts group's decisions

Status is the social ranking of individuals relative to others in a group based on the position they occupy. Status comes from factors the group values, such as achievement, personal characteristics, the ability to control rewards, or the ability to control information. Status is usually enjoyed by members who most conform to group norms. Higher-status members often exercise more influence in group decisions than others.

Status incongruence occurs when factors associated with group status are not congruent, such as when a younger, less experienced person becomes the group leader. Status incongruence can have a disruptive impact on a group. For example, isolates are members who have high external status and different backgrounds from regular group members. They usually work at acceptable levels but are isolated from the group because they do not fit the group member profile. Sometimes status incongruence occurs because the individual does not need the group's approval and makes no effort to obtain it.

The most important role in a group is the leadership role. Leaders are appointed for most formal groups, such as command groups, teams, committees, or task forces. Leaders in informal groups tend to emerge over time and in relation to the task to be performed. Some of the factors contributing to the emergence of leadership in small groups include the ability to accomplish the group's goals, sociability, good communication skills, self-confidence, and a desire for recognition. Guidelines for performing this leadership role are discussed later in this chapter.

Communication in Groups

Groups provide an important channel of communication in organizations. Members of high-performance work teams generally communicate openly, candidly, and clearly with one another about procedures, expectations, and plans. Communication is influenced by the status and roles of the individuals who dominate team discussions. High-status members who are fulfilling key roles in relation to a team's priorities are likely to exercise considerable control over communication in the group by determining topics, setting the tone of the discussion, and influencing how decisions are made.

Effective nurse managers can facilitate communication in groups by maintaining an atmosphere in which group members feel free to discuss concerns, make suggestions, critique ideas, and show respect and trust. An important leadership function related to communication is gate-keeping, that is, keeping communication channels open, refocusing attention on critical issues, identifying and processing conflict, fostering self-esteem, checking for understanding, actively seeking the participation of all group members, and suggesting procedures for discussing group problems.

How Groups Affect Individuals

Group relationships affect individual behavior in many ways. Organizational work groups affect the beliefs, knowledge, attitudes, values, emotions, and social behavior of individuals. Groups profoundly affect the nature and process of communication and interpersonal relationships. On the one hand, they may engender a higher degree of competition and political activity than individual behavior.

Group influence is greater than the sum of its parts. A group can bring out the best and the worst in individuals due to the stimulating presence of others. Frequently, this stimulation increases motivation, especially when an individual's potential contribution to the task is fairly clear or easily measured.

On the other hand, groups can lead to inordinate conformity among group members. Groups may be tyrannical toward members and ruthless toward nonmembers and thereby contribute to conflict in the organization. Some issues involved in intragroup, intergroup, and intraorganizational conflict are discussed in Chapter 12. The effect of groups on productivity, quality of work life (job satisfaction), and development and growth are discussed next.

GROUP PRODUCTIVITY AND COHESIVENESS

Productivity represents how well the work group or team uses the resources available to achieve its goals and produce its services. If patient care is satisfactorily completed at the end of each shift in relation to the levels of staffing, supplies, equipment, and support services used, the group has been productive. Productivity is influenced by work-group dynamics, especially a group's cohesiveness and collaboration.

Cohesiveness is the degree to which the members are attracted to the group and wish to retain membership in it. Cohesiveness includes how much the group members enjoy participating in the group and how much they are willing to contribute. Cohesiveness is also related to homogeneity of interests, values, attitudes, and background factors. Strong group cohesiveness leads to a feeling of "we" as more important than "I" and ensures a higher degree of cooperation and interpersonal support among group members.

Group norms may support or subvert organizational objectives, depending on the level of group cohesiveness. High group cohesiveness may foster high or low individual performance, depending on the prevailing group norms for performance. When cohesiveness is low, productivity may vary significantly. Although groups, in general, tend toward lower productivity,

nursing education and practice have especially high standards of performance that help to counter this tendency.

Groups are more likely to become cohesive when members:

- Share similar values and beliefs
- Are motivated by the same goals and tasks
- Must interact to achieve their goals and tasks
- Work in proximity to each other (on the same unit and on the same shift, for example)
- Have specific needs that can be satisfied by involvement in the group

Group cohesiveness is also influenced by the formal reward system. Groups tend to be more cohesive when group members receive comparable treatment and pay and perform similar tasks that require interaction among the members. Similarities in values, education, social class, gender, age, and ethnicity that lead to similar attitudes strengthen group cohesiveness.

Cohesiveness can produce intense social pressure. Highly cohesive groups can demand and enforce adherence to norms regardless of their practicality or effectiveness. In this circumstance, the nurse manager may have a very difficult time influencing individual nurses, especially if the group norms deviate from the manager's values or expectations. For example, operating room nurses may be used to arriving at the time their shift starts and then changing into scrubs. The nurse manager, in contrast, may expect the staff to be changed and ready for work by the time the shift starts. In addition, group dynamics can affect absenteeism and turnover. Groups with high levels of cohesiveness exhibit lower turnover and absenteeism than groups with low levels of cohesiveness.

For most individuals, the work group provides one of the most important social contacts in life; the experience of working on an effective work team contributes significantly to one's professional confidence and to the quality of work life and job satisfaction. The work group often provides the primary motivation for returning to the job day after day even when employees are dissatisfied with the employing organization or other working conditions.

Work groups not only perform tasks but also provide the context in which novices learn basic skills and become socialized and experts engage in clinical mentorship, standard setting, quality improvement, and innovation. Work-group relations influence the satisfaction of staff with their jobs, the overall quality of work life, and the quality of the environment for patient care. Managers play key roles in guiding the tasks of work groups and ensuring efficient and effective performance; managers also encourage relationships among members of work teams that will promote coordination and cooperation.

DEVELOPMENT AND GROWTH

Groups also can provide learning opportunities by increasing individual skills or abilities. The group may facilitate socialization of new employees into the organization by "showing them the ropes." The nurse manager must establish an atmosphere that encourages learning new skills and knowledge, creating a group-oriented learning environment by continuously encouraging group members to improve their technical and interpersonal skills and knowledge through training and development. Group cohesiveness and effectiveness improve as staff members take responsibility for teaching each other and jointly seeking new information or techniques.

The Nurse Manager as Team Leader

Influencing group processes toward the attainment of organizational objectives is the direct responsibility of the nurse manager. The nurse manager can do a great deal to foster effective individual and group performance by promoting the benefits of group membership and increasing interdependence. By publicizing group accomplishments, creating opportunities for group members to demonstrate new skills, and supporting group social activities, the manager can increase the perceived value of group membership. Indeed, this is one of the manager's primary functions in a nursing organization (Carroll, 2005; Lavoie-Tremblay, 2004). Members of groups who have a history of success are attracted to each other more than those who have not been successful.

The manager's communication style also affects group cohesiveness. Erecting barriers, that Kerfoot (2004) calls invisible "windshields," prevent the leader from hearing both positive and negative reports. By interrupting, changing the subject, monopolizing the conversation, or ignoring the feedback, problems escalate and the leader remains uninformed and both individuals in the group and the group's ability to function suffer.

In addition, the manager who maintains a high degree of information power controls not only what information is received but also who receives it. Directing information to only a few individuals represents a highly centralized communication structure. In a decentralized structure, the nurse manager shares information freely, encouraging a high degree of mutual communication and participative problem solving. In participative groups, each individual has the opportunity, and is encouraged, to seek and share information and to communicate frequently with anyone and everyone in the group. Managers and staff alike check with each other to ensure that information is clear, to offer suggestions, and to provide feedback.

GROUP TASK

The size of the group can influence its effectiveness, depending on the type of task: additive, disjunctive, divisible, or conjunctive (Steiner, 1972, 1976). The more people who work on an **additive task** (group performance depends on the sum of individual performance), the more inputs are available to produce a favorable result. For example, the game tug-of-war involves the combined effort of the team.

For a **disjunctive task** (the group succeeds if one member succeeds), the greater the number of people, the higher the probability that one group member will solve the problem. Consider the Olympics. The more athletes on one team, the greater the opportunity for a gold medal. Regardless of the event, a medalist from the United States team brings recognition to the country, and every citizen is able to share the honor.

With a **divisible task** (tasks that can break down into subtasks with division of labor), more people provide a greater opportunity for specialization and interdependence in performing the tasks. For instance, the construction of a car is a complex task. From design of the car to insertion of the last bolt, each individual involved has a specialized task. With a **conjunctive task** (the group succeeds only if all members succeed), more people increase the likelihood that one person can slow up the group's performance (e.g., jury trial).

On many tasks, interdependence is important (Thompson, 1967). There are three kinds:

- **Pooled interdependence**, in which each individual contributes but no one contribution is dependent on any other (e.g., a committee discussion)
- **Sequential interdependence**, in which group members must coordinate their activities with others in some designated order (e.g., an assembly line)

- **Reciprocal interdependence**, in which members must coordinate their activities with every other individual in the group (e.g., team nursing)

GROUP SIZE AND COMPOSITION

Groups with five to ten members tend to be optimal for most complex organizational tasks, which require diversity in knowledge, skills, and attitudes and allow full participation. In larger groups, members tend to contribute less of their individual potential while the leader is called on to take more corrective action, do more role clarification, manage more disruption, and make recognition more explicit. Groups tend to perform better with competent individuals as members. However, coordination of effort and proper utilization of abilities and task strategies must occur as well. Homogeneous groups tend to function more harmoniously, whereas heterogeneous groups may experience considerable conflict.

EVALUATING TEAM PERFORMANCE

The manager may be accustomed to evaluating individual performance, but evaluating how well a team performs requires different assessments. Patient outcomes and team functioning are the criteria by which teams can be evaluated (Barter, 2002). Using clinical pathway data, variances in critical paths, complication rates, falls, and medication errors are examples of outcome data that can help the manager evaluate team performance.

Group functioning can be assessed by the level of work-group cohesion, involvement in the job, and willingness to help each other. Conversely aggression, competition, hostility, aloofness, shaming, or blaming are characteristics of poorly functioning groups. Stability of members is an additional measure of group functioning.

See how one nurse handled his new assignment as manager for a multidisciplinary team in Case Study 11-1.

CASE STUDY 11-1   Introducing Multidisciplinary Teams

Bruce Shapiro was promoted 6 months ago to nurse manager for the stroke rehabilitation unit of a nationally owned rehabilitation hospital. Patient care delivery systems have been under intensive review at the corporate level, and major changes in staffing are underway. Previously, physical and occupational therapists were staffed out of a separate department and reported to the director of physical therapy. Now all therapists will be unit based and report to the nurse manager. Documentation will now be team centered instead of being split among nursing, therapists, and other care providers.

Janice Simpson has been a physical therapist for 25 years and has been at the rehab hospital for the past 6 years. She worked as a shift leader for physical therapy until the new unit-based staffing was implemented. Janice has been assigned to the stroke rehab unit and will report to Bruce. She is feeling uncomfortable in her new role and is concerned about how she will fit in with the established nursing staff. Janice is also concerned that with the new documentation system, the physical therapy patient evaluations will not be included in determining patient goals.

Bruce is eager for Janice to join the staff of the stroke rehabilitation unit. He schedules individual meetings with Janice and the three other therapists who will be assigned to his unit. Bruce outlines the roles and expectations of staff on the unit and listens attentively to their questions and concerns. He also reviews the physical and occupational therapy job descriptions and reviews their respective documentation standards.

At the monthly staff meeting, Bruce discusses the roles and responsibilities of the therapists with the nursing staff. A mentor is assigned to meet daily with each therapist for their first 2 weeks on the unit.

Manager's Checklist

The nurse manager is responsible to:

- Understand the new staffing policies and the impact on the unit
- Gain knowledge related to physical and occupational therapy practice
- Ease the transition of new staff into the existing staff group to help build trust and respect
- Educate all staff on the new staffing policies
- Ensure that all therapists and nurses attend mandatory documentation training and audit patient records for compliance with new documentation standards
- Communicate with human resources if there are any questions regarding performance evaluation, scheduling, or compensation
- Review the personnel files of new staff
- Establish roles for the therapists in the unit governance structure
- Facilitate open communication with therapists and nurses to discuss concerns or suggestions
- Provide appropriate feedback to nursing management related to the new staffing changes

Leading Committees and Task Forces

Committees are generally permanent and deal with recurring problems. Membership on committees is usually determined by organizational position and role. **Formal committees** are part of the organization and have authority as well as a specific role. **Informal committees** are primarily for discussion and have no delegated authority. **Task forces** are ad hoc committees appointed for a specific purpose and a limited time. Task forces work on problems or projects that cannot be readily handled by the organization through its normal activities and structures. Task forces often deal with problems crossing departmental boundaries. They tend to generate recommendations and then disband.

Nurses often are selected for leadership roles on committees and task forces. In these leadership roles and as unit managers and team leaders, they conduct numerous meetings. The following section provides guidance for leading and conducting meetings.

GUIDELINES FOR CONDUCTING MEETINGS

Although meetings are vital to the conduct of organizational work, they should be held principally for problem solving, decision making, and enhancing working relationships. Other uses of meetings, such as socializing, giving or clarifying information, or soliciting suggestions must be thoroughly justified. Meetings should be conducted efficiently and should result in relevant and meaningful outcomes. Meetings should not result in damaged interpersonal relations, frustration, or inconclusiveness.

Preparation

The first key to a successful meeting is thorough preparation. Preparation includes clearly defining the purpose of the meeting. The leader should prepare an agenda, determine who should attend, make assignments, distribute relevant material, arrange for recording of minutes, and select an appropriate time and place for the meeting. The agenda should be distributed well ahead of time, 7 to 10 days prior to the meeting, and it should include what topics will be covered, who will be responsible for each topic, what prework should be done, what outcomes are expected in relation to each topic, and how much time will be allotted for each topic.

Sometimes a "meeting before the meeting" is advisable (Sullivan, 2004). This is especially important if you are going into a meeting where you expect dissension. It may involve simply chatting with a few key people to identify any problems or issues they expect, or you may need to actually sit down with a key decision maker who has veto power. Also asking people you expect might have opposing points of view their opinion might be helpful as well.

Participation

In general, the meeting should include the fewest number of stakeholders who can actively and effectively participate in decision making, who have the skills and knowledge necessary to deal with the agenda, and who adequately can represent the interests of those who will be affected by decisions made. Too few or too many participants may limit the effectiveness of a committee or task force.

Place and Time

Meetings should be held in places where interruptions can be controlled and at a time when there is a natural time limit to the meeting, such as late in the morning or afternoon, when lunch or dinner make natural time barriers. Meetings should be limited to 50 to 90 minutes, except when members are dealing with complex, detailed issues in a one-time session. Meetings that exceed 90 minutes should be planned to include breaks at least every hour. Meetings should start and finish on time. Starting late positively reinforces latecomers, while penalizing those who arrive on time or early. If sanctions for late arrival are indicated, they should be applied respectfully and objectively. If it is the leader who is late, the cost of starting meetings late should be reiterated and an appropriate designee should begin the meeting on time.

Member Behaviors

The behavior of each member may be positive, negative, or neutral in relation to the group's goals. Members may contribute very little, or they may use the group to meet personal needs. Some members may assume most of the responsibility for the group action, thereby enabling less participative members to avoid contributing.

Group members should:

- Be prepared for the meeting, having read pertinent materials ahead of time
- Ask for clarification as needed

- Offer suggestions and ideas as appropriate
- Encourage others to contribute their ideas and opinions
- Offer constructive criticism as appropriate
- Help the discussion stay on track
- Assist with implementation as agreed

These behaviors facilitate group performance. All attendees should be familiar with behaviors that they may employ to facilitate well-managed meetings. All meeting participants must be helped to understand that they share responsibility for successful meetings.

A leader can increase meeting effectiveness greatly by not permitting one individual to dominate the discussion; separating idea generation from evaluation; encouraging members to refine and develop the ideas of others (a key to the success of brainstorming); recording problems, ideas, and solutions on a blackboard or flip chart; checking for understanding; periodically summarizing information and the group's progress; encouraging further discussion; and bringing disagreements out into the open and facilitating their reconciliation. The leader is also responsible for drawing out the members' hidden agendas (personal goals or needs). Revealing hidden agendas ensures that these agendas either contribute positively to group performance or are neutralized. Guidelines for leading group meetings are provided in Box 11-1.

MANAGING TASK FORCES

There are a few critical differences between task forces and formal committees. For example, members of a task force have less time to build relationships with each other, and, because task forces are temporary, there may be no desire for long-term positive relationships. Formation of a task force may suggest that the organization's usual problem-solving mechanisms have failed. This perception may lead to tensions among task force members and between the task force and other units in the organization. The various members of a task force usually come from different parts of the organization and, therefore, have different values, goals, and viewpoints. The leader will need to take specific action to efficiently familiarize task force members with each other and create bonds in relation to the task.

Preparing for the First Meeting

Prior to the task force's first meeting, the leader must clarify the objectives of the task force in terms of specific measurable outcomes, determine its membership, set a task completion date, plan how often and to whom the task force should report while working on the project, and ascertain the group's scope of authority, including its budget, availability of relevant information, and decision-making power. The task force leader should communicate directly and regularly with the administrator or governing body that commissioned the task force's work so that ongoing clarification of its charge and progress can be tracked and adjusted.

Task force members should be selected on the basis of their knowledge, skills, personal concern for the task, time availability, and organizational credibility. They should also be selected on the basis of their interpersonal skills. Those who relish group activities and can facilitate the group's efforts are especially good members. The group leader also should plan to include one or two individuals who potentially may oppose

---

BOX 11-1   Guidelines for Leading Group Meetings

- Begin and end on time.
- Create a warm, accepting, and nonthreatening climate.
- Arrange seating to minimize differences in power, maximize involvement, and allow visualization of all meeting activities. (A U-shape is optimal.)
- Use interesting and varied visuals and other aids.
- Clarify all terms and concepts. Avoid jargon.
- Foster cooperation in the group.
- Establish goals and key objectives.
- Keep the group focused.
- Focus the discussion on one topic at a time.

- Facilitate thoughtful problem solving.
- Allocate time for all problem-solving steps.
- Promote involvement.
- Facilitate integration of material and ideas.
- Encourage exploration of implications of ideas.
- Facilitate evaluation of the quality of the discussion.
- Elicit the expression of dissenting opinions.
- Summarize discussion.
- Finalize the plan of action for implementing decisions.
- Arrange for follow-up.

task force recommendations in order to solicit their input, involve them in the decision-making process, and win their support. By holding personal conversations with task force members before the first meeting, the group leader can explore individual expectations, concerns, and potential contributions. It also provides the leader with an opportunity to identify potential needs and conflicts and to build confidence and trust.

Conducting the First Meeting

The goal of the first meeting is to come to a common understanding of the group's task and to define the group's working procedures and relationships. Task forces must rely on the general norms of the organization to function. The task force leader should legitimize the representative nature of participation on the task force and encourage members to discuss the task force's process with the other members of the organization.

During the first meeting, a standard of total participation should be well established. The leader should remain as neutral as possible and should prevent premature decision making. Working procedures and relationships among the various members, subgroups, and the rest of the organization need to be established. The frequency and nature of full task force meetings and the number of subgroups must be determined. Ground rules for communicating must be established, along with norms for decision making and conflict resolution.

Managing Subsequent Meetings and Subgroups

In running a task force, especially when several subgroups are formed, the leader should hold full task force meetings often enough to keep all members informed of the group's progress. Unless a task force is small, subgroups are essential. The leader must not be aligned too closely with one position or subgroup. A work plan should be developed that includes realistic interim project deadlines. The task force and subgroups should be held to these deadlines. The leader plays a key role in coaching subgroups and the task force to meet its deadlines.

The leader also must be sensitive to the conflicting loyalties sometimes created by belonging to a task force. One of the leader's most important roles is to communicate information to both task force members and the rest of the organization in a timely and regular fashion. The leader should solicit feedback from other key organizational representatives during the course of the task force's work.

Completing the Task Force's Report

In bringing a project to completion, the task force should prepare a written report for the commissioning administrators that summarizes the findings and recommendations. Drafts of this report should be shared with the full task force prior to presentation. To identify any overlooked or sensitive information and reduce defensive reactions, it is especially important that the task force leader personally brief key administrators prior to presenting the report. This gives administrators a chance to read and respond to the report before making recommendations. The leader should consider involving a few task force members in the administrative presentation.

Patient Care Conferences

Patient-related conferences are held to address the needs of individual patients or patient populations. The purpose of the conference determines the composition of the group. Patient-focused meetings are usually multidisciplinary and used for case management to discuss specific patient care problems. For example, a multidisciplinary team may form to discuss the failure of a rehabilitation regimen to help a home care patient and to develop new plans for intervention.

Often nurses also are involved in activities associated with improving the quality of care for various patient groups and their families. For example, a nurse manager might organize meetings with primary care physicians and other managers to discuss how to improve discharge planning, to explore strategies to reduce the length of inpatient stays, or to improve coordination with outpatient clinics.

The team leader of a patient care conference often may not be a manager with line responsibility to supervise, evaluate, or hire employees. The team leader is, however, a coach, teacher, and facilitator. Thus the team leader needs to have excellent leadership skills. The task of a team leader varies according to the task and the skill level of the team members. Highly skilled registered nurses, for example, would not require, nor appreciate, a team leader who tries to micromanage their work, whereas less-experienced, technically trained individuals require more coaching and support (Barter, 2002).

Nurses may be members of teams as well as leaders. Understanding how groups and teams function (or do not) is essential to contribute to the organization, be successful in your position, and to garner satisfaction from your work.

What You Know Now

- A group is an aggregate of individuals who interact and mutually influence each other.
- Groups may be classified as real or task, formal or informal, permanent or temporary.
- A team is a group of individuals with complementary skills, a common purpose and performance goals, and a set of methods for which they hold themselves accountable.
- Groups have an impact on cohesiveness and productivity, as well as individual development and growth.
- A group's norms and roles directly influence the productivity and satisfaction of group members and their ability to develop and grow.
- Groups come together, build cohesiveness, complete their task, and disband or reform.
- Leading teams requires good communication and conflict resolution skills as well as the ability to plan, organize, facilitate, and evaluate group performance.
- Managing meetings involves preparing thoroughly, facilitating participation, and completing the group's work.

Tools for Building and Managing Teams

1. Notice how groups around you function. Use the best ideas with your own groups.
2. Watch effective leaders. Identify skills you could incorporate into your own leadership repertoire.
3. Review the problem behaviors of team members discussed in Table 11-1 and adopt solutions as appropriate.
4. Recognize that you can develop good team leadership skills. Practice those discussed in the chapter.
5. At the next opportunity be prepared to follow the directions for leading meetings.
6. Make a development plan to enhance your leadership skills.

Questions to Challenge You

1. Identify the groups that include you in your work or school. How are they different? Similar? Explain.
2. Describe an example of effective group leadership and an example of poor leadership.
3. Evaluate your own leadership performance. How could you improve?
4. Have you been involved in team building at work or school? Was it effective? Explain.
5. What roles do you usually play in a group meeting (or class)? What role would you like to play? Describe it.

Explore MediaLink 🌐

Additional interactive resources for this chapter can be found on the Website at http://www.prenhall.com/sullivan. Click on Chapter 11 to select activities for this chapter.

- Video Overview
- NCLEX® Review Questions
- Critical Thinking Activities
- Current Events
- Nursing Leadership and Management in Action
- MediaLinks

References

Barter, M. (2002). Follow the team leader. *Nursing Management, 33*(10), 54–57.

Carroll, T. L. (2005). Leadership skills and attributes of women and nurse executives: Challenges for the 21st century. *Nursing Administration Quarterly, 29*(2), 146–153.

Homans, G. (1950). *The human group.* New York: Harcourt Brace Jovanovich.

Homans, G. (1961). *Social behavior: Its elementary forms.* New York: Harcourt Brace.

Kerfoot, K. (2004). Leaders and windshields: The art of deflecting essential information. *Dermatology Nursing, 16*(6), 545–546.

Lavoie-Tremblay, M. (2004). Creating a healthy workplace: A participatory organizational intervention. *Journal of Nursing Administration, 34*(10), 469–474.

McNally, K., & Lukens, R. (2006). Leadership development: An external-internal coaching partnership. *Journal of Nursing Administration, 36*(3), 155–161.

Steiner, I. D. (1972). *Group process and productivity.* New York: Academic Press.

Steiner, I. D. (1976). Task-performing groups. In J. W. Thibaut, J. T. Spence, & R. C. Carson (Eds.), *Contemporary topics in social psychology* (pp. 94–108). Morristown, NJ: General Learning Press.

Sullivan, E. J. (2004). *Becoming influential: A guide for nurses.* Upper Saddle River, NJ: Prentice Hall.

Thompson, J. D. (1967). *Organizations in action.* New York: McGraw-Hill.

Handling Conflict

Learning Outcomes

After completing this chapter, you will be able to:

1. Describe why conflict can be positive or negative.
2. Discuss how conflict can help generate change.
3. Describe the components of conflict.
4. Identify different approaches that can be used to manage conflict.
5. Explain how to manage conflict.
6. Discuss how to handle bullying.

MediaLink

www.prenhall.com/sullivan

See the Companion Website for chapter-specific resources at
www.prenhall.com/sullivan.

Key Terms

Accommodating *p170*

Avoiding *p170*

Collaboration *p170*

Competing *p170*

Competitive conflict *p163*

Compromise *p170*

Conflict *p163*

Confrontation *p168*

Consensus *p168*

Disruptive conflict *p163*

Felt conflict *p166*

Forcing *p170*

Integrative decision making *p168*

Lose-lose strategy *p168*

Negotiation *p169*

Perceived conflict *p166*

Resistance *p170*

Resolution *p166*

Smoothing *p170*

Suppression *p166*

Win-lose strategy *p168*

Win-win strategy *p168*

Withdrawal *p170*

Conflict

A manager's communication often centers around conflict. In fact, nurse managers spend approximately 20 percent of their time dealing with conflict (McElhaney, 1996) and report that managing conflict is one of their top priorities (Cauldron, 2000). Conflict is a natural, inevitable condition in organizations, and it is often a prerequisite to change in people and organizations.

Conflict is defined as the consequence of real or perceived differences in mutually exclusive goals, values, ideas, attitudes, beliefs, feelings, or actions (a) within one individual (*intrapersonal conflict*), (b) between two or more individuals (*interpersonal conflict*), (c) within one group (*intragroup conflict*), or (d) between two or more groups (*intergroup conflict*). Conflict is dynamic. It can be positive or negative, healthy or dysfunctional.

A certain amount of conflict is beneficial to an organization. It can provide heightened sensitivity to an issue, further piquing the interest and curiosity of others. Conflict also can increase creativity by acting as a stimulus for developing new ideas or identifying methods for solving problems. Disagreements can help all parties become more aware of the tradeoffs, especially costs versus benefits, of a particular service or technique.

Conflict also helps people recognize legitimate differences within the organization or profession and serves as a powerful motivator to improve performance and effectiveness, as well as satisfaction. For example, during intergroup conflict, individual groups become more cohesive and task oriented, whereas communication between groups diminishes.

Aggressive behavior can occur (Briles, 2005). Groups placed in "win-lose" competition have the tendency to increase the in-group versus out-group bias between them. Scapegoating may occur, with each group viewing the other as an enemy. This may make it difficult for the groups to work together in the future. Finally, bullying requires specific intervention discussed later in the chapter.

Conflict may be covert and inappropriate. Anger may be displaced to innocent bystanders. Others may repress their frustration or anger, which may surface later in behavior (e.g., increased errors, accidents, or illness). Other inappropriate responses to conflict are retaliation, projection, rationalization, attention-seeking behaviors, repression, or escape tactics, such as resignation or flight into fantasy.

Conflict between the expectations of one generational cohort and another may disrupt group functioning. For example, generation X is more team oriented than their older counterparts, baby boomers. In addition, they expect to be treated as professionals, not technicians (Swearingen & Liberman, 2004). Conflict between the expectations of a baby boomer manager and a generation X staff could occur.

Competition, such as that which occurs between health care organizations, also is a frequent source of conflict. Competition occurs when two or more groups attempt the same goals and only one group can attain those goals. Filley (1975) defines **competitive conflict** as a victory for one side and a loss for the other side. The process by which the conflict is resolved is determined by a set of rules. The goals of each side are mutually incompatible, but the emphasis is on winning, not the defeat or reduction of the opponent. When one side has clearly won, competition is terminated.

Disruptive conflict, in contrast, does not follow any mutually acceptable set of rules and does not emphasize winning. The parties involved are engaged in activities to reduce, defeat, or eliminate the opponent. This type of conflict takes place in an environment charged with fear, anger, and stress. For example, a resident on night call may contribute to disruptive behavior by refusing to answer pages, turning off the beeper, or belittling nurses for calling with "minor" problems. Nurses often react to this type of behavior with their own disruptive behavior: frequent, "by the book," middle-of-the-night phone calls to get back at the offending resident. An example of a more subtle disruptive behavior would be the failure to extend minor work-saving courtesies to an unpopular resident. Disruptive conflict can, in unusual circumstances, result in irrational, upsetting, or even violent behavior.

Unresolved conflict can result in passive-aggressive behavior, chronic conflicts, frequent staff vacancies, or authoritarian management (Brandt, 2001). Afraid of confrontation, a manager may be unwilling to tackle a poor worker's behavior. This manager's incompetence harms both the employee, who fails to improve, and can result in dissatisfied employees and staff shortages (Sanford, 2004).

Conflict Process Model

Several authors have proposed models for examining conflict (Pondy, 1967; Filley, 1975; Thomas, 1976). All follow a generalized format for examining conflict. These models provide a framework that helps explain how and why conflict occurs and, ultimately, how one can minimize conflict or resolve it with the least amount of negative aftermath.

Conflict and its resolution develop according to a specific process (see **Figure 12–1**). This process begins with certain preexisting conditions (antecedent conditions). The parties are influenced by their feelings or perceptions about the situation (perceived or felt conflict), which initiates behavior, and conflict is exhibited. The conflict is either resolved or suppressed and the outcome results in new attitudes and feelings between the parties.

ANTECEDENT CONDITIONS

Antecedent conditions are associated with increases in conflict. Antecedent conditions propel a situation toward conflict; they may or may not be the cause. In nursing, antecedent conditions include incompatible goals, differences in values and beliefs, task interdependencies (especially asymmetric dependencies, in which one party is dependent on the other but not vice versa), unclear or ambiguous roles, competition for scarce resources, differentiation or distancing mechanisms, and unifying mechanisms.

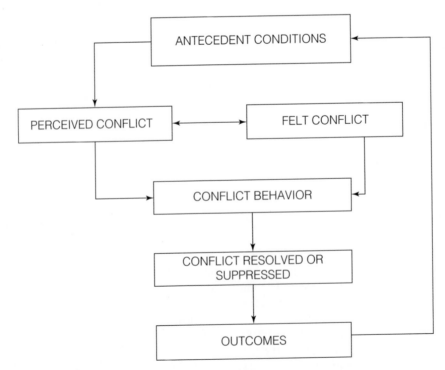

Figure 12-1 ● The conflict process.

Incompatible Goals

The most important antecedent condition to conflict is incompatible goals. As discussed in Chapter 2, goals are desired results toward which behavior is directed. Even though the common goal in health care organizations is to give quality patient care in a cost-effective manner, conflict in achieving these goals is inevitable because individuals often view this from different perspectives. In addition, individuals and organizations have multiple goals that change over time. A health care organization may have specific goals to achieve the best possible care for patients and control costs to stay within budget and, at the same time, to provide intrinsically satisfying jobs for its employees. These multiple goals will frequently conflict with each other, so they will have to be prioritized. Priority setting can be one of the most difficult but important activities a health care manager must face. Goals are important because they become the basis for allocating resources and thus become an important source (antecedent) of conflict in the organization.

Similarly, individuals themselves have multiple goals, and those goals may also conflict. Individuals allocate scarce resources, such as their time, on the basis of priority and, therefore, might achieve one goal at the expense of others. The inability to attain multiple (and mutually incompatible) goals—whether those goals are personal or organizational—can cause conflict.

An example of goal conflict in nursing is the dichotomy between health care providers and third-party payers. This issue can best be described as a conflict between groups with differing goals. Health care providers want to maximize the quality of care, whereas payers are concerned with minimizing health care costs.

Role Conflicts

Roles are defined as other people's expectations regarding behavior and attitudes. Roles become unclear when one or more parties have related responsibilities that are ambiguous or overlapping. A manager might experience conflict between his or her responsibilities as an administrator and responsibilities as a staff member. Similarly, unclear or overlapping job descriptions or assignments may lead to conflict. For example, there could be conflict over such mundane issues as who has responsibility to deliver a patient to the radiology department—the nurse or the transport staff?

Task interdependence is another potential source of conflict. Nursing and housekeeping, for example, are interdependent. Housekeeping cannot completely clean a room until nursing has discharged the patient.

Other examples of interdependence are the relationships among shifts and those between physicians and nurses. Interdependent relationships have the potential to initiate conflict.

Structural Conflict

One conflict commonly seen in the health care environment is structural conflict. Structured relationships (superior to subordinate, peer to peer) provoke conflict because of poor communication, competition for resources, opposing interests, or a lack of shared perceptions or attitudes. A nurse manager (superior) stimulates conflict with a staff member (subordinate) by reprimanding the staff member for some inappropriate act. If the nurse manager is unable to communicate to the staff member why the act was unacceptable, opposing interests develop, and the conflict is sustained. In this situation, positional power is often imposed. Positional power is the authority inherent in a certain position—for example, the nurse administrator has greater positional power than a nurse manager.

Competition for Resources

Competition for scarce resources can be internal (among different units in the organization) or external (among different organizations). Internally, competition for resources may involve assigning staff from one unit to another or purchasing high-technology equipment when another unit is desperate for staff.

Externally, health care organizations compete for finite external resources (e.g., managed-care contracts). Organizations are using a variety of means, such as developing new services and advertising, to try to capture the market in health care. With increased numbers of nurse practitioners, competition between nurses and physicians for patients also has increased.

Values and Beliefs

Differences in values and beliefs frequently contribute to conflict in health care organizations. Values and beliefs result from the individual's socialization experience. Conflicts between physicians and nurses, between nurses and administrators, or even between nurses with associate degrees versus those with baccalaureate degrees, often occur because of differences in values, beliefs, and experiences.

Distancing mechanisms or differentiation serve to divide a group's members into small, distinct groups, thus increasing the chance for conflict. This tends to lead to a "we–they" distinction. One of the more frequently seen examples is distancing between physicians and

MediaLink Recognizing Role Conflicts

nurses. Opposition between intensive care nurses and nurses on medical floors, night versus day shifts, and unlicensed versus licensed personnel also are examples. Differentiation among subunits also occurs and is due to differences in structure. The administrative unit may be bureaucratic, the nursing unit structured on a more professional basis, and staff physicians on an even different structure. Nonstaff physicians may be relatively independent of the health care organization.

Unifying mechanisms occur when greater intimacy develops or when unity is sought. All nurses might be expected to reach consensus over an issue, but they might experience internal conflict if they are forced to accept a group position even though individually they may not be wholly committed to the decision. A classic example of a unifying mechanism is the relationship between husband and wife. As intimacy increases, issues arise that would not normally cause conflict in a casual relationship but do affect closer relationships. A nurse manager's friendship with a staff member also may lead to this type of conflict.

PERCEIVED AND FELT CONFLICT

Perceived and felt conflict account for the conflict that may occur when the parties involved view situations or issues from differing perspectives, when they misunderstand each other's position, or when positions are based on limited knowledge. **Perceived conflict** refers to each party's perception of the other's position. **Felt conflict** refers to the negative feelings between two or more parties. It is characterized by mistrust, hostility, and fear.

To demonstrate how this process works, consider this situation. A nurse manager and a surgeon have worked together for years. They have mutual respect for each other's ability and skills, and they communicate frequently. When their subordinates clash, they are left with conflicting accounts of a situation, in which the only agreed-upon fact is that a patient received less-than-appropriate care. Now consider the same scenario if the nurse and doctor have never dealt with each other or if one feels that the other will not approach the problem constructively.

In the first situation (perceived conflict), their positive regard for each other's abilities makes the nurse and physician believe they can constructively solve the conflict. The nurse does not feel the physician will try to dominate, and the physician respects the nurse manager's managerial ability. With these preexisting attitudes, the physician and nurse can remain neutral while helping their subordinates solve the conflict. If

the nurse and physician were experiencing felt conflict, on the other hand, they might approach the situation differently. Each might assume the other will defend her or his subordinates at all costs and communication will be inhibited. The conflict is resolved by domination of the stronger person, either in personality or position. One wins; the other loses.

CONFLICT BEHAVIORS

Conflict behavior results from the parties' perceived or felt conflict. Behaviors may be overt or covert. Overt behavior may take the form of aggression, competition, debate, or problem solving. Covert behavior may be expressed by a variety of indirect tactics, such as scapegoating, avoidance, or apathy.

CONFLICT RESOLVED OR SUPPRESSED

In the next stage of the process conflict is resolved or suppressed. **Resolution** occurs when a mutually agreed-upon solution is arrived at and both parties commit themselves to carrying out the agreement. **Suppression** occurs when one person or group defeats the other. Only the dominant side is committed to the agreement, and the loser may or may not carry out the agreement.

OUTCOMES

The outcome affects how conflict will be addressed by the parties in the future. The optimal solution is to manage the issues in a way that will lead to a solution wherein both parties see themselves as winners and the problem is solved. This leaves a positive aftermath that will affect future relations and influence feelings and attitudes. In the example of conflict between the nurse manager and the physician, consider the difference in the aftermath and how future issues would be approached if both parties felt positive about the outcome, as compared to future interactions if one or both parties felt they had lost.

Managing Conflict

Managing conflict is an important part of the nurse manager's job. They often are involved in conflict management on several different levels. They may be participants in the conflict as individuals, supervisors, or representatives of a unit. In fact, they must often initiate conflict by confronting staff, individually or collectively, when a problem develops. They also may serve as mediators or judges to conflicting parties. There could be a conflict within the unit, between parties from different units, or between internal and external parties (for example, a nursing instructor from the university may have a conflict with staff on a particular unit).

Everyone must be realistic regarding the outcome. Often those inexperienced in conflict negotiation expect unrealistic outcomes. When two or more parties hold mutually exclusive ideas, attitudes, feelings, or goals, it is extremely difficult, without the commitment and willingness of all concerned, to arrive at an agreeable solution that meets the needs of both.

Conflict management begins with a decision regarding if and when to intervene. Failure to intervene can allow the conflict to get out of hand, whereas early intervention may be detrimental to those involved, causing them to lose confidence in themselves and reduce risk-taking behavior in the future. Some conflicts are so minor, particularly if they are between only two people, that they do not require intervention and would be better handled by the two people involved. Allowing them to resolve their conflict might provide a developmental experience and improve their abilities to resolve conflict in the future. When the conflict might result in considerable harm, however, the nurse manager must intervene.

Sometimes it is best to postpone intervention purposely to allow the conflict to escalate, because increased intensity can motivate participants to seek resolution. You could escalate the conflict even further by exposing participants to each other more frequently without the presence of others and without an easy means of escape. Participants are then forced to face the conflict between them. Giving participants a shared task or shared goals not directly related to the conflict may help them understand each other better and increase their chances to resolve their conflicts by themselves. Using such a method is useful only if the conflict is not of high intensity, if the participants are not highly anxious about it, and if the manager believes that the conflict will not decrease the efficiency of the department in the meantime.

If you decide to intervene in a conflict between two or more parties, you can apply mediation techniques, deciding when, where, and how the intervention should take place. Routine problems can be handled in either the superior's or subordinate's office, but serious confrontations should take place in a neutral location unless the parties involved are of unequal power. In this case, the setting should favor the disadvantaged participant, thereby equalizing their power.

The place should be one where distractions will not interfere and adequate time is available. Because conflict management takes time, the manager must be prepared to allow sufficient time for all parties to explain their points of view and arrive at a mutually agreeable solution. A quick solution that inexperienced managers often resort to is to impose positional power, making a premature decision. This results in a win-lose outcome, which leads to feelings of elation and eventual complacency for the winners and loss of morale for the losers.

The following are basic rules on how to mediate a conflict between two or more parties:

1. Protect each party's self-respect. Deal with a conflict of issues, not personalities.
2. Do not put blame or responsibility for the problem on the participants. The participants are responsible for developing a solution to the problem.
3. Allow open and complete discussion of the problem from each participant.
4. Maintain equity in the frequency and duration of each party's presentation. A person of higher status tends to speak more frequently and longer than a person of lower status. If this occurs, the mediator should intervene and ask the person of lower status for response and opinion.
5. Encourage full expression of positive and negative feelings in an accepting atmosphere. The novice mediator tends to discourage expressions of disagreement.
6. Make sure both parties listen actively to each other's words. One way to do this is to ask one person to summarize the comments of the other prior to stating her or his own.
7. Identify key themes in the discussion, and restate these at frequent intervals.
8. Encourage the parties to provide frequent feedback to each other's comments; each must truly understand the other's position.
9. Help the participants develop alternative solutions, select a mutually agreeable one, and develop a plan to carry it out. All parties must agree to the solution for successful resolution to occur.
10. At an agreed-upon interval, follow up on the progress of the plan.
11. Give positive feedback to participants regarding their cooperation in solving the conflict.

Conflict management is a difficult process, consuming both time and energy. Management and staff must be concerned and committed to resolving conflict by being willing to listen to others' positions and to find agreeable solutions.

FILLEY'S STRATEGIES

Filley (1975) identified three basic strategies for dealing with conflict according to the outcome: win-lose, lose-lose, and win-win. In the **win-lose strategy**, one party exerts dominance, usually by power of authority, and the other party submits and loses. Forcing, competing, and negotiation are techniques likely to lead to win-lose competition. Majority rule is another example of the win-lose outcome, especially within groups. It may be a satisfactory method of resolving conflict, however, if various factions vote differently on different issues and the group functions over time so that members win some and lose some. Win-lose outcomes often occur between groups. Frequent losing, however, can lead to the loss of cohesiveness within groups and diminish the authority of the group leader.

In the **lose-lose strategy**, neither side wins. The settlement reached is unsatisfactory to both sides. Avoiding, withdrawing, smoothing, and compromising may lead to lose-lose outcomes. One compromising strategy is to use a bribe to influence another's cooperation in doing something he or she dislikes. For example, the nurse manager may promise a future raise in an attempt to coerce a staff member to work an extra weekend. Using a third party as arbitrator can lead to a lose-lose outcome. Because an outsider may want to give something to each side, neither gets exactly what he or she desires, resulting in a lose-lose outcome. This is a common strategy in arbitration of labor-management disputes. Another strategy that may result in a lose-lose or win-lose outcome is resorting to rules. The outcome is determined by whatever the rules say, and confrontation is avoided.

The win-lose and lose-lose methods share some common characteristics:

1. The conflict is person-centered (we–they) rather than problem-centered. This is likely to occur when two cohesive groups that do not share common values or goals are in conflict.
2. Parties direct their energy toward total victory for themselves and total defeat for the other. This can cause long-term problems for the organization.
3. Each sees the issue from her or his own point of view rather than as a problem in need of a solution.
4. The emphasis is on outcomes rather than definition of goals, values, or objectives.
5. Conflicts are personalized.
6. Conflict-resolving activities are not differentiated from other group processes.
7. There is a short-run view of the conflict; the goal is to settle the immediate problem rather than resolve differences.

Win-win strategies focus on goals and attempt to meet the needs of both parties. Two specific win-win strategies are consensus and integrative decision making. **Consensus** involves attention to the facts and to the position of the other parties and avoidance of trading, voting, or averaging, where everyone loses something. The consensus decision is often superior to even the best individual one. This technique is most useful in a group setting because it is sensitive to the negative characteristics of win-lose and lose-lose outcomes. True consensus occurs when the problem is fully explored, the needs and goals of the involved parties are understood, and a solution that meets these needs is agreed upon.

Integrative decision making focuses on the means of solving a problem rather than the ends. They are most useful when the needs of the parties are polarized. Integrative decision making is a constructive process in which the parties jointly identify the problem and their needs. They explore a number of alternative solutions and come to consensus on a solution. The focus of this group activity is to solve the problem, not to force, dominate, suppress, or compromise. The group works toward a common goal in an atmosphere that encourages the free exchange of ideas and feelings. Using integrative decision-making methods, the parties jointly identify the value needs of each, conduct an exhaustive search for alternatives that could meet the needs of each, and then select the best alternative. Like the consensus methods, integrative decision making focuses on defeating the problem, not each other.

OTHER STRATEGIES

Several other strategies can be used to manage conflict. Some tend to be more successful than others depending on the situation, those involved, and the organization.

Confrontation is considered the most effective means for resolving conflicts. This is a problem-oriented technique in which the conflict is brought out into the open and attempts are made to resolve it through knowledge and reason. The goal of this technique is to achieve win-win solutions. Facts should be used to identify the problem. The desired outcome should be explicit. "This is the third time this week that you have not been here for report. According to hospital policy, you are expected to be changed, scrubbed, and ready for report in the lounge at 7:00 A.M." is an example.

Confrontation is most effective when delivered in private as soon as possible after the incident occurs. Employee respect and manager credibility are two important considerations when a situation warrants confrontation. A more immediate confrontation also helps both the employee and manager sort out pertinent facts. In an emotionally charged situation, however, it may be best for the parties to wait. Regardless of timing, the message is usually more effective if the manager listens and is empathetic.

Many other techniques besides intervention can be used to resolve conflict and are consistent with the problem-solving approach. Some of these include changing or clarifying goals, making appeals to the hierarchy, providing cooling-off periods, using intermediaries, and dividing the resources so each party can partially achieve its goals.

See how one nurse manager handled a conflict between two members of her staff in Case Study 12-1.

Negotiation involves give-and-take on various issues among the parties. Its purpose is to achieve agreement even though consensus will never be reached. Therefore, the best solution is not often achieved. Negotiation often becomes a structured, formal procedure, as in collective bargaining (see Chapter 21). However, negotiation skills are important in arriving at an agreeable solution between any two parties. Staff learn to negotiate schedules, advanced practice nurses negotiate with third-party payers for reimbursement, insurance companies negotiate with vendors and hospitals for discounts, and clinic managers negotiate employment contracts with physicians. Although negotiation involves adept communication skills, its usefulness revolves around issues of conflict. Without differences in opinion, there would be no need for negotiation.

CASE STUDY 12-1   Conflict Management

Mai Tran is the nurse manager of a 20-bed medical-surgical unit in a large university hospital. Her nursing staff is diverse in experience and educational background. Working in a teaching hospital, Mai believes that nurses should be open to new methods and work processes, with an emphasis on evidenced-based practice.

Ken Robertson, RN, has worked for 2 years on the unit and is in his final semester of a master's program focusing on geriatric care. Eileen Holcomb, RN, has worked on the same unit for the past 28 years and was a graduate of the hospital's former diploma program. Ken recently completed a clinical rotation in dermatology and has worked with the skin care team at the hospital to develop new protocols for preventing skin breakdown. During a recent staff meeting, Ken presents the new protocols to the staff. Eileen makes several comments during the presentation that simply getting patients out of bed and making sure they have adequate nutrition is easier and less time consuming than the new protocol. "All these new protocols are just a way to justify all those credentials behind a name," Eileen says, gathering a chorus of chuckles from some of the older nurses on the staff. Ken glares at Eileen and responds, "As nurses become educated we need to reflect a professional practice." Mai notices that several staff members are uncomfortable as the meeting ends.

Ken and Eileen continue to exchange sarcastic comments and glares over the next two shifts. The obvious disagreement is affecting their coworkers and gossiping is decreasing productivity on the unit. Mai

schedules individual meetings with Ken and Eileen to discuss their perspective. After reviewing the situation and determining that the issue is simply one of personality conflict, Mai brings Ken and Eileen together for a meeting in her office. Mai reviews the facts of the situation with them and shares her opinion that both have acted inappropriately and that their actions have affected not only their work, but that of the unit as a whole. She informs Ken and Eileen that they must act in a professional and respectful manner with each other or disciplinary action will be taken. She encourages them to work out any future problems in a cooperative manner.

Manager's Checklist

The nurse manager is responsible to:

- Understand how to manage conflict among staff members in a timely manner
- Understand generational perceptions and how they impact group dynamics
- Understand when disciplinary action is necessary
- Inform the human resource department of a potential personnel problem and the proposed solution
- Meet with staff to assist them in resolving conflict
- Determine whether all staff should be educated on respect in the workplace
- Document interventions and outcomes as appropriate

Levenstein (1984) lists ten commandments for negotiators:

1. Clarify the common purpose.
2. Keep the discussion relevant.
3. Get agreement on terminology.
4. Avoid abstract principles; concentrate on the facts.
5. Look for potential tradeoffs.
6. Listen.
7. Avoid debating tactics; use persuasive tactics.
8. Keep in mind the personal element.
9. Use logic logically.
10. Look for solutions that satisfy the other person's real interests.

Collaboration implies mutual attention to the problem, in which the talents of all parties are used. In collaboration, the focus is on solving the problem, not defeating the opponent. The goal is to satisfy both parties' concerns. Collaboration is useful in situations in which the goals of both parties are too important to be compromised.

Compromise is used to divide the rewards between both parties. Neither gets what she or he wants. Compromise can serve as a backup to resolve conflict when collaboration is ineffective. It is sometimes the only choice when opponents of equal power are in conflict over two or more mutually exclusive goals. Compromising also is expedient when a solution is needed rapidly.

Competing is an all-out effort to win, regardless of the cost. Competing may be needed in situations involving unpopular or critical decisions. Competing also is used in situations in which time does not allow for more cooperative techniques.

Accommodating is an unassertive, cooperative tactic used when individuals neglect their own concerns in favor of others' concerns. Accommodating frequently is used to preserve harmony when one person has a vested interest in an issue that is unimportant to the other party.

In situations where conflict is discouraged, suppression is often used. Suppression could even include the elimination of one of the conflicting parties through transfer or termination. Other, less effective techniques for managing conflict include withdrawing, smoothing, and forcing, although each mode of response is useful in given situations.

In **avoiding**, the participants never acknowledge that a conflict exists. Avoidance is the conflict resolution technique often used in highly cohesive groups. The group avoids disagreement because they do not want to do anything that may interfere with the good feelings they have for each other.

Withdrawal from the conflict simply removes at least one party, thereby making it impossible to resolve the situation. The issue remains unresolved, and feelings about the issue may resurface inappropriately. If the conflict escalates into a dangerous situation, avoiding and withdrawing are appropriate strategies.

Smoothing is accomplished by complimenting one's opponent, downplaying differences, and focusing on minor areas of agreement, as though little disagreement existed. Smoothing may be appropriate in dealing with minor problems, but in response to major problems, it produces the same results as withdrawing.

Forcing is a method that yields an immediate end to the conflict but leaves the cause of the conflict unresolved. A superior can resort to issuing orders, but the subordinate will lack commitment to the demanded action. Forcing may be appropriate in life-or-death situations but is otherwise inappropriate. Negotiation and confrontation are generally more effective modes of responding to conflict (Hader, 2007).

Resistance can be positive or negative. It may mean a resistance to change or disobedience, or it may be an effective approach to handling power differences, especially verbal abuse (Garon, 2006).

Bullying: A Unique Case of Conflict

Bullying in the workplace increases staff dissatisfaction, turnover, and litigation, and damages the organization's reputation and 70 percent leave the workplace (Dempster, 2006). Both students and practicing nurses report cases of workplace bullying (Stevenson, Randle, & Grayling, 2006). Such workplace aggression is similar to domestic violence in that it involves abuse of power (DelBel, 2003). Verbal abuse, such as publicly chastising or shaming, physical threats, intimidation, or sexual advances are just a few ways that bullies attempt to coerce their victims. To confront bullies, several strategies are suggested (Mladineo, 2006).

1. Don't blame yourself. Bullies tend to target those they feel threaten them or their status, and they use their superior position to try to make their victims blame themselves.
2. Learn how to bully-proof yourself. Know your rights and prepare answers in advance.

3. Confront the bully. Sometimes simply telling the bully that you find the behavior offensive and unacceptable will stop the behavior, especially if others you know are allies are present.
4. Avoid the bully if possible.
5. Keep a record. Detail each event with date, time, location, any others present, and what happened. This is invaluable should the situation escalate.

The manager has a special duty to protect staff from bullying by others, to each other, or to students. Take every report of verbal aggression seriously and use the appropriate conflict strategy to resolve it. Left on its own, bullying is likely to continue and escalate.

Managing conflict is an essential skill for the manager and, indeed, all nurses. Avoiding conflict or allowing it to fester and remain unresolved undermines the manager's effectiveness and can result in dissatisfied staff and nursing shortages. Resolving conflict, on the other hand, can lead to better outcomes both with the immediate situation and encourage the manager to resolve conflict in the future.

What You Know Now

- Conflict is a dynamic process, the consequence of real or perceived differences between individuals or groups.
- Conflict can be positive and the first step in initiating change or it may be negative and disruptive.
- Antecedent conditions that cause conflict include incompatible goals, role conflicts, structural conflict, competition for scarce resources, and differences in values and beliefs.
- A number of strategies exist to handle conflict; choosing the best one to use is based on the situation and the people involved.
- Learning to manage conflict, including bullying, is a requirement for all nurses and managers.

Tools for Handling Conflict

1. Evaluate conflict situations to decide if and when to intervene.
2. Understand the antecedent conditions for the conflict and the positions of those involved.
3. Enlist others to help solve conflicts.
4. Select a conflict management strategy appropriate to the situation.
5. Practice the conflict management strategies discussed in the chapter and evaluate the outcomes.
6. Identify bullying behavior promptly and intervene as appropriate.

Questions to Challenge You

1. How are conflicts handled at work or school? Are leaders good conflict managers? Use an example to explain.
2. Select a situation in which you have been involved in conflict. How did you handle your part in it? How about others involved? Did it turn out well? Explain.
3. What is the most difficult part of handling conflicts for you? Understanding others' positions? Devising a successful solution? Enlisting others' help? Encouraging participants to agree to a solution?
4. Study the chapter for help in improving your areas of weakness. Evaluate your performance.
5. Have you ever experienced bullying or seen others bullied? How did you or they handle it?

Explore MediaLink 🌐

Additional interactive resources for this chapter can be found on the Website at http://www.prenhall.com/sullivan. Click on Chapter 12 to select activities for this chapter.

- Video Overview
- NCLEX® Review Questions
- Critical Thinking Activities
- Current Events
- Nursing Leadership and Management in Action
- MediaLinks

References

Brandt, M. A. (2001). How to make conflict work for you. *Nursing Management, 32* (11), 32–35.

Briles, J. (2005). Zapping conflict builds better teams. *Nursing 2005, 35*(11), 32.

Cauldron, S. (2000). Keeping team conflict alive. *Public Management, 82*(2), 5–9.

DelBel, J. C. (2003). De-escalating workplace aggression. *Nursing Management, 34*(9), 30–34.

Dempster, M. (2006). Turning blind eye to bullies hurts business. Business Edge. Retrieved December 2007 at http://www.businessedge.ca/article.cfm/newsID/9505.cfm

Filley, A. C. (1975). *Interpersonal conflict resolution.* Glenview, IL: Scott, Foresman.

Garon, M. (2006). The positive face of resistance: Nurses relate their stories. *Journal of Nursing Administration, 36*(5), 249–258.

Hader, R. (2007). The power of saying no. *Nursing Management, 38*(1), 6.

Levenstein, A. (1984). Negotiation vs. confrontation. *Nursing Management, 15*(1), 52– 53.

McElhaney, R. (1996). Conflict management in nursing administration. *Nursing Management, 27*(3), 49–50.

Mladineo, C. (2006). How to survive a bully. *American Nurse Today, 1*(11), 44–45.

Pondy, L. R. (1967). Organizational conflict: Concepts and models. *Administrative Science Quarterly, 12,* 296–320.

Sanford, K. (2004). Become confident in confrontation. *Nursing Management, 35*(7), 14.

Stevenson, K., Randle, J., & Grayling, I. (2006). Inter-group conflict in health care: UK students' experiences of bullying and the need for organizational solutions. *Online Journal of Issues in Nursing, 11*(42). Retrieved September 2007 from www.nursingworld.org/MainMenuCategories/ANAMarketplace/ANAPeriodicals/OJIN/TableofContents/Volume112006/Number2May31/tpc30_516077.aspx

Swearingen, S., & Liberman, A. (2004). Nursing generations: An expanded look at the emergence of conflict and its resolution. *Health Care Manager, 23*(1), 54–64.

Thomas, K. W. (1976). Conflict and conflict management. In M. D. Dunnette (Ed.), *The handbook of industrial and organizational psychology.* Chicago: Rand McNally.

Managing Time

Learning Outcomes

After completing this chapter, you will be able to:

1. Identify time wasters.
2. Identify goals.
3. Set priorities.
4. Group activities and minimize routine work.
5. Manage personal organization and self discipline.
6. Minimize time wasters.

MediaLink

www.prenhall.com/sullivan

See the Companion Website for chapter-specific resources at
www.prenhall.com/sullivan.

Key Terms

Delegation *p176*
Goal setting *p175*
Goals *p175*

Interruption log *p177*
Job enlargement *p174*
Time logs *p175*

Time waster *p174*
To-do list *p176*

Time management is a misnomer. No one manages time: What is managed is how time is used. In today's downsized health care organization the pressure to do more in less time has increased. **Job enlargement** occurs when a flatter organizational structure causes positions to be combined and results in managers having more employees to supervise. In a horizontal organization structure few formal channels for communication exist so the time needed to communicate with staff increases (Arnold & Pulich, 2004).

Time can be used proactively or reactively (Carrick, Carrick, & Yurkow, 2007). If you focus your energy on people and events over which you have some direct or indirect control, you are using a proactive approach. If, on the other hand, the majority of your time is spent on what concerns you most about other people and events, you are focusing on those people and events that trouble you but your efforts will be less apt to be effective. For example, you can set and follow your goals and priorities or you can spend your time worrying, blaming, or making excuses about what you do not accomplish.

This chapter is designed to help you be proactive in targeting your use of time.

Time Wasters

Why do we waste time? It is one of our most valuable resources and yet everyone admits to wasting time. Box 13-1 answers this question by showing some of the constraints on an individual's ability to manage time effectively. These patterns of behavior must be understood and dealt with to be effective in managing time.

In addition to these patterns of behavior, certain time wasters prevent us from effectively managing time. A **time waster** is something that prevents a person from accomplishing the job or achieving the goal. Common time wasters include:

1. Interruptions, such as telephone calls and drop-in visitors
2. Meetings, both scheduled and unscheduled
3. Lack of clear-cut goals, objectives, and priorities

BOX 13-1　Why We Fail to Manage Time Effectively

- We do what we like to do before we do what we don't like to do.
- We do things we know how to do faster than things we do not know how to do.
- We do things that are easiest before things that are difficult.
- We do things that require a little time before things that require a lot of time.
- We do things for which resources are available.
- We do things that are scheduled (for example, meetings) before nonscheduled things.
- We sometimes do things that are planned before things that are unplanned.
- We respond to demands from others before demands from ourselves.
- We do things that are urgent before things that are important.
- We readily respond to crises and emergencies.

- We do interesting things before uninteresting things.
- We do things that advance our personal objectives or that are politically expedient.
- We wait until a deadline approaches before we really get moving.
- We do things that provide the most immediate closure.
- We respond on the basis of who wants it.
- We respond on the basis of the consequences to us of doing or not doing something.
- We tackle small jobs before large jobs.
- We work on things in the order of their arrival.
- We work on the basis of the squeaky-wheel principle (the squeaky wheel gets the grease).
- We work on the basis of consequences to the group.

4. Lack of daily and/or weekly plans
5. Lack of personal organization and self-discipline
6. Lack of knowledge about how one spends one's time
7. Failure to delegate, working on routine tasks
8. Ineffective communication
9. Waiting for others, not using transition time effectively
10. Inability to say no

TIME ANALYSIS

The first step is to analyze how time is being used. The second is to determine whether time use is appropriate to your role. You may find much of your time is taken up doing things that seem to be "busywork" rather than activities that contribute to a particular outcome. Job redesign places emphasis on ensuring that time is spent wisely and that the right individual is correctly assigned the responsibility for tasks.

Time logs, typically kept in intervals of 30 to 60 minutes, are useful in analyzing the actual time spent on various activities. These logs can be reviewed to determine which activities are essential to your job and which activities can be delegated to others or eliminated. Instead of a separate log, you can use your planner or appointment calendar to review patterns of time use.

THE MANAGER'S TIME

A significant difficulty in moving from a staff nurse position to a leadership position is the need to develop different time-management and organizational skills. In a staff nurse role, the registered nurse has little, if any, free or uncommitted time. Almost every minute of the shift is assigned to a task. For example, at 6:45 A.M., report is taken; at 7:00 A.M., insulin is administered; at 7:15 A.M., breakfast trays are distributed; from 8:00 A.M. to 10:30 A.M., morning care is administered; and so on. No planning is required, because every minute is taken. In contrast, when nurses move to a leadership position, they are responsible for defining how time will be spent. Learning to focus on setting goals, determining priorities, and evaluating time use is an important part of the analysis.

Setting Goals

Nurses are accustomed to setting both long- and short-range goals, although typically such goals are stated in terms of what patients will accomplish rather than what the nurse will achieve. A critical component of time management is establishing one's own goals and time frames.

Goals are specific statements of outcomes that are to be achieved. They provide direction and vision for actions as well as a timeline in which activities will be accomplished. Defining goals and time frames helps reduce stress by preventing the panic people often feel when confronted with multiple demands. Although time frames may not be as fast as the nurse manager would like (the tendency is to expect change yesterday), necessary actions have been identified.

Individual or organizational goals encourage thinking about the future and what might happen, what one wants to have happen, and what is likely to happen (Sullivan, 2004). **Goal setting** helps to relate current behavior, activities, or operations to the organization's or individual's long-range goals. Without this future orientation, activities may not lead to the outcomes that will help achieve the goals and meet the ideals of the individual or organization. The focus should be to develop measurable, realistic, and achievable goals.

It is useful to think of individual or personal goals in categories, such as:

- Department or unit
- Interpersonal (at work)
- Professional
- Financial
- Family and friends (outside of work)
- Vacation and travel
- Physical
- Lifestyle
- Community
- Spiritual

This partial listing is a guide to stimulate thinking about goals. Think about long-term goals, lifetime goals, and short-term goals. These should be divided into job-related goals and personal goals. Job-related goals may revolve around unit or departmental changes, whereas personal goals may include personal life and community involvement.

Short-term goals should be set for the next 6 to 12 months but need to be related to long-term goals. To manage time effectively, answer five major questions about these goals:

1. What specific objectives are to be achieved?
2. What specific activities are necessary to achieve these objectives?
3. How much time is required for each activity?
4. Which activities can be planned and scheduled for concurrent action, and which must be planned and scheduled sequentially?
5. Which activities can be delegated to staff?

Delegating tasks to others can be an efficient time-management tool. **Delegation** is the process by which responsibility and authority are transferred to another individual. It involves assigning tasks, determining expected results, and granting authority to the individual expected to accomplish these tasks. Delegation is perhaps the most difficult leadership skill for a nurse or a manager to acquire. Today, when more assistive personnel are being used to carry out the nurse's work and when manager's span of control has expanded, appropriate delegation skills are essential for success. Chapter 10 discusses delegation in detail.

DETERMINING PRIORITIES

To establish priorities, take into consideration both short- and long-term goals as well as the importance and urgency of each activity as shown in Table 13-1. Activities can be identified as:

- Urgent and important
- Important but not urgent
- Urgent but not important
- Busywork
- Wasted time

Activities that are both urgent and important must be completed. Activities that are important but not urgent may be those that make the difference between career progression or maintaining the status quo. Urgent but not important activities must be completed immediately but are not considered important or significant. Busywork and wasted time are self-explanatory.

DAILY PLANNING AND SCHEDULING

Once goals and priorities have been established, you can concentrate on scheduling activities. Prepare a **to-do list** each day, either after work hours the previous day or early before work on the same day. The list is typically planned by workday or workweek. If you have a combination of many responsibilities, a weekly to-do list may be more effective. Flexibility must be a major consideration in this plan; some time should remain uncommitted to allow you to deal with emergencies and crises that are sure to happen. The focus is not on activities and events, but rather on the outcomes that can be achieved in the time available.

A system to keep track of regularly scheduled meetings (staff meetings), regular events (annual or quarterly report due dates), and appointments is also necessary. This system should be used when establishing the to-do list; it should include both a calendar and files. The calendar might include information on the purpose of the meeting, who will be attending, and the time and place. Several commercial planning systems are available, including software packages for desktop or personal digital assistants (PDAs). Any such system includes a daily, weekly, or monthly calendar; a to-do section; a memo or note section; and an address component. An additional consideration is to have a calendar that is small enough to be taken to meetings or home. Files are maintained on the correspondence or reports related to the meeting. These files can be arranged by date so that they are readily retrievable when needed.

GROUPING ACTIVITIES AND MINIMIZING ROUTINE WORK

Work items that are similar in nature and require similar environmental surroundings and resources should be grouped within divisions of the work shift. Set aside blocks of uninterrupted time for the really important tasks, such as preparing the budget.

Group routine tasks, especially those that are not important or urgent, during your least productive time. For example, list what you can do in 5 minutes, such as scan your e-mail, confirm a meeting, or set up an appointment, or in 10 minutes, such as return a phone call, scan a website, or compose an e-mail (Winston, 2004). This helps to use the small bits of time productively.

TABLE 13-1	Importance–Urgency Chart
CATEGORY OF TIME USE	**EXAMPLES**
Important and urgent	Replacing two call-offs and ensuring sufficient staffing for the upcoming shift.
Important, not urgent	Drafting an educational program for nurses on the changes in Medicare reimbursement.
Urgent, not important	Completing and submitting the "beds available" list for a disaster drill.
Busywork	Compiling new charts for future patient admissions.
Wasted time	Sitting by the phone waiting for return calls.

Much time is spent in transition or waiting that can be turned into productive use. Commuting time can be used for self-development or planning work activities. We all have to wait sometimes; waiting for a meeting to start or waiting to talk to someone are just two examples. Bring along materials to read or work on in case you are kept waiting. View waiting or transition time as an opportunity, especially to think.

If you are having difficulty completing important tasks and are highly stressed, especially as the day winds down, doing routine tasks for a while often helps to reduce stress. Pick a task that can be successfully completed and save it for the end of the day. Reaching closure on even a routine task at the end of the day can reduce the sense of overload and stress.

Implementing the daily plan and daily follow-up is essential to managing your time. In addition, you should repeat your time analysis at least semiannually to see how well you are managing your time, whether the job or the environment has changed, and which requires changes in planning activities. This can help prevent reverting to poor time-management habits.

PERSONAL ORGANIZATION AND SELF-DISCIPLINE

Some other time wasters are lack of personal organization and self-discipline, including the inability to say no, waiting for others, and excessive or ineffective paperwork. Effective personal organization results from clearly defined priorities based on well-defined, measurable, and achievable objectives. Because the nurse manager does not work alone, priorities and objectives are often related to those of many professionals, as well as to objectives of patients and their families.

How time is used is often a matter of resolving conflicts among competing needs. It is easy to become overloaded with responsibilities and with more to do than should be expected in the time available. This is typical. There is never sufficient time for all the activities, situations, and events in which one might like to become involved.

To be effective, nurses and nurse managers must be personally well organized and possess self-discipline. This often includes the ability to say no. Taking on too much work can lead to overload and stress. Being realistic about the amount of work to which you commit is an indication of effective time management. If a superior is overloading you, make sure the person understands the consequences of additional assignments. Be assertive in communicating your own needs to others.

A cluttered desk, working on too many tasks at one time, and failing to set aside blocks of uninterrupted time to do important tasks also indicate a lack of personal self-discipline. Clean your desk, get out the materials you need to complete your highest-priority task, and start working on it immediately. Focus on one task at a time, making sure to start with a high-priority task.

One manager who felt overwhelmed by all of her responsibilities used the strategies shown in Case Study 13-1 to help her solve her problems.

Controlling Interruptions

An interruption occurs any time you are stopped in the middle of one activity to give attention to something else. Interruptions can be an essential part of your job, or they can be a time waster. An interruption that is more important and urgent than the activity in which you are involved is a positive interruption; it deserves immediate attention. An emergency or crisis, for instance, may cause the nurse manager to interrupt daily rounds.

Some interruptions interfere with achieving the job and are less important and urgent than current activities. As the nurse manager's role expands to a broader span of responsibility, more decision making is placed on the staff nurse. When a manager is interrupted to solve problems within the staff nurse's scope of accountability, the manager should not become responsible for solving the problem. Gently but firmly directing the individual to search for solutions will begin to break old patterns of behavior and help develop individual responsibility. Although time consuming in the beginning, this practice eventually reduces the number of unnecessary interruptions.

Keeping an **interruption log** on an occasional basis may help. The log should show who interrupted, the nature of the interruption, when it occurred, how long it lasted, what topics were discussed, the importance of the topics, and time-saving actions to be taken. Analysis of these data may identify patterns that you can use to plan ways to reduce the frequency and duration of interruptions. These patterns may indicate that certain staff members are the most frequent interrupters and require individual attention to develop problem-solving skills.

PHONE CALLS

Phone calls are a major source of interruption, and the interruption log will provide considerable insight for the nurse manager regarding the nature of telephone calls received. Although it is not possible to function

CASE STUDY 13-1   Time Management

For the past 6 years, Jane Schumann has been manager of staff development for three hospitals in a Catholic health care system. After the health care system suffered record operating losses last fiscal year, many middle management positions were eliminated. Jane was retained but had several other departments assigned to her. Now Jane has four hospitals and responsibility for staff development, utilization review staff, in-house float pool, night nursing supervisors, agency staffing, coordination of student nurse clinical rotations, and training of all nursing staff for the new hospital information system.

Jane has been overwhelmed with her new responsibilities. Wanting to establish trust and learn more about her staff, Jane has adopted an "open-door policy" resulting in many drop-in visits each day. She has been working much longer hours and most weekends. Frequently she has had to fill in for night supervisors, stretching her workday to 18 hours. Her desk is stacked with paperwork and her voice mail box is full of messages to be returned. On average, she returns 40 of the 60 e-mails received each day.

When Jane comes across information about a time-management seminar, she quickly signs up. At the seminar, Jane learns a number of strategies that she can use.

Back at work she makes a plan. First she makes a list of priorities for each of her departments and a time frame for completing each project. Then she completes daily plans for the next 2 weeks and a 3-month plan for the upcoming quarter. Jane also determines who among her new staff members can assume additional responsibilities and notes tasks that can be delegated. She sorts through paperwork and establishes a filing system for each department. Jane decides that she will train her administrative assistant to file routine paperwork and route other paperwork to Jane or delegated personnel. Jane also decides that at each departmental meeting she will establish specific times she will be available for drop-in visitors. She schedules a meeting with the senior nursing executive to discuss the staffing implications for training nurses at four hospitals to use the new hospital information system. Finally, she takes advantage of an upcoming 4-day weekend to catch up on some well-deserved rest.

Manager's Checklist

The nurse manager is responsible to:

- Prioritize workload
- Effectively delegate tasks and projects to others
- Respect own time and the time of others
- Request assistance when appropriate

---

today without a telephone, some people do not use the telephone effectively. A ringing telephone is highly compelling; few people can allow it to go unanswered. Nurses and nurse managers receive many telephone calls, some of them time wasters. Handling telephone calls effectively is a must:

- Minimize socializing and small talk. If you answer the phone with, "Hello, what can I do for you?" rather than, "Hello, how are you?" the caller is encouraged to get to business first. Be warm, friendly, and courteous, but do not allow others to waste time with inappropriate or extensive small talk. Calls placed and returned just prior to lunchtime, at the end of the day, and on Friday afternoons tend to result in more business and less socializing.
- Plan calls. The person who plans telephone calls does not waste anyone's time, including that of the person called. Write down topics to be discussed before making the call. This prevents the need for

additional calls to inform the other party of an important point or to ask a forgotten question.
- Set a time for calls. You may have a number of calls to return as well as calls to initiate. It is best to set aside a time to handle routine phone calls, especially during "downtime." Try not to interrupt what is being done at the moment. If an answer is necessary before a project can be continued, phone immediately; if not, phone for the information at a later time.
- State and ask for preferred call times and the purpose of the call. If a party is not available, state the purpose of the call, and provide several time frames when you will be available for a return call. Have those accepting messages ask for the same information. This makes it easier for the responder to be prepared for the call and helps to prevent "telephone tag."

Voice mail is an excellent way to send and receive messages when a real-time interaction is not essential.

For example, one person or a large group of people can be informed about an upcoming meeting in one voice mail message. They can phone their responses at their convenience, thus obviating the need to try to reach each other directly. Like other forms of communication, voice mail must be used appropriately. Long messages or sensitive information are better conveyed one-on-one. Also, another person (e.g., unit clerk) may be responsible for taking voice mail messages off the system, so it is important to state the message in a professional manner, omitting personal or confidential information.

E-MAIL

E-mail can enhance time management or it can be a time waster. E-mail minimizes wasted time trying to contact individuals, enables you to contact many people simultaneously, and allows you to code the urgency of the message. Tone, however, is difficult to convey by e-mail. Therefore it is better to use more personal forms of communication, such as the telephone or in-person contact, for potentially sensitive or troublesome issues.

Checking e-mail too often can waste time. Each time you read a message, you cannot help but think about it, thereby losing your concentration on the task at hand. It helps to turn off your e-mail alert and set specific times of day to check e-mail (Morgenstern, 2005).

DROP-IN VISITORS

Although often friendly and seemingly harmless, the typical "got-a-minute?" drop-in visit can last several minutes. Instead, direct the visit by identifying the issue or question, arranging an alternative meeting, referring the visitor to someone else, or redirecting the visitor's problem-solving efforts. An additional strategy is to stand up to greet the visitor and remain standing. The gesture appears gracious yet is obvious enough to encourage a short visit.

The nurse manager who is fortunate enough to have an office will find that open doors are open invitations for interruption. Although it is essential that you be available and accessible, concentration time also is necessary. Inform the staff that a specific block of time (a few hours at most) will be available to address issues.

Interruptions also can be controlled by the arrangement of furniture. The nurse manager whose desk is arranged so that immediate eye contact is made with passersby or drop-in visitors is asking for interruptions.

A desk turned 90 or even 180 degrees from the door minimizes potential eye contact.

Encouraging appointments to deal with routine matters also reduces interruptions. Regularly scheduled meetings with those who need to see you allow them to hold routine matters for those appointments. Holding such meetings in the other person's office places you in charge of keeping the time. It is easier to leave someone's office than to remove an individual from yours.

PAPERWORK

Health care organizations cannot function effectively without good information systems. In addition to telephone calls and face-to-face conversations, nurses and managers spend considerable time writing and reading communications. Increasing government regulations, measures to avoid legal action, stronger privacy requirements, new treatments and medications, data processing, work processing, and electronics place pressure on everyone to cope with increasing paperwork (including electronic "paperwork"). Some basic principles can help you process information while reducing it as a waster of time (Cohen, 2005).

1. **Plan and schedule paperwork.** Writing and reading reports, forms, e-mail, letters, and memos are essential elements of a job. They cannot be ignored. They will, however, become a major source of frustration if their processing is not planned and scheduled as an integral part of daily activities. Learn the organization's information system and requirements, analyze the paperwork requirements of the position, and make significant progress on that part of the job daily.
2. **Sort paperwork for effective processing.** A system of file folders either for paper mail or for e-mail can be very helpful. Here is one way to handle it.
   - Place all paperwork (or e-mail) requiring personal action in a red file or in an "action" folder on your computer's hard drive. It can then be handled according to its relative importance and urgency.
   - Place work that can be delegated in a separate pile, and distribute it appropriately.
   - Place all work that is informational in nature and related to present work in a yellow file folder or in an "informational" folder on the hard drive.
   - Place other reading material, such as professional journals, technical reports, and other items that

do not relate directly to the immediate work, in a blue file folder or a file labeled "R."

The informational file contains materials that must be read immediately, whereas the reading file materials are not as urgent and can be read later.

Do not be afraid to throw things away or erase them from your computer's memory. When they no longer have value, do not let them become clutter. Use trash receptacles in the office and on the electronic system.

3. **Send every communication electronically.** Unless a paper memo, report, or letter is required, send your work electronically.

4. **Analyze paperwork frequently.** Review filing policies and rules regularly, and purge files at least once each year. All standard forms, reports, and memos should be reviewed annually. Each should justify its continued existence and its present format. Do not be afraid to recommend changes and, when possible, initiate those changes.

5. **Do not be a paper shuffler.** "Handle a piece of paper only once" is a common adage, but impossible to follow if taken literally. It really means that each time a piece of paper or e-mail message is handled, some action should be taken to further process it. Paper shufflers are those who continually move things around on their desks or accumulate unread e-mails. They delay action unreasonably, and the problem

mounts. A desktop is a working surface; it is not for files and piles.

Respecting Time

The key to using time-management techniques is to respect one's own time as well as that of others. People who respect their time are likely to find others respecting it also. The same values and attitudes indicate respect for one's own time and for that of others. Using the above suggestions regarding time management communicates to those who interact with you that respect for time is demanded.

You, however, must reciprocate by respecting the time needs of others. If you need to talk to someone, it is appropriate to arrange an appointment, particularly for routine matters. One should continually ask, "What is the best use of my time right now?" and should answer in three ways:

- For myself and my goals
- For my staff and their goals
- For the organization and its goals

The effort to manage time may seem to take more time, but the reverse is true. Any activity that helps set goals, determine priorities, organize the workday, and minimize interruptions will pay off in increased efficiency and effectiveness.

What You Know Now

- The first step to manage time is to analyze how time is used by keeping a time log.
- Set goals and determine priorities to establish daily planning and scheduling.
- Personal organization strategies help to use time productively.
- An interruption log helps identify patterns that can be used to reduce unnecessary interruptions.
- Telephone calls can be controlled by minimizing small talk, planning calls, setting aside time for calls, stating preferred call times, and using voice mail.
- To control interruptions by drop-in visitors, meet visitors outside the office, keep visits short, encourage appointments, keep staff informed, and arrange furniture to discourage unscheduled visitors.
- Written communication also can cause interruptions. These can be minimized by planning and scheduling paperwork and e-mails, delegating, and using an effective filing system.
- People who respect their own time are likely to find others respecting it also.

Tools for Managing Time

1. Recognize that there will never be enough time to accomplish everything desired.
2. Use a time log to identify and reduce time wasters.
3. Use a planner to list goals, their priorities, and schedule the workday.
4. Set aside uninterrupted time to complete important tasks.
5. Group routine tasks and use short blocks of time to complete them.
6. Monitor interruptions and decide on ways to minimize them.

Questions to Challenge You

1. What are your major time wasters? Keep a time log for one week. Compare how you thought you wasted time with what your time log revealed.
2. Write down your goals for the next week. What action steps can you take to realize your goals? At the end of the week evaluate your progress. Then write down the next week's goals.
3. What is keeping you from accomplishing your goals? Think about how you can change the circumstances to better reflect your priorities.
4. Do you use a planner or other scheduling device? If not, investigate the choices and select the one that will work best for you. Use it!
5. Think about how you handle interruptions. During the next week try various strategies to minimize the effect of interruptions.

Explore MediaLink 🌐

Additional interactive resources for this chapter can be found on the Website at http://www.prenhall.com/sullivan. Click on Chapter 13 to select activities for this chapter.

- Video Overview
- NCLEX® Review Questions
- Critical Thinking Activities
- Current Events
- Nursing Leadership and Management in Action
- MediaLinks

References

Arnold, E., & Pulich, M. (2004). Improving productivity through more effective time management. *Health Care Manager, 23*(1), 65–70.

Carrick, L., Carrick, L., & Yurkow, J. (2007). A nurse leader's guide to managing priorities. *American Nurse Today, 2*(7), 40–41.

Cohen, S. (2005). Reclaim lost time with better organization. *Nursing Management, 36*(10), 11.

Morgenstern, J. (2005). *Never check e-mail in the morning: And other unexpected strategies for making your work life work.* New York: Fireside.

Sullivan, E. J. (2004). Becoming influential: A guide for nurses. Upper Saddle River, NJ: Prentice Hall.

Winston, S. (2004). *Organized for success: Top executive and CEOs reveal the organizing principles that helped them reach the top.* New York: Crown Books.

PART

3

Managing Fiscal Resources

CHAPTER 14

Budgeting and Managing Fiscal Resources

MediaLink

www.prenhall.com/sullivan

See the Companion Website for chapter-specific resources at
www.prenhall.com/sullivan.

Monitoring Budgetary Performance During the Year

    VARIANCE ANALYSIS

    POSITION CONTROL

    STAFF IMPACT ON BUDGETARY PERFORMANCE

Future Trends

Learning Outcomes

After completing this chapter, you will be able to:

1. Explain how health care is paid.
2. Describe how the budgeting process works.
3. Differentiate among types of budgets.
4. Demonstrate how to monitor and control budgetary performance.
5. Explain how to determine budget variance.
6. Describe how staff affect budgetary performance.

Key Terms

Benefit time *p190*	Fixed budget *p189*	Rate variance *p194*
Budget *p187*	Fixed costs *p190*	Revenue budget *p189*
Budgeting *p187*	Incremental (line-by-line)	Salary (personnel)
Capital budget *p192*	budget *p188*	budget *p190*
Controlling *p188*	Indirect costs *p190*	Variable budget *p189*
Cost center *p190*	Nonsalary expenditure	Variable costs *p190*
Diagnosis-related groups *p186*	variance *p194*	Variance *p193*
Direct costs *p190*	Operating budget *p189*	Volume variances *p194*
Efficiency variance *p194*	Personnel budget *p190*	Zero-based budget *p189*
Expense budget *p189*	Position control *p194*	
Fiscal year *p189*	Profit *p190*	

Budgeting is the process of planning and controlling future operations by comparing actual results with planned expectations. A budget is a detailed plan that communicates these expectations and serves as the basis for comparing them to actual results. The budget shows how resources will be acquired and used over some specific time interval; its purpose is to allow management to project activities into the future so that the objectives of the organization are coordinated and met. It also helps to ensure that the resources necessary to achieve these objectives are available at the appropriate time. Lastly, a budget helps management control the organization.

    Budgeting is performed by business, government, and individuals. In fact, nearly everyone budgets even though he or she may not identify the process as such. Even though a budget may exist only in an individual's mind, it is nonetheless a budget. Anyone who has planned how to pay a particular bill at some time in the future—say, 6 months—has a budget. Althought it is very simplistic, that plan accomplishes the essential budget functions. One now knows how much of a resource (money) is needed and when (in 6 months) it is needed. Note that the "when" is just as important as the "how much." The money has to be available at the right time.

    Managing a budget is a process of planning for a specified time in the future, usually one year, monitoring how well the plan is working during the budget time period, and adjusting the budget accordingly for the next budget cycle. The budgeting process allows the manager to visibly identify resource problems early and to adjust them to changing situations. Furthermore, a well-managed budget uses the organization's resources to best provide quality patient care.

The budget reflects how well you manage resources (Cohen, 2006). It is a visible record of your capability and your unit's productivity. Good budget management helps the manager gain confidence and the potential for promotion but, most importantly, managing resources translates into effective and efficient patient care.

Paying for Health Care

Between the years 1980 and 2004, health care spending grew faster than the economy (Stanton, 2005). As discussed in Chapter 1, health care is paid for by state or federal governments (Medicare, Medicaid, military and veterans' services), by private insurers, and by consumers directly. How to pay for the continually-escalating costs and for services to those citizens not covered under any third-party payer, such as those named above, is a concern for consumers, policy makers, and providers alike.

Medicare is the government's largest health care financing program, paying out more than $313.5 billion in 2006 (Forbes, 2007). The federal government has made several attempts to control Medicare costs. In the mid-1980s, a system of prospective, rather than retrospective, payment for health care was introduced for all Medicare recipients. Other third-party payers soon followed suit. This system, based on **diagnosis-related groups** (DRGs), pays a provider (individual or organization) a set amount for a specific condition. This amount is stipulated ahead of time, instead of paying the bill after care is rendered. In 1997 the Balanced Budget Act was passed by Congress in an attempt to control Medicare expenditures by reducing payments to providers. Deemed too radical, the 1999 Balanced Budget Reform Act and the Budget Improvement and Protection Act in 2000 restored some of these cuts. Providing adequate care to the uninsured, however, remains an unresolved problem.

Cost-Conscious Nursing Practice

With the economic climate of health care in turmoil, greater attention is being given to cost containment and operational efficiency. Mergers, integrated health care systems, the nursing shortage, and the scarcity of financial resources are key forces behind the current focus on financial accountability.

All nurses must be concerned about the cost of health care to ensure a viable health care system in the future (Vere-Jones, 2006). Because the nursing budget can account for as much as half of an organization's total expenses, nurse managers at all levels are facing significant pressure to become more cost conscious in the budgeting process, to allocate resources, and to control and monitor expenditures (Finkler & Kovner, 2007). This level of fiscal accountability is new to many managers and comes at a time when nursing must compete with other departments within the organization for limited resources.

Staff members may be unaccustomed to consider the cost of supplies, for example. The manager can share actual budget reports at staff meetings and show staff members printouts of commonly used items, leaving them readily available for future reference (Cohen, 2006). Labeling the cost of items alerts staff to the expense and encourages prudence (Vere-Jones, 2006). The goal is to make staff aware of costs, not to prevent use of appropriate supplies. Vere-Jones (2006, p. 15) suggests that nurses should strive to "use the right product for the right purpose."

In today's competitive environment, a higher level of performance is necessary. A focus on efficiency and effectiveness is essential (Porter-O'Grady, 2003), and the manager must help design the work to reduce extraneous and redundant tasks, making the best use of each individual's time and effort. Increased scrutiny of the cost of products, supplies, and new technology affects the expense budget, the capital budget, and patients' quality of care (Vere-Jones, 2006). These are no small tasks. Attention to the budgeting process is the first step to understanding how to use resources most effectively.

The Budgeting Process

A **budget** is a quantitative statement, usually in monetary terms, of the plans and expectations of a defined area over a specified period of time. Budgets provide a foundation for managing and evaluating financial performance. Budgets detail how resources (money, time, people) will be acquired and used to support planned services within the defined time period. The budget's purpose is to allow management to project action plans and their economic impact on the future so that objectives of the organization are coordinated and met (Finkler & McHugh, 2007).

The budget process also helps ensure that resources necessary to achieve these objectives are available at the appropriate time and that operations are carried out within the resources available. The budgeting process increases the awareness of costs and also helps employees understand the relationships among goals, expenses, and revenues. As a result, employees are committed to the goals and objectives of the organization, and various departments are able to coordinate activities and collaborate to achieve the organization's objectives. Budgets also help management control the resources expended through an organizational awareness of costs. Finally, budget performance provides management with feedback about resources management and the impact on the budget.

Budgeting is a process of planning and controlling future operations by comparing actual results with planned expectations (Finkler & McHugh, 2007). Planning first involves reviewing established *goals* and *objectives* of both nursing and the organization. Goals and objectives help identify the organization's priorities and direct the organization's efforts. To plan, the organization must anticipate the future by gathering information about the following (Foley, 2005):

- Demographics of the population served, community influences, and competitors
- Sources of revenue, especially managed-care contracts, as well as public payers such as Medicare, Medicaid, and commercial insurance companies, because payment arrangements and mechanisms determine the projected revenues of the organization
- Statistical data including:
  - Number of admissions or patient appointments
  - Average daily census
  - Average length of stay
  - Patient acuity
  - Projected occupancy or volume base for ambulatory or procedure-based units or home care visits
- Wage increases of market adjustments
- Price increases, including inflation rate, for supplies and other costs
- Costs for new equipment or technologies (e.g., wound vacs, sequential compression devices, monitoring equipment)
- Staff mix (e.g., RNs, LPNs, UAPs)
- Regulatory changes (e.g., Medicare, legislation mandating nurse-to-patient ratios, state board of health regulations) for the budgetary period
- Organizational changes (e.g., decentralization of pharmacy or respiratory therapy services) that result in salary and benefit dollars being charged in portion to the unit

The organization may use sophisticated and complex forecasting methods, including statistical techniques, to assist in making projections related to the budgetary period. Management normally uses the past as the common starting point for projecting the future, but in today's volatile payment environment, the past may be a poor predictor of the future. This is one of the major drawbacks of the budgeting process. In a rapidly changing industry, basing budgets on historical data often requires readjustment during the actual budget period.

Controlling is the process of comparing actual results with the results projected in the budget. (See later section on monitoring performance during the year.) Two techniques for controlling budgetary performance are variance analysis and position control. By measuring the differences between the projected and the actual results, management is better able to make modifications and corrections. Therefore, controlling depends on planning.

Approaches to Budgeting

Budgets may be developed in various formats depending on how the department is viewed by administration (Contino, 2001). They may be considered:

- **Cost centers.** Managers are responsible for predicting, documenting, and managing the costs (staffing, supplies) of the department.
- **Revenue centers.** Managers are responsible for generating revenues (patient volumes).
- **Profit centers.** Managers are responsible for generating revenues and managing costs so that the department shows a profit (revenues exceed costs).
- **Investment centers.** Managers are responsible for generating revenues and managing costs and capital equipment (assets).

Nursing units are typically considered cost centers, but they may also be viewed as revenue centers, profit centers, or investment centers. How the unit is considered is crucial in determining the manager's approach to budgeting.

Also, some nursing managers are responsible for service lines, and their staff are from multiple disciplines and departments. Other nurse managers are responsible for a single unit, such as a telemetry unit or the staff in a multiple physician office.

The organization may choose various approaches, or combinations of them, for requesting departmental managers to prepare their budget requests. These approaches are incremental (line-by-line), zero-based, fixed, and variable.

INCREMENTAL BUDGET

With an **incremental**, or **line-by-line**, **budget**, the finance department distributes a budget worksheet listing each expense item or category on a separate expense line. The expense line is usually divided into salary and nonsalary items. A budget worksheet is commonly used for mathematical calculations to be submitted for the next year. It may include several columns for the amount budgeted for the current year, the amount actually spent year-to-date, the projected total for the year based on the actual amount spent, increases and decreases in the expense amount for the new budget, and the request for the next year with an explanation attached.

The base or starting point for calculating next year's budget request may be either the previous year's actual results or projected expenditures for the current year. For salary expenses, the adjustment might be the average salary increase projected for next year. For nonsalary expenses, the finance department may provide an estimate of the average increase for supplies or opt to use a standard measure of cost increases, perhaps the consumer or medical price index projected for the next year.

To complete budget worksheets accurately, managers must be familiar with expense account categories. What type of expenses, such as instruments and minor equipment, are included under each line item? In addition, the manager has to keep abreast of different factors that have affected the expenditure level for each expense line during the current year. The projected impact of next year's activities will be translated into increases or decreases in expense levels of the nursing unit's expenditures for the coming year.

The advantage of the line-by-line budget method is its simplicity of preparation. The disadvantage of this method is that it discourages cost efficiency. To avoid budget cuts for the next year, an astute manager learns to spend the entire budget amount established for the current year, because this amount becomes the base for the next year.

ZERO-BASED BUDGET

The **zero-based budget** approach assumes the base for projecting next year's budget is zero. Managers are required to justify all activities and programs as if they were being initiated for the first time. Regardless of the level of expenditure in previous years, every proposed expenditure for the new year must be justified under the current environment and its fit with the organization's objectives.

The advantage of zero-based budgeting is that every expense is justified. The disadvantage is that the process is time consuming and may not be necessary. For that reason, organizations may not use this process every year. An adaptation of the zero-based budget is to start the budget with a lower base, for example, 80 percent of the current expenses. Managers then have to justify any budgetary expenses requested above the 80 percent base.

FIXED OR VARIABLE BUDGETS

Budgets also can be categorized as fixed or variable. Budgets are considered **fixed budgets** when the budgeted amounts are set without regard to changes that may occur during the year, such as patient volume or program activities, that have an impact on the cost assumptions originally used for the coming year. In contrast, **variable budgets** are developed with the understanding that adjustments to the budget may be made during the year based on changes in revenues, patient census, utilization of supplies, and other expenses.

The Operating Budget

The **operating budget**, also known as the annual budget, is the organization's statement of expected revenues and expenses for the coming year. It coincides with the **fiscal year** of the organization, a specified 12-month period during which the operational and financial performance of the organization is measured. The fiscal year may correspond with the calendar year—January to December—or another time frame. Many organizations use July 1 to June 30; the federal government begins its fiscal year on October 1. The operating budget may be further broken down into smaller periods of 6 months or 4 quarters; each quarter may be further separated into three 1-month periods. The revenues and expenses are organized separately, with a bottom-line net profit or loss calculated.

THE REVENUE BUDGET

The **revenue budget** represents the patient care income expected for the budget period. Most commonly health care payers pay a predetermined rate based on discounts or allowances. In many cases, actual payment generated by a given service or procedure will not equal the charges that appear on the patient bill. Instead, the health care provider will be reimbursed based on a variety of methods. These include

- Reimbursement of a predetermined amount, such as fixed costs per case (Medicare recipients);
- Negotiated rates, such as per diems (a specified reimbursement amount per patient, per day);
- Negotiated discounts; and
- Capitation (one rate per member, per month, regardless of the service provided).

Revenue projections for the next year are based on the volume and mix of patients, rates, and discounts that will prevail during the budget period. Projections are developed from historical volume data, impact of new or modified clinical programs, shifts from inpatient to outpatient procedures, and other influences. Projected revenues derived from Medicare, Medicaid, commercial insurance companies, HMOs, and other third-party payers also is taken into consideration.

Medicare payments for inpatient services are made at a predetermined specific rate for each Medicare recipient based on the patient's diagnosis. Care is classified into diagnosis-related groups (DRGs). Payments are made based on the assumption that patients with the same DRG use similar resources.

DRGs are based on primary and secondary diagnoses, age, and treatment received. Within each DRG is the assumption that a certain number of resources is required for a specific patient treatment. It also is assumed that the use of resources varies according to the patient's age, sex, primary and secondary diagnosis, and discharge status. The health care organization has a financial incentive to provide care at a cost below the fixed DRG price because it can keep the difference between the cost of treating the patient and the amount the organization is paid. Because of this incentive, organizations have used different methods to minimize the costs of caring for that patient, including reducing the patient's length of stay.

THE EXPENSE BUDGET

The **expense budget** consists of salary and nonsalary items. Expenses should reflect patient care objectives and activity parameters established for the nursing unit. The expense budget should be comprehensive and thorough; it should also take into consideration all available information regarding the next year's expectations. Described in the next section are several concepts and definitions related to the budgetary process in a health care setting.

Cost Centers

In health care organizations, nursing units are typically considered cost centers. A **cost center** is described as the smallest area of activity within an organization for which costs are accumulated. Cost centers may be revenue producing, such as laboratory and radiology, or non–revenue producing, such as environmental services and administration. Nursing managers are commonly given the responsibility for costs incurred by their department, but they have no revenue responsibilities.

In contrast, if managers are responsible for controlling both costs and revenues and if their financial performance is measured in terms of **profit** (the difference between revenues and expenses), then the manager is responsible for a profit center. Customarily, nursing is not directly reimbursed for its services. Nursing-related

costs usually are included in the room charge. In addition, nursing lacks a method to categorize its activities, although work has been done in developing a taxonomy and minimum data set for nursing.

Classification of Costs

Costs are commonly classified as fixed or variable. **Fixed costs** are costs that will remain the same for the budget period regardless of the activity level of the organization, such as rental payments and insurance premiums. **Variable costs** depend on and change in direct proportion to patient volume and patient acuity, such as patient care supply expenses. If more patients are admitted to a nursing unit, more supplies are used, causing higher supply expenses.

Expenditures also may be direct or indirect. **Direct costs** are expenses that directly affect patient care. For example, salaries for nursing personnel who provide hands-on patient care are considered direct costs. **Indirect costs** are expenditures that are necessary but don't affect patient care directly. Salaries for security or maintenance personnel, for example, are classified as indirect costs.

Determining the Salary (Personnel) Budget

The **salary budget**, also known as the **personnel budget**, projects the salary costs that will be paid and charged to the cost center in the budget period (see Table 14-1). Managing the salary budget is directly related to the manager's ability to supervise and lead the staff. Better managers tend to have more stable staff with fewer resources spent on supplementary staff, turnover, or absenteeism. Managing personnel costs are challenges for all managers, and a system to track needs and expenses is essential (Walsh, 2003).

In addition to anticipated salary expenses, factors such as benefits, shift differentials, overtime, on-call expenses, and bonuses and premiums may affect the salary budget as well.

BENEFITS

After the number of required full-time equivalents (FTEs) is determined (see Chapter 16 on scheduling), it is also necessary to determine how many FTEs are necessary to replace personnel for **benefit time** (vacations, holidays, personal days, and so on). This factor can be calculated by determining the average number of vacation days, paid holidays, personal days, bereavement days, or other days off with pay that the organization

TABLE 14-1	Monthly Salary Budget and Year-to-Date Budget Comparison Report Fiscal Year Ending June 30					
POSITION	**JUNE ACTUAL SALARY**	**JUNE BUDGETED SALARY**	**JUNE VARIANCE**	**YEAR-TO-DATE ACTUAL SALARY**	**YEAR-TO-DATE BUDGETED SALARY**	**YEAR-TO-DATE VARIANCE**
Nurse Manager	$6,250	$6,250	$0	$68,750	$75,000	$6,250
Registered Nurses	95,722	93,825	(1,897)	1,048,813	1,125,878	77,065
Licensed Practical Nurses	19,025	20,800	1,775	231,426	249,600	18,174
Nursing Assistants	14,886	13,200	(1,686)	159,500	158,400	(1,100)
Unit Clerks	5,483	5,495	12	60,391	65,273	4,882
Float Pool RNs	1,426	1,000	(426)	16,800	12,500	(4,300)
TOTAL SALARY:	**$142,792**	**$140,570**	**($2,222)**	**$1,585,680**	**$1,686,651**	**$100,971**

provides and the average number of sick days per employee as experienced by the cost center.

To determine FTEs required for replacement:

1. Determine hours of replacement time per individual.
2. Then determine FTE requirement.

Benefit time	Hours/shift	Replacement hours
15 vacation days	× 8 hours	= 120
8 holidays	× 8 hours	= 64
4 personal days	× 8 hours	= 32
5 sick days	× 8 hours	= 40
	Total	= 256

Divide replacement time by annual FTE base

$$\frac{256}{2,080} = 0.12$$

From the FTE calculations an FTE budget is calculated (Table 14-1). This budget provides the base for the salary budget. However, shift differentials, overtime, and bonuses or premiums also may affect budget performance and need to be considered.

SHIFT DIFFERENTIALS

Most facilities use a set percentage to determine shift differential. For example, 10 percent for evenings, 15 percent for nights, and 20 percent for weekends and holidays. If the hourly rate is $18.00, for instance, then the cost for a nurse working evenings would be $18.00 plus $1.80 for each hour worked. On an eight-hour shift, the total cost would be $158.40 and for the year, $41,184.

OVERTIME

Fluctuations in workload, patient volume, variability in admission patterns, and temporary replacement of staff due to illness or time off all create overtime in the nursing unit. A projection of overtime for the next year can be calculated by determining by staff classification (RN, LPN, nursing assistant, and other employee classifications) the historical or typical number of hours of overtime worked and multiplying that number by 1.5 times the hourly rate. For example, if the average number of overtime hours paid in a unit for RNs is 35 hours per 2-week pay period and the average hourly rate is $18.00, the projected overtime cost for the year would be $24,570 for the RN category.

To determine overtime costs:

1. Multiply average salary for classification		$18.00
by factor	×	1.50
to obtain overtime rate		$27.00
2. Multiply average overtime hours		35
by overtime rate	×	$27.00
to obtain expenditure per pay period		$945.00
3. Multiply number of pay periods		26
by overtime expenditure	×	$945.00
to obtain annual overtime costs		$24,570.00

Clearly, overtime can rapidly deplete finite budget dollars allocated to a nursing unit. The nurse manager should explore options to overtime such as using part-time or per diem workers in order to keep the cost per hour more in line with the regular hourly rates. A competent manager certainly would also evaluate unit productivity to decrease overtime.

ON-CALL HOURS

If the nursing unit uses a paid on-call system, the approximate number of hours that employees are put on call for the year should be estimated and that cost added to the budget. Typically under the on-call system, staff are requested to be available to be called back to work if patient need arises, and the number of hours on call are paid at a flat rate per hour.

PREMIUMS

Some organizations offer premiums for certifications or clinical ladder steps. In this situation, a fixed dollar amount may be added to the base hourly rate of eligible personnel; for example, an additional $1.00 per hour paid for professional certifications. This would result in the hourly rate of the employee being adjusted from a base of $18.00 to $19.00. In this case, if the employee is full time and works 2,080 hours a year (40 hours a week multiplied by 52 weeks a year), the annual new salary would be $39,520, or $19.00 multiplied by 2,080.

SALARY INCREASES

Merit increases and cost-of-living raises also need to be factored into budget projections. These increases are usually calculated on base pay. For example, if a 3 percent cost-of-living raise is projected and the base salary for an RN is $40,000, then the new base becomes $41,200.

ADDITIONAL CONSIDERATIONS

Other important factors to consider when developing the salary budget are changes in technology, clinical supports, delivery systems, clinical programs or procedures, and regulatory requirements. Changes in patient care technology or introduction of new equipment may influence the number, skill, or time that unit personnel may spend in becoming oriented to the new equipment and, later, operating and maintaining it. If significant, the projected number of additional labor hours for the new budgetary period should be incorporated into the request.

Joint Commission, the organization that accredits health care organizations, evaluates the institution to determine that it is adhering to the level of staffing it has determined is required to maintain a safe patient care environment. For example, the institution may have established a standard for critical care units and some other specialty units, that a minimum of two staff members are required at all times, regardless of patient number or acuity. Additionally, some states have mandated staffing levels.

Departments such as environmental services, dietary, escort, or laboratory may provide the nursing unit with support in performing certain tasks, such as transporting patients or specimens. Any change in the level of support they provide should be reviewed, and the effect of such change on the unit's staffing levels should be quantified for the next year's budget request. Changes in the method of delivering care (primary, team, differentiated practice, or functional nursing) or staff mix (RNs, LPNs, unlicensed assistive personnel) also will affect staffing patterns for the next year. Any changes in staffing can place new demands on the unit. Therefore, orientation and additional workload needs also should be considered.

In addition, changes might be made to the way the organization charges costs. For example, some direct or indirect costs formerly charged under other departments might now be allocated to the various units. You might find your unit charged its fair share of the heating or security budget. Major changes, of course, are planned ahead of time but some changes occur during the budget year and the unit might be expected to absorb those additional costs within its original budget.

Managing the Supply and Nonsalary Expense Budget

The supply and nonsalary expense budget identifies patient-related supplies needed to operate the nursing unit. In addition to supplies, other operating expenses, such as office supplies, rental fees, maintenance costs, and equipment service contracts, also may be paid out of the nursing unit's nonsalary budget.

An analysis of the current expense pattern and a determination of its applicability for the next budget period should be performed first. Any projected changes in patient volume, acuity, and patient mix also should be considered because they will affect next year's supply use and other nonsalary expenses. As an example, if patient days for a particular type of patient are projected to multiply and cause a 5 percent increase in the use of intravenous solutions, this increase should be addressed in the budget request by requesting an additional 5 percent for intravenous solution supplies for the next year.

Increases due to an inflation rate index, or at a rate estimated by the finance or purchasing department, are included as part of the budget request. A simple way of calculating the effect of a price increase is to take the estimated total ending expense for the year and multiply it by the inflationary factor.

To determine projected price increases:

Multiply current total line item expense	$12,758
by inflation factor plus 1.0	× 1.05
	$ 13,396

Increases in expenses, such as maintenance agreements and rental fees, should also be incorporated as part of the budget request. The introduction of new technology and changes in programs and regulatory requirements may require additional resources for supplies as well as increased salaries.

The Capital Budget

The **capital budget** is an important component of the plan to meet the organization's long-term goals. This budget identifies physical renovations, new construction, and new or replacement equipment planned within a specified time period. Organizations define capital items based on certain conditions or criteria. Usually, capital items must have an expected performance of 1 year or more and exceed a certain dollar value, such as $500 or $1,000.

The capital budget is limited to a specified amount and decisions need to be made how best to allocate available funds. Priority is given to those items needed most. Not all items that fall under capital budget will necessarily get funding in a given year.

Today few nurse managers are asked to prepare a capital budget because most organizations are buying through consortiums or negotiated agreements with one supplier. Many health care organizations have departments that coordinate bringing in selected vendors and items and limit equipment choices to those. The nurse manager would then be responsible for assisting in selecting and determining the amount of equipment needed. The capital pool is expensed out across all units who use the equipment.

The impact of the new equipment on the unit's expenses, such as the number of staff needed to run the equipment, use of supplies, and maintenance costs, needs to be considered as part of the operating budget, however. For example, if monitoring equipment is being requested, the cost of electrocardiogram paper and electrodes should be determined, documented, and included in the supply budget. Likewise, the need for additional nursing and nonnursing personnel to operate the new equipment, additional workload, and training of personnel should be quantified for the next year's budget.

Timetable for the Budgeting Process

Depending on the size and complexity of the organization, the budgeting process takes 3 to 6 months. The process begins with the first-level manager. The individual at this level of management may or may not have formalized budget responsibilities, but he or she is key to identifying needed resources for the upcoming budget period.

The manager seeks information from staff about areas of needed improvement or change and reviews unit productivity and the need for updated technology or supplies. The manager uses this information to prepare the first draft of the budget proposal.

Depending on the levels of organizational management, this proposal ascends through the managerial hierarchy. Each subsequent manager evaluates the budget proposal, making adjustments as needed. By the time the budget is approved by executive management, significant changes to the original proposal usually have been made.

The final step in the process is approval by a governing board, such as a board of directors or designated shareholders. Typically, the budget process timetable is structured so that the budget is approved a few months before the beginning of the new fiscal year.

Clearly articulating their budgetary needs is essential for budgetary success. Senior management must prioritize budget requests for the entire organization, and they base those decisions on strong supporting documentation. Nurse managers should not expect to receive all of their budget requests, but they need to be prepared to defend their priorities.

Monitoring Budgetary Performance During the Year

To manage your budget during the year requires ongoing attention to resource use (Cohen, 2006). The difference between the amount that was budgeted for a specific revenue or cost and the actual revenue or cost that resulted during the course of activities is known as the **variance**. In the case of nursing units, variance might occur in the actual cost of delivering patient care for a certain expense line item in a specified period of time. Nurse managers are commonly asked to justify the reason for variances and present an action plan to reduce or eliminate these variances.

Managers usually receive a monthly report prepared by the accounting department summarizing the expenses for the department (see Table 14-1). This report shows expense line items with the budgeted amount, actual expenditure, variance from budget, and the percentage from the budgeted amount that such variance represents. Commonly these monthly reports also show the comparison between actual year-to-date results and the year-to-date budget.

Once you receive the monthly report, you should:

- Identify items that are over or under budgeted amounts
- Find out why the variance occurred (e.g., a one-time event or an ongoing occurrence)
- Keep notes on what you have learned in preparation for next year's budget

In addition, on a weekly basis you should:

- Examine the payroll and note overtime or use of agency personnel
- Validate use of overtime or additional personnel and keep a note for your files

Keeping notes throughout the year will help prevent the annual budget process from becoming an overwhelming challenge. Trying to reconstruct what happened and why during the past 12 months is unlikely to be a complete and accurate picture of events and makes creating a future budget more difficult.

VARIANCE ANALYSIS

In the daily course of events, it is unlikely that projected budget items will be completely on target in all situations. One of the manager's most important jobs is to manage the financial resources for the department and to be able to respond to variances in a timely fashion (Kirkby, 2003).

When expenses occur that differ from the budgeted amounts, organizations usually have an established level at which a variance needs to be investigated and explained or justified by the manager of the department. This level may be a certain dollar amount, such as $500, or it may be a percentage, such as a 5 percent or 10 percent increase above the budget.

In determining causes for variance, the nurse manager must review the activity level of the unit for the same period. There may have been increases in census or patient acuity that generated additional expense in salary and supplies.

Also, in many situations, variances might not be independent of one another. Variances may result from expenses that follow a seasonal pattern, occurring only at determined times in the year; renewal of a maintenance agreement is one example. Expenses may also follow a tendency or trend either to increase or to decrease during the year. Even if the situation is outside the manager's usual responsibility or control, the manager needs to understand and be able to identify the cause or reason for the variance.

To determine when a variance is favorable or unfavorable, it is important to relate the variance to its impact on the organization in terms of revenues and expenses. If more earnings came in than expected, the variance is favorable; if less, the variance is negative. Likewise, if less was spent than expected, the variance is favorable; if more was spent, the variance is negative.

For instance, the nurse manager might receive the following expense report:

MEDICAL/SURGICAL SUPPLIES

Budgeted expenditures	Actual expenditures	Variance (in $)	Percent (in %)
$34,560	$36,958	(2,398)	(6.9)

This expense variance is considered unfavorable because the actual expense was greater than the budget. In this example, more money was spent on medical/surgical supplies than was projected in the budget.

If the variance percentage of the actual budget amount is not presented in the reports, it can be calculated as follows:

$$\frac{\$2,398}{\$34,560} = 0.069$$

Divide the dollar variance by the budget amount, then multiply by 100:

$$0.069 \times 100 = 6.9\% \text{ over budget}$$

Salary Variances

With salary expenditures, variances may occur in volume, efficiency, or rate. Typically these factors are related and have an impact on each other. **Volume variances** result when there is a difference in the budgeted and actual workload requirements as would occur with increases in patient days. An increase in the actual number of patient days will increase the salary expense, resulting in an unfavorable volume variance. Although the variance is unfavorable, concomitant increases in revenues for the organization should be apparent. Thus, the impact to the organization should be welcomed, even though it generated higher salary costs at the nursing unit level.

Efficiency variance, also called quantity or use variance, reflects the difference between budgeted and actual nursing care hours provided. Patient acuity, nursing skill, unit management, technology, and productivity all affect the number of patient care hours actually provided versus the original number planned or required. At the same time, if the census had been higher than expected, it would be understandable if more hours of nursing care were provided and paid. A favorable efficiency, or fewer nursing care hours paid, could suggest that patient acuity was lower than projected, that staff was more efficient, or that higher-skilled employees were used. An unfavorable efficiency may be due to greater patient acuity than allowed for in the budget, overstaffing of the unit, or the use of less experienced or less efficient employees.

Rate variances, also known as price or spending variance, reflect the difference in budgeted and actual hourly rates paid. A favorable rate variance may reflect the use of new employees who were paid lower salaries. Unfavorable rate variance may reflect unanticipated salary increases or increased use of personnel paid at higher wages, such as agency personnel.

Nonsalary Expenditure Variances

Nonsalary expenditure variances may be due to changes in patient volume, patient mix, supply quantities, or prices paid. New, additional, or more expensive supplies used at the nursing unit because of technology changes or new regulations also could influence expenditure totals.

POSITION CONTROL

Another monitoring tool used by nurse managers is the position control. The **position control** is used to compare actual numbers of employees to the number of budgeted FTEs for the nursing unit. The position control is a list of approved, budgeted FTE positions for the nursing cost center. The positions are displayed by category or job classification, such as nurse manager, RNs, LPNs, and so on. The nurse manager updates the position control with employee names and FTE factors for each individual with respect to personnel changes, new hires, and resignations that take place during the year.

STAFF IMPACT ON BUDGETARY PERFORMANCE

Staff can acutely affect the organization's finances. Misuse of sick time, excessive overtime or turnover, and wasteful use of resources can result in negative variance. The manager plays a key role in explaining the unit's goals, the organization's financial goals, and how each individual is responsible for helping the organization meet those goals.

Organizations have implemented a number of different programs and incentives for increasing employee awareness and minimizing costs. Techniques to decrease absenteeism and turnover may be instituted (see Chapters 22 and 23). Displaying equipment costs on supply stickers or requisitions and indicating medication costs on medication sheets increase staff awareness of costs. Participation in quality improvement and action teams also serves to inform staff of cost factors. Bonuses based on net gains have been shared with employees, in addition to cost-of-living raises. Case Study 14–1 illustrates how one nurse manager handled his budget.

Future Trends

A major trend in financial management of health care organizations is the shift from a revenue-based to a cost-based accounting system. Formerly, hospitals emphasized generating revenues to cover the costs of health care. With the shift to managed care, however, the focus is on decreasing costs to maintain adequate profit margins in an era of diminishing compensation. In the managed-care environment, payment is prospectively determined in a competitive arrangement between provider and payer.

In an effort to be a low-cost provider of health care, organizations are strongly motivated to be cost effective. This trend has serious implications for nursing. Nursing has always been considered a cost, not a source of revenue. It is nursing's challenge to be consistently cost conscious and to measure, manage, and document nursing's cost-effectiveness in this financial environment.

CASE STUDY 14-1   Budget Management

Byron Marshall is nurse manager for the Surgical Services department of a private orthopedic hospital. Byron has received notice from the vice president of Clinical Services that next year's budget will be due to her for review at the end of the month. Byron has kept careful records during the previous 12 months for use in preparing the Surgical Services department budget.

Each month, Byron has received and reviewed monthly reports of revenue and expense for his department. He validated each month's budget targets, carefully noting areas that didn't meet budget projections. For example, when April pharmacy charges were 15 percent above budget projections, Byron noted that surgery volume was up 30 percent over the previous year, accounting for the increase in preanesthesia drug charges. Nursing salaries were also over budget for the year, but again, increased surgery volume had resulted in the addition of two full-time surgery technicians to the department. When summer vacations resulted in agency staffing in the OR, Byron saved copies of the approval from the vice president and the Human Resources department and noted the total cost to his department.

Byron will use the budget information for the past 12 months to project the next fiscal year's budget for his department. Information from the Human Resources department provides data for cost of living and merit increases in salary, while Materials Management has projected a 20 percent across-the-board increase in surgical supplies and pharmaceutical charges. Byron will also request replacement of two OR tables and three gurneys as part of the capital budget. These items had been requested by staff during the last department meeting when Byron asked for changes and improvements in the budget. Budget discussion is part of each staff meeting and Byron provides copies of actual budget numbers to the staff each month. He has found showing revenue and expense reports to staff increases compliance with overtime expenses and supply usage.

With monthly preparation, good record keeping, and accurate analysis, Byron is confident his budget presentation will be on time and on target.

Manager's Checklist

The nurse manager is responsible to:

- Learn and understand the responsibilities of financial planning for your department
- Review monthly revenue and expense reports for accuracy and completeness
- Understand and track reasons why particular areas did not meet budget
- Communicate to staff the importance of fiscal responsibility
- Plan for capital items on an ongoing basis
- Identify and incorporate increasing or decreasing expenses into the department budget
- Prepare and present a complete departmental budget to administration

What You Know Now

- A budget is a quantitative statement, usually written in monetary terms, of plans and expectations over a specified period of time.
- The operating or annual budget is the organization's statement of expected revenues and expenses for the coming year.
- The revenue budget represents the patient care revenues expected for the budget period based on volume and mix of patients, rates, and discounts that will prevail during the same period of time.
- Nursing units are typically considered cost centers, but may be considered revenue centers, profit centers, or investment centers.
- Nurse managers may be responsible for service lines and staff from multiple disciplines and departments.
- Nurse managers have input into capital expenses and are responsible for salary and operating costs related to new equipment.
- A full-time equivalent (FTE) is a full-time position that can be equated to 40 hours of work per week for 52 weeks, or 2,080 hours per year.
- The position control is a list of approved, budgeted FTEs that compares the budgeted number of FTEs by classification (RN, LPN), shift, and status to the actual available employees of the unit.

- Variance is the difference between the amount that was budgeted for a specific revenue or cost and the actual revenue or cost that resulted during the course of activities.
- Monitoring the budget throughout the year requires weekly and monthly attention to variances and the reasons they occurred.
- The shift from a revenue- to a cost-based accounting system requires nurses to remain cost conscious and to demonstrate nursing's cost effectiveness.

Tools for Budgeting and Managing Resources

1. Understand the budgeting process in your organization.
2. Determine the number of full-time equivalents necessary to staff the unit.
3. Compute the salary and nonsalary budget, including salary increases and various additional factors.
4. Monitor variances over the budget period and identify negative variances, keeping notes in your files.
5. Understand that factors out of your control, such as changes in technology or indirect or direct costs that may be assigned to your budget, affect your budget and its performance.
6. Encourage staff to monitor resource use, including time and supplies.

Questions to Challenge You

1. Do you have a budget for your personal and professional income and expenses? If so, how well do you manage it? If not, begin next month to track your income and expenses for one month. See if you are surprised at the results.
2. How well does your organization manage its resources? Can you make suggestions for improvement?
3. Are there tasks or functions in your work that you believe are redundant, unnecessary, or repetitive or that could be done by a lesser-paid employee? Explain.
4. Does your organization waste salary or nonsalary resources? If not, think of ways that organizations could waste resources. Describe them.

Explore MediaLink 🌐

Additional interactive resources for this chapter can be found on the Website at http://www.prenhall.com/sullivan. Click on Chapter 14 to select activities for this chapter.

- Video Overview
- NCLEX® Review Questions
- Critical Thinking Activities
- Current Events
- Nursing Leadership and Management in Action
- MediaLinks

References

Cohen, S. (2006). Take the fear out of the figures. *Nursing Management, 37*(4), 12.

Contino, D. S. (2001). Budget training: It's overdue. *Nursing Management, 32*(8), 16–17.

Finkler, S. A., & Kovner, C. T. (2007). *Finanical management for nurse managers and executives* (3rd ed.). St. Louis, MO: Saunders.

Finkler, S. A., & McHugh, M. (2007). *Budgeting concepts for nurse managers* (4th ed.). St. Louis, MO: Saunders.

Foley, R. (2005). Learn to speak finance. *Nursing Management, 36*(8), 28–34.

Forbes. (2007). U.S. health care cost to top $4 trillion by 2016. Accessed July 2007 at http://www.forbes.com/forbeslife/health/feeds/hscout/2007/02/21/hscout602078.html.

Kirkby, M. P. (2003). Number crunching with variable budgets. *Nursing Management, 34*(2), 28–33.

Porter-O'Grady, T. (2003). A different age for leadership, Part 1: New context, new content. *Journal of Nursing Administration, 33*(2), 105–110.

Stanton, M. W. (2005). *The high concentration of U. S. health care expenditures*. Rockville, MD: Agency for Healthcare Research and Quality.

Vere-Jones, E. (2006). The business of nursing. *Nursing Times, 102*(23), 14–17.

Walsh, E. (2003). Get real with workload measurement. *Nursing Management, 34*(2), 38–42.

Recruiting and Selecting Staff

The Recruitment and Selection Process

Recruitment

WHERE TO LOOK

HOW TO LOOK

WHEN TO LOOK

HOW TO SELL THE ORGANIZATION

CROSS-TRAINING AS A RECRUITMENT STRATEGY

Interviewing

PRINCIPLES FOR EFFECTIVE INTERVIEWING

INVOLVING STAFF IN THE INTERVIEW PROCESS

INTERVIEW RELIABILITY AND VALIDITY

Education, Experience, Licensure, and Physical Examinations

Integrating the Information

Legality in Hiring

Learning Outcomes

After completing this chapter, you will be able to:

1. Describe how to recruit and select staff.
2. Perform a job analysis.
3. Describe how to interview prospective candidates.
4. Distinguish between appropriate and inappropriate questions to ask during an interview.
5. Discuss the legal issues involved in hiring.

MediaLink

www.prenhall.com/sullivan

See the Companion Website for chapter-specific resources at
www.prenhall.com/sullivan.

Key Terms

Recruiting and selecting staff who will contribute positively to the organization is crucial in the fast-paced world of health care and in the face of ever-increasing nursing shortages (U.S. Department of Labor, 2007). The cost of improper selection can be high (Jones, 2004). The visible cost is in recruiting, selecting, and training an employee who must later be terminated because of unsatisfactory performance. The hidden costs may be even more expensive and include poor quality of work, disruption of morale, and patients' ill will and dissatisfaction, which may contribute to later liability.

The Recruitment and Selection Process

The purpose of the selection process is to match people to jobs. Responsibility for selecting nursing personnel in health care organizations is usually shared by the human resources management (HRM) department, which may include a nurse recruiter, and nursing management. First-line nursing managers are the most knowledgeable about job requirements and can best describe the job to applicants. HRM performs the initial screening and monitors hiring practices to be sure they adhere to legal stipulations.

Before recruiting or selecting new staff, those responsible for hiring must be familiar with the position description. The **position description** (see Box 15-1) describes the skills, abilities, and knowledge required to perform the job. The position description should reflect current practice guidelines and include:

- Principal duties and responsibilities involved in a particular job

- Tasks inherent in those duties
- Personal qualifications (skills, abilities, knowledge, and traits) needed for the position
- May also include competency-based behaviors

The steps designed to acquire and retain personnel are:

1. Plan the number and types of personnel needed according to patient care delivery systems of the organization.
2. Determine the duties, requirements, tasks, and qualifications of each position.
3. Develop and implement a recruitment strategy to locate and attract enough qualified applicants to provide a pool of potential employees.
4. Interview, evaluate, and select needed staff.
5. Orient staff to the job.
6. Enhance employee performance through staff development and management of job performance.
7. Evaluate performance to provide feedback to the employee (see Chapter 18).
8. Manage absenteeism and other personnel problems (see Chapter 20).
9. Develop and implement strategies to retain staff (see Chapter 19).
10. Providing career counseling.
11. Develop exit strategies, such as preretirement counseling and exit interviews.

The purpose of recruitment is to generate a pool of qualified applicants, whereas the purpose of the selection process is to assess an applicant's ability, skills, and motivation related to the requirements and rewards of the job. When candidates are matched to the job, positive outcomes such as high job satisfaction, low turnover, and high-quality performance can result.

> ### BOX 15-1   Position Description: Registered Nurse Adult Medical Intensive Care Unit (MICU)
>
> **Job Overview**
>
> The medical intensive care unit registered nurse is responsible for direct patient care of adults admitted to the MICU for management of complex life-threatening illness. The RN reports directly to the MICU Nurse Manager.
>
> **Qualifications**
>
> - Current licensure in good standing in the state of practice.
> - Minimum of 1 year previous adult ICU experience within the past 3 years or 2 years telemetry experience within the past 3 years.
> - Current BLS mandatory, ACLS or TNCC preferred. ACLS must be obtained with 6 months of employment.
>
> **Responsibilities**
>
> - Performs complete, individualized patient assessment within unit time frames and determines patient care priorities based on assessment findings.
> - Completes additional patient assessments as required, based on patient status, protocols and/or physician orders.
> - Administers medications and appropriate treatments as ordered by the physician accurately and within specified time frames.
> - Initiates and maintains an individualized patient plan of care for each patient, using nursing interventions as appropriate.
> - Provides ongoing education to the patient and the patient's family.
> - Documents patient assessments, medication and therapy administration, patient response to treatments and interventions in an accurate and timely manner.
> - Initiates emergency resuscitation procedures according to ACLS protocols.
> - Maintains strict confidentiality of all information related to the patient and the patient's family.
> - Provides nursing care in a manner that is respectful and sensitive to the needs of the patient and the patient's family, and protecting their dignity and rights.
> - Communicates changes in patient condition to appropriate staff during the shift.
> - Maintains (or obtains within 6 months of initial hire) certification in ACLS.
> - Completes unit-based training modules for critical care competency on an annual basis.

Figure 15-1 shows a flowchart of the recruitment and selection process and suggested responsibilities. As indicated in the chart, this process is a joint effort among the nurse manager, the nursing department, and the HRM department. The recruitment and selection process begins with job analysis, which is a careful determination of job duties and requirements by nursing service, with technical assistance from HRM. Based on the job analysis and subsequent **job descriptions**, recruiting plans and selection systems are developed and implemented.

Once an applicant makes contact with the organization, HRM reviews the application and may conduct a preliminary interview. If the applicant does not meet the basic needs of the open position or positions, he or she should be so informed. Rejected applicants may be qualified for other positions or may refer friends to the organization and thus should be treated with utmost courtesy.

The next three stages include the selection instruments used: tests, reference checks, and managerial interviews. In most cases, the interview is last, but practices may vary. Even if an applicant does poorly on the selection test or receives poor references, it is prudent to carry out the interview so that the applicant is not aware that the test or reference checking led to the negative decision. In addition, applicants may feel they have a right to "tell their story" and may spontaneously provide information that explains poor references.

The nurse manager should participate in the interview process because the manager is:

- Best able to assess applicants' technical competence, potential, and overall suitability
- Able to answer applicants' technical, work-related questions more realistically. In some organizations, the candidate's future coworkers also participate in the interview process to assess compatibility.

After the managerial interview, the applicant is given a comprehensive medical examination to protect the organization from legal actions. For example, individuals with back problems should not be hired to

Figure 15-1 ● Flowchart of the typical recruitment and selection process.

work on a rehabilitation unit where a great deal of lifting of patients is required. In addition, state boards of health and other regulatory bodies require rubella, tetanus, and tuberculosis testing. The Occupational Safety and Health Administration (OSHA) requires that the hepatitis immune series be offered to health care workers who are not immune to hepatitis.

Once the medical examination has been completed, the nurse manager reviews the information available on each candidate and makes a job offer. The nurse manager must keep others involved in the selection process informed. The nurse manager is usually the first to be aware of potential resignations, requests for transfer, and maternity or family medical leaves that require replacement staff. The manager also is aware of changes in the work area that might necessitate a redistribution of staff, such as the need for a night nurse instead of a day one. Communicating these needs to HRM promptly and accurately helps ensure effective coordination of the selection process.

Recruitment

The purpose of recruitment is to locate and attract enough qualified applicants to provide a pool from which the required number of individuals can be selected. Even though recruiting is primarily carried out by HRM staff and nurse recruiters, nurse managers and nursing staff play an important role in the process. Recruiting is easier when current employees spread the recruiting message, reducing the need for expensive advertising and reward methods.

The best recruitment strategy is the organization's reputation among its nurses. Brady-Schwartz (2005) found that nurses in magnet hospitals demonstrated higher levels of job satisfaction than those in non-magnet hospitals. It follows that satisfied nurses are more likely to speak highly of the organization.

Kerfoot (2001) suggested ways in which the organization can attract potential employees by oft-ignored messages it sends. These are shown in Box 15-2.

Individual nurse managers also affect how well the unit is able to attract and retain staff. A nurse manager who is able to create a positive work environment through leadership style and clinical expertise will have a positive impact on recruitment efforts because potential staff members will hear about and be attracted to that area (e.g., hospital unit, home health team). In contrast, an autocratic manager is more likely to have a higher turnover rate and is less likely to attract sufficient numbers of high-quality nurses.

Any recruiting strategy includes essentially four elements:

1. Where to look
2. How to look
3. When to look
4. How to sell the organization to potential recruits

Each of these elements may be affected by market competition, nursing shortages, reputation, visibility, and location.

WHERE TO LOOK

For most health care organizations, the best place to look is in their own geographic area. During nursing shortages, however, many organizations conduct national searches. This effort is frequently futile because most nurses look for jobs in their local area. If the agency is in a major metropolitan area, a search may be

---

BOX 15-2   What Messages Does Your Organization Send?

- Does your lobby communicate a sense of inspiration?
- Are the work spaces organized and "humanized" so they are fit for human beings?
- Do your recruitment offices convey that you are serious about developing your staff and that you will guide them through the transitions of a professional career?
- Do the private spaces for staff areas clearly demonstrate concern about the stress levels of staff?

- When prospective employees interview in the workplace, do they quickly get the message that the growth of staff is important?
- Are continual educational and inspirational offerings available for growth?
- Do the opportunities to learn and grow clearly show?
- Will the candidate have a guide/preceptor who can help with the transition to the workplace?

From "On Leadership: It's Transformation, Not Patient Care!" by K. Kerfoot, 2001, *Nursing Economics, 19*(4), pp. 187–188. Reprinted with permission.

relatively easy; if it is located in a rural area, however, recruitment may need to be conducted in the nearest city. Organizations tend to recruit where past efforts have been the most successful. Most organizations adopt an incremental strategy whereby they recruit locally first and then expand to larger and larger markets until a sufficient applicant pool is obtained.

Because proximity to home is a key factor in choosing a job, recruitment efforts should focus on nurses living nearby. The state board of nursing can provide the names of registered nurses by zip code to allow organizations to target recruitment efforts to surrounding areas. Also, personnel officers in large companies or other organizations in the area can be asked to assist in recruiting nurse spouses of newly hired employees.

Collaborative arrangements with local schools of nursing offer opportunities for recruitment. Providing preceptors or mentors for students during their clinical rotation or offering externships or residencies postgraduation encourages students to consider employment in the organization. Nurses who work with students play a key role in recruitment. Students are more likely to be attracted to the organization if they see nurses' work valued and appreciated and perceive a positive impression of the work group.

Employing students as aides may provide another recruitment tool because it allows students to learn first-hand about the organization and what it has to offer. In turn, the organization can evaluate the student as a potential employee postgraduation. Some organizations provide assistance with student loan payments if the student continues to work after graduation. Of major importance to new graduates is the orientation program. Graduates look for an orientation that provides successful transition into professional practice. Other top factors they consider are the reputation of the agency, benefits, promotional opportunities, specialty area, and nurse–patient ratio.

HOW TO LOOK

Posting online on general job search sites (e.g., www. monster.com) or on nurse-specific job referral sites is a common practice. Nurse.com is one (www.nurse.com). Professional associations such as Sigma Theta Tau International (http://stti.monster.com) and the American Nurses Association (www.nursecareercenter.com) offer job search services.

Employee referrals, advertising in professional journals, attendance at professional conventions, job fairs, career days, visits to educational institutions, employment agencies (both private and public), and temporary help agencies are all recruiting sources. Advertising in professional journals or newspapers can be an effective recruiting tool, but it tends to be expensive. Numerous websites target nurses and may be free. On others, ads can be purchased.

In recruiting, both the **medium** and the message must be considered. The medium is the agent of contact between the organization and the potential applicant (e.g., online site, professional journal, newspaper). Obviously, it is desirable to find a medium that gives the widest exposure. Unfortunately, these media tend to be inefficient and low in credibility. The more influential media tend to be the more personal ones: present employees and recruiters. Acquaintances or friends of the recruit have prior credibility and the ability to communicate more subtle aspects of the organization and the job.

During extreme nursing shortages, some organizations offer bonuses to staff members who refer candidates, as well as bonuses to the recruits themselves. Direct applications and employee referrals are quick and relatively inexpensive ways of recruiting people, but these methods also tend to perpetuate the current cultural or social mix of the workforce. It is both legally and ethically necessary to recruit individuals without regard to their race, ethnicity, gender, or disability. In addition, organizations can benefit from the diversity of a staff composed of persons from a wide variety of social, experiential, cultural, generational, and educational backgrounds.

On the other hand, nurses referred by current employees are likely to have more realistic information about the job and the organization and, therefore, their expectations more closely fit reality. Those who come to the job with unrealistic expectations may experience dissatisfaction as a result. In an open labor market, these individuals may leave the organization, creating high turnover. When nursing jobs are less plentiful, dissatisfied staff members tend to stay in the organization because they need the job, but they are not likely to perform as well as other employees. Consequently, even where applicants are sought may have significant consequences later on.

WHEN TO LOOK

The time lag in recruiting is a concern to nursing because of the shortage. Positions in certain locations (e.g., rural areas) or specialty areas (e.g., critical care) may be especially difficult to fill. Careful planning is necessary to ensure that recruitment begins well in advance of anticipated needs.

HOW TO SELL THE ORGANIZATION

A critical component of any recruiting effort is marketing the organization and available positions to potential employees. The nursing department and/or HRM should develop a comprehensive marketing plan. Generally, four strategies are included in marketing plans and are called the **4 Ps of marketing**:

1. Product
2. Place
3. Price
4. Promotion

The consumer is the key figure around which the four concepts are oriented, and in the recruiting process, the consumer is the potential employee.

Product is the available position(s) within the organization. Consider several aspects of the position and organization, such as

- Professionalism
- Standards of care
- Quality
- Service
- Respect

Place refers to the physical qualities and location, such as

- Accessibility
- Scheduling
- Parking
- Reputation
- Organizational culture

Price includes

- Pay and differentials
- Benefits
- Sign-on bonuses
- Insurance
- Retirement plans

Promotion includes

- Advertising
- Public relations
- Direct word of mouth
- Personal selling (e.g., job fairs, professional meetings)

Developing an effective marketing message is important. Sometimes the tendency is to use a "scatter-gun" approach, sugarcoat the message, or make it very slick. A more balanced message, which includes honest communication and personal contact, is preferable. Overselling the organization creates unrealistic expectations that may lead to later dissatisfaction and turnover.

Realistically presenting the job requirements and rewards improves job satisfaction, in that the new recruit learns what the job is actually like. Promising a nurse every other weekend off and only a 25 percent rotation to nights on a severely understaffed unit and then scheduling the nurse off only every third weekend with 75 percent night rotations is an example of unrealistic job information. It is important to represent the situation honestly and describe the steps management is taking to improve situations that the applicant might find undesirable. The candidate can then make an informed decision about the job offer.

CROSS-TRAINING AS A RECRUITMENT STRATEGY

In today's rapidly changing health care environment, patient census fluctuates rapidly, and staffing requirements must be adjusted appropriately. These conditions may bring about layoffs and daily cancellations and contribute to low morale. Offering cross-training to potential employees may increase the applicant pool.

Cross-training has the benefits of increasing morale and job satisfaction, improving efficiency, increasing the flexibility of the staff, and providing a means to manage fluctuations in census. It gives nurses, such as those in obstetrics and neonatal areas, an opportunity to provide more holistic care. In addition, cross-training enhances the nurse's range of skills, adding expertise useful for career planning.

If cross-training is used, care should be taken to provide a didactic knowledge base in addition to clinical training. How broadly to cross-train is an important decision because training in too many areas may overload the nurse and reduce the quality of care. (See Chapter 19 on using floating to improve retention.)

Interviewing

The most common selection method, the interview, is an information-seeking mechanism between an individual applying for a position and a member of an organization doing the hiring. After the applicant's initial screening with HRM, the nurse manager usually conducts an interview.

The interview is used to clarify information gathered from the application form, evaluate the

MediaLink   The Employment Interview

applicant's responses to questions, and determine the fit of the applicant to the position, unit, and organization. In addition, the interviewer should provide information about the job and the organization. Finally, the interview should create goodwill toward the employing organization through good customer relations.

Research suggests that decision making is improved if the interviewer postpones reviewing information not needed for the interview, such as test scores, until after the interview. Reviewing such information before the interview may lead to ignoring data that disconfirm this information.

An effective interviewer must learn to solicit information efficiently and to gather relevant data. Interviews typically last for 1 or 1½ hours, and include an opening, an information-gathering and information-giving phase, and a closing. The opening is important because it is an attempt to establish rapport with the applicant so she or he will provide relevant information. Gathering information, however, is the core of the interview. Giving information also is important because it allows the interviewer to create realistic expectations in the applicant and sell the organization if that is needed. However, this portion of the interview should take place after the information has been gathered so that the applicant's answers will be as candid as possible. The interviewer should answer any direct questions the candidate poses. Finally, the closing is intended to provide information to the candidate on the mechanics of possible employment.

PRINCIPLES FOR EFFECTIVE INTERVIEWING

Developing Structured Interview Guides

Unstructured interviews present problems; if interviewers fail to ask the same questions of every candidate, it is often difficult to compare them. With any human skill or trait, no standard or true score exists that can serve as a basis on which to compare applicants. People can only be compared to other people. Consequently, the interview is most effective when the information on the pool of interviewees is as comparable as possible. Comparability is maximized via a structured interview supported by an interview guide. An **interview guide** is a written document containing questions, interviewer directions, and other pertinent information so that the same process is followed and the same basic information is gathered from each applicant. The guide should be specific to the job, or job category.

Instead of the traditional interview questions, such as "tell me about yourself, what are your strengths and weaknesses, and why do you want to work for us," specific questions that target job-related behaviors are more common today. **Behavioral interviewing**, also called competency-based interviewing, uses the candidate's past performance and behaviors to predict behavior on the job (Simonsen & Smith, 2007). The questions are based on requirements of the position. Examples of specific behaviors expected of staff nurses and related sample questions are found in Table 15-1.

TABLE 15-1	Examples of Behavioral Interview Questions
BEHAVIOR	**SAMPLE QUESTION**
Decision making	What was your most difficult decision in the last month and why was it difficult?
Communication	What do you think is the most important skill in successful communication?
Adaptability	Describe a major change that affected you and how you handled it.
Delegation	How do you make a decision to delegate? Describe a specific situation.
Initiative	What have you done in school or on a job that went beyond what was required?
Motivation	What is your most significant professional accomplishment?
Negotiation	Give an example of a negotiation situation and your role in it.
Planning and organization	How do you schedule your time? What do you do when unexpected circumstances interfere with your schedule?
Critical thinking	Describe a situation where you had to make a decision by analyzing information, consider a range of alternatives, and select the best one for the circumstances.
Conflict resolution	Describe a situation where you had to help settle a conflict.

In addition, develop additional questions based on the specific job. For example, you may want to add questions on teamwork and collaboration as they relate to position. Box 15-3 lists job-related questions for an oncology unit position that candidates could be asked.

Interview guides reduce interviewer bias, provide relevant and effective questions, minimize leading questions, and facilitate comparison among applicants. Space left between the questions on the guide provides room for note taking, and the guide also provides a written record of the interview.

Preparing for the Interview

Most managers do not adequately prepare for the interview, which should be planned just like any business undertaking. All needed materials should be on hand, and the interview site should be quiet and pleasant. If others are scheduled to see the applicant, their schedules should be checked to make sure they are available at the proper time. If coffee or other refreshments are to be offered, advance arrangements need to be made. Lack of advance preparation may lead to insufficient interviewing time, interruptions, or failure to gather important information. Other problems include losing focus in the interview because of a desire to be courteous or because a particularly dominant interviewee is encountered. This typically keeps the interviewer from obtaining the needed information.

In general, when time is limited, it is better to use part of it for planning rather than squander all of it on the interview itself. This is preferable to spending more time later trying to correct the performance of a poor employee. Before the interview, the interviewer should review job requirements, the application and résumé, and note specific questions to be asked. Planning should be done on the morning of the interview or the evening before for an early morning interview. If you are sure that time will be available, planning is best done immediately before an interview or between interviews. Unfortunately, a busy manager may have to deal with unexpected minor crises between interviews and may not be able to use the time to plan the next interview.

A cardinal rule is to review the application or résumé before beginning the interview. If the interviewee arrives with the résumé or application in hand, ask him or her to wait for a few minutes while you review the material. In doing a quick review, consider four things:

1. Are there clear discrepancies between the applicant's qualifications and the job specifications? If the answer is yes, then only a brief interview may be necessary to explain why the applicant will not be considered. (If a preliminary screening is performed by the HRM, such applicants should not be referred to nurse managers.)
2. Look for specific questions to ask the applicant during the interview.

BOX 15-3 Job-Related Questions for an Oncology Unit

Describe how you would intervene in the following situations:

- A patient whom you admitted with a diagnosis of lymphoma is going to begin chemotherapy, and you are preparing to hang the first dose. When you enter the room she says, "You know, I just can't believe that I have cancer. I know it is what the doctor says, but it just doesn't seem possible to me."
- The wife of a patient overhears some doctors caring for her husband say that the patient has received the incorrect dose of chemotherapy. You are caring for him.
- A young man is diagnosed with acute leukemia and expresses anger and frustration in the presence of his wife. You witness the frequent outbursts and become increasingly aware of the sense of hopelessness on the part of both him and his wife.

- A leukemia patient has been classified as a no-code. On the night shift, dyspnea develops. The patient becomes uncomfortable and anxious, and screams out periodically. The patient is on 100% oxygen already, but his wife insists that something more be done.
- A physician making rounds notices a discrepancy in your patient's intake and output record. The weights indicate that he has gained 10 pounds, but the intake records do not show how this could have happened.
- You are working nights and caring for a seriously ill man receiving platelets and antibiotic therapy. The patient's blood pressure is continuing to drop. You have talked to the resident on call twice by telephone, and he tells you to continue the present orders. The man's condition continues to decline. What would you do?

Adapted from a form used by Barnes-Jewish Hospital, St. Louis, Missouri. Used by permission.

3. Look for a rapport builder (something you have in common with the applicant) to break the ice at the beginning of the interview.
4. Remember that the résumé is prepared by the applicant and is intended to market an applicant's assets to the organization. It does not give a balanced view of strengths and weaknesses. So, examine the résumé critically and make notes about areas where you need more information.

To provide a relaxed, informal atmosphere, the setting is important. Both you and the applicant should be in comfortable chairs, as close as comfortably possible. No table or desk should separate you. If an office is used, arrange chairs so that the applicant is at the side of the desk. There should be complete freedom from distracting phone calls and other interruptions. If the view is distracting, do not seat the applicant so that she or he can look out a window.

Opening the Interview

The interview should start on time. Give a warm, friendly greeting, introduce yourself, and ask the applicant her or his preferred name. Try to minimize status; do not patronize or dominate. The objective is to establish an open atmosphere so applicants reveal as much as possible about themselves. Establish and maintain rapport throughout the interview by talking about yourself, discussing mutual interests such as hobbies or sports, and using nonverbal cues, such as maintaining eye contact. Finally, start the interview by outlining what will be discussed and setting the time limits for the interview.

Be careful not to form hasty first impressions and make equally hasty decisions. Interviewers tend to be influenced by first impressions of a candidate, and such judgments often lead to poor decisions. First impressions may degrade the quality of the interview by coloring the search for information to justify their first impressions, good or bad. If the first impression is negative and you decide not to hire a potentially successful candidate, you have wasted an hour or so and possibly lost a good recruit. If, because of a positive first impression, you hire an unsuccessful candidate, problems may continue for months. Conversely, your personal characteristics may influence the applicant's decisions. You create first impressions by tone of voice, eye contact, personal appearance, grooming, posture, and gestures.

Using the structured interview guide, take notes, telling the candidate that this is being done to aid recall and that you hope the candidate does not mind. There are various ways of asking questions, but only one question should be asked at a time and, where possible,

open-ended questions should be used, such as those found in Table 15-1. Open-ended questions cannot be answered with a single yes, no, or one-word answer and usually elicit more information about the applicant (Parrish, 2006). Closed questions (e.g., what, where, why, when, how many) should only be used to elicit specific information.

Work sample questions are used to determine an applicant's knowledge about work tasks and ability to perform the job. It is easy to ask a nurse whether she or he knows how to care for a patient who has a central intravenous line in place. An answer of yes does not necessarily prove the ability, so you might ask some very specific questions about central lines. Avoid leading questions, in which the answer is implied by the question (e.g., "We have lots of overtime. Do you mind overtime?"). You may also want to summarize what has been said, use silence to elicit more information, reflect back the applicant's feelings to clarify the issue, or indicate acceptance by urging the applicant to continue.

Giving Information

Before reaching the information-giving part of the interview, consider whether the candidate is promising enough to warrant spending time in giving detailed job information. Unless the candidate is clearly unacceptable, be careful not to communicate a negative impression, because evaluation of the candidate may change when the entire packet of material is reviewed or more promising candidates decline a job offer. You also must know what information you should give and what is to be provided by others. Detailed benefit or compensation questions are usually answered by HRM. If a promising candidate's questions cannot be answered, arrange for someone to contact the candidate later with the desired information.

Closing the Interview

In closing the interview, you may want to summarize the applicant's strengths. Make sure to ask the applicant whether she or he has anything to add or questions to ask related to the job and the organization. You may also want to mention the candidate's weaknesses, particularly if they are objective and clearly related to the job, such as lack of experience in a particular field. Mentioning a perception of a subjective weakness, such as poor supervisory skills, may lead to legal problems. Thanking the applicant and completing any notes made during the interview conclude the interview process.

INVOLVING STAFF IN THE INTERVIEW PROCESS

Today's trend toward decentralization of decision making may lead to sharing interview responsibilities with staff. Involving staff in interviews helps to strengthen teamwork, improves work-group effectiveness, increases staff involvement in other unit activities, and increases the likelihood of selecting the best candidate for the position.

If staff are involved in interviews, several steps must be taken to protect the integrity of the interview process. An organized orientation to interviewing should be given that includes:

- Federal, state, and local laws and regulations governing interviewing, as well as any collective-bargaining agreements that may affect the process
- Tips on handling awkward interviewing situations
- Time for rehearsing interviewing skills. Just as the manager does, staff should follow a structured interview guide to help standardize the process.

Graham Nelson is nurse manager of a dialysis center. Training a new renal dialysis nurse is an expensive process. To reduce turnover among nursing staff, Graham includes peer interviews as part of the overall interview process. Peer interviews can help ensure that potential employees will interact well with existing staff and ensure a cultural fit with the dialysis team. Additionally, an interviewee can gain a better understanding of the day-to-day workflow of the center.

INTERVIEW RELIABILITY AND VALIDITY

Numerous research studies have been performed on the reliability and validity of employment interviews. In general, agreement between two interviews of the same measure by the same interviewer (**intrarater reliability**) is fairly high, agreement between two interviews of the same measure by several interviewers (**interrater reliability**) is rather low, and the ability to predict job performance (**validity**) of the typical interview is very low. Research also has shown that:

1. Structured interviews are more reliable and valid
2. Interviewers who are under pressure to hire in a short time or meet a recruitment quota are less accurate than other interviewers
3. Interviewers who have detailed information about the job for which they are interviewing exhibit higher interrater reliability and validity

4. The interviewer's experience does not seem to be related to reliability and validity
5. There is a decided tendency for interviewers to make quick decisions and therefore be less accurate
6. Interviewers develop stereotypes of ideal applicants against which interviewees are evaluated, and individual interviewers may hold different stereotypes, thus decreasing interrater reliability and validity
7. Race and gender may influence interviewers' evaluations

Possibly the greatest weakness in the selection interview is the tendency for the interviewer to try to assess an applicant's personality characteristics. Although it is difficult to eliminate such subjectivity, evaluations of applicants are often more subjective than they need to be. Information collected during an interview should answer three fundamental questions:

1. Can the applicant perform the job?
2. Will the applicant perform the job?
3. Will the candidate fit into the culture of the unit and the organization?

The best predictor of the applicant's future behavior in these respects is past performance. Previous work and other experience, previous education and training, and current job performance all should be considered, not personality characteristics, which even psychologists cannot measure very accurately.

Education, Experience, Licensure, and Physical Examinations

Education and experience requirements for nurses have long been important screening factors and bear a close relationship to work sample tests. Educational requirements are a type of job knowledge sample because they tend to ensure that applicants have at least a minimal amount of knowledge necessary for the job. For nurses, educational preparation is particularly important. For example, nurses who are graduates of associate degree and diploma programs are prepared to care for individuals in structured settings and use the nursing process, decision-making process, and management skills in the care of those individuals. Baccalaureate graduates can provide nursing care for individuals, families, groups, and communities using the nursing process and decision-making process. Baccalaureate graduates also are prepared for beginning community health positions and possess the leadership and management skills needed for entry-level management positions.

Making assumptions regarding the type and number of years of experience should be avoided. Factors such as job requirements, patient acuity, clinic populations, autonomy, and degree of specialization vary from organization to organization. Therefore, careful interviewing is needed to determine the individual applicant's knowledge and skill level.

References and letters of recommendation also are used to assess the applicant's past job experience, but there is little evidence that these have any validity. Because few persons write unfavorable letters of recommendation, such letters do not really predict job performance. Criticisms are likely to be mild and may be reflected by the lack of positive language. Letters with any criticism should be verified with a telephone call, if possible, to avoid overreacting to an unusually honest author.

To avoid legal problems, many organizations include in letters of recommendation only employment dates, salary, and whether the applicant is eligible for rehire. Many organizations do not allow supervisors to write letters of recommendation. Negative references may be viewed as potential for slander or other legal recourse. Almost every organization will at least verify position title and dates of employment, which helps to detect the occasional applicant who counterfeits an entire work history. Unfortunately, omission of a position from the work history is more common than including a position not actually held. The only way to detect such omissions is to ask that candidates list year and month of all educational and work experiences. Caution is necessary when asking about time between jobs; be careful not to inquire about marital or family status.

In almost every selection situation, an applicant fills out an application form that requests information regarding previous experience, education, and references. Most applications also ask for the applicant's medical history and other personal data. As application forms are reviewed, the critical question to be asked is whether the applicant has distorted responses, either intentionally or unintentionally. Studies indicate that there is usually little distortion, at least not on the easily verifiable information. Applicants may stretch the truth a bit, but rarely are there complete falsehoods. Relative to other predictors, the application form may be one of the more valid predictors in a selection process.

Licensure status can be verified online with the state board of nursing, and most organizations obtain permission to do criminal background checks as well. The computerized NCLEX-RN® examination changed hiring practices for new graduates; because rapid notification (7 to 10 days) of licensure examination results are available, state boards no longer issue interim permits to new graduate nurses. Organizations generally wait for new graduates to obtain a license before starting employment.

Preemployment physical examinations can no longer be used to disqualify applicants for a job or benefits. Passage of PL 101-336, the Americans with Disabilities Act of 1990, protects individuals with physical or mental disabilities from discrimination. In fact, reasonable accommodations must be provided for an individual with disabilities. Regardless, disabled employees may be held to the same standards for employment (i.e., they must possess the necessary skills and experience to perform the job) as applicants without disabilities.

Integrating the Information

When comparing candidates, first weigh the qualities required for the job in order of importance, placing more emphasis on the most important elements. Second, weigh the qualities desired on the basis of the reliability of the data. The more consistent the observation of behavior from different elements in the selection system, the more weight that dimension should be given. Third, weigh job dimensions by trainability—consider the amount of education, experience, and additional training the applicant can reasonably be expected to receive, and consider the likelihood that the behavior in that dimension can be improved with training. Dimensions most likely to be learned in training (e.g., using new equipment) should be given the least weight so that more weight is placed on dimensions less likely to be learned in training (e.g., being emotionally able to care for terminally ill children).

Attempt to compare data across individuals in making a decision. It is more accurate to make decisions based on a comparison of several persons than to make a decision for each individual after each interview. Analysis of the entire applicant pool requires good interview records but lessens the impact of early impressions on the hiring decision because the interviewer must consider each job element across the entire pool.

One nurse manager used the recommendations in this chapter to hire a nurse as shown in Case Study 15-1.

Jack Turner is nurse manager of the emergency department in a large metropolitan area hospital. He has four full-time RN positions open in his department. There are three nursing programs located in the city: a state university program, a community college program, and an RN-to-BSN completion program.

Jack recently participated in a nursing job fair hosted by his hospital. The event was well attended by nursing students, and he received several promising résumés of soon-to-be graduate nurses. Jack notes that one of the applicants, Sabrina Ashworth, will graduate next month with a BSN. She has been working for the past year as a nursing assistant in the ER of another local hospital. In addition to her ER work, Sabrina has a high grade point average and indicates a strong interest in trauma and critical care. Jack contacts the human resource department to set up an interview with Sabrina.

Sabrina agrees to an interview for an RN position in the ER department. Jack schedules a conference room adjacent to the ER for the interview. Prior to Sabrina's arrival, he reviews her résumé and application, noting her educational background, previous work history, and recent volunteer trip to Mexico to assist with a vaccination program. Jack has assembled a packet for Sabrina, including job description and materials from human resources that outline the application process.

The interview begins promptly. Jack warmly greets Sabrina and establishes rapport. He follows the interview guide provided by the human resource department. Jack informs Sabrina that he will be taking notes during the interview process. After reviewing her educational and work history, Jack asks Sabrina several situational questions related to work in the ER. He also allows time for Sabrina to ask questions about the RN position. Jack also has two RN staff members give Sabrina a tour of the ER department. Finally, Jack outlines the next steps in the application process and indicates that he will follow up with Sabrina in 7 to 10 days.

Following the interview, Jack works with the human resource department and asks for transcript and reference checks for Sabrina. After verifying her transcript and receiving positive references, Jack extends an offer to Sabrina, which she accepts.

Manager's Checklist

The nurse manager is responsible to:

- Understand the organization's human resource policies and procedures related to selecting staff
- Work closely with the human resource department to facilitate the selection and hiring of qualified staff
- Know state and federal regulations related to the application and interview process
- Prepare for the interview process
- Conduct the interview
- Follow up with applicants in a timely manner

Legality in Hiring

As a result of Title VII of the Civil Rights Act of 1964, the Equal Pay Act of 1963, the Age Discrimination Act of 1967, and Title I of the Americans with Disabilities Act of 1990, recruitment and selection activities are subject to considerable scrutiny regarding discrimination and equal employment opportunity. Title VII of the Civil Rights Act specifically prohibits discrimination in any **personnel decision** on the basis of race, color, sex, religion, or national origin. "Any personnel decision" includes not only selection but also entrance into training programs, performance appraisal results, termination, promotions, compensation, benefits, and other terms, conditions, and privileges of employment.

The act applies to most employers with more than 15 employees, although there are several exemptions—among them, **bona fide occupational qualification** (BFOQ), business necessity, and validity of the procedure used to make the personnel decision (as discussed next). Discrimination is allowed on the basis of national origin (citizenship or immigration status), religion, sex, and age; for instance, if that discrimination can be shown to be a "bona fide occupational qualification reasonably necessary for the normal operation of a business." The classic example of a genuine BFOQ is a sperm donor. More realistic examples are a female part in a play, a Sunday school teacher of a certain religion, or a female correctional counselor at a women's prison. Claims of "customer preference" for female flight attendants or gross gender characteristics such as "women cannot lift over 30 pounds" have not been supported as BFOQs.

A BFOQ allows an organization to exclude members of certain groups (such as all men or all women) if the organization can demonstrate that a selection method is a **business necessity**. Business necessity is likely to withstand legal challenge only in the unusual instances when a selection method that discriminates against a protected group is necessary to ensure the safety of workers or customers.

The Equal Employment Opportunity Commission (EEOC) is charged with enforcing and interpreting the Civil Rights Act and has issued Uniform Guidelines on Employee Selection Procedures (43 Federal Register, 1978). The guidelines specify the kinds of methods and information required to justify the job relatedness of selection procedures. These guidelines are not described in detail here; however, the methods of selection discussed in this chapter do follow their specifications. Remember that the law does not say one cannot hire the best person for the job. What it says is that race, color, sex, religion, disability, national origin, or any other protected factor must not be used as selection criteria. As long as the decision is not made on the basis of protected status, one is complying with the Equal Employment Opportunity (EEO) law.

EEO law and successive court decisions have had three major impacts on selection procedures. First, organizations are more careful to use predictors and techniques that can be shown not to discriminate against protected classes. Second, organizations are reducing the use of tests, which may be difficult to defend if they screen out a large number of minority applicants. Third, organizations are relying heavily on the interview process as a selection device. Interviews also are subject to EEO and other regulations. Table 15-2 presents questions appropriate to ask in interviews. The basic rule of thumb in interviewing is: When in doubt about a question's legality, ask How is this question related to job performance? If it can be proved that only job-related questions are asked, EEO law will not be violated.

TABLE 15-2	Preemployment Questions	
	APPROPRIATE TO ASK	**INAPPROPRIATE TO ASK**
Name	Applicant's name. Whether applicant has school or work records under a different name.	Questions about any name or title that indicate race, color, religion, sex, national origin, or ancestry. Questions about father's surname or mother's maiden name.
Address	Questions concerning place and length of current and previous addresses.	Any specific probes into foreign addresses that would indicate national origin.
Age	Requiring proof of age by birth certificate after hiring. Can ask if applicant is over 18.	Requiring birth certificate or baptismal record *before* hiring.
Birthplace or national origin		Any question about place of birth of applicant or place of birth of parents, grandparents, or spouse. Any other question (direct or indirect) about applicant's national origin.
Race or color	Can request *after* employment as affirmative action data.	Any inquiry that would indicate race or color.
Sex		Any question on an application blank that would indicate sex.
Religion		Any questions to indicate applicant's religious denomination or beliefs. A recommendation or reference from the applicant's religious denomination.
Citizenship	Questions about whether the applicant is a U.S. citizen; if not, whether the applicant intends to become one. Questions regarding whether applicant's U.S. residence is legal; requiring proof of citizenship *after* being hired.	Questions of whether the applicant, parents, or spouse are native born or naturalized. Requiring proof of citizenship *before* hiring.
Photographs	May require after hiring for identification purposes only.	Requesting a photograph *before* hiring.

TABLE 15-2	Continued	
	APPROPRIATE TO ASK	**INAPPROPRIATE TO ASK**
Education	Questions concerning any academic, professional, or vocational schools attended. Inquiry into language skills, such as reading and writing of foreign languages.	Questions asking specifically the nationality, racial, or religious affiliation of any school attended. Inquiries as to the applicant's mother tongue or how any foreign language ability was acquired (unless it is necessary for the job).
Relatives	Name, relationship, and address of a person to be notified in case of an emergency.	Any unlawful inquiry about a relative or residence mate(s) as specified in this list.
Children		Questions about the number and ages of the applicant's children or information on child-care arrangements.
Transportation		Inquiries about transportation to or from work (unless a car is necessary for the job).
Organization	Questions about organization memberships and any offices that might be held.	Questions about any organization an applicant belongs to that may indicate the race, age, disabilities, color, religion, sex, national origin, or ancestry of its members.
Physical condition/ disabilities	Questions about being able to meet the job requirements, with or without some accommodation.	Questions about general medical condition, state of health, specific diseases, or nature/severity of disability.
Military service	Questions about services rendered in armed forces, the rank attained, and which branch of service. Requiring military discharge certificate *after* being hired.	Questions about military service in any armed forces other than the United States. Requesting military service records *before* hiring.
Work schedule	Questions about the applicant's willingness to work the required work schedule.	Questions about applicant's willingness to work any particular religious holiday.
References	General and work references not relating to race, color, religion, sex, national origin or ancestry, age, or disability.	References specifically from clergymen (as specified above) or any other persons who might reflect race, age, disability, color, sex, national origin or ancestry of applicant.
Financial		Questions about banking, credit rating, outstanding loans, bankruptcy, or having wages garnished.
Other qualifications	Any question that has direct reflection on the job to be applied for.	Any non-job-related inquiry that may present information permitting unlawful discrimination. Questions about arrests or convictions (unless necessary for job, such as security clearance).

Adapted from *Americans with Disabilities Act* (EEOC Publication #M-1A), Ohio Civil Rights Commission and United States Equal Employment Opportunities Commission, 1992, Washington, DC: Government Printing Office.

MediaLink Facts About Age Discrimination

The **Age Discrimination Act** prohibits discrimination against applicants and employees over the age of 40. Questions in recruitment and selection that are appropriate with respect to age are also presented in Table 15-2.

The **Americans with Disabilities Act** that took effect in July 1990 prohibits discrimination based on an individual's disability. A disability is defined as a physical or mental impairment that substantially limits one or more of the major life activities, or has a record of such impairment, or is being regarded as having such an impairment. A qualified individual is one who, with or without reasonable accommodation, can perform the essential functions of the position under consideration.

Employers with 15 or more employees are required to make accommodations to the known disability of a qualified applicant if it will not impose "undue hardship" on the operation of the business. Reasonable accommodations may include making existing facilities used by employees readily accessible to and usable by individuals with disabilities; job restructuring; part-time or modified work schedules; reassignment to a vacant position; acquiring or modifying equipment or devices; adjusting or modifying examinations, training materials, or policies; and providing qualified readers and interpreters.

Interview questions that may be asked of the disabled are also in Table 15-2. The law permits an organization to make an employment offer contingent on the applicant's passing a preemployment physical examination, but only if the examination is required of all applicants in similar jobs and is job related.

Organizations are liable for the character and actions of the employees they hire. To satisfy this requirement, the employer must check applicants' backgrounds before hiring in regard to licensure, credentials, and references.

Failure to do so constitutes **negligent hiring** if that employee harms a patient, visitor, or another employee. Furthermore, an employer is expected to properly train its employees.

Recruiting and selecting the most appropriate staff is one of the most important jobs in an organization. Candidates whose qualifications fit the job requirements are more likely to be productive and to remain on the job. The tendency, especially during times of shortages, is to shortcut the process, but this is ill advised. The effort to attract and select the best candidates pays off over time for the organization.

What You Know Now

- The selection of staff is a critical function that requires matching people to jobs, and responsibility for hiring is often shared by HRM and nurse managers.
- Position description is fundamental to all selection efforts because it defines the job.
- Recruitment is the process of locating and attracting enough qualified applicants to provide a pool from which the required number of new staff members can be chosen.
- Selection processes should be job related and most often include screening application forms, résumés, medical examinations, reference checks, and interviews.
- Interviewing is a complex skill that is intended to obtain information about the applicant and give the applicant information about the organization.
- Successful interviews require planning, implementation, and follow-up in order to make the best decisions.
- Developing a structured interview guide is a critical element in interviewing.
- Selection decisions are subject to provisions in the Civil Rights Act of 1964, Equal Pay Act of 1963, the Age Discrimination Act of 1967, and the Americans with Disabilities Act of 1990.

Tools for Recruiting and Selecting Staff

1. Conduct or modify a job description as needed.
2. Coordinate recruitment efforts with the human resource department.
3. Ensure your area of responsibility sends the message you want (see Box 15-1).
4. Prepare adequately for interviews.
5. Conduct interviews following recommendations presented in the chapter.
6. Process the information obtained in interviews and reference checks to make a final decision.

Questions to Challenge You

1. What approach does your organization use to recruit employees? Is it effective? How could the process be improved?
2. Imagine that a potential candidate asks you to describe your present workplace. What would you say?
3. Have you ever participated in a staff interview, either as a candidate or as a member of the staff? Describe your experience. Would you do anything differently now that you've read the chapter?
4. Cross-training has been used as a recruitment strategy. What are the pros and cons of using this strategy?
5. Consider the last interview you had for a job or school. Did the interviewer follow the principles discussed in this chapter? Explain.

Explore MediaLink 🌐

Additional interactive resources for this chapter can be found on the Website at http://www.prenhall.com/sullivan. Click on Chapter 15 to select activities for this chapter.

- Video Overview
- NCLEX® Review Questions
- Critical Thinking Activities
- Current Events
- Nursing Leadership and Management in Action
- MediaLinks

References

Brady-Schwartz, D. C. (2005). Further evidence on the Magnet Recognition Program: Implications for nursing leaders. *Journal of Nursing Administration, 35*(9), 397–403.

Jones, C. B. (2004). The costs of nurse turnover. *Journal of Nursing Administration, 34*(12), 562–570.

Kerfoot, K. (2001). On Leadership: It's transformation, not patient care!, *Nursing Economics, 19*(4), 187–188.

Parrish, F. (2006). How to recruit, interview, and retain employees. *Dermatology Nursing, 18*(2), 179–180.

Simonsen, P., & Smith, T. (2007). Competency-based behavioral interviewing. *The Career Trainer*. Retrieved December 2007 from http://www.careertrainer.com/Request.jsp?lView=ViewArticle&Article=OID%3A112413&Page=OID%3A112415

U.S. Department of Labor, Bureau of Labor Statistics. (2007). Employment projections. Retrieved October 2007 from http://www.bls.gov/emp/#outlook

Staffing and Scheduling

Learning Outcomes

After completing this chapter, you will be able to:

1. Determine staffing needs.
2. Demonstrate how to use patient classification systems to calculate nursing care hours necessary.
3. Calculate FTEs.
4. Determine the appropriate staffing mix and distribution of staff.
5. Describe the various ways to schedule staff.
6. Explain how to supplement staff when needed.

MediaLink

www.prenhall.com/sullivan

See the Companion Website for chapter-specific resources at www.prenhall.com/sullivan.

Key Terms

Block staffing *p218*

Demand management
p216

Full-time equivalent *p216*

Nursing care hours *p216*

Patient classification
systems *p215*

Pools *p220*

Self-staffing and scheduling
p218

Staffing *p215*

Staffing mix *p217*

Staffing and scheduling is an important responsibility of the nurse manager. The higher the proportion of registered nurses with more hours of care provided by them, the higher is quality care received by patients, according to a landmark study in the New England Journal of Medicine (Needleman, Buerhaus, Mattke, Stewart, and Zelevinsky, 2002). Another study demonstrated that the number of baccalaureate-prepared nurses affected surgical patient mortality (Aiken, Clarke, Cheung, Sloane, & Silber, 2003). Mortality was higher when the organization employed nurses with less than a baccalaureate degree. In addition, Potter, Barr, McSweeney, and Sledge (2003) found that adequate staffing levels positively affected patient outcomes. Thus, staffing and scheduling adequate numbers of competent staff to meet patients' needs is the focus of this chapter.

Staffing

The goal of **staffing** is to provide the appropriate numbers and mix of nursing staff (nursing care hours) to match actual or projected patient care needs (patient care hours) to provide effective and efficient nursing care. There is no single or perfect method to achieve this. In addition, variability in patient census requires continuous fine-tuning.

A hospital unit may experience a steady census during the 7 days of the week or a higher census from Monday to Friday. Its patient days may be distributed evenly during the year, or it may consistently experience peaks in occupancy in certain months (seasonality pattern) such as the months of April, July, and October. Outpatient clinics may be busier on days when specialists are available or vaccines are offered. Staffing is a challenge in all health care settings.

To determine the number of staff needed, managers must examine workload patterns for the designated unit, department, or clinic. For a hospital, this means determining the level of care, average daily census, and hours of care provided 24 hours a day, 7 days a week.

Joint Commission, health care's accrediting body, specifies that the right number of competent staff be provided to meet patients' needs based on organization-selected criteria (Joint Commission, 2005). Joint Commission does not identify specific levels of nursing care hours for specific patient populations or types of patient care units, or the type of patient classification system to be used. They do, however, require that the organization meets its own criteria for staffing.

The American Nurses Association (ANA, 2005) has developed principles for nurse staffing as shown in Box 16-1. ANA recommends that health care organizations shift from an industrial, technical model to a professional model and focus on the level of nurse competency required to provide quality nursing care.

Individual state boards of nursing may take a position on nurse staffing. For example, the Kansas State Board of Nursing advises that adequate staffing to meet safe, quality care should consider RN expertise, skill mix, and patient acuity as well as availability of support staff (KSBN, 2007).

PATIENT CLASSIFICATION SYSTEMS

Patient classification systems (PCSs), sometimes referred to as patient acuity systems, use patient needs to determine workload requirements and staffing needs objectively. To be most effective, patient classification data are collected midpoint for every shift by the unit nursing staff and analyzed before the next shift to ensure appropriate numbers and mix of nursing staff.

Ideally, this system would accurately predict the number and skill level of nurses needed for the next shift. In reality, much can go amiss. Some nurses may call in sick; the nurses scheduled may not have the skill set necessary for a new admission, for example; or, most important, the patient's condition may change.

MediaLink Patient Classification System

BOX 16-1	American Nurses Association's Principles for Nurse Staffing

A. Patient Care Unit Related
  1. Appropriate staffing levels for a patient care unit reflect analysis of individual and aggregate patient needs.
  2. There is a critical need to either retire or seriously question the usefulness of the concept of nursing hours per patient day (HPPD).
  3. Unit functions necessary to support delivery of quality patient care must also be considered in determining staffing levels.

B. Staff Related
  1. The specific needs of various patient populations should determine the appropriate clinical competencies required of the nurse practicing in that area.
  2. Registered nurses must have nursing management support and representation at both the operational level and the executive level.
  3. Clinical support from experienced RNs should be readily available to those RNs with less proficiency.

C. Institution/Organization Related
  1. Organizational policy should reflect an organizational climate that values registered nurses and other employees as strategic assets and exhibits a true commitment to filling budgeted positions in a timely manner.
  2. All institutions should have documented competencies for nursing staff, including agency or supplemental and traveling RNs, for those activities that they have been authorized to perform.
  3. Organizational policies should recognize the myriad needs of both patients and nursing staff.

From *Principles for Nurse Staffing*, copyright 1999. American Nurses Association, Washington, DC. Retrieved December 2007 from http://www.nursingworld.org/MainMenuCategories/HealthcareandPolicyIssues/Reports/ANAPrinciples/NurseStaffing.aspx

Picard and Warner (2007) suggest fine-tuning PCS systems to predict the demand for nursing expertise several days in advance. They complain that basing staffing on immediate patient needs is short-sighted and often results in failure as mentioned above. Their system, called **demand management,** uses best-practices staffing protocols to predict and control the demand for nurses based on patient outcomes. Based on historical data, a patient progress pattern typifies expected patient outcomes throughout a stay. Deviations are tracked and staffing adjusted accordingly. This system allows the manager to staff into the next few days with more assurance than predicting from one shift to the next. Whatever system is used, the next step is to determine the necessary nursing care hours.

DETERMINING NURSING CARE HOURS

Patient workload trends are analyzed for each day of the week (each hour in critical care) or for a specific patient diagnosis to determine staffing needs, known as **nursing care hours** (NCHs). For example, if 26 patients with the following acuities required 161 nursing care hours, then an average of 6.19 nursing hours per patient per day (NHPPD) are required. NHPPD are calculated by dividing the total nursing care hours by the total census (number of patients).

	Number of Patients	Acuity Level	Associated Hours of Care	Total Hours of Care
	3	I	2	6
	10	II	6	60
	11	III	7	77
	2	IV	9	18
Total	26			*161*

There are no specific standards for nursing care hours (NCHs) for any type of patient or patient care unit. NCHs may vary on the average from 5 to 7 hours of care for patients on medical and/or surgical units, to 10 to 24 hours of care for patients in critical care units, to 24 to 48 hours of care for selected patients, such as new, severely burned patients.

DETERMINING FTEs

Positions are defined in terms of a **full-time equivalent** (FTE). One FTE equals 40 hours of work per week for 52 weeks, or 2,080 hours per year. In a 2-week pay period, one FTE would equal 80 hours. For computational purposes, one FTE can be filled by one person or a combination of staff with comparable expertise. For example, one nurse may work 24 hours per week, and two other nurses may each work 8 hours per week. Together, the three nurses fill one FTE (24 + 8 + 8 = 40).

Several methods are available for determining the number of FTEs required to staff a unit 24 hours a day, 7 days a week. One technique incorporates information regarding the hours of work for the staff for 2 weeks, average daily census, and hours of care. The average daily census can be determined by dividing the total patient days (obtained from daily census counts for the year) by the number of days in the year.

■ **EXAMPLE**

$$\text{Total patient days} = \frac{9490}{365} = 26 \text{ patients per day}$$

Data

Number of hours worked per FTE in 2 weeks = 80
Number of days of coverage in 2 weeks = 14
Average daily census = 26
Average nursing care hours (from PCS) = 6.15

Formula

$$x = \frac{\text{average nursing care hours} \times \text{days in staffing period} \times \text{average patient census}}{\text{hours of work per FTE in 2 weeks}}$$

$$x = \frac{6.15 \times 14 \times 26}{80} = \frac{2238.6}{80} = 27.98, \text{ or } 28 \text{ FTEs}$$

A second technique uses nursing care hours and annual hours of work provided by one FTE:

Data

Number of hours worked per FTE in 1 year = 2080
Total nursing care hours (from PCS) = 161

Formula

$$x = \frac{\text{Total nursing care hours} \times \text{days in a year}}{\text{Total annual hours per one FTE}}$$

$$x = \frac{161 \times 365}{2080} = \frac{58,765}{2080} = 28.25, \text{ or } 28 \text{ FTEs}$$

One person working full-time usually works 80 hours (ten 8-hour shifts) in a 2-week period. However, to staff an 8-hour shift takes 1.4 FTEs, one person working ten 8-hour shifts (1.0 FTE) and another person working four 8-hour shifts (0.4 FTE) in order to provide for the full-time person's 2 days off every week. For 12-hour shifts, it takes 2.1 FTEs to staff one 12-hour shift each day, each week; two people each working three 12-hour shifts and one person working one 12-hour shift each week (0.9 FTE = 0.9 FTE = 0.3 FTE = 2.1 FTEs). Therefore, the same number of FTEs is required to staff a unit for 24 hours a day for 2 weeks, regardless of whether the staff are all on 8-hour shifts (1.4 FTEs × 33 shifts = 4.2 FTEs) or 12-hour shifts (2.1 FTEs × 32 shifts = 4.2 FTEs).

DETERMINING STAFFING MIX

The same data used to determine FTEs are used to identify **staffing mix.** For example, for patient care needs involving general hygiene care, feeding, transferring, or turning patients, licensed practical nurses (LPNs) or unlicensed assistive personnel (UAPs) can be used. For patient care needs involving frequent assessments, patient education, or discharge planning, RNs will be needed because of the skills required. A high RN-skill mix allows for greater staffing flexibility. Again, information on typical or usual patient needs is obtained by using trends from the patient classification system.

DETERMINING DISTRIBUTION OF STAFF

For many patient care units, the distribution of staff varies from shift to shift and by days of the week. Patient census on a surgical unit will probably fluctuate throughout the week, with a higher census Monday through Thursday and a lower census over the weekend. In addition, some surgical units may have more complex cases earlier in the week and short-stay surgical cases later in the week. Surgical patients may have a shorter length of stay (LOS) than many medical patients. The patient census on a medical unit rarely fluctuates Monday through Friday, but may be less on weekends, when diagnostic tests are not done.

The workload on many units also varies within the 24-hour period. The care demands on a surgical unit will be heaviest early in the morning hours prior to the start of the surgical schedule; mid-morning, when the unit receives patients from critical care units; late in the afternoon, when patients return from the postanesthesia recovery unit; and in the evening hours, when same-day surgical patients are discharged.

Critical care units may have greater care needs in the mornings when transferring patients to medical or surgical units and in the early afternoon hours when admitting new surgical cases. Medical units usually have the heaviest care needs in the morning hours, when patients' daily care needs are being met and physicians are making rounds. On skilled nursing and rehabilitation units, care needs are greatest before and immediately after mealtimes and in the evening hours; during other times of the day, patients are often away from the unit and involved in various therapeutic activities.

In contrast with the medical, surgical, critical care, and rehabilitation units that have definite patterns of patient care needs, labor-and-delivery and emergency department areas cannot predict when patient care needs will be most intense. Thus, labor-and-delivery and emergency department areas must rely on block staffing to ensure that adequate nursing staff are available at all times.

Block staffing involves scheduling a set staff mix for every shift. However, there may be trends in peak workload hours in emergency departments, when additional staff (RN, UAP, or secretary) beyond the block staff are necessary. Examples of peak workload hours within the emergency department may be from 6:00 P.M. to 10:00 P.M. to accommodate patient needs after physicians' offices close or from 12:00 A.M. to 3:00 A.M. to accommodate alcohol-related injuries. All these patterns of care needs must be known when staffing requirements and work schedules are established. Data reflecting peak workload times must be continuously monitored to maintain the appropriate levels and mix of staff.

Mandating staffing ratios is not as simple a solution to quality of care as one might think. Nursing care cannot always be so easily quantified, a problem revealed when the State of California mandated that specific nurse-to-patient ratios be established (Upenieks et al., 2007). The value-added occurs when nursing hours include not only direct care but also collaboration, communication with UAPs, and patient centeredness, among other indirect nursing activities that benefit the patient.

Federal policy staffing legislation mandating specific nurse-to-patient ratios may improve quality of care but may be unlikely for administrators to implement (Keeler & Cramer, 2007). Furthermore, the legislation would not address the overall supply of nurses so badly needed.

Scheduling

CREATIVE AND FLEXIBLE STAFFING

Nurse shortages and current restrictions in salary budgets have made creative and flexible staffing patterns necessary and probably everlasting. Combinations of 4-, 6-, 8-, 10-, and 12-hour shifts and schedules that have nurses working 6 consecutive days of 12-hour shifts with 13 days off, and staffing strategies such as weekend programs and split shifts are common.

Flexible staffing patterns can be a major challenge and, in some cases, a mathematical challenge. However, once a schedule is established and agreed to by the nurse manager and the staff, it can become a cyclic schedule for an extended period of time, such as 6 to 12 months. This allows staff members to know their work schedule many months ahead of time.

The use of 8-hour and 12-hour shifts is fairly straightforward. Problems with combined staffing patterns may include:

- The perception that nurses don't work full time when they work several days in a row and then are off for several days in a row
- Disruption in continuity of care if split shifts are used (7:00 A.M. to 11:00 A.M.; 11:00 A.M. to 3:00 P.M.; 3:00 P.M. to 7:00 P.M.; 7:00 P.M. to 1:00 A.M.; 1:00 A.M. to 7:00 A.M. shifts)
- Immense challenges for nurse managers to communicate with all staff in a timely manner

Advantages of using combined staffing patterns are that it:

- Better meets patient care needs during peak workload times
- Improves staff satisfaction
- Maximizes the availability of nurses

Ten-hour shifts provide greater overlap between shifts to permit extra time for nurses to complete their work; for this reason, 10-hour shifts may increase salary expenditures. There are a few specialty units in which 10-hour shifts would be cost-efficient: postanesthesia recovery areas, operating departments, and emergency departments are examples.

SELF-STAFFING AND SCHEDULING

Some hospitals have instituted **self-staffing**. This is an empowerment strategy that allows unit staff the authority to use their backup staffing options if the patient workload increases or if unscheduled staff absences occur. Likewise, staff can and must go home early if the patient workload decreases.

Self-scheduling allows the staff to create and manage the schedule. Self-scheduling can be positive for the staff and for the manager, but attention must be paid to balancing unit needs with individual requests (Bailyn, Collins, & Song, 2007).

Hospitals can no longer arbitrarily staff patient care units on weekends or at nights with marginal numbers or levels of qualified staff. The acuity of patients in hospitals, including medical and surgical patients, mandates staffing units on the weekends by the same principles used for weekdays. Thorough trend analysis of patient data can provide the justification necessary to appropriately decrease the number of RNs, at least for some levels, because of differences in patient care needs throughout the day. Another creative method for staffing includes a weekend program, in which a nurse agrees to work 24 hours every weekend (usually two 12-hour shifts) for full-time benefits and full-time salary or premium salary.

Whether the schedule is determined by the manager or by staff, the schedule can be transparent for all staff by posting it online (Bayhealth Medical Center, 2007). In this way the organization can demonstrate fairness in scheduling and leverage staff expertise in an equitable manner. Case Study 16–1 shows how one hospital used open scheduling to decrease its use of agency staff and improve staff morale.

SUPPLEMENTING STAFF

When there is a need for additional staff because of scheduled or unscheduled absences, increased workload demands, or existing staff vacancies, the nurse manager or staffing person must find additional staff. Options include using PRN staff (staff scheduled on an as-needed basis), part-time staff, internal float pools, or outside agency nurses.

Supplemental staff are needed when workload increases beyond that which the existing staff can manage, staff absences and resignations occur, and staff vacancies exist. Chronic staffing problems need to be addressed in a proactive manner involving the nurse manager, the chief nurse executive, and the nursing personnel on the unit having the problem. Strategies for dealing with turnover are given in Chapter 19, and strategies for managing absenteeism are discussed in Chapter 20.

CASE STUDY 16-1 Scheduling

Tori Abraham and Jillian Moore are both nurse managers of general Med/Surg units at separate hospitals that are part of a large metropolitan health care system. Staffing among the Med/Surg units has been problematic due to increased patient volume and cost control measures enacted by the health care corporation. Staff members have complained numerous times that extra shifts are only offered to part-time employees and premium pay shifts are given to those with more seniority. As the holidays approach, staff tension increases as a lottery system has traditionally been used to assign shifts for major holidays. Additionally, since employees are free to transfer within any of the eight metropolitan hospitals, there has been significant turnover on the Med/Surg units as employees decide to transfer to Ambulatory Care and Same Day Surgery facilities.

Tori and Jillian have volunteered to be part of a new scheduling system for their health care system. Nurses and nursing assistants will be able to view open shifts on each unit and e-mail Tori or Jillian with requests to staff shifts for which they are qualified. By allowing staff to have greater control over which additional shifts and at which facility they prefer to work, the nurse managers hope to decrease agency staffing and increase employee satisfaction. Additional units are expected to come online, which will also allow staff to have experience on oncology, skilled nursing, and orthopedic patients. The Education Department will provide a database of employee certifications to managers to ensure staff wishing to work away from their home units are qualified for the job.

After 90 days of using the new open shift scheduling system, Tori and Jillian are pleased with the results. Agency staff use has decreased by 60 percent and staff members report they are happier with the ability to schedule their own additional shifts as well as work at a different facility without having to transfer. Holiday staffing has been easier as those employees who prefer to work premium pay for holidays are able to self schedule. Tori and Jillian present their findings to the chief nursing officer and will be part of the team implementing systemwide use of open shift scheduling.

Manager's Checklist

The nurse manager is responsible to:

- Understand the scheduling and staffing needs for his or her areas of responsibility
- Analyze the economic impact of using agency staffing for open shifts and the financial impact on budget
- Ensure adequate staffing for safe and appropriate patient care
- Communicate with staff members regarding concerns or frustrations over scheduling and staffing
- Use creative problem solving to address scheduling and staffing issues
- Improve employee job satisfaction and patient care skills

Internal Pools

Acute staffing problems can be addressed by establishing internal float pools using nursing staff and unlicensed assistive personnel (UAPs). Internal float **pools** of nurses can provide supplemental staffing at a substantially lower cost than using agency nurses. In addition, internal staff are familiar with the organization. All staff participating in the internal float pool must be adequately trained for the type of patient care they will be giving.

Internal float pools can be centralized or decentralized. A centralized pool is the most efficient. A pool of RNs, LPNs, UAPs, and unit clerks are available for placement anywhere in the institution. However, it may be difficult to place the person with the correct skills for a particular unit at the needed time.

In decentralized pools, a staff member usually works only for one nurse manager or on only one unit. The advantages of decentralized pools include better accountability, improved staffing response, and improved continuity of care. Critical care units, operating rooms, maternal–child units, and other highly specialized or technical areas tend to use a decentralized system.

Also specific staff can receive cross-training in preparation for assignment to only one other unit (Wing, 2001). A critical-care nurse might be cross-trained for the step-down unit, for example. Dual-unit positions could be established in the recruiting phase to allow the organization the maximum flexibility in scheduling and the employee an opportunity to acquire additional skills.

Open Shift Management

Open shift management is an innovative technique to allow an organization's staff to self-schedule additional shifts (Bantle, 2007). With the schedule posted online, as described above, staff members can select assignments and shifts that fit their expertise and accommodates their personal schedules (Kulma & Springer, 2006; McKnight, McDaniel, & Ehmann, 2006). This strategy is especially valuable to health care systems with several hospitals in which nurses from any hospital can select assignments at any of the others (Bantle, 2007). The organization itself could establish an internal staffing agency as one hospital did (Blake, 2006).

External Pools

For some institutions, agency nurses become part of the regular staff contracted to fill vacancies for a specified period of time (e.g., traveling nurses). However, most agency nurses are used as supplemental staff. All agency nurses require orientation to the facility and unit; they must work under the supervision of an experienced in-house nurse. Management must verify valid licensure, ensure that either the agency or agency nurse has current malpractice insurance, and develop a mechanism to evaluate the agency nurse's performance. Although an agency nurse may meet an urgent staffing need, continuity of care may be compromised and there may be some staff resentment because these nurses may earn two to three times the salary of in-house nurses.

Concern about the quality of agency nurses appears to be unfounded, according to a study analyzing adverse events in Pennsylvania hospitals (Aiken, Xue, Clarke, & Sloane, 2007). Rather, adverse outcomes resulted from deficits in the hospital environments, not from the quality of agency nurse assigned there.

Nonetheless, quality concerns spurred Joint Commission to establish a certifying mechanism for staffing agencies (Evans, 2005). Although certification is voluntary, certified agencies may have a competitive advantage or reduce their liability.

Efficient Use of UAPs

Unlicensed assistive personnel, who may or may not provide direct patient care, may be able to expand their responsibilities. Be certain that UAPs are doing every task for which they are qualified. It may be that they can assume some tasks that could free up some additional nurses' time.

Ensuring that sufficient staff are available and that they are scheduled appropriately is a demanding task and one that is constantly in flux. Nevertheless, such activities are critical to achieving positive patient outcomes and providing safe, effective, and cost-conscious staffing.

What You Know Now

- The goal of staffing and scheduling is to provide an adequate mix of nursing staff to match patient care needs.
- Joint Commission requires that organizations determine criteria for nurse staffing and provide adequate numbers of competent staff to meet that criteria.
- Patient classification systems use patient needs to determine workload requirements and staffing needs.

- Scheduling involves assigning available staff in a way that patient care needs are met. Scheduling is always a challenge.
- Flexible and creative staffing and scheduling techniques are increasingly necessary.
- Self-staffing and scheduling is an option in which nursing staff participate in designing the schedule and accepting responsibility for ensuring attendance.

Tools for Handling Staffing and Scheduling

1. Familiarize yourself with the current patient classification or acuity system in use.
2. Determine the nursing care hours needed.
3. Determine FTEs needed.
4. Create or modify a schedule that best meets your patients' needs.
5. Supplement staff as needed.
6. Consider self-staffing if appropriate.

Questions to Challenge You

1. What has been your experience with staffing? Use any work setting where you are or have been an employee. How well did it work? Was there adequate coverage to meet the needs of the organization? Explain.
2. Using the formulas for calculating FTEs in the chapter, create your own examples and work the problems from them. Were you able to compute needed FTEs? Now calculate the hours needed when nursing staff work 8-hour or 12-hour shifts.
3. On occasion, there are more staff available than are needed. As a nurse manager, how would you handle this? How might the staff respond?
4. No one is ever completely satisfied with the schedule. How would you handle a staff member who repeatedly asks to have his schedule changed?

Explore MediaLink 🌐

Additional interactive resources for this chapter can be found on the Website at http://www.prenhall. com/sullivan. Click on Chapter 16 to select activities for this chapter.

- Video Overview
- NCLEX® Review Questions
- Critical Thinking Activities
- Current Events
- Nursing Leadership and Management in Action
- MediaLinks

References

Aiken, L. H., Clarke, S. P., Cheung, R. B., Sloane, D. M., & Silber, J. H. (2003). Educational levels of hospital nurses and surgical patient mortality. *JAMA, 290*(12), 1617–1623.

Aiken, L. H., Xue, Y., Clarke, S., & Sloane, D. M. (2007). Supplemental nurse staffing in hospitals and quality of care. *Journal of Nursing Administration, 37*(7/8), 335–342.

American Nurses Association. (2005). *Principles for nurse staffing.* Washington, DC: Author.

Bailyn, L., Collins, R., & Song, Y. (2007). Self-scheduling for hospital nurses: An attempt and its difficulties. *Journal of Nursing Management, 15*(1), 72–77.

Bantle, A. (2007). Automated workforce tracking keeps you flexible. *Nursing Management, 38*(9), 29.

Bayhealth Medical Center. (2007). BidShift: Bayhealth medical center first in Delaware to launch BidShift biotech week. (news release) *NewsRx.com.*

Blake, R. E. (2006). Scheduling software supports cost-saving staffing alternative. *Health Management Technology, 27*(12), 34.

Evans, M. (2005). Strong-arming agencies. *Modern Healthcare, 35*(45), 12.

Joint Commission. (2005). *Comprehensive accreditation manual for hospitals: The official handbook.* Oakbrook Terrace, IL: Author.

Kansas State Board of Nursing. (2007). Nurse staffing position statement. Retrieved January 2008 from http://www.ksbn.org/ positionstatements/Nurse%20Staffing%20.doc

Keeler, H. J., & Cramer, M. E. (2007). A policy analysis of federal registered nurses safe staffing legislation. *Journal of Nursing Administration, 37*(7/8), 350–356.

Kulma, M., & Springer, B. (2006). Easing the bottom-line impact of staffing shortages: A case study in shift bidding. *Healthcare Financial Management, 60*(4), 92.

McKnight, B., McDaniel, S., & Ehmann, V. (2006). Try point incentives for employee reward and recognition. *Nursing Management, 7*(12), 42–45.

Needleman, J., Buerhaus, P., Mattke, S., Stewart, M., & Zelevinsky, K. (2002). Nurse-staffing levels and the quality of care in hospitals. *New England Journal of Medicine, 346*(22), 1715–1722.

Pickard, B., & Warner, M. (2007). Demand management: A methodology for outcomes-driven staffing and patient flow management. *Nurse Leader, 5*(2), 30–34.

Potter, P., Barr, N., McSweeney, M., & Sledge, J. (2003). Identifying nurse staffing and patient outcome relationships: A guide for change in care delivery. *Nursing Economics, 21*(4), 158–166.

Upenieks, V. V., Akhavan, J., Kotlerman, J., Esser, J., & Ngo, M. J. (2007). Value-added care: A new way of assessing nursing staffing ratios and workload variability. *Journal of Nursing Administration, 37*(5), 243–252.

Wing, K. T. (2001). When flex comes to shove: Staffing and hospital census. *Nursing Management, 32*(1), 43–46.

Motivating and Developing Staff

A Model of Job Performance
- EMPLOYEE MOTIVATION
- MOTIVATIONAL THEORIES
- EMPLOYEE ABILITY

Staff Development
- HOW PEOPLE LEARN
- ORIENTATION
- STAFF DEVELOPMENT PROCESS
- STAFF DEVELOPMENT METHODS

Cultural and Generational Differences
- CULTURAL DIFFERENCES
- GENERATIONAL DIFFERENCES

Learning Outcomes

After completing this chapter, you will be able to:

1. Describe how motivation and ability affect job performance.
2. Describe how different theories explain motivation.
3. Discuss how different theories explain learning.
4. Explain why the goal of staff development should be to transfer learning to the job.
5. Demonstrate how educational programs enhance the organization's effectiveness.
6. Describe how cultural and generational differences affect learning.

MediaLink

www.prenhall.com/sullivan

See the Companion Website for chapter-specific resources at
www.prenhall.com/sullivan.

Key Terms

Adult education theory *p231*
Content theories *p225*
Equity *p227*
Equity theory *p227*
Evaluation *p236*
Expectancy *p227*
Expectancy theory *p227*
Extinction *p226*
Goal-setting theory *p228*
Implementation *p235*

Instrumentality *p227*
Motivation *p225*
Needs assessment *p234*
On-the-job instruction *p235*
Operant conditioning *p225*
Orientation *p232*
Peer coaching *p236*
Planning *p234*
Preceptor *p232*
Process theories *p225*

Punishment *p225*
Reinforcement theory (behavior modification) *p225*
Relapse prevention *p231*
Shaping *p226*
Social learning theory *p231*
Staff development *p230*
Valence *p227*

A continual and troublesome question facing nurse managers today is why some employees perform better than others. Making decisions about who performs what tasks in a particular manner without first considering individual behavior can lead to irreversible, long-term problems. Each employee is different in many respects. A manager needs to ask how such differences influence the behavior and performance of the job requirements. Ideally, the manager performs this assessment when the new employee is hired. In reality, however, many employees are placed in positions without the manager having adequate knowledge of their abilities and/or interests. This often results in problems with employee performance, as well as conflict between employees and managers. In addition, first-time managers are often uncomfortable with initiating motivational techniques (Strelecky, 2004).

Employee performance literature ultimately reveals two major dimensions as determinants of job performance: motivation and ability (Hersey, Blanchard, & Johnson, 2007). This chapter describes a model of job performance and presents techniques for evaluating performance.

A Model of Job Performance

Nurse managers spend considerable time making judgments about the fit among individuals, job tasks, and effectiveness. Such judgments are typically influenced by both the manager's and the employee's characteristics. For example, ability, instinct, and aspiration levels—as well as age, education, and family background—account for why some employees perform well and others poorly. Based on these factors, a model that considers motivation and ability as determinants of job performance is presented in Table 17-1.

This performance model identifies six categories likely to be viewed as important by the nurse manager:

1. Daily job performance
2. Attendance
3. Punctuality
4. Adherence to policies and procedures
5. Absence of incidents, errors, and accidents
6. Honesty and trustworthiness

TABLE 17-1   A Simplified Model of Job Performance

MOTIVATION	AND	ABILITY	=	EMPLOYEE PERFORMANCE
Compensation		Responsibilities		Daily job performance
Benefits		Education—basic/advanced		Attendance
Job design		Continuing education		Punctuality
Leadership style		Skills/abilities		Adherence to policies and procedures
Recruitment and selection				Absence of incidents/errors/accidents
Employee needs/goals/abilities				Honesty and trustworthiness

Although there is conceptual overlap in these categories, separate designation of each helps emphasize their importance.

When using this model, carefully consider several factors. First, the health care organization should establish and communicate clear descriptions of daily job performance so that deviations from expected behaviors can be easily identified and documented. Second, behaviors considered troublesome in one department may be acceptable in another department. Finally, some behaviors are viewed as serious only when repeated (e.g., being late to work), whereas others are classified as troublesome following only one incident (e.g., a medication error with severe consequences).

EMPLOYEE MOTIVATION

Motivation describes the factors that initiate and direct behavior. Because individuals bring to the workplace different needs and goals, the type and intensity of motivators vary among employees. Nurse managers prefer motivated employees because they strive to find the best way to perform their jobs. Motivated employees are more likely to be productive than are nonmotivated workers. This is one reason that motivation is an important aspect of enhancing employee performance.

MOTIVATIONAL THEORIES

Historically, motivational theories were concerned with three things:

1. What mobilizes or energizes human behavior
2. What directs behavior toward the accomplishment of some objective
3. How such behavior is sustained over time

The usefulness of motivational theories depends on their ability to explain motivation adequately, to predict with some degree of accuracy what people will actually do, and, finally, to suggest practical ways of influencing employees to accomplish organizational objectives. Motivational theories can be classified into at least two distinct groups: content theories and process theories.

Content Theories

In general, **content theories** emphasize individual needs or the rewards that may satisfy those needs. There are two types of content theories: instinct and need. Instinct theorists characterized instincts as inherited or innate tendencies that predisposed individuals to behave in certain ways. These theories were attacked for their difficulty in pinpointing the specific motivating behaviors and the acute awareness of the variability in the strengths of instincts across individuals. In addition, the development of need theories supported the concept that motives were learned behaviors.

Process Theories

Whereas content theories attempt to explain why a person behaves in a particular manner, **process theories** emphasize how the motivation process works to direct an individual's effort into performance. These theories add another dimension to the manager's understanding of motivation and help to predict employee behavior in certain circumstances. Examples of process theories are reinforcement theory, expectancy theory, equity theory, and goal-setting theory.

Reinforcement theory, also known as behavior modification, views motivation as learning (Skinner, 1953). According to this theory, behavior is learned through a process called **operant conditioning**, in which a behavior becomes associated with a particular consequence. In operant conditioning, the response-consequence connection is strengthened over time—that is, it is learned.

Consequences may be positive, as with praise or recognition, or negative. Positive reinforcers are used for the express purpose of increasing a desired behavior.

Kyle, a staff nurse, offered a creative idea to redesign work flow on the unit. His manager supported the idea and helped Kyle implement the new process. In addition, the manager praised Kyle for the extra effort and publicly recognized him for the idea. Kyle was encouraged by the outcome and sought other solutions to work-flow problems.

Negative reinforcers are used to inhibit an undesired behavior. **Punishment** is a common technique.

To get Rose to chart adequately, the manager required her to come to his office daily with her patient charts until she achieved an acceptable level of charting. Rose found the task laborious and humiliating. As a result, Rose soon was charting appropriately.

Because punishment is negative in character, an employee may fail to improve and also may avoid the manager and the job, as well. Research has shown that the effects of punishment are generally temporary. Undesirable behavior will be suppressed only as long as the manager monitors the situation and the threat of punishment is present. Conversely, research has demonstrated that positive reinforcement is the best way to change behavior.

Extinction is another technique used to eliminate negative behavior. By removing a positive reinforcer, undesired behavior is extinguished.

Consider the case of Jasmine, a chronic complainer. To curb this behavior, her manager chose to ignore her many complaints and not try to resolve them. Initially Jasmine complained more, but eventually she realized her behavior was not getting the desired response and stopped complaining.

A problem with operant conditioning (behavior modification) is that there is no sure way to elicit the desired behavior so that it can be reinforced. In addition, staff and the manager may view consequences differently.

Take Thad, for example. As a new employee, Thad conscientiously completed critical paths for his assigned patients. When the manager recognized Thad for his good work, his peers began to exclude him from the group. Although the manager was attempting positive reinforcement, Thad quit completing critical paths because he felt the manager had alienated him from his coworkers.

Another procedure is **shaping**. Shaping involves selectively reinforcing behaviors that are successively closer approximations to the desired behavior. Each successively closer approximation to the desired behavior is reinforced and well established before progressive reinforcement is given to closer approximations of the desired behavior. When people become clearly aware that desirable rewards are contingent on a specific behavior, their behavior will eventually change.

Behavior modification works quite well, provided that rewards can be found that, in fact, employees see as positive reinforcers and provided that supervisory personnel can control such rewards or make them contingent on performance. This does not mean that all rewards work equally well or that the same rewards will continue to function effectively over a long time. If someone is praised four or five times a day every day, the praise would soon begin to wear thin; it would cease to be a positive reinforcer. Care must be taken not to overdo a good thing.

Figure 17-1 illustrates the use of various schedules of reinforcement. *Partial schedules* of reinforcement, reinforcing behavior with every second or third occurrence, is more effective in changing behavior. This *fixed-ratio schedule* of reinforcement requires very close monitoring to reinforce every *n*th response and is obviously not very practical. Reinforcing on a fairly regular basis is known as a fixed-interval schedule of reinforcement; an example is the distribution of weekly or monthly paychecks.

A continuous schedule of reinforcement is the fastest method of establishing or learning a new behavior,

	Interval	Ratio
Fixed	Fixed interval Reinforcer given after a given time Weekly or monthly paychecks Regularly scheduled exams	Fixed ratio Reinforcer given after a given number of behavior occurrences Piece rate pay Commissioned salespeople; certain amount is given for each dollar of sales
Variable	Variable interval Reinforcer given at random times Occasional praise by boss on unscheduled visits Unspecified number of pop quizzes to students	Variable ratio Reinforcer given after a random number of behavior occurrences Random quality checks with praise for zero defects Commissioned salespeople; a varying number of calls is required to obtain a given sale
	Time based	Behavior occurrence based

Figure 17-1 ● Four types of intermittent reinforcement schedules. *From* Organizational Behavior, *8th ed. (p. 107), by J. R. Schermerhorn, J. G. Hunt, and R. N. Osborn, 2003, Hoboken, NJ: Wiley. Reprinted with permission.*

whereas any kind of partial schedule of reinforcement is much slower. On the other hand, behaviors learned under a continuous schedule also extinguish very quickly once reinforcement stops. Behavior learned on a partial schedule continues for a much longer time without being reinforced. In addition, continuous schedules of reinforcement are probably better when money is used rather than other reinforcers, such as praise.

Like reinforcement theory, **expectancy theory** (Vroom, 1964) emphasizes the role of rewards and their relationship to the performance of desired behaviors. Expectancy theory regards people as reacting deliberately and actively to their environment.

Vroom asserts that individuals are motivated by their expectancies (beliefs) about future outcomes (consequences of behavior) and by the value they place on those outcomes. Three components are important in predicting what and how much effort a person will exert:

1. **Expectancy** is the perceived probability that effort will result in successful performance, that is, the degree to which people expect they "can do" something.
2. **Instrumentality** is the perceived probability that performance will lead to desired outcomes.
3. **Valence** is the perceived value (attractiveness or unattractiveness) of an outcome.

The net effect of these three components is the amount of effort an individual will exert. Thus, when any one component is drastically reduced, so is motivation (effort). If staff members do not believe that they are capable of performing a task (expectancy), or if they believe there is little chance of reward for their work (instrumentality), or if the value of the outcome (valence) is low, motivation is reduced.

In an effort to improve the amount of delegation by the nurses on her unit, Andrea approached the situation from an expectancy theory perspective. She identified that the nurses wanted to assign more duties to assistive personnel but were reluctant because of concerns about liability. Once Andrea was able to clarify liability issues, the nurses were eager to delegate nonprofessional tasks in order to be able to devote more time to their professional responsibilities.

Expectancy theory also considers multiple outcomes. Consider the possibility of a promotion to nurse manager. Even though a staff nurse believes such a promotion is positive and is a desirable reward for competent performance in patient care, the nurse also realizes that there are possibly some negative outcomes (e.g., working longer hours, losing the close camaraderie enjoyed with other staff members). These multiple outcomes will influence the staff nurse's decision.

Expectancy theory is useful because of its clear managerial implications. First, managers can maximize expectancies by assigning to employees tasks that they are capable of performing or by providing them with the necessary training. In addition, removing obstacles (inadequate resources, lack of information or cooperation from others) increases employees' expectancies. Second, instrumentalities can be maximized by making certain that rewards (and punishment) are made contingent on performance. Finally, rewards must be perceived as desirable enough to make the effort toward high performance worthwhile. Similarly, to act as a successful deterrent to inappropriate job behavior, punishment must be regarded as sufficiently undesirable.

Similarly, **equity theory** suggests that effort and job satisfaction depend on the degree of equity, or perceived fairness, in the work situation (Adams, 1963, 1965). **Equity** simply means that a person perceives that one's contribution to the job is rewarded in the same proportion that another person's contribution is rewarded. Job contributions include such things as ability, education, experience, and effort, whereas rewards include job satisfaction, pay, prestige, and any other outcomes an employee regards as valuable.

Thus, equity theory is concerned with the conditions under which employees perceive their contributions to the job and the rewards obtained as fair and equitable. Equity does not in any way imply equality; rather, it suggests that employees who bring more to the job will receive greater rewards. Inequity occurs when an employee's effort and rewards are perceived to be disproportional to that of another person, whether a coworker or a person doing a similar job for a different employer. Inequity, then, motivates a change in behavior that may either increase or decrease actual effort and job performance. However, reducing inequity may or may not change performance.

Employees can try to restore what they perceive as equity in a variety of ways. First, they can increase or decrease effort. Nurses can attempt to increase their status by assuming more patient care assignments, spending more time on charting, or exhibiting other behaviors reflecting additional effort. Second, they may attempt to persuade the people to whom they are comparing themselves to increase or decrease their inputs—persuading nursing assistants to work less, for instance. Third, they may attempt to persuade the organization to change either their own rewards or those of the comparison persons (e.g., salary changes or perquisites). Fourth, they may psychologically distort the perceived importance and value of their own contributions and rewards ("How could they run this unit without me?"). Fifth, they may distort the perceived importance and value of the comparison persons' contributions or rewards ("What can you expect of assistants?").

Psychologically distorting the perceptions of a comparison person's outcomes or inputs is probably the easiest way to restore equity without actually changing one's effort. Alternatively, the staff member may select a different comparison person, someone who is seen as more relevant for the comparison being made, such as the nurse manager. Finally, the individual may actually leave the organization.

Perceived fairness of rewards affects the manner in which individuals view their jobs and the organization, and it can affect the amount of effort they expend in accomplishing tasks. Moreover, evidence indicates that inequitable rewards, especially underpayment inequity, lead to increased psychological tension, lower job satisfaction, and poor job performance. In times of economic retrenchment, when no one in the organization receives a salary increase, employees, for example, may perceive the situation as equitable if they believed it to be equitable prior to the retrenchment; thus, job satisfaction may not be adversely affected. However, simply distributing rewards equitably does not necessarily improve an otherwise poor motivational environment. In today's economic environment, with organizations being redesigned and reengineered and positions reduced, problems with perceived equity can be anticipated.

Unlike expectancy theory and equity theory, **goal-setting theory** suggests that it is not the rewards or outcomes of task performance per se that cause a person to expend effort, but rather the goal itself.

There are three basic propositions in goal setting (Locke, 1968):

1. Specific goals lead to higher performance than do such general goals as "Do your best."
2. Specific, difficult goals lead to higher performance than specific, easy goals, provided that those involved accept the goals.
3. Incentives such as money, knowledge of results, praise and reproof, participation, competition, and time limits affect behavior only if they cause individuals to change their goals or to accept goals that have been assigned to them.

Timothy was new to a home care hospice program. An important skill in care with the terminally ill is therapeutic communication. Timothy and his manager recognized that he needed help to improve his skills in communicating with these patients and their families. His manager asked him to write two goals related to communication. Timothy expressed a desire to attend a communications workshop and also indicated he would try at least one new communication technique each week. Within a month, Timothy's therapeutic communication skills had already improved. As a result, Timothy was more satisfied with his position, his patients received more compassionate care, and Timothy found his work more rewarding.

According to goal-setting theory, the function of rewards is to help ensure that the individual will accept an assigned goal or to set a more specific, difficult personal goal. The specificity and difficulty of the goal mobilize energy and direct behavior toward goal accomplishment. If the person sees tasks and duties as reasonable and specific, difficult goals are likely to produce higher performance as long as such performance is rewarded and the individual is held accountable for the task.

Obviously there is no single approach to motivating staff members. Some methods work better than others with different people or in different settings. However, each theory of work motivation contributes something to our understanding of, and ultimately our ability to influence, employee motivation.

Figure 17-2 illustrates a simple model of how the various motivational theories are related. First, there is a task to be accomplished. If this task is expressed in terms of a specific, difficult goal that is accepted by the staff member, a relatively high degree of performance may realistically be expected in most situations. How does this happen? Goals, perceived ability, and perceived situational constraints all combine to form the perceived likelihood that effort will lead to a given level of performance or goal accomplishment. This expectancy, when combined with the belief that valued rewards will follow from goal attainment (instrumentality), prompts the expenditure of effort (motivation). Thus, goal-setting and expectancy theory suggest not only that staff members should know exactly what they should be doing, but also that they should perceive rewards as contingent on performance of their assigned tasks.

Managers who are effective leaders draw from their knowledge of various motivational theories to create the environment in which their staff derive needs satisfaction from the work itself. No motivation theory provides a complete description of the motivational process;

MEDIALINK **Personal Motivation**

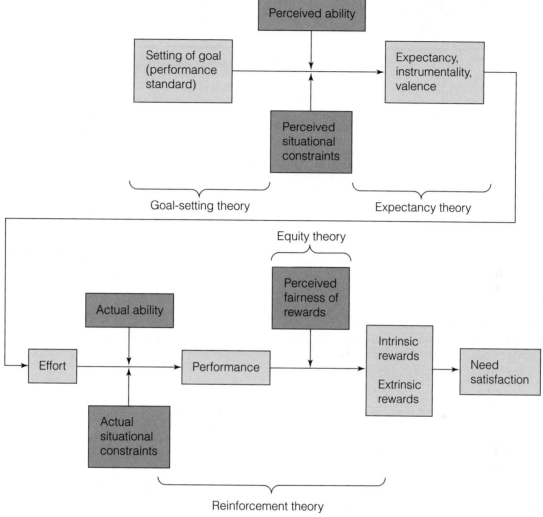

Figure 17-2 ● Integrated model of the motivational process.

each theory or technique brings a different perspective and contribution to understanding and influencing motivation. Effective staff motivation is best accomplished by judiciously combining theories and techniques so that their effects are complementary.

Case Study 17-1 illustrates how one nurse manager used her ingenuity to motivate staff.

EMPLOYEE ABILITY

Managers can arrange for staff to participate in development programs that upgrade the knowledge and skills of employees as job requirements change and in special programs, such as intensive workshops and continuing education. The nurse manager plays a crucial role in ongoing assessment and evaluation of employees, providing opportunities and encouragement for their advancement

and maintenance of abilities. In addition, the nurse manager is in the best position to communicate the department's educational needs to the administration so that adequate resources are allocated for this function.

Staff Development

Every individual is unique and, therefore, will vary in education, skills, and ability. There are a few common denominators; for example, all new staff nurses will have passed state board examinations. Yet educational preparation will vary, and some people will not have developed all of the skills and knowledge necessary to perform at the expected level. Furthermore, new nursing practice and technology call for ongoing staff education. One of the nurse manager's major responsibilities

CASE STUDY 17-1 Motivating Staff

Jamie Edgar is nurse manager of the mental health outpatient clinic for a large county health department. Her staff includes nurses, licensed clinical social workers, licensed mental health technicians, and clerical support staff. State funding for mental health services has been drastically cut. Jamie had a difficult decision to make regarding who on the staff would receive pay increases and who would not. Compounding her problem is the shortage of qualified psychiatric nurses and two vacant nursing positions she has been unable to fill due to the low starting salary.

Jamie decides that the nursing staff will receive a 4 percent raise and the licensed clinical social workers will receive a 3 percent raise. The mental health technicians and clerical staff will not receive a wage increase this year. The mental health technicians and clerical staff members are upset when Jamie tells them there will not be any pay increases this year. Kevin Adams, a licensed mental health technician, and Charlotte DuBois, an administrative assistant, have both expressed frustration about the disparity in pay increases. Over the past 2 workweeks, Kevin has been clocking in 10 minutes late each work day and taking longer lunch periods than scheduled. The quality of Charlotte's work has decreased, and she is using more business time for personal telephone calls and personal business.

Jamie is concerned that Kevin's and Charlotte's negative attitudes will continue to affect their work, as well as the morale of the staff. Initially, she tried more frequent praise of Kevin's and Charlotte's work, but after 3 weeks, noted no improvement in their attitude or performance. She counseled each employee individually about performance expectations; however, neither employee made an effort to improve his or her behavior. After receiving a final budget for her clinic, Jamie allocated $800 for training of clerical staff and mental health technicians. She met with Kevin, Charlotte, and two other staff members. Jamie asked the group to assist her in determining how to best spend the $800 training budget. The group agreed that time-management skills could be improved among many of the staff. After reviewing the cost associated with several time-management training programs, the group was surprised at the expense. Jamie challenged her group to think of alternative ideas other than sending staff members to a seminar and offered a restaurant gift certificate for the most creative ideas.

At their next meeting, Kevin produced reviews of several interactive CD-ROM training programs. Kevin had searched the Internet for the best price for the programs and brought in several demonstration CDs of the top two time-management programs. Charlotte proposed purchasing planners for those staff members who didn't already have a planner or personal digital assistant. Charlotte had spoken to the supplier who had the contract for county office supplies. They had agreed to a price of $12 per planner for a complete year of time-planning supplies. The group agreed that both Kevin and Charlotte's ideas were excellent, as well as coming in under the $800 limit.

Kevin and Charlotte were responsible for implementing their ideas with staff who requested training in time management. Although neither employee received a raise in base salary, Jamie was able to secure approval for both to work extra hours to complete training for the clinic staff. Jamie continued to praise both employees for their commitment to the clinic and their coworkers. Kevin began to arrive promptly for each work shift and kept his lunch periods to 30 minutes. Charlotte was eager to demonstrate to coworkers how her new planner helped her prioritize work and personal tasks. Her use of work time for personal business greatly decreased.

Manager's Checklist

The nurse manager is responsible to:

- Understand motivating factors for employees and how motivation affects job performance
- Use motivational techniques to enhance employee performance
- Utilize creative techniques to motivate staff when traditional rewards such as pay or benefit increases are unavailable
- Empower staff to use creativity to enhance job performance

is to enhance staff performance, an activity usually referred to as **staff development**.

HOW PEOPLE LEARN

Most early educational theories were based on the belief that the fundamental purpose of education was the transmission of the totality of human knowledge from one generation to the next. This is a workable assumption, provided that the quantity of knowledge is small enough to be managed collectively by the educational system and that the rate of change is small enough to allow the increase of knowledge to be packaged and delivered.

Today, however, these conditions do not exist. Instead, we live in a period of knowledge explosion in which cultural and technological change is rapid. For example, from the time a student enters nursing school to a few years after completing the educational program some of the early learning already is out of date. The implications of this are twofold. First, education must be viewed as a lifelong continuous process. Second, education must become a partnership between the learner and experts so that it occurs every day in an unstructured manner.

The process of education operates constantly during conscious human activity. How people learn, the content of what they need to learn, the processes of learning, and how to teach all are important to education. People even need to be taught how to learn so they can do their learning efficiently and are prepared to learn new information as it becomes available.

Every health care organization has specific goals, and their attainment requires trained personnel. Therefore, most organizations have specialized educational personnel who may be assigned directly to nursing service or be part of an organization-wide education department. These educators administer orientation programs, ongoing employee development, and specialized, unit-based programs. Regardless of the structure of the education department, the nurse manager remains extensively involved in the instructional process. A new employee, for example, must be taught specific work rules and tasks as well as new nursing or medical practices at the unit level. Properly educating employees usually results in higher productivity, fewer accidents or mistakes, better morale, greater pride in work, and better nursing care. Furthermore, continuing staff development is an investment with benefits for the organization, the individual, and the profession (Joyce & Cowman, 2007).

Educators must rely on principles of learning and basic knowledge about educational materials to develop instructional interventions. Also, theories of motivation can be applied to build the individual's desire to learn and to apply skills and concepts learned. Three learning theories help guide what we know about staff development. They are social learning theory, relapse prevention, and adult education theory.

Social Learning Theory

Bandura described **social learning theory** in 1977. It is a behavioral theory based on reinforcement. Bandura believed people learn new behaviors through direct experience or by observing other people performing the behaviors, which result in positive and negative outcomes. The observer learns that successful behaviors should be retained and behavior that is punished or not rewarded should be abandoned.

According to social learning theory, the anticipation of reinforcement influences what the person does or does not observe. This response suggests that observational learning is more effective when the observer is informed in advance about the benefits of adopting a certain behavior than when the observer is rewarded for imitative behavior. Knowing the benefits in advance also increases the observer's attentiveness to the model's actions.

After observing the model, the observer formulates how and in what sequence certain response components must be combined to produce the desired, new behavior. In other words, behavior is learned through cognitive processes before it is performed. Information is commonly conveyed by physical demonstrations, pictorial representations, verbal or written descriptions, and different media sources. ***Figure 17-3*** illustrates this theory.

Relapse Prevention

Relapse prevention emphasizes learning a set of self-control and coping strategies to increase retention of newly learned behaviors. The premise behind this model is that learners are:

1. Taught to anticipate high-risk situations
2. Taught coping strategies for avoiding high-risk situations
3. Taught that slight slips or relapses are predictable and need not become failures

As a result, learner self-efficacy increases because the learner anticipates potential problems and is confident in using coping strategies. In addition, this model minimizes the possibility of small relapses turning into absolute failure due to a violation of abstinence. Based on this model, learners should be encouraged to identify possible failure situations and ways to cope with them and practice such situations using new skills in the neutral environment of education.

Adult Education Theory

Knowles proposed the **adult education theory**, which described differences in the learning styles of adults and children; it was assumed that the same teaching principles could be used for both children and adults. Knowles suggested four basic conceptual differences between adult and child education: self-concept, experience,

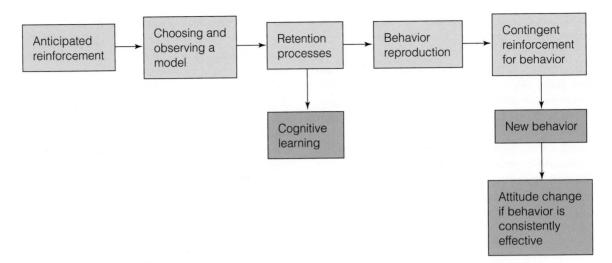

Figure 17-3 ● Social learning theory.

readiness to learn, and time perspective. These characteristics are described in Table 17-2. All of these learning theories are appropriate for adult students, such as nurses.

ORIENTATION

Getting an employee started in the right way is very important. Among other things, a well-planned **orientation** reduces the anxiety that new employees feel when beginning the job. In addition, socializing the employee into the workplace contributes to unit effectiveness by reducing dissatisfaction, absenteeism, and turnover.

Orientation is a joint responsibility of both the organization's staff development personnel and the nursing manager. In most organizations, the new staff nurse completes the orientation program, whereupon the nurse manager (or someone appointed to do this) provides an on-site orientation. Staff development personnel and unit staff should have a clear understanding of their respective, specific responsibilities so that nothing is left to chance. The development staff should provide information involving matters that are organization-wide in nature and relevant to all new employees, such as benefits, mission, governance, general policies and procedures, safety, quality improvement, infection control, and common equipment. The nurse manager should concentrate on those items unique to the employee's specific job.

New employees often have unrealistically high expectations about the amount of challenge and responsibility they will find in their first job. If they are assigned fairly undemanding, entry-level tasks, they feel discouraged and disillusioned. The result is job dissatisfaction, turnover, and low productivity.

So one function of orientation is to correct any unrealistic expectations. The nurse manager needs to outline very specifically what is expected of new employees. Such realistic job previews help prevent early departures from the organization and, possibly, the nursing profession.

Socializing new employees can sometimes be difficult because of the anxiety people feel when they first come on the job. They simply do not hear all of the information they are given. They spend a lot of energy attempting to integrate and interpret the information presented, and consequently they miss some of it. So repetition may be necessary the first few days or weeks on the job.

Because nurse managers are an extremely important part of the socialization process, they should discuss everything that they expect of the new employee openly and specifically. The new employee adapts more rapidly if this is done. The manager should address everything from standards of performance, attendance, and treatment of patients to the feedback the employee should expect in performance appraisals.

One method of orientation is the **preceptor** model, which can be used to assist new employees and to reward experienced staff nurses. The preceptor model provides a means for orienting and socializing the new nurse as well as providing a mechanism to recognize exceptionally competent staff nurses. Staff nurses who serve as preceptors are selected based on their clinical competence, organizational skills, ability to guide and direct others, and concern for the effective orientation of new nurses. The primary goal is for preceptors to assist new nurses to acquire the neces-

TABLE 17-2	Characteristics of Adult Learners and Educational Implications

ADULT LEARNER CHARACTERISTICS	IMPLICATIONS FOR ADULT LEARNING
1. *The need to know.*	Adults need to know why they need to learn something before undertaking to learn it. The first task of the facilitator of learning is to help the learners become aware of the "need to know." At the very least, facilitators can make an intellectual case for the value of the learning in improving the effectiveness of the learners' performance or the quality of their lives. Even more potent tools for raising the level of awareness of the need to know are real or simulated experiences in which the learners discover for themselves the gaps between where they are now and where they want to be. Personnel appraisal systems, job rotation, exposure to role models, and diagnostic performance assessments are examples of such tools.
2. *The learners' self-concept.*	Adults have a self-concept of being responsible for their own decisions, for their own lives. Once they have arrived at that self-concept they develop a deep psychological need to be seen by others and treated by others as being capable of self-direction. They resent and resist situations in which they feel others are imposing their wills on them. This presents a serious problem in adult education: the minute adults walk into an activity labeled "education," "training," or anything synonymous, they hark back to their conditioning in their previous school experience, put on their dunce hats of dependency, fold their arms, sit back, and say "teach me."
3. *The role of the learners' experiences.*	Adults come into an educational activity with both a greater volume and a different quality of experience from youths. The emphasis in adult education is on experiential techniques—techniques that tap into the experience of the learners, such as group discussion, simulation exercises, problem-solving activities, case method, and laboratory methods instead of transmittal techniques. Also, greater emphasis is placed on peer-helping activities.
4. *Readiness to learn.*	Adults become ready to learn those things they need to know and be able to do in order to cope effectively with their real-life situations. An especially rich source of "readiness to learn" is the developmental tasks associated with moving from one developmental stage to the next. The critical implication of this assumption is the importance of timing learning experiences to coincide with those developmental tasks.
5. *Orientation to learning.*	There are ways to induce readiness through exposure to models of superior performance, career counseling, simulation exercises, and other techniques.
	In contrast to children's and youths' subject-centered orientation to learning (at least in school), adults are life-centered (or task-centered or problem-centered) in their orientation to learning. Adults are motivated to learn to the extent that they perceive that learning will help them perform tasks or deal with problems that they confront in their life situations. Furthermore, they learn new knowledge, understandings, skills, values, and attitudes most effectively when they are presented in the context of application to real-life situations.
6. *Motivation.*	While adults are responsive to some external motivators (better jobs, promotions, higher salaries, and the like), the most potent motivators are internal pressures (the desire for increased job satisfaction, self-esteem, quality of life, and the like), but this motivation is frequently blocked by such barriers as negative self-concept as a student, inaccessibility of opportunities or resources, time constraints, and programs that violate principles of adult learning.

From: *The Adult Learner,* 6th ed. (pp. 64–68), by M. S. Knowles, E. F. Holton III, and R. A. Swanson, 1998, Woburn, MA: Butterfield-Heinemann. Reprinted with permission from Elsevier.

sary knowledge and skills so that they can function effectively on the job.

Preceptorships offer new nurses the advantage of an on-the-job instruction program tailored specifi-

cally to their needs. Staff nurses (preceptors) benefit by having an opportunity to sharpen their clinical skills and increasing their personal and professional satisfaction. The new nurse works closely with the preceptor for approximately 3 weeks, although the duration of the preceptorship may vary according to the nurse's individual learning needs or the organization's policies.

The primary function of the preceptor is to orient the new nurse to the unit. This includes proper socialization of the new nurse within the group as well as familiarizing her or him with unit functions. The preceptor teaches any unfamiliar procedures and helps the new nurse develop any necessary skills. The preceptor acts as a resource person on matters of unit functions as well as policies and procedures.

New nurses may need to use their preceptors as counselors as they make their transition to the unit. If new nurses experience discrepancy between their educational preparation or their expectations and the realities of working in the unit, the preceptor's role as counselor can prove invaluable in helping them cope with "reality shock."

The preceptor also serves as a staff nurse role model demonstrating work-related tasks, how to set priorities, solve problems and make decisions, manage time, delegate tasks, and interact with others. In addition, the preceptor evaluates the new nurse's performance and provides both verbal and written feedback to encourage development. The staff development department plays an integral role in the preceptor arrangement by providing the initial orientation, familiarizing the new employee with the organization and general policies and procedures before he or she begins work with the preceptor. The staff development department's function is to teach the experienced nurse the role of a preceptor, principles of adult education applicable to learning needs, how to teach necessary skills, how to plan teaching, how to evaluate teaching and learning objectives, and how to provide both formal and informal feedback.

Residency programs, 12 or 18 months in length, are designed to acclimate new graduates to the work environment and have been shown to be effective in reducing turnover (McPeck, 2006; Williams et al., 2007). These are discussed in Chapter 20.

STAFF DEVELOPMENT PROCESS

Needs Assessment

The first step in staff development is a **needs assessment** for an educational program. Too often, staff development programs are initiated simply because they have been advertised and marketed, because they have been done in the past, or because other organizations have offered them. Because only educational institutions can legitimately view education as an end in itself,

health care organizations must justify how an educational activity can achieve an organizational goal, such as better patient care, reduced operating costs, or more efficient or satisfied personnel. Systematic determination of educational needs based on organizational goals can be used as a basis for developing specific content. In this way, staff development programs are used in the most cost-effective and efficient manner.

The decision to offer educational programs should be based on teaching behaviors that:

1. Can be made more effective and efficient by educational efforts (e.g., a streamlined dressing technique)
2. Need maintenance (e.g., cardiopulmonary resuscitation, infection control)
3. New employees need to learn (e.g., required documentation)
4. Employees who are transferred or promoted need to learn (e.g., a nurse who transfers to intensive care and needs education about thermodilution catheters)
5. Are needed as a result of new evidence for practice or new technology (e.g., a new chemotherapeutic agent)

Staff development specialists and managers can identify learning needs through a variety of strategies: checklists, advisory groups, quality improvement data, professional standards, and group brainstorming.

Some educational programs are dictated by federal, state, or local regulations. Among these mandatory classes are the following:

- Infection control
- Employee fire and patient safety
- Quality assurance/quality improvement (QA/QI)
- Cardiopulmonary resuscitation (CPR)
- Handling of hazardous materials

Additional requirements may be established through professional organization standards. Joint Commission (2002) requires organizations to provide education and training necessary to maintain a knowledgeable and skilled staff.

Planning

After needs have been determined, the next step is to plan staff development programs. **Planning** is a four-stage process that includes establishing objectives, evaluating the present situation and predicting future trends and events, formulating a planning statement (means), and converting the plan into an action statement. It entails identifying learner objectives and matching them with educational methods. Learner objectives, like

BOX 17-1 Staff Development Learning Objectives

Infection Control – Hand Washing Unit

Following completion of the hand washing unit, the employee will be able to:

1. Understand and explain to the instructor why correct hand washing is important.
2. Correctly identify situations when the employee should wash hands.
3. Identify hand washing and hand sanitizing products used in the facility.
4. Demonstrate correct hand-washing technique.

client outcomes, should be specific, measurable statements about desired behaviors, skills, or knowledge to be acquired within a specific time frame. The strategy used to affect the desired outcome should be based on learning needs, the employee, and available resources. Box 17-1 illustrates learning objectives for an infection control unit on hand washing.

Nurse managers have a variety of resources at their disposal. The staff development or education department may use a variety of media, such as closed-circuit television, online Web-based instruction, satellite programs, competency-based programs, self-study, and traditional didactic programs. Other alternatives are using experienced staff members as teachers, preceptors, or mentors; unit-based educators; or off-site continuing education programs.

Three main questions should be considered in assessment and planning:

- Can the learner do what is required?
- How should the staff development program be arranged to facilitate learning?
- What can be done to ensure that what is learned will be transferred to the job?

Implementation

Implementation involves bringing together educators, learners, and the materials and methods needed for education. Although most staff development is carried out by the staff development or education department, staff development is also a unit responsibility.

STAFF DEVELOPMENT METHODS

Staff development can be divided into internal (on the unit) and external (off the unit) sources. Internal sources include on-the-job instruction, workshops for staff, and in-service programs. External sources are formal workshops presented by an education department within the hospital and educational activities outside the hospital, including college courses, conferences, Web-based learning, and continuing education workshops.

For effective adult education, the student needs, at a minimum:

1. Material to be presented
2. Practice using the new knowledge and/or skill
3. Feedback about performance

There must be opportunity for practice of the desired behaviors and feedback about it. For instance, if an individual is shown how to perform CPR, practices it, and is given feedback on his or her success, the person could be expected to be able to perform CPR. Reading about or listening to a lecture about how to do cardiopulmonary resuscitation provides no assurance that the recipient actually could resuscitate an individual in an emergency.

The most widely used educational method is **on-the-job instruction**. This often involves assigning new employees to experienced nurse peers, preceptors, or the nurse manager. The learner is expected to learn the job by observing the experienced employee and by performing the actual tasks under supervision.

On-the-job instruction has several positive features, one of which is its cost-effectiveness. Learners learn effectively at the same time they are providing necessary nursing services. Moreover, this method reduces the need for outside instructional facilities and reliance on professional educators. Transfer of learning is not an issue because the learning occurs on the actual job. However, on-the-job instruction often fails because there is no assurance that accurate and complete information is presented, and the on-the-job instructor may not know learning principles. As a result, presentation, practice, or feedback may be inadequate or omitted.

On-the-job instruction fulfills an important function; however, staff members involved may not view it as having equal value to more standardized and formal classroom instruction.

To implement effective on-the-job instruction, the following are suggested:

1. Employees who function as educators must be convinced that educating new employees in no way jeopardizes their own job security, pay level, seniority, or status.
2. Individuals serving as educators should realize that this added responsibility will be instrumental in attaining other rewards for them.

3. Pair teachers and learners to minimize any differences in background, language, personality, attitudes, or age that may inhibit communication and understanding.

4. Select teachers on the basis of their ability to teach and their desire to take on this added responsibility.

5. Staff nurses chosen as teachers should be carefully educated in the proper methods of instruction.

6. Formalize assignments so that nurses do not view on-the-job instruction as happenstance or second-class instruction.

7. Rotate learners to expose each learner to the specific know-how of various staff nurses or education department teachers.

8. Employees serving as teachers should understand that their new assignment is by no means a chance to get away from their own jobs but that they must build instructional time into their workload.

9. The efficiency of the unit may be reduced when on-the-job instruction occurs.

10. The learner must be closely supervised to prevent him or her from making any major mistakes and carrying out procedures incorrectly.

Other Educational Techniques

As technology continues to advance rapidly and the number of people requiring instruction increases, teaching is becoming more efficient and the learning process accelerating. Many organizations are using self-learning modules, such as online classes, closed-circuit television, computerized clinical simulations, interactive video instruction, satellite broadcasts (some of which are interactive), CDs, DVDs, and long-distance learning via cable television. These methods allow an instructor to convey information in a uniform manner on several occasions or at several locations at one time; many lessons can be repeated. These methods can enhance the instructor's presentation as well as reduce the need for an instructor to present every detail in person.

Evaluation

Few issues in education create as much controversy or discussion as evaluation. **Evaluation** is an investigative process to determine whether the education was cost-effective, the objective was achieved, and learning was applied to the job. Educators usually agree on the need for sound appraisal of educational programs, but they seldom agree on the best method to do evaluation and rarely do empirical evaluation. Typically, a program is initially reviewed at the corporate level before its implementation. The same program is used over and over until someone in authority decides the program is no longer useful or no longer effective, or, more commonly, until attendance decreases.

The purpose of evaluation is to determine whether the educational program has a positive effect on day-to-day operating problems and to identify elements of the program that need improvement. Designing sound evaluation tools is difficult and costly, though necessary.

Four evaluation criteria should be used:

1. Learner reaction
2. Learning acquired
3. Behavior change
4. Organizational impact

Learner reaction is usually ascertained through a questionnaire completed at the end of a program. The questionnaire may ask about the program's content, the educator, the educator's objectives, the methods used, physical facilities, and meals. Only required questions should be asked; irrelevant data should not be gathered.

Learner reactions are important because:

1. Positive reactions ensure organizational support for a program
2. Reactions can be used to assess the program
3. Reactions indicate whether the learners liked the program

Learning criteria assess the knowledge—the facts and figures—learned in the educational program. Knowledge is typically measured by paper-and-pencil tests that can include true–false, multiple-choice, fill-in-the-blank, matching, and essay questions.

But the acquisition of knowledge is not enough. Was that knowledge converted into behavioral change? One of the biggest problems in education is that instruction does not necessarily transfer from the classroom to the job—often because learners are taught the theory and the technique but never learn how to translate these into behavior on the job. There is a big difference between learning and doing; if behavior is not measured after the program (or on the job), it cannot be determined whether the instructional program has affected behavior or helped the employee transfer the new behavior to the job.

One technique to ensure transfer of learning to clinical practice is **peer coaching** (Waddell & Dunn, 2005). Peer coaching uses partners who have both participated in the educational program, observe each other practicing the skill, ask appropriate questions during the demonstration, and offer feedback about the performance.

The objective of many staff development programs can be expressed in terms of organizational impact, such as reduced turnover, fewer grievances, reduced absenteeism, improved quality of care, and fewer accidents. These are usually expressed in quantified data and can be easily tied to dollars.

It is often difficult to determine whether changes in such areas can be unequivocally attributed to the staff development program or to other variables in the organization, such as changes in management, increased pay, new equipment, better selection, or changes of some other kind. To rule out the effect of these variables, those who establish the program must take particular care in deciding the length of time for data collection, the unit of analysis, randomization, and other experimental design issues. The most important criteria for measuring results are those that are closely related to the key training behaviors. Despite all of the difficulties in collecting and analyzing such data, cost-related data should be collected because they can provide evidence to higher administration that educational efforts do affect organizational effectiveness.

Cultural and Generational Differences

CULTURAL DIFFERENCES

Addressing cultural differences, particularly those of the foreign-born nurse, is an important consideration in motivating staff and in planning educational programs. Some cultures outside the United States are more group-oriented than Americans and often place group needs over individual needs in an attempt to promote harmony and solidarity. In addition, some cultures avoid confrontation and emphasize group cooperation.

The goal of designing culturally sensitive programs is to eliminate stereotypes, remove barriers, prevent misinterpretations, and promote functioning. Common social barriers are language and cultural expectations. In some countries, nurses defer to physicians for all decision making, whereas in the United States such behavior would be viewed as inappropriate and inefficient. Therefore it is important to include during the orientation period information about the role of the nurse, including interdependent and independent functions, management expectations, and effective communication skills.

Cultural barriers also may exist. In many developing countries, needles and other disposable items are reused, families provide personal care, certain types of technology may not be available, or views on using technology to sustain life may differ. In addition, many foreign nursing programs do not incorporate psychosocial skills into their educational programs. Therefore, special programs may need to be developed to ensure a level of competence in this area. Basic nursing skills may need to be reviewed as well as safety procedures. Common components include:

1. Socialization into the nursing role
2. How to understand and be understood
3. The development of social skills
4. The use of preceptors

The manager must consider other cultural aspects of employees, especially religious beliefs and practices and family roles and obligations because these vary among and within cultures.

GENERATIONAL DIFFERENCES

Generational differences, as well, present challenges for managers. Baby boomers value collegiality and life-long learning and expect rewards for their work while generation X individuals tend to focus on outcomes rather than processes and prefer to learn on their own (Sherman, 2006). Generation X and millenials (also known as generation Y) both may be especially impatient with traditional teaching techniques (Weston, 2006). Individuals in these generations expect to access information immediately and most often online.

Goal-oriented millenials expect to be coached and mentored. They value self-development and feedback on their performance. Preceptorships and internships may be especially valuable for them (Halfer, 2004).

While it may appear that younger nurses would see little value in older nurses' experience, allowing exchanges of information between the two groups can help younger nurses value their older colleagues' expertise and, at the same time, these exchanges can help older nurses adapt to changes in technology and learn new evidence for practice (Weston, 2006).

To motivate staff and teach individuals with varying backgrounds, education, and experience is a challenge for all managers. Using the principles of motivation adapted to your work situation can increase productivity and satisfaction for both the manager and staff and enhance the organization's effectiveness as well.

What You Know Now

- Motivational theories (e.g., reinforcement, expectancy, equity, and goal-setting theories) describe the factors that initiate and direct behavior.
- Job performance is determined by motivation and ability.
- Learning theories appropriate for adult learning (e.g., social learning theory, relapse prevention, and adult education theories) help guide staff development activities.
- Orientation is the responsibility of the staff development and nursing managers.
- Staff development is used to enhance employee performance of specific job skills.
- The process of staff development includes needs assessment, planning, implementation, and evaluation.
- The most important outcome of staff development efforts is to transfer learning to the job in order to change work behavior.
- On-the-job instruction is the most widely used educational method.
- The purpose of educational programs should be to enhance the organization's effectiveness.
- Cultural and generational differences affect learning and should be considered when providing staff education.

Tools for Motivating and Developing Staff

1. Become familiar with various theories of motivation and use the information to help you motivate staff.
2. Recognize that an employee's job performance includes both ability to do the job and motivation.
3. Identify staff and department educational needs and communicate those to the appropriate decision makers.
4. Participate in in-service and/or staff development activities as appropriate.
5. Evaluate staff members' abilities to transfer learning to the job.
6. Become sensitive to the needs of a multicultural and multigenerational staff and design programs and activities to meet those needs.

Questions to Challenge You

1. What motivational theory appeals to your sense of how you learn? Why?
2. You are a new nurse manager:
   a. How would you discover what motivates the individuals on your staff?
   b. What would you do first to identify your staff's learning needs?
   c. What are the next steps you would take to meet those needs?
3. What has been your experience working with individuals from other cultures? Describe any problems that emerged and how they were handled.
4. Which generation best describes you? Consider traditionals, baby boomers, generation X, or millenials. Review Chapter 1 if needed.
5. What recommendations would you make to a new nurse manager regarding motivating staff? Have you seen any of these work? Explain.

Explore MediaLink

Additional interactive resources for this chapter can be found on the Website at http://www.prenhall.com/sullivan. Click on Chapter 17 to select activities for this chapter.

- Video Overview
- NCLEX® Review Questions
- Critical Thinking Activities
- Current Events
- Nursing Leadership and Management in Action
- MediaLinks

References

Adams, J. S. (1963). Toward an understanding of inequity. *Journal of Abnormal and Social Psychology, 67*, 422.

Adams, J. S. (1965). Injustice in social exchange. In L. Berkowitz (Ed.), *Advances in experimental social psychology* (Vol. 2). New York: Academic Press.

Bandura, A. (1977). *Social learning theory.* Englewood Cliffs, NJ: Prentice Hall.

Halfer, D. (2004, April 21). *Developing a multigenerational workforce.* Paper presented at the annual meeting of the American Organization of Nurse Executives. Phoenix, Arizona.

Hersey, P., Blanchard, K. H., & Johnson, D. E. (2007). *Management of organizational behavior* (9th ed.). Upper Saddle River, NJ: Prentice Hall.

Joint Commission. (2002). *Comprehensive accreditation manual for hospitals: The official handbook.* Oakbrook Terrace, IL: Author.

Joyce, P. & Cowman, S. (2007). Continuing professional development: Investment or expectation? *Journal of Nursing Management, 15*(6), 626–633.

Locke, E. A. (1968). Toward a theory of task motives and incentives. *Organizational Behavior and Human Performance, 3*, 157.

McPeck, P. (2006). Residencies ease new grads into practice. *NurseWeek*, September 11, 2006. Retrieved January 2008 from http://www.versant.org/item.asp?id=70

Sherman, R. O. (2006). Leading a multigenerational nursing workforce: Issues, challenges, and strategies. *Online Journal of Issues in Nursing, 11*(2), posted 06/29/2006.

Skinner, B. F. (1953). *Science and human behavior.* New York: Free Press.

Strelecky, J. (2004). Motivating unmotivated people. *Occupational Health & Safety, 73*(6), 20–22.

Vroom, V. H. (1964). *Work and motivation.* New York: Wiley.

Waddell, D. L., & Dunn, N. (2005). Peer coaching: The next step in staff development. *Journal of Continuing Education in Nursing, 36*(2), 84–89.

Weston, M. J. (2006). Integrating generational perspectives in nursing. *Online Journal of Issues in Nursing, 11*(2), posted 06/29/2006.

Williams, C. A., Goode, C. J., Krsek, C., Bednash, G. D., Lynn, M. R. (2007). Postbaccalaureate nurse residency 1-year option. *Journal of Nursing Administration, 37*(7/8), 357–365.

CHAPTER 18

Evaluating Staff Performance

The Performance Appraisal
COMPONENTS TO BE EVALUATED
SPECIFIC EVALUATION METHODS
POTENTIAL APPRAISAL PROBLEMS

The Appraiser
DOCUMENTING PERFORMANCE
DIAGNOSING PERFORMANCE PROBLEMS
THE PERFORMANCE APPRAISAL INTERVIEW

Improving Appraisal Accuracy
APPRAISER ABILITY
APPRAISER MOTIVATION

Evaluating Skill Competency

Rules of Thumb

Learning Outcomes

After completing this chapter, you will be able to:

1. Describe criteria that can be used to evaluate staff performance.
2. Discuss different methods used to evaluate performance.
3. Describe problems to expect when evaluating performance.
4. Explain how to use critical incidents to improve annual evaluations.
5. Explain how to conduct a performance evaluation.
6. Describe how to evaluate skill competency.

MediaLink

www.prenhall.com/sullivan
See the Companion Website for chapter-specific resources at
www.prenhall.com/sullivan.

Key Terms

Ambiguous evaluation
  standards problem *p245*
Behavior-oriented rating
  scales *p244*
Critical incidents *p247*
Essay evaluation *p243*

Forced distribution
  evaluation *p244*
Group evaluation *p247*
Halo error *p245*
Leniency error *p245*
Peer review *p246*

Performance appraisal *p241*
Recency error *p245*
Traditional rating
  scale *p243*
Written comments
  problem *p246*

A desired result of any employee's behavior is effective job performance. An important part of the manager's job is to define performance in advance and to state desired results. Performance-related behaviors are directly associated with job tasks and need to be accomplished to achieve a job's objectives.

Enhancing performance includes such actions as:

- Identifying performance problems
- Integrating, facilitating, and coordinating the work of employees
- Creating a motivational climate

Managers also may enhance an employee's performance by removing situational constraints, such as rotating shifts or providing assistance in overcoming constraints. Recognition also enhances performance. Careful management of these factors helps ensure that a staff member's effort or motivation is actively translated into effective job performance.

The Performance Appraisal

The **performance appraisal** process includes:

- Day-to-day manager–employee interactions (coaching, counseling, dealing with policy violations, and disciplining discussed in Chapter 19)
- Making notes about an employee's behavior
- Completing the performance appraisal form
- The formal appraisal interview
- Follow-up sessions that may involve coaching and/or discipline when needed

Performance appraisals are conducted for a number of reasons. The primary reason is to give constructive feedback. A good appraisal system ensures that staff know what they are to do and how well they are doing it.

Performance appraisals often serve as the basis on which administrative decisions, such as the size of a salary increase or who gets promoted, are made. Ideally, accurate appraisal information allows the organization to tie rewards to performance. However, accuracy is a skill developed only with experience.

A final reason for doing performance reviews concerns fair employment practice law. Performance appraisals and the decisions based on those appraisals, such as layoffs, are covered by several federal and state laws. In the past two decades, many employees have successfully sued their organizations over employment decisions that were based on questionable performance appraisal results.

There are several steps to help ensure that an appraisal system is nondiscriminatory.

1. The appraisal should be in writing and carried out at least once a year.
2. The performance appraisal information should be shared with the employee.
3. The employee should have the opportunity to respond in writing to the appraisal.
4. Employees should have a mechanism to appeal the results of the performance appraisal.
5. The manager should have adequate opportunity to observe the employee's job performance during the course of the evaluation period. If adequate contact is lacking (e.g., the appraiser and the appraisee work different shifts), then appraisal information should be gathered from other sources.
6. Anecdotal notes on the employee's performance should be kept during the entire evaluation period (e.g., 3 months, 1 year). These notes, called critical incidents and discussed later, should be shared with the employee during the course of the evaluation period.

MᴇᴅɪᴀLɪɴᴋ Performance Appraisal

7. Evaluators should be trained to carry out the performance appraisal process, including
   a. What is reasonable job performance,
   b. How to complete the form, and
   c. How to carry out the feedback interview.
8. As far as possible, the performance appraisal should focus on employee behavior and results rather than on personal traits or characteristics, such as
   a. Initiative
   b. Attitude
   c. Personality

Regardless of how an organization uses performance appraisals, they must accurately reflect the employee's actual job performance. If performance ratings are inaccurate, an inferior employee may be promoted, another employee may not receive needed training, or there may not be a tie between performance and rewards (thus lessening employee motivation). For appraisals to be successful, the needs of the staff and requirements of the organization must be bridged.

COMPONENTS TO BE EVALUATED

Nurses engage in a variety of job-related activities. To reflect the multidimensional nature of the job, the performance appraisal form usually requires a nurse manager to rate several different performance dimensions, such as use of the nursing process, professionalism, safety, continuing education, and initiative. In developing an appraisal device, an organization can focus on employee traits, results, behaviors, and/or some combination thereof. The specific focus of the form affects the whole appraisal process.

Traits and Personal Characteristics

Some appraisal systems focus on personal traits and characteristics, such as stability or ability to handle stress, because trait-oriented instruments are inexpensive to develop and can be used for a wide variety of positions. Today, however, employers seldom use trait-oriented systems, primarily because of charges that they discriminate against some groups. To satisfy legal requirements, the organization should be able to demonstrate the validity (job-relatedness) of the appraisal ratings.

Also trait ratings are not useful in helping to develop employees. In most health care organizations, a major reason for doing performance appraisals is to help employees improve. However, because most trait-rating dimensions are somewhat ambiguous (for example, what precisely is meant by "initiative"?), trait-oriented systems do not tell a staff nurse what to do differently in the future.

Results-Oriented System

All organizations need to be concerned with the bottom line. If a hospital has a 35 percent occupancy rate or a 20 percent employee absenteeism rate, its future is in jeopardy. In recent years, therefore, top management has turned to appraising some employees at least partly on results. With a results-oriented appraisal system, employees know in advance what is expected. Objectives are quantifiable, objective, and easily measured.

Sylvia is an experienced critical care nurse. Her goals for the year include:

- *Complete advanced cardiac life support (ACLS) recertification.*
- *Obtain CCRN credentialing.*
- *Preceptor one new graduate nurse.*
- *Serve on hospital shared governance committee.*

At Sylvia's annual performance review, her manager noted that she had:

- *Become ACLS recertified.*
- *Obtained CCRN credentialing.*
- *Preceptored a new graduate nurse who was functioning above expectations.*
- *Chaired subcommittee of hospital shared governance committee.*

Behavioral Criteria

In recent years, many health care organizations have adopted behavior-oriented performance appraisal systems rather than focusing on difficult-to-measure results or on vague traits that may cause legal problems. Behavior-oriented systems focus on what the employee actually does, as exemplified in **Figure 18-1**.

Such a system gives new employees specific information on how they are expected to behave and is less likely to lead to legal problems. The behavioral focus facilitates employee development. The major drawbacks of a behavior-oriented appraisal system are that it is relatively time consuming to develop and is tied to only one job or a narrow range of jobs. For example, the behavioral items presented in Figure 18-1 would be applicable only to staff nurses.

Combining Different Types of Criteria

As health care organizations have become more concerned with employee productivity in the last few years, some have developed appraisal systems that combine various types of criteria. In such a system,

	Outstanding (5)	Above average (4)	Average (3)	Needs improvement (2)	Unacceptable (1)
1. Performs and documents physical assessment according to unit standard.					
2. Completes patient plan of care according to unit standard on each assigned patient within 24 hours of admission.					
3. Administers medications in a safe and timely manner.					
4. Participates in all mandatory in-service programs.					
5. Dresses according to unit dress code.					
6. Adheres to universal precautions with each patient.					

Figure 18-1 ● Behavior-oriented performance appraisal items for the job of staff nurse.

each employee may have a few major objectives he or she is expected to accomplish. In addition to being evaluated on whether these results were attained, individuals are also evaluated in terms of both general personal characteristics and behaviorally specific criteria.

SPECIFIC EVALUATION METHODS

Traditional Rating Scales

Many organizations use a **traditional rating scale** for all employees in a class (e.g., staff nurse, clinical nurse specialist), regardless of their specific job setting (e.g., outpatient surgery, ambulatory clinic).

A traditional rating scale includes:

- General performance dimensions not necessarily based on a job description
- Equally weighted dimensions
- Absolute judgment standards
- Judgments based on the supervisor's idea of satisfactory performance

In filling out a traditional rating scale, the appraiser is required to reflect on the appraisee's performance over the entire evaluation period (usually 12 months) and rate the individual against the rater's internal standard of per-

formance. Individuals using trait-rating scales commonly complain either that the performance dimension (e.g., leadership) is irrelevant to the job in question or that they do not know exactly what is meant by the dimension. Such complaints arise because one appraisal form is being used across a variety of jobs and because the performance dimensions are not tied to concrete behaviors.

Essay Evaluation

With the **essay evaluation** technique, the nurse manager is required to describe the employee's performance over the entire evaluation period by writing a narrative detailing the strengths and weaknesses of the appraisee. If done correctly, this approach can provide a good deal of valuable data for discussion in the appraisal interview. If used alone, however, an essay evaluation is subject to a number of constraints that can limit its effectiveness. For example, essay evaluations can be time consuming to write, they depend on appraisers' abilities to express themselves in prose, and they can be difficult to defend in court because comments made by the manager may not be closely tied to actual job performance. Most organizations have found that essay evaluations are more useful when they are used in combination with other evaluation formats and when they are based on notes taken by the manager during the course of the evaluation period.

Forced Distribution Evaluation

The **forced distribution evaluation** is similar to grading on a curve. If the rating scale has five categories, the manager may be required to spread employees' ratings equally over the five categories.

Because this technique is constraining, most evaluators do not like it. One hears such complaints as:

"I have two exceptional employees, but this system only allows me to put one of them in the highest category."

"I don't have an employee who deserves to be rated in the lowest category."

Because of the general dislike of forced distribution systems, they are not commonly used. In those instances where they are used, forced distribution systems were generally implemented because managers were giving all of their employees high ratings.

Behavior-Oriented Rating Scales

As noted earlier, focusing on specific behaviors in appraising performance has tremendous advantages. For example, new employees have specific information on how they should behave. Although there are several varieties of **behavior-oriented rating scales**, they all share a number of things in common:

1. Groups of workers who are very familiar with the target job (generally, individuals doing the job and their immediate supervisors) provide written examples (*critical incidents*) of superior and inferior job behaviors.
2. These critical incidents are stated as measurable/quantifiable behaviors. (Examples are given in Figure 18-1.)
3. Critical incidents that are similar in theme are grouped together. These behavioral groupings (*performance dimensions*) are labeled, for example, nursing process or communication.
4. Statistical procedures are used to arrive at a subset of the original pool of critical incidents. These procedures eliminate items that do not clearly reflect the performance dimension into which they were grouped, overlap other critical incidents, or are poorly worded.

In view of the way that behavior-oriented rating scales are developed, it is apparent that such behavior-oriented

appraisal measures can be used only for one job or a cluster of very similar jobs and that these scales are time consuming and therefore expensive to develop. For these reasons, behavior-oriented systems are generally developed when a large number of individuals are doing the same job, such as staff nurses. Because employees and their managers actually develop the appraisal instrument, they have faith in the system and are motivated to use it.

Results-Oriented Evaluations

Whereas the other approaches to performance evaluation focus on an employee's personal characteristics (traits) or behavior, a focus on results requires setting objectives for what the employee is to accomplish. Although this technique has many variations, basically it involves two steps.

First, a set of work objectives is established at the start of the evaluation period for the employee to accomplish during some future time frame. These objectives can be developed by the employee's supervisor and given to the employee; however, it is better if the manager and employee work together to develop a set of objectives for the employee.

Each performance objective should be defined in concrete, quantifiable terms and have a specific time frame. For example, one objective may need to be accomplished in 1 month (e.g., "Revise the unit orientation manual to reflect the new Joint Commission standards"); another objective may not have to be met for 12 months (e.g., "Take and pass the CCRN examination within the next year"). In setting objectives, it is important that the employee perceive them as challenging yet attainable.

The second step involves the actual evaluation of the employee's performance. At this time, the supervisor and employee meet and focus on how well the employee has accomplished his or her objectives.

With increasing emphasis on outcomes, results-oriented assessments are becoming more commonly used in health care settings.

POTENTIAL APPRAISAL PROBLEMS

No matter what type of appraisal device is used, problems that lessen the accuracy of the performance rating can arise, such as leniency, recency, and halo errors; ambiguous evaluation standards; and written comments problems. These, in turn, limit the usefulness of the performance review. For example, if a performance rating can be shown to be inaccurate, it will be difficult to defend in court.

Leniency Error

Many nurse managers tend to overrate their staff's performance. This is called **leniency error**. For example, a manager may rate everyone on her or his staff as "above average." Although numerous reasons are given for inflated ratings (e.g., "I want my nurses to like me," "It's difficult to justify giving someone a low rating"), these reasons do not lessen the problems that leniency error can create for both the manager and the organization. For example, if you give a mediocre nurse lenient ratings, it is difficult to turn around and take some corrective action, such as discipline.

Leniency error can also be demoralizing to the best staff nurses, because they would have received high ratings without leniency. However, with leniency error, these outstanding nurses look less superior compared to their coworkers. Thus, leniency error tends to be welcomed by poorer performers and disliked by better ones.

Recency Error

Another difficulty with most appraisal systems is the length of time over which behavior is evaluated. In most organizations, employees are formally evaluated every 12 months. Evaluating employee performance over such an extended period of time, particularly if one supervises more than two or three individuals, is a difficult task. Typically, the evaluator recalls recent performance and tends to forget more distant events. Thus, the performance rating reflects what the employee has contributed lately rather than over the entire evaluation period. This tendency is called **recency error;** it too can create both legal and motivational problems.

Shelby Miller, RN, transferred from a medical unit to the telemetry unit 9 months ago. Overall, her performance has been good and she is an excellent team member. On two occasions, other nursing staff told the nurse manager, Lucinda Amos, about Shelby's quick and accurate assessment of critical changes in patient status. Last week, Shelby misread a physician's order and didn't administer preprocedure medications as directed. The procedure had to be rescheduled, resulting in surgical delays as well. The physician was angry and complained to both Lucinda and the cardiology nursing director. On her annual performance appraisal, Lucinda rated Shelby "below average" on patient care delivery.

Legally, if a disgruntled employee can demonstrate that an evaluation that supposedly reflects 12 months actually reflects performance over the last 2 or 3 months, an organization will have difficulty defending the validity of its appraisal system. In terms of motivation, recency error demonstrates to all employees that they only need to perform at a high level near the time of their performance review. In such situations, an employee is highly motivated (e.g., asking the supervisor for more work) just prior to appraisal but considerably less motivated as soon as it is completed.

As with leniency error, recency error benefits the poorly performing individual. Nurses who perform well year round may receive ratings similar to those mediocre nurses who spurt as their evaluation time approaches. Fortunately, a simple procedure (recording critical incidents, discussed later in the chapter) greatly lessens the impact of recency error.

Halo Error

Sometimes an appraiser fails to differentiate among the various performance dimensions (e.g., nursing process, communication skills) when evaluating an employee and assigns ratings on the basis of an overall impression, positive or negative, of the employee (Goffin, 2001). Thus, some employees are rated above average across dimensions, others are rated average, and a few are rated below average on all dimensions. This is referred to as **halo error**.

If a nurse is excellent, average, or poor on all performance dimensions, she or he deserves to be rated accordingly, but in most instances, employees have uneven strengths and weaknesses. Thus, it should be relatively uncommon for an employee to receive the same rating on all performance dimensions. Although halo error is less common and troublesome than leniency and recency error, it still is not an accurate assessment of performance.

Ambiguous Evaluation Standards

Most appraisal forms use rating scales that include words such as "outstanding," "above average," "satisfactory," or "needs improvement"; but different managers attach different meanings to these words, giving rise to what has been labeled the **ambiguous evaluation standards problem**. Organizations have attempted to address this problem in two ways. One approach is to have a group of nurse managers meet and discuss what each of them sees as outstanding performance, above-average performance, and poor performance on each dimension. The goal is to arrive at a consensus on what level of performance is expected on each dimension. Thus, the group of nurse managers may decide that to be rated excellent on the dimension of self-development, a nurse must attend at least 10 in-service meetings in a year. When agreement is reached on the behavior that reflects each level of a dimension, this information should be communicated to those being evaluated.

A more formal approach to dealing with the ambiguous evaluation standards problem is to develop rating forms that have each gradation along the performance continuum (e.g., excellent, satisfactory) anchored by examples of behavior that is representative of that level of performance. Although a detailed discussion of the process an organization would use for developing such performance standards is too complex to go into here (usually, a consulting firm works with the organization), it involves groups of knowledgeable employees (e.g., job incumbents and their managers) meeting to discuss the important performance dimensions (e.g., nursing process) of a job. Then examples of different levels of performance are developed for each performance standard. For example, a rating of excellent on the performance standard of nursing process/assessment might be anchored by "assessment documented on 95 percent of charts reviewed," whereas a rating of poor on the same standard might be anchored by "assessment completed on 75 percent of charts reviewed."

Written Comments Problem

Almost all performance appraisal forms provide space for written comments by the appraiser. The wise manager uses this space to justify in detail the basis for the ratings, to discuss developmental activities for the employee in the coming year, to put the ratings in context (e.g., although the evaluation period is 12 months, the appraiser notes on the form that he or she has only been the nurse's manager for the past 3 months), or to discuss the employee's promotion potential. Unfortunately, few nurse managers use this valuable space appropriately; in fact, the spaces for written comments are often left blank. When there are comments, they tend to be few and general (e.g., "Joan is conscientious"), focus totally on what the individual did wrong, or reflect only recent performance.

Dawn Stanley, RN, is director of nursing for an assisted living center. Two certified nurse aides transferred to her center from other facilities in the health care system. Both CNAs have struggled to meet performance expectations in the first 90 days of their new positions. In preparing performance appraisals for both employees, Dawn reviewed previous appraisals to see if other managers had indicated areas for improvement or performance trends. Both employees were rated as "marginal performers" but no written comments were provided, making the appraisal process more difficult for Dawn.

The existence of the **written comments problem** should not be surprising. Most nurse managers wait until the end of the evaluation period to make written comments; thus, the manager is faced with a difficult, time-consuming task. Small wonder, then, that the few comments tend to be vague, negative in tone, and reflect recent events. Fortunately, regular note taking can lessen the problems associated with written comments (see Documenting Performance).

The Appraiser

In most organizations, an employee's immediate manager is in charge of evaluating her or his performance. In many situations, this makes sense. The manager is familiar with the employee's work and thus is best able to evaluate it. If the immediate supervisor does not have enough information to evaluate an employee's performance accurately, alternatives are necessary. The manager can informally seek out performance-related information from other sources, such as the employee's coworkers, patients, or other managers who are familiar with the person being evaluated. The manager weighs this additional information, integrates it with his or her own judgment, and completes the evaluation.

Another alternative involves a formal use of other sources. Peer review, self-assessments, and group evaluations are growing in use and are appropriate for professionals. **Peer review** is a process by which registered nurses assess and judge the performance of professional peers against predetermined standards. Peer review is designed to make performance appraisal more objective because multiple ratings give a more objective appraisal. It is used frequently in clinical ladder programs, self-governance models, and evaluation of advanced practice nurses.

The steps for peer review are as follows:

1. The employee selects peers to conduct the evaluation. Usually, two to four peers are identified through a predetermined process.
2. The employee submits a self-evaluation portfolio. The portfolio might describe how he or she met objectives and/or predetermined standards during the past evaluation cycle. Supporting materials are included.
3. The peers evaluate the employee. This may be done individually or in a group. The individuals or group then submit a written evaluation to the manager.
4. The manager and employee meet to discuss the evaluation. The manager's evaluation is included, and objectives for the coming evaluation cycle are finalized.

Implementing a peer review involves several considerations. First, it is best to avoid selecting personal best friends for the review. Friends can provide poor ratings as well as inflated ratings, resulting in a negative experience. Second, consider how often to evaluate expert practitioners; for example, those nurses who have reached the top of a clinical ladder. The usual annual evaluations may not be necessary. Third, monitor the time needed for portfolio preparation. The object is to improve professionalism and quality of patient care, not to create more paperwork.

Self-assessments help the employee examine performance over the year and consider improvements to be made. It is difficult for anyone to accurately rate one's own performance so self-assessments tend to be overly positive or, in some cases, excessively negative. Nonetheless, it is a valuable exercise to require employees to focus attention on how well they have met the requirements of the job regardless of whether the appraisal is behavioral-oriented ("Completes patient care plan within 24 hours of admission") or results-oriented ("Presented one in-service on the unit").

Another technique is **group evaluation**. In group evaluation, several managers are asked to rank employee performance based on job descriptions and performance standards. Usually, one manager facilitates the process. In addition to evaluating individual performance, performance of groups of nurses can also be evaluated in this way and group variances can be benchmarked and evaluated. Using group evaluation reduces personal bias, is timely, and can be effective.

DOCUMENTING PERFORMANCE

Appraising an employee's performance can be a difficult job. A nurse manager is required to reflect on a staff member's performance over an extended period of time (usually 12 months) and then accurately evaluate it. Given that many nurse managers have several employees to evaluate, it is not surprising that they frequently forget what an individual did several months ago or that they may actually confuse what one employee did with what another worker did.

A useful mechanism for fighting such memory problems is the use of **critical incidents**, which are reports of employee behaviors that are out of the ordinary, in either a positive or a negative direction. Critical incidents include four items: name of employee, date and time of incident, a brief description of what occurred, and the nurse manager's comments on what transpired (**Figure 18-2**). Index cards or a PDA are best to use so that notes can be taken immediately without waiting until time is available to note information on a computer or paper file. Also this lag time increases the

---

1. Name of employee: Cindy Siegler

2. Date and time of incident: March 22, 8:22 A.M.

3. Description: Ms. Siegler came to work late. This was the third time in the past 2 weeks.

4. Comments: Ms. Siegler has only worked for the clinic for 4 months and her repeatedly late attendance is having an effect on the other clinic staff. I spoke with her privately and conveyed the above concerns on March 22 at 10:35 A.M. She acknowledged the problem she has had with baby sitters but reassured me that she has enrolled her child in preschool and that she should be on time from now on. We agreed to meet again in 2 weeks to evaluate her attendance.

Figure 18-2 ● Example of a critical incident.

likelihood of errors and the possibility that the manager will neglect to share the incident with the employee (see next section).

Recording critical incidents as they occur is bound to increase the accuracy of the year-end performance appraisal ratings. Although this type of note taking may sound simple and straightforward, a manager can still run into problems; for instance, some managers feel sheepish about this kind of record keeping. Many managers are uncomfortable about recording behaviors; they see themselves as spies lurking around the work area attempting to catch someone. What they need to remember is that this note taking will enable them to evaluate the employee more accurately and makes recency error much less likely.

The best time to write critical incidents is just after the behavior occurred. The note should focus specifically on what took place, not on an interpretation of what happened. For example, instead of writing, "Ms. Hudson was rude," write, "Ms. Hudson referred to the patient as a slob." The nurse manager is responsible for deciding what are critical incidents. In some departments, coming to work on time may be noteworthy; in other departments, coming to work late is. Once a critical incident has been recorded, the manager should share it with the employee in private. If the behavior is positive, this provides a good opportunity for the nurse manager to praise the employee; if the behavior is considered in some way undesirable, the manager may need to coach the employee (see Chapter 19).

Because most nurse managers are extremely busy, they sometimes question whether note taking is a good use of their time. In fact, keeping notes is not a time-consuming process. The average note takes less than 2 minutes to write. If one writes notes during the gaps in the day (e.g., while waiting for a meeting to start), little, if any, productive time is used. In the long run, such note taking saves time. For example, keeping and sharing notes forces a manager to deal with problems when they are small and thus are more quickly addressed. In addition, completing the appraisal form at the end of the evaluation period takes less time when one has notes for reference.

A key factor in effectively using this note-taking approach is how nurse managers introduce the technique to their staff. To get maximum value out of note taking, nurse managers need to keep in mind two important facts:

1. The primary reason for taking notes is to improve the accuracy of the performance review.
2. When something new is introduced, people tend to react negatively to it.

Managers should be open and candid about the first fact, admitting that they cannot remember every event associated with every employee and telling employees that these notes will make more accurate evaluations possible. Even then, employees will still be suspicious about this new procedure. One way to get this note-taking procedure off to a good start is for managers to make the first note they record on an employee a positive one, even if they have to stretch a bit to find one. By doing this, each employee's first contact with critical incidents is positive.

Three types of mistakes common with using notes are:

1. Some managers fail to make them specific and behavior oriented; rather, they record that a nurse was "careless" or "difficult to supervise."
2. Some managers record only undesirable behavior.
3. Some managers fail to give performance feedback to the employee at the time that a note was written.

Each of these errors can undermine the effectiveness of the note-taking process. If the notes are vague, the employee may not know specifically what was done wrong and therefore does not know how to improve. If only poor performance is documented, employees will resent the system and the nurse manager. If the nurse manager does not share notes as they are written, the employee will often react defensively when confronted with them at the end of the evaluation period. In sum, any nurse manager who is considering using this powerful note-taking procedure needs to take the process seriously and to use it as it is designed.

By increasing the accuracy of the performance review, written notes also diminish the legal liability of lawsuits. If a lawsuit is brought, written notes are very persuasive evidence in court. Sharing the notes with employees throughout the evaluation period also improves the communication flow between the manager and the employee. Having written notes also gives the manager considerable confidence when it comes time to complete the evaluation form and to carry out the appraisal interview.

The nurse manager will be less prone to leniency and recency error and will feel confident that the appraisal ratings are accurate. Not only does the nurse manager feel professional, but also the staff nurse shares that perception. In fact, it is typically found that with the use of notes, the performance appraisal interview focuses mainly on how the employee can improve next year rather than on how he or she was rated last year. Thus, the tone of the interview is constructive rather than argumentative.

One final issue needs to be addressed. Different employees react differently to the use of notes. Good employees react positively. Although the nurse manager records both what is done well and what is done poorly, good employees will have many more positive than negative notes and therefore will benefit from notes being taken. In contrast, poorer employees do not react well to notes being taken.

Whereas once they could rely on the poor memory of the nurse manager as well as on a leniency tendency to produce inflated ratings, note taking is likely to result in more accurate (i.e., lower) ratings for poor employees. The negative reaction of poor employees, however, tends not to be a lasting one. Generally, the poor performers either leave the organization, or when they discover that they no longer can get away with mediocre performance, their performance actually improves.

DIAGNOSING PERFORMANCE PROBLEMS

If the manager notes poor or inconsistent performance during the appraisal process, the manager must investigate and remedy the situation. Certain questions should be asked:

"Is the performance deficiency a problem?"

"Will it go away if ignored?"

"Is the deficiency due to a lack of skill or motivation? How do I know?"

The first step is to begin with accepted standards of performance and an accurate assessment of the current performance of the staff member. This means job descriptions must be current and performance appraisal tools must be written in behavioral terms. It also implies that employee evaluations are regularly carried out and implemented according to recognized guidelines. Also, the employee must know what behavior is expected.

Next decide whether the problem demands immediate attention and whether it is a skill-related or motivation-related problem. Skill-related problems can be solved through informal training, such as demonstration and coaching, whereas complex skills require formal training (e.g., in-service sessions or workshops). If there is a limit to the time an employee has to reach the desired level of skill, the manager must determine whether the job could be simplified or whether the better decision would be to terminate or transfer the employee.

If the performance problem is due to motivation rather than ability, the manager must address a different set of questions. Specifically, the manager must determine whether the employee believes that there are obstacles to the expected behavior or that the behavior leads to punishment, reward, or inaction. For example, if the reward for conscientiously coming to work on holidays (rather than calling in sick) leads to always being scheduled for holiday work, then good performance is associated with punishment.

Only when the employee sees a strong link between valued outcomes and meeting performance expectations will motivation strategies succeed. The manager plays a role in tailoring motivational efforts to meet the individual needs of the employee. Unfortunately, creating a performance–reward climate does not eliminate all problem behaviors. When the use of rewards proves ineffective, other strategies, such as coaching and discipline, are warranted (see Chapter 19).

To differentiate between lack of ability and lack of motivation, the manager can analyze past performance. If past performance has been acceptable and little change in standards of performance has taken place, then the problem results from a lack of motivation. In contrast, if the nurse has never performed at an acceptable level, then the problem may be primarily skill related. Different intervention strategies should be used, depending on the source of the problem. The objective should be to enhance performance rather than to punish the employee. *Figure 18-3* summarizes the steps to take.

THE PERFORMANCE APPRAISAL INTERVIEW

Once the manager completes an accurate evaluation of performance, he or she should arrange an appraisal interview. The appraisal interview is the first step in employee development.

Preparing for the Interview

Keep in mind what needs to be accomplished during the interview. If the appraisal ratings are accurate, they are more likely to be perceived as such by the employee. This perception should, in turn, make the employee more likely to accept them as a basis for both rewards as well as developmental activities. More specifically, to motivate employees, rewards need to be seen as linked to performance.

The performance appraisal interview is the key to this linkage. In the interview, establish that performance has been carefully assessed and that, when merited, rewards will be forthcoming. Developmental activities also need to be derived from an accurate evaluation. If an employee is rated as "needs immediate improvement" on

Figure 18-3 ● Decision tree for evaluating performance.

delegation skills, for example, any effort to remedy this deficiency must stem from the employee's acceptance of the need for improvement in delegation.

Even though nurse managers try to fill out the appraisal form accurately, they should still anticipate disagreement with their ratings. Most employees tend to see themselves as above-average performers. This tendency to exaggerate our own performance results from the fact that we tend to forget our mistakes and recall our accomplishments; we often rationalize away those instances where our performance was substandard (e.g., "I forgot, but with this heavy workload, what do you expect?"). Given this tendency to overevaluate one's own performance and the fact that most staff previously have had poor experiences with the evaluation process, expect that staff will lack confidence in the whole appraisal process.

A key step for making the appraisal interview go well is proper planning (Smith, 2003). Set up the performance appraisal interview in advance, preferably giving at least 2 days' notice. Schedule enough time: Most interviews last 20 to 30 minutes, although the time needed will vary considerably depending on the degree to which the nurse manager and the staff nurse have talked regularly during the year.

In preparing for the appraisal interview, have specific examples of behavior to support the ratings. Such documentation is particularly important for performance areas in which an employee receives low ratings. In addition, try to anticipate how the staff member will react to the appraisal. For example, will the individual challenge the manager's ratings as being too low? Anticipating such a reaction, one can respond by saying, "Before I made my ratings, I talked with two other unit managers to make sure my standards were reasonable."

The setting also should be considered in planning the meeting. It is critical that the interview take place in a setting that is private and relatively free from interruptions. This allows a frank, in-depth conversation with the employee. Although it is difficult to limit interruptions in a health care setting, choosing the meeting time carefully will help. You may be able to schedule the meeting when another manager can cover, or at a time when interruptions are least likely to occur. The most important point to remember is that a poor setting limits the usefulness of the interview. No one wants weaknesses discussed in public. Similarly, interruptions destroy the flow of the feedback session.

The Interview

The appraisal interview is most likely to go well if the nurse manager has written and shared critical incidents throughout the evaluation period. If such feedback has occurred, staff members go into the interview with a good idea of how they are likely to be rated, as well as what behaviors led to the rating. If the nurse manager has not kept notes throughout the year, it is very important to recall numerous, specific examples of behavior, both positive and negative, to support the ratings given.

The major focus of the feedback interview should be on how the nurse manager and the staff member can work together to improve performance in the coming year. However, establishing such an improvement-oriented climate is easier said than done. In giving feedback, be aware that every employee has a tolerance level for criticism beyond which defensiveness sets in. Thus, in reviewing an employee's performance, emphasize only a few areas—preferably, no more than two—that need immediate improvement.

Unfortunately, evaluators often exceed an employee's tolerance level, particularly if performance has been mediocre. Typically, the manager will come up with an extensive list of areas needing improvement. Confronted with such a list, the staff member gradually moves from a constructive frame of mind ("I need to work on that") after one or two criticisms are raised to a destructive perspective ("She doesn't like me," "He's nitpicking," "How can I get even?") as the list of criticisms continues.

Following are recommendations for conducting an appraisal interview:

1. **Put the employee at ease.** Many subordinates are nervous at the start of the appraisal interview, especially new employees who are facing their first evaluation or those who have not received frequent performance feedback from their manager over the course of the evaluation period. To facilitate two-way communication during the interview, some managers rely on small talk; others begin the interview by giving an overview of the type of information that was used in making the performance ratings, such as, "In preparing for this review, I relied heavily on the notes I have taken and shared with you throughout the year." Rather than trying to reduce the tension an employee may have at the start of the interview, it is better to ignore it. In many cases, if the manager has given the employee feedback throughout the evaluation period, the employee will not be unduly nervous at the start of the session.

2. **Clearly state the purpose of the appraisal interview.** This improvement-oriented theme should be conveyed at the beginning of the interview and will help the employee do the best possible job in the coming year.

3. **Go through the ratings one by one with the employee.** Provide a number of specific examples of behavior that led to each rating. Some nurse managers use only negative examples to support rat-

ings, and this can cause problems. Employees are more likely to become defensive because the entire focus is on problem areas. If the manager pays no attention to good performance in certain areas, the employee will pay less attention to these behaviors in the future.

In reviewing the ratings, be careful not to rush. By systematically going through the ratings and providing behavioral examples, the nurse manager projects an image of being prepared and of being a professional. This is important for getting the staff nurse to accept the ratings and act on them.

4. **Draw out the employee's reactions to the ratings.** More specifically, ask for the employee's reaction to the ratings and then listen, accept, and respond to them. Of the seven key behaviors for doing performance reviews, nurse managers have the most difficulty with this one. To carry out this phase of the interview effectively, you must have confidence in the accuracy of the ratings.

When asked to express their reactions, individuals who have received low ratings will frequently question the rater's judgment ("Don't you think your standards are a little high?"). Not surprisingly, the manager whose judgment has been questioned then tends to get defensive, cutting off the employee's remarks and arguing for the rating in question. Being cut off sends a contradictory message to the employee. The individual was asked for reactions, but when given, the supervisor did not want to hear them. You should anticipate that the ratings will be challenged and must truly want to hear the staff nurse's reaction to them.

After having listened to the employee's reactions, accept and respond to them in a manner that conveys the manager has heard what the employee said (e.g., paraphrase some of the comments) and accepts the individual's opinion ("I understand your view"). In addition, you may want to clarify what has been said ("I do not understand why you feel your initiative rating is too low. Could you cite specific behavior to justify a higher rating?"). Strive for a candid, two-way conversation to know exactly how the employee feels.

5. **Decide on specific ways in which performance areas can be strengthened.** The focus of the interview should now shift to the future. If a thorough review of an employee's performance reveals deficiencies, the manager and employee may jointly develop action plans to help the individual improve. An action plan describes mutually agreed-on activities for improving performance. Such developmental activities may

include formal training, academic course work, or on-the-job coaching. Together, the nurse manager and the staff nurse should write down the resulting plans.

Because of the possibility of defensiveness, only one or two performance areas needing improvement should be addressed. Choose only the areas that are most troublesome and focus attention on these. In arriving at plans for improving performance, begin by asking the staff member for ideas on how to enhance personal performance. After the individual has offered suggestions, you can offer additional suggestions. It is critical that such performance plans refer to specific behavior. In some cases, not only will the staff member be expected to do things in a different manner ("I will refer to a patient as Mr., Mrs., or Ms. unless specifically told otherwise"), but the manager may also be expected to change behavior ("I will post changes in hospital policy before enforcing them").

6. **Set a follow-up date.** After having agreed on specific ways to strengthen performance in problem areas, schedule a subsequent meeting, usually 4 to 6 weeks after the appraisal interview. At this later meeting, provide specific feedback on the nurse's recent performance. This meeting also gives the manager and the nurse an opportunity to discuss any problems they have encountered in attempting to carry out their agreed-on performance/improvement plans. In most cases, this follow-up session is quite positive. With only one or two areas to work on and a specific date on which feedback will be given, the nurse's performance usually improves dramatically. Thus, the follow-up meeting is one in which the nurse manager has the opportunity to praise the employee.

7. **Express confidence in the employee.** The final key behavior is simple but often overlooked. It is nevertheless important that the manager indicate confidence that improvement will be forthcoming.

Since no more than two problem areas should be addressed in the appraisal interview, other problem areas may be considered later in the year. If the targeted performance areas continue to improve significantly, then 1 or 2 weeks after this follow-up session, meet again with the staff member, this time raising an additional area that needs attention. As before, specific ways to improve the performance deficiency are developed and written down, and another follow-up meeting is scheduled. In short, performance deficiencies are not ignored, they are merely temporarily overlooked.

Improving Appraisal Accuracy

For the manager and employee to get maximum benefit from an appraisal, it needs to encompass all facets of job performance and be free from rater error. Although attempting to get totally accurate evaluations is much like the search for the Holy Grail, there are ways to greatly improve the accuracy of appraisals.

APPRAISER ABILITY

Accurately evaluating an employee's performance involves using the job description to identify behaviors required, observing the worker's performance over the course of the evaluation period and recalling it, and knowing how to use the appraisal form accurately (e.g., understanding what is meant by performance dimensions such as "initiative"). To the extent that any of these things are lacking, a manager's ability to rate accurately is limited.

Fortunately, a manager's ability to rate employees can be improved. An organization can develop detailed job descriptions and share them with the rater. Steps can be taken to give the rater greater opportunity to directly or indirectly observe an employee's behavior. For example, other supervisors can provide information on an employee's performance when the immediate supervisor is not present. Managers can be taught to take notes on an employee's behavior to facilitate recall. Also, managers can learn to use the appraisal form better through formal training.

Formal training programs help to increase appraiser ability by making raters aware of the various types of rating errors (the assumption being that awareness may reduce the error tendency), by improving raters' observational skills, and by improving raters' skill in carrying out the performance appraisal interview.

Simone Hurtado is team manager for the pediatric home services team. In previous years, Simone has struggled to adequately evaluate her employees. Since all of the patient care is delivered in client's homes, Simone relied on sporadic client feedback and review of patient care documentation to complete employee appraisals. Recently Simone attended an appraisal workshop. Using some of the suggested strategies, Simone and the other team managers have set up an observation schedule for their employees. Each employee will be randomly observed by a team manager in a client's home every 6 to 8 weeks. Additionally, employees will be asked to complete self-evaluations as well as evaluations of other team members they work with on a regular basis. Simone has also established a system for compiling ongoing employee performance documentation.

APPRAISER MOTIVATION

Although it is often assumed that managers are motivated to accurately appraise their employees, such an assumption is often fallacious. Nurse managers have a multitude of tasks to perform, often immediately. Not surprisingly, then, they often view performance appraisals as something that can be done later. Furthermore, many managers do not see doing appraisals as a particularly important task, and some question the need for doing them at all. This is especially true if all employees receive the same percentage salary increase. Thus, if nurse managers are to be motivated to do appraisals well, they need to be rewarded for their efforts.

A nurse manager may spend little time on appraisals for several reasons:

- The organization does not reward the person for doing a good job.
- The manager's superior spends little time on the nurse manager's own appraisal (thus sending the message that doing appraisals is not important).
- If a nurse manager gives low ratings to a poor employee, a superior may overrule and raise the ratings.

In short, in many health care organizations, the environment may actually dampen appraiser motivation rather than stimulate it. Given these reasons for not spending time on appraisals, it is fairly obvious how an organization can enhance appraiser motivation:

- The nurse manager needs to be rewarded for conscientiously doing performance reviews.
- The nurse manager's superior needs to present a good model of how an appraisal should be carried out.
- As far as possible, the nurse manager should be able to reward the highly rated staff.

This becomes more likely as outcomes are used as the basis for reimbursement to the organization and, subsequently, the organization bases rewards on productivity. For the organization and its employees to benefit from the performance appraisal system, pay increases should not be across the board, layoffs should not be based on seniority, and promotions should be tied to superior performance.

Learn how one manager used a performance evaluation to help a staff member and benefit the organization at the same time (see Case Study 18-1).

Evaluating Skill Competency

Health care organizations are required to assess their employees' abilities to perform the skills and tasks required for their positions (Joint Commission, 2005). Validation of competency is an ongoing process, initiated in orientation, followed up by development, and assessed on an annual basis and, possibly, remediation. Skill evaluation most commonly takes place in a skills lab, with simulation models, or by direct observation at the point of care (Ringerman, Flint, & Hughes, 2006; Whelan, 2006). The manager plays a key role in determining the competences required on the job, especially for unit or department-specific competencies.

Several programs are available for skills assessment. One system commonly used is the Performance-Based Development System (PBDS) created by Dorothy del Bueno (1979). PBDS is used to assess and validate skills for beginning nurses at orientation and skills required for nurses at advanced levels (Whelan, 2006). Skills days are another method to validate skills. A variety of stations can be set up and nurses can move from one to the other for assessment of that specific skill.

Another option is peer evaluation at the bedside or point of care (Ringerman, Flint, & Hughes, 2006). Specially selected staff complete a competency validator training program who observe, but do not coach, staff in clinical situations. For those staff unable to satisfactorily perform the skills required, the manager then follows up to ensure that the staff member receives the necessary remediation. Regardless of the system used, skills must be evaluated and updated regularly to reflect changes in evidence-based practice.

Rules of Thumb

For approximately 5 percent of employees, the prescriptions given in this chapter will not work, for reasons yet unknown. Additional suggestions or "rules of thumb" derived from practical experience include the following:

- **Go beyond the form.** Too often, people doing evaluations cite an inadequate form as an excuse for doing a poor job of evaluating their employees. No matter how inadequate an appraisal form is, managers can go beyond it. They can focus on behavior even if the form does not require it. They can set goals even if

CASE STUDY 18-1   Evaluating Staff

Brenda Tice has been nurse manager for the medical intensive care unit (MICU) in a large urban hospital for 6 months. The MICU rarely has staff openings and the average nurse has 12 years of experience on the unit. Brenda herself was a nurse on the unit for 10 years prior to her promotion to nurse manager.

Lori Cook has been an RN on the MICU day shift for the past 18 months. Lori is pleasant and tries hard to please her patients and coworkers. However, she consistently stays late to complete her charting, relies heavily on coworkers to help her throughout the shift, and has little confidence in her own ability to handle complex patients. Often Lori will break down and cry during a patient code and is seemingly overwhelmed by the code process. Although the other nurses are supportive of Lori, they are aware of her limitations. Several nurses have complained when they have been assigned two high acuity patients and Lori is assigned one lower acuity patient.

Brenda has arranged for Lori to attend several training programs designed specifically for ICU nurses, provided opportunities for experienced nurses to mentor Lori on more complex patients, and provided her with reference materials to reinforce Lori's skill set. Brenda also reviewed Lori's personnel records for the past 18 months. While Lori is rated high for attendance and her interpersonal skills, her clinical skills are rated as fair. Brenda notices three separate performance counseling documents dated within the past 12 months, with little improvement noted in her clinical performance.

Following another code incident in which Lori started crying and was asked to leave by a physician, Brenda determines that while Lori has many positive qualities, she does not have the clinical skills necessary to function independently in the MICU. After contacting the human resources department to discuss the transfer process, she schedules a meeting with Lori to discuss her performance issues. Brenda reviews the performance concerns with Lori and informs her that she has 30 days to accept reassignment within the hospital to a unit that more closely matches her clinical abilities. Lori decides to interview for positions in the geriatric psychiatric unit and the psychiatric day treatment program.

Manager's Checklist

The nurse manager is responsible to:

- Understand the performance appraisal process and appraisal tools used by the organization
- Provide honest and timely feedback to all employees
- Communicate as needed with the human resources department when performance issues arise
- Accurately and thoroughly document all performance-related issues
- Identify the impact of poor performers on the morale and productivity of staff
- Make staffing decisions in a timely manner

other supervisors do not. They can use critical incidents. In short, nurse managers should do the best job of managing they can and not let the form handicap them.

- **Postpone the appraisal interview if necessary.** Once the appraisal interview begins, there appears to be some natural law of management that the session must be completed in the time allotted, whether the session is going well or has degenerated into name calling. Managers forget the goal of the appraisal interview is not merely to get an employee's signature on the form but also to get the employee to improve performance in the coming year. Therefore, if the interview is not going well, a manager should discontinue it until a later time. Such a postponement allows both the manager and the employee some time to reflect on what has transpired as well as some time to calm down.

In postponing the meeting, the manager should not assign blame ("If you're going to act like a child, let's postpone the meeting"), but should adopt a more positive approach ("This meeting isn't going as I hoped it would; I'd like to postpone it to give us some time to collect our thoughts"). Most managers who have used this technique find that the second session, which generally takes place 1 to 2 days later, goes much better.

- **Don't be afraid to change an inaccurate rating.** New managers often ask whether they should change a rating if an employee challenges it. They fear that by changing a rating, they will be admitting an error. They also fear that changing a rating will lead to other ratings being challenged. A practical rule of thumb for this situation is if the rating is inaccurate, change it, but never change it during the appraisal interview. Rather, if an employee challenges a rating and the manager believes the employee has a case, the manager should tell the person that some time is needed to think about the rating before getting back to the employee.

The logic behind this rule of thumb is as follows: If a manager does a careful job of evaluating performance, few inaccurate ratings will be made. But no one is perfect, and on occasion, managers will err. When such an error occurs, the manager should correct it. Most employees respect a manager who admits a mistake and corrects it. By allowing for time to reflect on the ratings, a manager eliminates the pressure to make a snap judgment.

Karlene Kerfoot (2000) states that "Performance management systems are a way to hold a mirror up to employees and let them see their performance through the eyes of others" (p. 305). An effective performance evaluation contributes to the employee's development, improves job satisfaction, and enhances employee morale. Learning how to evaluate employees is one of the nurse manager's useful activities.

What You Know Now

- Doing performance appraisals is one of the most difficult and most important management activities.
- Accurate appraisals provide a sound basis for both administrative decisions (e.g., salary increases) and employee development.
- Criteria to be evaluated may include individual traits, outcome-oriented results, behavioral criteria, or a combination.
- Evaluation methods include rating scales, essays, forced distribution categories, behavior-oriented rating scales, and results-oriented evaluations.
- Problems with employee appraisal include leniency error, recency error, halo error, ambiguous standards, and the inadequate use of written comments.
- To enhance the accuracy of the performance appraisal, the manager should record critical incidents throughout the evaluation period.
- To improve the value of the appraisal interview, the manager should follow the key behaviors for conducting an appraisal interview.
- Self-evaluation, peer review, and group evaluation are additional appraisal methods that can be used.
- Validating skill competence can be conducted in the skills lab, in simulation, or at the point of care.

Tools for Evaluating Staff Performance

1. Become familiar with the evaluation process adopted by your organization.
2. Familiarize yourself with the appraisal instrument used for staff evaluation.
3. Learn to use critical incidents and include positive behaviors as well as those needing improvement.
4. Be alert to the chances for error in the appraisal process.
5. Prepare for an appraisal interview using the strategies suggested in the chapter.
6. Follow the key behaviors for conducting an appraisal interview.

Questions to Challenge You

1. What evaluation method is used at your workplace or clinical site? If you do not know, find out and share it with a colleague or class.
2. If you have been evaluated in the skills lab, on a simulator, or at the point of care, which assessment best evaluated your skills?
3. What components of your job (or clinical placement) are evaluated? Are they the appropriate ones?
4. What types of assessment methods have been used to evaluate you? Were they the best ones to evaluate your performance? What would you suggest?
5. If you have been evaluated as an employee, did your evaluator follow the key behaviors in this chapter? What improvements would you suggest?
6. Have you ever evaluated someone else's performance at work? How closely did your actions follow the suggestions in the chapter?

Explore MediaLink 🌐

Additional interactive resources for this chapter can be found on the Website at http://www.prenhall. com/sullivan. Click on Chapter 18 to select activities for this chapter.

- Video Overview
- NCLEX® Review Questions
- Critical Thinking Activities
- Current Events
- Nursing Leadership and Management in Action
- MediaLinks

References

del Bueno, D. (1979). Implementing a performance evaluation system. *Supervisor Nurse, 10*(2), 48–52.

Goffin, R. D. (2001). Is halo helpful? Effects of inducing halo on performance rating accuracy. Social Behavior and Personality. Retrieved January 2008 from http://findarticles.com/p/articles/mi_qa3852/is_200301/ai_n9198296

Joint Commission. (2005). *Comprehensive accreditation manual for hospitals: The official handbook*. Oakbrook Terrace, IL: Joint Commission Resources.

Kerfoot, K. (2000). On leadership: Leading from the inside out. *Nursing Economics, 18*(6), 7.

Ringerman, E., Flint, L. J., & Hughes, D. E. (2006). An innovative education program. *Journal for Nurses in Staff Development, 22*(5), 114–121.

Smith, M. H. (2003). Empower staff with praiseworthy appraisals. *Nursing Management, 34*(1), 16–17.

Whelan, L. (2006). Competency assessment of nursing staff. *Orthopaedic Nursing, 25*(3), 198–205.

Coaching, Disciplining, and Terminating Staff

Day-to-Day Coaching

Dealing with a Policy Violation

Disciplining Staff

Terminating Employees

Learning Outcomes

After completing this chapter, you will be able to:

1. Describe how to coach an employee.
2. Explain how to confront an employee about a policy violation.
3. Discuss how to discipline an employee.
4. Describe how to terminate an employee.

MediaLink

www.prenhall.com/sullivan

See the Companion Website for chapter-specific resources at
www.prenhall.com/sullivan.

Key Terms

One of the most challenging problems for managers is knowing what to do when employees fail to perform to expectations. Managers often want to ignore the problems, hoping they'll disappear, but that seldom happens. Instead the manager can learn how to handle these problems.

Day-to-Day Coaching

Coaching, the day-to-day process of helping employees improve their performance, is an important tool for effective nurse managers. Yet coaching is probably the most difficult task in management and often is neglected. In one short interaction, it encompasses needs analysis, staff development, interviewing, decision making, problem solving, analytical thinking, active listening, motivation, mentoring, and communication skills. Intervening immediately in performance problems on a day-to-day basis usually eliminates small problems before they become larger ones and the subject of discussion in performance appraisal interviews or disciplinary actions. Coaching also should be used when performance meets the standard but improvement can still be obtained.

The goal of coaching is to eliminate or improve performance problems, but few nurses are prepared to coach and often are hesitant to confront employee problems (Goggin, 2000; Lachman, 2000; Liebowitz, 2003). Coaching employees when the problem initially surfaces can potentially save time, prevent poor morale from occuring, and avoid later, more difficult action, such as discipline or termination (Cottringer, 2003; Palermo, 2007). Additionally, appropriate and timely coaching can help retain employees and reduce turnover (Murray, 2003; Stedman & Nolan, 2007). (See Chapter 20 for more on reducing turnover and retaining staff.)

Examples of problems that coaching can improve or eliminate are incorrect flow sheet documentation, excessive absenteeism, or frequent personal phone calls. Before entering into a coaching session, the nurse manager (coach) should prepare for the interaction and try to anticipate how the employee will react ("Everybody gets personal phone calls") in order to formulate an appropriate response ("I am here to talk about the number of personal phone calls you receive"). In general, coaching sessions should last no more than 5 to 10 minutes. The steps in successful coaching are:

1. **State the targeted performance in behavioral terms.** "For the past 2 days, the physical assessment portions of your flow sheets have not been filled out."

2. **Tie the problem to consequences for patient care, the functioning of the organization, or the person's self-interest.** "It's difficult for other nurses and physicians to know whether the patient's status is changing, and therefore it's hard to know how to treat the patient. Physical assessments are a standard of practice in our unit. Failure to document assessments could lead to legal problems should the patient's record go before a court of law." This is an important but often overlooked step because it cannot be taken for granted that the employee knows why the behavior is a problem. If employees are expected to act in a certain way, they need to understand why the behavior is important and be rewarded when it has improved. Also, avoid threatening language, such as "If you want to stay in this unit, you had better complete your documentation." This puts the employee on the defensive and makes the person less receptive to change.

3. **Having stated the problem behavior, avoid jumping to conclusions but instead explore reasons for the problem with the employee.** Listen openly as the employee describes the problem and the reasons for it. If the problem was caused by ignorance—for instance, lack of familiarity with the standard of care on performing and documenting assessments—simply inform the nurse of the appropriate behavior and end the coaching session.

4. **Ask the employee for his or her suggestions and discuss ideas on how to solve the problem.** In many cases, the employee knows best how to solve the problem and is more likely to be committed to the solution if it is his or her own. It is better to encourage employees to solve their own problems, but this does not mean that managers cannot add suggestions for improvement. It is essential to listen openly to understand the employee's perspectives.

5. **How formal should the coaching session be?** If the problem is minor and a first-time occurrence, you may simply state what actions will be taken to solve the problem and end the meeting. In most cases, however, you and the employee should agree on specific behavioral steps each will take to solve the problem; write down these steps for later reference.

6. **Arrange for a follow-up meeting, at which time the employee will receive performance feedback.** It is possible that an employee may bring up personal problems as a cause for the work problems. The coaching session then verges on becoming a counseling session. When the employee brings up personal problems, nurse managers should convey their concern and willingness to work with the employee to get help for the problems. In most cases, nurse managers will not be the direct source of the help but rather will help the employee seek out other, more appropriate, sources. Do not delve into potential personal problems ("Are there problems at home that I should know about?") unless staff raise them. The employee's personal life is not the manager's business.

Dealing with a Policy Violation

As with day-to-day coaching, prepare to confront an employee about a policy violation. The leadership style of the nurse is important in determining whether the employee perceives he or she is being told what to do versus being sold on the idea that she or he is an important contributor to the staff. The steps involved in **confrontation** are similar to coaching. These steps are outlined in Box 19-1.

The first key behavior is to determine whether the employee is aware of the policy. The employee should have received policy information at orientation, and an updated policy manual should be readily accessible to all employees. It is also important to know whether the policy has been enforced consistently. If policies regarding tardiness are not applied to everyone on a daily basis, efforts to change this behavior in one individual predictably will be unsuccessful. It is better to identify policies and procedures that the majority of staff accept and to determine which employees need direction in compliance.

Second, describe the behavior that violated the policy in a manner that conveys concern to the employee regarding the outcome. By focusing on the employee's behavior, you avoid making the interaction a personal issue.

After stating that the policy has been violated, have documents stating the policy so that interpretation issues can be clarified. For example, if the policy being violated is the requirement that nurses report to a peer about their patients when leaving the unit, have a copy of the policy in hand.

The next step is to solicit the employee's reason for the behavior (e.g., what is preventing the person from informing a peer about patients when leaving the unit). Allow sufficient time for the employee to respond while

BOX 19-1	Steps in Confrontation
1. Prepare before the meeting.	Is the employee aware of the policy and procedure? Desired behavior? Has the policy/procedure been consistently enforced? How will the employee react?
2. Without attacking the person, describe the undesired behavior. Tie that behavior to its consequences for the patients, organization, or employee.	Jane, were you aware that it is clinic policy to notify *both* the clinic manager and the hospital supervisor when you will be absent from work? Not only were we worried about you, but we had to reschedule patient procedures because we did not have the staff to attend to both clinic appointments and special procedures.
3. Solicit and openly listen with empathy to the employee's reasons for the behavior.	Why didn't you notify someone about your absence?
4. Explain why the behavior cannot continue, and ask for suggestions in solving the problem. If none are offered, suggest solutions. Agree on steps each will take to solve the problem.	In the future, you will need to notify both the clinic manager and the hospital supervisor if you cannot come in. How do you suppose you might do this since you do not have a phone?
5. Set and record a specific follow-up date.	Can we meet again in 1 month to review this plan?

at the same time guarding against the pursuit of extraneous, unrelated issues. In the latter event, redirect the employee's attention to the policy violation and suggest dealing with other issues at another time.

Convey to the employee that she or he cannot continue breaking an established policy. In the previous example, you could discuss the effects of the behavior, such as medications not given, IVs running dry, and patients being left unattended, as reasons for the policy.

Next, explore alternative solutions so that negative outcomes will be avoided. Ask the employee for suggestions for solving the problem, and discuss each of the suggestions. Offer help if it is appropriate. Decide and agree on a course of action. The last step in the process is to set up a reasonable date to follow up with the employee on adherence to the established policy.

Although dealing with policy violations in a distinct step-by-step sequence is not always possible, proceed in an orderly manner. Many policy violations require early and decisive interventions, and these must be handled in an immediate, forthright manner.

Disciplining Staff

Most nurses and managers dread having to **discipline** an employee (Hoffmann, 2005). Nevertheless, there will be occasions where discipline is necessary (e.g., when a regulation has been violated, jeopardizing patient safety). Managers may hesitate to discipline for many reasons, including:

- Lack of management support or training
- Letting past inappropriate behavior go by without mention
- Rationalizing to avoid disciplining
- Previous poor experience with attempting to discipline employees
- Fear that the employee will respond negatively (Anderson & Pulich, 2001; White, 2006)

Learning how to discipline effectively can reduce your concerns and improve morale for all employees. Keep in mind, though, that the primary function of discipline is not to punish the guilty party, but to teach new skills and encourage that person and others to behave appropriately in the future.

When faced with a disciplinary situation, maintain close contact with the organization's human resources department and administration. Before taking any disciplinary action, discuss the action he or she intends to take and seek approval for it. This close coordination with administration is essential to guarantee that any

---

BOX 19-2	**Guidelines for Effective Discipline**

1. Get the facts before acting.
2. Do not act while you are angry.
3. Do not suddenly tighten your enforcement of rules.
4. Do not apply penalties inconsistently.
5. Discipline in private.
6. Make the offense clear. Specify what is appropriate behavior.
7. Get the other side of the story.
8. Do not let the disciplining become personal.
9. Do not back down when you are right.
10. Inform the human resources department and administration of the outcome and other pertinent details.

---

disciplinary action is administered in a fair and legally defensible manner.

To further ensure fairness, rules and regulations must be clearly communicated, a system of progressive penalties must be established, and an appeals process must be available. To enforce rules or regulations, managers must inform employees of them ahead of time, preferably in writing. Guidelines for effective discipline can be found in Box 19-2.

Penalties should be progressive. **Progressive discipline** is the process of increasingly severe warnings for repeated violations that can result in termination. For minor violations (e.g., smoking outside in an unauthorized area), penalties may progress from an oral warning, to a written warning placed in the employee's personnel folder, to a suspension, and ultimately to termination. For major rule violations (e.g., theft of property), however, initial penalties should be more severe (e.g., immediate suspension). An appeals process should be built into an organization's disciplinary procedures to ensure that discipline is carried out in a fair, consistent manner. Case Study 19-1 shows how one nurse manager handled a disciplinary problem.

Terminating Employees

Unfortunately, some employees do not respond to either coaching or discipline and nurse managers will face the day when they must **terminate**, or fire, an employee (Bing, 2007). The steps in terminating an employee are similar to those for disciplining, except there are no plans to correct the behavior and no follow-up.

CASE STUDY 19-1   Progressive Discipline

Katie Connors is nurse manager of the birthing center in a metropolitan hospital. The hospital has several different nursing programs that utilize various patient care units for clinical instruction. A student nurse, Amber Schroeder, was assigned to work with Natalie Cole, RN, for the day shift. Natalie and Amber's patient arrives at the birthing center for induction of labor. During the admission process, the patient confides to Natalie and Amber that she is terrified that she might need a caesarian section. Amber tells the patient that a young woman and her baby recently died at the hospital during an emergency C-section. The patient begins to hyperventilate, refuses to let Natalie continue with the admission, and threatens to leave the birthing center. Natalie is so angry at Amber for scaring the patient she grabs her by the arm and pulls her out of the room. Natalie loudly berates Amber in the hallway to the point that Amber is crying.

Katie hears the commotion in the hallway and instructs Amber to sit in the staff lounge until her instructor can return to the unit. Katie and Natalie reassure the patient, who allows Natalie to complete the admission process. Throughout the shift, Natalie tells every staff member and physician about Amber's "stupid comment." Katie speaks with the nursing instructor and Amber about the incident. She also checks back with the patient and gently gathers facts about the incident.

Katie is concerned about Natalie's response to the situation. While Natalie has excellent nursing skills, she has often been abrupt or rude to other staff members. Katie has coached Natalie on her communication skills in three other specific incidents and verbally warned Natalie about her lack of professional communication. After discussing the incident with the human resources manager, Katie agrees that a written warning will be placed in Natalie's personnel file.

At the end of the shift, Katie requests that Natalie come to her office to discuss what happened with the student nurse. Katie informs Natalie she is disappointed in how she reacted to the inappropriate comment made by the student nurse. Specifically, physically grabbing the student and verbally attacking her in front of patients and staff was unacceptable and violates hospital policy. Further, Natalie continued to disparage the student to other staff and physicians, which is also unacceptable. Natalie expresses her frustration at the thoughtlessness of Amber's comment. Katie tells Natalie that while Amber's comment was inappropriate, Natalie's response was also inappropriate. Katie reinforces to Natalie the importance of professional communication at all times and reviews the communication points she had provided to Natalie in the past. She also informs Natalie that she will have a written warning placed in her personnel file. Natalie apologizes for her actions and assures Katie she will work on her communication skills. Katie documents the incident and follow-up action in Natalie's personnel file.

Manager's Checklist

The nurse manager is responsible to:

- Collect all necessary facts related to the disciplinary situation
- Communicate with the human resources department and nursing administration about the offense and appropriate penalty
- Discipline the employee in a timely manner
- Provide strategies to the disciplined employee to improve his or her behavior
- Clearly and firmly communicate expectations for appropriate behavior
- Document the outcome of the discipline as appropriate
- Follow-up with the human resources department and nursing administration regarding the outcome of the discipline

As with a disciplinary action, maintain close contact with the organization's human resource department and nursing administration. Again, discuss the termination and seek approval for it.

Preparation before terminating an employee is essential (Cohen, 2006; Michael, 2004). To prepare, answer the following questions:

1. Did you set your expectations clearly from the beginning? Did you review the job description, performance appraisal criteria, and pertinent policies and procedures with the employee? These expectations should have been in writing.
2. Did you document the employee's performance on a continuing basis using the critical incident or a similar method?
3. Did you keep the employee informed about his or her performance on a regular basis?
4. Did you conduct coaching sessions or deal with policy or procedure violations in a timely manner? Were the sessions and the agreed-on actions in these meetings documented?

5. Were you honest with the employee about the poor performance or the policy that was violated? Were you specific about behaviors that failed to meet expected standards? Was the expected performance stated in behavioral terms?

6. Were you consistent among employees in how you dealt with performance issues and policy or procedure violations?

7. Did you follow up? Did you deliver the actions you agreed to in the coaching sessions?

8. Did you document everything in writing? The importance of this cannot be overstated.

9. Have you notified security so that the terminated employee may be escorted out?

This checklist applies to almost every instance of termination. The few exceptions might be theft or physical abuse of a patient or assault on others. Even in the latter instances, observation and documentation are crucial to avoid legal challenges.

See how one manager handled terminating an employee in Case Study 19-2.

Terminating an employee affects the morale of the entire unit. Coworkers may take sides, and the man-

---

CASE STUDY 19-2   Terminating Staff

Carrie Lyle is nurse manager of a 20-bed medical–surgical unit in a suburban hospital. Six months ago, Margaret Johnson, LPN, transferred to the unit from the skilled nursing unit. Carrie noted that although Margaret had been an employee of the hospital for 12 years, her personnel record included several entries regarding substandard performance. Carrie also found gaps in her performance appraisals from other units. Carrie discussed these issues with Margaret prior to her transfer and clearly indicated performance expectations. However, Margaret often arrives late to work and leaves before report is finished for the day shift.

Claire Kindred, RN and night shift charge nurse, has worked with Margaret for the past 6 months. Claire requested a meeting with Carrie to discuss patient care concerns. Claire indicated that during most shifts, Margaret takes extended meal and break times. She has been found sleeping during her shift in empty patient rooms. Recently, Claire assisted one of Margaret's patients to the bathroom. When recording the patient's output, she noted that Margaret had charted the patient's IV intake for the entire shift even though it was only 3 hours into the night shift. When confronted, Margaret laughed and told Claire she was "just saving time." Claire had documented the dates of the incidents and provided them to Carrie.

Carrie met that evening with Margaret to discuss her performance and informed her that she will be on probation for the next 30 days. The next morning, Robert Adams, RN, brought one of his patient's charts to Carrie's office. The patient had been assigned to Margaret on the night shift. In addition to diabetes, the patient has bilateral below-the-knee amputations. On the patient's physical assessment, Margaret had charted positive pedal pulses. She also charted she had changed the patient's IV tubing and IV dressing. On closer inspection, Robert found that the date stickers had been covered over by new stickers and no IV tubing changes were noted on the patient's chart. Carrie immediately contacted the human resources department. She tells them that Margaret has falsified patient documentation in direct violation of her probation and hospital policy. The human resources department reviews Margaret's file and concurs that immediate termination is appropriate. Exit paperwork is initiated by the human resources department and forwarded to Carrie.

Carrie meets Margaret as she arrives for her scheduled shift. She asks Margaret to come into her office to discuss her immediate termination of employment. Margaret is visibly shaken. Carrie calmly outlines the performance problems and compliance issues that support Margaret's termination. She has a security officer escort Margaret to her locker to gather her personal items. Carrie documents the meeting outcome in Margaret's personnel file.

Manager's Checklist

The nurse manager is responsible to:

- Understand the organization's discipline and termination policies and procedures
- Review personnel files and identify past performance problems that may affect current or future performance
- Address employee performance issues in a timely manner
- Verify performance problems rather than personality problems
- Work with the human resources department when employee termination is indicated

ager may need to share pertinent facts if they relate to patient safety or acceptable behavioral standards. Not terminating poor performing staff, conversely, can hurt the manager's credibility and decrease performance on the unit (Hader, 2006).

Employees cannot be fired simply for being a member of a protected class, including their race, sex, national origin, or religion, or their disability as long as their disability does not prevent them from doing their job. Also a nurse, for example, cannot be fired for refusing to follow medical orders that he or she believes might harm a patient (Kleiner, 2003; Smith, 2002).

Even with careful documentation and the most conscientious adherence to organizational policies regarding termination, firing an employee may be followed by legal action, grievance procedures, and stressful and time-consuming hearings (Kleiner, 2003). A preferable alternative is that the employee voluntarily resign. Careful documentation may allow the manager to suggest that the employee voluntarily leave the organization. This allows the employee to leave without a record of termination.

Being a nurse manager is a challenging, ever-changing job and seldom more difficult than when employees must be disciplined, or terminated. Even coaching employees can be a stressful experience. Developing the skills to intervene early with employee problems and follow-up as necessary should the problem continue or escalate will help reduce incidents and improve performance and morale.

What You Know Now

- Coaching is the day-to-day process of helping employees improve their performance or eliminate a performance problem.
- When a policy violation occurs, confrontation is necessary.
- To confront an employee, make the employee aware of the violation and its consequences, elicit reasons for the behavior, and agree on steps to prevent future recurrence.
- When rule violations occur, disciplinary action is needed. Penalties should be progressive.
- When staff members do not respond to discipline, managers must terminate their employment.
- If an employee must be terminated, the manager must stay in close contact with the human resources department and administration when planning and carrying out the termination.

Tools for Coaching, Disciplining, and Terminating Staff

1. To prepare and conduct a coaching session
   a. Note the behavior and why it is unacceptable
   b. Explore reasons for the behavior with the employee
   c. Ask the employee for suggestions to solve the problem
   d. Arrange for follow-up
2. To conduct a discipline session
   a. Be certain you are calm before beginning
   b. Assure privacy before beginning
   c. Apply rules consistently
   d. Get both sides of a story
   e. Keep the focus on the problem, not the person
   f. Arrange for follow-up,
   g. Inform the human resources department and administration
3. To prepare to terminate a staff member
   a. Inform the human resources department and administration beforehand
   b. State the offending behavior and the reason for termination
   c. Explain the termination process
   d. Remain calm
   e. Arrange for employee to be escorted out
   f. Report back to the human resources department and administration

Questions to Challenge You

1. Have you ever been coached, confronted, or disciplined in your workplace or clinical site? How well did the intervenor handle the situation? How well did you handle it? Did you learn from it?
2. Have you ever had to coach, confront, or discipline someone? How did the person respond? How well did you do? What did you learn?
3. Do you think you could terminate a staff member? If not, how would you prepare yourself?
4. Select a colleague or classmate and role-play four situations:
   a. A coaching session
   b. A confrontation
   c. A discipline session
   d. A termination
   After you have completed these sessions, reverse positions and play the opposite role.
5. Critique each other's performance.

Explore MediaLink

Additional interactive resources for this chapter can be found on the Website at http://www.prenhall.com/sullivan. Click on Chapter 19 to select activities for this chapter.

- Video Overview
- NCLEX® Review Questions
- Critical Thinking Activities
- Current Events
- Nursing Leadership and Management in Action
- MediaLinks

References

Anderson, P., & Pulich, M. (2001). A positive look at progressive discipline. *Health Care Manager, 20*(1), 1–9.

Bing, S. (2007). A tale of three firings. *Fortune, 156*(2), 210.

Cohen, S. (2006). How to terminate a staff nurse. *Nursing Management, 37*(10), 16.

Cottringer, W. (2003). The abc's of employee discipline. *SuperVision, 64*(4), 5–7.

Goggin, M. (2000). I'm behind you! The manager as coach. *Nursing Economic$, 18*(3), 160–161.

Hader, R. (2006). Put employee termination etiquette to practice. *Nursing Management, 37*(12), 6.

Hoffmann, P. B. (2005). Confronting management incompetence. *Healthcare Executive, 20*(6), 28–30.

Kleiner, B. H. (2003). Principles and techniques for rightful termination. *Equal Opportunities International, 22*(6/7), 74–79.

Lachman, V. D. (2000). Enrich your performance coaching techniques. *Nursing Management, 31*(1), 14–19.

Liebowitz, B. (2003). Coaching managers. *Healthcare Financial Management, 57*(4), 108–112.

Michael, J. E. (2004). Investigate thoroughly to avoid wrongful termination suits. *Nursing Management, 35*(5), 20–22.

Murray, B. (2003). Positive discipline reaps retention. *Nursing Management, 34*(6), 19–22.

Palermo, J. C. (2007). Well-crafted worker discipline program diminishes risk. *Business Insurance, 41*(8), 9.

Smith, M. H. (2002). Protect your facility and staff with effective discipline and termination. *Nursing Management, 33*(7), 15–16.

Stedman, M. E. & Nolan, T. L. (2007). Coaching: A different approach to the nursing dilemma. *Nursing Administration Quarterly, 31*(1), 43–49.

White, K. M. (2006). Better manage your human capital. *Nursing Management, 37*(1), 16–19.

Reducing Turnover, Retaining Staff

Learning Outcomes

After completing this chapter, you will be able to:

1. Describe how nursing turnover affects the organization.
2. Explain how the hire decision affects nursing turnover.
3. Discuss what organizations can do to improve retention of nurses.
4. Discuss what managers can do to help retain nurses.
5. Demonstrate how clinical ladders, magnet recognition, mentors, coaches, and residency programs are effective in helping retain nurses.

MediaLink

www.prenhall.com/sullivan
See the Companion Website for chapter-specific resources at
www.prenhall.com/sullivan.

Key Terms

Coach *p272*
Horizontal promotion *p271*
Involuntary turnover *p267*

Mentor *p271*
Performance-driven clinical
    ladder *p270*

Salary compression *p268*
Turnover *p266*
Voluntary turnover *p267*

Reducing Turnover

Reducing turnover and retaining staff begins with recruitment and selection (see Chapter 15). Additionally, the overall shortage of nurses is expected to worsen (American Association of Colleges of Nursing, 2007; Joint Commission, 2007). An aging workforce coupled with an aging population and the spiraling cost of health care exacerbate the problem of too few nurses to care for many more patients. It behooves the nurse manager to make every effort to enhance the environment so that the best nurses remain.

Where nurses practice and what mix of nursing staff is required to adequately care for tomorrow's patients continue to shift (e.g., ambulatory care, home care). Regardless of the setting, reducing **turnover**, the number of staff members who vacate a position, is essential for the health care organization to thrive.

COST OF NURSING TURNOVER

The average nurse turnover rate in hospitals is estimated at 8.4 percent, but the average voluntary turnover of first-year nurses is 27.1 percent (PricewaterhouseCoopers, 2007). The cost, however, is more difficult to estimate. Suggestions range from $23,000 to $31,000 in one study (Waldman, Kelly, Sanjeev, & Smith, 2004) and $62,000 to $67,000 in another (Jones, 2005). Jones (2005) also reports that nurse turnover costs 1.2 to 1.3 times the RN salary at a study hospital. Given the numerous expenses incurred in hiring a new nurse (e.g., recruiting, selection, orientation, on-the-job training) and temporarily replacing a nurse who quits or is fired (e.g., paying other nurses to work overtime or filling the vacancy with a temporary replacement), the costs are certainly sizable.

Given its cost, nursing turnover clearly needs to be understood better and controlled more effectively. Turnover has been thought of in simplistic terms and seen as universally negative. Such a primitive view of

turnover is not helpful to managers as they attempt to deal with this costly problem. Rather, varieties of turnover need to be differentiated:

- Did the employee leave of her or his own accord, or was the person asked to leave?
- Was the departed individual's performance exceptional or mediocre?
- Did the employee leave for career development (e.g., return to school) or because of dissatisfaction with the organization?
- Will the departed nurse be easy or difficult to replace?

Turnover has consequences that go far beyond direct dollar costs. Turnover can have a number of repercussions among other nurses who worked with the departed nurse. If temporary replacements are used, problems still can result as the workflow of the unit is disturbed and communication patterns within the unit are disrupted.

Turnover can be interpreted by coworkers as a rejection of the job and a recognition that better job opportunities exist elsewhere. For those who remain, ways must be found to reconcile their decision to stay in light of evidence from others that the job may not be good. As a result, they may reevaluate their present position in the organization and develop more negative job attitudes. In addition, they may have to work longer hours (overtime) or simply work harder to cover for a departed nurse; this can cause both physical and mental strain and may result in additional departures. Thus, departed nurses may begin a cycle of nurses leaving, resulting in a turnover spiral.

Turnover, and the resultant decrease in the number of nurses, also may cause the organization to postpone, cancel, or not pursue potentially profitable new ventures. An organization may delay opening new clinics or services or even close existing units. In addition, turnover also can have undesirable effects on patients, coworkers, and others (Jones, 2005). Furthermore, what may be seen as a desirable departure by some (e.g., the nurse manager) may be viewed as a loss by others (e.g., a subset of coworkers).

Turnover is not always undesirable. Anyone with work experience can remember some individual (e.g., a coworker, a supervisor) whose departure would have improved the organization's functioning significantly. If the departed nurse was a poor performer, performance may improve. Recently-hired staff may be more enthusiastic, long-running conflicts between people may be reduced or eliminated, or administration may be challenged to improve the work environment (see Healthy Work Environment section).

CAUSES OF TURNOVER

Before turnover can be managed, its causes must be understood. Traditionally, organizations have attempted to determine the reasons for voluntary turnover through two sources: The exiting employee's supervisor is asked why the employee is leaving, and an exit interview with the departing employee is conducted by someone in the human resources department.

Such an approach for determining the cause of voluntary turnover is certainly straightforward, but departing employees may not give honest answers in their exit interviews because they know that future employers will ask for references. Thus, exiting employees may provide safe responses (e.g., "a better opportunity came along") during an exit interview.

Although this tendency for departing employees to make safe responses is understandable, it makes it difficult to determine why turnover is occurring. Surveys sent to former employees several weeks after they have resigned may be more useful. Former employees need to be assured that their responses will not influence any future reference information furnished about them, but rather will be used only to help the organization identify the reasons why nurses are leaving. Another way to attempt to discover the cause of nurse turnover is to conduct interviews with the former employee's coworkers, who often know why an employee left.

Turnover and employee absenteeism (see Chapter 21) have been referred to as withdrawal behaviors because they allow an employee to leave the workplace, in one case temporarily and, in the other, permanently. In many cases, these withdrawal behaviors share a common cause: job dissatisfaction.

UNDERSTANDING VOLUNTARY TURNOVER

The discussion in this chapter focuses on **voluntary turnover** (i.e., employees choose to leave). If an organization finds a significant amount of **involuntary turnover** (i.e., employees being terminated), then it needs to carefully examine the way it recruits, selects, trains, and motivates employees. (See Chapters 15, 16, and 17.)

The goal should be to reduce voluntary turnover. The manager's first opportunity to reduce turnover is when the decision to hire is made. An individual's length of stay at past employers is an indication of how long the person could be expected to stay on a new job.

Turnover is a direct function of a nurse's perceptions of both the ease and the desirability of leaving the organization. Perceived ease of movement depends on the nurse's personal characteristics, such as:

- Education
- Area of specialization
- Age
- Geographic mobility
- Contacts at other hospitals
- Transportation

As well as market forces, such as:

- Job openings at other organizations
- Non–health care organizations hiring nurses for nursing or nonnursing positions

As with ease of movement, perceptions of the desirability of movement can be affected by several factors. One is the opportunity for movement within the organization. If other positions exist within the organization, the less turnover there should be; that is, a nurse may be able to leave the current position by means of a lateral transfer, promotion, or demotion. For example, a nurse who is having problems with a coworker may be able to transfer to a new unit rather than leave the organization.

A number of studies have shown that the greater an employee's satisfaction level or level of organizational commitment, the lower the probability of the individual's quitting (Drenkard, 2004; Nedd, 2006; Roszak, 2006; Smith, Hood, Waldman, & Smith, 2005). Job satisfaction is affected by various facets of the work environment, including:

- Relationships with the nurse manager, other staff nurses and unit employees, patients, and physicians

- Shift worked (e.g., day versus evening, rotating versus fixed)
- Fit between nurse values and institutional culture
- Expectations of practice setting
- Compensation level
- Equal and fair distribution of rewards and punishments

In three national surveys Buerhaus and colleagues (2007) found that nurses believe that the shortage is caused by inadequate compensation and poor working conditions (Buerhaus, Donelan, Ulrich, DesRoches, & Dittus, 2007). Smith, Hood, Waldman and Smith (2005) found that a positive experience in the practice setting increased nurses' job satisfaction and reduced turnover even when they considered the pay and benefits inadequate. Similarly, Nedd (2006) reports that nurses were more likely to stay on the job if they had access to empowerment structures, such as the ability to affect decision making through serving on task forces, committees, and work groups.

Retaining Staff

HEALTHY WORK ENVIRONMENT

Gilmore (2007) suggests that a healthy work environment increases nurse job satisfaction, a necessary condition for retaining nurses. In contrast, unhealthy work environments lead to turnover and poor patient care (Barden & Distrito, 2005). Miracle (2008) posits that both nurse satisfaction and excellent nursing care is the product of a healthy work environment.

The American Association of Critical Care Nurses (AACN, 2005) established six criteria for a healthy work environment to "foster excellence in patient care" (p. 1). These criteria are:

- Skilled communication—as important as clinical skills
- True collaboration—between and among nurses and other health care professionals
- Effective decision making—involved as partners in making policy and leading organizations
- Appropriate staffing—effective match between patient needs and nurse competencies
- Meaningful recognition—for value of work
- Authentic leadership—leaders embrace, live, and engage others in it

Authentic leadership is required for a healthy work environment, according to Shirley (2006).

IMPROVING SALARIES

As the largest group of health care professionals, nurses' wages account for the majority of an organization's salary budget. It is reasonable (although not cost effective) that organizations imagine they can reduce expenses by constraining nurses' salaries or allowing open positions to go unfilled. Thus, nurses employed for many years find their salaries only slightly greater than (or even less than) nurses with only a few years of experience.

Salary compression is an ever-present problem in nurses' compensation (Greipp, 2003). **Salary compression** is the effect of higher starting pay of new nurses or rewarding those with fewer years of experience with higher increases that results in the salaries of long-term employees being at or below those of less-experienced nurses. Sign-on bonuses and loan-forgiveness programs are strategies used to attract new graduates. They are, however, only quick fixes that serve to disadvantage already-employed nurses whose salary ceilings remain fixed.

Pay scales must be reconfigured to reflect achievement and accomplishment. One institution has done just that. At the Methodist Hospital in Houston, Texas, a performance-driven clinical ladder program was developed and implemented (Triolo, 2003). The purpose was to integrate "organizational values, evidence-based practice, relationship-centered care" with pay for performance (Perry, 2003, p. 1). The American Nurses Credentialing Center magnet hospital criteria were used along with a differentiated practice model.

MANAGEMENT STRATEGIES TO RETAIN STAFF

In addition to the work environment, managers can use several strategies to help retain a valued employee in the organization. These include:

- Provide a realistic job preview to new hires
- Facilitate movement within the organization
- Improve the work environment
- Coordinate with other managers to influence organizational policy
- Adapt to turnover rate

Provide Realistic Job Preview and Follow-up

Drenkard (2004) suggests that new graduates' unmet expectations about the practice setting is the cause of the high rate of turnover (PriceWaterhouseCooper,

2007). Children's Memorial Hospital in Chicago reduced turnover among new graduates from 29.5 percent to 12.3 percent after implementing a multifaceted orientation program (Halfer, 2007). Providing a realistic job preview, orienting the new graduate to the practice setting, and monitoring the new graduate's adaptation can help prevent these early withdrawals (Parrish, 2006).

You may recall the example in Chapter 15 in which the manager included unit staff in peer interviews with applicants in order to provide realistic job previews. Another manager followed up with a new nurse in the next example.

Trina Prescott, RN, joined the pediatric oncology unit of a large university teaching hospital. Her nurse manager, Lily Yuen, scheduled a lunch with Trina 30 days after she started. Lily had a relaxed conversation with Trina about the first 30 days of her employment. Trina expressed how much she enjoyed her new job, but still felt uncomfortable accessing implanted vascular ports without assistance from her mentor. Lily makes a note to schedule one-on-one teaching for Trina with a nurse from the IV team. Scheduling a lunch with new employees approximately 30-days and 60-days into their employment has improved new employee retention and increased open communication between Lily and her staff.

Facilitate Intraorganizational Movement

If a staff nurse is "burned out" from working on an oncology floor, one option is to allow a transfer to another service area in the organization (e.g., home care). Unfortunately, some managers hinder or even prohibit such a transfer (particularly if the potential transferee is an excellent performer), not wanting to lose a good nurse. However, this perspective is shortsighted. If the staff nurse cannot transfer to another area (intraorganizational mobility), she or he may leave the organization entirely (interorganizational mobility).

Improve Management Practice

Some suggestions for managers to use are:

- Enrich or redesign the staff nurse's job
- Facilitate upward and downward communication
- Link rewards with performance (see next section on pay for performance)
- Develop group cohesiveness (see Chapter 11)
- Help resolve interpersonal conflicts (see Chapter 12)
- Provide training and educational opportunities (see Chapter 17)

The temptation is to look for a quick fix in dealing with turnover, but that is seldom effective. In fact, what appears to be a simple change (e.g., trying to enrich the job of a high-performing nurse) may not be. For example, providing additional duties to enrich a nurse's job may lead to complaints of favoritism from other nurses, or the human resources department may worry about assigning duties that are not included in the job description.

Such potential difficulties should not cause a nurse manager to revert back to status quo behavior. Rather, anticipate such potential problems and deal with them (e.g., be able to justify the differential treatment through the use of performance appraisal data, have the affected nurse agree to the additional duties in writing). One nurse manager decreased voluntary turnover on her unit without incurring additional costs (see Case Study 20-1).

Coordinate with Other Managers to Influence Organizational Policy

A manager wants to do everything possible to lessen the problem of turnover. Sometimes this involves coordinating efforts with other managers to change organizational policy. One example is changing an organization's policy concerning work schedules.

Work scheduling (self-scheduling, fixed versus rotating shifts, flexible work hours, job sharing) is a particularly important area not only because of its relationship to voluntary turnover but also because of its frequent linkage to unionization attempts. It should not be surprising that working conditions that lead to turnover also can motivate interest in unionization. Two key causes of turnover-related unionization are staff shortages and rotating work schedules.

Innovative work schedules have had positive impacts on both nurse recruitment and retention. Although changing to work schedules that staff nurses see as more advantageous (e.g., self-scheduling, bid-shifting, fixed shifts, flexible hours, job sharing) obviously involves costs (e.g., coordination time), it also provides benefits. Most nurses prefer fixed shifts. If possible, nurses also prefer flexible hours. For many nurses with child care responsibility, job sharing provides a perfect means for remaining in health care and, at the same time, fulfilling parental responsibilities.

Before implementing such innovative work schedules, considerable planning (e.g., cost–benefit analysis) clearly needs to take place. Unfortunately, many health care organizations, even those that are having trouble recruiting and retaining nurses, simply dismiss such schedules.

To increase their likelihood of a successful attempt, the group of managers may need to build a persuasive

Mona Karnes is nurse manager of labor and delivery at a suburban hospital. Over the past 12 months, the voluntary turnover rate among full-time RNs has been 15 percent for her unit and 25 percent for the hospital as a whole. Despite increasing starting salary rates and offering signing bonuses, turnover rates have remained high. Administration is in the process of conducting an annual salary review as well as a benefits review.

Mona has collected information from exit interviews conducted by the human resources department. From these data, Mona has developed three strategies to aid in retention for her unit:

1. Rotating leadership responsibilities on the unit to offer all nurses the opportunity to develop leadership and management skills. These responsibilities currently include a weekly charge nurse role for each shift, education committee chair, physician relations liaison, women's health service line representative, and information technology representative. Other leadership roles will be added as appropriate.

2. Surveying staff to determine interests and strengths and connecting staff members with a mentor. For example, Debbie Edwards, RN, enjoys developing patient education modules. Debbie will work with Heather Adams, GN, to develop her patient education skills.

3. Scheduling monthly CEU offerings during staff meetings that are free of charge and presented by staff members, physicians, or pharmaceutical company representatives. By attending monthly staff meetings, most RNs will complete 90 percent of state-required CEUs for license renewal.

All three strategies are at no cost to the unit or hospital. After 6 months, the voluntary turnover rate on Mona's unit has decreased to 8 percent.

Manager's Checklist

The nurse manager is responsible to:
- Understand the financial impact of voluntary turnover on the unit and the organization
- Gather and analyze data that provide insight into the reasons for voluntary turnover
- Utilize creative solutions to increase staff retention
- Establish open and effective communication with staff members
- Evaluate retention strategies in a timely manner and adjusting processes as appropriate
- Communicate successful strategies to colleagues and administration

case for the program they are suggesting (e.g., document the success of job sharing at other hospitals, cost out the possible financial gain—often, part-time nurses are paid at a lower rate and do not receive pension benefits). (Also see Chapter 16 on scheduling.)

Nurse managers from a small not-for-profit hospital meet each month with the vice president for nursing. Nursing staff retention has been an ongoing concern. The vice president recently began providing all of the managers with information gathered during exit or transfer interviews each month. The results are provided by the human resources department and do not identify any staff by name or department. The top three reasons nurses gave for leaving: high patient-to-nurse ratio, required overtime, and salary issues, have been identified and systemwide retention strategies are now being developed.

Adapt to Turnover Rate

Sometimes the organization may simply need to adapt to a high turnover rate. Even if this is the case, the manager may be able to lessen potential problems by doing two things:

1. Manage beliefs about why a nurse left. Sometimes, the reason is unclear, and the grapevine often will provide an inaccurate and less attractive reason from the organization's perspective (e.g., "She left for $1.05 more an hour at a competitor institution").

2. Provide human resources with a preferred list of replacement workers. One health care organization keeps an up-to-date list of former nurses who will fill in on an occasional basis. Such former employees are more familiar with organizational procedures and thus can handle things more efficiently.

CLINICAL LADDER PROGRAMS

The **performance-driven clinical ladder** program uses a system of performance indicators to advance an employee within the organization. An analysis of current salaries was conducted, using years of experience and performance ratings (Triolo, 2003). Then pay for performance replaced across-the-board increases. Three key concepts guided decision making:

1. Horizontal promotion
2. Clinical ladder
3. Clinical mentor

Horizontal promotion rewarded the excellent clinical nurse without promoting the nurse to management. A clinical ladder, based on Benner's (2001) novice-to-expert concepts, was designed. The five designations are:

1. Clinical apprentice—new nurse or nurse new to the area
2. Clinical colleague—a full partner in care
3. Clinical mentor—demonstrates preceptor ability
4. Clinical leader—demonstrates leadership in practice
5. Clinical expert—combines teaching and research with practice

The strength of the system is that superb, clinical nurses can remain at the bedside, clinical excellence can be rewarded, and nurses can move back and forth among the levels based on their personal and professional goals and needs.

Generational differences affect retention as well. Today's young nurses of generations X and Y (millenials) want to have challenging careers that offer opportunities for growth and advancement as well as time for lives outside of work. Flexible schedules and time off are valued by these cohorts, and organizations can expect high turnover if these expectations are not met (Clausing et al, 2003; Hart, 2006).

MAGNET HOSPITAL DESIGNATION

Magnet hospitals are those institutions that have met the stringent guidelines for nurses and are credentialed by the American Nurses Credentialing Center. Magnet hospitals are more successful in attracting and retaining nurses (Aiken, Havens, & Sloane 2000; Brady-Schwartz, 2005; Halfer, 2007; Upenieks, 2003a). Higher salaries are not the sole criteria that retained nurses in these institutions. Characteristics common in magnet hospitals include:

- Higher ratios of nurses to patients
- Flexible schedules
- Decentralized administration
- Participatory management

- Autonomy in decision making
- Recognition
- Advancement opportunities

To retain the current workforce and attract other nurses, health care organizations can take from the magnet program characteristics to improve work-life conditions for nurses. Encouraging nurses to be full participants and to share a vested interest in the success of the organization can help alleviate the nursing shortage in those organizations and in the profession.

MENTORING

Mentoring is another strategy to improve retention. Mentors take a greater role than preceptors in developing staff. Precepting usually is associated with orientation of staff, whereas mentoring occurs over a much longer period and involves a bigger investment of personal energy. Mentoring is suggested as a strategy to retain new graduates (Butler & Felts, 2006).

A **mentor** is a wiser and more experienced person who guides, supports, and nurtures a less experienced person. Mentors tell you what you need to know and show you how to get it. Preceptors and preceptees are assigned to each other, whereas the mentor and mentee find one another, generally outside formal development programs. Mentors trust you with a job by giving assignments that are important; they test your limits and provide opportunities for learning. Mentors help by talking to you. They introduce you to people who may be helpful to your career development. Having a mentor instills a sense of greater personal satisfaction, increased self-confidence, and enhanced self-esteem. The relationship usually is intensely personal and rarely is hidden.

Mentors are usually the same sex as the protégé, 8 to 15 years older, highly placed in the organization, powerful, and willing to share their experiences. They are not threatened by the protégé's potential for equaling or exceeding them. Protégés are selected by mentors for several reasons: good performance, loyalty to people and the organization, a similar social background or a social acquaintance with each other, appropriate appearance, opportunity to demonstrate the extraordinary, and high visibility.

Mentor–protégé relationships seem to advance through several stages. The initiation stage usually lasts 6 months to a year, during which the relationship gets started. The protégé stage is that in which the protégé's work is not yet recognized for its own merit, but rather as a byproduct of the mentor's instruction, support, and encouragement. The mentor thus buffers the protégé from criticism.

A breakup stage may occur from 6 months to 2 years after a significant change in the relationship, usually resulting from the protégé's taking a job in another department or organization so that there is a physical separation of the two individuals. It also can occur if the mentor refuses to accept the protégé as a peer or when the relationship becomes dysfunctional for some reason. The lasting friendship stage is the final phase and will occur if the mentor accepts the protégé as a peer or if the relationship is reestablished after a significant separation. The complete mentor process usually includes the last stage.

COACHING

Coaching is a strategy suggested to address nurses' job dissatisfaction (Stedman & Nolan, 2007). A **coach** helps the staff member focus on solving a specific problem or conflict that interferes with the employee's satisfaction at work. Coaches are often nurses or human resources staff within the organization prepared to help resolve conflicts. Conflicts could be between two nurses, between a nurse and a patient, or between a nurse and a physician. In a confidential environment, the coach helps the staff member explore the exact nature of the problem, consider various alternatives (e.g., transfer, quit, do nothing), delve into embedded issues (e.g., values conflict with organization, unmatched expectations), discover links (e.g., working with friends), and the disadvantages of leaving (e.g., start over with vacation time, benefits, leave friends). The goal is to reduce turnover from issues that can be resolved.

RESIDENCY PROGRAMS

Versant RN Residency™

An evidence-based program, designed to prepare new nursing graduates for practice and to reduce the RN turnover rate, is the Versant RN Residency Program™ (McPeck, 2006). The 18-month residency includes both educational and emotional components. Novice nurses receive lectures and online access to best practices as well as a nurse partner who maintains an ongoing relationship and teaches professional accountability and critical thinking. In addition, residents participate in emotional support groups to share experiences and feelings. New-grad turnover rates have gone from 35 percent to less than 6 percent, according to surveys of hospitals using the program (McPeck, 2006).

Additionally, a recent report documented the effectiveness of a 1-year residency program on retaining new graduates (Williams et al., 2007). The program was implemented at 12 sites and each involved a partnership between a school of nursing and a hospital. The program included a core curriculum, clinical guidance by a nurse preceptor, and a resident facilitator for professional role development assistance in addition to the usual orientation at the institution. The results showed that turnover of new graduates averaged 12 percent, more than half the national average. Although year-long residency programs are far from the norm today, these promising early results suggest that the investment in such programs might yield long-term positive results for health care organizations.

The strategies outlined in this chapter have been shown to be effective in reducing turnover. However, not all are equally applicable to all situations. Situational factors determine what is appropriate. For example, flexible work hours may be suitable for a clinic but not for an around-the-clock operation. By being creative, nurse managers not only can reduce the overall turnover rate but also can have an influence on which nurses leave by providing incentives for the exceptional nurse to stay and by doing less to retain mediocre nurses.

What You Know Now

- Turnover may be voluntary or involuntary, but it is always costly to the organization.
- Many factors cause voluntary turnover, including job dissatisfaction, undesirable work environment, and ease of movement.
- Organizations can help retain nurses by providing healthy work environments and improving salaries.
- Managers can help reduce turnover by providing realistic job previews and follow-up, facilitating intraorganizational movement, improving management practices, and coordinating with other managers to influence organizational policy.
- Pay-for-performance systems and performance-driven clinical ladder programs allow clinical nurses to be rewarded while staying at the bedside.

- Magnet hospital recognition programs have criteria, such as increasing the ratio of nurses to patients, flexible schedules, decentralized administration, participatory management, autonomy in decision making, recognition, and advancement opportunities, that help retain nurses.
- Mentoring, coaching, clinical ladders, and residency programs are additional strategies to help retain nurses.

Tools for Reducing Turnover, Retaining Staff

1. Monitor turnover and evaluate the causes.
2. Provide realistic job previews to new hires, especially new graduates.
3. Monitor new graduates performance and offer additional support and training as needed.
4. Consider ways to improve the work environment.
5. Try to resolve conflicts and deal with problems as they appear.
6. Consult with other managers for ideas and policy change opportunities.

Questions to Challenge You

1. Can you recall instances where an employee's leaving has benefited the organization? Describe what happened.
2. Have you voluntarily left a job?
   a. What was the reason? Was there more than one reason?
   b. What reason did you give your supervisor?
   c. Was it the same rationale that you answered in part *a* of this question?
3. In addition to ideas presented in the chapter, can you think of other ways to reduce voluntary turnover?
4. What suggestions to improve retention and reduce voluntary turnover would you recommend to administration of the organization where you work or have clinical experiences?
5. Have you seen managers be effective in retaining staff? What did they do that worked especially well?
6. If you were a manager, what specific actions would you take to retain staff?

Explore MediaLink 🌐

Additional interactive resources for this chapter can be found on the Website at http://www.prenhall.com/sullivan. Click on Chapter 20 to select activities for this chapter.

- Video Overview
- NCLEX® Review Questions
- Critical Thinking Activities
- Current Events
- Nursing Leadership and Management in Action
- MediaLinks

References

Aiken, L., Havens, D., & Sloane, D. (2000). The magnet nursing services recognition program: A comparison of two groups of magnet hospitals. *American Journal of Nursing, 100*(3), 26–35.

American Association of Colleges of Nursing. (2007). *Nursing shortage fact sheet*. Retrieved November 2007 from http://www.aacn.nche.edu/Media/pdf/NrsgShortageOct07.pdf

American Association of Critical Care Nurses. (2005). *AACN standards for establishing and sustaining health work environments: A journey to excellence*. Retrieved July 2007 from www.aacn.org/aacn/pubpolcy.nsf/Files/ExecSum/$file/ExecSum.pdf

Barden, C. & Distrito, C. Toward a healthy work environment. *Health Progress, 86*(6), 16–20.

Benner, P. (2001). *From novice to expert: Excellence and power in clinical nursing practice*. Upper Saddle River, NJ: Prentice Hall.

Brady-Schwartz, D. C. (2005). Further evidence on the magnet recognition program: Implications for nursing leaders. *Journal of Nursing Administration, 35*(9), 397–403.

Buerhaus, P. I., Donelan, K., Ulrich, B. T., DesRoches, C., & Dittus. (2007). Trends in the experiences of hospital-employed registered nurses: Results from three national surveys. *Nursing Economic$, 25*(2), 69–80.

Butler, M. R., & Felts, J. (2006). Tool kit for the staff mentor: Strategies for improving retention. *Journal of Continuing Education in Nursing, 37*(5), 210–213.

Clausing, S. L., Kurtz, D. L., Prendeville, J., & Wait, J. L. (2003). Generational diversity—the nexters. *AORN Journal, 78*(3), 373–379.

Drenkard, K. N. (2004). The clinical nurse leader: A response from practice. *Journal of Professional Nursing, 20*(3), 89–96.

Greipp, M. E. (2003). Salary compression: Its effect on nurse recruitment and retention. *Journal of Nursing Administration, 33*(6), 321–323.

Halfer, D. (2007). A magnetic strategy for new graduate nurses. *Nursing Economic$, 25*(1), 6–11.

Hart, S. M. (2006). Generational diversity: Impact on recruitment and retention of registered nurses. *Journal of Nursing Administration, 36*(1), 10–12.

Joint Commission. (2007). *Health care at the crossroads: Strategies for addressing the evolving nursing crisis.* Retrieved November 2007 from http://www.jointcommission.org/NR/rdonlyres/5C138711-ED76-4D6F-909F-B06E0309F36D/0/health_care_at_the_crossroads.pdf

Jones, C. B. (2005). The costs of nurse turnover, Part 2. *Journal of Nursing Administration, 35*(1), 41–49.

Miracle, V. A. (2008). A healthy work environment. (Editorial). *Dimensions of Critical Care Nursing, 27*(1), 41–42.

Nedd, N. (2006). Perceptions of empowerment and intent to stay. *Nursing Economic$, 24*(1), 13–18.

Parrish, F. (2006). How to recruit, interview, and retain employees. *Dermatology Nursing, 18*(2), 179–180.

Perry, G. (2003). A new performance-driven clinical ladder: Rewarding clinical excellence while keeping top nurses at the bedside. *Excellence in Nursing Administration, 4*(3). Retrieved September 2003, from www.nursingsociety.org/publication/EXCEL_NA3Q03.html

PricewaterhouseCooper. (2007). *What works: Healing the healthcare staffing shortage.* Retrieved November 2007 from http://www.pwc.com/extweb/pwcpublications.nsf/docid/674D1E79A678A0428525730D006B74A9

Roszak, D. (2006). Survey says hospitals must 'quickly transform' work environment to retain older nurses. *Hospitals & Health Networks, 80*(7), 119.

Rudy, S., & Sions, J. (2003). Floating: Managing a recruitment and retention issue. *Journal of Nursing Administration, 33*(4), 196–198.

Shirley, M. R. (2006). Authentic leaders creating health work environments for nursing practice. *American Journal of Critical Care, 15*(3), 256–268.

Smith, H. L., Hood, J. N., Waldman, J. D., & Smith, V. L. (2005). Creating a favorable practice environment for nurses. *Journal of Nursing Administration, 35*(12), 525–532.

Stedman, M. E., & Nolan, T. L. (2007). Coaching: A different approach to the nursing dilemma. *Nursing Administration Quarterly, 31*(1), 43–49.

Triolo, P. K. (2003). Designing and launching a performance-driven clinical ladder. *Excellence in Nursing Administration, 4*(3). Retrieved September 2003, from www.nursingsociety.org/publication/EXCEL_NA3Q03.html

Upenieks, V. (2003a). Recruitment and retention strategies: A magnet hospital prevention model. *Nursing Economics, 21*(1), 7–23.

Upenieks, V. (2003b). What's the attraction to magnet hospitals? *Nursing Management, 34*(2), 43–44.

Waldman, J. D, Kelly, R., Sanjeev, A., & Smith, H. L. (2004). The shocking cost of turnover in health care. *Health Care Management Review, 29*(1), 2–7.

Williams, C. A., Goode, C. J., Krsek, C., Bednash, G. D., & Lynn, M. R. (2007). Postbaccalaureate nurse residency 1-year option. *Journal of Nursing Administration, 37*(7/8), 357–365.

Managing Absenteeism and Other Staff Problems

Absenteeism

Employee Problems

Learning Outcomes

After completing this chapter, you will be able to:

1. Explain absenteeism.
2. Discuss ways to manage absenteeism.
3. Identify staff problems.
4. Explain how to manage staff with problem behaviors.
5. Explain how to handle staff with a substance abuse problem.

www.prenhall.com/sullivan

See the Companion Website for chapter-specific resources at
www.prenhall.com/sullivan.

Key Terms

Absence culture *p278*
Absence frequency *p276*
Attendance barriers *p277*

Family and Medical
  Leave Act *p280*
Involuntary absenteeism *p276*

Presenteeism *p280*
Total time lost *p276*
Voluntary absenteeism *p276*

A major challenge confronting managers today is not only improving individual performance and productivity, but also enhancing the efforts of the entire work group. Some of the general techniques for enhancing performance described in Chapter 17 are ineffective because individual problems affect group functioning.

Problems with absenteeism, marginal staff, disgruntled employees, lateral violence, incivility, or employees abusing alcohol or drugs are addressed in this chapter. There are no proven methods for managing these problems; the strategies presented here are a starting point. Assistance from administration and the human resources department often is needed.

Absenteeism

Although the extent or the cost of nurse absenteeism is difficult to determine, it is well established that absenteeism in health care organizations is both pervasive and expensive. The costs of absenteeism, however, go beyond its effects on patient care and dollar costs. Absenteeism can have a detrimental effect on the work lives of the other staff nurses. In some cases, they may have to work shorthanded; they are expected to cover the unit despite their missing colleagues. Working shorthanded, especially for an extended period of time, can create both physical and mental strain. These nurses may be forced to skip breaks, hurry through meals, work extended hours, abbreviate their interactions with patients, cancel scheduled nonwork activities, and so on. Even if temporary replacements are called in, the work flow of the unit will still be disrupted as hurried staff must take time to explain standard organizational procedures to replacement nurses.

Given the undesirable effects of absenteeism, it is not surprising that absenteeism has drawn a good deal of attention in the health care field. Before considering ways to manage absenteeism, we must understand its causes. The following section presents a useful model for understanding nurse absenteeism or, conversely, nurse attendance.

A MODEL OF EMPLOYEE ATTENDANCE

To understand employee absenteeism, it is important to distinguish voluntary from involuntary absenteeism. For example, not coming to work in order to finish one's income taxes would be seen as **voluntary absenteeism** (i.e., absenteeism under the employee's control). In contrast, taking a sick day because of food poisoning would be considered **involuntary absenteeism** (i.e., largely outside of the employee's control). Although this distinction seems reasonable in theory, in practice it is often difficult to distinguish these two categories because of a lack of accurate information (few employees will admit to abusing sick leave). In fact, 65 percent of employees call in sick for reasons other than illness (CCH Survey, 2007; Navarro & Bass, 2006).

Some organizations try to distinguish voluntary from involuntary absenteeism by the way they measure absenteeism. Traditionally, health care organizations have measured absenteeism in terms of **total time lost** (i.e., the number of scheduled days an employee misses). Given that one long illness can drastically affect this absenteeism index, total time lost is clearly not a perfect measure of voluntary absenteeism. In contrast, **absence frequency** (i.e., the total number of distinct absence periods, regardless of their duration) is somewhat insensitive to one long illness. Therefore, absence frequency has been used as an indirect estimate of voluntary absenteeism.

This distinction between absence frequency and total time lost should make sense to nurse managers. For example, an employee who missed nine Mondays in a row would have nine absence frequency periods as well as nine total days absent. In contrast, a person who missed nine consecutive days of work would have nine total days lost but only one absence frequency period. Intuitively, it seems likely that the first individual was much more prone to being absent voluntarily than the second.

Although there are many models of attendance/absenteeism behavior, a revised version of one developed by Rhodes and Steers (1990) is the basis of discussion in this chapter. According to this model (*Figure 21-1*), an employee's attendance at work is largely a function

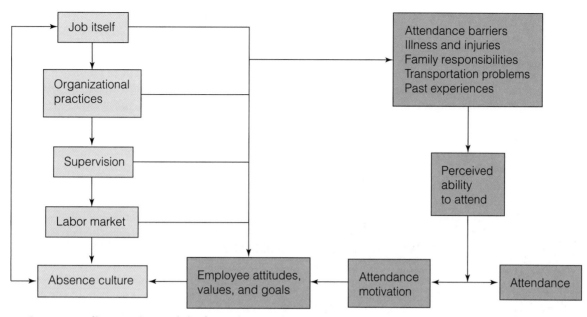

Figure 21-1 ● A diagnostic model of employee attendance.

of two variables: the individual's ability to attend and motivation to attend.

As seen in Figure 21-1, an employee's ability to attend can be affected by such **attendance barriers** as:

• Personal illness or injury
• Family responsibilities (e.g., a sick child)
• Transportation problems (e.g., an unreliable automobile)

Although it is natural to view such barriers as resulting in involuntary absenteeism, sometimes this is too simplistic a judgment. For example, an employee whose car was not running may consciously have not made alternative arrangements to get to work the next day because he or she was not motivated to attend. This example illustrates that some of the distinctions portrayed in Figure 21-1 are not always clear-cut. In trying to understand employee absenteeism, a manager will have to make assumptions about why the behavior is occurring (e.g., a manager cannot be certain that a person was actually ill).

According to the attendance model, an employee's motivation to attend is affected by several factors: the job itself, organizational practices, the absence culture, generational differences supervision, the labor market, and the employee's personal characteristics.

The Job Itself

In assessing the job itself, employees holding more enriched jobs are less likely to be absent than those with more mundane jobs. Enriched jobs may increase attendance motivation because employees believe that what they are doing is important and because they know that other employees are depending on the job holder (i.e., if the job holder doesn't do his or her job, other employees can't do theirs).

The nature of a job influences attendance through its effect on attendance motivation as well as on illness and injuries (i.e., attendance barriers). For example, a job that requires heavy lifting (e.g., moving patients from beds to stretchers) may increase the likelihood that a staff nurse will be injured. Similarly, a job that exposes a nurse to individuals with highly contagious conditions, such as in an outpatient clinic, may increase the likelihood of illness.

Organizational Practices

As portrayed in Figure 21-1, organizational practices also can influence attendance motivation. Some health care organizations have absence control policies that reward employees for good attendance and/or punish them for excessive absenteeism. An organization also may be able to increase attendance motivation by carefully recruiting and selecting employees (see Chapter 15). In addition to affecting attendance motivation, organizational practices may influence an employee's ability to attend. Organizational activities, such as offering wellness programs, employee assistance programs, van pools, on-site child care, or coordinating car pools could influence an employee's ability to attend work.

MediaLink Developing Policies and Procedures

Absence Culture

The **absence culture** of a work unit (or an organization) can also influence employee attendance motivation. Some work units have an absence culture that reflects a tolerance for excessive absenteeism. Other units have a culture in which being absent is frowned upon. Although an organization's absence culture can be affected by organizational practices (e.g., attendance policies) and the nature of the jobs involved (e.g., people in higher-level jobs tend to be less accepting of coworkers calling in sick), it is also affected by informal norms that develop among work-group members. For example, people in a cohesive work group may develop an understanding that missing work, except for an emergency or a serious illness, is unacceptable. Such an attendance culture is likely to emerge if the employees work in jobs that they see as important (e.g., providing direct patient care) and if an employee being absent causes a hardship for coworkers (e.g., forced overtime, being called in on a day off).

Generational Differences

As discussed in previous chapters, younger nurses from generations X and Y (also called millennials), have different expectations in the workplace. Milennials expect to have flexible scheduling (Clausing et al, 2003) and may use absenteeism to achieve it.

Supervision

Supervision also influences attendance motivation. A nurse manager can influence the nature of a staff nurse's job (e.g., the degree of responsibility given and participation in decision making), decisions about personnel, the consistency with which organizational practices are applied (e.g., whether sanctions are enforced for abuse of sick leave), and a work unit's absence culture by stressing the importance of good attendance.

Expectations of the younger generational cohorts affect supervision as well. They expect independence and to be involved in decision making (Hart, 2006). Thus, shared governance is an appropriate structure, and consultation is an effective management strategy.

Labor Market

Another factor that influences attendance is the labor market. To the extent that the local employment market for nurses leads an employee to perceive it would be easy to find an equivalent job if she or he lost or disliked the current one, one would expect a lower level of attendance motivation than if market conditions were less favorable. This might happen during a nursing shortage.

Personal Characteristics

Although features of the job itself, organizational practices, absence culture, generational differences, supervision, and the labor market can all have a direct effect on employee attendance motivation, these factors also can interact with an employee's attitudes (e.g., job satisfaction), values (e.g., personal work ethic), or goals (e.g., desire to get promoted). If a person who seeks variety works in a job that does not provide it, the employee may become dissatisfied and thus more likely to abuse sick leave. Employee attitudes, values, and goals also can have a direct effect on attendance motivation. For example, a staff nurse with a high personal work ethic or who has a goal of getting promoted should be more highly motivated to attend work than a nurse who lacks such a work ethic.

An employee's attendance behavior also is influenced by past experiences. For example, if an employee's perfect attendance in the previous year was not rewarded, we might expect the employee's attendance motivation to decrease in the coming year. Conversely, if a coworker with an outstanding attendance record received a promotion, peers who value a promotion and who witnessed this linkage between performance and reward would be more motivated to attend work in the upcoming year.

MANAGING EMPLOYEE ABSENTEEISM

The attendance model in Figure 21-1 is useful not only for understanding why absenteeism occurs, but also for developing strategies to control it. Some causes of absenteeism, such as transportation difficulties or child care problems, may be beyond the direct control of nurse managers. The manager, however, should try to do what is possible, either in interactions with staff nurses or by attempting to get the organization to change policies that may be interfering with a nurse's ability or motivation to attend work. On the other hand, a manager must be careful that the steps taken do not go so far as to discourage the legitimate use of sick leave. Clearly, one does not want sick nurses coming to work and exposing patients and coworkers.

To diagnose the key factors leading to absenteeism, the manager needs information from several sources, including staff, the human resources department, other nurse managers, and administration. Absence patterns can answer such questions as

- Is absenteeism equally distributed across staff nurses?
- In comparison to other units, does your area of responsibility have a high absenteeism rate?

- Are most absences of short or long duration?
- Does the absenteeism have a consistent pattern (e.g., occur predominantly on weekends or shortly before a person quits)?

Although a manager may not be able to do much to affect the staff's ability to attend, the organization can take several actions. For example, to lessen child care problems, the organization could set up or sponsor a child care center. To reduce transportation problems, an organization could provide shuttle buses or coordinate car pools. Health fairs, exercise programs, and stress-reduction classes could be offered to promote health. Given that alcoholism and drug abuse are widely recognized as important causes of absenteeism, it may be prudent for an organization to offer access to an employee assistance plan. In addition to these organizational actions, a nurse manager, through coaching, may be able to influence a staff nurse's attendance. (See Chapter 19 for information on how to coach staff.)

Clearly, the best way for nurse managers to control absenteeism is by encouraging their staff's motivation to attend. Other absenteeism management strategies that a nurse manager might consider include:

- Enriching the staff nurse's job by increasing its responsibility, variety, or challenge
- Reducing job stress (e.g., by providing timely and more concrete information)
- Creating a norm of excellent attendance (e.g., by emphasizing the negative impact of a nurse not coming to work)
- Enhancing advancement opportunities (e.g., by providing developmental experiences so that the best employees are promotable)
- Improving coworker relations (e.g., by considering coworker compatibility when scheduling work and/or creating work teams)
- Trying to select employees who will be satisfied with and committed to their jobs
- Being a good role model by rarely taking sick days
- Discussing the employee's attendance during the performance appraisal interview
- Rewarding good attendance with salary increases and other rewards
- Enforcing absenteeism control policies (e.g., carrying through on employee discipline when there is an attendance problem)

ABSENTEEISM POLICIES

Most organizational policies allow employees to accrue paid sick days—typically, 1 sick day for every month employed. Unused sick days accrue across time to some maximum number (e.g., 60 days). Typically, if an employee leaves the organization with accumulated sick leave or days above the maximum, the person simply loses it.

Although such a policy may seem reasonable, it may actually encourage unwanted behavior. For example, once a nurse has reached the maximum limit for accrued sick days, the person may see no reason for not using sick days that would otherwise be lost. Such a policy also encourages employees who know they will be leaving the organization (e.g., those about to retire or change jobs) to use accumulated sick leave.

An innovative approach for managing absenteeism is substituting personal days for unused sick days. Two problems arise if personal days are not given: Employees are forced to lie (i.e., say they are sick when they are not) to carry out what they see as legitimate activities (e.g., attending a conference with their child's teacher), and their manager has no warning and therefore may have difficulty covering for the absent employee.

By substituting personal days for sick days, the employee no longer has to lie, and the nurse manager may have time to plan for a replacement. In moving to a policy that incorporates the use of personal days, an organization typically allocates fewer paid sick days but adds personal days. For example, instead of 12 sick days, an employee may annually receive 9 sick days and 3 personal days. With the availability of personal days, a staff nurse can inform the nurse manager in advance of the need for a personal day off. In many cases, the two of them can arrive at a day off that is optimal for both of them.

Realizing that they have not been motivating good attendance, some progressive organizations have allowed sick days to accumulate without an upper limit. Then, when an employee leaves the organization, she or he is paid for unused sick days (e.g., one-half day's pay for each unused sick day). Other organizations allow retiring employees to add unused sick days to days worked. Still other organizations have paid employees for their sick days, or allowed the conversion of sick days to vacation days or additional pay.

Obviously, changing an organization's paid sick leave policy is beyond the control of the nurse manager. However, a concerted effort by an organized group of nurse managers can be effective in getting the human resources department and the administration to initiate such changes. Considering the high costs of absenteeism, these changes can be quite cost effective.

Most health care organizations have formal policies concerning how much absenteeism is allowed. Once this limit is reached, disciplinary steps are prescribed. In disciplining an employee, the nurse manager must follow the discipline policy carefully. The effectiveness of discipline as a strategy for reducing absenteeism is limited. Most discipline policies only take effect after excessive absenteeism. Not surprisingly, most employees know what this is and are careful not to exceed it. In effect, the nurse manager is left with an absenteeism problem but not one that she or he is able to address through the use of discipline.

SELECTING EMPLOYEES AND MONITORING ABSENTEEISM

Many of the managerial actions addressed in other chapters of this book are relevant to the control of absenteeism. For example, in recruiting employees, the use of a realistic job preview should increase the congruence between job characteristics and employee values and expectations. Similarly, basing merit pay and advancement opportunities on an employee's overall performance appraisal rating (which is partly based on attendance) will motivate better attendance. Also, leadership skills are important in getting the organization to change policy to lessen absenteeism (e.g., providing payment for unused sick days).

Two specific issues are relevant to employee selection: the use of personal characteristics and past behavior. Although personal characteristics (e.g., marital status, child care responsibility) have been linked to higher absenteeism rates, for legal reasons a nurse manager should not base a hiring decision on such personal characteristics.

On the other hand, the past behavior of a specific job candidate is potentially valuable information because absenteeism tendencies tend to be consistent from job to job. Although the reasons why some individuals have a higher level of absenteeism year after year are unclear (e.g., some people may be more susceptible to illness, others may have less of a work ethic), past behavior can be used as a predictor of future behavior. An applicant's previous absenteeism record may be acquired by written or telephone reference checks.

In a practical sense, nurse managers want strategies for dealing with employees with excessive absences. Several steps can be taken.

- Set expectations with each new employee. Give her or him the attendance policy in writing, and clarify any questions.
- Monitor each individual's attendance, and document it.

- Intervene early and consistently, coaching and dealing with policy or procedure violations as appropriate.
- If discipline is called for, use the key behaviors for disciplining in Chapter 19.
- Be sure to reward staff who have good attendance. Ensure that any organizational rewards are delivered, and give your personal reward through feedback in performance appraisals.
- Be a role model for good attendance yourself.

These steps will set a tone of intolerance for poor attendance. The opposite of absenteeism is **presenteeism** when the employee is at work although disabled by physical or mental illness. Those employees who were sick more often, who had heavier workloads, were highly skilled, enjoyed positive relationships with coworkers, or whose job status was precarious were more likely to be present at work even though ill (Biron, Brun, Ivers, & Cooper, 2006). Additionally, high psychological distress and psychosomatic illness were predictors of presenteeism.

FAMILY AND MEDICAL LEAVE

The federal **Family and Medical Leave Act** (FMLA) took effect in 1993 and has a significant impact on employers. Under this act, all public employers (federal, state, and local) and all private employers employing 50 or more individuals must provide their eligible employees with leave of up to 12 weeks during any 12-month period for the employee's own serious illness, the birth or adoption of a child, the placement of a foster child into the household, or the care of a seriously ill child, spouse, or parent.

The FMLA also allows eligible employees to maintain health insurance coverage while on leave and allows them to return to the same or equivalent position at the end of the leave period. The leave may be taken all at once, intermittently, or by working a reduced work schedule, if available. The employee must be allowed to take leave for qualified purposes without pressure or discouragement by the employer or manager. More generous collective-bargaining agreements or state laws supersede the FMLA, but the FMLA supersedes any inconsistent or less generous provisions. FMLA may run concurrently with other leaves, including state worker's compensation leave.

Employees are eligible to take leave if they:

- Have worked for the employer for at least 12 months
- Have worked at least 1,250 hours during the previous 12 months

- Are at a work site with 50 or more employees, or at a site where 50 workers are employed within 75 miles of the work site (50 employees/75 miles rule)

The FMLA is quite complex. Managers must be aware of multiple employee and employer responsibilities. State law and collective bargaining agreements may make the organization's leave policy unique. Furthermore, the overlap and interaction between the Americans with Disabilities Act and the FMLA is complicated. Although only a fraction of the FMLA leave is disability related, employers who integrate FMLA with disability programs are more likely to have workers return to work sooner than those who managed each program separately (Silva, 2006). It is important for the manager to work closely with the human resources department in executing the provisions of this law (Neuson, 2006).

Employee Problems

Managers and nurses are faced with any number of other problems presented by employees, including staff who are marginally competent, perpetually complaining, verbally abusive, or lack civility in the workplace. Still others may have a substance-abuse problem.

MARGINAL EMPLOYEES

Some staff, no matter how many times they are coached or disciplined, never seem to reach the level of competence expected of an experienced nurse. These are marginal employees. Work habits may be sloppy, communication skills poor, or decision making inadequate. Discipline does not help either in spite of the employee's attempts to improve.

Marginal employees present the manager with a unique challenge. The manager can ignore the problem and hope that the employee will improve, a largely ineffective strategy. Also this leaves the unit vulnerable to complaints from other staff who must cover for the marginal employee, and affects the unit's morale.

The manager could, in contrast, follow the organization's procedures for progressive discipline and termination (see Chapter 19), which may leave the unit understaffed. Furthermore, the nurse may move on to another institution, perpetuating the poor performance. Nonetheless, Baum (2000) recommends dismissal because of the negative effects on the organization.

In addition, in some organizations (e.g., government institutions and those with union contracts), the manager must follow strict guidelines for discipline and, especially, for dismissal. Because of the time and effort involved, managers in these organizations may allow the behavior to persist. We can all think of government agencies whose employees serve the public poorly.

DISGRUNTLED EMPLOYEES

Disgruntled employees are ones who are always complaining, behavior that affects morale on the unit. They complain about anything and everything, but they direct most complaints against the organization and may air them in public, which can affect how others view the organization. Although the temptation is to label this as an attitude problem, complaining is a behavior and as such can be addressed by the following:

- Remember to set standards of performance and communicate them to the employee.
- Keep notes about incidents of complaining in behavioral terms.
- Take action early, and be consistent among employees.
- Use key behaviors for coaching found in Chapter 19.
- Follow up as scheduled.

LATERAL VIOLENCE

Consider the following example:

Jeana Rossi, RN, is a staff nurse on a medical unit. At 0700, she took over care for five patients from Greg Robeson, RN, an agency nurse who had worked the 7p–7a shift. During her review of patient medication administration records, Jeana noted that an IV antibiotic scheduled to be administered at 2300 dose of IV had not been charted. Checking the IV bin, Jeana found the 2300 dose. Greg had already left the unit. Per hospital policy, Jeana completed a missing dose report and turned it in to her manager. Two days later, Greg corners Jeana in the staff lounge and loudly berates her in front of other staff members for completing a missing dose report. "You're so stupid!" Greg shouts. "You just wanted to make me look bad, didn't you?"

This example shows how difficult some staff problems can be to manage. If you were the manager on this unit, how would you handle the situation? Here are some alternatives. The manager could report Greg to the agency and request that he no longer be assigned to the unit, but then a replacement must be found. The manager now worries about the competency of other nurses this agency might send. Remember, Greg was the only nurse on the night shift. In the end, the manager reported the situation to her supervisor and called the director of the agency, who assured the manager that they would provide a competent nurse for the next shift.

LACK OF CIVILITY

Another complex problem in the workplace is lack of civility (Hutton, 2006). Uncivil behavior creates a culture of rudeness that can permeate the workplace and become the norm of behavior (Peck, 2006). Low morale, high turnover, and declining patient care can ultimately result.

Lack of civility includes any behavior that is:

- Rude
- Disrespectful
- Impolite
- Ill-mannered

Examples are aggressive behaviors, such as:

- Yelling
- Swearing
- Spreading rumors
- Destroying or taking another's property

Here's an example.

Reid Martin, nurse manger, has encouraged new graduate nurse Joy Gabriel, to develop an informational presentation as a strategy to improve her self-confidence. At the next monthly staff meeting, Joy is presenting information about a new occlusive dressing. Joy is shy and public speaking is difficult for her. Her voice shakes and she drops the box of new dressings she brought to demonstrate. Kristi Sanderson, RN, has been rolling her eyes and sighing loudly throughout Joy's presentation. At the end of the meeting, Kristi makes a point of telling several other staff members that it was "painful" to sit through Joy's presentation. Joy overhears Kristi's comments.

This example is a situation that does not quite rise to the level of bullying, described in Chapter 12. Nonetheless, the manager must confront Kristi and explain why nonverbal signals are inappropriate. (Remember you learned in Chapter 9 that nonverbal communication is more powerful than verbal communication.) Also Kristi must be told that *sotto voice* criticisms will not be tolerated. Following the suggestions on coaching and progressive discipline, the manager must explain the consequences for repeated instances of discourtesy to her fellow staff members and insist that Kristi conduct herself in a civil manner.

Here is another example of a complex staff problem.

The staff at the outpatient imaging center all share a common break room. Over the past several months, several staff members have complained to their nurse manager, Julie Fredrickson, that their lunches are missing from the break room refrigerator or particular items such as desserts or cans of soda are missing out of their lunches. One afternoon, Julie enters the break room to get a cup a coffee and sees one of the radiologists, Dr. Gibson, eating a brownie and looking through several lunch bags. "I never get a chance to get out for lunch," Dr. Gibson said. "I'm sure your staff doesn't mind sharing with a hungry physician."

If you were the nurse manager at this outpatient center, how would you handle this situation? Dr. Gibson was committing theft, albeit the items he stole were inexpensive. Nonetheless, his behavior caused nurses to go without some of their own food, and, more importantly, it was disrespectful to them. It implied that he thought his needs were more important than any of theirs. When informed, the manager alerted his supervisor and then confronted Dr. Gibson who, after threatening to report the manager to administration, calmed down, and agreed to donate pizza for the staff the next day and to stop stealing (yes, the manager used the word "stealing").

Case Study 21-1 describes one manager's experience with an employee with another problematic behavior.

THE EMPLOYEE WITH A SUBSTANCE ABUSE PROBLEM

As substance abuse has become increasingly prevalent in society, nursing has not remained immune. Substance abuse not only is detrimental to the impaired nurse, but also jeopardizes patients' care, thereby also exposing the employing agency to greater liability.

Early recognition of alcohol or drug dependency and prompt referral for treatment are generally recognized as responsibilities of the nurse manager, although the role of the nurse manager varies according to organizational policy.

Identifying the Employee with a Substance Abuse Problem

It is not easy to identify anyone who is abusing substances (Ponech, 2000; West, 2002). The primary symptom is denial, which is present in the sufferer as well as in those around him or her. The person in denial really does not believe what seems obvious. Furthermore, alcohol or drug problems in women in general,

CASE STUDY 21-1 Problem Staff

Gene Marshall is the nurse manager for a general medical–surgical unit in a veteran's hospital. His busy unit primarily serves elderly male patients. Felicia Ralston, RN, has worked on the medical–surgical unit for 3 years. Since her hiring, Felicia has obtained several body piercings, including her nose, eyebrow, and tongue. She usually wears large hoops or bars in her facial piercings. Felicia added a visible tattoo to the back of her neck and upper shoulder. Often her uniforms allow visualization of a tattoo on her lower back. Recently, she came to work after adding purple highlights to her hair.

As the number and prominence of Felicia's piercings and body art have increased, several patients and their family members expressed to Gene that they were "uncomfortable" having Felicia as their nurse. Some patients have felt intimidated by her unusual appearance. Gene spoke with Felicia about the patient and family member concerns and reviewed the hospital's dress code with her. Felicia became angry and told Gene that hair color, body piercings, and tattoos were a form of individual expression and had nothing to do with her performance as a nurse.

Later, Felicia told everyone on the unit about her discussion with Gene, speaking loudly and inappropriately in patient care areas. She asked the unit clerk if she knew which patients or family members had complained to Gene about her appearance. The following day, Felicia asked each of her assigned patients if they had a "problem with her." Felicia reported back to Gene that none of her patients expressed they had any problems with her or her appearance. After discussing the situation with the human resources department, Gene met with Felicia and provided her with a written warning regarding her body piercings, tattoos, and hair color, as well as her unprofessional behavior following their initial meeting. Gene told Felicia that she must remove jewelry from her nose and eyebrows prior to reporting for work and her hair color must be a natural color. He also told her that her tongue jewelry must be small and unnoticeable. Felicia's uniforms were to cover her tattoos completely.

Gene also provided Felicia with a copy of the federal court ruling in which the court ruled that body piercings and tattoos were not considered protected as free speech and employers had the right to set standards of dress and appearance for their employees. Finally, Gene emphasized to Felicia that she should directly speak with him regarding any performance issues or problems and not involve staff or patients in the situation. If Felicia does not comply with these standards within 10 working days, she will be terminated from her position.

Manager's Checklist

The nurse manager is responsible to:

- Understand the human resources policies for their organization
- Consistently apply policies to all employees
- Provide timely and appropriate feedback when an employee is in violation of policies
- Remain professional at all times when dealing with an irate or angry employee
- Maintain accurate and thorough documentation of performance issues
- Follow up with the human resources department as necessary

---

as well as in nurses in particular, are stigmatized in today's society. This stigma, added to the profession's own negative attitudes regarding the disorder, encourages nurses—even those who break through their own denial—to continue to conceal their problem. The result is that nurses dependent on alcohol or drugs may continue practicing nursing, endangering both patients' and their own lives. Before obvious serious consequences take place, some general signs and symptoms may become evident as a nurse's dependency progresses (Boxes 21-1 and 21-2).

In addition to the signs and symptoms listed in Boxes 21-1 and 21-2, the nurse manager should be alert for frequently incorrect narcotics counts, alteration of narcotics vials, patient reports that their pain medications are ineffective, inaccurate recording of pain medication administration, discrepancies in narcotics records, large amounts of narcotic wastage, and marked shift variations in the quantity of drugs required on a unit.

If the manager discovers signs or symptoms in an employee or becomes aware of the unit changes described, further investigation is warranted, and administration should be informed. Often, with unit discrepancies, that simply means checking the schedule to see who was working when most of the errors occurred. Usually, one or two people emerge as those most likely to have been available during the time of the discrepancies. Further checking and observation may reveal

BOX 21-1	Signs of Alcohol or Drug Dependency

- Family history of alcoholism or drug abuse
- Frequent change of work site (same or other institution)
- Prior medical history requiring pain control
- Conscientious worker with recent decrease in performance
- Decreased attention to personal appearance
- Frequent complaints of marital and family problems
- Reports of illness, minor accidents, and emergencies
- Complaints from coworkers
- Mood swings/depression/suicide attempts
- Strong interest in patients' pain control
- Frequent trips to the bathroom
- Increasing isolation (night shift request; eating alone)
- Elaborate excuses for tardiness
- Difficulty in meeting schedules/deadlines
- Inadequate explanation for missing work

From: *Chemical Dependency in Nursing: The Deadly Diversion,* by E. J. Sullivan, L. Bissell, and E. Williams, 1988, Menlo Park, CA: Addison-Wesley Nursing. Reprinted by permission of Pearson Education, Inc., Upper Saddle River, NJ.

BOX 21-2	Physical Symptoms of Alcohol or Drug Dependency

- Shakiness, tremors of hands, jitteriness
- Slurred speech
- Watery eyes, dilated or constricted pupils
- Diaphoresis
- Unsteady gait
- Runny nose
- Nausea, vomiting, diarrhea
- Weight loss or gain
- Blackouts (memory losses while conscious)
- Wears long-sleeved clothing continuously

From: *Chemical Dependency in Nursing: The Deadly Diversion,* by E. J. Sullivan, L. Bissell, and E. Williams, 1988, Menlo Park, CA: Addison-Wesley Nursing. Reprinted by permission of Pearson Education, Inc., Upper Saddle River, NJ.

individual behaviors suggesting a person has a substance abuse problem.

Even if the manager is unsure of her or his perceptions or if the actions are so vague that the manager has many doubts about the identity of the person, the situation will be clarified in time. Untreated, addiction continues; as tolerance increases, use will increase, and the person will become increasingly careless about covering up actions. Thus, the manager will become more certain about a person's abuse problem. However, the longer it takes to identify the problem, the longer the nurse may continue to practice, jeopardizing both patients and self. Thus, the manager should carefully assess information about possible dependency problems

but not wait too long. How long is a matter of judgment for the manager and administration.

State Board of Nursing

State boards of nursing are charged with protecting the public, including the practice by nurses impaired by substance abuse. Reporting laws vary from state to state, as do consequences, but most state boards require the nurse manager to report an impaired colleague under threat of one's own license.

Diversion programs offering referral, assistance, and monitoring may be offered in lieu of disciplinary action in some states. For example, the Kansas Nurse Assistance Program (KNAP) is offered to nurses whose practice is impaired by substance abuse (Sidlinger & Hornberger, 2008). Nurses who successfully complete the program are not reported to the Kansas State Board of Nursing (Kansas State Board of Nursing, 2008).

Strategies for Intervention

Once the manager has identified a nurse with a substance abuse problem, intervention with that nurse must be planned. With the assistance of administration, the manager should examine the organization's policies and procedures and licensure laws as well as determine if a diversion program exists (see above).

Before intervening, the manager should collect all documentation or information about the nurse's behavior that would suggest an abuse problem. Documentation includes records of absenteeism and tardiness (especially recent changes), records of patient complaints about ineffective medications or poor care, staff complaints about job performance, records of controlled substances, and physical signs and symptoms noticed at different times. Dates, times, and behaviors should be carefully noted. Any one behavior means very little; it is the composite pattern that identifies the problem.

Next, the manager should identify appropriate resources to help the nurse. Internal resources include an employee assistance program (EAP) counselor, if the organization has one, or other nurses recovering from alcohol or drug dependency who have offered to help. External resources include the names and phone numbers of treatment center staff, other recovering nurses (if known), and Alcoholics Anonymous or Narcotics Anonymous. It is absolutely essential that several sources be provided so that the nurse knows that help from someone who knows how he or she feels is available and how to get it. This support cannot be emphasized enough. Failing to offer this assistance is like telling the diabetic he has diabetes and failing to tell him where he can get insulin.

In addition to assistance for the nurse, the manager should check on health insurance provisions for substance abuse treatment. Many insurance carriers have recognized that successful treatment reduces the use of other health care services and, thus, reduces the cost of health care. Accordingly, they offer coverage for treatment to encourage participants to enter recovery programs. Others, unfortunately, do not. Because many of an organization's employees may be covered under the same health care plan, the manager should be able to check these provisions. Few policies cover any but brief inpatient care, usually only for detoxification, but they may cover outpatient treatment, which is considerably less expensive. Even when there is little or no insurance coverage, the nurse may be able to afford outpatient care. Alcoholics Anonymous and Narcotics Anonymous are effective alternatives, and both are free.

Before initiating the intervention, the manager must examine his or her own attitudes about the abuse problem. Probably, the drug or alcohol abuse has gone on for some time, and both the manager and the staff may have lost patience with the person whose performance and attendance may have forced others to do more than their fair share of the work. If substance abuse was suspected, others may have felt that the person should just "pull herself together," "stop doing it," and, as a last resort, should "know better." Once they understand that alcohol or drug dependency is an illness, however, they realize that none of these behaviors is possible; willpower and education have not prevented others from becoming addicted. The manager will need to deal with the staff's feelings later, but at this time it is enough to be certain that his or her own attitudes will not imperil the intervention. It is important that the message be clearly one of help and hope.

The goal of the intervention is to get the nurse to an appropriate place for an evaluation of the possible problem. Treatment centers or therapists who specialize in substance abuse are recommended to conduct the evaluation. They have the necessary experience for diagnosing and, if indicated, treating the disease.

The manager and administration must also decide beforehand what action on the part of the nurse will be acceptable. If the nurse refuses to go for an evaluation, what will be the consequences? The organization's policies and the state board of nursing regulations must be met, and the manager must be clear about the consequences (e.g., discipline, termination) and willing to carry them out. Most experts in treating addictions in nurses recommend that the nurse be offered the option of substance abuse evaluation and, if needed, treatment. If she or he does not agree to that, then the manager should follow the usual disciplinary process and make a report to the state board of nursing, if indicated.

Once preparations have been made, the intervention should be scheduled as soon as possible. Others may be asked to join the manager, but the group should be small and restricted to only those involved in past problems, a substance abuse or human resource staff person, or the manager's supervisor. In some organizations, the top nursing administrator conducts all substance abuse interventions and, in that case, the nurse manager must fully inform the administrator of all circumstances leading to the intervention and provide all the documentation needed. Also, the manager should participate in the intervention so that all relevant information is presented and denial is kept to a minimum.

The intervention should be scheduled at a time and place when interruptions can be avoided. It is best to surprise the nurse with a request to come to the office. Denial can build, rationalizations can be developed, and defensiveness can increase if the nurse is given time to consider the problem.

The manager should present the nurse with the collected evidence showing a pattern of behaviors that suggests an abuse problem might be occurring and that an evaluation must be undertaken to know for sure. It is important to focus on the problem behaviors, not on the inadequacy of the person. The individual has already experienced shame and guilt about the use. The manager has an opportunity to help the nurse recognize that substance abuse is an illness that needs treatment; then the nurse will be better able to accept that a problem exists.

In the best-case scenario, the nurse admits the problem, is grateful to be getting help, and goes willingly to treatment. It is best to go directly to treatment from the work site if this can be arranged beforehand. It is important to move quickly before denial resurfaces.

Some nurses, of course, will continue to deny the obvious, in which case the manager must continue to confront the nurse with the reality of the circumstances. If the nurse refuses to go for an evaluation, the manager must follow the organization's disciplinary process. If the nurse is using alcohol or drugs at the time, immediate removal from patient care is necessary. The manager should arrange to have someone (either a family member or another staff member) drive the nurse home, whether the nurse is going to treatment or not. Not only do alcohol or drugs make the nurse an unsafe driver, but the stress of the intervention may distract the nurse even more.

If the nurse agrees to go for an evaluation and/or treatment, specific plans must be made. It should be clear to all parties when the nurse will contact the treatment center (the sooner the better, even if mood-altering chemicals are not being used at the time) and when the nurse will report back to the manager the recommended course of action. It is possible to arrange with a treatment facility for reports to be made directly to the manager, but federal regulations regarding confidentiality prohibit treatment staff from reporting a patient's status to anyone without that person's written consent. Because the goal of treatment is recovery, which includes returning to work, most facilities request that the nurse give this consent.

Treatment

As with other forms of medical treatment, treatment for substance abuse has moved from the inpatient to the outpatient setting. Whereas a few years ago a patient could be expected to be admitted to a month-long hospitalization for substance abuse, today treatment is offered in several different formats along a continuum of care. These include:

- Inpatient treatment for detoxification (3 to 5 days)
- Partial hospitalization (day treatment for 1 to 2 weeks)
- Intensive outpatient treatment (e.g., 3 nights a week for 3 hours each night)
- Traditional outpatient treatment (e.g., 4 hours a week, including some group therapy and one-to-one sessions)
- Weekly aftercare group sessions for 3 months

The choices of treatments and their order ideally are based on the patient's status, environmental supports, and potential for relapse. Unfortunately, the decision is usually based on insurance coverage, which varies considerably among insurers.

The decision to allow an employee to return to work or even to require the employee to avoid returning for any period of time will be based on the recommended treatment. Withdrawal from narcotics very likely will require inpatient detoxification; partial hospitalization also may be recommended. If the employee needs time off for these treatments, sick leave can be used, or the employee may be given an unpaid leave of absence (see the section on the Americans with Disabilities Act and substance abuse).

Reentry

Reentry to the workplace must be carefully planned, whether the employee has been absent for any length of time or not. It is especially important for the manager and administration to recognize the threat that access to the category of drugs the nurse was addicted to (e.g., narcotics) poses to recovery. Return to work is usually recommended, but not all treatment staff are familiar enough with nursing to be aware of the danger of putting the nurse in constant, daily contact with the drugs that may have been abused in the past. However, it is vitally important to the nurse's recovery that he or she return to work, preferably in the same setting.

This dilemma has often been dealt with in two ways. One method is to reassign the nurse for a period of time (possibly as long as 2 years) to a job or a unit where few mood-altering drugs are given, such as the nursery, department of education, rehabilitation, home care, or patient care audits. Although reassignment presents a problem for the organization and may be disappointing to the nurse, it is far better to make this accommodation than to jeopardize the nurse's recovery by providing access to drugs too soon. This is less a concern with nurses who abused only alcohol.

Another method is to retain the nurse on the unit but not allow administration of mood-altering medications. In fact, state law or organizational policy may require that recovering nurses in the early posttreatment period be restricted from handling controlled substances, carrying narcotic keys, being in charge, or working overtime. This method requires that other staff not only know about the nurse's problem but also be willing to give pain and sleep medications to that nurse's patients. Because this involves disclosing the nurse's addiction, management and staff must decide whether this is reasonable, and the nurse must agree.

Recovering nurses may be discouraged from working evening or night shifts. A reentry contract may be used to specify these restrictions. The contract also may require documentation of participation in recovery groups and random urine drug tests. Ideally, the reentering nurse should have an identified support person available at work.

These restrictions are usually necessary only for the nurse who was addicted to narcotics, but each case should be individually decided based on the amount of stress in the job, the need for rotating shifts, and other factors that may inhibit recovery.

Health care today requires that every employee function at peak efficiency and effectiveness. Health care organizations cannot afford to protect an employee whose professional functioning is impaired by substance abuse. Discharging the employee and allowing the person to go to another institution to continue practicing and endangering patients, as well as himself or herself, cannot be allowed. The nurse manager is the frontline contact with staff and can be alert to the signs and symptoms of substance abuse problems, learn intervention techniques and skills, and help recovering nurses return to the workplace. Concern for patients' safety requires intervention, and humane concern for nurse colleagues mandates that such assistance be made available.

The Americans with Disabilities Act and Substance Abuse

The Americans with Disabilities Act (ADA) went into effect in 1990 and applies to employers of 15 or more people. This law prohibits discrimination in personnel policies (such as hiring and firing) and other employment-related issues if an individual has a qualifying disability. Because alcohol or drug dependency limits one or more of the nurse's activities, it is considered a disability under the ADA. Only those who have been identified with substance abuse disorders, either diagnosed or self-reported, are protected under the law. A person using drugs or who is under the influence of alcohol in the workplace is not protected from the job-related consequences of that use.

The same consideration must be given to the nurse addict as to a nurse with a hearing impairment. This means providing sick leave and treatment opportunity, as well as making reasonable job accommodations. Several reasonable job accommodations have been mentioned previously: assignment to a unit where narcotics and sedatives are not given or are given infrequently, exemption from shift rotation, exemption from charge duties, and the like. Furthermore, the employee's drug abuse history must be kept private. The ADA confidentiality provisions require the employer to keep records on employee substance abuse (i.e., disability) in separate, locked files with access limited to a need-to-know basis.

As with other chronic diseases, alcohol and drug dependency is a disorder prone to relapse. How relapses will be treated under this law is not clear. As with many other personnel issues, it is wise for the nurse manager to consult with human resources and administration about ADA requirements.

Dealing with absenteeism and employee problems are ongoing challenges for the nurse manager, but the steps are similar to those described in Chapters 17 and 19. That is, identify the problem, intervene appropriately, and follow up as necessary (Flowers, 2005).

What You Know Now

- Employee attendance is affected by the job, organizational practices, generational cohort, supervision, absence culture, labor market, and the employee's characteristics.
- An organization can improve employee attendance by addressing specific barriers, such as adding a child care center, coordinating car pools, or offering health promotion and employee assistance.
- Innovative solutions to absenteeism problems include substituting personal days for sick days, allowing sick days to accrue and unused days to be paid to the employee, or converting unused sick days to paid days at retirement.
- The behaviors of employees who are frequently absent, marginal, disgruntled, practice lateral violence, lack civility, or abuse substances affect work-group functioning.
- Nurse managers need to identify staff problems early and intervene if necessary.
- Identifying, intervening, and returning nurses with substance abuse problems to the workplace help the organization, the manager, and the affected nurse.
- Substance abuse not only is detrimental to the impaired nurse but also jeopardizes patient care and places the organization at increased liability.

Tools for Managing Absenteeism and Other Staff Problems

1. Be familiar with your organization's policies on employee attendance.
2. Identify potential problems and monitor their progression, if necessary.
3. Document all instances of problem behavior.
4. Consult administration and human resources before intervening in serious problems, such as substance abuse.
5. Follow up with coaching, disciplining, or terminating if needed, using the guide in Chapter 19.

Questions to Challenge You

1. Have you ever worked or shared a class with a person who caused problems? (Most of us have.) How did the problem manifest itself? How was it handled? How do you wish the problem had been handled?
2. Are you familiar with the signs and symptoms of substance abuse? Have you seen someone exhibit these characteristics? What signs or symptoms did they exhibit? What happened?
3. For what reasons have you been absent from work or class?
4. As a nurse manager, what would you do to reduce absenteeism?

Explore MediaLink 🌐

Additional interactive resources for this chapter can be found on the Website at http://www.prenhall. com/sullivan. Click on Chapter 21 to select activities for this chapter.

- Video Overview
- NCLEX® Review Questions
- Critical Thinking Activities
- Current Events
- Nursing Leadership and Management in Action
- MediaLinks

References

Baum, G. (2000). Ready, aim, fire. *Forbes, 165*(8), 174–175.

Biron, C., Brun, J., Ivers, H., & Cooper, C. L. (2006). At work but ill: Psychosocial work environment and well-being determinants of presenteeism propensity. *Journal of Public Mental Health, 5*(4), 26–37.

CCH survey finds most employees call in "sick" for reasons other than illness. (2007). Wolters Kluwer Press Release (October 10, 2007). Retrieved November 2007 from http://www.wolterskluwer. com/WK/Press/Product+Press+Releases/2007/Oct/pr_11oct07_2. htm

Clausing, S. L., Kurtz, D. L., Prendeville, J., & Wait, J. L. (2003). Generational diversity—the nexters. *AORN Journal, 78*(3), 373–379.

Flowers, L. (2005). A plan for managing problem employees. *OR Manager, 21*(11), 29–30.

Hart, S. M. (2006). Generational diversity: Impact on recruitment and retention of registered nurses. *Journal of Nursing Administration, 36*(1), 10–12.

Hutton, S. A. (2006). Workplace incivility: State of the science. *Journal of Nursing Administration, 36*(1), 22–27.

Kansas State Board of Nursing. (2008). The Kansas nurses assistance program. Retrieved January 2008 from http://www. ksbn.org/knap.htm

Navarro, C., & Bass, C. (2006). Are sick days contagious? Connecting the relationship between employee absence and corporate benefits. *Employee Benefit Plan Review, 61*(6), 14–15.

Neuson, B. A. (2006). What you don't know about the FMLA can hurt you. *Nursing Management, 37*(5), 14–15.

Peck, M. (2006). Workplace incivility: A nurse executive responds. *Journal of Nursing Administration, 36*(1), 27–28.

Ponech, S. (2000). Telltale signs. *Nursing Management, 31*(5), 32–37.

Rhodes, S. & Steers, R. (1990). *Managing employee absenteeism.* Reading, MA: Addison-Wesley.

Sidlinger, L., & Hornberger, C. (2008). Current characteristics of the investigated impaired nurse in Kansas. *The Kansas Nurse, 83*(1), 3–5.

Silva, C. (2006). *Big-picture benefits integrating FMLA and disability claims data helps employees reduce absenteeism.* Employee Benefit News (press release, September 1, 2006), p. 1.

Sullivan, E. J., Bissell, L., & Williams, E. (1988). *Chemical dependency in nursing: The deadly diversion.* Menlo Park, CA: Addison-Wesley.

West, M. M. (2002). Early risk indicators of substance abuse among nurses. *Journal of Nursing Scholarship, 34*(2), 187–193.

Preventing Workplace Violence

Violence in Health Care
- INCIDENCE
- CONSEQUENCES
- FACTORS CONTRIBUTING TO VIOLENCE IN HEALTH CARE

Preventing Violence
- ZERO-TOLERANCE POLICIES
- REPORTING AND EDUCATION
- ENVIRONMENTAL CONTROLS

Dealing with Violence
- VERBAL INTERVENTION
- A VIOLENT INCIDENT
- POST-INCIDENT FOLLOW-UP

Learning Outcomes

After completing this chapter, you will be able to:

1. Explain why violence can occur in health care settings.
2. Discuss what health care organizations can do to prevent violence.
3. Identify threats and threatening behaviors.
4. Describe how to recognize escalating violence.
5. Discuss how to respond to a violent incident and handle the follow-up.

MediaLink

www.prenhall.com/sullivan
See the Companion Website for chapter-specific resources at
www.prenhall.com/sullivan.

Key Term

Workplace violence *p290*

Violence in Health Care

Workplace violence is any violent act, including physical assaults and threats of assault, directed toward persons at work or on duty (Ray, 2007). Those working in health care are among the most vulnerable to attack (Nachreiner et al., 2007). Most assaults in health care are by patients, but attacks are also made by disgruntled family members, coworkers, vendors, employers, or even colleagues (Gilmore, 2006). Some assaults are episodes of domestic violence that occur at work.

Violence includes:

- Threating actions, such as waving fists, throwing objects, or threatening body language
- Verbal or written threats
- Physical attacks, including slapping, hitting, biting, shoving, kicking, pushing, beating
- Violent assaults, including rape, homicide, and attacks with weapons, such as knives, firearms, or bombs (Gilmore, 2006; Clements et al., 2005)

Violence can range in intensity and cause physical injuries, temporary or permanent disability, psychological trauma, or death (Ray, 2007). In health care violence is more likely to occur in psychiatric settings, emergency rooms, waiting rooms, and geriatric units, while clinics are reported to be less likely sites of violence (Nachreiner et al., 2007; National Institute for Occupational Safety and Health [NIOSH], 2003).

INCIDENCE

Violence in health care occurs more often than in other workplace setting with 8.3 assaults per 10,000 health care workers (U.S. Department of Health and Human Services, 2002). Clements and colleagues (2005) found that between 35 and 80 percent of hospital staff had been victims of at least one assault during their careers. Nurses are more likely than others in health care to experience violence (Nachreiner et al., 2007), and women report violence more often than men (Findorff, McGovern, Wall, & Gerberich, 2005). Additionally, May and Grubbs (2006) report that fewer than 50 percent of nurses who were victims reported their assault. Such underreporting may be due to an erroneous belief

that experiencing violence simply goes along with the job (Ray, 2007).

CONSEQUENCES

In addition to harm to employees, violence in the workplace can affect worker morale, increase staff stress, cause a mistrust of administration, and exacerbate a hostile work environment (NIOSH, 2003). Furthermore, absenteeism and turnover are expensive, and the organization may incur additional health costs for care of injured workers (AACN, 2006).

FACTORS CONTRIBUTING TO VIOLENCE IN HEALTH CARE

Working with the public carries with it inherent risks, and the added stress by staff, patients, and families in health care settings increases that risk (Gilmore, 2006). Also hospitals today have an "open door" policy for visitors. Visiting hours are not restricted, and visitors are often not required to check in when they enter.

Patients with head trauma, seizure disorders, dementia, alcohol or drug withdrawal, or who are homeless may lash out in violence. Crime victims and the perpetrators might be admitted to the same hospital, and gang violence could spill over into the hospital (Keely, 2002). Also family members' stress and fear as well as long waits can contribute to the possibility of violent actions. Finally, the absence of visible, armed, and adequately trained security personnel may make the setting less secure.

Although no workplace can be certain to be free from violence, especially random violence, some additional risk factors for potential violence in health care organizations are:

- Working understaffed, especially at meal times and visiting hours
- Long waiting times
- Overcrowded waiting rooms
- Working alone
- Inadequate security
- Unlimited public access
- Poorly lit corridors, rooms, and parking lots (NIOSH, 2003)

MEDIALINK   Center for the Study and Prevention of Violence

MEDIALINK Violence Prevention

Preventing Violence

Chavez (2003) suggests that inadequate policies to address violence in the workplace may simply be the result of the employer's lack of awareness. Nonetheless, health care organizations are required to provide a safe environment for their employees (NIOSH, 2003; OSHA, 2004). The Emergency Nurses Association and the American Association of Critical Care Nurses agree (AACN, 2004; ENA, 2006).

ZERO-TOLERANCE POLICIES

The health care organization should cultivate a culture of intolerance to violence (Gilmore, 2006) and set its violence prevention policies to reflect that position. Appropriate personnel policies must state clearly what will happen if violence or the threat of violence occurs (Findorff, McGovern, & Sinclair, 2005). Policies regarding patients and visitors must do the same. Specifically, anyone who becomes violent or who exhibits threatening behavior must be removed from the setting and the authorities contacted.

Questions to ask when developing policies regarding violence prevention are shown in Box 22-1.

REPORTING AND EDUCATION

Employees must be educated to recognize the warning signs of violence and potential assailants or agitators, and be taught conflict resolution skills and de-escalation tactics. Also they should be alerted to use care when storing health instruments (stethoscopes, hemostats, scissors) that could be used as weapons.

Once adequate policies are in place, employees must be adequately informed about the policies so that they are prepared in case of an event and not trying to find out at the time of crisis. Also they need to know how to report and to whom to report as well as how to document problem situations (Keely, 2002). Employees should be reassured that reporting threatening behavior will not result in reprisals (Runy, 2006).

ENVIRONMENTAL CONTROLS

The organization should institute environmental controls to ensure patient, visitor, and employee safety. These include:

- Adequate lighting
- Security devices
- Bullet-resistant barriers in the emergency department
- Curved mirrors in hallways

In addition, safe work practices should be implemented, such as:

- Escort services
- Adequate staffing
- Judicious use of restraints or seclusion
- Alerting staff about patients with histories of violent behavior, dementia, or intoxication

Dealing with Violence

VERBAL INTERVENTION

Verbal threats often precede a physically violent event so all employees need to know techniques for reducing aggression in people who are making verbal threats as shown in Box 22-2.

Try to keep calm even when another person is screaming threats or abuse. Also try to get the person away from others. A crowd might encourage the abuser, or the person might be afraid to "lose face" in the presence of others. As you learned in Chapter 9, nonverbal communication is more powerful than your words so watch your body language and keep a distance from the person. Use clear and direct words; anxiety could make it difficult for the person to comprehend. Reflect the person's words back; this lets the person know that you hear him or her. Silence is often effective because it forces the person to think about what is being said and may be calming in itself. Finally, keep your tone of voice

---

| BOX 22-1 | Preventing Violence: Questions to Ask |

- Does your facility have a clear reporting procedure in the event that there's a workplace aggression incident?
- Whom does the staff inform of its concerns?
- What are the repercussions should individuals report an incident that makes them uneasy?
- Does your facility offer a mental health support program for staff? Is it effective in helping to reduce employee stress?
- When someone voices a concern to supervisory staff, is action taken to address the problem quickly?

From: "De-Escalating Workplace Aggression," by J. C. DelBel, 2003, *Nursing Management, 34*(9), pp. 30–34.

BOX 22-2	Verbal Intervention Strategies

1. Remain calm.
2. Isolate the individual.
3. Watch your body language.
4. Keep it simple.
5. Use reflective questioning.
6. Embrace silence.
7. Maintain moderation in speech.

From: "De-Escalating Workplace Aggression," by J. C. DelBel, 2003, *Nursing Management, 34*(9), pp. 30–34.

calm, your volume normal, and your slow your rate of speech. Together, these strategies may reduce the person's anxiety and aggression (DelBel, 2003).

A VIOLENT INCIDENT

In spite of all that an organization and individuals do to try to prevent violence, the person's aggression may escalate. In the event that such a situation occurs, the organization should make certain that all employees are prepared. Each employee should:

- Recognize signs of escalating violence
- Know the organization's violence policies
- Be prepared to protect their patients, visitors, and themselves

Every employee should learn how to watch for threatening behaviors to evaluate when a person is likely to become violent. Law enforcement personnel recommend watching for these behaviors:

- Clenched fists
- Blank stare
- Fighting stance (one foot back with arm pulled back ready to strike)
- Arms raised in a fighting position
- Standing too close or advancing toward you
- Holding anything that might be used as a weapon, such as a pen, letter opener, heavy object, or any actual weapon—a gun or knife
- Overt intent (say that they intend to "kick your—" or similar statements)
- Movement toward the exit to prevent you from leaving (Sullivan, 2004)

BOX 22-3	How to Handle a Violent Incident

1. Notify security immediately.
2. Never try to disarm someone with a weapon.
3. If not armed, enlist staff help in restraining a violent person.
4. Put a barrier between you and the violent person.

When these threatening behaviors are present or when the person becomes physically violent, you must protect your patients, visitors, other staff, and yourself. Box 22-3 lists the steps to take.

POST-INCIDENT FOLLOW-UP

After a violent incident, everyone involved will suffer some degree of emotional, if not physical, trauma. Post-incident follow-up is essential for patients', visitors', and staff members' well-being. The steps to take are shown in Box 22-4.

A nurse manager used the steps in handling a violent incident and its follow-up in Case Study 22-1.

Violence in the workplace is a reality of life today, but organizations and individuals can take steps to reduce potential threats. Because the nursing shortage is continuing and because nurses and women are more likely to be attacked, organizations must take all the necessary steps to ensure that their nurses are kept safe from harm. Additionally, nurses themselves must be informed about how to recognize potential threats and how to prevent violence from escalating. In this way violence may be prevented or, at the least, reduced.

BOX 22-4	How to Handle Post-Incident Follow-up

1. Be certain that everyone is safe following a violent event.
2. Arrange immediate treatment for the injured.
3. Complete injury and incident reports.
4. Follow up with human resources regarding the worker's compensation process for the injured employees.
5. Contact security to determine if a police report should be filed.
6. Contact the injured employee at home to express concern for the person's well-being and follow up with any questions the person may have.

CASE STUDY 22-1 　Workplace Violence

Melanie Sanchez is nurse manager of a 30-bed skilled nursing unit (SNU) in an urban hospital. Patient confusion and aggression are not uncommon occurrences for her staff. Nursing and assistive staff have been trained on conflict resolution and methods for dealing with aggressive patients.

Sandra Porter, RN, has worked in the SNU for the past 6 years. Today while administering medication to patients prior to lunch in the common dining room, Sandra noticed a newly admitted patient, Mr. B, yelling obscenities at another staff member. Sandra secured her medication cart and came to the aid of the nursing assistant. Sandra attempted to verbally de-escalate the situation, but Mr. B became increasingly aggressive. When Sandra turned to instruct the nursing assistant to clear patients from the dining room, Mr. B. picked up a chair and struck Sandra in the arm and shoulder. The nursing assistant alerted Melanie and several nurses to the problem. Melanie immediately called the hospital operator requesting security to respond to a violent patient on the SNU. Upon entering the dining room, nursing staff were able to restrain Mr. B while Melanie accompanied Sandra to the emergency department for treatment of her injuries. Sandra sustained a broken arm, a laceration to her shoulder and several contusions.

As soon as Sandra's injuries were treated and she was released from the emergency department, Melanie contacted the medical/surgical nursing division director and the human resources department regarding the assault and completed an incident report. She also completed an injury report for Sandra's worker's compensation claim. Melanie contacted the security department and requested a meeting with the security director to determine if a police report should be filed regarding Mr. B's assault of Sandra Porter. The next day, Melanie contacted Sandra at home and informed her that a case manager from human resources would call her within the week regarding her worker's compensation claim. Melanie also checked to see how Sandra was doing and encouraged her to call Melanie directly if she had questions or concerns.

Manager's Checklist

The nurse manager is responsible to:

- Ensure appropriate action is taken to secure the safety and well-being of the injured employee, patients, and other staff immediately following the workplace violence incident.
- Secure immediate and appropriate treatment for the injured employee.
- Inform administration and human resources departments of the incident.
- Complete required injury and incident reports in a timely manner.
- Follow up with human resources regarding the worker's compensation process for the injured employee.
- Contact security to determine if a police report should be filed regarding the incident.
- Contact the injured employee at home to express concern for their well-being and follow up with any questions they may have.
- Ensure any scheduling problems due to the injured employee's absence are resolved.

What You Know Now

- Health care organizations are vulnerable to violence in the workplace.
- Risk factors for violence in health care organizations include understaffing, patient conditions, family members' anxiety, unlimited public access, inadequate security, and an unsafe environment.
- The organization should establish a zero-tolerance for violence policy and make certain that all employees know it.
- All employees should be able to recognize potential threats and the warning signs of violence.
- All employees should know how to report threats and threatening behavior, to whom to report such episodes, and how to document the incidents.
- Employees should be assured that reporting potential threats will not result in reprisals.
- Organizations should institute environmental controls to reduce and prevent opportunities for unmonitored violence.
- All employees should know the steps to take if a violent incident occurs.

Tools for Preventing Workplace Violence

1. Recognize potential threats and threatening behavior and how to report them.
2. Alert staff and administration to these threats.
3. Know how to respond to a person who becomes violent.
4. Know what to do following a violent incident.
5. Monitor the environment for dangerous areas and report your observations to administration.
6. Remain alert for potential violence and instruct staff to stay vigilant.

Questions to Challenge You

1. Evaluate your current workplace or clinical site. See if you can find potential opportunities that would allow violence to occur. Describe them.
2. Ask to see the workplace violence policy at your school, clinical site, and/or workplace. Evaluate them. Are they adequate? Can you suggest changes?
3. Have you ever been the victim of violence or threats of violence? How did you handle the event and its aftermath? Would you do something differently now? How did the authorities respond? Could you suggest changes for them?
4. Are you aware of specific action that your school, workplace, or clinical site has done to protect people from violence? What more could you suggest?

Explore MediaLink 🌐

Additional interactive resources for this chapter can be found on the Website at http://www.prenhall.com/sullivan. Click on Chapter 22 to select activities for this chapter.

- Video Overview
- NCLEX® Review Questions
- Critical Thinking Activities
- Current Events
- Nursing Leadership and Management in Action
- MediaLinks

References

American Association of Critical Care Nurses (AACN). (2004). *Workplace violence prevention.* Retrieved December 2007 from www.aacn.org/AACN/pubpolcy.nsf/vwdoc/workenv

Chavez, L. J. (2003). *Workplace violence 101: Latest findings on workplace violence.* Retrieved December 2007 from http://members.aol.com/Endwpv/statistics.html

Clements, P. T., DeRanien, J. T., Clark, K., Manno, M. S., & Kuhn, D. W. (2005). Workplace violence and corporate policy for health care settings. *Nursing Economic$, 23*(3), 119–124.

DelBel, J. C. (2003). De-escalating workplace violence. *Nursing Management, 34*(9), 30–34.

Emergency Nurses Association (ENA). (2006). Emergency Nurses Association position statement. *Violence in the emergency care setting.* Retrieved December 2007 from http://ena.org/about/position/PDFs/45BFF88286AF4167B3C59D4AFE655DC7.pdf

Findorff, M. J., McGovern, P. M., & Sinclair, S. (2005). Work-related violence policy: A process evaluation. *AAOHN Journal, 53*(8), 360–371.

Findorff, M. J., McGovern, P. M., Wall, M. M., & Gerberich, S. G. (2005). Reporting violence to a health care employer: A cross-sectional study. *AAOHN Journal, 53*(9), 399–406.

Gilmore, J. (2006). Violence in the workplace. *Nephrology Nursing Journal, 33*(3), 254–255.

Keely, B. R. (2002). Could your patient—or colleague—become violent? *Nursing2002, 32*(12), 1–5.

May, D. D. & Grubbs, L. M. The extent, nature and precipitating factors of nurse assault among three groups of registered nurses in a regional medical center. *Journal of Emergency Nursing, 28*(1), 11–17.

Nachreiner, N. M., Hansen, H. E., Okano, A., Gerberich, S. G., Ryan, A. D., McGovern, P. M., Church, T. R., & Watt, G. D. (2007). Difference in work-related violence by nurse license type. *Journal of Professional Nursing, 23*(5), 290–300.

National Institute of Occupational Safety and Health (NIOSH). (2003). *Developing and implementing a workplace violence prevention program and policy.* Retrieved December 2007 from www.cdc.gov/niosh/violdev.html

Occupational Safety and Health Administration (OSHA). (2004). *Guidelines for preventing workplace violence for health care and social services workers.* Retrieved December 2007 from www.osha.gov/Publications/osha3148.pdf

Ray, M. M. (2007). The dark side of the job: Violence in the emergency department. *Journal of Emergency Nursing, 33*(3), 257–261.

Runy, L. A. (2006). Dangerous jobs. *Hospitals & Health Networks, 80*(2), 24–26.

Sullivan, E. J. (2004). *Becoming influential: A guide for nurses.* Upper Saddle River, NJ: Prentice Hall.

U.S. Department of Health and Human Services. (2002). *Violence: Occupational hazards in hospitals*(DHHS Publication No. 2002-101). Retrieved December 2007 from www.cdc.gov/niosh/2002-101.html

Handling Collective-Bargaining Issues

Learning Outcomes

After completing this chapter, you will be able to:

1. Discuss the laws that govern collective bargaining.
2. Explain how a union is formed.
3. Explain how a contract is administered.
4. Describe what is involved in the grievance process.
5. Discuss how recent legal decisions have changed nurses' roles in collective bargaining.
6. Describe the nurse manager's role.

MediaLink

www.prenhall.com/sullivan
See the Companion Website for chapter-specific resources at www.prenhall.com/sullivan.

Key Terms

Bargaining agent *p297*
Certification to contract *p298*
Collective bargaining *p296*

Decertification *p298*
Grievances *p298*
Ratification *p298*

Representation election *p297*
Strike *p300*

Collective Bargaining

Before federal laws governing labor relations in this country were enacted, disputes between the owners or managers of a company and the company's labor force were settled by the judiciary branch of government. During this period of American history, the courts often ruled that **collective bargaining**, collective action taken by workers to secure better wages or working conditions, was illegal. Today, however, labor laws enacted by Congress, decisions by the U.S. Supreme Court, and the National Labor Relations Board (NLRB) guide labor relations between employers and employees.

LAWS GOVERNING UNIONS

Since enactment of the National Labor Relations Act in 1935, nurses and other employees of private, for-profit health care institutions have been protected in their right to organize for collective bargaining purposes. Under the provisions of the act, as amended in 1974, employees of voluntary, not-for-profit health care institutions also were granted the same rights and protections.

In the United States, a *closed shop* is a business in which union membership (often of a specific union and no other) is a precondition to employment. The *open shop* is a business in which union membership is not a component in hiring decisions and union members don't receive any preference in hiring. The federal government operates under open shop rules nationwide, although many of its employees are represented by unions. The *union shop* does not require employees to be union members as a condition of employment, but it does require that they join the union within a set period of time following their hire. Finally, in the *agency shop*, employees must pay the equivalent of union dues, but the employee does not have to officially join the union.

A *right-to-work state* is a state in which no person can be denied the right to work because of membership or nonmembership in a labor union. Trade unions and employers cannot make membership in a union or payment of union dues or "fees" a condition of employment, either before or after hiring. Under the open shop rule, an employee cannot be compelled to join or pay the equivalent of dues to a union, nor can the employee be fired if he or she joins the union. In other words, the employee has the right to work, regardless of whether he or she is member or financial contributor to such union. Twenty-eight states do not have right-to-work laws. The lack of a right-to-work law does not mean an employee has to join a union if one is formed in his workplace.

PUBLIC VERSUS PRIVATE COLLECTIVE BARGAINING

Collective bargaining laws differ depending on if the nurses are employed in the private sector in either non-profit or for-profit organizations or if they are employed in the public sector as city, county, state, or federal employees. Most of this chapter deals with private sector employees, but it explains the differences for public sector employees.

The Civil Service Reform Act of 1978 gave certain federal employees the right to organize, bargain collectively, and participate through labor organizations of their choice in decisions affecting their work environment although it depends on what federal agency is their employer. State or local employees, however, fall under state regulations, which vary greatly from state to state. Nurses in state hospitals, for example, would be governed by their state laws. Some states don't allow employees to strike or form collective bargaining units; other states don't allow wages or overtime pay to be part of a union contract.

There are usually three broad categories into which negotiations may be classified: mandatory, prohibited, and permissive. All three categories are addressed in both public and private sector bargaining. However, the subjects in each category can vary greatly depending on applicable law and judicial interpretation.

Parties are obligated to negotiate on mandatory subjects of bargaining. In the private sector, wages, hours and other terms and conditions of work are considered mandatory subjects. In the public sector, the scope of mandatory subjects of bargaining is often far narrower. Legislatures may decide that certain subjects may not be appropriate for bargaining.

In the federal sector, for example, wages—a mandatory item in the private sector—is a prohibited subject. One example of a prohibited subject in the private sector is a closed shop clause. It is illegal to negotiate a union agreement requiring union membership as a condition of obtaining a job.

Why Do Nurses Join Unions?

Dissatisfaction with working conditions and administration has been cited as contributing to nurses' propensity to form unions, and first-line managers have the most impact on employee satisfaction (Friedrich, 2001). According to a study by Bilchik (2000), hospital administrators make their organizations more likely to unionize if they make three erroneous assumptions:

1. Believe that low wages cause the most job dissatisfaction
2. Believe that supervisors understand how front-line employees think about unionizing
3. Are ineffective in communicating with employees

More recently nurses concerns about the practice environment and decisions about quality care have prompted collective bargaining efforts (Budd, Warino, & Patton, 2004). Regardless of the reasons, health care organizations are susceptible to unionizing efforts, and nurses and nurse managers are often involved in the process of unionization and deal with grievances.

Process of Unionization

SELECTING A BARGAINING AGENT

The process of establishing a union in any setting begins with the selection of a **bargaining agent** certified to conduct labor negotiations for a group of individuals. This process is known as a **representation election** and is presided over by the National Labor Relations Board. For an election to occur, the union must demonstrate that interest is shown by at least 30 percent of the employees affected by this action. Unions seldom move forward, however, without a much higher card signing count due to their reluctance to expend resources where

there are such limited data regarding support for an election. In this process, the union will ask eligible employees to sign a card authorizing an election. Once the 30 percent level is reached, the union can petition the NLRB to conduct an election. The NLRB then meets with both the union and the employer. At the conclusion of this meeting the NLRB will have determined three things:

1. Who is eligible to participate in the union. This is a problematic issue and not easily resolved, because registered nurses employed as staff nurses are eligible for collective bargaining, but registered nurses employed as managers are not. Registered nurses who work for an organization, but in a capacity outside the traditional nursing department, such as a clinic, home health care, or in education, may or may not be eligible for membership. This issue alone can take many days or weeks to resolve and is more complicated these days by recent legal decisions (see section Recent Legal Decisions).
2. Whether the signatories are employees of the organization.
3. A date for union election.

The election is conducted by the NLRB within 45 days, using a secret ballot. All individuals eligible for representation by the union are notified of the election time and date. On election day, eligible employees are asked to choose if they wish to be represented by a union. A simple majority of the votes cast is required for the nurses to form a union.

Many unions represent RNs in collective bargaining. To place its name on the ballot to become the bargaining agent, a union needs to show that at least one person eligible to vote in the election has signed an authorization card requesting that this union represent the organization's nurses. At the time of voting, nurses are also asked if they want the union on the ballot to be their representative. Again, a simple majority of those eligible to vote is required. Then this union is certified to enter into contract negotiations with the employer.

The process of selecting a bargaining agent produces a tense, emotional climate that affects everyone in the organization. It is important for both nurse managers and staff nurses to remember that during this period, the rules of unfair labor practice apply. Nurse managers must refrain from any action that could be seen as interfering with the employees' right to determine their collective bargaining representative. Such actions include individually questioning staff nurses about their knowledge of collective bargaining activities and making promises or threats to individual staff members based on the outcome of the election. Promising raises or promotions if the union is defeated or promising pay cuts and demotions if the union succeeds are examples of unfair practices.

Staff nurses also must be careful that their discussions regarding collective bargaining take place away from the work site and not on work time. In a recent ruling, the NLRB specified that employees may not use their employer's e-mail system to communicate about unionizing activities (NLRB, 2007).

CERTIFYING THE CONTRACT

Certification by the NLRB of a union to be the bargaining agent does not automatically mean employees have a contract. It does mean that a group of people have the right to enter into a contract with an employer, a concept known as **certification to contract**. The actual contract and its provisions must be written and voted on by the union membership, a process that may take some time.

Issues considered mandatory subjects of bargaining are:

1. Rates of pay
2. Wages
3. Hours of employment
4. Conditions of employment
5. Grievance procedures

In addition, the contract may specify other areas provided that both parties agree they should be included. These can include:

1. Union security clause
2. Management rights clause
3. Seniority
4. Fringe benefits
5. Layoffs and reductions in work
6. Floating procedures
7. Insurance provided
8. Retirement policies
9. Professional issues

The contract is considered to be in effect when both management of the organization and employees agree on its content. The final agreement is subject to a ratification vote by the affected employees. Passage of the contract, or **ratification**, is obtained by a simple majority of eligible members who vote.

ADMINISTERING THE CONTRACT

The role of administering the contract then falls to an individual designated as the union representative. This individual may be an employee of the union or a member of the nursing staff. It is the duty of the union representative to provide fair and equal representation to all members of the unit. The role of the union representative is to explain the provisions of the contract to the union membership and be available to help in the grievance process.

DECERTIFYING THE CONTRACT

Occasionally, members of a particular unit may decide that the union they have chosen to represent them may not be the union they want or that no union at all is needed. In such a case, the members of the bargaining unit have the right to either change their union affiliation or remove the union by using a process known as **decertification**. This process is essentially the same as that followed by the NLRB for a representation election. Once again, an employee who is a member of the bargaining unit must submit to the NLRB signed documents showing that at least 30 percent of the bargaining unit membership request an election to remove a union as their representative. Then the NLRB will review the signatures for authenticity, set a date and time, and conduct an election by secret ballot. The winner is determined by a majority of the cast ballots. Once an election has been conducted, the NLRB will not return to the same work site for a vote by the same group for a period of 1 year (National Labor Relations Act [NLRA], Sec 9[e]2).

THE NURSE MANAGER'S ROLE

The nurse manager in a health care organization where nurses are organized into a collective bargaining unit needs to be aware of the five categories of unfair labor practices described by the NLRA:

1. Interference with the right to organize
2. Domination
3. Encouraging or discouraging union membership
4. Discharging an employee for giving testimony or filing a charge with the NLRB
5. Refusal to bargain collectively

Another responsibility of the nurse manager is to participate in resolving **grievances**, using the agreed-upon grievance procedure. Grievances can usually be classified as:

1. Contract violations
2. Violations of federal or state law
3. Failure of management to meet its responsibilities
4. Violation of agency rules

Grievances may be caused by misunderstandings that usually stem from circumstances surrounding the grievance, a lack of familiarity with the contract, or an inadequate labor agreement.

The grievance procedure used will be negotiated and clearly described in the labor agreement. Most likely, it will contain a series of progressive steps and time limits for submission/resolution of grievances.

THE GRIEVANCE PROCESS

The typical grievance process follows these steps.

Step 1. The employee talks informally with her or his direct supervisor, usually as soon as possible after the incident has occurred. A representative of the bargaining agent is allowed to be present. If the grievance is not adjusted in the informal discussion, a written request for the next step is given to the immediate supervisor within 10 work days. A written response must be received within 5 work days. The employee, supervisor, and agent will be present for any discussion.

Step 2. If the response to step 1 is not satisfactory, a written appeal may be submitted within 10 work days to the director of nursing or her or his designee. The employee, agent, grievance chairperson, and the top nursing administrator or designee can be present for discussion. Again, written response will be provided in 5 work days subsequent to these meetings. In most bargaining units, the positions of agent and grievance chairperson are separated. Generally, the grievance chairperson is an officer in the bargaining unit.

Step 3. The employee, agent, grievance chairperson, nursing administrator, and director of human resources meet for discussions. The 10- and 5-day time limits for appeal and answer are again observed.

Step 4. This final step is arbitration, which is invoked when no solution suggested is acceptable. An arbitrator who is a neutral third party is selected and is present at these meetings. The submission of a grievance may be required within 15 days after step 3 is completed.

Often, a statement included in each of the steps states that if the time limits are not observed by one party, the grievance may be considered resolved and further action barred. The contract also usually specifies how an arbitrator is selected.

Here are some suggestions that may be helpful in handling grievances:

1. The objective of the grievance procedure is not to achieve conquest. You have to work with one another after resolution of the grievance, so treat each other with courtesy and respect. Don't threaten or bluff. Don't withhold facts or information relating to the grievance.

2. Do not, whatever your position, allow disagreements or disputes among members of your team (e.g., management) to be public. Both the bargaining unit and the management team must present a solid front when faced with one another.

3. Expedience is a must; delaying tactics serve only to heighten emotions. However, allow time to consider all of the facts.

4. Stay objective. Emotionalism usually leads to further problems. If discussions escalate into angry exchanges, adjourn and reschedule later.

5. Implementing decisions or filing grievances requires planning. Get all the facts and information, witnesses, and documentation. Evaluate and anticipate the other party's position and possible response. Know the strengths and weaknesses of the issue for both sides. Find out whether any similar situations occurred and what decision was reached. Use all the resources available. Seek guidance from those higher in administrative positions.

6. Never refuse to meet with the grievant's representatives. The right to representation is one of the advantages of being under the auspices of a collective bargaining unit.

7. The bargaining unit representative, though in a unique position, is not immune from reprimand or discipline. When not involved in bargaining unit activities, the agent is an employee who must observe the rules and regulations of the organization, and the employer has the right to a full day's work and an acceptable level of performance. However, while handling grievances, the employee/agent is not really considered an employee. She or he is considered the representative and advocate of the employee who filed the grievance.

8. Integral to bargaining are solutions that may also accommodate future changes and needs. Therefore, think ahead. Once a grievance is filed, a chain reaction may occur, and almost any imaginable outcome may end up as the solution. However, a carefully written grievance procedure should obviate this possibility.

9. Be prepared to give or take acceptable compromises and alternative solutions within the framework of the contract, no matter which party suggests them. Know your bottom line for compromise. Do not submit to emotional appeals as to what is fair. The contract is the sole determinant of what is fair; if necessary, a neutral third party will

be called on to interpret the contract. What one person considers fair may not necessarily be seen in the same light by the other.

10. Pat formulas do not settle grievances or solve problems. A formula would negate the needed judgment and flexibility that are so necessary to grievance handling.

11. Observe the time limits. If you do not, the bargaining unit may lose the right to continue the grievance to the next level, or both the bargaining unit and management may lose in an eventual arbitration.

12. In adjusting a grievance, knowledge is very important. As with any interaction between people, your statement is colored by your temperament and is interpreted by the other party in accordance with his or her own temperament.

13. Gloating over a win is human, but remember that you may lose the next one; don't become overconfident. Similarly, don't blame the other side for taking advantage of your mistakes. Learn from them, and don't repeat them the next time.

The Grievance Hearing

In the grievance hearing, remember these key behaviors:

1. Put the grievant at ease. Do not interrupt or disagree. Let the grievant have her or his say.

2. Listen openly and carefully. Search for what the employee is trying to say. Take notes.

3. Discuss the problem calmly and with an open mind. Avoid arguments, avoid antagonizing others, and avoid the urge to win. Negotiate.

4. Get the story straight. Get all the facts. Ask logical questions to clarify doubtful points. Distinguish fact from opinion.

5. Consider the grievant's viewpoint. Do not assume she or he is automatically wrong.

6. Avoid snap judgments. Do not jump to conclusions. But be willing to admit mistakes.

7. Make an equitable decision, then give it to the grievant promptly. Do not pass the buck.

Strikes

When an agreement cannot be reached through collective bargaining, employees usually **strike.** A strike is an organized stoppage of work by employees within the union. Striking is not commonly used by nurses. By law, a 10-day notice must be given to allow hospitals the opportunity to prepare for striking nurses' absences. Also, employers have the right to permanently replace striking employees.

Collective Bargaining for Nurses

To ensure the balance between the rights of employees and the rights of the public to health care, Congress passed a special set of dispute-settling procedures to be applied in the health care industry:

1. Before changing or terminating a contract, one party must notify the other of its intent to do so 90 days prior to the contract expiration date. This is 30 days more than specified for other industries.

2. If after 30 days of this notification both sides cannot agree, then the Federal Mediation and Conciliation Service (FMCS) must be notified.

3. The FMCS will appoint either a mediator or an inquiry board within 30 days.

4. The mediator or board must make recommendations within 15 days.

5. If after 15 more days both sides cannot agree, then a strike vote can be conducted and a strike scheduled.

If a strike vote is affirmed, then a 10-day written notice must be given to management indicating the date, time, and place of the strike. This is to ensure that a hospital has adequate time to provide for continuity of patient care in the event of a strike.

To enforce these amendments, the NLRB established separate provisions for the health care industry. These provisions include

1. Recognition of appropriate bargaining units for health care employees so that the hospital would not have to conduct separate contract negotiations with many different unions. Registered nurses are a separate bargaining unit in health care.

2. Determination of locations where unions could solicit members and distribute literature in the hospital without disrupting patient care or interfering with work time. Currently, solicitation of members can occur in hospital cafeterias, gift shops, and main lobbies.

RECENT LEGAL DECISIONS

Three areas of supervision over subordinates have been under debate for a number of years. These are:

1. The responsibility to assign
2. The responsibility to direct
3. Independent judgment

The NLRB recently issued several landmark decisions regarding the supervisory status of nurses (NLRB, 2006). Three cases were considered together and have become known as the *Kentucky River* trilogy. They are *Oakwood Healthcare, Inc.*, *Golden Crest Healthcare Center*, and *Croft Metal, Inc.* These rulings are important to nurses because those employees deemed as supervisors are prohibited from joining a union.

The NLRB clearly defined the supervisory status of nurses in its ruling (NLRB, 2006). They ruled that:

1. The responsibility to assign includes nurses' responsibility to assign other nurses and assistants to patients.
2. The responsibility to direct includes the responsibility for the actions of those to whom tasks have been assigned.
3. Independent judgment includes the nurse's decision to match staff skills to patient needs.

This ruling has an impact on the eligibility of many nurses who heretofore were not considered supervisors and thus were eligible to be members of a collective bargaining unit. Nurses who are charge nurses either permanently or part-time on a regular basis and who meet the above criteria for assigning, directing, and using independent judgment, are not eligible to join a union. While health care employers have lauded the decision (The Health Care Employer, 2006), the United American Nurses, AFL-CIO has decried it (United American Nurses, 2006).

THE ANA AND COLLECTIVE BARGAINING

Since its inception, the American Nurses Association (ANA) has had an active interest in the economic security of nurses. One of the purposes of ANA was "to promote the usefulness and honor, the financial and other interests of the nursing profession" (Flannigan, 1976, p. 169). Although this statement was useful in helping to shape the role of the profession in supporting collective bargaining for nurses, the ANA did not officially adopt an economic security program that included collective bargaining until 1946 (Flannigan, 1976). ANA has actively promoted collective bargaining for nurses through the Economic and General Welfare Program, which became the Department of Labor Relations and, finally, the Commission on Workplace Advocacy.

In 1999 the ANA House of Delegates changed its bylaws to create the United American Nurses (UAN) as the labor arm of the ANA. UAN held its first National Labor Assembly (NLA) in June 2000 and became an affiliate of the AFL-CIO in 2001.

Complicating the collective bargaining issue today are numerous other efforts to organize nurses. Established unions in a variety of fields (e.g., steelworkers, textile workers, food workers, UAW Teamsters, AFL-CIO) are attempting to recruit nurses. Employees of individual health care organizations are forming their own collective bargaining organization and include nurses. So collective bargaining in nursing runs the gamut from national collaboration of state organizations to coordination with other employees in health care to individual units of nurses.

FUTURE OF COLLECTIVE BARGAINING

The use of collective bargaining as a way for nurses to influence the practice environment and to ensure their economic security holds both concerns and promises, especially with the radical changes occurring in health care today. The concerns are that the very processes of collective bargaining separate rather than unite nurses, notably between staff nurses and those in management. What the future holds for collective bargaining in nursing is uncertain and unknown.

What You Know Now

- Nurse dissatisfaction with working conditions and the care environment are often the impetus for establishing a union.
- The process of achieving unionization involves selecting a bargaining agent, developing a contract between the employer and the employees, and ratifying the contract.
- The contract specifies workplace policies and employee benefits, among other conditions.
- Disagreements between employees and employers are handled by a structured, formal arrangement known as the grievance process.
- A collective-bargaining unit can be decertified in much the same way it was originally certified.
- Certain conditions of labor law apply in health care to protect patients and the public.
- The American Nurses Association, through its constituent member associations and the United American Nurses, provides collective bargaining services to nurses, but other unions also represent nurses.

- Recent decisions by the National Labor Relations Board have clarified the supervisory status of nurses and increased the number of nurses now classified as supervisors, making them ineligible to join a union.
- The future of collective bargaining for nurses is uncertain and unknown.

Tools for Handling Collective Bargaining Issues

1. Determine if your organization has a collective bargaining arrangement with its registered nurse employees.
2. If so, become familiar with provisions of the policy and grievance procedure.
3. Contact administration for any questions you may have with contract policies.
4. If your organization does not have a union contract, be aware of the possibility that efforts to establish a collective bargaining unit may be initiated.
5. If attempts are made to unionize your workplace, obtain information on the legal obligations you have as an employee and/or manager.
6. Remember, collective bargaining is an agreement between an employer and its employees; it does not need to be adversarial.

Questions to Challenge You

1. Are you a member of a collective bargaining unit? Do you know anyone who is?
2. Have you been involved in union organizing? What happened during and after the process?
3. If you have not been involved in union organizing, find someone who has been and ask him or her what happened.
4. What is your opinion of unions for nurses? Name the pros and cons.
5. You are negotiating a union contract on behalf of the nurses. List your demands in priority order.
6. You are negotiating a union contract on behalf of administration. Respond to the demands on your list generated in question 5.

Explore MediaLink 🌐

Additional interactive resources for this chapter can be found on the Website at http://www.prenhall.com/sullivan. Click on Chapter 23 to select activities for this chapter.

- Video Overview
- NCLEX® Review Questions
- Critical Thinking Activities
- Current Events
- Nursing Leadership and Management in Action
- MediaLinks

References

Bilchik, G. S. (2000). Norma Rae, RN. *Hospitals and Health Networks, 74*(11), 40–44.

Budd, K. W., Warino, L. S., & Patton, M. E. (2004). Traditional and non-traditional collective bargaining: Strategies to improve the patient care environment. *Online Journal of Issues in Nursing, 9*(1). Retrieved October 2007 from http://nursingworld.org/MainMenuCategories/ANAMarketplace/ANAPeriodicals/OJIN/TableofContents/Volume92004/Number1January31/CollectiveBargainingStrategies.aspx

Flannigan, L. (1976). *One strong voice: The history of the American Nurses Association.* Kansas City, MO: American Nurses Association.

Friedrich, B. (2001). Staying power: Unions. *Nursing Management, 32*(7), 26–28.

National Labor Relations Board. (2007). NLRB finds no statutory right to use employer's e-mail system for "section 7 communications." Retrieved January 2008 from http://www.nlrb.gov/shared_files/Press%20Releases/2007/R-2652.pdf

National Labor Relations Board. (2006). Statement of national labor relations board regarding "Kentucky River" cases. Retrieved January 2008 from http://www.nlrb.gov/shared_files/Press%20Releases/2006/r2596.htm

The Health Care Employer. (2006). What the change in supervisory status will mean in the health care setting. *The Health Care Employer, 32*(4), 2–3.

United American Nurses. (2006). UAN's statement on the NLRB's decisions on the Kentucky River cases. Retrieved February 2008 from http://www.uannurse.org/media/press.html?view=press_release&press_id=159&year=2006

Managing Stress

Learning Outcomes

After completing this chapter, you will be able to:

1. Explain why stress is necessary.
2. Describe the organizational, interpersonal, and individual factors that cause stress.
3. Explain the consequences that result from stress, including burnout and compassion fatigue.
4. Discuss how individuals can manage stress.
5. Discuss how managers can help themselves and their staff manage stress.
6. Explain how organizations can help reduce stress in the workplace.

MediaLink

www.prenhall.com/sullivan

See the Companion Website for chapter-specific resources at www.prenhall.com/sullivan.

Consider the following scenario:

Keandra is a medical nurse with 10 years of experience. She is married and has two children under the age of 6 who attend preschool while Keandra is at work. As a nurse manager, Keandra has 24-hour responsibility for supervision of two 30-bed medical units. She frequently receives calls from the unit nurses during the evenings and nights, and approximately once a week she has to return to the unit to intervene in a situation or to replace nurses who are absent. Keandra is responsible for scheduling all nurses on her unit and has no approval to use agency nurses, in spite of a 20 percent vacancy rate. In addition, Keandra serves on four departmental committees and the hospital task force on consumer relations. She consistently takes work home, including performance appraisals, quality assessment reports, and professional journals. Although provided with an office, Keandra has little opportunity to use it because of constant interruptions from nurses, physicians, other departmental leaders, and her clinical director. Recently, Keandra saw her family physician, complaining of persistent headaches, weight loss, and a feeling of constant fatigue. After a complete diagnostic workup, Keandra was found to have a slightly elevated blood pressure, with a resting pulse of 100. Her physician prescribed an exercise program, and she was advised to lighten her workload, take a vacation, and reduce her stress level.

Stress is the nonspecific reaction that people have to demands from the environment that pose a threat (Steers, 1991). Stress results when two or more incompatible demands on the body cause a conflict. Selye (1978), recognized as the pioneer of stress research, suggests that the body's wear and tear results from its response to normal stressors. The rate and intensity of damage increase when an organism experiences greater stress than it is capable of accommodating.

Selye maintains that the physiological response to stress is the same whether the stressor is positive, *enstress*, or negative, *distress*. It is easy to see how negative events, such as job loss, can cause stress. However, positive events also may cause stress.

Anthony was the director of nursing for critical care in a 400-bed hospital. He was offered the opportunity to develop a hyperbaric unit. In assuming the additional responsibility, Anthony began putting in long hours and working weekends. As the project progressed, Anthony became unable to sleep and gained 10 pounds. After the unit opened, Anthony's sleep pattern and weight returned to normal. Clearly, Anthony displayed emotional and physical signs of stress although he was experiencing a "positive" promotion and career opportunity.

A certain amount of stress is essential to sustain life, and moderate amounts serve as stimuli to performance, but overpowering stress can cause a person to respond in a maladaptive physiological or psychological manner.

The Nature of Stress

A balance must exist between stress and the capability to handle it. When the degree of stress is equal to the degree of ability to accommodate it, the organism is in a state of equilibrium. Normal wear and tear occur, but sustained damage does not. When the degree of stress is greater than the available coping mechanism, the individual experiences negative aspects of stress. The situation is often described metaphorically through such statements as "carrying a load on one's shoulders" or "bearing a heavy burden." This often leads to physiological and psychological problems for the person and poor performance for the organization. When the degree of stress is not stimulating enough, lack of interest, apathy, boredom, low motivation, and even poor performance can result.

The experience of stress is subjective and individualized. One person's stressful event is another's challenge. One individual can experience an event, positive or negative, that would prove overwhelming for someone else. Even a minor change in organizational policy may cause some individuals to experience stress, whereas others welcome it. Some nurses seem to thrive on the demands of work, family, school, and community involvement, whereas others find even minimal changes in their expectations a source of great discomfort. In the current health care environment, where constant change is the norm, some nurse managers may choose a less demanding position because they find the stress level too high in their current position.

For nurses, stress in the workplace can develop from several sources and may be due to organizational, interpersonal, or individual (intrapersonal) factors.

Causes of Stress

ORGANIZATIONAL FACTORS

Stress can result from job-related factors, such as task overload, conflicting tasks, inability to do the tasks assigned because of lack of preparation or experience, and unclear or insufficient information regarding the assignment. Nurses' jobs are often performed in life-or-death situations; emergencies may cause periods of extreme overload.

The physical environment may also be stressful. Consider the intensive care unit with its constant alarms, beeps, and other noises. Besides noise levels, lighting and other comfort factors may increase stress within the environment. Tight quarters, poorly organized work environments, and lack of equipment also augment stress levels.

The manager's behavior also can be a factor in stress. Authoritarian or punitive supervisory behavior is closely related to stress levels. Participative management, in contrast, can reduce job stress.

Other organizational factors that can lead to stress include organizational norms and expectations that conflict with an individual's needs. Managers trying to do more with less, overworked staff, and more acutely ill patients can lead to an organizational environment that by its very nature is stressful.

Managed care, cost containment, the creation of integrated organizations, and reorganization are creating dramatic changes in health care that are contributing to stress in nursing. New technology, increased expecta-

tions from patients and their families, liability concerns, and competition among health care providers, and increased pressures for efficiency have made the role of nurses more difficult, conflicting, and stressful.

INTERPERSONAL FACTORS

To add to the pressures created by organizational changes, nurses must contend with strained interpersonal relationships within the nursing profession and between nursing and other professions (e.g., medicine, administration). Relationships are strained even further as pressures mount. Shorter lengths of stay for patients, supervision of assistive personnel, job redesign, and case management challenge relationships among nursing care providers.

Interdisciplinary difficulties may precipitate tension. For example, in one rehabilitation setting, therapists expect the patients to be bathed, to have eaten breakfast, and to be dressed and ready to start therapy by 8:30 A.M. This expectation places undue stress on rehabilitation nurses, who must motivate patients who complain that they have had far too little sleep. Another example of stress due to interdisciplinary conflict is: A radiology technician responds to a 9:00 P.M. page for a chest X-ray examination and informs the registered nurse that the patient will have to be brought back down because the radiology department is understaffed.

Interactions between physicians and nurses often are not characterized by open communication. Most nurses have experienced an irate response from a physician who is awakened during the night for something the physician thinks should have been handled earlier or might have waited until morning. In one small community hospital, an internist was well known for his outbursts during middle-of-the-night calls. One experienced nurse dealt with necessary calls to him by directly stating when he answered the phone, "This is Jane Jones from St. Matthew's. I have two important things to tell you about Mrs. Smith. . . ." This helped the internist focus on the problem at hand and reduced his outbursts.

The need to fulfill multiple roles is another source of stress. A **role** is a set of expectations about behavior ascribed to a specific position in society (e.g., nurse, spouse, parent). Conflict between family roles and professional ones results in stress. Adding to stress is the shift and weekend work required in nursing jobs in hospitals that must be staffed 24 hours a day, 7 days a week. Nurses who work on evening or night shifts may experience family problems if their spouse and children are on different schedules, especially if the nurse rotates shifts. It takes several weeks to adjust physiologically to a change in shifts; however, rotation patterns often require nurses to change shifts several times a month. Managers can reduce the physiological pressure through ensuring that nurses receive adequate rest and work breaks, rotating staff only between two shifts, and never scheduling "double backs" (working 8 hours, off 8 hours, working 8 hours).

INDIVIDUAL FACTORS

Stress can result from personal factors as well. One of these factors is the rate of life change. Changes throughout life, such as marriage, pregnancy, or purchasing a new home, generate stress. Each individual responds to stress differently, but the cumulative effects of stress often lead to the onset of disease or illness. The ways people interpret events ultimately determine whether the person sees the event as stressful or as a positive challenge.

Deficiency Focusing

Deficiency focusing is the habit of focusing on the negatives at the expense of the positives. There is a tendency to exaggerate weaknesses and disregard strengths. Deficiency focusing can lead to an increased sense of threat and a diminished sense of optimism, immobilizing individuals and limiting their ability to solve problems. They become so overwhelmed with what might go wrong that they don't look at options and opportunities that also are present.

As resources in health care continue to shrink, nurses are being asked or told to assume responsibility for tasks that had been performed by other departments (e.g., phlebotomy, electrocardiography, respiratory therapy). Nurses can see these responsibilities as an overwhelming amount of work that can't possibly be accomplished given the existing number of staff or as work that is not appropriate for nurses to do. But if nurses approach the task as a means to improve continuity of care or deliver patient-focused care, they can focus energy on skills in which nurses excel: managing patient care.

Necessitating

Necessitating is the belief that it is imperative or necessary that a particular task be done by a specific person; it is a belief structure that limits choice. Tasks become inflexible demands that must be met. Nurses are especially prone to this type of thinking. Many nurse managers continue to believe that it is necessary to be as clinically competent as their staff. There are

many tasks that nursing staff believe only nurses can do. Then, as patient care loads become heavier, their stress level increases.

Nurses must begin to question old ways of thinking and to evaluate what tasks should belong to the nursing profession in the future. Core competencies for nurse managers include a different set of managerial skills (e.g., facilitation, negotiation, team building), not excelling at clinical skills. By continually questioning whether the usual activity continues to be appropriate, both the manager and members of the staff can reduce stress.

Low Skill Recognition

Low skill recognition is perhaps the least stress producing of the three habits but may be the one that needs the most attention in an unstable and unpredictable environment. Low skill recognition is a tendency not to recognize the role one's own ability has played in producing one's successes; it affects both managers and staff nurses when they face something unfamiliar. Rushton (2007) suggests that nurses' performance improves when they work in organizations that recognize their accomplishments and offer assertive suggestions.

New graduates, for example, often do not recognize that they have demonstrated a definitive set of skills and knowledge in having passed all the requirements to become a registered nurse. The stress they experience when changing from the student role to the professional practitioner role has been explained by Kramer (1974) as **reality shock**. It is the surprise and disequilibrium experienced when moving from the familiar school culture to the work culture, where values, rewards, and sanctions are different and often seem illogical.

Moving from a staff nurse position to a management position also creates surprise and disequilibrium. The reward structure is totally different for managers. New managers often experience a sense of isolation from the peer group of staff nurses who previously provided support. In each of these cases, the individual often questions her or his abilities to make the transition to the new role. Therefore, low skill recognition is not to be overlooked as a key element in developing stress resiliency.

Stress can also result from incongruence between one's expectations for performance and one's perception of the resulting performance **(intrarole conflict)**. Similarly, conflict between the roles of nurse manager and nurse can be a source of stress **(interrole conflict)**. Doing a job and directing others to do the job are different. Directing others is stressful, and a person may be tempted to believe that it will be faster to complete a task by doing it herself or himself.

Past experience in coping with stress provides insight into an individual's ability for successful coping in current experiences. People tend to repeat coping behaviors in similar situations, regardless of whether the initial behavior reduced stress.

One's self-esteem also affects coping. Individuals with low self-esteem often have difficulty coping with role conflict and role ambiguity. **Role ambiguity** results from unclear expectations for one's performance. Individuals with high tolerances for ambiguity can deal better with the strains that come from uncertainties and, therefore, are likely to be able to cope with role ambiguity.

Certain personality traits either positively or negatively influence one's responses to stress. Individuals who believe that their life is controlled largely by events external to themselves often perceive less stress and are less likely to react negatively to surrounding events. However, those who perceive factors as being internal react more negatively to situations that are beyond their control. They are more likely to be proactive to situations within their control and engage in positive coping behaviors to change the environment and reduce stresses on themselves.

Role Conflict

Role conflicts occur when an individual has two competing roles, such as when a nurse manager both assumes a patient care assignment and needs to attend a leadership meeting. Another example is the conflict between nurses' personal roles as parents or spouses versus their roles as professional nurses.

Individual role conflict is the result of incompatibility between the individual's perception of the role and its actual requirements. Novice nurse managers experience this type of conflict when they find that administration expects primary loyalty to the organization and its goals, whereas the staff expects the nurse manager's first loyalty to be to their needs.

Role conflict within the profession places nursing at a distinct disadvantage in its relationship with other health care workers. Strife within the profession, differences in educational preparation, the structure of practice settings, and the role of labor and professional organizations contribute to the environment in which nurses must function. This conflict has its roots in a perceived poor regard for nurses. The felt lack of worth is complicated by divisiveness within the profession and the image nursing presents to others.

Role underload and *underutilization* can also occur. Being underutilized or not having much responsibility may be seen as stressful by a person who is a high achiever or who has high self-esteem.

Consequences of Stress

What happens to a person when stress overload occurs? Both physiological and psychological responses can cause structural or functional changes or both. Warning signs of too much stress are:

- Undue, prolonged anxiety, phobias, or a persistent state of fear or free-floating anxiety that seems to have many alternating causes
- Depression, which causes people to withdraw from family and friends, to be unable to experience emotions, and to feel helpless to change the situation
- Abrupt changes in mood and behavior, which may be exhibited as erratic behavior
- Perfectionism, which is the setting of unreasonably high standards for oneself and thereby being under constant stress
- Physical illnesses, such as an ulcer, arthritis, colitis, hypertension, myocardial infarction, and migraine headaches

Ineffective coping methods for reducing stress include excessive use of alcohol and other mood-altering substances, which can result in substance abuse or dependence. Some people become workaholics in an attempt to cope with real or imagined demands.

The term **burnout** refers to the perception that an individual has used up all available energy to perform the job and feels that he or she doesn't have enough energy to complete the task (Sherman, 2004). Burnout is a combination of physical fatigue, emotional exhaustion, and cognitive weariness. As a result, the individual may reduce hours worked or change to another profession.

Compassion fatigue is secondary traumatic stress experienced by caregivers (Figley, 2003; LaRow, 2008). Similar to posttraumatic stress disorder, the term originated in nursing in 1992 (Joinson, 1992). Today the term includes those involved in caring for others who are suffering from physical or emotional pain (Figley, 2003). Symptoms are similar to those of burnout but may be more severe if the caregiver is providing care to those traumatized by crime, war, and war-related traumatic stress or are emergency workers or first responders (Figley, 2008).

Job performance suffers during times of high stress; so much energy and attention are needed to manage the stress that little energy is available for performance. Also increased absenteeism and turnover may result. Although there are various causes of absenteeism (see Chapter 21) and turnover (see Chapter 20), both may occur when the individual attempts to withdraw from a stressful situation. Such a situation is financially costly in industry but even more costly in human health and well-being.

One director of nursing at a 120-bed nursing home stated that she could no longer handle the overwhelming needs of the patients; the ever-present shortage of qualified, caring nurses; and consistently dwindling resources. When a for-profit chain purchased the home and further reduced economic resources, the director of nursing left to become a real estate agent.

Managing Stress

We will always have factors in our lives that create stress. To manage those factors effectively and keep stress at levels that enhance one's performance rather than deplete energy, the key is to develop some resiliency. To accomplish this requires a comprehensive approach to managing stress, which involves planning, time, and energy.

PERSONAL METHODS

One of the first steps in managing stress is to recognize stressors in the environment (Graner, 2007). Nurses tend to think they can be "all things to all people." Therefore, it is important to improve one's self-awareness regarding stressors.

Keeping your life in balance is difficult, but it can be done (Heckerson & Laser, 2006). Caring for yourself physically (e.g., eating a well-balanced diet, exercising regularly, getting adequate sleep) and developing effective mental habits are also important for coping with stress. These effective habits include role redefinition, time management, and self-care. Development of interpersonal skills and identifying and nurturing social supports can also facilitate stress management.

Role Redefinition

Role redefinition involves clarifying roles and attempting to integrate or tie together the various roles individuals play. If there is role conflict or ambiguity, it is important to confront others by pointing out conflicting messages. Role redefinition may also involve renegotiation of roles in an attempt to lessen overload.

Much of the stress nurses and nurse managers experience results from the perception that staff, patient, and work-group needs must be met immediately and simultaneously. A notable method of coping with and reducing the stress of time is through time management. We determine how, where, and when our time is used. Time

is the essence of living, and it is the scarcest resource. Because the nurse manager has a limited amount of time, it is essential that time be used expeditiously. One lost hour a day every day for a year results in 260 hours of waste, or 6.5 weeks of missed opportunity, annually. (Time management is explained in Chapter 13.)

Self-care is, according to Sherman (2004, p. 52), "insulation against stress." Replenishing themselves and relaxation are essential for nurses to be able to care for others. This is not easy, especially for an individual with a high-stress job. Some relaxation methods are listening to music, reading, and socializing with friends. Developing outside interests, such as hobbies and recreational activities, can provide diversion and enjoyment and also can be a source of relaxation. Taking regular vacations, regardless of job pressures, is important for renewal and revitalization.

ORGANIZATIONAL METHODS

Nurse managers are often in the position of helping others identify their level of stress and stressors. If staff appear to be under a great deal of stress, the manager must help identify the source and decide how these can be reduced or eliminated. In addition to suggesting the techniques previously delineated, the manager should explore work-related sources of stress.

The manager must ask these questions:

- Is role ambiguity or conflict creating the stress?
- Can the manager help clarify individual staff members' roles, thereby reducing the conflict or ambiguity?
- Is the manager using an appropriate leadership style? (See Chapter 4.)
- Does the manager need to clarify a staff member's goals and eliminate barriers that are interfering with goal attainment? Involving staff in decision making is one way to identify and reduce such stress.
- Is the stress due to feelings of low self-worth?
- Would additional training or education help reduce the stress?
- Can I help by recognizing and reinforcing positive behaviors and accomplishments?
- Can other sources of support, such as the work group, help the individual deal with stress?
- Are counseling services available in the organization?

When stress is job-related, several strategies can be used. First, proper matching of the job with the applicant during the selection and hiring process is an important step in reducing stress (see Chapter 15). Skills training also reduces stress and promotes better performance and less turnover (see Chapter 17). Developing a program of job enrichment matched to the individual's goals and desires often increases autonomy and participation. In turn, greater participation in decisions increases job commitment and reduces stress.

Communication and social support are additional factors in reducing stress. Both upward and downward communication channels should be open. Keeping personnel informed about what is going on in an organization helps reduce suspicion and rumor. Team building encourages staff to build a network of support with each other.

Policies that reduce the stress of shift work also are important. The number of hours in the night shift, weekend, and holiday work assignments also affects the level of stress. Providing adequate opportunities for breaks and meals is an important function of the organization.

Leaders must manage their own stress and assist staff to manage theirs as well as work with the organization to reduce stress in the environment. See Case Study 24-1 for an example of how one nurse managed her own stress and helped her staff manage theirs.

Regardless of the work or life situation, everyone experiences stress, both positive and negative. It is how stress is handled that makes life interesting or excessively difficult. Stress-management strategies enable nurses to improve job performance and satisfaction.

CASE STUDY 24-1   Managing Stress

Madeline Mears, RN, is nurse manager of emergency services and critical care units at two corporately owned suburban hospitals. The corporation recently purchased three not-for-profit hospitals located in the urban center of the metropolitan area. Madeline and several other nurse mangers at the suburban hospitals were informed by the vice president for patient care services they will now be responsible for managing the same service lines at the newly acquired hospitals. Managers at the urban hospitals will move into charge nurse roles on their respective units.

Madeline has the challenge of effectively and efficiently managing emergency services and critical care units at five separate facilities all located within a 60-mile metropolitan radius. Her past experience in merging the management responsibilities at the two suburban hospitals will be extremely useful as she works to transition the new hospitals into the health care system.

Madeline anticipates that staff at the hospitals will be concerned over the changes in ownership and management. Some staff may be fearful of the unknown, worried about their jobs, while others may be excited at the opportunity for increased pay and job mobility in the health care system. Former managers at the hospitals may be angry about their demotion. Human resources representatives have indicated they will offer former managers the opportunity to apply for open management positions in the health care system.

Myriad reactions among the staff members are expected, as well as the potential for increased stress. Madeline and the other nurse managers meet and develop a transition plan. The transition plan defines the tasks, time frames, and expectations for merging the patient care units. Additionally, the plan helps decrease the stress Madeline and her fellow managers experience by organizing and delineating roles and responsibilities. Consistency in implementing change will help decrease stress among the staff at the urban hospitals. Each manager is committed to meeting with staff on each unit to address questions, concerns, and morale issues. Madeline plans to schedule a lunch meeting with each former manager to discuss the unit's strengths and weaknesses as well as her goals for the unit.

Three months into the transition, Madeline's units have had low turnover and staff members report they are satisfied with the new management structure. In particular, staff nurses enthusiastically accepted the clinical ladder promotion program and evidence-based practice implementation. Two of the former managers have moved into management roles in the health care system. The transition has been stressful but Madeline has enjoyed the opportunity to stretch her leadership skills.

Manager's Checklist

The nurse manager is responsible to:

- Recognize the impact of stress, both positive and negative, on themselves and their staff
- Utilize personal and professional strategies to identify stressors and develop a plan to manage stress
- Communicate openly and honestly with employees who are stressed in their work environment
- Use creative solutions to address stress so employees are able to effectively perform their jobs
- Assess the effectiveness of solutions and adjust as necessary

What You Know Now

- Stress is a person's reaction to demands from the environment.
- Stress can be both positive and negative; regardless, the physiological response is the same.
- Causes of stress come from organizational, interpersonal, and individual factors.
- Stress can cause physical and psychological problems, including burnout and compassion fatigue.
- Individuals can help manage stress by recognizing stressors, redefining roles, time management, and self-care.
- Managers can help their staff and themselves manage stress.
- Organizations can support employees to manage work-related stress by matching applicants to appropriate jobs, providing skills training, offering support, using participative management, and referring over-stressed employees for counseling.

Tools for Managing Stress

1. Recognize that stress is necessary for life.
2. Acknowledge the impact of stress, both positive and negative, on professional and personal life.
3. Review your stress-management strategies and evaluate them for effectiveness.
4. If you are experiencing an exceptional amount of stress, try to identify the source and try various ways to reduce your stress.
5. Pay attention to your stress levels and try to create opportunities to help deal with stress.

Questions to Challenge You

1. What causes you the most stress?
2. What methods do you use to cope with stress?
3. Have you seen others respond negatively to stress? Explain what happened.
4. Have you experienced any of the consequences of stress described in the chapter? How did you handle it? Explain.
5. Have you experienced role ambiguity or role conflict? Describe the situation. How did you handle it?
6. What ways do you care for yourself? What other ways might you add to your repertoire of self-care skills?

Explore MediaLink 🌐

Additional interactive resources for this chapter can be found on the Website at http://www.prenhall.com/sullivan. Click on Chapter 24 to select activities for this chapter.

- Video Overview
- NCLEX® Review Questions
- Critical Thinking Activities
- Current Events
- Nursing Leadership and Management in Action
- MediaLinks

References

Figley, C. R. (2003). *Treating compassion fatigue.* New York: Routledge.

Figley, C. R. (2008). Compassion fatigue: An introduction. Retrieved February 2008 from http://mailer.fsu.edu/~cfigley/CFintro.html

Graner, B. (2007). Break the cycle of stress with PBR [3]. *American Nurse Today, 2*(5), 56–57.

Heckerson, E. W., & Laser, C. S. (2006). Just breathe! The critical importance of maintaining a work-life balance. *Nurse Leader, 4*(6), 26–28.

Joinson, C. (1992). Coping with compassion fatigue. *Nursing, 22*(4), 116–122.

Kramer, M. (1974). *Reality shock.* St. Louis, MO: Mosby.

LaRow, K. D. (2008). *Breath of relief: Transforming compassion fatigue into flow* (2nd ed.). Boston, MA: Acanthus.

Rushton, C. H. (2007). Meaningful recognition: Make it happen! *American Nurse Today, 2*(1), 33–34.

Selye, H. (1978). *The stress of life* (2nd ed.). New York: McGraw-Hill.

Sherman, D. W. (2004). Nurses' stress & burnout: How to care for yourself when caring for patients and their families experiencing life-threatening illness. *American Journal of Nursing, 104*(5), 48–56.

Steers, R. (1991). *Introduction to organizational behavior* (4th ed.). Santa Monica, CA: Goodyear.

CHAPTER 25

Advancing Your Career

Learning Outcomes

After completing this chapter, you will be able to:

1. Describe how you envision your future.
2. Discuss how to obtain your first job.
3. Build a résumé.
4. Explain how to find and use mentors.
5. Explain how to find your next job.
6. Discuss what to do when your plans fail.

MediaLink

www.prenhall.com/sullivan
See the Companion Website for chapter-specific resources at
www.prenhall.com/sullivan.

Key Terms

Envisioning Your Future

The future is always uncertain, which leads many to believe they cannot do anything about it. The future, however, is shaped by human decisions and actions, including our own, made daily. What any one person cannot do is control the future. Nonetheless, we are affecting the future by what we do today or what we fail to do.

The future seems like something over which we have so little control that it isn't realistic to plan for it. Wait to see what happens, try to handle the circumstances, and hope for the best, is as much planning as most people do.

Instead, imagine yourself in one year, creating in your mind the life you most desire. What are you doing? What have you done over the course of the past year?

Now imagine what you are doing in 5 years. How about what you are doing in 10 years? Finally, what will you be doing right before you retire? Will you be satisfied with what you've done? What do you wish you had done?

A nurse met with the advisor in a baccalaureate program designed for RNs. After talking about the requirements of the program, the classes she needed, and her own schedule, they concluded that by taking one course a semester, it would take the nurse 5 years to complete the program. The RN looked discouraged. The advisor asked her what was wrong.

"If I enroll in this program I'll be 35 in 5 years," she said.

The advisor smiled. "Yes, and you'll be 35 in 5 years if you don't."

Acquiring Your First Position

The first step, after you've completed your basic nursing education, is to select your first job. The purpose of this job is to learn as much as you can and to perfect your clinical skills. Additionally, you will make contacts among your colleagues and supervisors.

Here are some criteria for choosing your first job.

- You will have opportunity to hone your skills in a clinical area of interest.

- You will learn from more experienced clinicians who are willing to teach you.
- The culture of the organization and, especially, the administration are supportive of nursing.
- The organization's mission fits your values (e.g., a teaching hospital that serves the poor).
- There are opportunities for advancement.

No job is perfect, just as no relationship, home, career, or family is perfect. Use the above criteria to assess the position and the organization. If the position and the organization fit most of them, especially the criteria most important to you, consider the following additional criteria.

- The schedule fits your lifestyle.
- The institution is near your home.

The least important criteria for selecting your first job is the salary. A small amount more in your hourly pay is worth much less than opportunities to help meet your future goals. Remember, you have a long time to be in your career; don't sacrifice opportunities in the future for a slight difference in salary now.

APPLYING FOR THE POSITION

Some organizations ask you to fill out an application, either online, by mail, or in person; others request a résumé. A **résumé** is a written record of your educational achievements, employment, and accomplishments. (See Sample Résumé.) Your résumé might also include your immediate professional goal, such as "gain clinical experience" and/or your long-term goal, such as "become a manager."

Education includes:

- Degrees, institutions, years attended, graduation date (actual or expected)
- Specialty training
- Continuing education

Employment includes:

- Positions held
- Names of employers
- Dates of employment

Accomplishments might include:

- Volunteer service, such as helping in a homeless shelter
- Organizational service, such as serving as student body president

- Awards won, such as Outstanding Junior Student

See Box 25-1 for an example of a résumé of a new graduate.

Once you have applied for a position and the organization contacts you to say a representative is interested

---

BOX 25-1   Sample Résumé

Chloe R. Stevenson, R.N., B.S.N.
5625 Summit Lane
Overland Park, Kansas 66222
913.555.2222
chloestevenson@anyprovider.net

Objective
To obtain a position as a professional registered nurse in dynamic intensive care unit which will utilize my strong clinical skills, work ethic, problem solving ability, and passion for providing superior patient care.

Work Experience

Registered Nurse

May 2007–Present Telemetry Unit, Memorial Hospital, Overland Park, KS

- Currently providing direct patient care to a variety of cardiac and post-operative cardiac patients on a 30-bed telemetry unit.
- Clinical duties include assessment, medication administration, including titration of cardiac IV medications, cardiac monitoring, and all other aspects of nursing care.
- Actively develop, implement, and monitor individualized patient plans of care as well as documenting patient response and outcomes.
- ACLS certified and leader of unit Critical Response Team.
- Member of Evidenced Based Practice Committee for Cardiology Services.

Patient Care Technician

January 2006 – May 2007 Telemetry Unit, Memorial Hospital, Overland Park, KS

- Worked under the supervision of an RN, provided direct patient care, including taking vital signs, dressing changes, bathing, ambulation of patients, and assisting with the admission and discharge process.
- Responsible for appropriate clinical documentation.
- Trained to perform 12-lead EKGs as well as cardiac monitoring.
- Served on unit Quality Improvement Team.

Education

- Bachelor of Science in Nursing, May 2007
  University of Kansas, Lawrence, KS
  GPA: 3.7/4.0
- Registered Nurse, State of Kansas, June 2007
- Advanced Cardiac Life Support (ACLS) certified, August 2007

Awards

Jane Smith Award for Excellence in Clinical Nursing, May 2007

- Awarded by faculty to the senior nursing student who demonstrates excellence in clinical skills and academic coursework.

References available upon request

in meeting you, you will agree on a time and place for an interview. The interview is your chance (sometimes your only chance) to sell yourself to a potential employer. Make no mistake: if you can't sell yourself, no one can. You need to prepare for your interview just as you would for any other important meeting. That includes knowing who you are meeting, learning as much as you can about the organization, and anticipating questions you might be asked.

THE INTERVIEW

The purpose of an interview is twofold: for a potential employer to learn about you and for you to learn about the organization. Ideally, the two of you will discover if there is a role for you in the organization, what is known as a good "fit."

To prepare for the interview itself, identify:

- What you want to know about the position and the organization
- What questions you might be asked about your education or past experiences. Be prepared to describe briefly your achievements.
- What you think your strengths and weaknesses are and how those fit with your potential employer's needs
- What additional information you want about the organization and the job

Find out who will be interviewing you and ask the person's position and role in the organization. You may interview with someone in the human resources office as well as the person who would be your supervisor.

Be especially courteous to office staff; they have the power to smooth your way or report your behavior to their boss. Try to schedule your interview for a time when you can be rested and unhurried, not right after a long day at work or when you must be somewhere else immediately afterward.

You will probably be sent some information about the organization or you can ask for it if not. A position description is essential. You can use it to compare to your qualifications. Also, the organization's mission statement, vision for the future, and goals might be included. (See Chapter 2 for examples.)

An organizational chart also is helpful, but not always available. The important information for you is where this position fits in the organizational structure. That will tell you to whom you would report and that person's reporting relationship. The most direct line to top administration is the most powerful.

For the interview, take along a copy of your résumé even if you filled out an application. You can refer to it if you are asked to explain an item. Ask for explicit directions to the building and office where you will go and plan to arrive a few minutes early. Prepare yourself mentally by reminding yourself of the qualifications you bring to the position, noting items on the position description that fit you. Enter the office with confidence, smile, and shake hands firmly.

To consider what questions you might be asked in an interview, see examples of general questions in Table 25-1 and review Table 15-1 for examples of behavioral interview questions. In addition, you will be asked questions about your education and work history. Answer questions honestly, but don't feel you must explain anything you are not asked. You will have an opportunity to ask your questions about the position and the organization. Be sure you are prepared to do so. A candidate who has no questions suggests lack of interest or expertise.

Most interviewers today understand what questions are legal to ask and what are not. You are not required to answer questions about how many children you have, their ages, or your marital status, for example.

TABLE 25-1	Examples of Interview Questions

YOUR CURRENT JOB

What do you do in your present job?

What do you like best about your present job?

What do you like least?

Why do you want to leave your present job?

YOUR ACHIEVEMENTS AND GOALS

What are you most proud of accomplishing?

What do you think you do especially well?

What are your areas of weakness?

What are your long-term goals?

What do you plan to do to meet your goals?

YOUR INTEREST IN THE POSITION

Why are you interested in this position?

What do you see yourself doing next?

Why do you think you are right for this position?

Is there anything you would like to add about your qualifications that we haven't already discussed?

From *Becoming Influential: A Guide for Nurses* by E. J. Sullivan (2004). Upper Saddle River, NJ: Prentice Hall Health. Used with permission.

(See Table 15-2 for questions that are illegal to ask.) Just being asked such questions indicates an organizational bias, and you might want to reconsider your interest in the organization. Chapter 15 also includes information about interviewing from the employer's position.

After the Interview

Send a post-interview thank you letter within 24 hours of the interview, says career guru Donna Cardillo (2001), to everyone who interviewed you. Your letter can be handwritten on nice quality note paper (nothing cutesy) or word processed on nice stationery. It should be brief, thanking the interviewer for interest in you and saying that you enjoyed the meeting. Include a few words summing up your qualifications that fit the position and end by saying that you are looking forward to hearing from her or him soon.

A Second Interview

It is not unusual to have a second interview if you have passed initial scrutiny and appear to be an appropriate candidate for the position. The second interview usually includes colleagues and managers with whom you will work. You will probably tour the unit and meet potential coworkers, giving you an opportunity to assess the environment.

Situational questions are often asked at this time. For example, you are given a scenario and asked how you would handle the situation. Take your time to think through an answer. Obviously they think you can handle such situations because you have been asked back. Keep your answer short and to the point. Your goal is to show you are a competent, confident professional (Cardillo, 2002a).

Interviewing with potential coworkers is also your opportunity to find out what you want to know about the specific responsibilities and challenges of the position. You might ask, "What are the most pressing problems facing the unit?" or "What do you need most from a nurse practitioner in this clinic?"

You will probably be asked if you are still interested in the position. If you are, ask when a hiring decision will be made. Following this interview, again send thank you letters but only to the new people who have interviewed you.

ACCEPTING THE POSITION

When you are offered the position, you have an opportunity to negotiate. Don't ignore this opportunity in your excitement of getting the job.

Salary is usually the main topic for negotiation. Most employers have some flexibility with salary if they have a justifiable reason for it, but they will seldom tell you that. It is much more common to offer the lowest salary they think they can and see if the candidate asks for more. Ask for more than you would accept, but don't get carried away. Asking for a salary way above comparable amounts is not only unprofessional, but it makes you appear to be more interested in the money than the job.

You can negotiate for scheduling as long as it doesn't make you too different from others in similar positions. You might also negotiate for other perks, such as a parking place or vacation days, but acquiring those are unlikely unless others have them too. Management cannot appear to give you such obvious perks that are more than other employees who have been with them longer receive. You want to start your new job on an even footing with coworkers.

Follow up your verbal agreement accepting the position with a formal letter of acceptance to the administrator who hired you. Thank the individual for having confidence in you and your potential, and state again how pleased you are to be joining the organization.

DECLINING THE POSITION

Sometimes you will decide not to accept a position offered to you. It might not be the right job, at the right time, or in the right organization. Be sure to let the appropriate person know your intention as soon as possible. Thank him or her for the offer and the confidence the organization has in you. Explain briefly why you cannot accept at this time and state that you hope the organization will keep you in mind in the future. Follow up with a letter as well. Even if you are not interested in this position or this organization, someone there might prove valuable in referring another organization to you in the future, for example. Your career will be long; never alienate potential connections.

Building a Résumé

Once you have accepted your first position, it is time to think about what you will need to advance in your career.

The first step is to assess yourself. Identify:

- Your personality, values, beliefs, likes, and dislikes
- Your lifestyle
- Your family
- Your friends and social life

- Your hobbies and personal activities
- Your vision of your future
- Your skills
- Your knowledge
- Your nursing preferences

The last item refers to the areas of nursing that suit you best. This may take some time and experience in practice. Then ask yourself:

- Do you like a fast-paced environment, such as an ER, OR, or trauma care?
- Do you prefer to have time with your patients? Rehabilitation nursing, a medical floor, or long-term care might suit you better.
- Which patient conditions and treatments do you prefer?
- What patient conditions intrigue you the most? Cardiac problems, psychiatric conditions, or diagnostics (e.g., GI lab)?
- Would you like to work in a clinic, medical office, in home care, or in public health?
- Would you enjoy school nursing or occupational health?

This assessment is not done quickly; it involves a period of time in practice, introspection, asking friends and family members for their thoughts about you, and learning from reading or attending programs. It is also flexible and responsive to ways in which you grow and change. Your family and social life changes also, sometimes making adjustments in your plan necessary.

The next step is to assess the environment.

Consider what might change in the health care system, a change that has come more and more rapidly. Does the country's economic or political system portend a major change in health care financing? Are any new medications or vaccines pending that might eliminate current jobs or create new opportunities for you? Are any new educational programs being proposed?

The clinical nurse leader, as explained in Chapter 4, is an example. As advances in transplant technology proliferate, new specialties of nurses and physicians are created. Today's noninvasive technology for monitoring and treating patients for a variety of ills and from a distance suggests that many changes in clinical care may be on the horizon.

There are many ways to learn about the environment. Certainly, paying attention to popular media reports on scientific breakthroughs and advances in technology is one way. Reading your professional literature or attending programs in your interest area is another.

Joining a professional or specialty organization and receiving its newsletters and journals is especially useful because those target your interests.

Observing others may prove worthwhile. Many people chose their career path after watching more experienced members of the profession. Nurses who pursue teaching and administration often do so after working with an especially competent role model.

Talking with experts, colleagues, and administrators is also valuable. Keep alert to what you hear, evaluate its credibility, and assess its usefulness to you. Gathering information is an ongoing process. Your plan will not be fixed; it will change in response to changes in your life, your goals, and the environment.

Once you have assessed yourself and the environment, determine what your options are. Include legal constraints or possibilities (e.g., is the nurse practice law in your state going to be changed to allow more privileges for nurse practitioners?), new programs proposed (e.g., a local university is starting an acute care nurse practitioner program), your own desires (e.g., doctoral education to become a nurse researcher), and how willing you are or might become to relocate, go into debt, or sacrifice the time to reach your goal. The latter issues are likely to change over time as your family life or lifestyle changes.

Evaluate what experiences you need and where you might get those from a continuing education program, on-the-job training, a certificate offered by your institution's education department, or a graduate degree. Is there a license or certification you need? What organizations, such as working at a trauma center or accepting a leadership position in your chapter of Sigma Theta Tau International, could help you achieve your goals? Are there publications or online resources that would help?

Nursing offers an incredible array of opportunities in clinical areas as diverse as cardiac surgery and trauma care to home health and rehabilitation nursing. You can be a clinician or a specialist, a teacher, administrator, or researcher. You can become an entrepreneur, an information systems specialist, branch into pharmaceutical sales, or, for that matter, write books about nursing, all the while being a nurse. See how one nurse advanced his career in Case Study 25-1.

Consider your plan long-term and flexible. No one knows what will happen in his or her own life or in the environment over time, or what opportunities may emerge. Keep an open mind; talk to other professionals; explore your interests. What we do know is that we are contributing to our own future by what we do today or what we fail to do.

CASE STUDY 25-1 — Advancing Your Career

Trevor Briggs, RN, BSN, has worked as the operating room supervisor for the past 4 years. The department has used a stand-alone clinical information system for the past 2 years and Trevor has been an integral part of the successful implementation of technology in the OR. In addition to training staff to use the system, Trevor has worked with the IT vendor to enhance the system's capabilities. Recently, Trevor was appointed by his nurse manager to serve on a hospital-wide clinical information system selection committee. Administration has initiated the process of selecting an integrated clinical information system and is seeking input from each service line.

Trevor enjoys working with the committee and learning about the implementation processes. The chief information officer met with the committee and announced the creation of a new role, clinical systems team leader. Team leaders will be nurses who are specially trained to work with the IT department in implementing the new clinical information system. Trevor's background with the OR system makes him an excellent candidate for the team leader position. After interviewing with the IT department manager, Trevor is selected as a clinical systems team leader. Trevor also learns the hospital is willing to pay for specialized training, including tuition reimbursement for graduate classes.

To increase his knowledge of information systems, Trevor enrolls in a master of information management systems program at the city university. After completing the initial 12 hours of his masters program, Trevor must decide whether to pursue a specialty track in software development or project management. Trevor reviews market trends to determine the best option and also considers his personal preferences. He also takes the time to meet with an instructor in the masters program who is an informatics nurse specialist and has worked in the IT field for 10 years. Trevor decides to pursue a track in project management, which will allow him to utilize his strong leadership and people management skills. After completing his masters degree, Trevor is promoted to clinical systems nurse manager and is pursuing certification in nursing informatics.

Manager's Checklist

The nurse is responsible to:

- Determine what career track best suits individual skills, talents, and interests.
- Look for opportunities to enhance skills and knowledge outside of your current career.
- Analyze market trends for emerging roles.
- Network with experts and mentors in the field that may present opportunities.

TRACKING YOUR PROGRESS

Keep an **activity log** to track everything you are doing so that when the time comes to apply for a new position you are not frantically trying to remember your accomplishments, what continuing education programs you took, or when you completed a course at your hospital. Note the name of the program, activity, certification, or accomplishments, add the dates, who sponsored it and where, and note anything special you received or learned. Include a list of accomplishments on your job, such as teaching a class or preceptoring students, or skills you've acquired. Include any cross-training as well. Table 25-2 shows an example of a format you could use.

Every item on your activity log will not go on every résumé. A résumé must be crafted to meet the purpose you have for submitting it. For example, the résumé you submit to an organization to be considered for membership differs from one you would use to apply to graduate school. Having a comprehensive list of all your activities and accomplishments helps ensure that

when you put together an application or submit your résumé, you will be less likely to forget some of your achievements.

You will want to keep track of your expenses as well. Those can be noted in your activity log or in a separate file noted by year; they come in handy at tax time. A document on your computer or a notebook can be used, and it helps to keep continuing education (CE) certificates and receipts in a file as well.

Another advantage of keeping a record of your activities is that you can quickly see if you are meeting your goals (see Chapter 13). A quick perusal of your list might show you what else you need to do.

IDENTIFYING YOUR LEARNING NEEDS

Pursuing a career involves lifelong learning (Smalley, 2005). You can learn in many ways. Online courses, graduate school, short-term certificate programs, books, journals, and professional meetings are just a few of the ways you can acquire the knowledge you need.

TABLE 25-2	Activity Log for Career Progress
ACTIVITY	**CONTENT**
Education earned	Include names of schools, location, dates attended, degrees
Employment	Include all positions, including summer jobs and part-time or full-time work while in school
Licenses	Include license number and state
Certificates/Credentials	Include name, date earned, sponsoring organization
Professional Organizations	Include name, date joined, any committees or offices held with dates
Publications	Include title, name of publication, date
Volunteer Activities	Include name of organization and your participation
Accomplishments	Include accomplishments from your job, professional activities, volunteer experiences

From *Becoming Influential: A Guide for Nurses* by E. J. Sullivan (2004). Upper Saddle River, NJ: Prentice Hall Health. Used with permission.

To develop skills, however, you need experience. Several options are possible.

Baccalaureate Education for RNs

Today, many RNs have added a baccalaureate degree in nursing to their basic education from a hospital diploma program or an associate degree from a community college. They recognize that a baccalaureate degree will help qualify them for management positions and, for many, prepare them for graduate education. Most baccalaureate programs in nursing have an option for RNs to complete their degrees without repeating content from their basic program. Many even offer their programs online for busy professionals.

Graduate Education

Graduate school, in either a masters or doctoral program, offers both didactic content and experience, which might be clinical for a practitioner program or research in a doctoral program, depending on your goals. If you want to be a nurse practitioner, teach nursing, become a nurse researcher, or advance as an administrator, you need graduate education.

Choosing a graduate program is a difficult and time-consuming endeavor. You must learn as much as you can about the program, its requirements, and its graduates' success to determine if the program will meet your needs. Gather literature, meet with admissions staff and faculty, and talk to students and colleagues. Compare national rankings of the schools that interest you. Request names of recent graduates to contact for references for the program and interview them. Ask advice from your teachers, supervisors, and preceptors.

This is one of the most important decisions you will make in your career. It can also be the most valuable.

Take your time, consider your options, and be fully committed before you enroll.

Many options are available to pay for graduate school education. As with the decision to select a school and a program, finding sources of funding takes perseverance. The school's financial aid office can help you locate loans and scholarships. Service clubs, such as Rotary International, support nursing scholarships.

Knowing your long-term goal helps, especially if you are interested in an area of need. For example, a nursing faculty shortage is increasing as retirements thin the ranks of today's teachers. Nurse practitioners to work in disadvantaged areas are also needed, and some scholarships exist for nurses who agree to provide care in these areas for a period of time after graduation. The military, also, offers scholarships in return for a service commitment.

Continuing Education

Finding continuing education to further your career is not difficult; determining the quality of the program is not as easy. If you receive information about a program that interests you and fits with your career goals, evaluate the information using the following:

- Is the program sponsored by a known organization, such as a college or professional association?
- Who are the speakers? Are their credentials appropriate to their presentations?
- Is the content appropriate to you at this stage in your development, neither too advanced nor too elementary?
- Can you obtain financial assistance to attend and, if you do, what do you owe the organization? Bringing back a report of a program you've attended

is an excellent way to reinforce your own learning, and it gives you an opportunity to speak in public as well.

- Consider attending even if you must pay your own way. You may be able to deduct the expense on your taxes and, after all, you and your career are the beneficiary.
- Can you arrange to be off work, if necessary, and afford the time and expense?

Professional Associations

Membership in professional associations offers many opportunities for learning. Journals, newsletters, e-mails, conventions, programs, and books are just the beginning. The opportunity to meet and network with your colleagues and senior people in the profession and to learn by serving on committees, task forces, and boards is immense. Many successful nurses began their career by participating in a professional association.

Nursing associations cover every specialty and interest. Membership in the American Nurses Association is open to all registered nurses through its constituent member associations. Sigma Theta Tau International has more than 400 chapters affiliated with schools of nursing around the world. Specialty organizations exist for nurses who work in many clinical areas, such as the American Association of Critical Care Nurses or the American Psychiatric Nurses Association. Each of these organizations has divisions, committees, and boards where your time and talents are welcomed.

Finding and Using Mentors

One of the most important tasks in your career is to identify and cultivate mentor relationships. A **mentor** is a person who has more experience than you and is willing to help you progress in your career. A mentor introduces you to key people, and tells you what you need to know and do to move ahead. A mentor provides opportunities for learning, counsels you on mistakes, and takes pride in your successes.

A mentor may be a senior nurse or in another closely aligned profession, mostly because the mentor must have contacts that can be useful to your career. Often you work for the same organization, but that is not a requirement. You can have more than one mentor but usually not at one time.

You might identify someone you would like to be your mentor or the mentor might select you. The arrangement of mentor and mentee, however, is rarely named as such. Usually, you find yourself relying more and more on one or two people for advice, or a mentor singles you out for special opportunities or assignments. If any of those do not work out especially well or if the two of you don't seem to be compatible, nothing is lost. You both go on your way without any bad feelings. A person becomes a mentor when positive experiences accumulate, bringing satisfaction to you both.

A number of benefits accrue for both you and your mentor. You gain a sense of accomplishment by working with a mentor, and the mentor acquires fulfillment from contributing to you, and by extension, to your profession. People senior in the field have a responsibility to pass along what they've learned and to prepare those who come after them. These are the satisfactions of a career done well.

The time will come, however, when you move away from your mentor. You take a new job or your mentor does. Your relationship changes as a result. You may then become colleagues and friends, and you may acquire a new mentor in the new organization. Sometimes you will move ahead of the mentor, a situation that requires tact and commitment from both of you. Accomplished professional people know that they will always owe a debt to their mentor, and they will continue to show their appreciation in large and small ways.

Considering Your Next Position

The time to think about your next job is when you accept the first one. Begin to assess how much you can learn in this job and think about your next step. Take every opportunity you can to learn.

One new grad had already determined that she wanted to teach nursing but she knew she needed clinical experience before she went on to graduate school. She used each clinical experience as a learning opportunity. She made notes on the patients she cared for and later looked up their conditions, treatments, and meds on her time off from work. In less than a year, she had compiled a study guide full of her own notes. She began graduate school full-time and continued to work part-time, continuing to add notes throughout her graduate school experience. By the time she graduated, she was an experienced clinician although the actual hours she spent in clinical work were less than most of the other new nurse faculty.

FINDING YOUR NEXT POSITION

Because jobs are plentiful in nursing today and into the foreseeable future, you have many opportunities for finding the next job in your career. This move must not be taken lightly, however, no matter how many jobs are available. This is where your self-assessment is essential. You want to be certain you are ready to leave your current job, that you have learned and accomplished what you came there to do, that you will not be leaving at a crucial time (e.g., imminent Joint Commission visit), and that you have selected the job that fits your needs now.

When you are ready, there are many ways to find potential positions. Online sources are plentiful. Nurse.com is one (www.nurse.com/jobs). Professional associations offer job search services: Sigma Theta Tau International at http://stti.monster.com, and the American Nurses Association at www.nursecareercenter.com.

Career fairs, ads in newspapers and nursing publications, and faculty from the school where you graduated are additional ways to inquire about opportunities and to let others know you are interested in considering future options.

LEAVING YOUR PRESENT POSITION

Just as there is a way to finding a job, so too is there a best way to leave a job, says nursing career expert Donna Cardillo (2002b). First, check to see how much notice your employer requires. Tell your supervisor as soon as you have accepted the new position, and follow up with a formal letter of resignation. It is a good idea, Cardillo says, to add some friendly comments, regardless of how you feel about the organization, your coworkers, or the supervisor. Your goal is to leave on good terms.

Resist the urge to just walk out, regardless of the situation. The only reason for doing this would be that you are in physical danger, and the organization is not providing adequately for your safety, a rare, though not unknown, situation.

Always be polite in your interactions with your coworkers and your supervisor. Resist, also, the urge to belittle the organization or the administration. Negative comments about others reflect mostly on you. Of course, don't say anything that is untrue. If the situation is difficult, the other employees know it as well. You needn't say anything at all, even if you're asked. You never know what the future will bring, and ending relationships politely is best for your future.

When Your Plans Fail

Be assured that the future you envision will not work exactly as you hope (it might work out better), and you will make mistakes. All successful people take risks, and all have failed at some point in their careers. What makes their career progress significant, however, is that they learn from their mistakes and are willing to go on when external events affect their plans.

TAKING THE WRONG JOB

Sometimes you will take a job that is not the right one for you. Maybe you thought you were ready for a management job, but you were overwhelmed with the responsibility. No job turns out exactly the way we thought it would, but sometimes the disconnect between our expectations and what actually happens is so far apart that we cannot continue.

Maybe you took the right job but for the wrong reason. You wanted a faster-paced environment and accepted a position in a busy surgical ICU, working nights. You soon discover that the pressure, your loss of sleep, and the acuity of your patients is more than you can handle.

When you think you may have made a mistake, try to get some advice from someone you trust. An advisor, teacher, or a mentor may be able to help you sort out what's wrong. It may not be the job. Maybe you need a brief period of counseling or to learn better ways to handle stress. (Also see Chapter 24, "Managing Stress.")

If you decide you must leave this job, do so with as much care as you can. You will undoubtedly be leaving your employer in a difficult position so you want to do everything you can to help. Also, having a short-term employment on your résumé is generally seen as negative, so you want to be able to explain this experience in the future and have your employer able to report that you did all you could to help the organization once you realized you did not fit the job.

ADAPTING TO CHANGE

Every day change is occurring in health care, and the pace of change seems to come faster and faster. To pursue the career you want and to find satisfaction in that career requires you to be able to adjust and respond to change. The most important attribute you can bring to this effort is to remain flexible. The courage to change

MediaLink Taking the Wrong Job

direction is essential for nurses, according to Shaffer (2006).

Marika, experienced in psychiatric nursing and home care, entered a masters program, intending to apply as a mental health clinical specialist for a home health care agency. During graduate school she learned that the agency's reimbursement for the service had dropped, and they were discontinuing the position. Fortunately, Marika had a backup plan. She changed course, continued on in graduate school, and obtained her doctorate. She became a nursing faculty member and researched mental health problems in patients with home care needs.

Other events can change your future. Your spouse is offered a job in another part of the country. You find you're going to become a parent. Your parents need more care than you have been providing. When events intrude on your plan, you may need to adjust your time schedule, taking graduate classes slower, for example.

Life is a work in progress. We never know what our future will bring. Allow for unplanned events, such as illness, pregnancy, or your hospital closing. Plan for contingencies, but keep your eye on your vision. Remain flexible. You might discover that new opportunities await you, bringing a better future than one you had imagined.

What You Know Now

- You have learned how to envision your future.
- You have learned how to select your first position, and how to apply, interview, and accept or decline the position.
- You have learned how to create and build a résumé.
- You have learned how to track your progress and identify your learning needs.
- You have learned how to find and use mentors.
- You have learned how to find your next position and leave your current one.
- You have learned that flexibility is needed to adapt to change.

Tools for Advancing Your Career

1. Select positions and professional activities that further your short- and long-term goals.
2. Keep a log of your activities and accomplishments.
3. Keep abreast of the health care and policy environment, noting possibilities for your future.
4. Evaluate educational opportunities for their appropriateness for your learning needs and career advancement.
5. Identify and cultivate mentor relationships.
6. Evaluate your progress periodically and update with new information or interests.

Questions to Challenge You

1. Answer the questions posed in the chapter about how you envision your future. Is the study or work you are currently doing helping you progress toward that future? If not, what do you need to do to help yourself?
2. Create or review your résumé. Is it up to date? If not, add the necessary information. Take a few moments to ponder your accomplishments.
3. Do you have a mentor? Evaluate that relationship. What more might you want from your interactions with your mentor? How might that occur?
4. What educational needs do you have? Investigate potential opportunities to acquire the necessary education.
5. Have you ever had your professional plans fail? What, if anything, would you do differently in the future?

Explore MediaLink 🌐

Additional interactive resources for this chapter can be found on the Website at http://www.prenhall. com/sullivan. Click on Chapter 25 to select activities for this chapter.

- Video Overview
- NCLEX® Review Questions
- Critical Thinking Activities
- Current Events
- Nursing Leadership and Management in Action
- MediaLinks

References

Cardillo, D. (2001). Dear Donna delivers plain FAQs. *Nursing Spectrum*, 2(3), 12.

Cardillo, D. (2002a). Dear Donna delivers plain FAQs. *Nursing Spectrum*, 3(3), 16mw.

Cardillo, D. (2002b). How to resign with style. *Nursing Spectrum*, 3(2), 11.

Shaffer, J. (2006). Cultivating personal courage. *American Nurse Today*, 1(10), 52–53.

Smalley, J. (2005). What's your nursing philosophy? *Nursing Management*, 36(12), 59–61.

Sullivan, E. J. (2004). *Becoming influential: A guide for nurses.* Upper Saddle River, NJ: Prentice Hall Health.

GLOSSARY

4 Ps of marketing   Four strategies included in marketing plans: product, place, price, and promotion.

A

Absence culture   The informal norms within a work unit that determine how employees of that unit view absenteeism.

Absence frequency   The total number of distinct absence periods, regardless of their duration.

Accommodating   An unassertive, cooperative tactic used in conflict management when individuals neglect their own concerns in favor of others' concerns.

Accountability   The act of accepting ownership for the results or lack thereof.

Achievement-oriented leadership   A leadership style that includes goal setting and maintaining high levels of performance in order to motivate employees.

Activity log   An ongoing record of professional progress, including educational programs, training, certifications, and accomplishments.

Adaptive decisions   The type of decisions made when problems and alternative solutions are somewhat unusual and only partially understood.

Additive task   A task in which group performance depends on the sum of individual performance.

Adjourning   The final stage of group development in which a group dissolves after achieving its objectives.

Adult education theory   A theory, described by Knowles, that children and adults learn differently.

Age Discrimination Act   A law prohibiting discrimination against applicants and employees over the age of 40.

Ambiguous evaluation standards problem   The tendency of evaluators to place differing connotations on rating scale words.

Americans with Disabilities Act   A law prohibiting discrimination against qualified individuals who have physical or mental impairments that substantially limit one or more of the major life activities.

Artificial intelligence   Computer technology that can diagnose problems and make limited decisions.

Assignment   Allocating tasks appropriate to the individual's job description.

Attendance barriers   The events that affect an employee's ability to attend (e.g., illness, family responsibilities).

Authority   The right to act or empower.

Autocratic leadership   A leadership style that assumes individuals are motivated by external forces; therefore, the leader makes all the decisions and directs the followers' behavior.

Avoiding   A conflict management technique in which the participants deny that conflict exists.

B

Bargaining agent   A union certified by the NLRB to conduct labor negotiations for a group of individuals.

Behavioral interviewing   Interview questions that use the candidates's past performance and behaviors to predict behavior on the job.

Behavior-oriented rating scales   A type of scale used in evaluation that focuses on specific behaviors and uses critical incidents grouped into performance dimensions.

Benchmarking   A method of comparing performance using identified quality indicators across institutions or disciplines.

Benefit time   Paid time, such as vacation, holidays, and sick days for which there is no work output.

Block staffing   Scheduling a set staff mix for every shift so that adequate staff is available at all times.

Bona fide occupational qualification (BFOQ)   A characteristic that excludes certain groups from consideration for employment.

Brainstorming   A decision-making method in which group members meet and generate diverse ideas about the nature, cause, definition, or solution to a problem.

Budget   A quantitative statement, usually in monetary terms, of the expectations of a defined area of the organization over a specified period of time in order to manage financial performance.

Budgeting   The process of planning and controlling future operations by comparing actual results with planned expectations.

Bureaucracy   A term proposed by Max Weber to define the ideal, intentionally rational, most efficient form of organization.

Bureaucratic leadership   A leadership style that assumes individuals are motivated by external forces; leader trusts neither followers nor self to make decisions and therefore relies on organizational policies and rules.

Burnout   The perception that an individual has used up all available energy to perform the job and feels that he or she doesn't have enough energy to complete the task.

Business necessity   Discrimination or exclusion that is allowed if it is necessary to ensure the safety of workers or customers.

C

Capital budget   A component of the budget plan that includes equipment and renovations needed by an organization in order to meet long-term goals.

Capitation   A fixed monthly fee for providing services to enrollees.

Case management   A model for identifying, coordinating, and monitoring the implementation of services needed to achieve desired patient care outcomes within a specified period of time.

Certification to contract   A process by which a union, certified by the NLRB as a bargaining agent, can enter into a contract with an employer that has been voted on by the union membership.

Chain of command   The hierarchy of authority and responsibility within the organization.

Change   The process of making something different from what it was.

Change agent   One who works to bring about change.

Charge nurse   An expanded staff nurse role with increased responsibility and the function of liaison to the nurse manager.

Charismatic leadership   Leadership based on valued personal characteristics and beliefs.

Clinical microsystems   A small unit of care that maintains itself over time.

Clinical nurse leader   A lateral integrator of care responsible for a specified group of clients within a microsystem of the health care setting.

Coach   An individual who helps the staff member focus on solving a specific problem or conflict that interferes with the employee's satisfaction at work.

Coaching   The day-to-day process of helping employees improve their performance.

Cohesiveness   The degree to which the members are attracted to the group and wish to retain membership in it.

Collaboration   All parties work together to solve a problem.

Collective bargaining   Collective action taken by workers to secure better wages or working conditions.

Committees or task forces   Groups that deal with specific issues involving several service areas.

Communication   A complex, ongoing, dynamic process in which the participants simultaneously create shared meaning in an interaction.

Compassion fatigue   Secondary traumatic stress experienced by caregivers.

Competing   An all-out effort to win, regardless of the cost.

Competing groups   Groups in which members compete for resources or recognition.

Competitive conflict   A type of conflict that is resolved through competition, in which victory for one side and loss for the other side is determined by a set of rules.

Compromise   A conflict management technique in which the rewards are divided between both parties.

Concurrent audit   A nursing audit conducted during the patient's course of care.

Conflict   The consequence of real or perceived differences in mutually exclusive goals, values, ideas, attitudes, beliefs, feelings, or actions.

Confrontation   The most effective means of resolving conflict, in which the conflict is brought out in the open and attempts are made to resolve it through knowledge and reason.

Conjunctive task   A task in which the group succeeds only if all members succeed.

Connection power   Power based on an individual's formal and informal links to influential or prestigious persons within and outside an organization.

Consensus   A conflict strategy in which a solution that meets everyone's needs is agreed upon.

Content theories   Motivational theories that emphasize individual needs or the rewards that may satisfy those needs.

Contingency planning   The reactive or proactive identification and management of problems that arise.

Continuous quality improvement (CQI)   The process used to improve quality and performance.

Controlling   The process of comparing actual results with projected results.

Cost center   The smallest area of activity within an organization for which costs are accumulated.

Creativity   The ability to develop and implement new and better solutions.

Critical incidents   Reports of employee behaviors that are out of the ordinary, either positive or negative.

Critical pathways   Tools or guidelines that direct care by identifying expected outcomes.

Critical thinking   A process of examining underlying assumptions, interpreting and evaluating arguments, imagining and exploring alternatives, and developing reflective criticism for the purpose of reaching a reasoned, justifiable conclusion.

D

Decertification   The process of changing union affiliation or removing the union altogether.

Decision making   A process whereby appropriate alternatives are weighed and one is ultimately selected.

Deficiency focusing   The habit of focusing on the negatives at the expense of the positives.

Delegation   The process by which responsibility and authority are transferred to another individual.

Delphi technique   A decision-making technique in which judgments on a particular topic are systematically gathered from participants who do not meet face to face.

Demand management   A system that uses best-practices protocols to predict the demand for nursing expertise several days in advance.

Democratic leadership   A leadership style that assumes individuals are motivated by internal forces; leader uses participation and majority rule to get work done.

Descriptive rationality model   A decision-making process that emphasizes the limitations of the rationality of the decision maker and the situation.

Diagnosis-related groups   Systems of prospective payment used by Medicare that pay a provider a set amount for a specific condition.

Diagonal communication   Communication involving individuals at different hierarchical levels.

Dialectical inquiry   A technique used to minimize groupthink through the use of a formal debate format.

Differentiated practice   A nursing care delivery system that maximizes nursing resources by focusing on the structure of nursing roles according to education, experience, and competency.

Direct costs   Expenses that directly affect patient care.

Directing   The process of getting the work within an organization done.

Directive leadership   A leadership style that involves telling employees expectations, giving guidance, ensuring adherence to rules, and scheduling work efforts.

Discipline   The action taken when a regulation has been violated.

Disjunctive task   A task in which the group succeeds if one member succeeds.

Disruptive conflict   A type of conflict in which winning is not emphasized and there is no mutually acceptable set of rules; parties involved are engaged in activities to reduce, defeat, or eliminate the opponent.

Diversification   The expansion of an organization into new arenas of service.

Divisible task   Tasks that can be broken down into subtasks with division of labor.

Downward communication   Communication, generally directive, given from an authority figure or manager to staff.

Driving forces   Behaviors that facilitate change by pushing participants in the desired direction.

E

Efficiency variance   The difference between budgeted and actual nursing care hours provided.

Electronic health record   An integrated record that includes information from all medical sources and can be accessed from multiple locations by sanctioned providers.

Empirical-rational model   A change agent strategy based on the assumption that people are rational and follow self-interest if that self-interest is made clear.

Equity   The perception that one's work contribution is rewarded in the same proportion that another person's contribution is rewarded.

Equity theory   The motivational theory that suggests effort and job satisfaction depend on the degree of equity or perceived fairness in the work situation.

Essay evaluation   An evaluation method in which an employee's performance is described through a detailed written narrative.

Evaluation   The investigative process to determine whether outcomes were achieved and to what extent.

Evidence-based practice   Applying the best scientific evidence to a patient's unique diagnosis, condition, and situation to make clinical decisions.

Expectancy   The perceived probability that effort will result in successful performance.

Expectancy theory   The motivational theory that emphasizes the role of rewards and their relationship to the performance of desired behaviors.

Expense budget   A comprehensive budget that lists salary and nonsalary items that reflect patient care objectives and activity parameters for the nursing unit.

Experimentation   A type of problem solving in which a theory is tested to enhance knowledge, understanding, or prediction.

Expert power   Power based on the manager's possession of unique skills, knowledge, and competence.

Expert systems   Computer programs that provide complex data processing, reasoning, and decision making.

Extinction   The technique used to eliminate negative behavior, in which a positive reinforcer is removed and the undesired behavior is extinguished.

F

Family and Medical Leave Act   A federal law stating that employers must provide employees with leave when serious illness or family issues arise, while maintaining insurance and an equal position within the organization.

Felt conflict   The negative feelings between two or more parties.

First-level manager   The manager responsible for supervising nonmanagerial personnel and day-to-day activities of specific work units.

Fiscal year   A specified 12-month period during which operational and financial performance is measured.

Fixed budget   A budget in which budgeted amounts are set regardless of changes that occur during the year.

Fixed costs   Expenses that remain the same for the budget period regardless of the activity level of the organization.

Fogging   A communication technique in which one agrees with part of what was said.

Followership   Interactive and complementary relationship to leadership.

Forced distribution evaluation   An evaluation method in which employees are rated in a fixed method, similar to grading on a curve.

Forcing   A conflict management technique that forces an immediate end to conflict but leaves the cause unresolved.

Formal committees   Committees in an organization with authority and a specific role.

Formal groups   Clusters of individuals designated by an organization to perform specified organizational tasks.

Formal leadership   Leadership that is exercised by an individual with legitimate authority conferred by position within the organization.

Forming   The initial stage of group development, in which individuals assemble into a well-defined cluster.

Full-time equivalent (FTE)   The percentage of time an employee works that is based on a 40-hour workweek.

Functional nursing   A nursing care delivery system in which the needs of patients are broken down into tasks and assigned to caregivers.

G

Goal setting   The relating of current behavior, activities, or operations to the organization's or individual's long-range goals.

Goals   Specific statements of outcomes that are to be achieved.

Goal-setting theory   The motivational theory that suggests that the goal itself is the motivating force.

Grievances   Formal expressions of complaints, generally classified as misunderstandings, contract violations, or an inadequate labor agreement.

Group   An aggregate of individuals who interact and mutually influence each other.

Group evaluation   An evaluation process whereby managers compare individual and group performance to organizational standards.

Groupthink   A negative phenomenon occurring in highly cohesive, isolated groups in which group members come to think alike, which interferes with critical thinking.

H

Halo error   The failure to differentiate among the various performance dimensions when evaluating.

Hawthorne effect   The tendency for people to perform as expected because of special attention.

Heterarchy   A relational design based on the concept of connections.

Hidden agendas   A group member's individual, unspoken objectives that interfere with commitment or enthusiasm.

Horizontal integration   Arrangements between or among organizations that provide the same or similar services.

Horizontal promotion   A program to reward a high-performing employee without promoting the employee to a management position.

I

Implementation Bringing together materials, methods, speakers, and learners for education.

Incident report An accurate and comprehensive report on unplanned or unexpected occurrences that could potentially affect a patient, family member, or staff.

Incremental (line-by-line) budget A budget worksheet listing expense items on separate lines that is usually divided into salary and nonsalary expenses.

Indicator A tool used to measure the performance of structure, process, and outcome standards.

Indirect costs Necessary expenditures that do not affect patient care directly.

Informal committees Committees with no delegated authority that are organized for discussion.

Informal groups Groups that evolve from social interactions that are not defined by an organizational structure.

Informal leadership Leadership that is exercised by an individual who does not have a specified management role.

Information power Power based on an individual's access to valued data.

Innovative decisions The type of decisions made when problems are unusual and unclear and creative solutions are necessary.

Instrumentality The perceived probability that performance will lead to desired outcomes.

Integrated health care networks Organizational health care structures that deliver a continuum of care, provide coverage for a group of individuals, and accept fixed payments for that group.

Integrative decision making A conflict strategy that focuses on the means of solving a problem rather than the ends.

Interrater reliability Agreement between two measures by several interviewers.

Interrole conflict Conflict resulting from incongruence between the different roles an individual might play, such as doing a job and directing others to do the job.

Interruption log Journal of specific information regarding interruptions, analysis of which may help identify ways to reduce interruptions.

Intersender conflict Difficulty in interpreting the intended meaning of a message due to two conflicting messages received from differing sources.

Interview guide A written document containing questions, interviewer directions, and other pertinent information so that the same process is followed and the same basic information is gathered from each applicant.

Intrarater reliability Agreement between two measures by the same interviewer.

Intrarole conflict Conflict resulting from incongruence between one's expectations for performance and one's perception of the resulting performance.

Intrasender conflict Difficulty in interpreting the intended meaning of a message due to incongruity between verbal and nonverbal communication.

Involuntary absenteeism Absenteeism that is not under the employee's control.

Involuntary turnover The employee is terminated by the employers.

J

Job description Describes the skills, abilities, and knowledge required to perform the job.

Job enlargement A flatter organizational structure that causes positions to be combined and results in managers having more employees to supervise.

Joint venture A partnership in which each partner contributes different areas of expertise, resources, or service to create a new product or service.

L

Laissez-faire leadership A leadership style that assumes individuals are motivated by internal forces and should be left alone to complete work; leader provides no direction or facilitation.

Lateral communication Communication that occurs between individuals at the same hierarchical level.

Leader Someone who uses interpersonal skills to influence others to accomplish specific goals.

Lean Six Sigma A quality program that focuses on improving process flow and eliminating waste.

Legitimate power A manager's right to make requests because of authority within an organizational hierarchy.

Leniency error The tendency of a manager to overrate staff performance.

Line authority The linear hierarchy of supervisory responsibility and authority.

Lose–lose strategy A conflict strategy in which neither side wins; the settlement reached is unsatisfactory to both sides.

Low skill recognition The tendency not to recognize the role one's own ability has played in producing one's successes.

M

Magnet recognition program Recognition by the American Nurses Credentialing Center that the organization provides quality nursing care.

Manager An individual employed by an organization who is responsible for efficiently accomplishing the goals of the organization.

Medium The agent of contact between the organization and the potential applicant.

Mentor A more experienced person who guides, supports, and nurtures a less experienced person.

Metacommunications Nonverbal messages in communication, including body language and environmental factors.

Mindguards A feature of groupthink in which the group is "protected" from controversial information.

Mission A general statement of the purpose of an organization.

Motivation The factors that initiate and direct behavior.

N

Necessitating The belief that it is imperative or necessary that a particular task be done by a specific person.

Needs assessment An evaluation of learning needs in a select population.

Negative assertion A communication technique in which one accepts some blame for what was said.

Negative inquiry A communication technique used to clarify objections and feelings (e.g., I don't understand . . .).

Negligent hiring Failure of an organization, responsible for the character and actions of all employees, to ascertain the background of an employee.

Negotiation A conflict management technique in which the conflicting parties give and take on various issues.

Nominal group technique (NGT) A decision-making technique that elicits written questions, ideas, and reactions from group members.

Nonsalary expenditure variance Deviation from the budget as a result of changes in patient volume, supply quantities, or prices paid.

Normative-reeducative strategy A change agent strategy based on the assumption that people act in accordance with social norms and values.

Norming The third stage of group development, in which group members define goals and rules of behavior.

Norms Informal rules of behavior shared and enforced by group members.

Nursing care hours (NCHs) The number of hours of patient care provided per unit of time.

O

Objective probability The likelihood that an event will or will not occur based on facts and reliable information.

Objectives Statements of specific outcomes within a component of the organization.

On-the-job instruction An educational method using observation and practice that involves the employees learning new skills after being employed.

Operant conditioning Process by which a behavior becomes associated with a particular consequence.

Operating budget The organization's statement of expected revenues and expenses for the upcoming year.

Ordinary interacting groups Common types of groups; generally have a formal leader and are run according to an informal structure with the purpose of solving a problem or making a decision.

Organization A collection of people working together under a defined structure to achieve predetermined outcomes.

Organizational culture The basic assumptions and values held by members of the organization.

Organizational environment The systemwide conditions that contribute to a positive or negative work setting.

Organizing The process of coordinating the work to be done within an organization.

Orientation A process by which staff development personnel and managers ease a new employee into the organization by providing relevant information.

Outcome standards Standards that reflect the desired result or outcome of care.

Outcomes management A system in which costs and quality are concurrently and retrospectively measured and evaluated in order to improve clinical practice.

Overdelegation A common form of ineffective delegation that occurs when the delegator loses control over a situation by giving too much authority or responsibility to the delegate.

P

Participative leadership A leadership style that involves consultation with subordinates in decision making.

Patient classification systems (PCSs) Systems developed to objectively determine workload requirements and staffing needs.

Patient-centered care A nursing care delivery system that is unit-based and consists of patient care coordinators, patient care associates, unit support assistants, administrative support personnel, and a nurse manager.

Peer coaching Using partners, who have both participated in the educational program, to observe each other practicing the skill, ask appropriate questions during the demonstration, and offer feedback about the performance.

Peer review A process by which other employees assess and judge the performance of professional peers against predetermined standards.

Perceived conflict One's perception of the other's position in a conflict.

Performance appraisal The process of interaction, written documentation, formal interview, and follow-up that occurs between managers and their employees to give feedback, make decisions, and cover fair employment practice law.

Performance-driven clinical ladder A system of using performance indicators to advance an employee within the organization.

Performing The fourth stage of group development, in which group members agree on basic purposes and activities and carry out the work.

Personal power Power based on an individual's credibility, reputation, expertise, experience, control of resources or information, and ability to build trust.

Personnel decisions Decisions that affect the terms, conditions, and privileges of employment.

Philosophy The mission, values, and vision of an organization.

Planning A four-stage process that includes establishing objectives, evaluating the present situation and predicting future trends and events, formulating a planning statement (means), and converting the plan into an action statement.

Policy Decisions that govern action and determine an organization's relationships, activities, and goals.

Political decision-making model A decision-making process in which the particular interests and objectives of powerful stakeholders influence how problems and objectives are defined.

Politics A means of influencing the allocation of scarce resources, events, and the decisions of others.

Pooled interdependence A type of interdependence in which each individual contributes to the group but no one contribution is dependent on any other.

Pools Internal or external groups of workers that are used as supplemental staff by the organization.

Position control A monitoring tool used to compare actual numbers of employees to the number of budgeted FTEs for the nursing unit.

Position power Power of an individual that is determined by the job description, assigned responsibilities, recognition, advancement, authority, the ability to withhold money, and decision making.

Power The potential ability to influence in order to achieve goals.

Power-coercive strategies Change agent strategies based on the application of power by legitimate authority, economic sanctions, or political clout.

Power plays Power plays are attempts by others to diminish or demolish their opponents.

Practice partnership A nursing care delivery system in which senior and junior staff members share patient care responsibilities.

Preceptor An experienced individual who assists new employees in acquiring the necessary knowledge and skills to function effectively in a new environment.

Premature concurrence seeking A result of groupthink caused by pressure to conform, self-censorship, mindguards, and apparent unanimity.

Presenteeism An employee is at work although disabled by physical or mental illness.

Primary nursing A nursing care delivery system in which one nurse is responsible and accountable for the nursing care of specific patients for the duration of their stay.

Probability The likelihood that an event will or will not occur.

Probability analysis A calculation of the expected risk made to accurately determine the probabilities of each alternative.

Problem solving A process whereby a dilemma is identified and corrected.

Process standards Standards connected with the actual delivery of care.

Process theories Motivational theories that emphasize how the motivation process works to direct an individual's effort into performance.

Productivity A measure of how well the work group or team uses the resources available to achieve its goals and produce its services.

Profit The difference between revenues and expenses.

Progressive discipline The process of increasingly severe warnings for repeated violations that can result in termination.

Punishment A process used to inhibit an undesired behavior by applying a negative reinforcer.

Punishment (coercive) power Power based on penalties a manager might impose if the individual or group does not comply with authority.

Q

Quality management A preventive approach designed to address problems efficiently and quickly.

Quantum leadership A leadership style based on the concepts of chaos theory.

R

Rate variance The difference between budgeted and actual hourly rates paid.

Ratification Passage of the contract by a simple majority vote of the union membership.

Rational decision-making model A decision-making process based on logical, well-grounded, rational choices that maximize the achievement of objectives.

Real (command) groups Groups that accomplish tasks in an organization and are recognized as legitimate organizational entities.

Reality shock The stress, surprise, and disequilibrium experienced when shifting from a familiar culture into one whose values, rewards, and sanctions are different (e.g., from school culture to work culture).

Recency error The tendency of a manager to rate an employee based on recent events, rather than over the entire evaluation period.

Reciprocal interdependence A type of interdependence in which members must coordinate their activities with every other individual in the group.

Redesign A technique that examines the tasks within each job with the goal of combining appropriate tasks to improve efficiency.

Reengineering A complex and often radical approach to the organization of patient care in which new relationships and expectations are adopted.

Referent power Power based on admiration and respect for an individual.

Re-forming A stage of group development in which the group reassembles after a major change in the environment or in the goals of the group that requires the group to refocus its activities.

Reinforcement theory (behavior modification) The motivational theory that views motivation as learning and proposes that behavior is learned through a process called operant conditioning.

Relapse prevention A model that emphasizes learning a set of self-control and coping strategies to increase the retention of newly learned behavior.

Relational (connective) leadership A leadership style that values collaboration and teamwork; interpersonal skills are used to promote collegiality in achieving organizational goals.

Remote care Using technology to provide medical and nursing services from afar.

Reportable incident Any unexpected or unplanned occurrence that affects or could potentially affect a patient, family member, or staff.

Representation election The process of establishing a union through the selection of a bargaining agent certified to conduct labor negotiations for a group of individuals.

Resistance A behavior that can be positive or negative and may mean a resistance to change or disobedience, or it may be an effective approach to handling power differences.

Resolution The stage of conflict that occurs when a mutually agreed-upon solution is arrived at and both parties commit themselves to carry out the agreement.

Responsibility An obligation to accomplish a task.

Restraining forces Behaviors that impede change by discouraging participants from making specified changes.

Restructuring An examination of a health care organization's structure to improve the organization's productivity.

Résumé A written record of your educational achievements, employment, and accomplishments.

Retrospective audit A nursing audit conducted after a patient's discharge that involves examining records of a large number of cases.

Revenue budget A projection of expected income for a budget period based on volume and mix of patients, rates, and discounts.

Reverse delegation A common form of ineffective delegation that occurs when someone with a lower rank delegates to someone with more authority.

Reward power Power based on inducements offered by the manager in exchange for contributions that advance the manager's objectives.

Risk management A program directed toward identifying, evaluating, and taking corrective action against potential risks that could lead to injury.

Risky shift   A phenomenon seen in groups in which riskier, more controversial decisions are made.

Robotics   Using robots to deliver supplies and remote care.

Role   A set of expectations about behavior ascribed to a specific position.

Role ambiguity   The frustrations that result from unclear expectations for one's performance.

Role redefinition   The clarification of roles and an attempt to integrate or tie together the various roles individuals play.

Routine decisions   The type of decisions made when problems are relatively well defined and common and when established rules, policies, and procedures can be used to solve them.

S

Salary (personnel) budget   A budget that projects salary costs to be paid and charged to the cost center during the budget period.

Salary compression   The effect of higher starting pay of new nurses or rewarding those with fewer years of experience with higher increases that results in the salaries of long-term employees being at or below those of less-experienced nurses.

Satisficing   A decision-making strategy whereby the individual chooses a less than ideal alternative that meets minimum standards of acceptance.

Self-staffing and scheduling   A staffing model whereby managers and their staff completely manage staffing and schedules.

Sequential interdependence   A type of interdependence in which members must coordinate their activities with others in some designated order.

Servant leadership   The premise that leadership originates from a desire to serve; a leader emerges when others' needs take priority.

Shaping   The selective reinforcement of behaviors that are successively closer approximations to the desired behavior.

Shared governance   An organizational paradigm based on the values of interdependence and accountability that allows nurses to make decisions in a decentralized environment.

Shared leadership   An organizational structure in which several individuals share the responsibility for achieving the organization's goals.

Six Sigma   A quality management program that uses measures, goals, and management involvement to monitor performance and ensure progress.

Smoothing   Managing conflict by complimenting one's opponent, downplaying differences, and focusing on minor areas of agreement.

Social learning theory   A behavioral theory based on reinforcement theory that proposes new behaviors are learned through direct experience or observation that can result in positive or negative outcomes.

Span of control   The number of employees that can be effectively supervised by a single manager.

Staff authority   The advisory relationship in which responsibility for actual work is assigned to others.

Staff development   The process of enhancing staff performance with specific learning activities.

Staffing   The process of balancing the quantity of staff available with the quantity and mix of staff needed by the organization.

Staffing mix   The type of staff necessary to perform the work of the organization.

Stakeholders   People or groups with a direct interest in the work of an organization.

Standards   Written statements that define a level of performance or a set of conditions determined to be acceptable by some authority.

Statistical aggregation   A decision-making technique in which individuals are polled regarding a specific problem and their responses are tallied.

Status   The social ranking of individuals relative to others in a group based on the position they occupy.

Status incongruence   The disruptive impact that occurs when factors associated with group status are not congruent.

Storming   The second stage of group development, in which group members develop roles and relationships; competition and conflict generally occur.

Strategic planning   A process of continual assessment, planning, and evaluation to guide the future.

Strategies   Actions by which objectives are to be achieved.

Stress   The nonspecific reaction that people have to threatening demands from the environment.

Strike   The organized stoppage of work by employees within the union.

Structure standards   Standards that relate to the physical environment, organization, and management of an organization.

Subjective probability   The likelihood that an event will or will not occur based on a manager's personal judgment and beliefs.

Supportive leadership   A leadership style that focuses on the needs of employees.

Suppression   The stage of conflict that occurs when one person or group defeats the other.

T

Task forces   Ad hoc committees appointed for a specific purpose and a limited time.

Task group   Several individuals who work together to accomplish specific time-limited assignments.

Team building   A group development technique that focuses on task and relationship aspects of a group's functioning in order to build team cohesiveness.

Team nursing   The most common delivery system; nursing staff are divided into teams, which are responsible for the care of a group of patients.

Teams   Real groups in which people work cooperatively with each other in order to achieve some goal.

Terminate   To fire an employee.

The Leapfrog Group   A coalition of public and private employers organized to bring attention to consumers about quality indicators in health care and mobilize employers to reward health care organizations that demonstrate quality outcome measures.

Time logs   Journals of activities that are useful in analyzing actual time spent on specific activities.

Time waster   Something that prevents a person from accomplishing a job or achieving a goal.

To-do list   A list of responsibilities to be accomplished within a specific time frame.

Total patient care   The original model of nursing care delivery, in which one RN is responsible for all aspects of one or more patients' care.

Total quality management (TQM)   A management philosophy that emphasizes a commitment to excellence throughout the organization.

Total time lost   The number of scheduled days an employee misses.

Traditional rating scale   An evaluation method that uses performance dimensions to rate employees.

Transactional leadership   A leadership style based on principles of social exchange theory in which social interaction between leaders and followers is essentially economic, and success is achieved when needs are met, loyalty is enhanced, and work performance is enhanced.

Transformational leadership   A leadership style focused on effecting revolutionary change in organizations through a commitment to the organization's vision.

Transitions   The periods of time between the current situation and when change is implemented.

Trial-and-error method   A method whereby one solution after another is tried until the problem is solved or appears to be improving.

Turnover   The number of staff members who vacate a position.

U

Underdelegation   A common form of ineffective delegation that occurs when full authority is not transferred, responsibility is taken back, or there is a failure to equip and direct the delegate.

Upward communication   Communication that occurs from staff to management.

Utilization reviews   Reviews mandated by the Joint Commission, based on the appropriate allocation of resources.

V

Valence   The perceived value of an outcome.

Validity   The ability to predict outcomes with some accuracy.

Values   The beliefs or attitudes one has about people, ideas, objects, or actions that form a basis for behavior.

Variable budget   A budget developed with the understanding that adjustments to the budget may be made during the year.

Variable costs   Expenses that depend on and change in direct proportion to patient volume and acuity.

Variance   The difference between the amount that was budgeted for a specific cost and the actual cost.

Vertical integration   An arrangement between or among dissimilar but related organizations to provide a continuum of services.

Vision statement   A description of the goal to which an organization aspires.

Volume variances   Differences in the budget as a result of increases or decreases in patient volume.

Voluntary absenteeism   Absenteeism that is under the employee's control.

Voluntary turnover   The employee chooses to leave the organization.

W

Win–lose strategy   A strategy used during conflict in which one party exerts dominance and the other submits and loses.

Win–win strategy   A conflict strategy that focuses on goals and attempts to meet the needs of both parties.

Withdrawal The removal of at least one party from the conflict, making it impossible to resolve the situation.

Work sample questions Used to determine an applicant's knowledge about work tasks and ability to perform the job.

Workplace violence Any violent act, including physical assaults and threats of assault, directed toward persons at work or on duty.

Written comments problem The tendency of evaluators not to include written comments on appraisal forms.

Z

Zero-based budget A budgetary approach that assumes the base for projecting next year's budget is zero; managers are required to justify all activities and every proposed expenditure.

Page numbers followed by *f* indicate figures and those followed by *t* indicate tables or boxes.